"*Drummer* was a map of leather culture, and Fritscher and his books are unabashed and uninhibited tour guides." —**Chuck Renslow, founder, Leather Archives & Museum and International Mr. Leather (IML)**

"I invite you all to join us in this extraordinary walk down memory lane." —**Jeanne Barney, First and Founding LA Editor-in-Chief of** *Drummer*

"What rollicking fun...to reopen old friendships and even some ancient hostilities of that golden age. To be a bystander to those vibrant talents and hear again those voices.... Can you imagine the pleasure in being able to put one's arms around some of those people, just like you maybe should have done back then when they were still around and available?"
—**John Embry, founding publisher of** *Drummer*

"Those concerned with the preservation of GLBT history are very fortunate that Fritscher has such a remarkable memory for the people, places, and pivotal events he has witnessed. His long association with *Drummer* in San Francisco placed him at the center of the revolution."
—**Catherine Johnson-Roehr, The Kinsey Institute**

"There is no written account of Old Guard leather. Fritscher's detailing of the *Drummer* Boom is unparalleled and we need it."
—**Dave Rhodes, publisher,** *The Leather Journal*

"Fritscher is about as informed as anyone on the history of erotic writing, its importance, and the state of erotic publishing today. According to him, religion and nipple clamps were invented for the same reason, namely that everyone likes being bottom of the domination pile."
—**Bruno Bayley,** *Vice Magazine*

All-around leatherman Jack Fritscher chronicles our leather lifestyle. His books on people, places, events, and ideas in our world are accurate, and seethe with the fervor of our lives in those bygone days."
—**Mr. Marcus,** *Bay Area Reporter*

"Fritscher invented the South of Market prose style and its magazines."
—**John F. Karr,** *Bay Area Reporter*

Fritscher "added journalistic realism to the magical thinking and masturbatory desires of *Drummer* readers. It was the original bible of leather culture." —**Lauren Murrow, "Jack Fritscher, Peter Berlin, Annie Sprinkle, and the Cockettes: The Pioneers of San Francisco's Sexual Heyday,"** *San Francisco Magazine*

"Jack Fritscher is the prolific author who since the late Sixties has helped document the gay world and the changes it has undergone."
—**Willie Walker, founder, GLBT Historical Society, San Francisco**

"Fritscher brings a loving ear, erotic eye, and lyric voice to American Gay Popular Culture, and is an archivist active in researching, recording and preserving the heritage of gay history."
—**Ron Suresha, author,** *Bears on Bears*

"Fritscher is a key player...This is must reading for those who want to know more about their past and for those who simply want to relive the days when it was fun to be gay."
—**David Van Leer, author,** *The Queening of America*

"In 1977 Jack Fritscher became editor-in-chief of *Drummer* and introduced into 'mainstream' gay media such artists as Tom of Finland, Robert Mapplethorpe and David Hurles (Old Reliable), and showcased talents such as Robert Opel, Arthur Tress, Samuel Steward (Phil Andros), Larry Townsend, John Preston, Wakefield Poole, Rex, and A. Jay. Through Fritscher's work with *Drummer* the gay-identity word *homomasculinity* was coined as well as redefining S&M as 'Sensuality and Mutuality' (1974). Documenting on page the dawn of the 'Daddy' and 'Bear' movements, Fritscher was the first writer and editor to feature 'older men' (*Drummer* 24, September 1978) and 'Mountain Men Bears' (*Drummer* 119, July 1988) in the gay press."
—**BacktoStonewall.com**

"Fritscher preserves the history, passions, troubles, and dreams of our departed brothers, and living elders, from back in the day of our very best as a Leather Tribe. *Drummer* magazine should be required study material at colleges worldwide because *Drummer* was our first loud voice when the whole world wanted to shut us up and shut us down."
—**Papa Tony, Tribal Elder, http://tribalvibept.blogspot.com**

"Jack Fritscher is the firebrand writer who made the 1970s leather scene happen in a big way. His Drummer Salon introduced many artists and photographers like Tom of Finland and Robert Mapplethorpe into our Fey-Way Gallery stable. As leatherman and academic, Fritscher writes definitively about gay pop culture like no one else can. His books are always a revelation!"
—Camille O'Grady, author, multi-media artist, partner, Robert Opel's Fey-Way Gallery

"Jack Fritscher took a dreary newsprint bar guide called *Drummer* and transformed it into a major publication that revolutionized gay publishing to become the international gay magazine to be reckoned with—the one all the others imitated but could never match.. As editor, Fritscher single-handedly discovered and promoted with great passion, an amazing string of artists, writers, performers, filmmakers and photographers who went on to become Porn Royalty in gay culture—legends whose names still resonate with the public thirty years later. His unstinting faith in these fledgling talents by showcasing them in *Drummer* was an integral part of their success. In an era of dumbed-down, politically correct gay rags passing themselves off as magazines today, their editors would be well advised to study Fritscher's memoir and discover just what it really means to 'march to a different *drummer*' in publishing."
—The Artist REX, Rexwerk

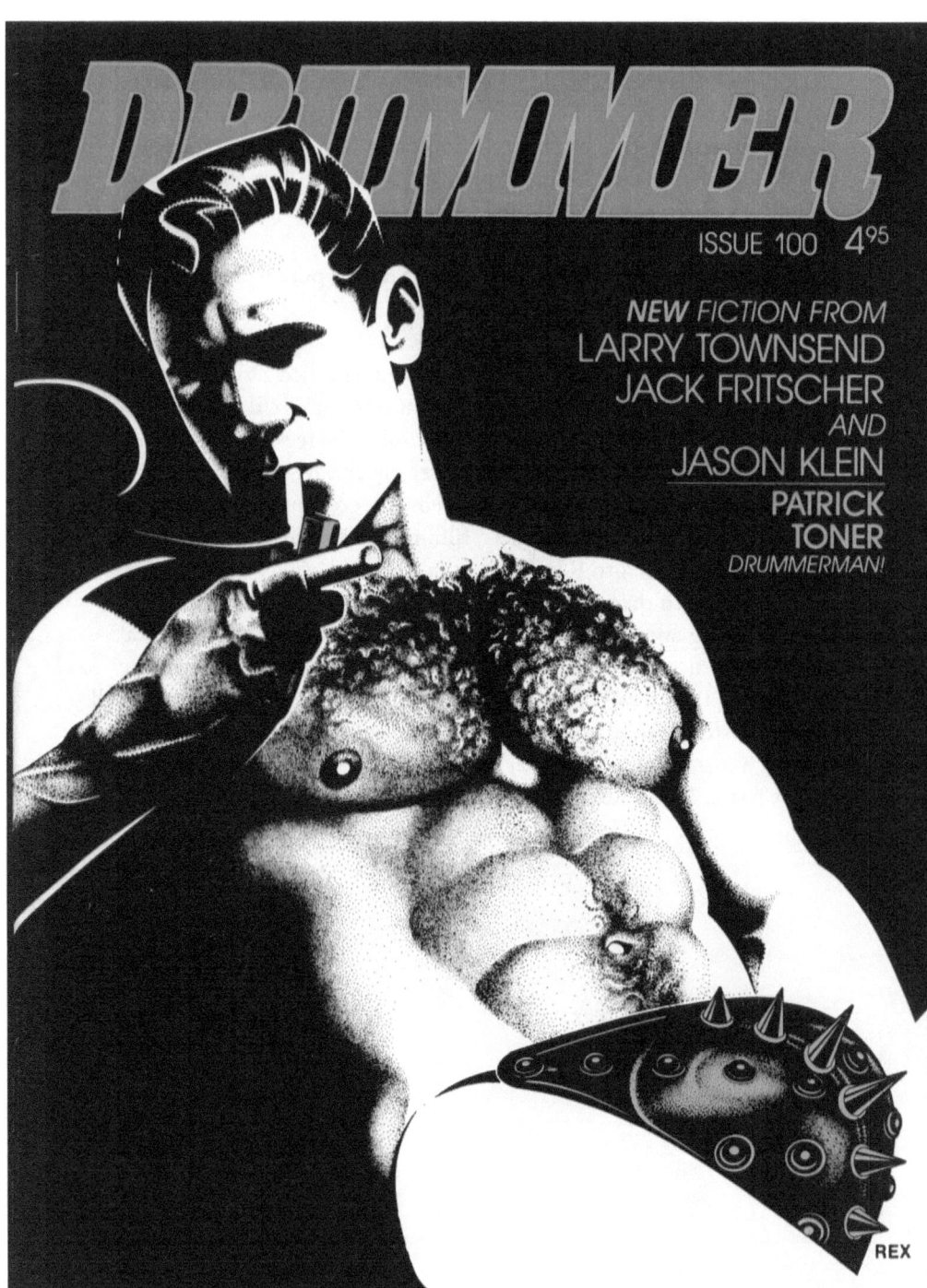

REX, Cover Art, *Drummer* 100

Other Works by Jack Fritscher

Novels

*Some Dance to Remember:
A Memoir-Novel of San Francisco 1970-1982*
The Geography of Women
What They Did to the Kid
Leather Blues

Short-Fiction

Rainbow County
Corporal in Charge
Stand by Your Man
Titanic
Stonewall: Stories of Gay Liberation
Sweet Embraceable You: Coffee House Stories

Non-Fiction

Gay San Francisco: Eyewitness Drummer
Mapplethorpe: Assault with a Deadly Camera
Popular Witchcraft
Love and Death in Tennesssee Williams
When Malory Met Arthur: Camelot
Television Today
California Dreamin'

www.JackFritscher.com

DRUMMER

ISSUE 108

4^{95}

ZEUS PHOTOGRAPHS OF
MR. DRUMMER
CONTEST FINALS

LARRY TOWNSEND
RUN, LITTLE LEATHER BOY!

LOVE AND PAIN
BY THOMAS L. DAWSON

THE TROUGH
PART 2
BY ADOLPH

BEER-BELLIED BRUISERS
BY RICHARD A. WHITE

Cover Photograph by Mikal Bales, Zeus Studio

GAY PIONEERS:
How *Drummer* Magazine Shaped Gay Popular Culture 1965-1999

Volume 4

Jack Fritscher, Ph.D.
Founding San Francisco
Editor-in-Chief of *Drummer*

Collected and Edited by Mark Hemry

A Narrative Timeline, Analysis, and Archive of Art,
Sex, Erotica, Obscenity, Homophobia, Identity Politics,
the Culture War, and the Salon around *Drummer* Magazine

Based on internal evidence in *Drummer* magazine,
and in journals, diaries, letters, photographs,
interviews, recordings, magazines, and newspapers
in the Jack Fritscher and Mark Hemry Archive

Palm Drive Publishing ™
San Francisco

Copyright ©2017 Jack Fritscher

All rights are reserved by the author. Except for brief passages quoted in newspaper, magazine, radio, television, internet review, or other electronic media, or academic paper, no part of this book may be reproduced or transmitted in any form or by any means, electronic or mechanical, including photocopy, recording, web posting, or any information storage-and-retrieval system now known or to be invented, without permission in writing from the publisher.

For author history and for historical research www.JackFritscher.com

Cover and book design by Mark Hemry. Cover photography by Jack Fritscher.

Published by Palm Drive Publishing, San Francisco
Email: publisher@PalmDrivePublishing.com

This memoir is a product of the author's recollections and is thus rendered as a subjective accounting of events that occurred in his life. This is a memoir book of humor, comedy, and satire meant to refract the author's eyewitness experience of what might otherwise be objective history. While all of this written "oral history" may be true, none of it may be. It must be emphasized that the text and allegations are provisional. With the first pages written in 1977, this is the first history to begin the difficult documentation of *Drummer* magazine. The text, the lists, the quotations, the illustrations, the credits for the illustrations, and the annotated bibliography in this "work in progress" are as thoroughly fact-checked as possible from internal evidence in *Drummer* itself, as well as, where possible, from journals, diaries, letters, photographs, interviews, recordings, magazines, and newspapers found in the personal collection of the Jack Fritscher and Mark Hemry Archive. Text may or may not be true and accurate, and does not reflect the sexual orientation of persons mentioned or depicted therein. The opinions, views, and allegations expressed are those of the author, or of the individual writers and speakers quoted, who themselves, in turn, do not represent the views or opinions of the author or the editor or the publisher; these opinions, views, and allegations may differ substantially from the opinion, views, and allegations of those who are referenced as personalities in this historical survey. The author, regretting any misrepresentation or misinformation or violation of copyright, apologizes; and he encourages documented corrections for future editions be sent to the publisher. Any person who is mentioned in these pages, or is an eyewitness to this history, or is a copyright owner, or is somehow concerned, is invited to correct or add or subtract from this book by contacting the publisher@ PalmDrivePublishing.com

Library of Congress Control Number: 2008920734
Fritscher, Jack 1939-
Gay Pioneers: How Drummer Magazine Shaped Gay Popular Culture / Jack Fritscher
p.cm
ISBN 978-1-890834-17-3 Print
ISBN 978-1-890834-18-0 Ebook
1. Biography/Autobiography, 2. Personal Memoirs, 3. Homosexuality, 4. Masculinity, 5. Gay and Lesbian Studies, 6. Gay Studies (Gay Men), 7. Popular Culture, 8. Editors, Journalists, Publishers, 9. Sadomasochism, 10. American Literature—20th Century, 11. Feminism, 12. Homomasculinity.

First Printing 2017
10 9 8 7 6 5 4 3 2
www.PalmDrivePublishing.com

Dedication

Gay Pioneers:
How Drummer Magazine Shaped Gay Popular Culture 1965-1999

Gay Pioneers is dedicated to the following essential contributors to *Drummer* magazine: Jeanne Barney, Robert Mapplethorpe, A. Jay (Al Shapiro), David Sparrow, Larry Townsend, Robert Opel, Chuck Arnett, Phil Andros (Samuel Steward), Fred Halsted, Val Martin, Old Reliable (David Hurles), Jim Stewart, Rex, Tom Hinde, Lou Thomas, Mikal Bales, Wakefield Poole, Patrick Califia, Gene Weber, Bob Zygarlicki, Max Morales, Steven Saylor, John Preston, Richard Hamilton, M.D., Anthony F. DeBlase, Andrew Charles, Tim Barrus, JimEd Thompson, J. D. Slater, Mark Thompson, The Hun, Mason Powell, Robert Davolt, Ronald Johnson, Race Bannon, Mr. Marcus Hernandez, Skipper Davis, Mark I. Chester, Efren Ramirez, Ed Menerth, Guy Baldwin, Ken Lackey, Joseph W. Bean, and John H. Embry

Special dedication and thanks
to my stoic editor Mark Hemry
without whose remarkable diligence over thirty-seven years
this material would have been
impossible to collect, analyze, and present

With gratitude to
Jeanne Barney,
Jim Stewart, Mark Thompson
Chuck Renslow, Rick Storer
and The Leather Archives & Museum

How to Use This Text in the Printed Book and on the Internet

Initiated in 1977, this is the first history to begin the documentation of *Drummer* magazine. This book may be read as a narrative stream beginning with page one and continuing to the end. However, for both the fun of browsing and the ease of research, the book is designed with an index, and may be opened and entered on almost any page. Because each section is written to stand alone, what sometimes may seem like repetition is instead a refrain and rephrasing of a statement or a theme. The reader, who must be his or her own best critic, can turn the text like a chunk of Labrador spar to see the facets.

Responsibility and Transparency in This Book

For thirty years this book has been a work in progress. I was not paid, nor was I given grants, nor lunch, nor sex to write this book, nor do I expect much if any commercial return for the joy and labor required to fill in some big blanks in previously ignored and censored gay history. No agent or corporate publishers enforced spin, revisionism, or censorship. Asking the readers' indulgence, I assert that in my opining content and style, what is accurate is mine; what is inaccurate is also mine, and will be revised in future editions. What is here written is the eyewitness documentary and the oral history I have transparently offered for years to GLBT ethnographers. As a gay community service, my goal is to offer *Gay Pioneers: How Drummer Magazine Shaped Gay Popular Culture* simultaneously both as a low-cost-plus trade paperback, and as a free research document on the Internet. Visit www.JackFritscher.com

Research Materials

All research materials including publications, personal journals, letters, audio and video recordings, art, artifacts, photographs, and graphics are from the Jack Fritscher and Mark Hemry Archive Research Collection. Every reasonable effort has been made to acknowledge all copyright holders. Any errors or omissions that may have occurred are inadvertent, and anyone with any copyright queries is invited to write to the publisher, so that full acknowledgment may be included in subsequent editions of this work.

Authorship

Except for the quotations of others, Jack Fritscher is the author of all the writing in this book.

The Sexual Revolution of the Titanic 1970s

Epigraphs

Whoever did not live in the years
neighboring the revolution
does not know
what the pleasure of living means.
—Charles Maurice de Talleyrand

Bliss was it that dawn to be alive,
but to be young was very heaven.
—William Wordsworth,
The Prelude

DRUMMER

ISSUE 126

4^{95}

MOTORCYCLE MEN
3 leathermen
bikes
hard rods

The Denim Raiders
fiction by Jack Ricardo

COLT THOMAS
The Fifth International Mr. Leather
finally shows it!

**Cover Photograph
by Jim Wigler**

A Leathermans Legacy:
A Hero's Welcome
by Hoddy Allen

ROGER EARL
S/M AUTEUR
on The Dungeons of Europe,
Born To Raise Hell, & his other videos

Introducing
MAX BEAR

DISTRIBUTION TO MINORS PROHIBITED

Contents

Introduction	Chasing *Drummer*	1
Chapter 1	A Master's Thesis: *Drummer*'s Big Bang	15
Chapter 2	Dirty Issues: Some *Drummer* Covers	55
Chapter 3	Leather Perversatility	77
Chapter 4	Founding *Drummer*	89
Chapter 5	Sex, Race, and Gender	105
Chapter 6	Dutch Treat: Who's Driving *Drummer*	135
Chapter 7	The *Drummer* Salon	159
Chapter 8	The Mafia: Straight and Gay and Maybe Not	193
Chapter 9	Stealing *Drummer*	217
Chapter 10	The *Drummer* Curse	251
Chapter 11	Raiders of the Lost Archives	275
Chapter 12	*Drummer* Roots	297
Chapter 13	Annus Mirabilis 1979	311
Chapter 14	*Back Stab!* The Back-Stage *Drummer* Musical	353
Chapter 15	Required Reading	365
Chapter 16	*Drummer*: First Victim of the Culture War	389
Chapter 17	When Queers Collide	411
Chapter 18	Venom Never Dies: The *Drummer* Blacklist	433
Chapter 19	Virtual *Drummer*	485
Appendix 1	A Quick Who's Who in *Drummer*	495
Appendix 2	*Drummer* Magazine Timeline Bibliography	507
Index	....	533

CELTIC KNOT

HOW TO READ THIS BOOK
IN PAPERBACK AND ON-LINE

To do justice to the way *Drummer* drew roots from 1960s gay popular culture and shaped fin de siecle gay popular culture and leather history from as many points of view as possible, and to assist readers scrolling piecemeal through the text on the internet, this book contains nineteen interconnected chapters.

I designed them purposely to build and loop around one another, like a Celtic Knot, sometimes telling the same story twice or three times as the different points of view of all the eyewitnesses' testimony affirm or contradict each other.

I hope this *frisson* encourages readers to peruse the rich text and fire up their own critical thinking.

Three players key to the founding of *Drummer* magazine. "Jack Fritscher, Jeanne Barney, and Larry Townsend," Dorothy Chandler Pavilion, Los Angeles, January 10, 2007. Photograph by Mark Hemry. ©Mark Hemry

DRUMMER EXPANDS TO BRING YOU THE SAME FILTH, BUT NOW DISGUISED WITH SOCIALLY REDEEMING SCHOLARLY SIGNIFICANCE

MER exists by popular demand. Readers need their DRUMMER fix. We can't come out fast enough. If DRUMMER didn't exist, we'd have to be invented. DRUMMER's lucky enough to be a distinct medium for a genuine level of popular consciousness in the gay community. DRUMMER assures guys it's okay not to be locked into a 21-year-old all-American boy image, because our readers (you) are not boys. You're adult men.

EVEN BLUEBOYS GET THE COWS

You prefer hard sex the way you prefer men. You're not afraid of your rich fantasy life. You're not afraid of actualizing your fantasies. You've begun to notice that some gay periodicals are little more than soft-focus clones from erotic-photo mailorder catalogs. DRUMMER has always had a different, harder beat. DRUMMER isn't *Vogue* in butch drag. DRUMMER is increasingly a voice of a now less-closeted part of gay society. DRUMMER is a forum for men who enjoy authentic Sensuality and Mutuality.

We want to touch the way you really are after dark. When you've gone beyond the pretty-baby stage, you want articles, interviews, and fiction that stroke your head. We're not the last word on gay pop culture; but we're the first, and we're working to be the best. We dare to publish attitudes others repress. First, because you want our point of view which we picked up from you. Second, because certain subjects need to be printed to give full dimension to the genuinely alternate ways of being an adult, masculine, gay man in this country at this time.

DRUMMER IS AGGRESSIVE

Just you mention DRUMMER in a roomful of guys. You'll get a heavy feedback of attitude. They either love us or hate us. They either understand us (meaning themselves) or they refuse to understand us (again, meaning themselves). Some of them have every issue from Number One. Some of them wouldn't let DRUMMER sully their art-deco coffee tables. But lots of them interestingly enough, are closet-DRUMMER-boys: they keep their secret copy of our latest issue hidden handily under the bed next to the grease, the poppers, and the clothespins.

YOU ARE OUR VOICE

DRUMMER is a duo-purpose magazine. As we slowly evolve, we want to get your head off as much as we've always gotten your, uh, other head off. In short, DRUMMER has the balls to assume to report, rehash, and reshuffle at a certain expressive level of gay pop culture, because you keep buying and demanding this certain stuff issue after issue. You keep telling us what you want to see and read. We go beyond "models" — hot as they are. We prefer to reflect more authentic, real-life men. You ask for the same in our articles and fiction. It's you after all, who puts the *popular* in pop culture. Your very special, adult, masculine voice gives DRUMMER its very definite responsibility, purpose, and direction. ▲

Jack Fritscher wrote his activist editorial "Getting Off" in May 1978 for *Drummer* 23 (July 1978). In the 1970s, the first liberated decade after Stonewall, he added to *Drummer* the tag line, "The American Review of Gay Popular Culture." He was planting a flag for a declaration of gay independence, an assertive vision of the new direction and new character of a San Francisco *Drummer* that reflected its grassroots readers, and how those national and international readers lived real-time in the emerging gay pop culture of the 1970s before that Titanic Decade hit the iceberg of AIDS. The illustration was custom created for this editorial by *Drummer* art director, Al Shapiro/A. Jay. This page can be read in larger point size later in this book. —Mark Hemry, editor

Alright. So where's DRUMMER get the leather balls to assume, yeah, assume to track, report, and chronicle what's happening in the masculine world of gay men? How legit can a rag get without losing its j/o quality? Pretty g.d. legit and pretty hardassed. No other mag sticks it into the gay subculture the way DRUMMER sticks it for you. No other gay mag touches the same raw nerve of what goes on in a wide cross-section of gay heads after midnight, after the lights go down low. DRUMMER dares to reassure you that even with the extremes that you fantasize about in your most secret heart of hards: you are not alone.

GAY POP CULTURE

DRUMMER is no plastic fantasy. Every issue increasingly reflects what our readers want, as they send us more of what and where they're coming from: photos they snap, stories and articles they write, artwork they draw. DRUM-

INTRODUCTION

Hundreds of People Created *Drummer*
Millions of People Read *Drummer*

CHASING *DRUMMER*

**In the Golden Age of Leather,
It Took a Village to Raise a Magazine**

Toward an Autobiography of *Drummer*

"My Heart's a Drummer!"
—Barbara Streisand,
"Don't Rain on My Parade"

This book of investigative journalism is an eyewitness oral history about a soon-to-be-lost generation of a once-important subculture of gay pioneers.

This is a gay Origin Story.

This is a guide not a gospel.

Drummer was a first draft of leather history.

This popular culture memoir about *Drummer* is a second draft in nineteen fluid chapters of interwoven eyewitness testimony. As in Akira Kurosawa's film *Rashomon* or Lawrence Durrell's novels in *The Alexandria Quartet*, what may seem like repetition is the quantum build of testimony from many *Drummer* eyewitness insiders experiencing the same things and coming away with differing truths, even as, over time, each is also changing his or her own memory's spiraling point of view. What happened depends on whom you ask. I hope this *frisson* encourages readers to peruse the rich text and fire up their own critical thinking. This is oral history about the institutional memory of *Drummer* written down for remembrance. This is memoir ricocheting off Gertrude Stein's *Everybody's Autobiography*.

Readers may understand the huge task of writing history that includes the melodrama of so many of our own lives lived in the first liberated decades of gay life and gay publishing after Stonewall. The legacy of *Drummer* has many sides and to ignore one or the other because it is untidy is to subtract from the total. Willie Walker, the founder of the San Francisco GLBT Historical Society wrote: "*Drummer* was a center of a whole cultural phenomenon....and its editor Jack Fritscher is a prolific writer who since the late sixties has helped document the gay world and the changes it has undergone....if queer people do not preserve our own history, most of it will simply disappear."

Drummer helped create the very culture it reported on. *Drummer* was a revolutionary idea in motion. In our leather archetribe, *Drummer* vicariously portrayed our desires to organize our thoughts to inform our practices.

Drummer published 214 issues from June 1975 to April 1999, and quit business on Folsom Fair weekend, September 30, 1999. A stack of 214 issues of *Drummer* is a coffee-table sculpture 3.5 feet tall weighing 120 pounds. Laid flat, top-to-bottom, *Drummer* stretches sixty-four yards: two-thirds of the length of a football field.

Drummer was the autobiography of us all, or at least a lot of us, written and drawn and photographed by many of us to entertain the rest of us from 1975 to its end in 1999.

At a rough ninety pages per issue, *Drummer* comprised a total 20,000 pages of advocacy journalism created by hundreds of writers, artists, photographers, and designers including even more thousands of revealing autobiographical Personals ads written by readers, with advertisers displaying their own commercial wares as pop-culture signifiers of the times. It took a village to fill *Drummer*. It took the Village People to act it out.

A group photo of every person who helped create *Drummer* would rival the cover of *Sgt. Pepper's Lonely Hearts Club Band*.

So how does this "J. Alfred Prufrock" dare to eat a peach, and wear my leather trousers rolled?

As its founding San Francisco editor-in-chief for nearly three years (March 17, 1977-December 31, 1979) and its most frequent contributor of writing and photography during twenty-four years, I enjoyed backstage access that over time made me one of many eyewitnesses of its evolving institutional history under the three publishers, John Embry (1975-1986), Anthony DeBlase (1986-1992), and Martijn Bakker (1992-1999). Keeping notes during 24 years, I observed *Drummer* for 2.5 times longer than Embry who owned *Drummer* for only 11 years, and fought with it for 13 years; and 4 times longer than DeBlase who struggled with *Drummer* for 6 years, and Bakker who killed *Drummer* in an assisted suicide that took 7 years.

Editing monthly *Drummer* daily in real time was a wild literary ride in gay popular culture when readers demanded authenticity and truth in reporting the emergence of BDSM rites and rights. Near the end of *Drummer*'s first five years at the end of 1979, by chance of good fortune, I had edited half of the *Drummer* issues in existence.

SHOULD AULD ACQUAINTANCE BE FORGOT

"What rollicking fun...to reopen old friendships and even some ancient hostilities of that golden age. To be a bystander to those vibrant talents and hear again those voices.... Can you imagine the pleasure in being able to put one's arms around some of those people, just like you maybe should have done back then when they were still around and available?"

"What happened in 1977 could fill a book. We hired A. Jay's friend, Jack Fritscher, as editor-in-chief, and bought a building on Harriet Street."

—John Embry, *Manifest Reader* 33 (1997) and *Drummer* 188 (September 1995), 20th Anniversary Issue

---

With a 42,000 copy press run for each issue in the 1970s, and with a pass-along rate of at least one reader in addition to each subscriber, approximately 80,000 people handled each issue of *Drummer* for an estimated total nearing twenty million people. The mobbed Folsom Street Fair in San Francisco hosts 100,000 leather guests every September. Even if publisher Embry, the self-appointed antagonist in this history, exaggerated his claim of 42,000 monthly copies and did a press run of only 21,000 copies, each issue of *Drummer* would have passed through the hands of nearly 50,000 people. In gay book publishing, 5,000 copies sold is considered a best seller.

Drummer was a people's magazine that helped invent modern gay publishing as we know it. First came the magazines in the 1970s and then the book publishers in the 1980s. More eyes have likely read one issue of *Drummer* than have read any one book by any deeply established GLBT author on the top hundred list of best-sellers in the gay literary canon, including James Baldwin, John Rechy, Rita Mae Brown, Edmund White, and Larry Kramer.

A book is published once while a magazine renews its lively connection to readers monthly. That's why, having been a young and tenured university professor and a founding member of the American Popular Culture Association in 1968, I added the tag line to the masthead of *Drummer* 23 (July 1978): "The American Review of Gay Popular Culture."

Drummer was a home and a home run. For thirty years, among the millions of leatherfolk in North America and Europe, there was hardly a player alive who had not heard of or read *Drummer*. Years after *Drummer* closed, readers continue to report that as teenagers they had managed to find *Drummer*, even in Iowa and Arkansas, and that the assertive primer that was *Drummer* had mentored, shaped, and emboldened their gender and kink identities. There was political empowerment in erotic representation.

MARCHING ORDERS
Printed on the Contents Page
in every issue except 4-12

"If a man does not keep pace with his companions, perhaps it is because he hears a different drummer. Let him step to the music which he hears, however measured or far away.
—Henry David Thoreau, *Walden: Or, Life in the Woods* (1854)

The liberal beauty of *Drummer* was its social permissiveness anchored in marching to one's own drummer. Self-reliance was the *Drummer* philosophy. *Drummer* was descriptive—not prescriptive—about leather behavior. Descriptive *Drummer* was non-judgmental in simply reporting how grass-roots leather lives were actually lived without commandments. Even though the *Drummer* editorial voice was a "Top" seducing subscribers who mostly liked to read from a deliciously overpowered "bottom" point of view, *Drummer* was no domineering Dutch uncle demanding, "Thou Shalt" or "Thou Shalt Not." *Drummer* never prescribed that there was a politically correct way to live leather because while there may be rules around sex, nobody's sure what they are.

Drummer was never Old Guard or New Guard.

Drummer was always Avant Garde.

SINGING SONGS FROM A TIME SOME DANCE TO REMEMBER

For those aching with a personal nostalgia for the Auld Lang Syne of Leather, think of where you were when you first read *Drummer*.

For those born in 1980 as the speeding Titanic 1970s cruised into the iceberg of HIV, you were nineteen when *Drummer* closed; but if you have intellectual or emotional or erotic curiosity about the way we were, and how high we flew, during the last twenty-five years of the twentieth-century, consider how the black-box flight recorder I have recovered from the take-off, cruising altitude, and crash of *Drummer* may reveal how *Drummer* shaped the gay popular culture of leather and kink for the twenty-first century.

David "Trooper" Vargo
Mr. Florida Drummer 1992, and
International Mr. Drummer, First Runner-Up

Drummer was my bible, my textbook for Life. I still have every issue in my possession (safely tucked away in an air-controlled storage unit). Yes, there are pages that are covered in notes, and some pages are still sticky. Some pages have tears and rips and holes. But so do I. I learned how to be a Man from *Drummer*. I learned how to "play" from *Drummer*. I learned how to conduct myself as a Leatherman from *Drummer*, and most importantly I discovered who I was and who I continue to be from the pages of *Drummer* magazine. It came at a time when I was just coming out not only as a gay man but as a Leatherman. It all happened at once. I was young and impressionable, and *Drummer* resonated deep within my psyche, a mystical union between a boy and the printed page. I followed it to the letter. And when it died, I mourned its loss like the death of a best old friend. Thank you, Jack, in many ways, you raised me.
—David Vargo, Mr. Florida Drummer 1992, International Mr. Drummer First Runner-Up, June 20, 2012

Richard Hunter,
Owner, Mr. S Leather Co.
San Francisco

Most of us may never have had the introduction to this Leather scene had it not been for John Embry and the Original *Drummer* Magazine....I know it's how I first realized I wasn't alone in all my perverted fantasies. Finding that *Drummer* magazine on a news stand in New Orleans in 1981 changed my life....and you can see where it all led for me [into a stylish leather goods business serving the community]. Tens of thousands of guys worldwide read *Drummer* every month and felt a bonding connection to each other because of it.
—Richard Hunter, Owner, *Mr. S Leather Co. Newsletter*, October 13, 2010

Erotic writing begins with one stroke of the pen and ends with many strokes of the penis. Paying my dues while editor-in-chief, I had by the end of 1979 contributed 147 pieces of writing and 266 photographs under my own byline or my pen names for writing, using "Denny Sargent" and "Eric van Meter" once each, and for photography, "Larry Olson" once, and "David Sparrow" and "Sparrow Photography" many times, as well as beginning in the mid-1980s, "Palm Drive Video." Estimating that each ninety-page issue of *Drummer* equaled a nearly four-hundred-page trade paperback book, I edited 942 pages of *Drummer* 18-33, the equivalent of a 3,778-page book.

Following the popular 1960s style of the New Journalism of American writers Tom Wolfe, Norman Mailer, Gay Talese, and George Plimpton who immersed themselves in a subject or an experience to write what they knew with authenticity and authority, *Drummer* created, coached, validated, and enabled the authentic voices of many leatherfolk who, freely outing themselves as eyewitnesses inside the kink BDSM scene, reported what they knew in their grass-roots and first-person you-are-there articles, stories, drawings, and photographs.

"The *Drummer* Salon" was so named by member Samuel Steward/Phil Andros who was part of Gertrude Stein's Salon. Included variously among many talents identified with *Drummer* were Jeanne Barney, Robert Mapplethorpe, Tom of Finland, Al Shapiro, Larry Townsend, Etienne, Anthony DeBlase, A. Jay, Rex, Chuck Arnett, Mark I. Chester, Joseph W. Bean, Lou Thomas, Bill Ward, Mikal Bales, David Sparrow, Steven Saylor, Old Reliable David Hurles, Domino, Jim Kane, Roger Earl, Patrick Califia, Hank Trout, Guy Baldwin, Jim Wigler, Olaf, Rick Leathers, Judy Tallwing McCarthy, The Hun, Fred Halsted, Robert Opel, George Birimisa, Tim Barrus, Rick Castro, Mr. Marcus Hernandez, Rick Leathers, Jim Stewart, Wickie Stamps, and Robert Davolt.

FOUNDING LA EDITOR-IN-CHIEF JEANNE BARNEY, WOMEN IN *DRUMMER*, AND GENDER

At Stonewall in 1969, gay character changed. At the founding of *Drummer* in 1975, leather character changed. In that first decade of gay liberation after Stonewall, homosexuality itself changed from not daring to speak its name to shouting out its many erotic identities.

Drummer led the gay liberation stampede out of the closet with transformational erotica. To write about the new psychology as well as emerging sex acts previously unnamed in polite society, we introduced or created new images and new concepts, and coined new vocabulary that advanced the gay cultural conversation with words like *homomasculinity* with its complement *homofemininity*.

Starting with Jeanne Barney, the founding Los Angeles editor-in-chief, *Drummer* began as a men's magazine, but it was never separatist. Even as our core subscribers identified themselves in the Personals ads as masculine men whose point of desire was masculinity itself, *Drummer* continued to evolve editorially to include in its innate reader-responsiveness leatherwomen and leatherfolk of diverse gender-fluid identities in our leather archetribe. Of its two founding activist editors, Barney showcased gender-bender drag in *Drummer* 9, and I authored the first article on women in *Drummer* in my feature essay on Society of Janus founder Cynthia Slater in *Drummer* 27.

In fact, much of *Drummer*'s early tone came from the generous heart and inventive mind of Jeanne Barney (issues 1-11) whose brave eyewitness testimony in this book is essential and brilliantly honest. Barney envisioned the Los Angeles infant *Drummer* as a kind of *Evergreen Review*. I thought of the San Francisco teenaged *Drummer* as the gay love child of the New Journalism in *Esquire* and the straight pulp S&M of men's mid-century adventure magazines featuring bondage, kink, and sex, like *Argosy*, *Saga*, *Soldier of Fortune*, and *True: The Men's Magazine*.

Barney, whose relation to Embry caused her to want to quit during production of issue two, edited only those first eleven issues before she split from the contentious publisher whose personal *Drummer* Blacklist bullied contributors, destroyed reputations, and triggered shameful partisan infighting that, to this day, causes covetous and abusive separatist elites to continue to duke out what leather persons or leather groups own leather culture which is too diverse to be claimed by anyone.

Even so, for many years, Pat Califia, who transitioned into Patrick Califia, was an associate editor and wrote a popular and educational monthly pan-sexual advice column. Cynthia Slater, co-founder of the female-piloted Society of Janus, was often consulted, interviewed, and reported on importantly. Anne Rice, who, despite feminist fantasy, never wrote for *Drummer*, was represented three times with brief excerpts from her novels. Frequent contributor Judy Tallwing McCarthy, International Ms. Leather 1987, wrote about the politics of gender in the landmark issue, *Drummer* 100, and her "Gay Birds" S&M cartoons ran for more than a year. The second female managing editor and editorial director was gothic novelist and filmmaker Wickie Stamps who bravely fashioned *Drummer* issues 183 to 208 against all odds during its crash in the 1990s.

Susie Bright, founding editor of the lesbian magazine *On Our Backs*, wrote, "The gay men who edited *Drummer* were our mentors in many ways:

John Rowberry, John Preston, and Jack Fritscher." *(Susie Bright's Journal*, "A Brief History of *On Our Backs*, 1984-1991," November 15, 2011)

Leather pioneer and historian Viola Johnson, founder of the resource-rich Carter/Johnson Leather Library, recalled a delightful gender friendly story in her *C/JLL Newsletter*, March 2011, about kink-identified women in Greenwich Village discovering *Drummer* in the 1970s during what happened to be my three-year tenure as editor-in-chief creating issues 18 to 33, March 1977 to December 31, 1979.

> In the...1970s, Jill and I sporadically read hand-me-down copies of *Drummer*. Yes, I was a woman married to another woman, but I still loved looking at the male form. Beauty is beauty regardless of sex or gender. I knew the date and the time *Drummer* would hit the only newsstand in the Village that sold it....I couldn't wait to get my hands on the latest adventures of Mr. Benson and his slave Jamie. Then one night after a Eulenspiegel (TES) meeting a group of us went out to eat and one of the dominants at the table asked if anyone would loan her their *Drummer*.... Within a few minutes all the women at the table, dominant and submissive were talking about *Drummer* and what they liked or read in the magazine. We were all surprised to know that there were other women who read *Drummer* also. It didn't matter that *Drummer* was a gay men's magazine. We read *Drummer*, learned from it and enjoyed it.

MAGICAL THINKING, TOM OF FINLAND, AND THE ALGORITHM OF THE MARLBORO MAN

Masturbation is magical thinking. So, initially, what we did to make *Drummer* pulsate hard was add realism and availability to the spank bank fantasies of one-handed readers who wanted a virile magazine that made the frontiers of newly liberated sex seem possible, accessible, and boundless. What they wanted they found in the homomasculine media image of themselves as newly minted leathermen come alive in the *cinema verite* stories and the *reality-show* photos and drawings reflecting what gay men really did at night.

Drummer changed the homophobic image of queers into the Platonic Ideal of the masculine-identified new gay man. And the algorithm of the new label "Leatherman" went viral in American popular culture, films, and fashion.

The Tom of Finland Foundation, headed by Durk Dehner, declared that "*Drummer*, groundbreaking for its time, set precedence for all homomasculine representation to come."

Years ago when I was thirty-seven, I arrived at *Drummer* with seventeen years' experience in magazine publishing. In the Swinging Sixties of Andy Warhol and Pop Art, I had taken my cue from one of the most successful, influential, and erotic popular-culture advertising campaigns in history. I mindfully took scissors and cut dozens of Marlboro Man ads from magazines and glued the iteration of icons, like a meaningful repetition of Warhol Soup Cans, into studied meditation collages to reveal their masturbatory essence. So, in the 1970s, I based the algorithm of "the Platonic Ideal of the Leatherman" in *Drummer* on that quintessentially American image of the self-reliant Marlboro Man whose rugged existential appeal as homomasculine avatar was his cool independence because he marched to no drummer but his own.

WARHOL, SHILTS, KEPNER: THE TRADITION OF BOOKS WRITTEN ABOUT THE INSTITUTIONAL MEMORY OF GAY MAGAZINES

Knowledge accumulates. We each contribute our bit, and history selects what evolution needs to enlighten itself. During the twenty years of sleuthing, interviewing, studying, researching, and writing for this book, and its companion volume, *Gay San Francisco: Eyewitness Drummer* (2008), I found good company in several books written specifically about the institutional memory of magazines, especially *Interview* magazine editor Bob Colacello's *Holy Terror: Andy Warhol Close Up*, Mark Thompson's and Randy Shilts' *The Advocate History of the Gay and Lesbian Movement*, and the great Jim Kepner's *Rough News, Daring Views: 1950s Pioneer Gay Press Journalism* (1998), a memoir of politics, philosophy, and personalities inside gay publishing at *ONE* magazine that led to the founding of the ONE National Gay and Lesbian Archives in virtually the same way that *Drummer*, steered by its publisher DeBlase in concert with pioneer photographer Chuck Renslow, led to the founding of the Leather Archives & Museum.

Because testimony can be hearsay without corroboration from a second witness, the fact-checked investigative journalism in this book is constructed 1) on the testimony of dozens of eyewitnesses, to whom I am forever grateful, as well as 2) on the internal evidence found in *Drummer* itself, and 3) in the journals, diaries, letters, photographs, interviews, recordings, magazines, and newspapers in the gay popular culture and leather archives my husband Mark Hemry and I, following the advice of the American Popular Culture Association, have collected and curated since the early 1960s.

My labor of love is not the last word on *Drummer* because *Drummer* is as mysterious a creation as the "Mona Lisa" whose creator and smile are as enigmatic as *Drummer*'s own creators and mystique. Each artwork has penetrated cultural consciousness. So many mysteries remain inside *Drummer*'s acculturations of journalism, fiction, poetry, stage plays, film scripts, art, and photography, that even I who have read every page, can only begin to introduce the *Drummer* Origin Story of who created what with whom, where, when, how, and, maybe, why.

Riffing on closeted poet T. S. Eliot's existential gay man, "J. Alfred Prufrock" who dares question everything, I penned these analogous lines to explain my concerns and motivations for the Sisyphean challenge of writing this book.

> Sometimes iconoclasm is a good thing.
> Sometimes a memoir is a portrait
> in a fun house mirror.
> Sometimes it pays to investigate
> where truth lies.
> Sometimes it's wise to dare
> to wear one's trousers rolled,
> and to eat a peach,
> because in the empty rooms
> the queerfolk come and go
> speaking of Michael and Angelo.

Against all odds, *Drummer* survived twenty-four years of stress not only from mismanagement, but also from censorship, plague, and politics that, in one early plot twist of bad luck becoming good luck, got the *Drummer* staff and forty subscribers arrested by the LAPD in 1976, causing the ten-month-old infant *Drummer* to move from disaster in Los Angeles to destiny in San Francisco. *Gay Pioneers* is a living history of leatherfolk written in human blood tattooed on tribal skin.

ARCHIVING *DRUMMER*

Drummer is the Rosetta Stone of leather heritage.

"Who'd a thunk it?" Vanilla author Andrew Halloran snapped in *Christopher Street*, Issue 231, November 1995. "Who'd a thunk that one day back issues of *Drummer* would be displayed in glass cases at a library like this (the John Hay Library at Brown University)?"

Or that *Drummer* would be represented in the permanent collections of many institutions including the John Hay, the Getty Museum and Research Center, the Kinsey Institute, the Los Angeles County Museum of Art, the San Francisco GLBT Historical Society Museum, the Leslie-Lohman Museum in New York, the Leather Archives & Museum of Chicago, and the ONE National Gay & Lesbian Archives at the University of Southern California.

Or that *Drummer* would be featured fearlessly and prominently on screen as a driving cultural force in Fenton Bailey and Randy Barbato's award-winning HBO documentary, *Mapplethorpe: Look at the Pictures* (2016).

HAIL AND FAREWELL

The rise and fall of *Drummer* happened during the best of times after Stonewall and the worst of times after the onslaught of AIDS.

My writer-hero Jack Kennedy, for whom I campaigned and voted in 1960, was president for only thirty-four months of accomplishment while I, as editor-in-chief for thirty-three months, just before the news of HIV, was also granted a once-in-a-lifetime gift to shape the monthly "leather community diary" that was *Drummer* during that exciting first decade of gay liberation when masculine gay men first uncloseted a sex-positive homomasculine identity before Anita Bryant's fundamentalist culture war, and politically correct Marxism, and separatist feminism, and killer plague ripped at the human heart of gay society.

> "I know what I have given you. I do not know what you have received."
> —Antonio Porchia, Argentinian poet, 1886-1968

I like to think I authored some good writing of my own in *Drummer*, and more, that, as editor-in-chief, I encouraged and nurtured and published some of the next generation of beginning writers in that first decade of liberated neophytes learning the self-shaping words of self-identifying sex.

I enjoy dancing to remember the authors, artists, and photographers who came to me with their first uncloseted work in their hopeful hands, and the looks on their faces when I accepted them for their first publication. I thank them all as much as I thank the readers who sent so many wonderful letters to the editor.

Because history is *Rashomon* in its many points of view, I've written three books around the richly diverse *Drummer* experience including this one, plus *Gay San Francisco: Eyewitness Drummer*, and *Some Dance to Remember: A Memoir-Novel of San Francisco 1970-1982*.

Oh! Allegedly. I must mention *allegedly*.

In the vertigo of memory, I wrote these eyewitness objective notes and subjective opinions about all these public personalities, and the public lives they led, *allegedly*, because in my finite limits I can only analyze events, manuscripts, and how we people all seemed when we were thrown together, and not the true hearts of persons.

In a sense, writing *Drummer*'s institutional history keeps these 20th-century gay pioneers and players alive in a kind of group eulogy. As a survivor of the Titanic 1970s, I enjoy sharing my own nostalgia for that golden age of gay sex and *Drummer*. While nothing compares to Proust nibbling on his madeleine, I love the smell of old magazines.

It's too sentimental, but, sometimes at night, sitting by the fire, nearing eighty, I love the feel of *Drummer* in my hands while leafing through the stories and articles and photographs of how we were when we were creating the way we were before things fell apart.

What heroes. What villains. What fun.

I adore Jeanne Barney.

I cherish Tony DeBlase.

I'd still shake John Embry's hand.

On his eightieth birthday in 2010, I sent him roses.

Jack Fritscher
San Francisco

* * * *

The thoughts and opinions expressed and alleged in this book are those of the individual contributors alone and do not necessarily reflect my views any more than my own alleged opinions and allegations reflect theirs. To all of them, especially the one and only Jeanne Barney, founding Los Angeles editor-in-chief of *Drummer*, I remain forever grateful.

"Flash back, not too far back, to one of our favorite resources:
Drummer Magazine."
—Leather Archives & Museum of Chicago, July 9, 2012

"*Drummer* was map of leather culture.
Fritscher and his book are unabashed and uninhibited tour guides."
—Chuck Renslow, Founder, Chicago Leather Archives & Museum,
and of the International Mr. Leather Contest (IML)

* * * *

"Proust was transported by his tea and his petite madeleine.
I love the damp yellow smell of old magazines
that take me back in time to the way we were."
—Jack Fritscher

"A shady business never yields a sunny life."
—B. C. Forbes, founding publisher, Forbes Magazine

DRUMMER

ISSUE 133 / $5.95

JACK FRITSCHER ON
ROBERT MAPPLETHORPE
"INTELLIGENT PEOPLE MAKING EXCELLENT..."

FAKIR MUSAFAR
EXPLORING THE SEXUAL-SPIRITUAL FRONTIER

MEN WITH NO NAME
PART II OF THE DUNGEONS OF E...

THE MEN OF
MOTORSEXUAL

DISTRIBUTION TO MINORS PROHIBITED

Cover Photograph by Jim Wigler

CHAPTER 1

A MASTER'S THESIS
DRUMMER'S BIG BANG

Its Creation. Its Evolution.
Its Civil War. Its Culture War.
Its Origin Story.

A Popular Culture Magazine of Gay Gender Identity

Who Did What to Whom When Where and Sometimes Why
How the Leather Boys in the Band Played on

- Who Founded and Created *Drummer*? An Eyewitness Narrative Timeline Featuring the Cast of Characters at *Drummer*
- The Drummer Slave Auction, Saturday, April 10, 1976, Publisher John Embry Arrested for the Crime of Slavery; Val Martin, the First Mr. Drummer, Tells All
- How Los Angeles *Drummer* Became San Francisco *Drummer*
- Blood, Fingerprints, and DNA: History Is the Internal Evidence Printed in the *Drummer* Text
- Buyer's Remorse and Seller's Remorse; the Cloning of *Drummer*
- Blood Feud: How the Second and Third Publishers of *Drummer*, Anthony DeBlase and Martijn Bakker, Reviled First Publisher John Embry Who Reviled Them Both; The Contempt between John Embry and Larry Townsend

With its cast of writers, artists, and photographers, the *mise en scene* of *Drummer* was important to gay identity because in its 214 issues over twenty-four years, *Drummer* created the very post-Stonewall leather culture it reported on. *Drummer* helped readers examine their boundaries, step into the closeted heartland of their erotic identities, find the true north of their homomasculine gender identities, and make their own new narratives.

In March 1977, John Embry hired me as editor-in-chief to assist his move from Los Angeles to San Francisco, and to write the *Drummer* story inside the magazine.

Drummer was a first draft of leather history.

This memoir of *Drummer* is a second.

This is a story of some talented artists and some unsympathetic persons, with some discomfiting eyewitness testimony about the pressures of art and commerce on the moral actions of writers and publishers during the first decade of gay liberation after the Stonewall Rebellion in 1969. *Drummer* was to me what Chawton village was to Jane Austen who also wrote about "a world in small" with characters reflecting the human condition.

> "I never foresaw the impact that *Drummer* would have.
> It was a big surprise to me....I'm amazed."
> —John Embry to Robert Davolt, 2003

John Embry was not a pure bully only because nobody's perfect.

This is a backstage story born of a whisper, anchored in evidence, and told by many insiders interested in the truths rather than the legends about *Drummer*.

It is a cautionary tale about esthetic, psychological and financial abuse, as well as betrayal in the gay community.

It is a representative history, universal in its specifics, of the 1% of publishers exploiting the 99% of writers, artists, and photographers. An internet search for "bad publishers" yields 74,800,000 results in 0.23 seconds.

In our transparent age of social communication, nothing is secret anymore.

This book was ninety percent written when its present-tense immediacy changed the morning John Embry died in his sleep on September 16, 2010.

John Embry (1926-2010), born a Methodist in Winslow, Arizona, moved to Los Angeles to study art, was drafted into the U.S. Army (1949), and sold advertising in Hawaii and LA before his involvement with H.E.L.P., the Homophile Effort for Legal Protection that rescued gay men entrapped by the Los Angeles Police Department. The slick life in LA suited his business style perfectly. In 1971, his fledgling mail-order business, the "Leather Fraternity," selling poppers and leather wristbands, needed a small-format brochure whose sales pitch he cleverly insinuated within his editorial and advertising coverage of bars and restaurants such as the Glass Onion, the Sewers of Paris, the Bitter End West, and the Bla Bla Café in Studio City. In December, he debuted his first mini-mag "trial balloon" and titled it

Drummer, listing himself (and not his alter-ego "Robert Payne") as managing editor, and Dagmar King (*Drummer*'s first female employee) as art director, with fiction by Larry Townsend.

Always controversial and frequently exposed in the press because of his trickster business practices, Embry, the publisher who had two faces, quickly became a Los Angeles character whose twenty-five-cent bi-weekly magazine, in the end, ran away from him to San Francisco where it achieved an international cultural reach beyond his LA vision.

Drummer was a noble undertaking, but with the rebellious hubris of a bottom taunting a top, founding *Drummer* publisher Embry provoked the Los Angeles Police Department so relentlessly in the first pages of the first issue of his bi-weekly zine *Drummer* (December 1, 1971, page 31) and in the first issue of monthly *Drummer* (June 20, 1975) that he nearly destroyed the magazine when he caused the LAPD to arrest him and forty-one other leatherfolk at the infamous Drummer Slave Auction in 1976.

For years, the relentless Police Chief Ed Davis was Embry's Inspector Javert, but Embry, who taunted Davis personally in print, was no innocent Jean Valjean. He stuffed *Drummer* with shady topics that drove Davis crazy. Former *Drummer* editor Joseph W. Bean observed in *Drummer* 188, page 17: "The first four issues of monthly *Drummer* featured slavery, SM, incest, phone sex, piss play, fist fucking, art, movies, plays, porn, and, to see what buttons really could be pushed, a piece on necrophilia as a fetish." He could have added the bestiality themes and underage sex ads and Nazi display ads that Embry fancied made him and his petulant *Drummer* politically relevant in that first decade of gay liberation after Stonewall.

In 1973, the American Psychiatric Association declared that homosexuality was not a mental illness. In 1975, the future mayor of San Francisco, Willie Brown, personally moved civilization forward with the passage of the "California Consenting Adults Law." During the founding of *Drummer*, gay sex was changing into something psychologically defensible and legal. Thus thwarted, LAPD Police Chief Ed Davis had to scramble to invent new constitutional grounds for arresting queers. Davis decided the best way to destroy *Drummer* was to use its contents against itself—in the same way I use *Drummer* contents to find its identity and prove its history. His approach was biblical: "Out of their own mouths they shall be condemned." Davis, convinced that *Drummer* was subversive, studied the writing in *Drummer* so he could destroy *Drummer* and the "sick" leather culture that threatened Davis more than did effete drag culture.

It was easy for a fundamentalist like Davis to deconstruct the text of *Drummer* which had those references to underage sex, as well as an emerging gay vocabulary where the words *boy* and *slave* were evolving to new meanings beyond the linguistic ability of the LAPD. To destroy the upstart *Drummer*, Davis decided to arrest publisher Embry for committing the crime of, not sodomy, but slavery. At the "Great Slave Auction" on Saturday night, April 10, 1976, at the Mark IV Health Club, Davis and his stormtroopers rounded up 125 leatherfolk and arrested forty-one men, and one woman, *Drummer* editor-in-chief, Jeanne Barney.

The infant *Drummer* was only five issues and ten months old.

Ten years later, John Embry, still shaken but not stirred to greatness by adversity, sold *Drummer* in 1986 to Anthony F. DeBlase who sold it in September 1992 to the Dutch publisher, Martijn Bakker, who Amsterdamned the American classic.

In fact, *Drummer* had been in such deep trouble with the law when Embry asked me to become the editor-in-chief in March 1977, I must have been out of my mind to ink our deal. The entire time I was editor of *Drummer*, Embry was on probation, continuously in court, and sentenced to community service.

Drummer had a dangerous history.

If I play "pinball" with *Drummer*, shooting the silver ball past the kick-up holes through the chase lights, using the flippers, risking TILT, all to make the score add up on the back glass, well, it lights up with something like the following facts and opinions.

If there is a point here, it is first to establish the history of *Drummer* itself, as well as the vast archive of leather history incidentally hidden in its pages.

Second, it is to answer the call to "Save Leather Culture" sounded at the height of the AIDS epidemic by Anthony DeBlase who with Chuck Renslow founded the Leather Archives & Museum of Chicago. Embry himself wrote in *Alternate Reader* (1995): "These days it is up to the survivors to pick up the mantle and fill in some of our terrible voids."

Third, it is also up to the critical thinking of discerning readers as well as of literary historians, culture critics, and queer theorists to examine the role of *Drummer*, its owners, and its contributors, as well as its evolving content that helped create and shape leather culture itself. Readers who had never considered smoking a cigar as a fetish changed their minds in May 1978 upon discovering the feature-article instructions of "Cigar Blues" in *Drummer* 22 which ignited the cigar fetish in bars beginning that summer.

During the magazine's twenty-four years and through all three owner-publishers, I was the fated eyewitness participant who was in sum the most frequent contributor of editing, writing, photography, and display advertising to *Drummer*. My observations are those of a pioneer, a participant, and a university trained detective of literary history. I have a resume tied to media innovation in academia as well as in magazines, books, and video. As a critical thinker, I hope I am both objective and intimate enough eyewitness to be a professional keeper of the institutional memory of *Drummer*.

As a journalist, I have taken care to interview multiple eyewitnesses and to fact-check everything possible because *Drummer* is a vastly underestimated treasure trove of leather history and gay popular culture. I have studied every issue of *Drummer* to find in its pages the internal evidence needed to support a revealing narrative of *Drummer* history, using the magazine text itself.

Nevertheless, because I am a fallible human writing about other fallible humans, I wish to give the benefit of the doubt to all the living and dead involved, and, so, what I write in this book I write allegedly.

THAR HE BLOWS! EMBRYONIC YOUNG *DRUMMER*

If Embry was cruisin' for a bruisin', he got it. He published heated accusations against the LAPD in both *Drummer* 6 (May 1976), and in the nuclear challenge of "Getting Off" in *Drummer* 9 (October 1976). All gays love the bravado of I-Am-Who-I-Am Broadway anthems. But, if not his gay fear, where was his gay caution?

After the arrests, most of the small *Drummer* staff fled. Because of telephone taps at their homes, search warrants for their houses, police cars tailing them, and ka-*ching* lawyers for the prosecution and defense, *Drummer* went into—what I call—its "First Coma" and for a year was on life support.

Founding Los Angeles editor-in-chief of *Drummer*, Jeanne Barney wrote to me on July 1, 2006:

> I did not "flee" because of the phone taps. My telephone had been tapped since the early 1970s when I first began writing for the original *Advocate*. I "fled" *Drummer* because I was tired of having to deal with John Embry's middle-of-the-night revisions, and because he owed me $13,000 in unpaid salary and for out-of-pocket payments to talent who would otherwise not have worked for us—and because I finally realized what a crook John Embry was, and I no longer wanted my name linked with his.

She added on November 12, 2006: "I left because of ethical and moral differences" with Embry.

During issues 6 to 11, legal, creative, and personal tensions ran high. The first Mr. Drummer was the Hispanic Vallot Martinelli, a native Argentinian, chosen, not in a contest, but in a business decision made in the *Drummer* office by John Embry, Al Shapiro, and me. "Val Martin" recalled his own Embry-caused stress in his interview with *Drummer* artist, Olaf Odegaard, in "Serving Two Masters, Or: The Great Slave Auction Bust," *Connection* (October 10-24, 1984): "From 1976 until 1979, we [Embry *et al.*] used to go to court almost every other week, every three weeks, every month [while Fritscher was editor]. On Christmas we had to go to court."

In *Drummer* 6, Embry wrote his own eyewitness version of the LAPD raid in a three-page essay with photographs, "*Drummer* Goes to a Slave Auction." Embry's first paragraph is an exercise in self-defense claiming—and this was always the controversial point—that his Slave Auction was a "private fund-raiser for charity." Always scheming, Embry was trying to out-trick the LAPD charge that he had planned the Slave Auction for "commercial reasons" to fund his own private "Leather Fraternity" club in *Drummer*, and that it was not "private," but open to the paying public. Noting that the aggressive LAPD bust that night was traumatic, Embry more importantly revealed the terrorizing ten months of LAPD harassment that the staff of *Drummer* suffered during the first year of publication. In *Drummer* 7 and *Drummer* 8, Embry continued his angry narrative in his publisher's column "In Passing." In *Drummer* 8, editor Jeanne Barney devoted her "Getting Off" column to the back story of the raid that so obsessed Embry she called it "a burning issue" in *Drummer* 6.

In San Francisco, I inherited this "burning" climate which was not sexy "hot" and asked Embry either to turn his emotions into an S&M porn story or give it a rest. His major complaint in a minor key was a turnoff. He rather much caused his legal troubles himself. National readers seeking erotica hardly cared about an old Los Angeles bathhouse raid that was not the Stonewall Rebellion Embry wanted to galvanize it into. From March 1977 through December 31, 1979, the entire time I was editor-in-chief, Embry was more than less absent because he had to drive his van round-trip from San Francisco to LA for his many court appearances with the legendary defense attorney Al Gordon, and he usually returned ranting, angry, and exhausted. Nerve-wracking legal problems, I think, contributed psychosomatically to his colon cancer in 1978. During the four months of his treatment, he was again absent from the *Drummer* office, leaving the production and creation of *Drummer* to art director Al Shapiro and me who created a new *Drummer* by coloring outside Embry's lines.

Embry was peeved that Al Gordon, and not Embry himself, became a quiet gay folk hero because of the Drummer Slave Auction. Embry always feared being upstaged by anyone helping him. In San Francisco, Embry refused to talk about Gordon who saved his skin. Embry never liked to admit he needed help. When the famous Gordon, 94, died in 2009, a year before the infamous Embry died at 83, the *Los Angeles Times* observed on September 6.

Albert L. Gordon, an attorney who helped advance gay rights in the 1970s and 1980s by challenging discriminatory practices and laws, including a successful effort to decriminalize consensual homosexual acts, died August 10 in Los Angeles. He was 94. Gordon, a heterosexual whose twin sons were gay, became a lawyer in his late 40s and devoted most of his practice to defending the rights of homosexuals and battling the bigotry of law enforcement...."Before there was a straight-gay alliance in America, there was Al Gordon," the Rev. Troy Perry, a longtime activist and founder of the gay-friendly Metropolitan Community Churches, said in an interview last week. "When other people wouldn't touch us, he did. He was a hero."

...One of Gordon's most memorable cases stemmed from a notorious raid on a gay bathhouse [the Mark IV] on Melrose Avenue in 1975 [actually, 1976], when scores of Los Angeles police officers broke up a mock slave auction staged as part of the entertainment for a gay community fund-raiser [*sic*]. Apparently not amused by the gimmick, the police treated the [*Drummer* magazine] event as actual human slave trafficking, a felony, and arrested 40 participants. Gordon helped win their release. He supported a second mock auction, organized by Perry to raise defense funds, by going on the auction block himself. He went for $369 to his wife, Lorraine.

Only gay historians may care, but this timeline of facts is wrong in the book *Gay L. A.* (2006) written by Stuart Timmons and Lillian Faderman in the way that is typical of vanilla authors confused by the texture of the leather subculture of which they are not a part, especially when they live in LA culture and do not understand at all the *mise en scene* of gay San Francisco history.

The first editor-in-chief, Jeanne Barney, exited *Drummer* with issue 11 although some of her completed work ran on through Los Angeles/San Francisco hybrid issues, *Drummer* 12 and 13. For a year after the arrest, April 1976 to April 1977, issues 11 to 18 were published with "Robert Payne" (aka John Embry) listed as "editor." It was a ritual that the fictitious "Robert Payne" always rode to the rescue when *Drummer* had no actual editor.

FRITSCHER TIMELINE INSIDE CLASSIC *DRUMMER*

1. Beginning in March 1977, I was editor-in-chief working out of my home at 4436 25th Street because Embry was still working out of his 311 California Street home. While he found and readied a San Francisco office, I studied *Drummer* and initiated my editorial make-over on theoretical and practical fronts. Proving no good deed goes unpunished, Embry, absentee because of court and cancer (1978-1979) seemed to feel that my make-over was a take-over.

2. My first association with *Drummer* was in *Drummer* 5 and *Drummer* 6, producing Phil Andros' aka Sam Steward's first stories for *Drummer*: "Baby Sitter" and "Many Happy Returns." Steward who was sixty-six, alcoholic, and depressed was grateful for my help in resurrecting in *Drummer* his earlier mid-century European publishing career inside *Der Kreis* magazine.

3. My first writing in *Drummer* appeared in *Drummer* 14 (May 1977) when I produced and wrote: "Men South of Market," page 46;

4. My second writing in *Drummer* 16 (June 1977) included producing and co-writing: "Tom Hinde Portfolio," pages 39-46;

5. My first *Drummer* byline was in *Drummer* 18, (August 1977) when I directed the photography and wrote the feature "The Leatherneck Bar," pages 82-85.

6. As needed, I worked as a producer on the intermediate Los Angeles/San Francisco hybrid issues, *Drummer* 14 to *Drummer* 18, assuming with each issue more responsibilities, and ghost-editing the entirety of *Drummer* 18. After I put *Drummer* on an August-December hiatus in order to collect its hysterical wits, I produced my first full issue, credited on the masthead as editor-in-chief, with *Drummer* 19 (December 1977).

7. The last of my work as editor-in-chief, but not of my writing and photography, appeared in *Drummer* 33 (December 1979). Embry was miffed that in August 1979 I had given early notice, not to strand him, but to phase out, and exit officially on December 31, 1979. Angry that I demanded my wages for my editing work, he fixed his face into a slow burn that exploded in flames. He was still a dubious newcomer from Los Angeles to San Francisco, and had depended on me, who had first arrived in San Francisco in 1961, as his best reference and introduction to local writers, artists, photographers, and models. By *Drummer* 33, he had completed the cleansing of my name which he had begun exorcizing in *Drummer* 31 (September

1979). All that autumn we played office tug-of-war negotiating contents, credit lines, and cash until we came to loggerheads.

8. Although in *Drummer* 31 Embry published two of my bylined articles, "Mr. International Leather" and "Do-ers Profile: Tony Plewik," he deleted my name twice in that issue: as editor-in-chief, and, most important to me, as photographer of the twenty-some centerfold photos of Val Martin and Bob Hyslop which I shot alone on Sunday, May 20, 1979. He also deleted my credit line for my final edit and serialization of the draft of John Preston's novel *Mr. Benson*.

9. By *Drummer* 32 and 33, I was disappearing until I was "disappeared." However in some instances, Embry published my unsigned work as he had Jeanne Barney's after she exited. Knowing Embry's tactics, I signed a couple of my pieces internally, one in *Drummer* 32 (October 1979) by using my birth day and month in the opening paragraph: "A Confidential *Drummer* Dossier: 20 June 1979," page 19. His "cleansing" plus his effort to "backfill" 31, 32, and 33 delayed *Drummer* 33, the Christmas issue, until late January 1980.

10. After six years on Embry's Blacklist, I was invited to return as a private paid consultant by new publisher Anthony F. DeBlase in *Drummer* 100 (October 1986). I continued contributing for a total run of 65 issues, and was listed on the masthead, till the end of *Drummer*, as both "contributing writer" and "photographer" along with my Palm Drive Video company named as "contributor," also to the end of *Drummer*.

11. As noted, during twenty-four years under all three owner-publishers, I was the most frequent contributor of editing, writing, and photography to *Drummer*, and thus intimate enough eyewitness to be keeper of the institutional memory of *Drummer*.

The last issue was *Drummer* 214 (April 1999). The business closed officially on Folsom Fair weekend, September 30, 1999. Happily, in the mid-1990s, while I continued contributing to *Drummer*, Embry and I reconciled in a Mexican stand-off when he asked to publish my writing in his new *MR* brand magazines, *Manifest Reader, Manhood Rituals,* and *Super MR*.

On the one hand, I had to admire Embry's brazenness in subject matter and bravado against censorship in 1975. But realistically, his brass balls meant the infant *Drummer* could barely survive, and certainly not in LA.

As founding San Francisco editor-in-chief, I was given my head to remodel Los Angeles *Drummer*, to re-box, and re-brand the product with—and here was the challenge—heat, guts, and aggressive masculinity, but in a new erotic way that was legal in most places. My desire was to reflect the niche tastes of its masculine-identified readers living, not only in regional LA, but also out in the diversity of our national American popular culture.

That was a hard dance on the killing ground. Without prejudice to other genders, it had to be done for love of men, love of writing, and not love of money, because the money at *Drummer* always evaporated mysteriously.

DIALING FOR DOLLARS

Warhol Superstar Joe Dallesandro recalled that at Andy's Factory in 1969, "A $100.00 was two-weeks salary for a forty-hour week and a movie or two." By 1979, worker income was the only thing that had not changed in the underground world of alternative art. To illustrate the salary scale and the Jurassic degree of clerical difficulty in the pre-computer age of 1977-1979, consider this. As full-time *Drummer* editor-in-chief, writing on yellow legal pads and a manual typewriter, I began at $200 a month. The minimum wage was $2.10 an hour. As the press run climbed to 42,000 copies per issue (Embry's statistic told to me when I asked him directly), I negotiated my salary to $400 a month.

Jeanne Barney told me about herself: "I was supposed to be paid $200 a week [$800 a month]." Atypically, the female editor-in-chief earned twice as much in 1976 as the male editor-in-chief did in 1977-1979. Barney continued: "Not only did I rarely receive that amount or anything close to it, as I've told you before, I frequently paid talent out of my own pocket."

The pay was exclusively for editing, and did not include my writing and photography for which in those sixty-five issues over twenty-four years I was never paid money, never once, not a cent, not by any *Drummer* publisher. (DeBlase paid me not for writing or photos, but as his personal creative consultant.) After I began my Palm Drive Video company in earnest in 1984, I opened to accepting ad space in dozens of magazines in trade for my writing and photography. My first Palm Drive Video display ad in *Drummer* appeared in issue 116 (May 1988), page 39, and the ads, with photos changing to keep them editorially fresh, continued virtually to the end of *Drummer*.

As a "zero-degrees of separation" autobiographical subtext to *Drummer*, my 1960s roots were deep in Chicago with my longtime friend Andy Charles, whom I knew years before he partnered with Anthony DeBlase. When the wealthy psychiatrist Andy Charles bought *Drummer* from Embry to amuse his lover DeBlase in 1986, Andy Charles wanted me involved to help float DeBlase's novice experience in publishing, particularly in publishing *Drummer*.

Andy Charles remained grateful to the day he died because of a chilling tale of a true-life capture-and-revenge story of a rapist-sadist who in 1969 held Charles, long before he met DeBlase, captive in bondage in Charles' high-end designer apartment on the North Shore. Working one hand free, Andy Charles reached his bedside telephone and called for rescue from his friends Dan Baus, my lover David Sparrow, and me who, because Chicago police were the enemy, had to break into the apartment and like gay vigilantes subdue the rapist and hold him until Andy Charles' then-lover returned from a business trip to take care of the situation.

But that's another outlaw story in the *Drummer* salon.

GAY PSEUDONYMS: NAMES ON THE CLOSET

Embry was two people in one. So with whom was I, a Gemini, dealing? Embry had legitimate right to his gay pseudonym "Robert Payne," but Embry could not have picked a more dangerous legal moment to market, in a mail-order sex business, what the LAPD had reason and prejudice to suspect was his "criminal alias."

Over time, as Embry alienated people with his Blacklist, as did David Goodstein with his Blacklist at *The Advocate*, I've noticed that through arrest, scandal, legal battles, bad reviews, collapsed creative relationships, cash problems, catastrophic illness, personal brickbats, erotic abandonment, and death, John Embry always relied on his alter-ego: Robert Payne.

Pseudonyms are a part of the split-case identities in gay life caused by homophobia. Because of onward-marching Christian soldiers, many gay folk have traditionally altered their names for privacy and safety against Inquisitions. In my first meeting as editor-in-chief with first-time *Drummer* author, John Preston, I advised him against using "Jack Prescott" for erotica such as his one-off novel *Mr. Benson*. I wonder if New Englander Preston, because of his sexual interest in domination, actively or subliminally chose the name because he was mesmerized by its closeness to his own as well as to the vertiginous power of New England politician Prescott Bush, father of President George Bush and grandfather of President George W. Bush? Other pseudonyms that seem real are: Larry Townsend, Aaron Travis, and Phil Andros; "Pat Califia" is a pseudonym that became the second pseudonym "Patrick Califia"; "Anne Rice" is also pseudonymous for "Howard Allen Frances Rice née O'Brien" as is "A. N. Roquelaure" who, despite urban legend, never wrote for *Drummer*, although her work was excerpted.

I make note that for all the bravado of the first two issues of *Drummer*, the closeted staff was so circumspect that, while they were bylined, they dared list no responsible names on the masthead: no publisher, no editor, no art director. It was *Drummer* 3 that first listed John Embry as publisher and Jeanne Barney as editor-in-chief.

Jeanne Barney told me:

> I, at least, was not "closeted." Indeed, I was the only writer to use her real name at the old *Advocate* so my name could not appear on another masthead. I was hands-on and off-site until we put together *Drummer* 3. John Embry put *Drummer* 1 and 2 together on his kitchen table. We didn't even have an office until it was time for *Drummer* 3. My name, however, did appear as a byline in each of those first two issues.

Before my friend, Al Shapiro, became art director whose work first appeared in *Drummer* 17 (July 1977), he had introduced me to Embry in March 1977. During that spring, *Drummer*, I observed subjectively, was hysterical, and still arriving in bits and pieces from LA, fleeing for sanctuary in San Francisco where Embry set up his home and office at 311 California Street. Traveling between two cities, while trying to escape one and set up business in the other, Embry produced his first hybrid LA-San Francisco issue with *Drummer* 12, February 1977. He had completely cleansed its pages of Jeanne Barney.

In truth, Embry hired me because I had twenty years' experience in editing magazines and books, because I had drawers-full of my original writing and photography to feed *Drummer*, and because I was socially and sexually connected into the grass-roots liberation leather culture of San Francisco. As a stranger in town, he figured the way to move forward was to climb on the back of anyone who mattered.

I knew people. He knew I knew people. One time I joked with him about bringing meat from farm to table: "I live it up to write it down. I have sex with all the men I write about. I fuck them in July, photograph them in August, and they're published in September." When I dedicated my gay popular-culture novel *Some Dance to Remember* to "the 13,000 veterans of the liberation wars," I was referencing John Rechy's concept in *Numbers*. Those 13,000 men were my sex partners with whom I balled and talked the truths of pillow talk during the positive and educational sex orgy of the Titanic 1970s. I might not have had an orgasm with each of them; but, with those 13,000 men in two-ways and three-ways and parties and orgies and sleep overs, the identity-revealing sex I remember so fondly was intimate enough—I swear to show how real and risky all this was—to have been able to catch, at worst, a temporary disease and, at best, the grass-roots temper of gay male psychology as grist for magazine articles, fiction, and photographs.

As a professionally educated journalist erotically identified with leather, patrolling the bars and baths and bistros of San Francisco and sexing my way into fuck-and-talk contact, I worked to employ my 1950s and 1960s magazine skills, ripening my reporter's factual insight and my documentarian's intuitive discernment into what gay men liked and what they wanted in the 1970s. Perhaps, my version of *Drummer* worked because it helped define the pop-culture of leathermen inventing a new lifestyle. As published inside *Drummer*, readers responded that my editing and writing reflected their grass-roots leather culture as it blossomed, making 1970s *Drummer*, the peoples' *Drummer*. The beauty of *Drummer* was that *Drummer* helped create the very leather culture it reported on, thus spreading leather identity farther. What *Drummer* started locally spread internationally.

Editor's Note

1971-1977: A *DRUMMER* TIMELINE

How *Drummer* was invented in Los Angeles and San Francisco and found its slowly emerging international character during the tumultuous first decade after Stonewall, helping create the very leather culture it reported on during the 1970s Golden Age of Leather.

I
Gestation and Birth

I. 1. 1971: In December, *Drummer* appears as a small "zine" on yellow newsprint reporting on bars, restaurants, and hairpieces in West Hollywood.

I. 2. 1973: *Drummer* appears as the samizdat political *H.E.L.P./Drummer Newsletter* slamming the LAPD for harassment, bar raids, and arrests.

I. 3. June 20, 1975: *Drummer* official first issue of 214 issues in large format with slick cover.

1.4. 1977: "The Year *Drummer* Nearly Died," fighting for survival, and virtually out of business while being retooled during two stoppages of four months (February-May) and five months (August-December).

II

On Hiatus: Four Near-Death Stoppages

II. 1. 1976 HIATUS #1 (April-December) is caused by the April 10 Slave Auction arrest by the LAPD whose continuing harassment, including court hearings against John Embry and *Drummer* staff, virtually stop the presses for eight months when the infant *Drummer* was less than a year old.

II. 2. 1977 HIATUS #2 (February to May) is caused by *Drummer* moving incrementally in John Embry's van from Los Angeles to San Francisco; founding LA editor-in-chief Jeanne Barney quits with *Drummer* 11; replacing her with no one, the distressed Embry lists himself as editor of *Drummer* 12-18; founding San Francisco editor-in-chief Jack Fritscher, having produced features and fiction by Sam Steward for teenage *Drummer*, is hired full-time March 1977 after ghost-editing parts of Embry's "half-LA and half-San Francisco hybrid" issues *Drummer* 15 through *Drummer* 18; Fritscher is first credited as the founding San Francisco editor-in-chief in *Drummer* 19.

Eyewitness Rewind: As a sex refugee in the culture wars, Embry assessed his own state of mind at the time and wrote about his tension-filled "Tale of Two Cities": "The change from 'LAPD Land' to San Francisco was like abandoning East Berlin for Oz." (January 29, 2008 email to Jeanne Barney). He repeated his psychology in his *Super MR* 5, page 39, and in his *Manifest Reader* 26, page 53: "The day we took the final load [of months' of loads] from LA and drove across the Bay Bridge for keeps, I felt like we had finally made it out of East Berlin." Upon its arrival, *Drummer* needed to get its bearings.

II. 3. 1977 HIATUS #3 (August-December) begins after publication of *Drummer* 18 (August) when new editor Fritscher quiets down production for four months with no new issues of *Drummer* until the first fully San Francisco issue of *Drummer* 19 (December), taking time to reorganize production operations, hire local staff, compose a style guide, and create new and emerging content and format while deleting references to minors, bestiality, and pro-Nazi ads; soon after, in early Autumn 1978, Embry, gut-sick with anxiety about his arrest, is diagnosed with colon cancer, goes absent from the office, has surgery on March 16, 1979, and again goes absent for recovery for four months leaving Fritscher and art director Al Shapiro the space and time of many months to reshape, reinvent, and revive LA *Drummer* into the San Francisco *Drummer* that resultantly went international, turning *Drummer* from a fledgling LA magazine into a thriving San Francisco magazine reflecting and amplifying the first

Golden Age of Leather: 1977-1979; with *Drummer* 21 as the Platonic Ideal of *Drummer*, those classic issues are *Drummer* issues 19-30.

III. 4. HIATUS #4 (October 1989-January 1990) happens without warning on October 17 when the Loma Prieta earthquake destroys the *Drummer* office, as well as the fiscal foundation of the Anthony DeBlase-Andrew Charles ownership of *Drummer*; monthly issues struggle out saved by editor Joseph W. Bean; the earthquake is also a metaphor of AIDS tectonically shifting the tone and contents of the magazine, and of DeBlase's faltering and unsustainable business model causing him to advertise inside *Drummer* 140 (June 1990) that the magazine is for sale to anyone; soon after Martijn Bakker of Amsterdam becomes the third and final, and foreign, publisher, closing the quintessentially American *Drummer* forever in September 1999.

DRUMMER AS PRIMARY HISTORICAL DOCUMENT

My father grew up as a child laborer on a Minnesota farm and escaped on an athletic scholarship to a small Illinois town where my mother was a cheerleader. Later they both worked in sales and marketing, surveying demographics. There is a show business axiom in Hollywood: "Will it play in Peoria?" Growing up there with that test-market consciousness, I was taught a heartland insight into American popular culture: Give the audience what it wants. So, synergistically, *Drummer* to me was a piece of cake. I was gay. I was leather. I was a writer. I was a founding member of the American Popular Culture Association in 1968. I aimed to gather, write, and publish what my leather pals wanted. *Drummer* was a way to put real stuff about real guys monthly between two covers.

Having taught magazine journalism as a tenured university professor for fifteen years, and then working as a corporate marketing professional from 1977 onwards with a full-time career at Kaiser Engineers the entire thirty-two months I edited *Drummer*, I felt I owed respect enough to Embry and to *Drummer* to be completely familiar with every form-and-content aspect of the magazine. So, as editor-in-chief, I paid to modernize my mid-century graphic skills at a UC Berkeley seminar conducted by Anthony Dubovsky and Marc Treib: "New Graphic Presentation Techniques for the Design Professional," June 1978. At Stanford University on March 24, 1979, this *Drummer* editor also won two Bay Area Golden Gate awards for technical writing and advertising design of corporate marketing brochures for Kaiser Engineers in Oakland.

I think there ought to be qualifications for being a gay publisher or gay author or gay critic or queer theorist other than just taking it up the ass. The pope's Pontifical College Josephinum taught me how to study the texts of Aquinas, Descartes, Marx, Jung, and even the Bible as a collection of folk tales told by an ancient tribe around campfires. The progressive Jesuit professors at Loyola University graduate school taught me how to limn literary analysis on Chaucer, Malory, Faulkner, and Woolf, with the vast dramas, short stories, and poetry of Tennessee Williams as the proving ground of my doctoral dissertation.

Internal evidence is always the best place to start.

Readers needn't get an "A" in "Literary Interpretation" or "History 101" to examine *Drummer* for forensic evidence, finger prints, blood stains, semen, DNA, skid marks in the underwear, and Sartre-like no-exit wounds.

In the spring of 1977, I studied *Drummer*'s first dozen issues and found that Embry's embryonic baby *Drummer* had repeatedly attempted suicide by its fourth issue.

The subject matter of *Drummer* 4 would have put any erotic magazine out of business, even if Embry's noble goal was to advance gay liberation through First Amendment freedom of the press. Having always fought for that same principle, I would have directed Los Angeles *Drummer*'s raw aggression differently from the first issue onwards in the way that I redirected San Francisco *Drummer*'s raw passion by serving up sex and sadomasochism with a masturbatory heartbeat, minus politics, beginning with *Drummer* 19.

With my gay gaze, I grew up as a wide-eyed witness of the connection of World War II veterans' biker culture to the gay leather culture of the 1950s and 1960s. At 1970s *Drummer*, my goal was to transport that straight outlaw street esthetic into a gay art setting: from the roads and racetracks to the pages of a new lifestyle magazine. I had the bona fides. I grew up on the roar of engines, the smell of exhaust, and the vision of bikers. In Peoria, during the juvenile delinquent craze of the 1950s, I hung out as a teenager every summer ogling the rugged bikers who scooted into town to hit the dirt track at the annual three-day AMA Flat Track championship races started by the Peoria Motorcycle Club in 1947, the same year Hollister, California, hosted its first Gypsy Tour run made famous in 1953 by *The Wild One*. By 1964, I was twenty-five, and was enough of a homomasculine man to pass hassle-free among heteromasculine men. Hiding in plain sight, I shot my first 35mm transparencies of straight outlaw bikers while I was a participant in the rise of us outlaw gays as leather bikers. My first novel, *Leather Blues* (1969), was about a boy coming out into leather, and was based on those days of dirt-bike scrambles in my small town. Leather is a language, and I was intent on speaking and writing it fluently, as much as I was enjoying coining new leather vocabulary to write about gay masculine concepts that before Stonewall had been afraid to speak their names.

THE LAPD GAY-BASHES *DRUMMER*

Between Embry's flame-throwing *Drummer* 4 (January 1976) and *Drummer* 6 (May 1976), the LAPD's high-profile and political raid on the Drummer Slave Auction (April 10, 1976) struck *Drummer* with a vengeance.

What were Embry and Barney thinking?

Barney wanted *Drummer* to be a leather *Evergreen Review*.

Embry wanted *Drummer* to be a leather *Advocate*.

I wanted *Drummer* to be the gay-identity version of 1940s and 1950s men's adventure magazines like *Argosy* and *Saga* mixed with the substance of *Esquire*, *Time*, and *The Journal of Popular Culture*.

So why did *Drummer* aggravate and bedevil the LAPD?

Were the pioneering Embry and Barney living up to some last hurrah from the Revolutionary 1960s? Were they drumming up some ersatz Stonewall incident in LA? Embry first mentions Stonewall in *Drummer* 2 (August 1976), the same issue in which Barney made the first mention of "adult-child sex."

Were they trying to be shocking like Sally Bowles?

Didn't they know that in 1967 the S&M favorite, Jim Morrison, the black-leather singer of the Doors, had been maced and arrested on stage in Florida, not for exposing his penis as charged, but for bad-mouthing the police in his act and in his interviews?

Had Embry misinterpreted Thoreau and his drum?

Every gay person should own *Walden* (1854): "If a man does not keep pace with his companions, perhaps it is because he hears a different drummer. Let him step to the music which he hears, however measured or far away."

Embry was well aware that Thoreau's quote had appeared on *Drummer*'s 1965 predecessor, *Drum* magazine, published by Clark Polak in Philadelphia. In Los Angeles in 1971, Embry published a small-format *Drummer*, costing twenty-five-cents. It was, historically the first issue of "little" *Drummer*, December 1, 1971, and Thoreau was not mentioned. "Little" *Drummer*, issue two, December 10-24, featured articles on restaurants and where to buy hairpieces. Thoreau was not mentioned. On September 15, 1972, Embry created "Little *Drummer*, Volume 2, Number 1, in a *Time* magazine size on cheap newsprint. It was published by H.E.L.P. Incorporated whose president was Larry Townsend. Thoreau was not mentioned.

In May 1973, *Action* magazine published author Phil Cooper's two-page feature condemning John Embry's handling of H.E.L.P, At the same time, in *California Scene*, Steve Shoch/Shock, an intimate at H.E.L.P, wrote a scathing indictment of both Embry and Townsend with particular emphasis on Embry's mishandling funds, and his claiming that H.E.L.P owed *Drummer* money. In a hostile takeover not forgotten years later by an unforgiving Townsend, Embry replaced Townsend as president of H.E.L.P. Exiting the organization he had founded, Townsend channeled Sun Tzu, and in his cynical resignation letter "praised" his enemy Embry in *The Advocate*, December 19, 1973.

In the first issue of the slick-format *Drummer* (June 1975), Embry, well into blacklisting his partners and contributors, took his characteristic revenge trashing Townsend's latest work in the first and only book review in that first issue. Embry and Townsend famously hated each other. In 1997, I wrote a narrative of this feud which Larry Townsend published as the "Introduction" to the twenty-fifth anniversary edition of his classic, *The Leatherman's Handbook*.

Finally, reaching for socio-political relevance, Embry printed Thoreau's marching orders for the first time on the masthead of *Drummer* 1, 2, and 3. Thoreau's quote then mysteriously disappeared from the next nine Los Angeles issues 4-12, reappearing inside San Francisco *Drummer* 13 and thenceforth in every issue.

RACE AND RACIALISM: HOW THE LAPD BUSTED *DRUMMER*

Note that it only took six—count 'em, *six*—lines in the *first* article in the *first* issue of *Drummer* to use the word *nigger* erotically in the same way Mapplethorpe did in the 1970s.

That may be "racial," but is it "racist"? It is a curious "compliment" within gay culture that the very ethnicity of a person, even a howdy white redneck, can be objectified by himself or others into a sexual fetish without prejudice. Page through all the *Drummer* stories, and read the revealing Personal sex ads, lusting with equal opportunity after Blacks, Latinos, Asians, Southern white trash, and the disabled during that taboo-busting heyday when Robert Mapplethorpe, Rex, and Tom of Finland were fetishizing blond Nazis. *Drummer* thrived on erotic racialism that confused and angered the white racist LAPD.

John Embry's longtime partner was the immigrant from Spain, Mario

Simon. The first Mr. Drummer was the Colombian/Argentinian immigrant Vallot Martinelli aka *Drummer* signature model Val Martin, the star of *Born to Raise Hell*, who was featured on the cover of five issues: 2, 3, 8, 30, 60, and centerfold, 31.

Drummer 1 and 6 featured the Blacks of *Mandingo*. *Drummer* 17: Japanese artist Goh Mishima. *Drummer* 21, 23: ex-con rednecks. *Drummer* 41, 65, 164: Swedish leather. Special 1978 issue, *Son of Drummer*: "Chico Is the Man." *Drummer* 93: erotic disability, "Maimed Beauty," with photos by George Dureau and Mark I. Chester. *Drummer* 103: Indians. *Drummer* 105: Scotsman in Leather. *Drummer* 118: An Indian Trucker's Revenge. *Drummer* 127: Vietnamese story, "Shadow Soldiers." *Drummer* 131: Black uncut soldier. *Drummer* 137: Un Señor Tambor, "Mr. Northeast Drummer," Anthony Citro. *Drummer* 155: Mexican "Attitude of Jose Del Norte." *Drummer* 174: cover and lead feature, African-American Graylin Thornton, "International Mr. Drummer 1993." The cover of *Drummer* 177 produced by associate editor Patrick Califia featured Asian leather hunk Ken Chang for the Jim Wigler photo feature, "Men of the Mystical East: A Whole New Image of Asian Masculinity."

Drummer was in good gay literary company. The always racially progressive Tennessee Williams made a sex fetish of an African-American in "Desire and the Black Masseur"; and, in *A Streetcar Named Desire*, he created an enduring archetypal blue-collar sex fetish in what his script called the "Polack," Stanley Kowalski, archetypally acted by Marlon Brando (1951) who continued to play the Kowalski character in the first Hollywood biker movie so formative to the style of leather popular culture, *The Wild One* (1953).

For eyewitness notes on racial diversity and on *Drummer* whose text and photographs were keenly and positively aware of the erotic appeal of race, turn to the "Timeline Bibliography" in this book.

Drummer's patron saint, Henry David Thoreau, famously spent a night in jail.

John Henry Embry never mentioned Thoreau's stretch as any consolation for his own six-hour night in the poky after the Slave Auction.

After Thoreau left jail, he wrote *Civil Disobedience*.

After Embry left jail, he wrote a rant in *Drummer* 6 (June 1976, page 12) titled "*Drummer* Goes to a 'Slave Auction'...And So Do 65 LA Police Officers." Even this flaming did not cool his distemper. He was already toying with fleeing fascism in LA to freedom in San Francisco. He wrote on page 14: "People in San Francisco say you have to be a masochist to live in Los Angeles."

For a Rorschach of the magazine's post-raid state of mind, study the rattled cover design of *Drummer* 6, the second worst *Drummer* cover. It was a scrawl of busy and bad design too metaphorical and unsexy for readers wanting the newly uncloseted images of frank leather action. You can judge a magazine by its cover. In *Drummer* 7 (July 1976, page 68), Embry keened, "The LAPD understands no minority's lifestyle."

In *Drummer* 9, (October 1976), Jeanne Barney editorialized on page 4 that the LAPD Vice Squad had been very interested in *Drummer* changing its address; subpoenas, she wrote, were served by officers

> ...involved in the Slave Auction caper.... these visits always seem to occur after we've taken Ad Vice's [sic] Lloyd Martin or "Crazy Ed" Davis to task in print for malperformance. The last raid on our offices took place a matter of hours after the issue which reported on police outrages at the Slave Auction. (Issue No. 6). The most recent drop-in came about within seven days of *Drummer* No. 8 hitting the stands...the issue in which we blew the whistle on the deal made by the Deputy District Attorney....

With issues of *Drummer* always hungry for fill, why did Embry never create a special "Drummer Slave Auction Issue" in the regular run of *Drummer* or in any of the fifty-something extra issues of *Drummer*? If not immediately after the bust, then some time during the eleven years he personally owned *Drummer*? In endless complaints he referenced his famous arrest, but was he unable to deal creatively with his abuse by cops? Embry was no artist. He was incapable of lifting his reality to the level of erotic creative expression. He was so angry with the LAPD that he could not handle the idea of creating a thematic issue dedicated in words and illustrations to exorcizing the raid by eroticizing the leathermen, the slaves, the sex, the bondage, the whips, the cops, the uniforms, the arrest, the jail, and the fetishes in play that April night. At one time, I wanted to dramatize that LAPD "Mark IV Bath" bust the same way I did the NYPD "Stonewall Inn" bust in my story "Stonewall: June 27, 1969, 11 PM."

Herein lies an essential evaluation of Embry as a publisher and historian. Any publisher who is a real journalist would have interviewed *Rashomon* eyewitnesses Jeanne Barney, Val Martin, Terry LeGrand, and the Libertarian, Fred Halsted, a co-auctioneer, who wrote his own eyewitness in *Package* 1 (July 1976), pages 28-29, and in *Package* 2 (September 1976), page 3. A crusading journalist would also have subpoenaed the LAPD for return of *Drummer*'s confiscated photographs, and would have purchased news-media photographs and TV footage for its single frames. A good publisher could have done all this while skating figure 8's on an ice cube in hell. The issue would have spontaneously created its sensational self—with breathless commentary by activist Robert Opel, and with sexy re-staged "erotic arrest photos" upon which Embry's dreaded "camp cartoon-dialogue balloons" might have for once been suitable.

Embry, during the age of Woodward and Bernstein, owned a gay magazine and missed a triumphant opportunity for GLBT investigative journalism, political commentary, and exciting satire, particularly of *The Advocate* which, while owned and published by the rich-born heir to a family fortune, the bourgeois David Goodstein, did nothing significant to support the annoying leather freaks against the LAPD. Even as some LA political activists, including the Reverend Troy Perry, galvanized around the Slave Auction at fund-raisers, West Coast journalists failed in their responsibility to jump all over this 1976 liberation story unlike East Coast writers who elevated a similar 1969 raid on the Stonewall Bar into a benchmark myth. The two raids were very different. At Stonewall, the NYPD purpose was to bust the Mafia—with gays being no more than collateral damage. At the Slave Auction, the LAPD goal was to bust queers.

Will a GLBT queer studies conference ever host a panel investigating why there is an inherent queerstream double-standard against S&M leatherfolks who tend to embarrass the mainstream *Advocate* culture? Twelve years after the Slave Auction, my colleague Eric Rofes, writing in *Drummer* 115 (April 1988), raised a *cri de couer* wondering why leathermen, and the "feckless press," rarely fight back against anti-leather raids. He cited LAPD harassment specifically against leather bars such as the One Way, Griff's, and the Gauntlet which the cops, not liking shoulder-to-shoulder men, limited to only fifty-seven patrons. Rofes claimed nothing had changed since the 1976 Slave Auction. "This isn't 1978 [sic]," he wrote in his "Rough Stuff" column. "It's 1988 and the issues that these bar raids raise for our specific [leather] community are great." On the cusp of becoming executive director of the Shanti Project in San Francisco, he meant that especially because the AIDS epidemic was raging at its height, leather culture seeking collective safety needed to be "especially protective of our community spaces."

Rofes was the author of *Dry Bones Breathe: Gay Men Creating Post-AIDS Identities and Cultures*. He was an informed voice of the times. In a sense in post-Embry *Drummer*, Rofes faulted former publisher Embry for agonizing way too personally over the Slave Auction arrests, and for failing to use the power of his press to turn that horrible event into a game-changing West Coast Stonewall. Embry was too cash crazy to become a leather Patrick

Henry. In his last days, Embry was kicking himself for not having the intellectual and literary gifts to raise the personal to the political, the specific to the universal. That failure, if anything, is a measure of Embry's greatest flaw, as well as of his hubris.

Luckily, Val Martin told us friends what happened that traumatic, comic, and ironic night when he was the main auctioneer for the Slave Auction. Perhaps Embry didn't get that Val Martin was a smart man and not just a pretty sex object on the cover of *Drummer*.

When *Drummer* artist, Olaf Odegaard, interviewed Val Martin in 1984, one year before Val Martin's death, one can only speculate why that "eyewitness *Drummer*" interview between one of Embry's superstar models and one of his superstar artists about a subject burning a hole in his guts was published in the now-disappeared news weekly, *Connection*, and not in *Drummer* where Embry and his staffer John Rowberry sat contemplating their navels? Had one of the usual Blacklist enmities, jealousies, or estrangements arisen between *Drummer*'s top model and its publisher?

Were Val and Olaf, like Fred Halsted and Robert Opel, just two more of the many former intimates of Embry who turned against him? Did they have to use other magazines to do an end-run around him to give voice to their testimony? Val told Olaf:

> So, that night [Saturday, April 10, 1976] we started the show and I started selling slaves.... We kept the slaves in a special room [off stage] where they were all in cages. In shackles and everything. We brought them one by one from the room to the stage....We tied some people up and spot-lighted them, took their clothes off... I had seventy slaves in the cages.... I was up to about my seventh slave, and I was selling him; a very groovy guy comes up to me with a leather jacket and a leather cap, torn jeans, very good-looking. And he...asks...the price of these slaves....He asked me if (the slave) was a good cocksucker; I said "sure" and he said, "Well, I have a big dick, do you think he can suck my big dick?" So, I said, "Sure, as a matter of fact they call him 'Jaws.'" I was just kidding...finally the guy bid the highest and I said, "sold." And...as soon as I said "sold" and received the money from him, the whole thing comes down.
>
> He gives a signal to the rest of the police and a couple of helicopters, two or three busses, three or four TV cameras, and 120 policemen surrounded the premises.... The police came in [to the cages]...and said, "We've come to free you. We know you've been sold, abused, beaten up and we've come here to free you." One of

the slaves said, "I don't want to be freed. I am here because I want to be."...We repeated many times what the [charitable and playful] purpose of the slave auction was.... They made us lay on the ground, hands on our necks;....they actually booked 380 people, and they took 40 to jail. They just went you..you...you.... They treated us like animals.... The funniest thing was this friend of mine was wearing a dildo. And when they made us strip, a cop was standing in front of him, and when he took his pants off, his dildo fell out. The cop just freaked out....for the cops it was like a carnival. They must have called everybody in the building to come in and take a look at us. They were taking pictures, calling us names....

Of the 40 [charged], they dropped 36. They left only four:... John Embry, myself, my helper [Douglas Holiday] and a lady who bought one of the slaves, Jeannie [*sic*] Barney....I think the sentence [for "slavery" which was changed to "prostitution"] could have been 5-10 years. They gave me ten days in jail and three years probation. John Embry and Jeannie [*sic*] Barney, the same. My helper didn't go to jail. He had to pay a $500 fine and got three-years probation. My lawyer fought back and we [all] got off with 100 hours of volunteer work instead of ten days in jail, and three-years probation. It cost the community [LA taxpayers] something like $160,000... Most of the people [had] paid bail... For the 40 it was half a million dollars.... The bail was reduced from half a million to $100 a piece, to $50. But those who went earliest paid $1,000, even $2,000.... [The LAPD] spent over $150,000 that night....[Coincidentally] a lady was killed ten blocks away, at the same time they were doing the raid. She was mugged and killed. —Selections from and © 1984 Olaf Odegaard, "Serving Two Masters, Or: The Great Slave Auction Bust (1975): An Interview with Val Martin," *Connection*, October 10-24, 1984

So infamous was the bust worldwide that the Slave Auction was reported on immediately, with some sexual detail, as far away as in the mimeographed newsletter, *South Africa Gay Scene*, No.21-21, May-June, 1976, who found their information in the straight newpaper, the *Rand Daily Mail*.

Hollywood. About 39 men were charged with "Suspicion of Slavery" recently under a state law going back to 1901....The 30 officers who raided the Mark IV Health Club one Saturday night around midnight confiscated leashes, chains, ropes...harnesses, studded arm bands...labeled in a police report as "sado-masochistic" paraphernalia.

...about 175 people were attending the "auction." ...the slave then became the property of the buyer for 24 hours. Captain Wilson said...."you can rent paddles there so you keep your slave in line. You can put them in leather harnesses fashioned in a bizarre manner for restraint. It's a very humiliating experience." Another police spokesman said about 65 officers took part in the raid and witnessed acts of copulation and sodomy before the auction... Bail was set at about R 4 250 [South African currency]. Conviction could bring a prison sentence of one to 10 years. "Gay community" spokesman, Mr. Morris Night [*sic*; Morris Kight, Los Angeles gay pioneer, one of the founders of the Gay Liberation Front]...denounced the raid as politically motivated and termed it "appalling and excessive." He said the event was "harmless fun" to raise money for "gay" activities...similar to high school and college slave auctions....

As a footnote, gay historians might find a legal insight into the Drummer Slave Auction in the *ACLU Gay Rights Newsletter*, September 1977, which featured the Slave Auction in its cover article, "The $200,000 Tragic Farce," with a photograph of Jeanne Barney and Thomas Hunter Russell, calling "The Notorious 'Mark IV Forty Slave Auction' episode...one of the more blatant landmarks in the history of [LAPD] police paranoia with regards to the gay community."

Nearly twenty years later, Ben Attias published his analysis "Police Free 'Gay Slaves': Some Juridico-Legal Consequences of the Discursive Distinctions Between the Sexualities," California State University, June 10, 1995.

John Embry, after penning many short versions, finally wrote his own eyewitness narrative of the Slave Auction which he excerpted from his unpublished memoir, *Epilogue*, in *Super MR* #5 (2000), pages 34-39.

EYEWITNESS: *DRUMMER* TIMELINE & SCORE CARD

Drummer ran 214 issues from *Drummer* 1 (June 1975) to *Drummer* 214 (April 1999); *Drummer* officially quit business on Folsom Fair weekend, September 30, 1999.

A QUARTET FOUNDED *DRUMMER*; HUNDREDS OF PEOPLE CREATED *DRUMMER*; MILLIONS OF PEOPLE READ *DRUMMER*

A stack of 214 issues of *Drummer* is a coffee-table sculpture 3.5 feet tall weighing 120 pounds. Laid flat, top-to-bottom, *Drummer* stretches sixty-four yards which is two-thirds of the length of a football field. At approximately ninety pages per issue, *Drummer* comprises a total 20,000 pages filled by hundreds of writers, artists, designers, and photographers, including even more thousands of revealing personal ads voiced and written by readers, with commercial advertisers displaying precise pop-culture signs of the times.

Drummer surged beyond calculation.

A *Drummer* group photo would look like the album cover of *Sgt. Pepper's Lonely Hearts Club Band*.

With a 42,000 copy press run for each issue in the 1970s, and with a pass-along rate of two readers in addition to the subscriber, approximately 100,000 people handled each issue of *Drummer* for an approximate total of 21 million people.

The mobbed Folsom Street Fair in San Francisco hosts 100,000 leather guests every September.

Even if Embry exaggerated the press run by fifty percent, each issue of *Drummer* would have been in the hands of 50,000 people. In gay book publishing, 5,000 copies sold is considered a best seller, and books fall far short of the pass-along rate of magazines.

Drummer was huge.

For the last quarter of the 21st century, among the millions of leatherfolk, there was hardly a person alive who had not heard of or read *Drummer*. Years after *Drummer* closed, readers continued to write to me that as young teenagers they had managed somehow to find *Drummer*, even in Sweet Home, Alabama, and it had answered their incipient needs and shaped their masculine identities.

More people have read one issue of *Drummer* than have read any one book by any deeply established GLBT author in the "Top 100" list of literary best-sellers in the gay canon.

That's why I added the line to the masthead of *Drummer* 23 (July 1978): "The American Review of Gay Popular Culture."

During that same year, Richard Labonté and Norman Laurila founded the revolutionary bookstore, A Different Light, in the Silver Lake district of LA. In his eyewitness recall, the trend-spotting Labonté noted that during ADL's first months in 1979 while I was editor-in-chief, he had to increase his monthly order for San Francisco *Drummer*. Labonté's amusing eyewitness email sent December 21, 2006, paints a sweet picture of the ADL startup which coincided with a moment in time, that I remember fondly, when I had edited more than half of the existing issues of *Drummer*.

> I think our magazine supplier (a Venice Beach independent, not one of the Larry Flynt or Mafia companies [who published so many gay magazines]) started us with 5 copies of *Drummer* the first couple of weeks. At the same time, we were dropping [our cash-drawer] quarters into *The Advocate* vending machines in front of the YMCA in Glendale and the old Bodybuilders Gym in Silver Lake and liberating five or six copies from each box, because *The Advocate* was one mag our supplier couldn't supply. Within a few weeks, our draw for *Drummer* went from 5 to 10 to 25 and finally to 50 for each new issue, with fill-ins ordered in as required until the next issue. I soon learned to keep as many back issues in stock as our supplier could provide (often returns from other outlets), so that customers from out of town could buy three or four months' worth of *Drummer* at a time.

In the zero degrees of separation, Richard Labonté and A Different Light helped *Drummer* succeed in its significant 1979 growth spurt. Labonté's statement reveals how periodical literature grew in the 1970s before small gay book publishers arose in the 1980s. *Drummer* had fled LA and had become a San Francisco magazine whose reintroduction to LA was greatly goosed because Labonté in Silver Lake exhibited hard copies at A Different Light where browsers could sample the redesigned *Drummer* before becoming subscribers. The British actor and leather personality, Peter Bromilow, who emceed leather events at LA bars and starred in many big-budget films including *Camelot*, recalled that Los Angeles leather queens, as he called them, were amazed at the change made in *Drummer* by the move to San Francisco.

DRUMMER RESTORATION SUPPER: WHAT CAME AFTER

Having purchased *Drummer* from John Embry on August 22, 1986, new *Drummer* publisher Anthony F. DeBlase and his lover, the psychiatrist Andrew Charles, president of their Desmodus, Inc. corporation, ending the Blacklist, personally invited me to return to the landmark issue 100 of the Embry-free *Drummer*. In fact, DeBlase, cued and funded by Charles, quietly hired me as a private personal advisor for the next three years because they wanted to return *Drummer* to its roots and its core themes while at the same time changing its attitudes to accommodate the safe-sex exigencies of HIV.

Here is "inside" eyewitness history.

Their invitation to rejoin *Drummer* occurred in tandem with the significant "*Drummer* Restoration Dinner Party" hosted Folsom Fair weekend, September 28, 1986, 2:30 PM, by the erotic artist Rex and by Trent Dunphy and Robert Mainardi, owners of the archival San Francisco store, "The Magazine." If ever a *Drummer* Salon dinner party for ten gay men was ripe for a screenplay, this sit-down summit had characters, wit, and intrigue enough for a Merchant-Ivory production scripted by Parker Wilde, the love child of Dorothy and Oscar.

Celebrating the exit of the old regime of Embry and the new purchase of *Drummer* by DeBlase and Charles, the eight guests at the supper table in the photography-filled Dunphy-Mainardi Victorian included the intentionally forward-planning boys in the band: Anthony DeBlase, Andrew Charles, Rex, Al Shapiro and his partner Dick Kriegmont, Mark I. Chester, Mark Hemry, and me.

Two months later, in a letter to Al Shapiro, dated November 20, 1986, I wrote:

> Dear Al, All this *nuevo Drummer* stuff, starting with our pasta supper at Trent and Bob's, has reminded me, as issue 100 sits next to me, and your name and mine are so entwined, that I might not have become editor of *Drummer* if you as art director hadn't been so insistent [to me and to Embry]....Those were some days when you were the once-and-future famous A. Jay and I got to watch you work, designing issue after issue! Embry was a curse and a disaster, but he never was able to divide and conquer and come between us....I just wanted you to be the first to know that Gay Sunshine Press has today signed me to a contract for an anthology of my writing titled *Stand by Your Man* due out in late 1987, and, on page 1, I'm dedicating the book to you, because when I moved to San Francisco, you were one of three guys who tried to help me find suitable work, and you succeeded....So what the hay! We can lift our heads and blow raspberries at all the small-minded, cheating, conniving Embrys, because, truly, we have been artists and friends together.

Six months later, Allen J. Shapiro died May 30, 1987, ten years after we first marched together into *Drummer*. I wrote his eulogy in *Drummer* 107 (August 1987). In that eulogy built on my interviews with him, he explained how he, like *Drummer*, had evolved out of the pioneering gay publishing of the 1960s. So important was his art to Embry that when A. Jay quit *Drummer*, Embry tried to claim for himself the copyright ownership of *Harry Chess*. When A. Jay threatened legal action, Embry was forced to cease and desist.

> **A. Jay:** *Drummer* was the first magazine for masculine gay men, not for embarrassed leather queens....I once heard John Embry called the "Marie Antoinette of Gay Publishing." He didn't really have much respect for the intelligence of the readers. Let them eat cake. The same pictures and models, especially the beloved Val Martin, the same tired beefcake recycled monthly for the public to eat. I don't really agree with all that, but I am used to working with publishers with balls. At the beginning, John Embry was an innovator. *Drummer* started back after poppers hit big [actually poppers in mesh capsules hit around 1966, nine years before *Drummer*] and the leather market was ripe for its own publication, and not just for another mimeographed underground bike club monthly newsletter printed on typing paper.
>
> Embry and I did lock horns numerous times, but I do give him credit for giving me, as "A. Jay," great exposure, and an opportunity to do my art-director thing for almost three years. I did uncover budding genius artists like Matt and Domino. [New Yorker Don Merrick/Domino's first West Coast show opened March 24, 1979.] Embry, as the cartoon fanatic he is, had the good taste of recognizing the pulling power of my *Harry Chess* and taking it on. Also Embry picked up Bill Ward's wonderful cartoon panels, *Drum*, before he took on *Harry Chess*. So as a fan of gay cartoons, he did some real good.
>
> **Jack:** How did you launch *Harry Chess*? That strip led you to *Drummer*, yes?
>
> **A. Jay:** *Harry Chess* got started because one of the world's most daring publishers, Clark Polak, put an ad in the *New York Times* twenty-five years ago, saying he needed an art director for his gay magazine. He actually used the word *gay* in the ad! He nearly caused a couple hundred heart attacks at the *Times* when they found out what it meant. Anyway, I was considering drawing a gay comic strip then, so I proposed *Harry Chess* to him.

Jack: The rest is gay pop history.

A. Jay: Back in those closeted days, Clark dared to put in a special slip-sheet mailed only to his subscribers. Frontal nudes. No sucking and fucking. Men who bought his mag called—guess what, guys, *Drum*—on the news stand missed out on that hot stuff. How times have changed! I did *Harry* in *Drum* for five or six years. Long before *Drummer*. One episode a month. Clark reprinted the whole thing once as a pocket book.

Jack: That would have been *The Original Adventures of Harry Chess*. It's now out of print. A collector's item, right?

A. Jay: I wish I had a couple dozen copies....Uh, let me see, where was I in the Decline and Fall of Practically Everybody Who Was Anybody? Oh yeah. Like Sebastian Venable, you see, I traveled a lot. I left *Drum* for a year to live in Mexico City for the 1968 Olympics. Sniffing around the wrestlers, picking up used international jockstraps, and pumping my tits up at the local gym. Always hoping the yummy bodybuilder and movie star, Jorge Rivera, the Mexican Steve Reeves, would come in and sit on my face.

While I was feasting on dark meat, *Drum* magazine died. Clark chose to move on to something better that made him, I think, rich. So *Harry Chess* became "Little Orphan Harry." Then Hanns Ebensten [the pioneer of gay group travel] told me about *Queen's Quarterly*. Can you imagine a mag being called *that* in 1987? Back then you could. Anyway, publisher George DeSantis hired me freelance and *Harry* had a new home.

I talked George into changing his two-word camp title to the sleeker, more designer-like "QQ" to try to butch it up. I could tell sissies were on the way out and sleaze-macho was on its way in.

DeSantis then started two more mags: *Body* and *Ciao*. DeSantis was a great publisher. A kind man. I learned a great deal from him about magazine production, which prepared me, really, to take over the art direction of *Drummer*.

At a meeting with a struggling DeBlase at *Drummer* on Friday, February 12, 1988, I made a proposal offering to further help lift his load producing his monthly periodical. Besides my discreet hand-holding, I suggested reviving my 1970s concept of creating "theme" issues for *Drummer* featuring underwear, rubber, bears, mud, and tit torture. To me, the announcement of upcoming themes was a pro-active way to encourage writers and artists with enough lead time to submit materials on the themes. To make the point, I showed DeBlase a portion of my Palm Drive Video photographic portfolio and its themes. On March 1, 1988, DeBlase wrote me a letter confirming our plan:

Dear Jack,
 Life as usual is amazingly hectic.... With your proposals in mind [i.e.: my theme thumbnails and thematic photos which I left in his hands to cue his issues], upcoming fetish features are:
 Issue 116, Underwear: Your shot of Curtis James in his long-johns is great. Do you have more of these that we could use along with a review of this tape? [The video was *Redneck Cowboy in Black Leather*, and he published three of my underwear fetish photos on pages 48 and 98.]
 Issue 117, Daddies: I plan to use your *Dave Gold's Gym Workout* [still photographs taken during the video shoot] here; do you have others that you'd like included? [DeBlase published two of Dave Gold, page 45.]
 Issue 118, Rubber: A natural for your new Keith Ardent video [*Pec Stud in Black Rubber*, during which I shot two hundred photos, including a special *Drummer* cover and a photo spread of eleven centerfold pictures (pages 2, 3, 11-18, 32), as well as authoring the cover feature article "Rubberotica"].
 Issue 119, Bears and Mountain Men: Curtis James again, as well as many of your models. You pick the ...[models] you'd like emphasized here. [DeBlase printed twenty-one of my photographs of straight mountain men and gay bears and published my lead cover feature article, "Bears! How to Hunt Buckskin Mountain Men."]
 Issue 120, Mud, Oil, Grease, and Grunge: Naturally, your *Mud Pillow Fight* video and photographs will be featured. Anything else you have that is appropriate? [I provided three interior photographs of "mud" for "Sodbuster," *Drummer* 148, page 61.]
 Issue 121, Tits: Again a natural for your *Tit Torture Blues* tape. [DeBlase printed one of my photographs of Jason Steele.]
 Any more recommendations for upcoming fetish features?

At DeBlase's request, I suggested "solo sex and video" as the theme for *Drummer* 123 and wrote the lead feature, "Solo Sex: Who's Who in J/O

Video," to accompany my twenty-two photographs (pages 34-36, 38-41). I offered "bodybuilding" for *Drummer* 124 and wrote the lead feature with DeBlase selecting an excerpt from *Some Dance to Remember: A Memoir-Novel of San Francisco 1970-1982*, plus five of my photos (pages 16-17, 35). Following up in 1989, because my former lover Robert Mapplethorpe, whom I had featured in *Drummer* 24 and *Son of Drummer*, had recently died, I nominated Mapplethorpe as the hook for *Drummer* 133 and wrote the lead feature article, "Pentimento for Robert Mapplethorpe: Fetishes, Faces, and Flowers of Evil." Additionally, because "safe sex" was the new buzz word, I tendered "nostalgia for the way we were in the Titanic 1970s" as the theme for *Drummer* 139 with my lead feature article, "Remembrance of Sleaze Past."

Editor's note:

See DeBlase's editorial credit for themes created by Fritscher in *Drummer* 139, p. 35: "So, inspired by Jack Fritscher's theme, we decided to do a photo shoot with a hot leatherman nibbling on...cake..." which referenced both Proust's cookie and the title of the "Remembrance" feature article. See also Tim Barrus' posting of this re-instituted "theme approach" as a way to solicit and build issues out of the grass roots readership in *Drummer* 120, page 19.)

DeBlase continued:

Do you mind having your name mentioned in conjunction with your Palm Drive Video company? I was going to name you in the review I did of your *Gut Punchers* [*Drummer* 115], but since you didn't include your name in your own literature [because I was keeping my literary identity separate from my photographic identity], I didn't do it. What is your feeling on the subject? I think *Drummer* readers will take your name as a badge of quality and be more likely to purchase from a company they haven't dealt with before—if they knew of your association. [A couple weeks later, on Saint Patrick's Day, March 17, over lunch at Original Joe's, DeBlase said, "Let me give you this business advice. Your name is a brand name. People are still learning the name of Palm Drive Video. You should start calling it 'Jack Fritscher's Palm Drive Video.'" [And so, on DeBlase's marketing recommendation, the name was changed, and thousands of Palm Drive videos were sold by DeBlase at *Drummer*, by Beardog Hoffman at *Bear* magazine's Brush Creek Media, and by John Embry's Wings and Alternate distributing through *Super MR* mail-order.]

Sincerely,
Tony DeBlase

In September, 1992, when Martijn Bakker, residing in Amsterdam, purchased *Drummer*, he globalized the name of the uniquely American *Drummer* into *International Drummer*. Not understanding American gay pop culture and *Drummer*'s place within the psychology of leatherfolk, Bakker destroyed its homomasculine American mythology, and foolishly replaced its "personal contents" with "corporate contents" interchangeable with other newer glossy mags in cahoots with video companies pushing their corporate photographs as soulless centerfolds. Even as Bakker intended to produce an online version of *Drummer*, the site never functionally happened. He closed *Drummer* forever. He added high-profile insult to injury when he worsened the indignity by shuttering *Drummer* during the highest American Leather Festival of the year, Folsom Fair weekend, September 30, 1999.

San Francisco leather-heritage historian, Mister Marcus wrote in his online column, "Leather Bazaar," May 26, 2005, at www.mamasfamily.org/MisterMarcus: "Martijn Bakker, the Dutchman...was the sole killer of *Drummer* and all it stood for." However, Bakker was hardly the sole "killer"; he had competition from villainous accomplices, including John Embry and Robert Davolt, the last editor of *Drummer*, who both reviled Bakker publicly. Did Bakker hate Embry and Davolt? Whereas Embry and DeBlase fought privately, this threesome fought publicly in a passionate blood feud that broke out into print. Bakker relished that he had scored internationally when he purchased *Drummer* which was the Holy Grail Embry had sold to DeBlase in the biggest mistake of both their publishing lives. Bakker, in a neck-snapping duel, fought back, for instance, in a Press Release announcing that the new Dutch *International Drummer* was in fine shape for the year 2000, and that

> a well-known American publisher [Embry] moons wistfully over the *Drummer* era as if it were past and shows up only in old copies of former issues. Gentlemen, it is not so. Anyone who actually believes *Drummer* is dead, is simply not paying attention."

In return, Embry's talking head Robert Davolt ranted back against Bakker in the rival *Super MR* 7 (2001):

> ...*Drummer*, as we knew it, is plainly gone. It is particularly embarressing [sic] to [Embry's] Alternate Publishing who originated the title [*Drummer*] 25 years ago...

Why would Embry's Alternate Publishing be "embarrassed"? It was ironic. Why would Embry, notorious for years for ripping off subscribers to *Drummer* and its "Leather Fraternity" want to fulfill the subscriptions of *Drummer* subscribers when there was a new publisher of *Drummer* in Amsterdam? Embry wasn't even the previous publisher. He had bowed out of *Drummer* in 1986; he hated everything that DeBlase did; and then he hated everything that Bakker did in the way he had hated everything Jeanne Barney and I had done.

Just as DeBlase, surprised that he had to pay the debts Embry owed, had buyer's remorse, Embry had a major case of seller's remorse. Perversely, Embry abused *Drummer* when he owned it, and when he got rid of it, he loved it. Embry fancied he was *Drummer* incarnate, but he wasn't, Blanche, he wasn't, and that fact fried his *cojones* for the rest of his life.

Embry was first motivated to start the infant *Drummer* (gestation was from the twice-monthly little "zine" of 1971 to the slick monthly magazine of 1975) mainly as a medium for his mail-order business: "The Embry Company, PO Box 3843, Hollywood." In the last issue Embry published, *Drummer* 98 (June 1986), he bitterly tried to destroy the future mail-order business that DeBlase would be running in his own version of the *Drummer* business. In his "so-long-suckers" issue, Embry penned a two-page diatribe against poppers in the "*Drummer* Forum" section titled "Death Rush" which he illustrated with a drawing Rex had created to sell the popper brand "Bolt: New from the makers of Rush." Ironically, Embry had for eleven years courted popper manufacturers like W. Jay Freezer who made "room odorizers" with names like "Rush" and "Aroma." Poppers kept *Drummer* flying high. Popper dealers paid a huge chunk of advertising dollars buying full-page display ads including expensive inside covers and back covers, often illustrated by identified *Drummer* artists like Rex. Embry's sudden "abstinence from poppers" was no epiphany of social consciousness about the health effects of poppers. He wanted to injure DeBlase enough by alienating advertisers to drive *Drummer* out of business so that Embry would be able to crow that *Drummer* could not exist without him. He ended his diatribe with this sentence naming all the commercial brands of poppers:

"I...went around the house [meaning *Drummer*], seeking out anything with a RUSH, RAM, THUNDERBOLT, LOCKER ROOM HARDWARE, DOUBLE EAGLE, CLIMAX, QUICKSILVER, HEAD, or CRYPT TONIGHT [his caps] label and tossed them into the garbage. Room odorizers indeed!"

With the popper companies boycotting the issue, *Drummer* 98 had no ads either inside the front cover or on the back cover which instead promoted Embry's mail-order video company. The inside back cover was an antidote-to-poppers ad for VitaMen and Immunitab vitamins.

At the height of the AIDS epidemic, "Death Rush" was the last piece Embry wrote for *Drummer*. Thirty days later, in his first issue of *Drummer* (*Drummer* 99, August 1986), DeBlase was so fiercely angry at this attack and, by extension, at all of Embry's skullduggery that he reprinted in his own first "*Drummer* Forum: The Popper Wars Continue" an article by Dr. Bruce Voeller to rebut Embry with Voeller's feature noting that while poppers may have health risks, the studies were not scientific, and anti-popper crusaders were often too politically motivated to discuss the issue. Professor Voeller was the founder of the National Gay Task Force and the Mariposa Foundation and was the man who coined the phrase "acquired immune deficiency syndrome." DeBlase's laissez faire attitude of choice around drugs was not too different from what I learned at San Francisco General when my longtime friend Tony Tavarossi, one of the founding pioneers of Folsom Street culture, was dying of some mysterious ailment in ICU in 1981. I asked his doctor, "What's the matter with him?" "We don't know," she said in that summer when no one had heard of AIDS. She added, "We've never seen a patient so distressed." Tony was on a ventilator. I asked, "Could poppers have caused this?" She looked up and said, "Poppers are an insult to the lungs, but, no, poppers did not cause this."

The several times when I could have bought the *Drummer* business, I did not, because I knew as an insider, there was nothing for sale but the *Drummer* name, and a lot of ongoing debt.

Embry's fake embarrassment at Bakker's *Drummer* was nothing more than a sniffy attack of the "vapors," trying to remind everyone of his one-time connection to *Drummer*.

So confused is the timeline of leather history, and so bad were the internecine vendettas that a blogger wrote in his inflated obituary for Embry, "The *young* [italics added] John Embry founded *Drummer*." In truth, on the day that the first issue of *Drummer* was published, John Embry was forty-five years old, and not at all part of the youth revolution of the 1960s and

1970s that trusted no one over thirty. When I crossed swords with Embry and resigned from editing *Drummer* on New Year's Eve, December 31, 1979, Embry was turning fifty years old, was distracted by lawsuits and cancer, was obsessed with draining *Drummer* to fund his real estate holdings, and was no participant in the nighttime culture of leather in San Francisco.

The best objective correlative of how Embry's on-going colon cancer subtracted him for almost a year of functional creativity at *Drummer* is an editorial he wrote after he fell and broke his hip in 2001.

I spent...the past weeks recuperating from a broken hip... Now, months later, I'm still not completely functional, but at least I'm mobile...I am now propped up in my own bed...still embroiled in an experience [health crisis] that threatens to go on for some time more. *The healing process takes a lot of energy, leaving little for the creative process.* [Italics added] (*Super MR #7*, page 5)

Against the culture-changing tide of HIV, Bakker was riding high. He had recently purchased the legendary company, Rob of Amsterdam, founded by the person, Rob of Amsterdam, whom Mark Hemry and I—in the zero degrees of separation—videotaped in an hour-long interview in his leather shop in Amsterdam on June 22, 1989. Ravaged by HIV, Rob told us his eyewitness story in his last interview before his assisted suicide.

Whether it was against Bakker or DeBlase or anyone who ever told him "no," John Embry carried grudges. Jeanne Barney said that Embry oftentimes sat on his porch at one of his Russian River houses repeating, over and over, the long lists of those who had done him wrong.

Embry was nothing but trendy. At the very same time, like a bitter queen escaped from *The Boys in the Band*, Truman Capote, another obsessive-compulsive, was sitting in Manhattan repeating over and over his infamous Hate List of all the rich and famous folk who had dropped him after he betrayed their personal secrets in his scandalous 1970s *Esquire* articles which became chapters in his troubled book, *Answered Prayers.* Like Embry's Blacklist, Capote's Hate List of hundreds of socialites and artists who had made the young Truman their darling included Jackie Kennedy Onassis' sister, Princess Lee Bouvier Radziwill; his arch-enemy Gore Vidal; designer Gianni Versace; society hustler Denham Fouts; and

Anderson Cooper's mother, heiress Gloria Vanderbilt. Capote's magazine-generated trouble started with his tattletale article, "La Côte Basque 1965," in *Esquire* (November 1975), the same month that the infant *Drummer* published issue number three, which was the first issue to dare to list the names of staff on the masthead.

In his own exit from *Drummer* in 1992, former editor DeBlase, enjoying a big-fat-cigar moment in *Drummer* 159, adopted the title for himself that I had suggested for my own situation when he asked me how I defined my professional relationship to *Drummer*. When as a retired university associate professor emeritus, I suggested "Editor Emeritus," DeBlase followed suit. After he sold *Drummer*, he went on to list himself as *Drummer* "Publisher Emeritus" and "Editor Emeritus." Doesn't almost every former *Drummer* editor deserve the title?

Jeanne Barney laughed when I suggested she was "*Drummer* Editrix Emerita."

Embry, who was no Edith Piaf, might have best solved his regrets and his identity crisis over *Drummer* by simply naming himself *Drummer* founding publisher emeritus, and then moving on to publish his *Drummer* clones: *Manifest Reader*, *MR*, and *Super MR*. Although DeBlase had made Embry sign a non-compete clause in the 1986 sales contract, Embry would not stop competing. Even so, after selling *Drummer*, Embry never stopped fantasizing about the original *Drummer* which had made him a success, and not vice versa. From start to finish, it took not just Embry, but hundreds of us to create *Drummer*.

The history of the rise of *Drummer* was a birthing, nursing, and teething process of three years of angst (1975-1978) accomplished by a parental quartet consisting of one publisher (John Embry), and two editors-in-chief (Jeanne Barney and Jack Fritscher), and one art director (Al Shapiro) who founded and evolved *Drummer* from a pulp-paper LA tabloid to a glossy San Francisco magazine read internationally as a gay-identity journal.

After that, came all the other publishers and editors who creatively repeated the themes and memes of original-recipe *Drummer*, particularly the crucial leather identity and gender identity issues of *Drummer* 19 to *Drummer* 33. Nearly everything contained in *Drummer* from 1980 to 1999 was a reprise of the themes that the late-1970s *Drummer* had introduced—which is not to say that the later versions are not original, entertaining, valuable, and historic issues in their own right. *Drummer* is like wine. When someone says they love *Drummer*, ask what was the year and who was the editor of their favorite issue.

APPENDIX

The *Drummer* Origin Story
Morally Speaking

In the *Drummer* Origin Story, the founding Big Bang of *Drummer* resembled the tumultuous founding of *The Advocate*, Andy Warhol's *Interview*, and Facebook. Derived out of the Clark Polak's 1960s magazine, *Drum*, founded in 1963 and published by the Janus Society of Philadelphia whose motto was the "different drummer" of Henry David Thoreau, *Drummer*—which did not become iconic overnight—evolved during the four rocky years of its trial-balloon emergence from a Hollywood bimonthly chapbook "zine" (December 1, 1971) to its first glossy monthly issue of *Drummer* 1 (June 1975). *Drummer* finally found its leather character and homomasculine voice in both form and content in perhaps its most platonically perfect issue, the breakthrough and brand-making *Drummer* 21 (January 1978).

During its four-year gestation in Los Angeles (1971-1975), *Drummer* struggled to be born in the hands of advertising man John Embry, assisted by his archenemy leather author Larry Townsend who, when he withdrew his support from Embry in 1973, nearly put the fledgling *Drummer* out of business. Driven out of Los Angeles by the LAPD, *Drummer* was finally fully birthed in San Francisco in 1977.

In the tale of two cities, and in the tumultuous years of its delivery from 1975-1978, it took a village to create the legendary *Drummer*.

John Embry started *Drummer*, yes, in Los Angeles, yes, but he could not achieve liftoff. LA was the runway for *Drummer*, yes, but San Francisco, yes, was where *Drummer* achieved liftoff, yes, and cruising altitude, yes, that took it national and global.

Historically, Embry went to his grave protesting, perhaps too much, claiming *Drummer* was his immaculate conception, and his solitary conception, writing in his must-read editorial in *Manifest Reader* 26: "Unlike popular conceptions [which he was actively refuting], *Drummer* magazine was not something we all got together on, like in an Andy Hardy movie, with lots of enthusiasm and offers of Judy Garland's father's barn for a theater. Or even like Shel Silverstein's wonderful concept of *Playboy*'s beginning with all the fellas standing around the steps of a Chicago brownstone deciding who was going to be the editor, the art director, and who would recruit the broads [*sic*]." In addition to writing this "broad" sexism that he thought was "cool," Embry also confessed to his "unnatural aversion...

[to] drag and female impersonation." Pulling his wizard's curtain back, he confirmed his naivete that at the beginning in LA he had "little, if any, idea what it [*Drummer*] should look like."

So, like a designer baby whose four parents decide "what it should look like," the *Drummer* that readers nationwide first responded to in June 1975, and came to love internationally by 1979, was gestated by a Jedi Council of four mitochondrial people: founding Los Angeles publisher John Embry, founding Los Angeles editor-in-chief Jeanne Barney, founding San Francisco editor-in-chief Jack Fritscher, and founding San Francisco art director Al Shapiro aka the artist A. Jay who had been hired in 1977 by Embry who was seeking publishing roots and design magic in A. Jay himself because Shapiro had been the art director of the original *Drum* magazine and *Queen's Quarterly* in the 1960s.

Embry acknowledged this evolution, from nothing to something, when he wrote ingenuously in *Manifest Reader* 26 (1995): "*Drummer*'s first issue had 48 pages, a cover price of $2.50, and was made up of whatever."

Made up of w*hatever?*

"Later [after moving to San Francisco] we were [he was] amazed at how much there was available to us."

Embry, in actuality, paired Barney and Fritscher with equal billing, crediting each as editor-in-chief, the only two *Drummer* editors distinguished with that title, although he did bend history in *Manifest Reader* 26 when he lied, despite absolutely no evidence at all on any masthead in *Drummer*, that "John Rowberry, after Jack Fritscher's exit, went on to become editor-in-chief." He depended on both Barney and me for the magazine's survival during the founding process made convulsive by three formative events: the arrest of Embry and Barney by the LAPD at the Drummer Slave Auction (April 1976); and the character-changing relocation of *Drummer* from LA to San Francisco (March 1977) when Embry, still on two years' parole, left only after the court gave permission; and, finally, Embry's nearly year-long absence from the *Drummer* office because of his long bout with cancer. (1978-1979).

He wrote in his *Super Manifest Reader* (2000), that his Los Angeles "*Drummer* was so limited in its subject matter....Moving from Los Angeles to San Francisco was like," in a comparison he made repeatedly like an angry man obsessed, "leaving East Berlin." He had earlier confirmed the fact of the magazine's evolution between two cities in his column in *Drummer* 26 (January 1978) published while I was his editor having accomplished the previous eight issues: "*Drummer* has had a number of renovations [geographically and editorially] in these three years, most of them, we assume, being in the right direction."

Strictly speaking, it is also noteworthy that in the dreamtime of *Drummer* pre-history (1971-1975), Embry had early on, two years before Barney exited *The Advocate*, also hired a "Ron Harris," who left little or no DNA, as the *first* Los Angeles editor of *H.E.L.P./Drummer* in April 1973 while Embry was publishing that first chapbook "zine" and 32-page tabloid version of *Drummer*. Even earlier in 1971, wanting to expand his Leather Fraternity *NewsLeather* into entertainment coverage, he sketched out a magazine called *Drumsticks* which in 1975 became the fully fledged *Drummer* in which "Drumsticks" became a column featuring campy news items.

In the village it took to raise a magazine, the one thing John Embry personally invented about *Drummer* was its title.

Even his ambitious masthead tag line grasping for the gravitas of marching to Henry David Thoreau's "different drummer" was shoplifted from *Drum* magazine.

Coincidentally, at the very same time in New York, Andy Warhol's *Interview* magazine was having its identity invented by its own Jedi Council of six parents led by its editor Bob Colacello who wrote about the group genesis of *Interview* in his insider biography *Holy Terror: Andy Warhol Close Up*.

In Los Angeles, *The Advocate*, first named *The Los Angeles Advocate*, published by the Pride Foundation as its newsletter until 1968 when bought from Pride by Richard Mitch and Bill Rau, was also founded through its emerging period of more than seven years (1967-1974) by a cast of at least six characters: the founding publishers Richard Mitch ("Dick Michaels"), Bill Rau ("Bill Rand"), with artist Sam Allen, and Aristede Laurent, plus their all-important editor Rob Cole who professionalized the magazine's character, and their columnist Jeanne Barney—as well as by Wall Street banker David Goodstein who bought Mitch and Rau out in 1974. Goodstein, firing his inherited staff as "too radical," changed, with his new staff, the form and content of *The Advocate*, and turned its editorial politics bourgeois and conservative.

It took the competitive Embry only seven months after Goodstein bought *The Advocate* in November, 1974, to rush his startup of glossy *Drummer* in June 1975. Envious of Goodstein's growing media power at *The Advocate*, Embry purposely in San Francisco in November 1977—and at the expense of his cash-cow *Drummer*—dubbed his newest magazine with the mirror title *The Alternate: What's Happening in Your World*. When the talented Rob Cole started his new magazine *NewsWest* (1975-1977) which became *Dateline*, he and Embry could come to no accord because of Embry's fear of Cole's strength as an editor who might outperform him. So Embry worked to destroy the competition and frequently bragged in early

Drummer issues about how he had trounced the "inept" Cole at *NewsWest* and *Dateline*. He even coopted the title *Dateline* into the *Drummer* column "Dateline." Continuously jealous of Goodstein, Embry slammed him and his controversial *"Advocate* Experience" by publishing a scathing feature, written to order by frequent contributor to *The Advocate*, Dan Gengle, titled "The Thing That Ate *The Advocate*," in *Alternate* 9 (May 1979). Embry had by then poached as many "left-leaning" *Advocate* staff as possible, including, early on, Jeanne Barney and Aristede Laurent, and, later, *Advocate* editor John Preston and transman columnist Patrick/Pat Califia.

Embry, who denied he depended on the kindness of strangers, reached to the virgin-birth that Mark Zuckerberg later wanted at *Facebook*. Playing rock-paper-scissors, Embry was the only person ever to suggest himself as the sole creator of *Drummer*. Sometimes in the convenient shorthand of leather history timelines, people not familiar with the *Drummer* Origin Story name him as the founder of *Drummer*. In truth, he was the principal of the founders in the village that created *Drummer*. He was also the man most responsible for nearly all of the unnecessary drama and bad luck that always threatened the destruction of *Drummer* even after he sold the magazine to the second publisher of *Drummer*, Anthony DeBlase whose own point of view invented, after 1986, yet another version of *Drummer*, beyond our original *Drummer*, in order to cope with AIDS and political correctness.

In the way that George Washington, the "Founding Father of Our Country," depended on the six other Founding Fathers, Embry, the founder of *Drummer*, depended morally on the two other Founding Fathers and one Founding Mother.

> "The past is never dead; in fact, it's not even past."
> —*Requiem for a Nun*, William Faulkner

CHAPTER 2

DIRTY ISSUES:
Some *Drummer* Covers Selected
by Artist, Photographer, and Model

- The *Drummer* Salon in the Titanic 1970s: The Power of the *Drummer* Editorial Desk, Sam Steward, Jim Kane, Robert Opel, Al Shapiro, and an Iconic Dinner Party Hosting Tom of Finland
- Shooting *Drummer* Covers: Robert Mapplethorpe, Lou Thomas, Robert Opel, David Sparrow, and Jack Fritscher
- Why Tom of Finland Never Appeared on the Cover of *Drummer* While Embry Owned It
- Gay Marriage, Leather-Style: 1976
- Gay Face Uncloseted: "Tough Customers" and "Tough Shit"

"The past is never where you think you left it."
—Original Cockette Rumi Missabu (James Bartlett), 2014

Editor's Note:
Jack Fritscher was the only *Drummer* editor to shoot *Drummer* covers: eight in total. As a photographer, he was also the only *Drummer* editor to shoot photographs for the interior and centerfold of the magazine, beginning with *Drummer* 21 (March 1978) through *Drummer* 204 (June 1997).

Drummer covers, at least some of them, provide handy hooks in the timelining of *Drummer* history. Drawings graced the covers of many of the first issues because well into the Titanic 1970s gays remained as afraid of cameras as they had been before gay liberation when cops used cameras as powertools to gather facial recognition for legal prosecution. As a result, there are not many early cover photos displaying the faces of the first-class partypeople who innocently cruised on at full speed not knowing that ahead lay the iceberg of HIV. In the way that John Embry shied away from outing the gay "face," so did his successor Anthony DeBlase for his first few covers (*Drummer* 99, 100, etc.)

To me, the essence of movies is the human face. The perfect photo for a magazine cover is also the human face. Seven of the eight cover photos I shot for *Drummer* between 1977 and 1993 all feature face. Three were shot with David Sparrow: *Drummer* 21, *Drummer* 25, and *Drummer* 30; the other five I shot solo: *Drummer* 118, *Drummer* 140, *Drummer* 157, *Drummer* 159, and *Drummer* 170. I also shot two covers for *Drummer*'s sibling, *Mach* (*Mach* 20, April 1990, and *Mach* 22, December 1990).The *Drummer* 24 cover I cast, designed, and assigned to photographer Robert Mapplethorpe is also all about the human face of my friend, Elliot Siegal. *Time* and *Newsweek* proved that nothing sells a magazine like a face.

Branding in *Drummer* 29, page 64, my original "Tough Customers" feature which I had debuted in *Drummer* 25 (December 1978), I created my *Drummer* Outreach program and asked invisible readers to shoot and share the personality of their own faces. As a gay activist journalist, I specifically crafted "Tough Customers" to help guys come out of the closet. If Harvey Milk's Castro Camera was among the first photo shops to develop gay men's sex pictures of themselves, I figured the next step was to out those grass-roots selfie photos in *Drummer* which in the 1970s was that decade's New Media:

> KeeRIST! If youse guys are gonna send us your hot pictures for publication, at least include your FACE. Who wants to look at a disconnected cock? *Drummer* is a magazine, not a gloryhole....This is almost the Eighties, doncha know!

At the request of publisher DeBlase, I also shot the "color-revival" cover and centerfold photographs of Palm Drive Video model Keith Ardent for *Drummer* 118 (July 1988) which was, DeBlase wrote, "the first color nude photography *Drummer* has offered in years...and more full color than the magazine has ever had before." (*Drummer* 118, page 4) His words were one of his many passive-aggressive digs at Embry for publishing *Drummer* on the cheap by dropping the beautiful interior color that had graced many of the early issues.

SELECT *DRUMMER* COVERS AND "THEME" ISSUES:
A BACK-STORY NARRATIVE OF ORAL HISTORY

The survey of the following select *Drummer* covers shows how face and bodies and drawings and photographs evolved in early *Drummer* into the "theme covers" shot by Fred Halsted, Robert Opel, Sparrow and Fritscher, and in one instance, Mapplethorpe.

Drummer 1 Cover: drawing by Bud; drawing also used as symbol of Embry's "Leather Fraternity" mail-order club.

Drummer 2 Cover: publicity photo by Fred Halsted from his film, *Sextool*; no faces showing; however, the face and torso of Val Martin, the star of *Sextool*, are featured on the back cover.

Drummer 3 Cover: uncredited publicity photo from the film, *Born to Raise Hell* (1974); with his face showing, this is the first *Drummer* front cover for Val Martin who became a star in *Born to Raise Hell*; Martin appeared on the front covers of *Drummer* 3, 8, 30, and 60.

Drummer 4 Cover: photo by Robert Opel of model's face obscured into a "virtual drawing" referencing a leatherman on acid.

Drummer 5 Cover: drawing by Chuck Arnett, the man who introduced the needle into Folsom Street sex, profiled in a feature article by Robert Opel and produced by Jack Fritscher, "Lautrec in Leather,"*Drummer* 4, January 1976; also in "Chuck Arnett: His Life, Our Times," by Jack Fritscher, *Drummer* 134, October 1989, reprinted in Mark Thompson's anthology *Leatherfolk: Radical Sex, People, Politics, and Practice*.

Drummer 6 Cover: drawing by British artist, Bill Ward, who, from his *oeuvre* as large as Tom of Finland's, contributed his serial-cartoon strip, *Drum*, as well as other erotic heroes, to so many dozens of issues he became the artist with the most pages published in *Drummer*.

Drummer 7 Cover: documentary photo by Robert Opel of faces, partially obscured, of two grooms kissing at a gay wedding—leather style in Los Angeles. The Philadelphia magazine, *Drum*, profiled a "Gay Marriage in Rotterdam" on the cover of *Drum* #26, September 1967; *Queens Quarterly Magazine*, Volume 2 #4, Fall 1970, also featured "Gay Marriage."

Before I made David Sparrow my *Drummer* photographer in 1977, he and I were married on the roof of 2 Charlton Street, New York, on David's birthday, May 7, 1972, to mark the third year of our ten-year domestic relationship. The wedding was performed by the Catholic priest, Jim Kane, the nationally popular leatherman who was four times featured in *Drummer*:

1. in two stories by our mutual friend, Sam Steward aka Phil Andros: "Babysitter" (*Drummer* 5) and "Many Happy Returns" (*Drummer* 6);

2. in one photo feature "Dungeons of San Francisco" (*Drummer* 17); and

3. as "Frank Cross" in my feature article "The Janus Society" (*Drummer* 27).

In my zero degrees of separation within *Drummer*, I should disclose that from 1968-1972 I had an S&M affair with my lifelong friend, the Reverend Jim Kane, who also in 1970-1971 commissioned and published my media columns, such as "The Chicago Seven" and "You're in the Midst of the Second American Revolution," in his monthly Catholic newspaper *Dateline Colorado* (Colorado Springs), for which he was priest-editor. Through Kane, I met Sam Steward/Phil Andros whose stories I agented and produced for *Drummer* 5 and 6. Seeing how much in love the Sparrow and I were, Kane, feeling a tad jealous, began actively to seek his own lover. In that hunt, I was Kane's "advisor" during his difficult year-long courtship of former football player, Ike Barnes, as chronicled in dozens of his signed and archived letters to me.

> February 2, 1971. Dear Jackanddave [*sic*], The razor strop you sent [as a gift] is great...plan to use shortly on Ike Barnes, my new m from N.Y. state...1959 Rose Bowl half-back for Ohio State...muscled, and out of his gourd on my style....—Jim

In San Francisco, during 1971 and 1972, the Fritscher-Sparrow duo were house mates with the newly partnered Kane-Barnes duo in a flat owned by Anthony (Tony) Perles at 4131 19th Street, four doors from 19th and Castro Streets. Perles was the author of *The Peoples' Railway: History of the San Francisco Muni* (1980); when he was unemployed in 1978, I hired him on my staff when I managed the proposals department at Kaiser Engineers, where I also hired John Trojanski, a fellow seminarian, whom I groomed as a *Drummer* writer and photographer in *Drummer* 25, "In the Habit: Sex in the Seminary," December 1978. After *Drummer*, when I was seconded from Kaiser Engineers to manage the writing for the San Francisco Municipal Railway's Muni Metro Light Rail Vehicle Startup Program, I hired another writer, a man-about-town known publicly as Roger of San Francisco who soon after began his ball-busting S&M company, Shotgun Video.

At the San Francisco Municipal Railway, I quickly learned that Muni at that time was rather much managed by a dedicated infrastructure of leather-identified homosexuals trying to solve the perpetual problems of mass transit and buses and trains running on time. As a new broom from Kaiser Engineers, I wrote from scratch for the San Francisco Muni Metro all the safety and procedures manuals, and the bus billboards introducing the new Muni Metro rail cars and station layouts to a city learning how to use it, as well as the *Elderly and Handicapped Guide to Muni Metro*. It was amusing to me to be a gay author writing *Drummer* while writing billboards for buses, and a leather writer penning brochures instructing people where to go. Within the rules of equal opportunity hiring in late 1979, I fell to one knee at the desk of Muni personnel director Al Schaaf begging him to hire the college-qualified David Sparrow—who in solidarity with me had quit as *Drummer* photographer—for a permanent position that he kept until he died of AIDS in 1992.

Our *Drummer* Salon encompassed writing, photography, sex, art, and real estate. David Sparrow and I helped Kane and Barnes remodel their newly purchased fixer-upper home at 11 Pink Alley. That silly address caused much hilarity in our leather Bloomsbury. The *pink* sounded gay and the two words together sounded like the G. I. American-in-Paris thrill: the sex district *Pigalle* pronounced as "Pig Alley." Because Kane was a famous priest *whipmeister* and a founder of the Society of Janus, it became a sexual and social code: "Have you been to Pink Alley?"

The Kane-Barnes living space was built above a garage and became famous for their first-floor garage dungeon, entered through a hidden door upstairs in the kitchen floor, as well as for their upstairs dinner parties where we sat around the table with artists such as author, artist, and tattooist, Sam Steward; my lover Robert Mapplethorpe; my longtime playmate, the German commercial photographer, Gerhard Pohl, the director of scatological films, who became a *Drummer* contributor; my fuckbuddy, who was also the art director of *Drummer*, Al Shapiro aka the artist A. Jay, and Touko Laaksonen aka Tom of Finland. At this Pink location, my friend and travel companion, photographer Gene Weber, shot black-and-white pictures documenting Kane and Barnes in their dungeon for *Drummer*.

That season, Tom was traveling with his longtime lover, Veli, who spoke only Finnish. It was Tom's first trip to the United States in February-March 1978 for his first American exhibitions. Tom opened at Robert Opel's Fey-Way Gallery in San Francisco at an invitation-only 8 PM reception on Friday, February 3, with a second personal gallery appearance by Tom on Saturday, 3-6 PM, February 4, for the opening of the show running February 4-15. Tom appeared at Fey-Way courtesy of Eons Gallery in Los Angeles where he and his show opened on Friday, February 17, 1978.

It was a singular high point of the *Drummer* Salon, when for February 9, 1978, I arranged a dinner party, aided by Al Shapiro, to cross-pollinate the best of the *Drummer* talent at that moment present in San Francisco. Because I employed all the guests in one way or another from my editorial desk at *Drummer*, I took a kind of glee in anticipating the needs of gay icons who wished to meet other icons back in that first decade of liberation when icons were colliding for the first time. In the carousing melodrama that was the *Drummer* Salon, it was like setting up a gentlemen's Algonquin Club supper, clever and agreeable and toned not at all like a scene from *The Boys in the Band*.

The February 9 soiree was such a *Drummer* triumph that in his letter to Douglas Martin, my ever-ascending friend Sam Steward, who hungered for his own charmed circle ala Gertrude Stein, shrewdly overstepped and attributed to himself the creation of my dinner party. Sam, at that time, was an unlikely host of anything. He was nearly seventy, and old for his age. He was a drug-and-alcohol-addicted hermit of melancholy hiding in Berkeley, and he was pretty much grandfathered—through his being published in *Drummer*—into post-Stonewall culture for his S&M writing penned in earlier decades for *Der Kreis* (*The Circle*) whose closing in 1967 troubled him deeply. Sam Steward, who always depended on the kindness of strangers to drive him and feed him and fuck him, never organized much more than his 1950s *spintriae* orgies of sailors. Hung up on straight rough-trade hustlers, he famously had little regard for other gay men. I met him in 1969, and I doubt if he ever served a trick a sandwich, much less hosted a dinner party. I am certain that Sam had not met Al Shapiro, Tom of Finland, Robert Opel, or Robert Mapplethorpe until I introduced them to him, as I also did to Kane and Barnes. In fact, Sam Steward had no connection to any one of the dinner party guests except to his caretakers Kane and Barnes who were social-climbers enough to agree to my invitation that they, in their own striving to collect a Pink Alley salon, would be foolish not to entertain such an iconic gay summit of leather artists, photographers, and writers.

Present on my editorial guest list for that February 9 dinner party were hosts Kane who swanned at the head of the table and Barnes who skivvied in the kitchen; my lover Robert Mapplethorpe; my pal, Fey-Way Gallery owner and Oscar streaker Robert Opel; my creative partner and erotic intimate, Al Shapiro, the art director of *Drummer*; and the editor-in-chief of *Drummer*, who happened to be me, a New Journalist swimming in history and taking notes of the forces I had unleashed to sit together for the first and only time at one dinner table.

This one evening indicates how powerful was the *Drummer* editorship (no matter who was editor) in organizing all the disparate talents who filled its pages. My motive was to see, out of my editorial curiosity, at least, what the talented guests, combined or collaborating, might come up with to refresh the ongoing hungry issues of the magazine. The power of *Drummer* pulled Mapplethorpe unbidden by me to my desk. It pulled Tom of Finland and Sam Steward as well. In that time on the international leather scene, *Drummer* was the only game in town.

It is worth noting that *Drummer* publisher John Embry never met Sam Steward, or cared to figure out who Steward's pseudonymous Phil Andros was. Jeanne Barney also never met Sam. But she was most gracious to him when I suggested he submit his stories to *Drummer*, and she published him, in the midst of the April Slave Auction turmoil, in *Drummer* issues five and eight (March 1976 and September 1976).

Justin Spring quoted Sam Steward's self-focused letter, dated "Valentino's Day [February 14], 1978," about this February 9 dinner party in his biography, *Secret Historian: The Life and Times of Samuel Steward, Professor, Tattoo Artist, and Sexual Renegade*. Sam Steward was, even as a friend I admired, a wise and wizened queen who could control an arcade of rough sailors with an eyebrow, but a dinner party? He had the certain kind of Ionesco absurdist gravitational pull that comes when sexual bottoms in search of a center try to balance their subordinate lives by claiming to be the primal cause of other peoples' efforts on the self-styled "power bottom's" behalf.

As a resurrectionist of Steward's writing under Jeanne Barney in *Drummer*, I was never one of my dear Sammy's controllable sailors. Inside his demure demeanor, he was a Napoleonic banty of a man who tried to trump everyone, and hustle his hustlers and friends and 1980s acolytes, such as John Preston, to get the future canonization he wanted by giving the upcoming generation what they wanted: their ancestral connection to him. When the obsessive Sam Steward tied up loose ends, he was always the center of the knot. I adored him as an intellectual friend and as an old gent whom I respected as a pioneer gay writer, but I was always careful of his diktats because after I interviewed him on audiotape in 1972, he abruptly told me, who became aghast, I could not do what I had a grant for: publish an article about him. As an alcoholic with a taste for hustlers, he had impoverished himself, and out of his poverty, he decreed: "You can't publish anything I told you until after I'm dead. I have to live off these stories." I understood his concerns and complied even as I had to explain to the grant giver that I could not publish my research. Nevertheless, I didn't drop him because I truly liked him, and we remained pals for twenty-four years, but his request warned me to be ever analytic of him and his motives.

TOM OF FINLAND AND *DRUMMER*

Below: The [single brackets] are insertions by Justin Spring into his own quotation from Sam Steward's letter; the [[double brackets]] are my observations.

On February 9, 1978, on one of his increasing rare nights out, [[the agoraphobic]] Steward had the pleasure [[because of my invitation]] of meeting Tom of Finland...Steward [[who was a starfucker of Valentino, Stein, and Toklas]] wrote Douglas Martin that "the living legend Tom of Finland...is actually a Finn named Tuoko [[*sic*; Touko]] Laaksonen—a nice old geezer, my age bracket, with a kind of long horsey face...[Since] Jim Kane and Ike Barnes wanted to meet him...[[Sam begins the structure of his little prevarication]] I arranged [another] dinner [with him] and [the art dealer] Robert Opel and [[my lover]] Robert Mapplethorpe. Anyway, Tom and I were toasted [[by the *Drummer* editor, as I well recall doing]] as the two dirtiest men in the Westron [[sic]] world, and as responsible for an ocean of cum deep enough to float a battleship....

During dinner, Steward had a long conversation [[it was little more than a sentence or two tossed off by Sam at the sometimes condescending New Yorker Mapplethorpe who fended Sam off with his business card]] with the photographer Robert Mapplethorpe, who apparently [[Apparently? As an eyewitness, I rest my case.]] told him that his erotic studies of black males had been partly inspired by similar studies by George Platt Lynes....[[as well as, and even more so, the studies of black males shot by Miles Everitt and George Dureau. It is meaningful that Mapplethorpe, shooting leather personalities and players in San Francisco, never bothered to lens a portrait of Sam.]]

Four days after Sam Steward wrote to Douglas Martin, Tom of Finland, acknowledging the actual source of the dinner party, wrote to Al Shapiro and me on February 18, 1978, from New York where he continued his American tour:

Many thanks for the dinner party which we both, Veli and I, enjoyed very much. I'd liked to stay in San Francisco much longer, but even those few days made me feel happy. Seattle [where he visited between San Francisco and LA] was interesting and L-A rainy. N. Y. Is cold but warmer weather has been promised in the next days. After two busy weeks here [in New York where he had a sold-out exhibition at Stompers Gallery], I'll fly back to Finland to start working again.—All the best..., Tom.

On July 27, 1978, Tom of Finland once again wrote to Al Shapiro and me at *Drummer* saying thanks to us all for squiring him around San Francisco. Tom was also very pleased with Robert Opel's "Interview of Tom of Finland" in the four-page layout that Al and I produced and edited for my *Drummer* 22 (May 1978):

...thank you personally for your hospitality during my visit to San Francisco. I enjoyed meeting you and being around in places with you. And I must say I envy you being able to live and work in a city like San Francisco. I found it very inspiring. I also want to tell my thanks for the *Drummer* issue 22 which I received some days ago. I liked Robert Opel's interview, the photos were well selected and the whole article looked good, much better than those in local L.A. papers. I am very pleased.....Best wishes, Tom

Has anyone ever asked why Tom of Finland never appeared on the cover of *Drummer* while John Embry owned it? Tom was a surefire draw for readers. Like Robert Mapplethorpe's duality of "art and commerce" and very like Peter Schjeldahl's great assessment of Frieda Kahlo in *The New Yorker* (May 25, 2015), Tom of Finland existed in gay pop culture somewhere "between sainthood and a brand": gay sainthood as sweet man and artist, as well as brand name selling Tom of Finland Company cologne and clothing on fashion runways sponsored by Absolut Vodka in the way Robert Mapplethorpe sold art calendars and calla lily plates and appeared in print ads for Rose's Lime Juice. Even before Tom's first arrival in the United States, Al Shapiro and I invited his work into *Drummer* in 1977. Tom was, in fact, so accomplished professionally that for seventeen years until 1973 when he retired to devote his time to his own art, he was senior art director at the Helsinki branch of the global ad agency McCann Erickson featured years later on the television series *Mad Men*.

In my archives exist three letters from Tom of Finland to Al Shapiro which tell the tale of how Tom's offer to publisher Embry went nowhere because of Embry's lack of response to the reticent and overly modest Tom who was willing to sell his Tom of Finland original to *Drummer* for $300, or lease the use of his *Drummer*-specific drawing for $50. It is indicative of how out of touch Embry was with the erotic heart and heritage purpose of *Drummer*. For fifty bucks, thirty-seven years before Tom was honored with an iconic Finnish postal stamp, and forty years before the major motion picture *Tom of Finland* (2017), the skinflint Embry missed the "roots" chance to publish what would have been a gay history coup: the legendary Tom of Finland on the cover of the legendary *Drummer*. The cavalier Embry, always choosing favorites, blew Tom off because he had already contracted an equally brilliant European artist, the British Bill Ward, who over the years, as the artist most published in *Drummer*, created hundreds of *Drummer* pages with his ongoing graphic-novel, *Drum*.

Tom of Finland wrote on September 12, 1977:

Touko Laaksonen, Tehtaankatu 7 D 29, 00140 Helsinki 14, Finland.

...Well, I'd make a cover to *Drummer* with pleasure. I am busy now a couple of months, but in the end of November I should have time. I charge $300 for the original. I have not signed yet the contract with Eons, but if it is fixed by then, the price will be more. If *Drummer* prefers buying only the reproduction rights, I could also consider it. In that case, I'd like to know how much the magazine pays for that.... —Tom

Ninety days later on December 12, 1977, Tom of Finland noted *Drummer* dragging its feet. He also enclosed a photocopy of the crayon drawing he had specially designed to accommodate the *Drummer* cover logo and headline:

Even though I haven't heard from you since my last letter, I've made this drawing thinking of *Drummer*'s cover. It is drawn with wax crayons (in colors) in size about 17"x22" and in the layout space [around the figure of a leatherman], I have left layout space for the title and usual headlines. Perhaps you'd talk with *Drummer* people [Code: meaning the intractable, stubborn Embry] of this and let me know if the magazine wants the picture or not. As I mentioned earlier, I am willing to sell the original to *Drummer* (because it is specially made for the purpose) for $300.00, but if they prefer to buy only the right to use the picture on the magazine's cover, it is also OK. As I said, I don't know what the prices are at *Drummer* in that case, so let me know. Anyway I don't give it under $50.00....I am coming to San Francisco in early February for a week or two. I hope I can meet you then.... —Sincerely, Tom

Ten months later, just before his New York, October 28, 1978, double show with Etienne, Tom of Finland wrote to Al Shapiro. Tom was hoping he could move permanently to America, and he was patiently awaiting for Embry to respond to his many inquiries. He wrote on October 16, 1978:

> Dear Al, ...I hope to be able to come to California some time next year, but probably not for good even if I wished so. I can write again to John Embry about the publication [of the drawing(s)] if you think he is interested. I on my side should like the idea because there are several in my opinion very good drawings which are never published before....and also because I know that the technical quality in printing is good at Alternate Publishing.... —Tom

Embry was my "Original-Recipe Tough Customer." When Tom of Finland died, Embry managed to cobble up a half-page generic obituary of Tom featuring a murky reprint of one of Tom's drawings in *Manifest Reader* 16 (1992) page 77. As if he begrudged Tom's talent and success, Embry never once mentioned any connection at all of the legendary Tom of Finland to the legendary *Drummer* which Embry had sold in 1986. Thus does an unrequited grudge in an obituary change the bits of history. Embry's obituary for Tom of Finland was a passive-aggressive "revision by omission" of what tension and drama historically occurred between the two men. It was characteristic of Embry's lifelong "Los Angeles modus operandi," or, what San Franciscans postulate about LA, that "LA gays fight over everything in the gay world because, it seems, so little is of any value." If the LAPD had not driven John Embry out of LA, his revolving door of unpaid talent contributing to *Drummer*, backed by his erstwhile frenemies, including Larry Townsend, Ed Menerth, and even Jeanne Barney, would have gladly given him the gate.

Tom of Finland triumphed over Embry's Blacklist when Tony DeBlase, giving the finger to Embry's shunning of Tom, published a boot drawing by Tom on the cover of *Drummer* 113 (February 1988).

When the Sparrow and I split up after ten years in 1979, Kane—happy I had given up saving Sparrow—was finally able to fulfill his desire to "have and own" David, and to "fix" his alcohol and drug dependency. He rented David an apartment he and Barnes owned next door to their Pink Alley house, at 42 Pearl Street, where David lived until he died February 20, 1992. Kane, ever the leather parish priest, rented to "bottom" S&M males and females because they were easy tenants to counsel and control; he also rented a flat to Society of Janus founder Cynthia Slater who was also a famous "pain" bottom. When elderly, Jim Kane and Ike Barnes also bought a second home in Sebastopol, on Blank Road, one mile from my home and ten miles from John Embry, where, selling Christmas trees six weeks each year at the nearby Sorenson Farm, they both died, but not before a smirking Kane told me to "hang on to your Mapplethorpe pictures because someday they might be worth something."

Gene Weber, who shot Kane and Barnes with me (top page 17) for "Dungeons" (*Drummer* 17, July 1977), documented deep inside the secret truths of San Francisco S&M. Even as we balled frequently, I kept him artistically involved with *Drummer* and he lensed me in the underwater fisting shots of my "Gay Sports" feature in *Drummer* 20 (January 1978), as well as with my longtime playmate and "co-star" bottom, the redheaded Russell Van Leer, in *Blood Crucifixion*. That was one of Gene Weber's famous mixed-media 35mm S&M extravaganzas which he frequently screened for invited audiences of gentlemen in his luxury apartment on Buena Vista West Avenue. He was a millionaire living in the only high-rise Art Deco building on the street. Guests enjoyed his view overlooking the sex trails in Buena Vista Park to the east across the street. Very high-tech for the time, he projected his images on his art-theater-sized 20-foot-wide roll-down screen using a bank of nine projectors programmed so fluidly that his presentation looked like a movie when, in fact, it was a series of 35mm slides dissolving at different speeds into each other. When Gene Weber died, October 2, 1992, he bequeathed his vast 35mm-color transparency collection to the GLBT Historical Society of San Francisco where our *Blood Crucifixion* and his other erotic photography may be viewed.

Besides having vacationed together in the Carribean (1977) for the *Drummer* 20 scuba sex shots, Gene Weber and I had traveled together to Japan in October 1975, spending time in the outskirts of Tokyo at a Samurai house of bondage where the vibe was polite but a bit cool because the owners remembered World War II. The model in Gene Weber's photos for "Cock Casting" (*Drummer* 15, May 1977) and for "Plaster Casting" (*Drummer* 18, August 1977) was our friend, Max Morales, the handsome and spiritually centered athlete who was great friends with Paul Gerrior aka Ledermeister, the archetypal Colt leather-bear model. In North Beach theater-clubs and cabarets featuring "Live Topless Girls," Max appeared nightly, or at least, regularly, oozing male sex appeal, as the exotic-erotic dance partner of several female dancers. Max Morales was fictionalized in *The Holy Mountain* section of *Some Dance to Remember*, Reel 6, Scene 4.

This is the kind of salon of S&M and talent that *Drummer* fell into when *arriviste* Embry found himself exiled from LA to San Francisco late in 1976 and early 1977. Cut to the quick by his banishment by the LAPD, Embry was like a man who had lost his country. He never became a "San Franciscan." He had left what heart he had in Los Angeles, and his arrest and exile and PTSD may have so eaten at his guts that the stress may have contributed to the colon cancer he suffered soon after he set up the *Drummer* office where I worked at 1730 Divisadero Street in San Francisco.

Distressed in his long move from LA and from illness, Embry was absent from *Drummer* for seven formative months in 1978 (February-May while moving, and again, August-December while ill) during which time Al Shapiro and I, eager to please this new publisher we had just met, created the San Francisco version of *Drummer* that changed it from an LA magazine into an international success. In an almost ironic coincidence in Autumn 2000, John Embry, heading for the International Mr. Drummer Contest which he had scorned and sold in 1986, ran down the stairs on his way to the airport and fell, breaking his hip. He observed about that illness what was true about his earlier long bout with cancer: "The healing process takes a lot of energy, leaving little time for the creative process." (*Super MR 7*, page 5) Even when physically healthy, Embry was far from a creative force behind *Drummer*. At best, he was a show-runner seeing to the mechanics and commercial accounts of publishing. He never understood the soul of *Drummer*. The hiatus caused by his colon cancer, sad to say for him, left open a wonderful door for the creative staff to invent a magazine that Embry never understood. That wasn't the intent, but it was the result.

So confused and jealous was Embry by the diverse reasons for the success of our re-imagined *Drummer* that he obsessively filled his subsequent magazines such as *Super MR* with page after page of reprints from 1970s *Drummer*, and often, with reprints of the very features and fiction, like "Prison Blues," that I had penned for the *Drummer* he so misunderstood he sold it. For twenty-four years, he groused and regretted that sale until his death in 2010.

As an eyewitness of his regrets, I offer his *Super MR 7* which contains nearly a dozen pages nostalgic for the early *Drummer* whose lightning caught in a bottle he never really understood anymore than he understood the rainmakers who turned *Drummer* into a perfect storm of sex, masculine identity, and sadomasochism.

One wonders if Embry so loved *Drummer*, why did he plunder the profits, sell it, and, then, why did he try to reinvent a new *Drummer* inside the magazines he later created? While Embry's sale of *Drummer* saddled

DeBlase with Embry's old debts, it freed *Drummer* from his fiscal tyranny that caused *Drummer* staff and contributors so much hardship because, when it came to paying the talent, or honoring subscriptions, Embry was a deadbeat who was notorious in LA, according to *Drummer* editor-in-chief Jeanne Barney, as "Robert Ripoff."

The reason Embry sold *Drummer*, according to DeBlase, was that Embry owed so many writers, artists, photographers, printers, suppliers, and staff so much money, siphoned off for his many real estate and publishing ventures, that he had no choice but to sell and run. Insulted when he discovered Embry's hidden debts, DeBlase felt betrayed at Embry's failure of "leather fraternity," and expressed his bitterness in several of his *Drummer* editorials.

Drummer 8 Cover: photo by Roy Dean of model Val Martin body-painted by tattoo artist, Cliff Raven, to look like a virtual drawing; Raven (*Drummer* 14, p. 47) was named after a bird by his mentor, the tattooist Sam Steward who was the tough old bird known as Phil Sparrow aka Philip Sparrow aka Phil Andros whose story "Many Happy Returns" appeared in the same issue; within the Chuck Renslow Family, Raven tattooed me in Chicago in 1969; David Sparrow's true surname, *Sparrow*, was his family name, and his mother's name was "Nellie" which caused him to be terribly teased among the queens when he came out in Evansville, Indiana. I used my lover, David Sparrow, as basis for the fictitious characters named "Arrow" in my 1969 novel, *I Am Curious (Leather)* aka *Leather Blues*, and "Teddy" in my 1990 book, *Some Dance to Remember: A Memoir-Novel of San Francisco 1970-1982*.

Drummer 9 Cover: photo by Robert Opel of the male "Gloria Hole" in gender-bender drag, face obscured by makeup, from the LA Cycle Sluts performance-art troop which included Mikal Bales, founder of Zeus Studio later featured in *Drummer* for its bondage-nipple-whipping videos; this was *Drummer* magazine's most unpopular cover ever. Leather animus against gender-fucking anima began in the next issue with "Letters to the Editor" and simmered for years: in *Drummer* 134 (October 1989), an angry reader wrote on page 7:

> GENDERFUCK LIVES. In your latest issue of *Drummer*, I saw a listing for "Fantasia Fair Provincetown" listed in the "Leather Calendar." For your information, "Fantasia Fair" is a national convention for transvestites; far from a leather event. Better do some more checking into what you list as "leather events." —BL, Provincetown

Publisher DeBlase alluding to Embry's misstep responded: "The genderfuck was unintentional (this time)."

Drummer 10 Cover: drawing by Rex; his last for Embry's *Drummer* until invited back by DeBlase to draw the milestone cover of *Drummer* 100, recalling at that time that Rex had drawn the illustrations for covers of two of my books, *Leather Blues*, which was excerpted in *Drummer*, and for *Corporal in Charge of Taking Care of Captain O'Malley and Other Stories*, which was the first book anthology of *Drummer* fiction.

Drummer 13 Cover: photo by Lou Thomas aka "Jon Target"; my longtime (beginning October 1968) friend, Lou Thomas, co-founder of Colt Studio with Jim French, split off Colt in 1968-69 to found Target Studio in New York; in his startup of Target Studio and wanting to print a *Target* magazine, Lou Thomas did a publishing trial balloon by printing a limited edition of my 1969 novel, *I Am Curious (Leather)* aka *Leather Blues*. Using low-tech hectograph, he published one hundred copies in the popular, and very underground, samizdat style of gay "magazines" created with unfolded pages of typing paper printed both sides and bound with two staples. Other pertinent examples I collected in the 1960s of this leather-and-fetish format pre-dating *Drummer* are: *Justice Weekly*, a tabloid published in Canada 1949-1972; *SMADS*, Old Chelsea Station, New York; *Wheels* published at 254 West 25th Street in New York by the Cycle Motorcycle Club; *The Inner Tube* published by the V (Five) Senses, Murray Hill Station, Manhattan; and *Buddy Riders* published by Essem Enterprises, San Francisco. Years later, *I Am Curious (Leather)* was excerpted in *Son of Drummer* (1978), and announced by Embry as "a forthcoming *Drummer* novel." That did not happen.

Leather Blues, the "1960s Leather Novel That Could," had a gypsy-biker history. After its publication by Target and its excerpt in *Son of Drummer*, it was published in book form by Gay Sunshine Press (1984) and sold 10,000 copies. It was also serialized in eight issues of *Man2Man Quarterly* 1980-1982; and was excerpted as the premiere fiction in the first issue of *Skin* (January 1979), and in *Inches*, Volume 1 #3 (July 1985), and in the Magcorp magazine, *Stroke*, Volume 4 #4, 1985. When gay pop-culture critic Michael Bronski reviewed both *Leather Blues* and my *Corporal in Charge and Other Stories* along with a short fiction anthology by Sam Steward and the novel I had edited for print, *Mr. Benson* by John Preston, he declared *Drummer* writing and *Drummer* writers as essentially romantic in his essay, "S&M: The New Romance: Cruelty without Pain," *Gay Community News*, Boston, Issue 30, February 16, 1985.

On June 4, 1981, Lou Thomas wrote a letter on Target Studios stationery asking me to contribute to his *Target Album* magazine: "Dear Jack: ...As you know, I've long admired your writing ability—it was a sad day for *Drummer* when you and A. Jay left." On August 21, 1981, Lou wrote a similar letter of invitation to Al Shapiro. Both letters are in my leather archives. The story which I sent him was "The Dirtiest Blond Contractor in West Texas."

Drummer 14 Cover: photo by Lou Thomas, Target Studio.

Drummer 15 Cover: drawing by A. Jay aka Al Shapiro, founding San Francisco *Drummer* art director; A. Jay's only *Drummer* cover.

Drummer 19 Cover: publicity photo by Joe Gage from his film *El Paso Wrecking Corp.*

Drummer 21 Cover: photo by Fritscher-Sparrow of San Francisco cabaret pianist, John Trowbridge; together, he and I wrote the S&M song, "Masochist Stomp," for *Drummer*.

Drummer 23 Cover: photo by Lou Thomas; Target Studio photo of homomasculine "Barry" whom I chose to place on the *Drummer* cover because he typified my "Redneck" theme issue; Barry exuded universal sex appeal as a tattooed Southern model also for Colt Studio and for David Hurles' Old Reliable Studio. As a photographer, I wanted to shoot Barry, but he was one model who got away. My longtime friend David Hurles, usually so generous in sharing his models, was oddly possessive of his "exclusive" on Barry Hoffman who was also a Colt and Target model, and I dropped the subject. Before he was a porn film star, Barry was, in fact, the real person on whom James Leo Herlihy based his character Joe Buck in his 1965 novel *Midnight Cowboy*. Jon Voight who played Joe Buck in the 1969 film, the only X-rated movie to win the Oscar for Best Picture, was cast because of his resemblance to Barry who was more sexy and handsome. Voight was no Joe Buck, and, with his anti-gay conservative Republican Party politics, he eventually made his entire acting career impossible to watch.

Drummer 24 Cover: photo by Robert Mapplethorpe is the quintessential Mapplethorpe leather portrait; I cast and designed the photograph and commissioned Mapplethorpe to shoot it, requesting the portrait be in color which was unexpected for Mapplethorpe who usually shot people in black and white, and flowers in color. I cast my New York playmate, Elliot Siegal, who had never modeled, because I thought him an Emersonian representative man dripping with the *verite* of "dirty Mineshaft appeal." After meeting Elliott Siegal, Mapplethorpe fell in lust and shot him several times: "Elliot and Dominick 1979," Photograph 11 in *Robert Mapplethorpe: Ten by Ten* (1988). Elliott lived at 58 Charles Street where Mapplethorpe lensed him.

Drummer 25 Cover: photo by Fritscher-Sparrow of pre-steroid Mike Glassman, the future Colt model "Ed Dinakos," armpits rampant, and smiling which was then unusual in leather photography.

Drummer 30 Cover: photo by Fritscher-Sparrow; a carefully coded "fisting" two-shot of Val Martin and his lover, Bob Hyslop aka the model "Leo Stone." This is the last *Drummer* cover shot by the team of Fritscher-Sparrow. We staged it in Sonoma County. Its design was inspired by our annual October visits to the International Arm-Wrestling Championships in Petaluma, California, one hour north of the Golden Gate Bridge.

The *mano-a-mano* eye-stare and arm-wrestle signify how my first love, David Sparrow, and I were struggling at the end of what had been our mostly wonderful ten-year affair. The pose is also symbolic of how David Sparrow and I were arm-wrestling Embry over the esthetics and payment for our photos in *Drummer*. As David Sparrow struggled with his addictions and depression during our divorce, he was increasingly angry at Embry and unavailable for shoots.

Conditions dictated that, solo, I shot Val Martin and Leo Stone one more time for the "Spit" centerfold of *Drummer* 31. The weekend shoot again occurred at the Sonoma ranch of Ed Linotti, one of the founding members of the Pacific Drill Patrol (PDP), the first uniform club founded in San Francisco (1972). When published in *Drummer*, my Martin/Stone centerfold, because of Embry's dirty math subtracting "Fritscher," was bylined "by David Sparrow."

Drummer 118 Cover: photo by Jack Fritscher of Keith Ardent (real name, Coleman Jones) from the Palm Drive Video feature, *Pec Stud in Black Rubber*. I shot this 35mm transparency on November 22, 1987, at the urgent request of the model, Keith Ardent, whose HIV bucket list included the hope of being made immortal on the cover of *Drummer*. (Keith Ardent also modeled for Christopher Rage and Zeus Studio.) True to Ardent's wish, this July 1988 cover shot was designed in studio to be an archetypal and representative *Drummer* cover.

In content, it showcases a true-life *verite Drummer* player encircled with fetish items covering his frontal nudity and presenting the *hauteur* of a top.

In design, the purposely vertical shot is composed by shooting up at the standing figure to empower him. At the top of the frame, I left air-space for the *Drummer* title, and at the side for a stack of cover copy. The photo is lit with off-camera electric spotlights to enhance the "outdoor shoot" which is signature of the early "Fritscher-Sparrow" and later "Fritscher solo" covers shot outdoors in contrast to most *Drummer* covers shot indoors.

On April 18, 1988, I again photographed Keith Ardent, who was a lovely man, in his quintessential leather video, *Let's Play Doctor*. Keith Ardent, wish-fulfilled and thereafter known as "a *Drummer* cover model," lived until September 9, 1992.

Drummer 140 Cover: photo by Jack Fritscher of Randy Rann from the Palm Drive Video feature, *Daddy's Tools*. In this June 1990 issue, DeBlase announces *Drummer* is "For Sale" on page 5.

Drummer 157 Cover: photo by Jack Fritscher of "Moustached Bodybuilder" inserted on lower left of cover next to photograph by Steve Savage of the model Brutus who was the star of four Palm Drive Video features. Printed twice on the cover and on page 10, this Fritscher photograph is mistakenly uncredited in *Drummer* 157; its provenance is that Fritscher's "Moustached Bodybuilder," shot in 1978, was also the cover of *California Action Guide* (August 1982).

Drummer 159 Cover: photo by Jack Fritscher of Larry Perry, the most famous 1980s bartender at the Spike in LA who had appeared in *Drummer* 132, page 45. My photo, shot October 3, 1990, is a production still from my Palm Drive Video feature, *Naked Came the Stranger*, starring Larry Perry. This photo shared the cover with a larger photo of IML winner, Lenny Broberg, shot by Scott Beseman. My agreement with the second publisher of *Drummer*, Tony Deblase, was that Larry Perry was to be solo on the cover. But Deblase sold *Drummer*, to its third publisher, Martijn Bakker, and agreements, as they always did at *Drummer*, shifted. According to editor Joseph W. Bean, Perry had somehow offended Bakker who allegedly said, "That man will never be on the cover of my magazine." I figure, according to the divine right of porn kings, new owner Bakker, who is a mystery, may have demanded sex and Larry Perry said, "Fuck you."

Nevertheless, the brilliant Bean managed to print the extremely popular Perry's appearance on this first cover of the first issue published by Martijn

Bakker, known perhaps unfairly, as the last of the assassins who murdered *Drummer*.

Drummer 170 Cover: portrait photo by Jack Fritscher of Donnie Russo. I cast and directed Donnie Russo during the first six weeks of his meteoric video career in my features *Homme Alone, When Bodybuilders Collide,* and *Rough Night at the Jockstrap Gym*. I immediately pitched him and his videos to the new regime of Martijn Bakker's "Dutch" *Drummer*. Every porn director in America wanted to shoot Russo. I hired him as the new, younger, *fin de siecle Drummer* man. Playing on the pop-culture provenance of Beatlemania and Wrestlemania, I submitted my concept of a "Russomania" theme issue to Joseph W. Bean who, as he exited *Drummer,* relayed the baton to Marcus-Jay Wonacott who was progressing from editorial manager to editor. Ten minutes later, I felt the freshness of the punch line inherent in my proposed pun lose its dewiness when the word *Wrestlemania* was suddenly and gratuitously added to the very next cover of *Drummer* 161 (March 1993) featuring a depressingly drab shot of a joyless leather model that had nothing at all to do with wrestling. My proposal of "Russomania" for the future issue (170) was the trigger that had shot the theme word *Wrestlemania* to the cover of that very next issue. This cloning wasn't Bean's or Wonacott's fault during that stressful period of in-house confusion as *Drummer* changed owners. For years staff had struggled to fill the next hungry issue with little regard to future issues. Fixated on the minutiae of one issue, editors, who came and went, often could not see the bigger picture of the long game. To them, *Drummer* was a bunch of separate issues. To me, *Drummer* was a very long book in which each issue was a continuing chapter documenting an eyewitness and narrative arc of gay culture and human drama very like an episodic television show with its long-form storyline that spans the series. But, then, I have congenital *Drummer*mania.

The minute *Drummer* 161 hit the stands, the World Wrestling Federation (WWF), the owner of the word *Wrestlemania* threatened suit against *Drummer* for copyright infringement unless *Drummer* pulled the issue off the newsstands. The principle involved was similar to the "Gay Olympics" copyright fiasco in 1986 when the homophobic United States Olympic Committee won its suit prohibiting Dr. Tom Waddell, the gay Olympic athlete, from calling the first "Gay Games," which he founded, the "Gay Olympics." Just so, the WWF had owned its coined word long before *Drummer*'s not-so-fair use made it seem as if the WWF had suddenly come out of its obvious closet into a gay leather magazine! Coincidentally, while protecting its intellectual property from the clutches of *Drummer* in

1993, the WWF itself was sued in 1994 by the "World Wide Federation for Nature" for using the initials "WWF," and had to re-brand itself as the "WWE," World Wrestling Entertainment.

Intellectual property historians might note that *Drummer* 161 was so scofflaw that Maya Angelou might also have sued because the entire text of her poem written for Bill Clinton's 1993 Presidential Inaugural, "On the Pulse of Morning" was boldly published across pages 6 and 7 with no note of permission or copyright.

In *Drummer* 185 (May 1995) on page 51, editorial manager Wickie Stamps published a photo-spread titled "Forbidden *Drummer*" featuring pictures from *Drummer* 161 and confirming the WWF law suit.

> A legal wrangle over the use of a trademarked name [Wrestlemania] on the cover [of *Drummer* 161] forced all copies of that issue off the newsstands and into the shredder. Only a few copies of #161 ever made it into public hands.

All that notwithstanding, on the cover of *Drummer* 170 (December 1993), my word *Russomania* was pasted in large letters next to my cover photograph of Donnie Russo.

Drummer 188 Cover: photo by Ram Studios/Franco of model Ted Downer. In what should have been a classic and gorgeous "Twentieth Anniversary Issue" in *Drummer* 188, Wickie Stamps was, according to my interview with her on January 20, 2011, rather coerced by circumstances into producing an issue that in art design looked like a ransom note cut-and-pasted from previous *Drummer* issues. Frankly, I saw Embry's characteristic reprint fingerprints and his revisionist history of *Drummer* all over the issue created at the precise time Embry and Robert Davolt were conspiring together over Davolt returning *Drummer* to Embry even as the Dutch publisher Martijn Bakker found he could not control San Francisco *Drummer* from Amsterdam. At my home in 2014, Dutch leather historian Pieter Claeys told me that Bakker said: "I couldn't fly to San Francisco every week to put out the fires. (Ik kon neit elke week naar SF vliegen on de brandjes daar te blussen.)" The issue also was full, not of leather photographers's warm and personal erotic work, but of corporate video photographs, and a grinding agenda to sell its soul for money that moved away from what it had been in the gay liberation 1970s and what it had become in the politically correct 1980s into the queer feminism of the 1990s. In the magazine's tortured last three years (1996-1999), Embry seemed obsessively dedicated to regaining his control of *Drummer* and its institutional memory through his operatives such as John W. Rowberry and Robert Davolt, who termed himself the "last publisher" of *Drummer*.

In 1999, as *Drummer* died, Davolt claimed to have delivered to Embry, who by then had no connection to *Drummer* for thirteen years, the coveted treasures of the *Drummer* files of manuscripts, photographs, and drawings which, in fact, belonged to the authors, photographers, and artists who since 1975 had expected to have their original work returned to them. In return, Embry hired Davolt to work on Embry's *Super MR* magazine. Davolt appeared as an editorial writer in *Super MR* 7 where he wrote this amazingly cheeky propaganda statement about the shameless Embry's obsession with "seizing the legacy" of the magazine he dumped as a losing proposition in 1986:

> When the magazine [*Drummer*] ceased publication, employees, advertisers and subscribers were left dangling in the wind....It was *Super MR* [i.e.: John Embry] who, as a good will gesture, offered *Drummer* subscribers and advertisers a credit equal to their unfulfilled subscriptions and advertising. It may be difficult to seize the legacy....It is particularly embarrassing [*sic*] to Alternate Publishing [John Embry] who originated the [*Drummer*] title 25 years ago, the name is now just an empty trademark.

I am not an attorney, but as far as I have been able to research, there is no paper trail to indicate that the *Drummer* title was ever a registered trademark. In Summer 1977, after the 1976 copyright laws were significantly changed about ownership of the contents in magazines, I specifically asked Embry if he were going to trademark the title of the two-year-old *Drummer*. I was inside *Drummer* and concerned for its future. *Drummer* was my job and had become my love. Embry was spending so much money on his court case regarding the 1976 Slave Auction, he shrank from even more legal expenses, and seemed to think his titles, like his content, were covered by simple copyright under "*Drummer* Publications" (*Drummer* 3, p. 3) and then "Alternate Publishing" (*Drummer* 7, p. 1, the First Anniversary Issue). On the masthead of *Drummer* 39 (August 1980), Embry tried to invoke a kind of "trademark" protection by claiming instead "copyright" protection.

> *Drummer, Drumsticks, Drumbeats, Tough Customers, Tough Shit, Leatherman's Notebook, Man to Man, Astrologic, In Passing*, and *Drum* are copyrighted names of departments appearing in *Drummer* Magazine. Copyright 1980 by Alternate Publishing.

Trademark and copyright are two different categories. Names and titles are not protected by copyright law. Embry may, however, have been relying on the laws about "unregistered trademarks." Therefore, besides the *Drummer* magazine founded in 1975, there exists *Modern Drummer* magazine founded in 1977. One is about gay leather and the other is about musical percussionists.

INNOVATIONS INSIDE *DRUMMER*:

Fritscher Kickstarts the Grass-roots *Drummer* Outreach Program
to Relate Directly to Readers with "Tough Customers" and "Tough Shit."

Editor's Note: In *Drummer* 25 (December 1978), Fritscher invented the "Tough Customers" photo feature to liberate recently closeted readers' primal fear of the camera, and to make the pages of *Drummer* reflect genuine gay faces rather than only models. No other person was involved with creating "Tough Customers."

In 1990, *Tough Customers* became its own magazine created by the astute *Drummer* editor Joseph W. Bean. *Drummer* publisher Anthony DeBlase wrote in *Drummer* 128 (May 1989), that Jack Fritscher's "'Tough Customers'" concept "is obviously one of the, if not the, most popular feature in *Drummer*." In the first issue of *Tough Customers*, DeBlase acknowledged on page 4 the grass-roots outreach Fritscher invented to reflect the readers: "When we asked *Drummer* readers what they liked best about each monthly issue of *Drummer*, the response was overwhelming: 'Tough Customers!'"

As a companion to "Tough Customers," Fritscher also created the news-clipping column, "Tough Shit," which was announced on the contents page of *Drummer* 22 (May 1978), but not included; "Tough Shit" appeared for the first time in *Drummer* 23 (July 1978). It parodied human foibles from a leather humor point of view.

CHAPTER 3

LEATHER PERVERSATILITY

What Makes Redneck Cops Erotic?
The LAPD Busts the Drummer Slave Auction
Anita Bryant, Arnold Schwarzenegger, and the Culture War

- Counter-phobic Lust: How Gay Men Sexualize "Bully Cops" as "Fetish Tops" from the LAPD to the Academy Training Center
- Charles Manson, Patty Hearst, and the Great Drummer Slave Auction Raid
- Anita Bryant Ignites the Culture War; *The Advocate* and *The National Enquirer* Trash *Drummer*
- Photographic Censorship in Cincinnati, the Most Puritan City in the USA
- Mapplethorpe and Schwarzenegger: Political Censorship on eBay

Los Angeles in the leather-*noir* 1970s was a mysteriously conservative city. Think of the LA politics, danger, and corruption in the 1974 film, *Chinatown*, directed by Roman Polanski who learned plenty about the LAPD after the Manson Family murdered his wife, Sharon Tate, and six others in 1969. The Manson-Tate killings made LA's conservative police chief Ed Davis nationally infamous over night. Conscious of his media image as a star "technical advisor" to popular television shows glamorizing right-wing cops such as *Dragnet* (1967-1970) and *Adam*-12 (1968-1975), he was dedicated to preserving the values of "Old Los Angeles" even as he was driven, in the "New Los Angeles "of the 1970s, to set straight the twisted press his LAPD had earned over his handling of the Manson-Tate bloodbath executed by Charles Manson's Family of sex slaves whom he and the media confused with BDSM leather behavior.

In March 1977, the same month that John Embry hired me to edit *Drummer* at the moment the magazine was fleeing from LA to San Francisco, Polanski learned even more when arrested by the LAPD and charged with the drugging and raping of a minor female at the home of Jack Nicholson. Polanski fled LA and the United States forever.

All during 1974, with Davis (popularly derided as "Crazy Ed") chasing the glamorous and elusive high-society fugitive, Patty Hearst, around LA, the LAPD called in its public relations team with camera and a helicopter to cover the LAPD's furious gun battle and fiery attack on the mixed-race Symbionese Liberation Army which had kidnaped and radicalized their white "sex slave," San Francisco heiress Patty Hearst, who, after prison and pardon, went on to camp stardom in John Waters' films, *Cry-Baby* and *Serial Mom*.

The brutal LAPD attack on the SLA terrorists on May 17, 1974, forecasted exactly the way Davis alerted the media and brought in the guns and troops, and two buses to haul his quota of queers, and to get TV cameras rolling for his staged media attack on the Drummer Slave Auction, April 10, 1976. Davis had stalked the easy prey of the three-person *Drummer* staff for months harassing them with gumshoe detectives tailing cars, home phone taps, and surprise visits to the tiny office. Like a Hollywood mogul manufacturing publicity, he planned the arrest of the *Drummer* leather queers. He could not arrest them for simply being gay. So he doubled down and dug deep, like the fundamentalist he was, to resurrect the ancient charge of practicing "slavery" which had been abolished by the Thirteenth Amendment to the United States Constitution in 1865. Davis set up the raid as a photo opportunity to prove during that decade of great social change, and drugs and gangs and politics, that he was a true blue cop fighting vice in the good old City of Angels. The *Orange County Register* headline crowed: "Police Free Gay Slaves." Davis, who went on to be elected a California State Senator, had the nerve to say that he had used extreme force because he and his men were being bullied by queers, declaring that for years the LAPD had been "cowed by being too lenient with the most powerful lobby in the city, the homosexual community."

The institutional homophobia of the LAPD was traditional, voter-approved, and sick. The long-term psychological effects on LA gay people being debased and brutalized in a second-class life of entrapment and harassment, and on leathermen being abused down to a third-class lifestyle, are revealed in John Embry's brazen reaction to gay persecution in which he purposed *Drummer* as a very risky political assault weapon against the LAPD.

Was the often violent and always intimidating Police Chief Ed Davis, who was no stranger to the choke hold, the ideal "Bully Top" of Embry's personal BDSM dreams? Counter-phobic behavior is a precise "survival response" to anxiety that gay men use to turn the bullies they fear into the gods they worship. BDSM provides both metaphor and mechanism for this kind of erotic transubstantiation. In *Drummer*, where Embry insistently poked fun at Davis in years of monthly issues, nearly every story and article centered on some insecure "daredevil" bottom seeking out and eroticising the man and behavior he fears enough to obey. This counter-phobic BDSM attitude is endlessly perverse in twirling pain into pleasure. In *Brideshead Revisited*, when Anthony Blanche is threatened with a dunking by bullies of the kind who tossed Cecil Beaton into a river at one of Stephen Tennant's famous parties, Blanche, as articulated by Evelyn Waugh, said: "Nothing would give me greater pleasure than to be manhandled by you meaty boys. It would be ecstasy of the naughtiest kind."

A core concept to examine is how erotic the LAPD Slave Auction bust was to the heart of the magazine's psyche and autobiography. Embry, arrested by the LAPD in 1976, may have suffered from "Stockholm Syndrome," wherein the arrested or captured person develops a strong emotional connection to the captor, in the way that Patty Hearst, rescued from the Symbionese Liberation Front in 1975, had her life shaped by her oppressors. From the night he was arrested in 1976 until his death in 2010, John Embry could not quit Ed Davis with whom he was obsessed, and on whom he wasted so many pages in *Drummer*.

In *Drummer* 6, pages 12-14, *Drummer* 7, page 68, and *Drummer* 11, page 76, and *Super MR* #5 (2000), pages 34-39, Embry, greasing up the inherent eroticism, wrote virtual porno S&M details of how on that Slave Auction night forty-two leatherfolk were arrested, bound in handcuffs, hauled off in full leather—and in one dress—on two police busses, locked in crowded cells, and forced to soil and wet their leather pants during the long transport and the longer time they spent on the crowded floor of the booking center cells.

The "Slave Auction Arrest" story is an archetypal *Drummer* tale of capture wherein, through magical thinking, the pushy bottom sets himself up erotically to be bullied and bound in service to fetishized alpha males in authority.

An observer doesn't need to juggle the archetypes of Joseph Campbell's *The Hero with a Thousand Faces* to recognize that the Slave Auction bust also doubles as a kind of hero's journey into the sort of S&M counter-phobic jerkoff fantasy that *Drummer* and its personals ads specialized in. In fact, the following archetypal "Services" ad with a photo of a straight dominant cop ran for years in *Drummer* personals. This was probably the most popular classified ad in *Drummer* history. It offered an ultimate *Drummer* fantasy: a real weekend with real straight cops. Many *Drummer* readers took out their charge cards and booked their vacations at the Academy Training Center. Secretly aided and abetted by my longtime friend and Training Center founder Chip Weichelt (1952-2003), and cheered on by publisher Tony DeBlase, I went undercover at the Academy as an eyewitness reporter for *Drummer*. In fact, I was the first and only editor or writer of *Drummer* to go under deep cover to get a *Drummer* exclusive. In *Drummer* 145 (December 1990), editor Joseph W. Bean published my upbeat gonzo feature on straight cops role-playing rough but consensual BDSM games with gay men behind bars: "Incarceration for Pleasure: The Academy Training Center."

This is Chip Weichelt's monthly ad as it appeared in *Drummer* 123 (September 1988):

> The [Academy] Training Center, Inc, now a full-time staffed facility [first in Washington, Missouri, and then in Alpharetta outside Atlanta], continues to offer men with a serious interest a unique alternative service. TC can design and implement each detail of your experience in various environments and scenarios for weekend or week-long sessions. Special situations such as public arrest, hostage, and other complex programs are executed in a realistic correctional or military atmosphere. Cell confinement, immobilization, isolation, interrogation, sensory control, and endurance situations are all offered in a safe, sane, discreet [that is, no sex with the straight cops; shaming words like *gay* and *faggot* were never uttered in a Training Center scene] and monitored environment. All TC programs are administered by professionally trained military, corrections, and LE [law enforcement] personnel. Written inquiries should include a phone number for contact, or call (314) 281-4345. Reservation and deposit are required. References available worldwide. TC cannot offer sexual situations as part of their programs. Training Center, PO Box 672, Bridgeton MO 63044. Special programs for guest instructors now available.

The counter-phobic stretch from the negative psychology of the LAPD arrests (1976) to the positive Academy Training Center experience (1988) is a way for queer historians to measure how erotic archetypes of dominance and submission in gay liberation evolved forward inside leather culture. This delicious fatal attraction led to the publication ten years earlier of my feature, "Prison Blues: Confessions of a Prison Tour Junkie," in *Drummer* 21 (March 1978), as well as Frank O'Rourke's "Prison Punk," serialized in many issues of *Drummer*. Embry's personal "take" on being topped by real cops was typical of a pivotal universal drama within mid-century gay liberation in which the hero struggles on his journey as the ancient procreation myths of tribal eros evolve into new modern kinds of complicated personal sexualities that replace procreation with recreation.

In those twelve years, attitudes changed 180 degrees.

Before that evolution, however, Embry suffered from the conservative fascism in the LA scene that Larry Townsend had fought in founding the Homophile Effort for Legal Protection (H.E.L.P.) in 1968 to assist gays entrapped by cops. After the Slave Auction bust, Embry, beaten but unbowed, acknowledged the opening of the culture war, a year before Anita Bryant came down with Full-Blown Crazy Syndrome, in *Drummer* 11 (December 1976), page 76: "Chief Edward M. Davis is at war with the gay community. He is basing many of his political aspirations on the battle." Yet, faced with the dangerous Ed Davis who had the usual political ambitions of a fundamentalist conservative, Embry seemed, in some expiatory act of self-immolation, to have been asking for trouble by publishing wild articles, seductive stories, and feel-good coverage of very risky topics. Was it to goad Davis? Or to harass the LAPD? Was it Embry's masochistic hubris? Was it radical sex journalism? What was Embry's motive?

The mechanics of the Drummer Slave Auction arrest can be explained simply: Embry tried to stage an event to increase business and publicity for his "Leather Fraternity" mail-order scheme, and when the LAPD took notice, Embry—to make himself appear a gay victim—claimed, post factum, that his commercial party which was for his own business gain was, in his telling, a charity benefit for the gay community. But was it a private event, or was it open to the public? In short, when caught, Embry lied his way to an alibi, redundantly casting Ed Davis as the villain. Embry, thinking fast on his feet, hoped to link the Slave Auction raid to the legendary Stonewall arrests in New York. But, even in LA, he could not gin up the kind of sympathetic traction that the Black Pipe bar defendants received after two LAPD raids in 1967 and 1972. A year before the Slave Auction, Embry prefigured his motivation and his model for grabbing his fifteen minutes of fame when in *Drummer* 3, page 37, he salivated over the almost "Stonewall-level" headlines *The Advocate* had screamed when connecting the Black Pipe raid to LAPD excess: "Biggest Raid in LA Since Prohibition." Even though the *Drummer* essay, "Triumph of the Black Pipe," was Embry at his most cogent, the reach of rhetoric he sought was impossible in 1976 because in 1975 *The Advocate* was sold by its progressive founders who had covered the Black Pipe in liberal ways the uptight new owner would never cover the Slave Auction. Embry found an enemy as shameless as himself in David Goodstein, the new and very conservative publisher of *The Advocate*, who was passive-aggressively sucking up to the LAPD by condemning in print the same "outrageous" gay leather behavior hated by Ed Davis. In his editorials, Goodstein dismissed Embry and the leather community. He did not buy Embry's self-serving "spin" as witnessed in several articles, beginning immediately after the Slave Auction, with *The Advocate*, issue 190, May 19, 1976. As an unintended side effect of Goodstein profiling leathermen as bad-boy outlaws, sales of *Drummer* took off, and Embry banged the drum of the Slave Auction bust as if he were setting the beat for a gay Pride parade.

In *Out for Good: The Struggle to Build a Gay Rights Movement in America*, authors Dudley Clendinen and Adam Nagourney noted the conservative righteousness of David Goodstein trying to social engineer gay culture by denouncing a diversity of gay identities in *The Advocate*, issue 243, June 14, 1978. In his editorial, David Goodstein addressed "Proposition 6: The Briggs Initiative" which was on the upcoming California ballot for November 7, 1978, banning homosexuals from teaching in schools. It was spawned by singer Anita Bryant's "Save the Children" campaign in Dade County, Florida, that had nationally ignited the Culture Wars in 1977 by repealing an ordinance banning discrimination based on sexual orientation.

Goodstein wrote:

> This is one of those times when the truth we have to report is very unpleasant. The bottom line is that it is most unlikely that the Briggs initiative can be defeated in the November election....We may lose even in San Francisco. We can expect a multi-million-dollar media campaign of lies and hate directed at us. Some gay people will likely commit suicide under this onslaught of hate.

In their analysis, Clendinen and Nagourney commented:

> Goodstein proceeded to offer his by now familiar prescription to minimize the damage. The "gay extermists" and "hedonists"—the drag queens, the advocates of man-boy sex, the feminist-separatists, the *leather enthusiasts* [italics added], the sexual liberationists, the Marxists—must keep out of sight and leave it to the professionals [Goodstein] to salvage the campaign. Straight people are put off by homosexuals, Goodstein said, so "almost all gay people [Really, All?] could help best by maintaining very low profiles." [Closets in

1978?]... The "gay media freaks' had to 'get off the television and let our [straight] friends and allies speak to the non-gay issues."

Goodstein's editorial promoting gay self-hate concluded:

Constructively, we should assist in registering gay voters, stuffing envelopes in the campaign headquarters, and keeping out of sight of non-gay voters, except for persuading straight friends and relatives. Destructively, we can do a lot to assist John Briggs [Brigg's political victory] by being *visible* and in any way *stereotypical*. [Italics added]

Bitter rivals Embry and Goodstein both exploited the axiom: "The freedom of the press belongs to those who own one." Embry wanted gays to act up and Goodstein wanted gays to shut up. The wild political times turned both *The Advocate* and *Drummer* into important eyewitnesses as each rival magazine published in each issue its own first draft of the epic gay history exploding all around in that exciting first decade of gay liberation from Stonewall in 1969 to Harvey Milk's murder in 1978 to the first cases of AIDS in 1981. Not to be dismissed as dated ephemera of gay pop culture, both magazines are immense repositories of descriptive and prescriptive grammars and primers of gay history told first hand by eyewitness writers, artists, and photographers.

CONTROVERSY IS FREE PUBLICITY

Embry, having read his First Amendment rights, seemed politically masochistically self-destructive in his constant pushing of forbidden erotica to taunt the cops. Two months before he offered me to become, in his flattering words, "the founding San Francisco editor of *Drummer*," he wrote in *Drummer* 12 (January 1977), an ill-advised full-page ad for the upcoming extra issue, *The Best and the Worst of Drummer* (January 1977), bragging that the post-arrest issue would contain pages of writing, images, and "items we felt were too much even for *Drummer*." To the relief of the LAPD desk sergeant assigned to read *Drummer*, the extra issue contained little that was new. As was Embry's unpopular custom of selling the same text and pictures twice or thrice, nearly everything in *The Best and the Worst of Drummer* was a reprint of previous *Drummer* features. Readers so disliked re-runs, and wrote so many "Letters to the Editor" about Embry's recycling, that I changed the course of *Drummer* by including only all-new materials in my first issues beginning with *Drummer* 19, including my special New York arts issue, *Son of Drummer* (September 1978), showcasing the artist Rex and Robert Mapplethorpe in his *Drummer* debut.

Eleven months after the Slave Auction arrests, Embry used his "In Passing" editorial column in *Drummer* 13 (March 1977 to protest too much the arrest of straight publisher, Larry Flynt, whose *Hustler* magazine had just been busted for pornography in Cincinnati, the most puritan city in American fundamentalism. Stretching to identify with Flynt on page 76, and claiming permission from the *L. A. Free Press*, Embry reprinted novelist Harold Robbins' article defining the censorship of *Hustler* as "another example of fascism in America."

When Mapplethorpe died eleven years after *Son of Drummer*, I updated this American Fascist censorship battle with my obituary feature article, "Pentimento for Robert Mapplethorpe: Faces, Fetishes, and Flowers of Evil," in *Drummer* 133 (September 1989). It was in censorious Cincinnati where seven of leatherman Robert Mapplethorpe's *Drummer*-style photographs were put on trial in 1990 as dramatized in the feature film, *Dirty Pictures* (2000), a docudrama focused on museum director Dennis Barrie and his attempt to exhibit Mapplethorpe's photographs at the local Contemporary Arts Center. Although the jury ruled in favor of Barrie, the Mapplethorpe case had a nationwide impact debating the role of government in supporting the arts. After censuring the recently deceased Mapplethorpe on the floor of the U. S. Senate, Culture War conservatives slashed almost all the government funding for the National Endowment for the Arts. Conversely, as soon as a New York editor read the *Drummer* obituary, I was contracted to turn the essay into the book, *Mapplethorpe: Assault with a Deadly Camera* (1994), which was followed by my entry, "Mapplethorpe," in *Censorship: A World Encyclopedia* (2001). I also contributed photographs, personal letters to me from Robert, and onscreen eyewitness testimony for Fenton Bailey and Randy Barbato's HBO documentary, *Mapplethorpe: Look at the Pictures* (2016).

Censorship from the outside plagued *Drummer* as much as did insider complaints from passionate subscribers. In that same *Drummer* 133, a disgruntled reader wrote to publisher Anthony DeBlase accusing *Drummer* of politically correct self-censorship on the one hand and the glorification of drugs on the other:

> ...sorry to see so much has become a no-no in your fiction. You claim your distributors threaten you to be sweet and clean and pure like *Family Circle* magazine or *Reader's Digest*. However, it seems that you still promote the use of drugs in your safe-sex vanilla

fiction. Many of the characters (maybe the authors?) can't function in sex...unless they are stoned blind? —HM, Bridgeport CT

Drummer assistant editor Paul Martin, an eyewitness bear who defined himself in *Drummer* 143, page 59, responded that only four stories depicted drug use. One was an excerpt from my pal Geoff Mains' *Gentle Warrior*, and another was an excerpt from my own *Some Dance to Remember: A Memoir-Novel of San Francisco 1970-1982*. As for *Drummer* self-censoring and turning "vanilla," Martin wrote: "I don't call the for-real POW torture in 'Shadow Soldiers' [*Drummer* 127] by Jack Fritscher 'vanilla.'" Indeed, the landmark *Drummer* 100 also dared publish my non-consensual S&M story "The Lords of Leather" which was later included in the anthology *Rainbow County and Other Stories* (1999) and subsequently optioned by *The Advocate* through its Alyson Publishing. Alyson's book editor, however, freaked out over the sex-torture of American soldiers and censored the "men's adventure magazine" story by asking to drop it in favor of one of my consensual stories. After that judgmental snip, writer Simon Sheppard dignified "The Shadow Soldiers" in his canonical anthology *Homosex: 60 Years of Gay Erotica* (2007).

Regarding the "Great Slave Auction," Embry must have felt he had won the free- publicity lottery when *The National Enquirer* ran a two-page spread titled "The Real Hollywood—Wild, Wicked, & Wide Open." The authors were Barbara Stemigin and Malcolm Boyes whose name is similar to venerable gay author, Malcolm Boyd, the partner of then *Advocate* editor, Mark Thompson. Malcolm Boyes was the British journalist who, after working for the *Enquirer*, became the producer of television "tabloid gossip" programs such as *Inside Edition* and *Extra*.

Embry so relished the *Enquirer* Slave Auction details and photos that he photostated its two-page coverage and reprinted its copyrighted material without permission in *Drummer* 18 (August 1977), page 6. He even feigned indignation in his introductory essay about the very existence of the *Enquirer* feature, but was he bragging or complaining? It was a major counter-phobic *coup* to be covered by the scandal-sucking tabloid, *The National Enquirer*, that was published in Florida where Anita Bryant, second runner-up to Miss America, had revved her Christianist self up with a 1969 "Rally for Decency" in which she had protested Jim Morrison's exposing his rock-star penis on stage before launching her culture-changing Dade County Children's Crusade in 1977. As sure as karma can be a pie in the face, Bryant's homophobia ended her singing career and her commercial endorsements; her straight marriage split into divorce amidst gay rumors imagining her first husband was gay—he wasn't; and she later declared bankruptcy which the straight former husband allegedly blamed on gay people not playing "fair."

Years later in its longtime alliance with the Republican Party, *The Enquirer* allegedly created a deal with the onward-marching Arnold Schwarzenegger not to publish trash journalism about him during 2003 when he was campaigning for the governorship of California. Just four days before the election, eBay, the corporation headed by Republican Meg Whitman, "censored" my "performance-art auction" of my Schwarzenegger and Mapplethorpe photographs and memorabilia on the very same weekend that several women were suddenly coming forward at the last minute accusing Schwarzenegger of pushing his unwelcome sexual advances on them. The eBay "bust" of my "Schwarzenegger Shrine" auction, with its Mapplethorpe connection, made headlines around the globe, exposing yet one more way how anti-gay and anti-women corporations and publications protect politicians.

After he was elected the following Tuesday, the hateful Schwarzenegger, who, as a young bodybuilder, had been photographed by Mapplethorpe, became the one and only person standing between gays and gay marriage in California. He alone twice refused to sign his name to the done deal of Assemblyman Mark Leno's gay marriage bill passed by the California legislature. Schwarzenegger was a duplicitous Republican hypocrite defending the sanctity of straight marriage. At the very moments he vetoed gay marriage, he was an active adulterer. While famously married to the Kennedy family's Maria Shriver, and father to four children with her, Schwarzenegger impregnated the family's Hispanic maid who lived inside the action "hero's" family with the illegitimate child the maid and he were rearing without Shriver's knowledge of paternity.

The Advocate, October 7, 2003
eBay Shuts Down "Schwarzenegger Shrine"

Artist Jack Fritscher wanted to "start a dialogue" with fellow Californians about actor Arnold Schwarzenegger's views on gay rights, censorship, and government funding of art, so he gathered nine items from his pop culture collection and auctioned them on eBay.

The 64-year-old author of erotic fiction and San Francisco gay history launched his "Schwarzenegger Shrine" in late September with an opening bid of $24,000. The menagerie, dedicated to the front-runner in California's October 7 gubernatorial recall election, included a postcard of Schwarzenegger's torso that was photographed and signed by the late Robert Mapplethorpe. The controversial photographer used the postcard to invite friends to a "Hot Dirty Man" party in New York in 1979.

More than 61,000 people visited Fritscher's auction. But on Thursday afternoon, with two days left in the bidding, eBay shuttered the site and took away all references to it in its search engines. The San Jose, Calif.-based auction giant still hasn't offered Fritscher any explanation. "It was taken down because it's gay-themed, period," Fritscher said Friday. "It's censorship of what's gay. There's no nudity or politics here. There might be a political question asked, but it's only because the piece for sale is curious and I was trying to distinguish it from the other Schwarzenegger items for sale."...

"I was the bicoastal lover of the notoriously gay Robert Mapplethorpe, who photographed Arnold Schwarzenegger," Fritscher's listing began. "In a national scandal in 1989 to 1990, Sen. Jesse Helms denounced Mapplethorpe on the floor of the U.S. Senate and took away government funding of art.... Considering Arnold's posing for Mapplethorpe, one wonders what is the Schwarzenegger position on government taxes paying for uncensored art?"

...Fritscher, a longtime pop culture enthusiast who has listed his novels on eBay, said the site has evolved into a social phenomenon beyond a simple catalog of goods for sale. It is a platform for people to market not only products but the values that accompany them, he said. "eBay is a public forum," Fritscher said. "If Fox can take a political spin, why can't a seller on eBay pitch political materials any way they want to?"

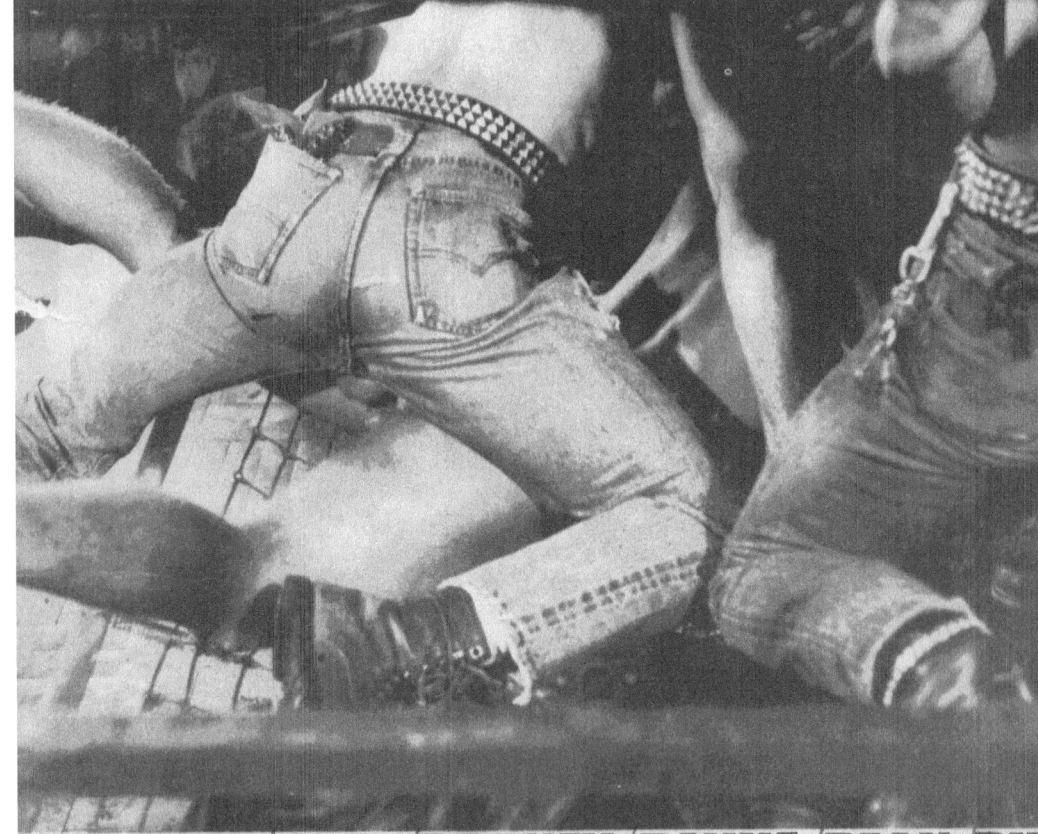

DRUMMER
the leather fraternity

HALSTED/OPEL/BARNEY/PAYNE/DEAN/BU

THE ONE PUBLICATION DEDICATED TO THE LEATHER LIFESTYLE

25

Cover Photograph by Fred Halsted

CHAPTER 4

FOUNDING *DRUMMER*

West Hollywood Bitch Fight
When Embry Met Townsend
and the Slaves of the LAPD

- How the *H.E.L.P. Newsletter* for Legal Protection Morphed into *H.E.L.P./Drummer*, and Evolved into *Drummer* Itself
- When Frenemies Collide: The Feud between the Heroic Larry Townsend and the Hubristic John Embry
- The LA Postal Inspector; Jeanne Barney, the Woman Who Was Not A Drag; and the Missing TV Footage of the Slave Auction Raid
- Gay Cannibalism: Steve Schoch's Eyewitness Testimony about Embry and Townsend at *H.E.L.P./Drummer*
- The Con-Man Shell Game: the Black Pipe Bar, the Mark IV Baths, and Making a Private "Slave Auction" Public

---

Los Angeles Times, April 14, 1955
UCLA Student Gets Medal for Rhine Heroism

Irvin T. Bernhard, 24, UCLA sophomore [name changed to "Michael Lawrence 'Larry' Townsend," July 19, 1972], was presented with a medal and scroll yesterday by Dr. Richard Hertz, German Consul General in Los Angeles, for saving a 9-year-old German boy from drowning in the Rhine River at Bonn last August.

Gov. Karl Arnold of the German state of Nordrhein-Westfalen sent the scroll and medal to Dr. Hertz for presentation to Bernhard, who was a member of the U.S. Air Force when he performed the heroic feat.

The youngster had been riding along a Rhine River road on his scooter when he had an accident and fell into the deep river. As a swift current spun the boy around in the water, Bernhard, who was eating at a nearby sidewalk café, got up, raced to the river, and dived in fully dressed.

"I swallowed an awful lot of the Rhine, but the two of us made it back to shore all right," Bernhard, who lives at 624 Veteran Ave, West Los Angeles, recounted yesterday in the German Counsulate at 3450 Wilshire Blvd. Accompanying the young man to the Counsulate was his sister, Mrs. Ralph J. Tingle of 621 S. Barrington Ave., who proudly looked on as Dr. Hertz gave the awards.

THE 1972 BLACK PIPE RAID AND ARRESTS: LARRY TOWNSEND'S *H.E.L.P. NEWSLETTER* BECOMES *DRUMMER*

How John Embry's spit hit the fan! Let me count the ways. Was it Embry's act-up content and politicking what done him in? In the *mise en scene* of gay LA, Embry was sketchily involved with the August 1972 fund-raiser for H.E.L.P. headed up by leather author Larry Townsend. The title of the "Homophile Effort for Legal Protection," founded in 1968 (three years before Embry's arrival) was designed so its acronym would announce its mission: *Help*. Its campy tap root in 1960s popular culture was the Beatles film, *HELP!* (1965). Its main purpose was to bail out gays entrapped in tea rooms and arrested in bar raids by the LAPD. Townsend was particularly motivated. In his FBI file, I found he had been arrested three times: Sex Perversion and Fellatio (1963); Failure to Register as Sex Offender (1964), followed by a 1968 ruling that his registration was no longer required; and for Lewd Conduct at the H.E.L.P. fund-raiser that was dismissed for insufficient evidence the same year he first published his *Leatherman's Handbook* (1972). Held at LA's then-leading leather bar called the Black Pipe, the H.E.L.P. charity event suggested a two-dollar donation at the door. One of the booths on the open-air patio "auctioned off leathermen for a date" to raise money to open a gay Community Center. This mini-event was a Slave Auction that preceded the more famous Drummer Slave Auction four years later in 1976.

Proving no good deed goes unpunished, the cops targeted their so-called "Black Pipe 21" arrests on the President of H.E.L.P. who was Larry Townsend, and on H.E.L.P.'s board of advisors, including, almost Fascistically, the astonished guy at the card table registering voters. In 1975, Larry Townsend became the founding president of the Hollywood Hills Democratic Club which was the first openly gay political club in LA. But, in 1972, political activist Townsend's name, with ad man John Embry's, appeared for the first time together on the masthead of the first issue of the newsprint magazine combining Townsend's *H.E.L.P Newsletter* with Embry's small zine-version of *Drummer* which Embry had first published in November 1971. The new merged title was *H.E.L.P./Drummer*. The Black Pipe itself was bothering no one out on La Cienega near Venice in West LA, a deserted light industrial area similar to San Francisco's South of Market.

The Advocate headlined "Massive Bar Raid," September 12, 1972.

Gay activists, Morris Kight and the leathery Reverend Troy Perry, helped raise bail; and H.E.L.P. carried the costs. The charges against Larry Townsend were dropped and the last defendant cleared on June 21, 1974, one year before *H.E.L.P./Drummer*, with its personal ads, evolved through a civil war with Townsend into Embry's iteration of the slick, large-format *Drummer* magazine on June 20, 1975. In those early years, Embry had shown up at H.E.L.P. riding his Trojan High Horse and announced to Townsend that he could design the group a much better-looking newsletter. He took over like a Greek bearing gifts, but without the charm.

It was a tectonic shift.

During the four-year period 1971-1975, Embry wrested *Drummer* into and out of *H.E.L.P./Drummer* while the H.E.L.P. organization disintegrated with internal political strife stoked by him because he used the LAPD mess with the Black Pipe to further the destruction of H.E.L.P. Even so, his internecine actions with Townsend continued. In 2008, a week after Townsend died, I was helping his sister Tracy Tingle archive his papers, and found a revealing file of clippings and letters documenting what Townsend hated to admit was the "bitch fight" that Embry had plotted to check-mate him.

In the late autumn of 1973, the deposed president of H.E.L.P., Townsend, resigned as an ex-officio member of the H.E.L.P. board of directors with a cynical letter he sent to Embry, the new president of H.E.L.P. He was making his competitive moves against Embry, and landing on his feet politically. In its October 10, 1973 issue, *The Advocate* reported that Townsend was chosen by David B. Goodstein, president of the San Francisco Whitman-Radclyffe Foundation, as its Southern California representative. Even then, Goodstein's name set Embry's teeth on edge, a full year before the bourgeois Goodstein bought *The Advocate* so envied by the scofflaw Embry who could not afford to buy it.

Carefully crafting his air-kiss-off, Townsend coded his "press release" with ironic praise that partially revealed the politics of how quickly Embry had moved in on him and made him redundant. He described the H.E.L.P. coup that took Embry only eight months, referring to "the very fine leadership of yourself [Embry] and your fellow board members for over eight months," adding, in the smirk of simmering lifelong indignation he was known for, that he was convinced that "this organization, which means so much to me, is in exceptionally capable and dedicated hands....my continued work and assistance are no longer necessary to the furtherance of the goals of H.E.L.P."

Embry, in turn, air-kissed back. To hitch his own little-known wagon to that of the star author Townsend, Embry turned the resignation letter into a self-serving press release that he sent to *The Advocate* which headlined "Townsend Resigns from H.E.L.P. Board." The six-paragraph "spin" reported: "Embry said H.E.L.P. 'is heavily in debt to Larry Townsend for his years of service to us, and we wish him well in his new endeavors.'" Pulling his frenemy close to capture his voice and to link to his fame, Embry trumpeted that he "...understood that Townsend would continue to write a column for *H.E.L.P./Drummer*, the organization's official newspaper."

Embry's press release was like a birth announcement: this was the first ever mention of *Drummer* in *The Advocate*, December 19, 1973. This recognition gave him the "win" he longed for: validation by Dick Michaels and Bill Rand's popular Los Angeles magazine. Yet within two years of becoming president of H.E.L.P., Embry's machinations finally helped kill that organization because he was litle interested in H.E.L.P. except as a hijacked platform to launch *Drummer* as his political power tool. Ever the High Priest of Calumny, Embry scared off even the last sympathizers of H.E.L.P. when he reported, warned, and bragged in *Drummer* 3 (October 1975), page 43: "The word was out: to have anything to do with H.E.L.P. was to invite disaster."

FEUDING, FUSSING, AND FIGHTING

History is like Akira Kurosawa's 1951 classic Japanese film, *Rashomon*, which in eighty-eight minutes tells the same story four times, each time from a different participant's point of view. When Embry and Townsend squared off at H.E.L.P., eyewitnesses of their power struggle sometimes felt like collateral damage in their ego issues. Steve Schoch, the vice-president of H.E.L.P., became so frustrated that in 1973 he turned whistle-blower and bought four pages of advertising space in the Los Angeles magazine, *Action*, to publish his essay, "A Time for Truth." His insider and specific accusations seem prescient because the management of H.E.L.P. by Embry and Townsend foreshadowed Embry's management style at *Drummer*. Schoch testified:

> Due to the tremendous controversy which has emerged concerning the battle which has been raging for some time now over the

activities of H.E.L.P. Inc., I have decided that it is time for me to speak frankly about some of the practices and people involved. My name is Steve Schoch. I was personally involved with H.E.L.P. Inc. by serving two years as Vice Chairman of the T.G.A. (Tavern & Guild Association of H.E.L.P. Inc.), and eight months as Vice President of the Board of Directors of H.E.L.P. Inc.

Schoch stated that because the rank and file at H.E.L.P. were apathetic about the operations of the organization, the control of it fell "...into the hands of a select few who can control and manipulate." He admitted his own complicity:

> I know; I participated in some of these decisions....All it really takes is for a few individuals to contact their friends and solicit or even mark their ballots for them. I know, because this was how Larry Townsend and I defeated Cliff Lettieri in last year's elections.
>
> I ran in the most recent election...and because I refused to be a lackey of Larry Townsend's and refused to participate in ballot stuffing and refused to write a mud-slinging campaign letter to the members, I was defeated. So be it.

Even if disgruntled from eating sour grapes, Schoch accepted his personal loss by rising to the larger issue of conceptualizing, organizing, and preserving pioneer organizations: "But H.E.L.P. Inc. as a concept and *H.E.L.P./Drummer* as a concept and the T.G.A. must somehow be preserved from what is happening to them because either the members do not care or will not participate." Digging into specifics of pride, prejudice, class, gender, and embezzlement, Schoch passionately alleged:

> Now we have H.E.L.P. in its present form, purporting to represent many thousands of very conservative and upper-middle-class Gays!!! Bunk...H.E.L.P. is a mixture of everybody including 'the long-haired Hippy freaks' that Larry Townsend is so afraid of. Afraid to the point that he and Jerry Howard did everything they could to discourage the Gay Community Services Center's "Funky Dance" held for awhile at the H.E.L.P. Center. The income derived from the rental of the Center's facilities was $75.00 per week. Gone now, it went quite a way in defraying the $750.00 per month rent on the Center.
>
> While working for both the California Committee for Sexual Freedom law reform and The Whitman-Radclyffe Foundation, I

came to know, like, and respect the Women's Movement. The static I received from H.E.L.P., mainly from Larry, regarding the Lesbian Feminists and others was not to be believed. He told me he wanted no more Communist or Socialist Workers Party people (both male and female) in the Center. I do not belong to either party, but I'll defend their right to exist, even though the vast majority of our Sisters and Brothers are not affiliated with those political parties either.

Schoch's intuition about Townsend's taste for intrigue and select conservatism had some basis in his family history. His father had been an anti-Nazi spy before the outbreak of World War II. When, freshly demobbed from the Air Force, Townsend was seeking work in the early 1960s with the System Development Corporation, he had to explain why, in the 1950s, his Secret Security Clearance had been suspended. Still identifying himself as "Irvin Townsend Bernhard, Jr.," a name he did not change until 1972, he explained, as witnessed by Frances Lias, in his Personnel Security Questionnaire:

> While on duty with USAF Intelligence Service (7050th AISW, Rhein Main ABF), my SECRET clearance was revoked for a period of approximately two weeks, due to the fact that my father (Irvin T. Bernhard, Sr.) had been active in collecting information for the FBI on German Bundest activities in New England during 1940. His name had been recorded on some subversive list at that time. A letter from J. Edgar Hoover, instructing him as to field offices and indicating that his help was appreciated is on file with security office, SDC. Also, refer to Mr. J. Frank Mothershead, 5241 42nd Street NW, Washington. D. C. This gentleman is former head of Patent Law Division, Dept. of Justice, and is aware of details to greater extent than I, since I was only ten years of age at the time.

Even as the H.E.L.P. battle received coverage in *The Advocate*, Schoch confessed how he supported Embry and Townsend in that fundamentalist Puritan custom of ostracizing anyone who disagreed with them at H.E.L.P., especially of Jeff Buckley, the publisher of *California Scene* which Embry saw as a competitor to his new *H.E.L.P./Drummer*. Schoch's paragraph is the first published evidence of Embry's famous Blacklist.

> The worst thing I feel I participated in was the shutting up [silencing] at Board meetings of Jeff Buckley, publisher of *California Scene*. Jeff

can and does get carried away and can be very coarse and demanding, but Jeff has, and still does have, many questions to ask about the conduct of H.E.L.P. business....None have been answered to his or anybody else's satisfaction, nor have Phil Cooper's. Contrary to a statement published in *The Advocate*, Phil wrote his own letter without any prompting from me as Larry Townsend intimates.

When Embry wrested the presidency of H.E.L.P. from Townsend, Schoch wrote: "The current regime under John Embry is nothing more than an extension of Larry's policies of private control and manipulation." As would be the future with Embry at *Drummer*, Schoch pinpointed the problems of bills unpaid because of dodgy ledgers and cash gone missing:

> For the members' edification, there is much they should be concerned about:
> 1. H.E.L.P. keeps no general ledger.
> 2. Expenses have often been posted in the same entry as both "net" and "gross" with no breakdown as to profit or loss.
> 3. The so-called "Black Pipe 21 War Chest" is a sham. With over $2000.00 collected, there is no money left...because all H.E.L.P. funds are in one account and H.E.LP. is practically broke.
> 4. *H.E.L.P./Drummer* is owed over $3000.00 for ads, many of which were never authorized or were incorrectly run. (I owe *Drummer* for ads, myself!)
> 5. As of early April [1973], H.E.L.P. had less than $700.00 in the bank and over $1500.00 owed to creditors—plus $750.00 due for April 15 for rent and five or six hundred dollars to print the April issue [of *H.E.L.P/Drummer*], plus whatever the issue cost to typeset.

Finally, Schoch addressed the general duplicity through which Townsend and Embry engaged in public politics in order to advance their own private mail-order businesses. He was particularly accurate in 1973 in exposing Embry's grift as a con-artist running his business and finances as a kind of shell game that he would use to confuse matters with the LAPD around the exact public or private nature of the 1976 Slave Auction.

> ...Is this fiscal responsibility? I cannot be blamed nor can other former Board members...because when I asked questions about our finances, both Larry and Jerry Howard told me it was none of my concern...OK...now let them answer to the members.

Let them also explain why a large number of members received their ballots too late to vote and some not at all. Let them explain why they have used the confidential H.E.L.P. membership list [as Embry would later use the "Leather Fraternity" list] for their own personal use in promoting mail-order sales!!! (John Embry aka Robert Payne) And why does Larry hide behind that name when his real name is Irvin Bernhard. This is liberation?

...I feel the future of H.E.L.P. and what it has done and can still do for the Gay Community is far too important to keep quiet.... Let's clean up this mess. I feel that together we can overcome this incompetency and gross neglect of your interest. How? Under the By-Laws, we can force a new election and make a clean sweep of the despots who hold power.

The editor of *Action* magazine made a point in ALL CAPS: "THE ENTIRE CONTENTS OF THIS LETTER ARE THE EXPRESSED OPINION OF STEVE SCHOCH AND DO NOT NECESSARILY REPRESENT THE OPINIONS OF ANY OTHER INDIVIDUAL OR ORGANIZATION."

In the 1970s "Los Angeles Party Game of Gay Cannibalism," Embry, in the next issue of *H.E.L.P./Drummer*, published a letter rebutting Schoch. In the anonymous fashion that would become typical of John Embry aka Robert Payne in "Letters to the Editor" in *Drummer*, the style and content of the letter, signed only as "J. R. Santa Monica (H.E.L.P. Member)," would fairly much have fingered the name-changing Embry as the author.

However, in this instance, because the nine-paragraph letter was indignantly specific in defending Townsend without ever mentioning Embry, its author may well have been Townsend himself.

The caustic letter drips with the writer's intimate access to biographical details and inner thoughts of a "noble" Townsend who refuses to lower himself to rebut Schoch. It even directly quotes Townsend with a warm and fuzzy sentence that Larry, lit up or sober, would not likely have said, except for the dig that Schoch was mentally ill. "[Schoch]...has done some good things in the past. I think he's just going through a little emotional problem. It'll all work out." This early-days version of a "proto" *Drummer*, published monthly by Embry via *H.E.L.P./Drummer*, listed a "Ron Harris" as the editor who titled the response: "Bullshit Is Not the Truth." J. R. wrote:

I am sending this to *H.E.L.P./Drummer* because I am not saying things which the *Action* [magazine] people want to hear, and thus know they wouldn't be willing to swap checks with me, or whatever they're doing to pretend that people like Steve Schoch are actually paying for their articles [paid advertisements].…The reason I am writing at all is because Larry refuses to involve himself in what he calls a "bitch fight."

J. R. defended Townsend's name change, and launched a litany of offenses "committed" by Schoch, alleging his ripping off the gay clients of his own heating and air-conditioning business, being too drunk and too sick to acquit his own H.E.L.P. duties as vice president, and hampering Townsend's effectiveness as president.

Despite the fact that he was unwilling (or unable) to do the work, Steve wanted the titles that went with these [political] jobs. For months, Larry was after him to carry his share of the load, and eventually got pretty pushy about it.…There is a hell of a lot of difference between a man doing the work and taking some pride in his accomplishments, and the one who simply seeks the title while avoiding the work. If Larry had gone through the year in his presidency with a dependable, supporting vice president, he would have accomplished more than he did.

EMBRY ECLIPSED BY THE SHADOW OF TOWNSEND

During that first decade of gay liberation after Stonewall, the competition was fierce in LA among emerging publishers eager to catch the gay market, the pink dollar, and the leather crowd. If I were writing a byzantine LA screenplay fictionalizing this transition in leather history, I could dramatize moves on this chessboard that would shock Iago. And Iago, with his motiveless malignancy, would be too easy to cast.

The rift opened up further between leather impresarios Embry and Townsend who poured himself a double when the LAPD drove Embry out of LA in 1977. For six years, Townsend was conspicuously absent from *Drummer* until the 1980s. In 1978 when I was editor-in-chief, I took Townsend to supper at the cozy Haystack Restaurant on San Francisco's 24th Street and tried to persuade him to write for *Drummer*. He said he did not want to endure thirty-day deadlines, and, in any case, he wanted nothing to do with Embry.

Strictly speaking, Townsend never really wrote "for" *Drummer*. Townsend was never what was known as "a *Drummer* writer." He was larger than *Drummer*. He refused to be defined by *Drummer*. He was simply, and perfectly, the marquee identity of "Larry Townsend, author of *The Leatherman's Handbook*." Although he was part of the wider *Drummer* Salon, Townsend always worked from outside *Drummer* as a guest "contributing editor" whose fiction and advice columns—which he also wrote freelance for a variety of publications—were printed in *Drummer*.

His "Leather Notebook" column ran from *Drummer* 38 (1980) through *Drummer* 156 (1992) when Dutch publisher Martijn Bakker bought *Drummer*. Typically, magazine editors, eager for his famous byline, welcomed Townsend who shuffled the deck of his writing and dealt it out strategically to publicize his new books. In the landmark *Drummer* 100 which published Townsend's story "Board of Inquiry," his "Leather Notebook" Q&A column appeared "in trade" for his full-page mail-order ad, page 93.

Famous for mining leather and S&M themes, Townsend liked *Drummer* hosting occasional excerpts from his fiction as well as from his "Ask Larry" column which was also published in other magazines. As an author in a kind of early gay syndication, he finally acquiesced to write monthly columns as synergistic promotions for his yearly books. His self-referential column in *Drummer* was in effect "advertising in trade" for his mail-order business through which he sold his independent L. T. Publication titles from 1972 to 2008. With the startup of his publishing company in 1970, Townsend was one of the first founders of a gay small business, and Embry scrambled to emulate him with his Alternate Publishing. Through *Drummer*, Townsend found value writing for several magazines with a masculine-identified demographic. With *Drummer* dead for the nine years since 1999, I remember in 2008 when he went apoplectic on the telephone because his long-running column in *Honcho* was suddenly cancelled; he died six weeks later, July 29, 2008.

In short, although Townsend and Embry despised each other like karmic star-crossed lovers to the day they died, Townsend liked the mail-order publicity in *Drummer*, and Embry needed the endorsement of Townsend's marquee name. It was a Hollywood marriage made in hell, and eyewitness Jeanne Barney was its eyewitness bridesmaid.

Jeanne Barney wrote to me on September 8, 2006:

> I rather imagine that John envied Larry's reputation as The Last Word in Leather. I know for sure that Larry was (and still is) really bothered by Embry's dishonesty, the reason that he declined when approached to kick in with *Drummer* in the beginning. [Some men on the mailing list confused "Embry" and "Payne" and "Townsend"

into one person the way others later confused "Robert Mapplethorpe" and "Robert Opel" into "Robert Opelthorpe."] Because John and Larry both used the same mail drop at 525 Laurel, Larry continually received complaints that "he" [Townsend] had not sent merchandise ordered from "Robert Payne." Larry printed something explaining the difference. John also was very late in paying Larry for his books that he sold mail order.

Compare both *The Advocate* and Embry each spinning a *Rashomon* eye-witness perspective of this history, "Triumph of the Black Pipe: Cops and Leathermen Clash in the Biggest Raid of All Time," *Drummer* 3 (October 1975), page 36.

Six months after his Black Pipe H.E.L.P. feature article, Embry set about hosting two of his own "Slave Auctions."

1) Larry Townsend told me, "Embry tossed his own first little Slave Auction at the Detour on New Year's Eve 1975 and hardly anyone showed up but the LAPD who warned him, 'Don't ever try this in LA again.'" Those were fighting words. The LAPD acted. Embry reacted, and double-dared them. In the best laid plans of mice and men, a raid would be good for business because it could create a newsworthy Stonewall-like event to earn the then six-month-old *Drummer* free publicity, and gain Embry a crusading publisher's reputation in gay history.

2) Despite the LAPD warning, Embry, Jeanne Barney remembered, proceeded to advertise a second, even bigger, Slave Auction for Valentine's Day, February 14, 1976, which was bumped to April 10, and into history as the "Great Drummer Slave Auction."

Embry mailed "invites" to his private membership list, the "Leather Fraternity" list, and then he broadened the mailing to his general direct-mail list. That maneuver shifted the shifty private event into a shiftier public event, and alerted a Postal Inspector who alerted the LAPD. See *Drummer* 6 (June 1976), page 14, for details about one Kenneth Elesser aka Kenneth Schmidt of Post Office Box 71002, Los Angeles.

Jeanne Barney added on September 5, 2006:

> As for an eyewitness that would be me [Barney]. He went public with the invitations because the Leather Fraternity members, being mostly out-of-towners, were not responding in the $ amount Embry had hoped for. In a "what-the-heck" attitude, he told me that he was going to send to the direct mail list. The Postal Inspector was not on the Fraternity list, but on the direct-mail list. [*Drummer*

6, page 14] As for going to the bars to solicit attendees, I was with him and Mario [Simon] and, I believe, Val on at least one occasion when he hit the Stud, among other bars.

Eyewitness Val Martin said:

Everything was private, only for the Leather Fraternity, and people who were into leather. Everybody who came was on a private mailing list, by invitation....The whistle was blown by an undercover cop on the mailing list of [both] *Drummer*, [which was a commercial mailing list] and the Leather Fraternity [which was private]. —Olaf Odegaard, "Serving Two Masters, Or: The Great Slave Auction Bust: An Interview with Val Martin," *Connection*, October 10-24, 1984

Embry was ambiguous in his sleight of hand. Did he or did he not decide in some hardon of hubris to allow this private fund-raiser to admit the public, and to charge admission—or was it a donation?—at the door?

His was an ambiguity whose subtlety was lost on the flat-earth LAPD. Police Chief Davis did not like disobedient pansies, especially the insidious ones geared up like masculine men, thumbing their nose at the law. And, the political being personal, he did not like Embry, the perceived agitator with a printing press, in particular.

Little did Embry know that his Slave Auction would turn into a high-profile photo op for his arch rival, the Christian crusader Davis, to feast upon. Davis knew Hollywood. Raiding a fabulous leather party on a Friday night had so much more dramatic appeal than a sad afternoon bust of a shabby little fag-mag office with a woman editor, an obese chain-smoking typesetter lady, and a nearsighted male paste-up artist.

In LA, on a slow news night, the Hollywood headline of "Sex Slaves" seemed so much better with photos of the Beautiful People in handcuffs. Under arrest, the immortal Jeanne Barney in a black-and-white gown snapped at a cop questioning her gender: "Honey, if I were a drag queen, I'd have bigger tits."

In *Drummer* 4 (January 1976), Embry had foolishly cued sixty-five Keystone Cops when he wrote dangerous hints of under-age human sex-traffic in his "coming attractions" for the Slave Auction scheduled for *Drummer* 5: "See Val Martin parade tender young...," Embry wrote, "...stuff for sale...," Embry continued, "...to the highest bidder." He was practically lip-synching Cole Porter's "Love for Sale" with its lyric of "appetizing young love for sale." In the cocktail lounges and taverns in which men of Embry's vintage came out during the 1940s and 1950s, "Love for Sale" was a staple on every juke box. When it came to male prostitution, Davis ran a fierce ongoing policy of targeting male hustlers and gay johns cruising Santa Monica Boulevard. To Davis, the Slave Auction was commercial sex trafficking. What an opportunity! Davis must have fallen to his fundamentalist knees. It was as if Embry had rounded up all the fag barflies and hustlers and johns from a dozen blocks of Santa Monica Boulevard, and penned them up at the Mark IV Baths for the convenience of Ed Davis and the LAPD.

In addition, the straight logic of the LAPD—who half-suspected that leathermen were also Hell's Angels outlaws—gave Davis reason to believe that the elusive S&M serial killer responsible for the "Orange County Torso Murders" of gay men was to be a guest at the Slave Auction party.

My own eyewitness experience in LA at the time was that every gay man knew some gay man who knew the killer. (See *Drummer* 9, 10, 11: "The 'S&M' Murder Mystery.")

In her eyewitness files, Jeanne Barney quoted *Los Angeles Magazine* (June 1976) which reported under the headline, "Love Ya to Pieces":

> A string of unsolved murders was the real reason for Ed Davis' raid of that gay Slave Auction, according to LAPD insiders. Police believe a local S-M ring may be responsible for savagely dismembering at least 17 persons, some of whom haven't been identified because investigators haven't been able to find enough pieces. At the auction, Davis' raiders were said to have observed spectators twisting rings affixed to the slaves' breasts and dragging them by chains attached to their genitals. Police claim they were hampered from giving their version of the raid by gag restrictions.

Three years after the Black Pipe H.E.L.P. raid, Embry, beating a drum no one marched to, tried in vain to rally the troops by invoking the Lavender Standard of "Stonewall" as an emblem of freedom in *Drummer* 3, page 43. The difference was that it took a Greenwich Village of authors to raise their neighborhood news of the Stonewall raid into legend, whereas *Drummer*, lost in the vast grid of Los Angeles had only three staff members, a couple of freelance writers, and only Embry himself to care about reviving the ancient history of the Black Pipe arrests. From inside his West Hollywood bubble, Embry wrote: "One would think that, more than the Stonewall incident which happened 3,000 miles away and still spawned Christopher

Street West, the Black Pipe raid would be the rallying point of the Southern California gay community."

In that sentence, he signaled his model, his scheme, and his lust for a second, bigger, historical raid. This time on *Drummer* itself.

Val Martin commented to Olaf Odegaard:

> Stonewall was different, but they have similarities. Stonewall was the greatest thing that happened to the community. In a way, thank God, this [Drummer Slave Auction] happened, too. We learned how to cope with it, fight back, stand up for our rights....There was more unity after people began to find out what was really going on; what the image of the leather person was. —Olaf Odegaard, in "Serving Two Masters, Or: The Great Slave Auction Bust: An Interview with Val Martin,," *Connection* (October 10-24, 1984

Jeanne Barney noted that the LAPD had confiscated all the gay cameras and film that night at the Mark IV Baths, leaving her with no photographs of the Slave Auction to publish. One of Embry's purposes for the Slave Auction was to shoot cost-free photos of leathermen for future issues of *Drummer*. The droll Barney editorialized in *Drummer* 6 (May/June 1976), page 4:

> We had considered running their [the LAPD's] version of what happened at the slave auction in place of our usual fiction section, for the finest writer in town could not begin to approach the fabrications of the LAPD. We had thought to reprint the Arrest Report in its entirety, faithfully retaining every misspelling, every grammatical and factual error. We decided against this, however. Not because we fear retribution or continued harassment at the hands of Los Angeles' Blue Meanies, but because we benevolently hesitate to make the ridiculous even more so. Instead, we have reported on the events of the evening and the days following. Sadly, we are unable to use photographs of the "slave auction." The police [destroying gay culture] not only robbed us or our dignity but confiscated our film as well. We hope that they enjoy the pictures.

Thirty years later she told me about film footage that should be pursued by an attorney for some Leather Heritage GLBT Society:

> At the same time our own photographs were taken by the LAPD, never to be seen again, there was a French television crew in LA

doing a Bicentennial special titled, *American Mores and Forays*. A producer named Jean-Jacques—I think he had abbreviated himself to that—contacted me about photographs and film footage. So I steered him to the people hired by the police [to shoot the raid]. They were more than willing to sell 370 feet of film at 13 cents a foot.

In the ONE Archive at the University of Southern California, filed under the "Mark 40 Defense Fund" there is a nine-folder collection of ephemera and police reports from several participating undercover officers. The materials about the excessive and oppressive "police action" around the Slave Auction include the LA City Council's findings from its investigation headed by councilman ZevYaroslavsky, a longtime Democratic member of the Los Angeles County Board of Supervisors, and a straight opponent of Chief Ed Davis and of all the anti-gay excesses in the LAPD from 1975 to 2014.

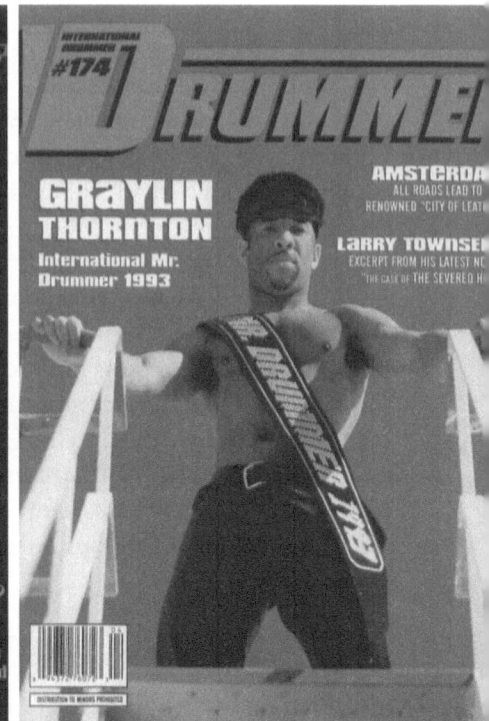

CHAPTER 5

SEX, RACE, AND GENDER

Publisher John Embry versus Los Angeles Police Chief Ed Davis

25 Subversive Ways *Drummer* Angered Law, Morality, Gay Nazis, and the LAPD

- *Drummer* Tests Community Standards: Sex, Race, and Gender; Fisting; Coprophagia; the Gay Nazi Party That Sued *Drummer*; and the Effeminists
- Oscar-Streaker Robert Opel, Photographer and Writer for *Drummer*, Is Murdered
- The S&M Murder Mystery and S&M Sex Rings: LA Serial Killer Outwits LAPD Chief Ed Davis Who Confuses the Manson Family Sex Slaves and the Symbionese Liberation Front with Emerging Gay Leather Biker Culture
- Censorship and Forbidden BDSM Films: Fred Halsted's *Sextool*, Roger Earl and Terry LeGrand's *Born to Raise Hell* (1974), and Steve Toushin's Videos Defended by *Drummer*
- *Bound for Europe*: Reality-TV Video Series of Extreme BDSM
- Arthur Evans and the Politically Correct Begin to Notice the Pioneering Uncloseting of "Masculinities" and "Homomasculinity" in the Masculine-Identified *Drummer*

HE SAID/HE SAID

1

"I enjoy inflicting homosexuality on them [straight men]."
—"Male Rape," *Drummer* 12 (January 1977)

2

> Folks, one of many "elephants in the room" of politically incorrect topics that most people dare not discuss in debating homosexuality is that—for self-described "gay" men—homosexuality is a masculinity [gender] crisis...The converse is also true: lesbianism is a femininity crisis....You cannot be a masculine nation and support homosexuality....[Consider]... the pitiable homosexual "leathermen," with their "overkill" attempt at being "macho men,"—even as they engage in the most degrading (and unmanly) sexual perversions known to the human race—not the least of which is male-to-male anal sodomy. —"Fake Masculinity of Homosexuality," Peter LaBarbera, President of Americans For Truth about Homosexuality (AFTAH), June 5, 2014 Americansfortruth.com

---

In principle, no one can condemn John Embry's own eyewitness testimony concerning his corporate publishing choices based on Freedom of Speech which is not absolute in any nation on Earth. My historical purpose is to analyze the way some of *Drummer*'s "youthful indiscretions" pissed off the LAPD who perceived the emerging tribe of 1970s leathermen as a suspicious cult not unlike the Manson Family sex slaves (1969) or a gang not unlike the Symbionese Liberation Army (1973-1975) who kidnaped and raped San Francisco heiress Patty Hearst. Both sex-driven outlaw groups provoked media coverage on television and in newspapers that framed the LAPD as inept at a time when they could not catch two prolific serial-killer-rapists who had been terrorizing LA for years. Embarrassed while policing clueless, and desperate to appear pro-active to the media, the LAPD responded by searching for suspect killers in sadomasochistic sex bars like the Black Pipe. When Police Chief Ed Davis first saw *Drummer,* he figured he'd found the secret text of an outlaw leather cult that would help him get ahead of sex crimes he had not gotten ahead of with Manson and the SLA. Upon reading the first free-speech issues of *Drummer* in 1975, Davis ordered surveillance of the magazine staff, and in a great display of helicopters and cameras raided the Drummer Slave Auction in April 1976, arresting forty-two people including John Embry and editor-in-chief Jeanne Barney.

Los Angeles Magazine
June 1976

> In addition to Embry's personal baiting of Ed Davis inside *Drummer*, the 1970s "...string of unsolved murders was the real reason for Ed Davis' raid of that gay Slave Auction, *according to LAPD insiders*. [Italics added] Police believe a local S-M ring may be responsible for savagely...."

In terms of free speech, my erotic writing was once censored by Embry in *Drummer* which was itself banned in uptight towns across the nation. My novel *Leather Blues*, introduced in *Drummer*, was confiscated by Canadian customs. And my frontal photographs from my *Drummer*-inflected photo book *American Men* were censored by British puritans as reported in Edward Lucie-Smith's article in the *Index on Censorship for Free Expression* (Volume 28, No. 6 Nov/Dec 1999, Issue 191). As an eyewitness activist experienced in the intersection of censorship, art, and politics, especially around Robert Mapplethorpe, I wrote about collisions in that intersection in several books, *Television Today*, *Popular Witchcraft*, and *Mapplethorpe: Assault with a Deadly Camera*, as well as in my essay "Mapplethorpe: Censored" in *Censorship: A World Encyclopedia* (2002). My stand on the relativity of freedom of the press is different from Embry touting absolutely, inside Los Angeles *Drummer*, the following twenty-five risky and often illegal topics which were all more dangerous in Davis' Fascist Los Angeles than in liberated San Francisco.

Embry and Davis were like two antagonistic Hollywood monsters meeting their match in one another. In their relationship lies a major motion picture, a moody crime thriller about the LA sex wars in the 1970s, shot in the neo-noir tradition of *Chinatown* which was about the LA water wars of the 1930s.

In all cases, I have tried to substantiate my analysis with suitable internal evidence directly from the pages of *Drummer* itself.

1. PEDOPHILIA WITH AND WITHOUT WHITE SLAVERY

Embry allowed publication of advice, names, and addresses of magazines featuring minors, including younger children *(Drummer* 2); poem, "Boys" (*Drummer* 5); 17-year-old boy in Scott Masters' serial-book, *Five in the Training Room* (*Drummer* 6); and "Robert Payne" ad for Embry's own novel, *The Story of Q*, with its "Love for Sale" pitch about minors: "Sold into slavery at 16..."; plus a half-page under-age chicken ad (*Drummer* 9); then, twice in *Drummer* 18, page 74, and *Drummer* 19, Embry published a quarter-page ad titled "Photos of Male High School Students" sold mail-order by

Leland Wiegert, Jr., which he would not let me delete from my first full issue (*Drummer* 19), but which, after I had insistent words with Embry, was never published again.

Some things keep reoccurring. In *Drummer* 123 (September 1988), publisher Anthony DeBlase published a letter from the ACLU on page 4, and then, in a first-person confession titled "Thinking," allowed a writer named "Spunk" to rant on about performing forbidden sex "as a fantasy, as a thought" with "women, kids, dogs, horses; killing sex; hanging, castration, fucking to death....Hey, it's FANTASY." Analysis of both the writing and the photographs of this avowed "self-sucking sex performer" convinced me that the writer "Spunk" and the "model" were one and the same: the headstrong blond porn actor Scott O'Hara, a *Drummer* slave model famous for auto-fellatio, who in the 1980s in his *Steam* magazine singlehandedly ruined tearoom sex in the United States by publishing, for all law enforcement to see as Ed Davis had seen in *Drummer*, a list of the best spots for public gay sex; in what appear to be his fingerprints in an "ad in trade," O'Hara was pictured in *Drummer* 123, page 63, demonstrating a penis pump available through mail order. O'Hara's *Steam* appeared in a display ad in *Drummer* 166, page 29.

2. NECROPHILIA

Sex with the dead is one of those things one doesn't notice right away on Quaaludes, especially the original Rorer 714 edition. Nevertheless, Embry (who as far as I know never took a Quaalude) published the feature article "Fetish: Necrophilia" by the sensationalist writer William Wulfwine checking out a dead blond surfer, with Embry editorializing dangerously with camp irony Davis could not comprehend on page 9, that "The active partner can, and often does, carve up his [dead] subject...and he need not relate at all. He doesn't even have to say, 'I love you.'" (*Drummer* 4); the snuff poem by the night porter at the Ramada Inn on Santa Monica, John Rowberry (*Drummer* 5); and Satan sexing it up in a graveyard in Bill Ward's graphic novel, *King* (*Drummer* 9).

3. BESTIALITY

"Man's Best Friend: Bestiality" (*Drummer* 9) reprinted as "Bestiality" (in *The Best and the Worst of Drummer*) featuring 14-and-16-year-old farm boys; plus the pop culture of San Francisco's famous "Lion Pub" man-and-beast posters which are featured on two pages, 54 and 55, in *The Best and the Worst of Drummer* as well as in many pages throughout early *Drummer*. Embry fully acknowledged controversy and censorship over animal sex: "A couple of the [Lion Pub] drawings were rejected by some [other] publications.... Here they are, intact."

4. PISS

"Golden Shower Festival" (*Drummer* 2, pages 8-9); photo, cock pissing in mouth (*Drummer* 3); Orlando Paris' "Water King": enema, piss, scat; the homomasculine *Kansas City Trucking Company* (*Drummer* 10), a film by the Gage Brothers, Sam and Joe Gage aka Sam Christensen and Tim Kincaid.

5. SCAT

Lead feature, "Scat Anyone?" with drawing (*Drummer* 5); two "Letters to the Editor," almost too coincidentally seeming to share the tone of other letters, praising earlier scatology article in *Drummer* 5 ("Hooray for Scat" *Drummer* 8; *Drummer* 10). Did Embry himself write or ask "Robert Payne" or staff to pen letters to the editor to make a point or sell a product? (Yes. He did. Repeatedly.) Positive review (*Drummer* 6, page 36) of the scatological graphic novel, *Timmy*, RFM Productions, 1976, 40 pages, fully illustrated. *Timmy* was "full of the most graphic scenes of shit and piss.... there is something to offend anyone (unless you are an atheist) [Later, Embry would not be so flip about theology.]....It's so bizarre that, like the Master DeSade himself, it is utterly fascinating."

6. EDGE PLAY

The then shockingly new avant garde of tit piercing and blood licking in Fred Halsted's 1975 film, *Sextool* (*Drummer* 1, *Drummer* 3), starring Val Martin in which Halsted pierces twinkie-blond Joey Yale's nipple. The LA Halsted "quotes" New Yorker Sandy Daley's film, *Robert Gets His Nipple Pierced* (1970), shot at the Chelsea Hotel, and featuring my soon-to-be lover, Robert Mapplethorpe, the scourge of US government censorship, with his then-partner punk rocker, Patti Smith, spieling on the soundtrack; "Branding, Piercing, Tattooing" (*Drummer* 6).

7. SATANISM

Hints of sulphur in Bill Ward's homomasculine cartoon strip, *King*, with its "Satan's Boy" (*Drummer* 6); leather-bar festivities with occult and

Satanic-themed names like "Full-Moon Party" and "Leather Sabbat(h)" (*Drummer* 9, page 44) made worse by being pasted above the ad for the Scandinavian "chicken magazine" titled *Boy* sent mail order from Denmark.[1]

8. HALSTED, FRED

Age and consent problems in "Rape," a narrative of a "young blond twinkie in bondage" (over 21, of course) written by notorious LA sex-scofflaw and filmmaker, Fred Halsted (*Drummer* 4, page 48) who was cover photographer for *Drummer* 2, featuring his controversial film, *Sextool* (1975), which opened in New York and San Francisco, but was forbidden to open in LA, during the same June 1975 that *Drummer* debuted its first issue. *Variety* reviewed Halsted as "the Ken Russell of S&M homoerotica." In 1969, the outrageous British director Ken Russell had startled mainstream filmgoers with his sensuous *Women in Love*, based on the novel by D. H. Lawrence from a script by gay activist Larry Kramer; the taboo-busting film became famous for its iconic nude scene of two homomasculine men, Oliver Reed and Alan Bates, wrestling in front of a blazing fireplace.

When Halsted and Embry fell out after they were both arrested in the Slave Auction raid, Halsted turned competitor and immediately founded his own magazine called *Package* (1976) to replace in Los Angeles what *Drummer* had been to local LA leather before *Drummer* went national in San Francisco. Halsted, along with Academy Awards Oscar Streaker Robert Opel, continued Embry's mistake of challenging Ed Davis in the pages of *Package* which was quickly driven out of business after only six issues.

Because of Davis, *Package* died the way *Drummer* would have died in its infancy if it had not exited LA to be reborn in San Francisco.

Eighteen months later, Opel died mysteriously, shot in the head execution-style in his new Fey-Way art gallery in San Francisco.

9. MALE RAPE

Lead feature article introduces the scary concept of gay sex used as an assault weapon against straight men; it's a revenge fantasy against straight bullies,

---

1 Editor's Note: For more insider eyewitness information about 1960s and 1970s black-leather culture, Folsom Street phallic worship, S&M ritual, Goth sex, Satanism, wicca, and witchcraft, see *Popular Witchcraft: Straight from the Witch's Mouth* written by *Drummer* editor-in-chief, Jack Fritscher, in late 1960s and early 1970s, and published 1972, three years before *Drummer* debuted; new edition, 2005.

titled "Male Rape" with the kind of aggressively provocative and shocking sentence that puts real *phobia* into *homophobia*: gays no longer take abuse, and they rape and recruit. The challenging fantasy sentence that drove Davis wild is "I enjoy inflicting homosexuality on them." (*Drummer* 12) Consider also the "Rape" drawing by Rex (*Drummer* 12, page 8); cops who know prisons fear this rape taboo because straight guys in their vanity often fantasize and flatter themselves that they are irresistible to gay men, especially the scary new-breed of masculine leather bikers straddling Harley hogs, who desire them and will attack them sexually.

10. FISTING

Fisting was considered illegal in LA; Halsted's fist-suggestive cover photograph of butts, hankies, and rough sex was from his fisting film, *Sextool* (*Drummer* 2); the lead feature article, "FF of A," coopted the wholesome "Future Farmers of America" initials into the decadent "Fist Fuckers of America" (*Drummer* 3).

11. HOMOMASCULINITY IN FICTION, FEATURES, AND PERSONAL ADS

"Leather Fraternity" personals profiled the emerging identity of the new homosexual not as a sissy but as a masculine man resisting bullies and thus threatening straight masculinity; by my sweeping survey inside the texts of the 214 issues of *Drummer*, the keyword most used from the first issue of *Drummer* to the last is *masculine* (including *masculinity*). *Drummer* 12 (January 1977), pages 70 and 73, trumpeted the Eagle bar in Boston with the tag line *If You're Man Enough*. That slogan in Boston had appeared much earlier in San Francisco as written by artist/dancer/junkie Chuck Arnett, founder of the Tool Box, in his poster for the Red Star Saloon at the Barracks bath on Folsom Street. That classic Red Star poster was printed several times in *Drummer* with Arnett spelling *you're* as *your*. In that same *Drummer* 12, page 74, the legendary One Way bar in LA advertised itself simply as "A Man's Bar."

As soon as Anthony DeBlase bought *Drummer*, his second editorial confirmed this explicit homomasculinity in *Drummer* 99 (page 5) when he wrote:

> What kind of man reads *Drummer*? Leathermen is one obvious answer...but it does not go far enough...Not everyone is into leather.

The only common denominator among *Drummer*men is a cock-hardening interest in masculine men, masculine images, masculine fantasy, and masculine reality.

Joseph W. Bean wrote in the 20th Anniversary Issue, *Drummer* 188, page 18, that "The move toward masculinity by gay magazines happened more because of *Drummer* than any other publication....The very existence of *Drummer* magazine...began to undermine the monopoly of inexperienced, shiny smooth, and tiresomely youthful models."

The original tag line for *Drummer* was "America's Mag for the Macho Male." Also to be interpreted: Opel's historic obituary for the homomasculine "Tool Box" (*Drummer* 2); Bernie Prock's and Toby Bailey's very-XYY-chromosome "Leather Journal" column (*Drummer* 6) which is the exact kind of "Masculinist Manifesto" I fictionalized in *Some Dance to Remember* to chronicle this theme of homomasculinity in *Drummer*. In addition, some of the Prock-Bailey topics confirmed LAPD suspicions about "Compulsive Public Sex." The centerfold with Durk Parker aka Durk Dehner was titled "Studies in Masculinity," *Drummer* 15, page 39. (Canadian Durk Dehner early on worked in advertising with *The Advocate* and then in 1984 as founder of the Tom of Finland Foundation; see photograph of Dehner with "homomasculine art pioneer Tom of Finland," *Drummer* 137, page 35.)

Years later in *Drummer* 131 (July 1989), a letter to the editor, page 5, complained that the twenty-one-year-old "Mr. Drummer 1988" Ron Zehel (1966-2016) was too soft and too young to represent "all around masculinity" which was the purported aim of the Mr. Drummer Contest. I was one of the Mr. Drummer judges who voted for Ohioan Zehel because he seemed something new and healthy on the leather scene. On the surface, he was handsome and minted off the Eagles' *Hotel California* album—he *was* the "New Kid in Town" and he seemed to the judges to be what *Drummer* marketing needed to keep its demographic fresh for its so-called "old guard" readership.

What a dismissive term. *Drummer* loyalists never used it. There never was an "old guard." Leather is always "avant garde."

Unfortunately, the leather community assessment of Zehel was that he turned out to be rather much a leather mirage during the AIDS plague of wishful hope. Even though he advertised his photos and services in "Models Nationwide" in *Drummer* 125, he seemed too shy and immature, even though his modeling ad promised to give a portion of his profits "to fight AIDS," to shoulder the public relations responsibilities of a proper Mr. Drummer on the order of the glorious Michael Pereya, winner of the 1988

International Mr. Leather title. At the 1987 Mr. Drummer Contest at the Warfield Theater on Market Street, Michael Pereya in a leather raincoat walked up to me during rehearsals and flashed me, standing in the orchestra pit, in a total grinning "reveal" of his torso and leather codpiece that to me was like a thousand paparazzi bulbs shooting off unforgettably in my wondrous eyes. Pereya had the zeal and razzle that Zehel's dazzle lacked.

Drummer editor, Joseph Bean, concurred when he wrote about the "publishing wars" in *Drummer* 188 (May 1989), the 20th Anniversary Issue:

> The newly bold gay mags of the mid-1970s scared distributors, retailers, and buyers who were a little nervous about them. Many of the mags were "macho" gay, a phrase that was no longer oxymoronic [as in the 1950s and 1960s] and not yet humorous.

The humor came later, in 1977, when the Village People debuted their first hit, "San Francisco." The Village People "leatherman," Glenn Hughes, often partied with our *Drummer* Salon in San Francisco and in our summer retreat in Sonoma County. I published a photograph of David Hodo, the construction worker from the Village People, in *Drummer* 30 (June 1979), page 7; the caption reading "One David Hodo pic, cuming up! —Editor" illustrates that my style guide for *Drummer* spelled *cuming* with one *u* and one *m*, and not as *coming*, or *cumming*. After rising triumphant as *cum* in large point in *Drummer* 121, page 34, the spelling of *cum* and *cuming* slipped to *cumming* and then under the Dutch owner *Drummer* returned to the distinctive *cuming* as in *Drummer* 186, page 6. In the language-shaping world of advertising, nearly all video companies whose money is made on *cum* shots have adopted the sexier, raunchier spellings, *cum* and *cuming*, as have many "wink-wink" leather bar ads inviting customers to "Cum to our beer bust."

The use of language in *Drummer* is addressed in the *Gay San Francisco: Eyewitness Drummer* article: "Homomasculinity: Framing Keywords of Queer Popular Culture in *Drummer* Magazine" from the Queer Keyword Conference, University College Dublin, Ireland, April 2005. In the culture war over emerging gay vocabulary, it may be worth noting that I headlined a "prison punk" feature on the cover of my *Drummer* 24 (September 1978) with the defiant word *fag* as in "We Abuse Fags!" *Vis-a-vis* the S&M keywords words *slave* and *boy*, confer *Drummer* 174, page 5, for the editorial, "The Slavery of Words," by Graylin Thornton who happened to be both Mr. Drummer 1993 and African-American, as well as the actor-producer of the film *Foucault Who* (2002) directed by Wickie Stamps who was the editor of *Drummer* in the mid-1990s.

In 1984 when Embry was secretly looking to sell *Drummer*, he tried to up its capital value by cashing in on the popularity of masculinity as an emerging gender identity. He published *Drummer* 82 with the monetizing tag line printed with big red letters: "Manhood Rituals Issue." The subhead read: "This Issue Is Devoted to the Ordeals of Becoming a Man!" The issue featured a lead article, "Manhood Rituals"; an anti-Fascist screed, "Naked Threats," written by the tempestuous video director T. R. Witomski against the radical feminist censor, Andrea Dworkin; and page after page of prose in praise of male secondary sex characteristics that are the basis of sex appeal. Working that theme, he also included masculine-fetish news about a shaving newsletter out of Reno titled *Stubble*; and he repeated my early homomasculine concept, "*Drummer* Daddies," which he tagged with my original line: "In Praise of Older Men." In his opening editorial, he wrote ingenuously: "This issue of *Drummer* is devoted to 'Manhood Rituals,' a subject dear to my heart...."

In fact, at this time, he was already preparing and expanding his publishing empire to create some career to retreat to after he dumped *Drummer* on some unsuspecting buyer, as he did eighteen months later, in 1986, when he sold it to Anthony DeBlase. There was a seeding purpose inside that "Manhood Ritual" theme of *Drummer* 82 that was another one of his business schemes. Like a Trojan Horse inside *Drummer*, he was introducing the names of his new clones of *Drummer* which were, *quelle surprise*, the magazines, *Manhood Rituals* and *Manifest Reader*, which he combined into a third title, *Super MR Magazine*. In those post-*Drummer* doppelgängers he frequently published features and stories using my coinage, *homomasculinity*. Most often the articles were written by his longtime Alternate Publishing staffer, Rick Leathers aka Dane Leathers aka Mike Leathers who, despite openly loathing Embry, understood him and kept his office enterprises afloat for eleven years so he could collect a regular paycheck. See Rick Leather's essay in *Manifest Reader* 23, "Bullwhips, Bullshit, & Ballot Boxes."

From the first issue of *Drummer* to the last, such considerations of masculinity and gender freaked out LAPD Chief Ed Davis who till then thought gay men were sissies who wanted to be women, not authentic men who enjoyed being male, and not just male, but macho and rugged as a way to italicize their natural-born masculine identity.

12. GENDER-FUCK

The Cycle Sluts gender-fuck cover photo (*Drummer* 9) and interviews of leathermen gussied up in glitter like *The Rocky Horror Show*, included my colleague in the *Drummer* Salon, Mikal Bales (1939-2011), who soon after reinvented himself as "Daddy Zeus," founding owner and director of the masculine Zeus Studio, whose steamy underground videos fleshed out the kind of man-on-man whipping, bondage, and torture scenes Hollywood action movies only dared suggest. Robert Opel's campy, but unsuitable, "Cycle Sluts" photo is winner of the "Worst *Drummer* Cover Ever" because it missed the marching beat of *Drummer*. Its "drag queen camp" is 180 degrees from readers' personals ads seeking that keyword *masculinity*, emphatically followed by a repeated separatist mantra of "no fats, no fems, no phonies." A personal classified in *Drummer* 1, page 14, threw down the gauntlet of authentic gender identification: "No fags playing butch."

Because *Drummer* was at that time the only magazine aimed at masculine men, readers became justifiably anxious about any invasion by privileged drag queens favored by and featured in all the other vanilla magazines that excluded leathermen. In the "Letters to the Editor," after the Cycle Sluts' gooey "thank-you" note, there was a letter complaining:

> The Cycle Sluts cover picture and the associated article you used in your latest issue, *Drummer* 9, disgusted me beyond words. I thought when you started out, that this was to be a unique magazine—for men—not for campy bar queens. I was wrong. The Cycle Sluts have no place in my lifestyle or that of my friends. If I want to read that kind of trash, I will subscribe to *After Dark* or *The Advocate*.... — Bruce, Seattle (*Drummer* 11).

That tell-tale reader response rang true enough to be reprinted *con brio* and in full in *Drummer* 188 (June 1995), the 20th Anniversary Issue, page 6. In 1997, twenty-one years after the dragazine of *Drummer* 9, Embry dedicated the "Parting Shot" page (98) in his *Manifest Reader* 33 to a frontal nude photograph of the bearded transman Loren Cameron. Embry being Embry announced this portrait on his Contents page with his reductive gender-insensitive line: "Loren Cameron. A bodybuilder complete with pussy? Who says it can't be done." His photo caption read: "Loren Cameron, author/photographer of *Body Alchemy* shows off his/her accomplished male physique and fully female attributes."

13. ROBERT OPEL: OSCAR STREAKER, LEATHER ICON, PHOTOGRAPHER

Multiple photos were shot and articles written by frequent *Drummer* contributor, Robert Opel. If ever any one person should have been the editor-in-chief of *Drummer*, although he lacked the endurance and long-view oversight needed, it was the creative, inventive Robert Opel who had bigger fish than *Drummer* to fry in the performance art that was his life and ultimately his death.

Former LA school teacher, Opel, was a 1960s gay radical who was Police Chief Ed Davis' *bete noir*, famous for stripping naked at City Council meetings and showing his cock to Ed Davis (photo of Opel and Davis: *Drummer* 26, page 19) and even more famously streaking a billion viewers during the 1974 Academy Awards when David Niven and Elizabeth Taylor were on camera (*Drummer* 3); and finally famous for being shot to death Sunday evening, July 8, 1979, by—according to the intuitive gay grapevine of allegations—vengeful cops, pals of Dan White, in his SOMA gallery Fey-Way (*Drummer* 31, *Drummer* 32). Opel's murder is dramatized in *Some Dance to Remember*, Reel 3, Scene 1 and Scene 9. Embry also published ads for Opel's own LA magazine venture titled *Finger* (*Drummer* 7, page 3) with satiric "endorsements" by Embry's nemeses, "E. Davis" and "D. Goodstein."

In 1977, Opel asked me to write on spec for his next new magazine whose title was too perfect for its own good. He never got to publish his *National Pornographic* because of objections from *National Geographic*. If his story were not true, by now some other porn publisher would have used that title. There is an interview of the amazing Robert Opel that should have appeared in *Drummer*; instead it appeared in the "Virtual *Drummer*" of Fred Halsted's *Package* magazine. Stopping his own contributions to *Drummer*, Halsted competed with Embry to steal *Drummer*'s thunder in the publishing wars. He released *Package* 1, July 1976. Confer author, Bill Arseneaux, "Bob Opel: An Interview," *Package* 6, January 1977. Is *Arseneaux* ("arse nose") another camp pen name? Was it a pseudonym for entrepreneur Opel, the perfect publicist, who, with the esthetic introspection of a Modernist, interviewed himself?

Separation is not six degrees. In August, 2001, working as an associate producer with Andy Perrott to create a television documentary on Robert Opel for the LA cable series, *Fame for 15*, I set up on-camera interviews with Opel's pals, Durk Dehner of the Tom of Finland Foundation and with Mark Thompson. Former *Advocate* editor Thompson had previously interviewed me for a book he was writing on the glamorously notorious life of Robert Opel whom I interviewed at Fey-Way Gallery with Patti Smith's avowed rival, Camille O'Grady—who was Opel's lover—just three weeks before his murder. In 2008,Thompson invited me to collaborate on his screenplay about Robert Opel that he was writing with Andy Perrott. In 2009, Robert

Opel's young nephew, Robert Oppel (the family spelling), interviewed O'Grady, Thompson, and me for his documentary film, *Uncle Bob*, which in 2010, was featured at the Frameline San Francisco International Gay and Lesbian Film Festival. In 2014, thirty-five years after our first interview, O'Grady once again sat down with me for a long chat in my studio as I filmed her intimately spelling out her own eyewitness details of that night of horror in Fey-Way when she was held at gunpoint and saw her boyfriend Opel terminated.

14. "THE GREAT 'S/M' MURDER MYSTERY"

This loudly touted "cover" essay, serialized in three issues (*Drummer* 9, *Drummer* 10, *Drummer* 11) was an expose of the S&M murders in LA that the LAPD could not solve. Embry published it as "Murder in California, The Golden State's Gay Victims: The Great 'S/M' Murder Mystery?!" Jeanne Barney told me in 2006 that she and John Rowberry, who spent fifteen years in a sine wave of loving her and trashing her, had interviewed people from West Los Angeles to San Diego who were "99 percent certain of the identity of the murderer."

It was, according to *Los Angeles Magazine* (June 1976), that "...string of unsolved murders [that] was the real reason for Ed Davis' raid of that gay [Drummer] Slave Auction, according to LAPD insiders. Police believe a local S-M ring may be responsible for savagely...."

15. RACE WRITING; THE "N" WORD

The provocative use of the word, *nigger*, to describe a convict "top man" who is threatening to defecate on a prison punk's face—not a good idea in itchy-twitchy LA where cops, since the 1965 Watts Riots, were under pressure to keep the peace in prisons and in the streets, as well as in the Pantages Theater on trashy, draggy, funky Hollywood Boulevard where *Mandingo* (1975) was screening to throngs of charged-up audiences of Blacks and the whites who love them; photographs of the beautiful boxer Ken Norton from *Mandingo* appear repeatedly as a main theme in early *Drummer* (*Drummer* 1, "Whips, Paddles, Pitchforks, Pain Dominate *Mandingo*"; *Drummer* 6, "*Mandingo*: Revisiting Falconhurst"). See photographer Roy Dean's color photograph of a Black "Mr. Drummer" in *The Best and the Worst of Drummer*, page 41. Dean's "Mr. USA" could be one of Emerson's "Representative Men." The statuesque photo is about the sweet-looking man's nonchalant masculinity. He is nude but for his brown boots and a drum strategically hanging against his groin. The sides of the round drum are pasted up with a series of three *Drummer* front covers: *Drummer* 2, *Drummer* 5, and *Drummer* 9. By the date of the latest cover, the photo was likely shot in 1976. It is good commercial art meme because the use of the literal drum idealizes the brand name. The photo prefigures the first Mr. Drummer Contest by three years.

16. INTER-RACIAL SEX ADS

Classified ads promoting inter-racial sex with Blacks as tops and whites as bottoms eroticised the urban legend behind straight white fears about the alleged omni-sexuality of predatory Black men who rape both women and men—which in the never-politically-correct *Drummer* is considered "dinner and dancing." (*Drummer* 1, and "Leather Fraternity" personals)

Swabbing the DNA of popular culture, I figured serial author Embry in his youth wanted to be Kyle Onstott, the author of the Falconhurst trilogy of novels which included *Mandingo* (1957), *Drum* (1962), and *Master of Falconhurst* (1964). In *Drummer* 2, Embry proclaimed in the "Coming Up" column on the contents page, "Falconhurst: The 'Mandingo' Series of American Slavery." In "Revisiting Falconhurst" in *Drummer* 6, across pages 10 and 11, he reviewed and showcased his alter-ego with nine photos from the movie, *Mandingo*, plus eleven photos of Onstott's book covers. *Mandingo* sold ten million copies even before adaptation into a 1961 Broadway play and a 1975 Hollywood movie. The influence of *Drum* on the name *Drummer* is obvious. Onstott was the master of best-selling campy potboilers of race, sex, and violence. And, well, the entire text of *Drummer* was always sex, race, gender, and consensual action some misdefined as violence.

Onstott, with Lance Horner, also authored the story of Elagabalus, a young gay Roman who would become emperor. The novel, *Child of the Sun*, appeared in 1972 with advertising cashing in on the new fad of gay liberation. Directly influenced by Onstott, Steven Saylor, a 1980s fiction editor at *Drummer*, became a prolific best-selling historical novelist in his series of sexy detective novels set in ancient Rome.

17. FORBIDDEN FILMS IN LA: BAD BUSINESS—HOW GAY MOVIES AND VIDEO SHAPED *DRUMMER*

Reviews, covers, and pictorials razzing the LAPD about *Born to Raise Hell* while tub-thumping that S&M film so specifically forbidden in LA that producer, Terry LeGrand, and director, Roger Earl, had to premiere it one morning in Summer 1974 for a specially invited leather audience of us San

Franciscans at the Powell Theater on Powell Street at the Market Street cable-car turnaround (*Drummer* 3). Thereafter the film screened for over a year at the San Francisco Century Theater. There was also Embry's publication of a *Drummer* "extra" book of stills from *Born to Raise Hell* which, again, fails to print masthead credits for the responsible publisher or the filmmakers, LeGrand and Earl; the cover of *Drummer* 3 leads to two pages of six movie stills including piss flowing from a dick into a mouth, sex torture in bondage, and two men raping a third with a police baton. In Embry's first issue of his "Virtual *Drummer*," *Mach* 1 (1980), pages 54-56, he published a photo spread titled "*Born to Raise Hell* Revisited." He camped it up with his cartoon balloons pasted on the sex photographs from the film; and in his introduction, he aired his endless digs at Davis: "*Born to Raise Hell* played everywhere except Los Angeles, then finally after three years in release, opening and closing in Hollywood in one night, the LAPD being what it is."

Historically, the LAPD went gunning for the film because LeGrand and Earl went very *cinema verite* and dared shoot on location in bars that were already under heavy scrutiny from the vice squad who figured gay bars were inherently dens of iniquity. To use bars to shoot porn films went way beyond the pale of community standards for right-wing LAPD Captain Edward M. Davis whose hobby was raiding gay bars and gay movie theaters. Roger Earl told me, "We shot most of the interiors in a bar in the Valley called 'The Truck Stop.' We also shot at a bar on La Brea Avenue in Los Angeles called 'The Falcon's Lair,' but the scene in the bedroom was shot in my bedroom." When I first saw that bedroom in 1989, the industrial-strength wooden four-poster that Roger used for his own fun and games looked as rugged and ready as it did in the film. Roger added, "We also used a straight dungeon on Cahuenga Boulevard called 'The House of Dominance.' The Mistresses who worked there were all crazy about Val."

As an eyewitness then, I remained an eyewitness. Eighteen years later, much to *Drummer*'s delight and DeBlase's hunger for photos, Mark Hemry and I, as Palm Drive Video for hire, traveled in the summer of 1989 through Holland and Germany with LeGrand and Earl giving them their first "two-camera shoot" on the six new videos we lensed for their Marathon Films under the omnibus title, *Bound for Europe.*

Our June-July 1989 European video shoot turned into a treasure trove of articles, photographs, and advertising for American *Drummer* faltering for editorial material after the September 17, 1989, earthquake that destroyed the *Drummer* office and panicked publisher DeBlase into selling *Drummer* in what would amount to a "fire sale."

In 1990, DeBlase's post-earthquake *Drummer* began featuring, reviewing, advertising, and selling our six "sex-education" films with enthusiasm. These S&M video features were not fiction. They were "Reality TV." Each of the six was an American *verite* documentary of real European leathermen exhibiting themselves in real Art Brut scenes. That kind of intercontinental blood transfusion in an age of AIDS enlivened the shaken, ailing *Drummer*. DeBlase chose one of the color photographs I shot for LeGrand and Earl in the iconic Argos Bar, Amsterdam, for the cover of the "*Drummer* Super Publication," *Mach* 20, April 1990. Ten other of my Argos photos appeared on pages 41-45.

Bound for Europe
The Six "Reality TV" Video Series of Extreme BDSM
Directed by Roger Earl, Produced by Terry LeGrand of
Marathon Films
Cinematography by Jack Fritscher and Mark Hemry of
Palm Drive Video
Production Date: June-July 1989
Released serially: 1990-1994

1. *Argos: The Sessions* shot in Amsterdam
2. *Fit to Be Tied* shot in Hamburg
3. *Marks of Pleasure* shot in Dusseldorf
4. *The Knast* shot in West Berlin
5. *The Berlin Connection* shot in West Berlin
6. *Loose Ends of the Rope* shot in Hamburg, Dusseldorf, and West Berlin

After Amsterdam, the British painter, David Pearce, had to be called in to become our translator and still photographer because Mark Hemry and I told LeGrand and Earl that it was too much to expect us two to do three things at once: shoot the two High-8 video cameras as well as the 35mm still camera for publicity photographs. When LeGrand introduced us three, Pearce's first words were his unforgettable pick-up line: "Are you two the gentlemen I was expecting?" David Pearce became our intimate pal while shooting together in dungeons in Hamburg, Dusseldorf, and West Berlin. Six months later, in 1990, he flew from London to San Francisco because he wanted to capture the anxiety and risk he saw around me as an author, made naked to the world, he said, by the first publication of *Some Dance to Remember: A Memoir-Novel of San Francisco 1970-1982*. He decided to paint me nude, bearded like a mountainman, and standing with elbows upright alongside my head as in the statues and paintings of "The Flaying of Marsyas." Beside me, he painted Mark Hemry, fully clothed in buckskins, his long blond "Buffalo Bill" hair flowing, seated with his black-powder rifle on his lap: the warrior-lover protecting the author going naked in public with so much historical information. The painting was very *Drummer*.

Drummer was too down on its luck and was suffering with too much post-traumatic stress by that time to bother with the very erotic and real journal I had written of the making of the *Bound for Europe* films that Mark Hemry and I dubbed *Trouble in the Rubble*. But, what fun! We had traveled Europe inside a gonzo leather fantasy, shooting *verite* S&M sex scenes with the most *verite* leathermen in the most *verite* locations in legendary leather bars, the cellars of bars, and high-tech dungeon bordellos.

In fact, in the early months of the epic AIDS year of 1989, I had a choice of shooting porn, or defending porn, when Tony DeBlase, for whom I was an editorial consultant, queried me about my availability for testifying for the trial of pioneer Steve Toushin who had been arrested in 1988 on Federal obscenity charges for producing and distributing S&M videos, including films *Drummer* loved like the perfect fisting film *Erotic Hands*. I had first encountered Toushin's work in the 1960s during my graduate school nights cruising Chicago's Old Town where he managed the Aardvark Theater Cinematheque and screened underground movies like Jack Smith's *Flaming Creatures*, and Kenneth Anger's *Scorpio Rising*—despite the censorious six police widows, mothers and grandmothers, who ran the Chicago Film Board out of police headquarters at 11th and State Street until public resistance killed it in the mid-1970s.

In the *mise en scene* of grief in 1989, a person could not be involved in every cause and had to choose. My former sweetheart, Robert Mapplethorpe, died of AIDS in March, and by June, the censorious United States Senator Jesse Helms, was launching his government attack on what he called Mapplethorpe's pornographic photographs. I countered my grief with extra busy-ness. I was proofing the final galleys for *Some Dance to Remember* which Knights Press was publishing, and was also in pre-production for several video projects. I told DeBlase that having six video features to shoot on location in Europe for Roger Earl at Marathon Films, and twelve features to lens for my Palm Drive Video, I had no time to testify, but that I would be pleased to address censorship alternatively by writing a feature obituary about Robert Mapplethorpe, the most famous, and most censored, leather photographer in history. DeBlase published that "Pentimento for Robert Mapplethorpe: Fetishes, Faces, and Flowers of Evil" in *Drummer*

133 (September 1989) which was one month before the disastrous 6.9 Loma Prieta Earthquake on October 17.

Eleven days earlier, on October 6, the SFPD added to San Francisco's AIDS misery of that year, and that decade, with a police riot that swept the Castro, beating anyone marching among ACT UP signs reading "Living with AIDS & Fighting Back." Bullhorns announced the "news" that the street and sidewalks from Market Street to 18th Street were suddenly an illegal assembly area, and the cop attack, worthy of Fascists worldwide, began. Fighting back, marchers switched the chant from demanding AIDS funding to the hail-and-call Jody chants resisting the cops' brutal street censorship of free speech: "First Amendment under attack!/What do we do?/Act up!/ Fight back!"

Nevertheless, in a fine moment in leather history, *Drummer* rode to the defense of Toushin in the persons who did testify: *Drummer* publisher DeBlase and his partner and co-publisher, the psychiatrist, Dr. Andrew Charles; *Drummer* columnist and psychotherapist, Guy Baldwin; *Drummer* editor, John Rowberry; *Drummer* writer and biochemist, Dr. Geoff Mains (author of *Urban Aboriginals* who died of AIDS June 21, 1989); as well as *Drummer* contributor and anthropologist, Dr. Gayle Rubin, and Jim Ward, founder of the Gauntlet piercing company featured in *Drummer*, and Barry Douglas from the Gay Men's S&M Association (GMSMA).

That August 1989, Toushin was sentenced to five-years' probation and fined $500,000. The *Adult Video News* awards immediately bestowed on him the "Reuben Sturman Award for Legal Battles on Behalf of the Adult Industry" at the same moment the legendary Sturman, a true pioneer of the adult industry who died in prison, was convicted of tax evasion as the government's way to censor his porn empire. Sturman, who had Mafia connections, became connected to *Drummer* in 1980 when John Embry bought the back-alley property at 15 Harriet Street to house *Drummer* and then, very quickly because of his shaky finances, rented extra office and storage space to *Stars Magazine* and its publisher Glenn Turner who was funded by Sturman.

That emotion-packed year of AIDS, earthquake, and censorship battles in court and on the streets made the idea of escaping to shoot erotic films on location in Europe all the more attractive.

That beautiful summer of 1989 was remarkable. The population of West Berlin was locked down by the Russians: no American could enter unless one American exited. As uptight as it was, no one sensed it was to be the last summer that West Berlin existed. No one knew the Berlin Wall would come down ninety days later. Casting severe, real-life German sadists and masochists in West Berlin that summer was easy and hot because sadistic sex and masochistic endurance was one way gay West Berliners felt destressed and free even while completely surrounded on their West Berlin "island" by Communists with guns. Our star from East Berlin, Christian Dreesen, had twice been caught escaping across the Wall and had twice done time in a gruesome Stasi prison cell. His third try he reached freedom, and the silver screen.

While filming on location in Der Knast bar and the newly opened Connection bar, both on Fuggerstrasse, we passed though Checkpoint Charlie, which still gives me chills, to scout the ruins of East Berlin for additional location shooting we decided not to do because of the political danger. On our last night in West Berlin, we were taken to the underside of the bridge where, to release their Weimar tension, Liza Minnelli and Michael York, on location for *Cabaret*, had screamed with the train roaring overhead. So, of course, we waited, and waited, and laughed, and waited, and finally with a train rushing overhead and our backs pressed against the stone wall, we screamed our own primal scream releasing our tension about porn, plague, and politics.

Drummer, however, having perforce become politically correct in its fantasies by 1989, could not scream out its lust. It was past its journalistic zenith of 1970s activism and realism. It sought refuge from the horror of AIDS and sexual politics by retreating into self-help advice, fantasy fiction, and leather contest reports. In *Drummer* 21 (March 1978), the magazine published the true New Journalism feature article about San Quentin, "Prison Blues." But by the 1990s, when bought by the Dutch, *Drummer* could not handle the true story of how the handsome Christian Dreesen's homomasculine sex appeal, obvious even to resentful homophobes, had itself made more intense the brutal sex abuse he suffered at the hands of East German and Russian jailers fueled by the jealous passions of Cold War politics against gay decadence.

Expressing the zero degrees of our creative salon life around *Drummer*, the blue-eyed Teuton, Christian Dreesen, whom Mark Hemry and I also shot for our own Palm Drive Video in West Berlin, shared the cover of *Drummer* 147 (March 1991) with my other Palm Drive Video model, Glenn Marsh aka Blue Blake, one of the stars of my "twincest" feature, *The Blake Twins Raw*. Both actors appeared in my British coffee-table photo book edited by Edward Lucie-Smith, *American Men*: Christian Dreesen, who was "Mr. Germany Drummer," page 36, and Blue Blake, who was "Mr. UK Drummer," page 61.

18. POLICE HARASSMENT

Taunting the cops were the many articles riding the LAPD about their harassment (*Drummer* 6, pages 4, 12-14, *Drummer* 7, page 68; *Drummer* 11, page 76) and their arch stupidity for raiding the gay play, *What Do You Say to a Naked Waiter?* The LAPD rushed on stage and arrested the cast, who each took campy bows to much audience applause, while the pissed-off cops rousted them off the stage and down the theater aisles in real handcuffs (*Drummer* 4).

19. LAPD RAID ON LEATHER BAR, THE BLACK PIPE

To summarize the previously analyzed LAPD bust of the Black Pipe, the *Drummer* feature rather much characterized the police raid as a kind of Keystone Cops' invasion of the clowns (*Drummer* 3); perhaps this verbal provocation was the "beyond which not" for the LAPD that caused Ed Davis to retaliate by busting the April 10, 1976, Slave Auction as if to show the antagonizing Embry how a garden-variety gay raid could be escalated to operatic proportions that would cause regret and post-trumatic stress and bankruptcy. Embry's column "In Passing" continued to exorcise his dudgeon at Ed Davis and the LAPD, *Drummer* 7 (July 1976), page 68. Also in *Drummer* 7, page 13, Embry published an unflattering photo of Ed Davis in a hell-fire preacher's God-Has-Spoken pose shot by Bob Selan of the *L. A. Free Press*, and wrote the caption: "...in Los Angeles, EDWARD M. DAVIS [sic] is seldom challenged at all, by anyone." Were Davis and Embry two peas in a pod who could not countenance one another? In the brawl around the Slave Auction, Embry's imperial character and hubris emerged. Embry would brook no one telling him what to do whether it was the LAPD or his *Drummer* staff. I could not have morphed LA *Drummer* into San Francisco *Drummer* if Embry had not been distracted by his legal problems and had not been absent from the office for months before, during, and after his onset of cancer.

20. LAPD IN THE CLOSET: GAY VICE COP

In huge "red type" on a "yellow band" on the "dark cover" of *Drummer* 13 appeared the screaming gay banner "Interview with a Gay Vice Cop," a fiction (I think) published as a "true confession" to bedevil the LAPD by making them seem internally gay and corrupt. Embry's passive-aggressive cover design was a red flag that kept the bulls angry.

21. KEYWORDS OF S&M & HOMO-LEXICOLOGY: THE NEED TO CREATE LEATHER VOCABULARY IN ORDER TO WRITE ABOUT THE NEW WAYS TO HAVE SEX

Gay vocabulary is more than Polari or S&M code. *Drummer* tried to formulate its own "Leather Style Guide" of gay vocabulary because gay people, and their subset of leatherfolk, speak a second language that is always changing because of previously unheard-of ways to have sex, and to talk and write about sex. Jeanne Barney updated leather readers with the latest linguistics and semiotics in "The ABC's of S&M," but the feature alarmed the LAPD who were challenged by continuously evolving new gay code words (like *boy* and *slave*) and hanky codes that seemed like gang colors (*Drummer* 1, page 31).

When *Drummer* staff were not skirmishing with each other, it is interesting to see them reporting the new keywords of leather culture in order to write about uncloseted topics never before named by the love that dare not speak even its own name. Barney had learned the "sex alphabet" at *The Advocate* whose "Pink Section" personal classifieds was written in gay shorthand: GWM seeks CBT, TT, WS, FF, & VA. (Decoded, that means "Gay White Male seeks Cock and Ball Torture, Tit Torture, Water Sports, Fist Fucking, and Verbal Abuse.) In *Drummer* 1, she composed a leather dictionary, "The ABC's of S&M Sex." Crossing Alfred Kinsey and Margaret Mead, pop-culturist Barney interviewed players in the scene and sorted the new semiotics. She told me, "I did not make this shit up as I went along."

At the Stonewall dawn of leather culture, the character of kinky folk changed.

Out of silent closets came the need for new codes. There was the colorful semaphore of the hanky code. There was a mini-civil war over the meaning of wearing keys, hankies, and chains worn on the *left* or *right*. There was debate over the significance of "dressing" left or right: that is, the "meaning" of displaying one's cock and balls tucked down the left leg or right through tight Levi's. For a long while at the dawn of leather when distinctive signals for *top* and *bottom* needed invention and negotiation, *left* meant one thing on the East Coast and the reverse on the West Coast.

In Barney's "ABC's of S&M Sex," at that time "TT" meant "toilet training." Soon it meant "tit torture" as in CBTT which was shorthand for "cock-ball-and-tit torture." Seventeen issues later, "The Official Handkerchief Color Code" was sorted by Gary Barnhill, and published in *Drummer* 18 (August 1977), page 80.

When leatherfolk came out of the closet in the 1960s, it required an entrance exam to insure fluency. Sucking and fucking were not enough. For the first time, gay men were writing openly about gay men. There was a vocabulary and reading list for incoming students.

In 1968, San Francisco author Bill Carney's psychological novel, *The Real Thing*, educated beginners in S&M language, codes, rituals, and relationships in an elegant way that 1993 MacArthur Genius and leather poet Thom Gunn termed "brilliant" because Carney modeled his book on Pierre Choderlos de Laclos' *Dangerous Liaisons* (1782).

Beginners and Old Hands both, in 1972, immediately bonded with Larry Townsend's leather primer and catechism, *The Leatherman's Handbook*, the best-seller that educated leatherfolk for thirty years. "Old Hand," as in "I'm an Old Hand who is experienced," was a perfectly affectionate term to show how one generation can gently nurture another with out either being *en garde*. It is very different from the hard new term "Old Guard" which implies uptight old leather warhorses demanding new leather dudes genuflect to the old ways.

In the 1970s, Sam Steward (1909-1993), who was the *Drummer* author Phil Andros, also weighed in to teach beginners about our leather roots in his nostalgia for the simpler 1930s and 1940s of sexual outlaws like himself, and like Jean Genet (1910-1986) who created a whole new sadomasochistic language around sex. Identifying some roots of pre-Stonewall leather, Sam pined for bygone values and times, all lost, all gone with the winds of change, in his *Chapters from an Autobiography*, page 101:

> [This was] ...long before [1960s and 1970s] leather mania had codified and ritualized itself into leather-drag posturings, studied gestures, codes of dress and behavior that Genet had partially described and analyzed earlier in *Querelle de Brest*.

Fred Halsted claimed in *Drummer* to have invented the gay keyword, *twink*, to describe his "twinkie blond" slave, Joey Yale, who was the business brains behind Halsted's ventures in publishing *Package* magazine and in opening his short-lived LA bar called "Halsted's." *Twink*, from the name of the "Twinkie" brand cupcake, gained a second gay meaning when assassin Dan White plied his "Twinkie Defense," claiming too much junk food had caused him to kill Harvey Milk and Mayor George Moscone.

As editor-in-chief, I tried to create a *Drummer* "style guide" for punctuation, grammar, and spelling, sort of an X-rated version of Strunk and White's *Elements of Style*, but a bit more descriptive than prescriptive. Is an erection a *hard on* or a *hardon*? Is ejaculate *jism* or *jizm*? I wanted a word like *come* to be spelled consistently the hot and dirty looking way as *cum*. Later, DeBlase honored that spelling of *cum* which is also favored by the internet. A *cum rag* is so much hotter than a *come rag*.

I am no Eleanor come from the Aquitaine to Henry's court to clean up ballsy Anglo-Saxon with polite French circumlocutions, but I have spent a career designing sex words that connect with the reader's Id. Erotic spelling might best be based on the grass-roots spellings on toilet walls that are primal art galleries and dictionaries of gay linguistics.

On Halloween, October 31, 1988, I wrote a letter to DeBlase and his editorial assistant, Ken Lackey, regarding formalizing the *Drummer* and "Desmodus Style Guide" with spelling, punctuation, picture-credit format, etc., to help remedy consistency errors caused by the constant turn-over of inexperienced staff trying to copyedit, typeset, proof, and create layout. In the temperamental gypsy world of gay publishing, the average length of employment for dissatisfied office help at *Drummer* was six minutes to six months. What style-guide standards were set in the 1970s became scrambled in the Dark Ages of the 1980s when death by AIDS caused a generation gap that caused a consistency gap, as a new breed of leatherfolk emerged with New Media sensibilities that didn't give a fig about old-school publishing standards or the kind of spelling consistency on which internet searches depend. As a result, few noticed in the 1990s that *Drummer* slipped from literacy and became a photo magazine and video catalog. Its literary model was no longer the *Evergreen Review* that founding editor-in-chief Jeanne Barney had envisioned in 1975.[2]

22. ACLU

With ads for the American Civil Liberties Union, Embry took a liberal stance during the beginning of the American culture war begun by Holy Bully Right-Wing Fundamentalists ignited by Florida Orange Juice Queen Anita Bryant, and fueled by the hate-monger Jerry Falwell who founded his Moral Majority in 1979, the first year of the national peak of *Drummer* popularity. The *Drummer* ACLU ads angered the LAPD as much as did the National Socialist League ads (*Drummer* 6, page 18; *Drummer* 9).

23. GAY NAZI PARTY

---

2 For expanded detail on leather linguistics: "Homomasculinity: Framing Keywords of Queer Popular Culture in *Drummer* Magazine" in *Gay San Francisco: Eyewitness Drummer* (2008).

Ads for the gay National Socialist League, with the Nazi insignia (the first issue, *Drummer* 1, page 26; *Drummer* 2, page 43; *Drummer* 3, page 38) featuring a "camp" line spun off the 1972 anti-Nazi film, *Cabaret*. The song "Tomorrow Belongs to Me" became the Nazi tag line "Tomorrow Belongs to You!"

Jeanne Barney told me:

> John ran the first ad without my knowledge. I loudly protested running the ad in *Drummer* 3, but John told me that it had been pre-paid. I told him to refund their money. He removed the ad, sneaking it back in after I'd read the flats and before they went to the printer.

Finally, with Jeanne Barney and with "Letters to the Editor" protesting the gay Nazi ad (*Drummer* 3, *Drummer* 5, *Drummer* 9), Embry bowed to reader pressure and stopped running it. As a result, the National Socialist League sued Embry who claimed he lost the case (*Drummer* 13, page 4). Hemorrhaging cash for legal fees from this suit and his Slave Auction court hearings, Embry groused that somehow the LAPD was behind this second expensive lawsuit brought by the "Gay Nazis" (whom he couldn't afford to fight), writing "you can't do business with Hitler." It seemed he also included LAPD Chief Ed Davis in the "Hitler" epithet he threw. Twenty issues later, in *Drummer* 33 (December 1979), page 6, the fight over whether *Drummer*—as a champion of free speech—could print the Nazi advertisement continued in a letter to the editor from F. K. L. Meir, a subscriber in Germany who thought Embry needed to be "less right wing." Embry responded with the courtroom lessons he had learned which had cost the *Drummer* development fund so much cash:

> *Drummer* does not accept advertising from any political organization that bases its philosophy on fascism. A long and bitter court case resulted from our [Embry's] past attitude that anyone had the right to believe in whatever they wish; and that *Drummer* could not act as a censor. We no longer feel that way."

In 1981 in *Drummer* 49, professional man-hater and scold, Arthur Evans, who made a career sucking joy out of homomasculine leather culture, wrote to Embry: "In issue 47, you try to justify your recent Nazi sex fantasy [story] on the grounds that it was a joke, and not meant to be taken seriously....What kind of people think Nazis are funny, anyway?" The answer: Bars full of gay men watching Charlie Chaplin in *The Great Dictator* and Mel Brooks in the original *The Producers.* At 1970s film nights at the Ramrod on Folsom Street, the clip repeatedly screened precisely for Nazi "camp" was "Springtime for Hitler." The myopic Evans, born minus a humor gene, obviously missed other pop-culture entertainments such as the camp exploitation film, *Ilsa: She-Wolf of the SS* (1974), or the sexual seductiveness of Oscar-nominated director Lina Wertmueller's *Seven Beauties* (1975), or Liliana Cavani's sexually transgressive BDSM classic *The Night Porter* (1974).

All of these very popular, controversial, and libido-lifting films, two directed by famous women, mirror exactly the *Drummer* fetish for and obsession with forbidden Nazis, no more and no less, because nearly all the men in 1970s bars had been young American boys traumatized and fascinated by Nazi terror during the Second World War in the same way that the young Tom of Finland, in clutched erotic anxiety, in the 1930s and 1940s had feared and fetishized Nazis in his glamorous uniform drawings.

Regarding the erotic temper of the mid-1970s, these smartly reviewed Nazi-lust films all debuted at the same moment that the first issue of *Drummer* hit the stands in 1975. In the Christmas issue, *Drummer* 25 (December 1978), to peg the shrill Evans, I had published one of his typical flaming tirades, "Afraid You're Not Butch Enough?," written under his pseudonym, the "Red Queen." During that same year, Evans interested me because following my 1972 book on women and gays and the occult, *Popular Witchcraft*, he published in 1978 his anti-male book *Witchcraft and the Gay Counterculture.*

Earlier in *Drummer* 20 (January 1978), I wrote a feature about Pier Paolo Pasolini's film *Salo,* explaining to pitchfork-and-torch villagers like Evans the erotic appeal of the forbidden, as well as the social good that esthetic analysis can do with art about Fascists and Nazis, especially when erotic desire itself is stridently politically incorrect. Evans committed the very social sins he complained about. He was trapped in binaries. He used the historic persecution of women and gays by straight men, including the Inquisition and Nazis, to justify his politically correct attacks on sadomasochism and innocent masculine-identified gay men he and the Effeminists mistook for the enemy. Everything is of a piece in the puzzlement of this universe. Later writing about "The Cult of Masculinity" in the *White Crane Journal* #58, he remained not unlike Richard Goldstein who wrote a seminal attack screed, "S&M: The Dark Side of Gay Liberation," in *The Village Voice,* July 7, 1975, seventeen days after the publication of the first issue of *Drummer.*

In 1973, *The Effeminist Manifesto,* published in *Double-F: A Magazine of Effeminism,* was written by self-described "gynarchists" Steven Dansky,

John Knoebel, and Kenneth Pitchford who were also the publishers of *Double-F*. It raised more red flags than a bullfight because, earlier, in 1968, two months after the hit Broadway premiere of the dissident sexualities in *The Boys in the Band*, radical lesbian separatist Valerie Solanas had published her *SCUM Manifesto* for her "Society for Cutting Up Men," and had then shot two famous gay men, Andy Warhol and Mario Amaya, two days before Robert Kennedy was assassinated in Los Angeles, and twelve months before Stonewall.

"Masculinist" Police Chief Ed Davis, self-defined as the protector of red-blooded American masculinity, was no more a fan of gay identities proclaimed by Dansky and the Gay Liberation Front than he was of macho "leather-cult" bars or, worse, the "menacing" gay-identity publications, *The Advocate* or *Drummer*, founded in "his" Los Angeles in 1969 and 1975. Both agitated Davis' Gay Panic Disorder.

That *Effeminist Manifesto*, censoring masculinity, did not need an anti-Fascist film like *Salo* to expose its aggressive Fort Sumter fireworks at the startup of the post-Stonewall civil war over gender that was so outrageously biased against all men, straight and gay, that it awakened a genuine gay-male need for "self defense" that called out for the necessary invention of the kind of practical "masculine manifesto" that *Drummer* effectively became despite Embry's first issues promoting gay Nazis (*Drummer* 1), leather weddings (*Drummer* 7) and "inflicting homosexuality" on straight men (*Drummer* 12).

To lampoon *The Scum Manifesto* and *The Effeminist Manifesto* outside of *Drummer*, I responded fictively to manifestos proliferating everywhere when the protagonist of my novel, *Some Dance to Remember*, wrote a spiraling "Masculinist Manifesto" that was the character's brisk opinion, not mine, inside the storyline.

Of the radical Effeminists' "quintessential Thirteen Principles," two of their statutes, revealing their anti-BDSM and anti-male disdain, were "Sado-Masculinity: Role Playing and Objectification" and "Masculinism" which they did not understand as a reciprocal term with "Feminism," the way the word *mother* cannot be understood without the reciprocal term of *child*. Did the men who were the Effeminists realize that they had internalized the aggressive hatred of males that radical lesbian feminism was championing to the ruin of GLBT harmony in the civil war that turned the joys of 1970s gay liberation into the struggles of 1980s gay politics?

Long lives can be blessed with change. By 2013, Steven Dansky reconfigured his position as a gay pioneer by producing, directing, and shooting his brilliant video series, *Outspoken: Oral Histories from LGBTQ*

Pioneers, which he opened up to every possible diverse political voice. In 2014, he conducted a two-hour interview in San Francisco about my work at *Drummer*; and nearly a year later, we took supper together in Santa Rosa with Mark Hemry, and Steven mentioned in his dignified and soft-spoken voice, that, without losing his larger humanist principles, he had evolved inclusively, away from the hot topics of the primal separatism of his early days as a pioneer member of the Gay Liberation Front in 1969 and a founder of Effeminism in 1973. Such philosophical conversations between friends who can differ and evolve without personal animosity is one of the reasons being an inclusive humanist seems existentially more open than being either a feminist or a masculinist.

In *Drummer* 115 (April 1988), Anthony DeBlase continued Mel Brooks' anti-Nazi camp when he published a full-page ad picturing a uniformed German with riding crop and tall boots disciplining a floored *Drummer* reader. Soliciting subscriptions, the tag line read with the stereotypic comedy accent, "You Vill [*sic*] Read *Drummer*."

A classified ad on page 53 in *Drummer* 123 (September 1988) revealed how one man, among many, eroticized history that may have frightened him as a child: "Leather Nazi, 38, 5' 8," seeks same or redneck cop type. Heavy-duty Nazi conversation. Fucking around. Relationship....Concord CA."

In *Drummer* 147 (March 1991), two of the worst-written "Nazi S&M stories" in the history of the world were published by DeBlase: "Hot Poker" by Jeff Kincaid illustrated with a Nazi drawing by the All-American Etienne, and "Dance Master" by DeBlase himself writing as Fledermaus.

Drummer 169 (November 1993) featured Nazi uniforms and concentration-camp still photographs from Falcon's *The Abduction Series*.

In *Manifest Reader* 15 (1991), Embry, continuing to merchandise the underground S&M lust around Nazi uniforms and dominance, featured a Nazi on the dramatic cover. The color photograph of two blond men, one wearing a Nazi uniform, was from the gay video, *The Abduction*. Embry's reviewer John F. Karr, even while fluttering over the eroticism of Aryan beefcake, tried to make his dick stand politically correct, writing on page 89: "MR [*Manifest Reader*] is sure to hear from some who believe its *Abduction* cover is peopled by Nazis. The uniforms are more in the tradition of *The Student Prince*."

And the Brown Shirts are more in the tradition of the Boy Scouts....

Tom of Finland told me on his first visit to the United States that, despite his teenage conscience, he was so fascinated by Nazis that he could not stop drawing them because, he said, "They had the sexiest uniforms." Romancing them with his pencil in single frames and storyboards, he introduced dominant Nazi attitude, sex, and style directly into the erotic iconography of gay leather art and culture.

Hitler's politically correct Nazi party founded at the Furstenfelder Hof pub in Munich on January 5, 1919, was centered around beer halls, homosexuals, camaraderie, uniforms, and short leather pants—just like *Drummer*.

24. GAY MARRIAGE, LEATHER WEDDING

Gay marriage was the *piece de resistance* that drove conservatives like Ed Davis crazy. A cover and photo feature, by Robert Opel, pictured a gay marriage in Los Angeles: a leather wedding with a minister (*Drummer 7*, pages 8-11; reprinted in *The Best and the Worst of Drummer*). In our gay roots history, gay marriage in the 1970s was such a rising threat and controversial topic that in 1977 the California State legislature outlawed it by defining marriage as the union of a man and a woman. At the same moment, the gay-evolving Dianne Feinstein married two lesbians in the garden of her Pacific Heights mansion.

The more we make ourselves similar or equal to heterosexuals the more they freak about their own identity, and the more they falsify their invented victimization by us who "force" government workers, who happen to be conveniently Christian, to do their civil job and issue state documents registering same-sex marriages. We reveal their lesser angels. It's the same psychology as the plot of *Forbidden Planet* (1956) wherein the audience learns the monster is inside themselves. To heterosexuals with a defensive "Ego" and a moralistic "Superego," homosexuals play the forbidden "Id." Homosexuality represents everything "natural" they deny about their "normal" heterosexualized selves. It's easier to censor in others what it is hard to repress in oneself.

As Truman Capote said, "I'd rather be natural than normal."

In *Popular Witchcraft*, I wrote on page 111:

> Again comes the unavoidable theme, and the horror-inducing existential twist, that the Devil rises from inside humans. Metro-Goldwyn-Mayer's little classic, *Forbidden Planet*, a camp retelling of William Shakespeare's *The Tempest*, offered the ultimate horror to the Freudian mindscape: the amok monster, unbridled of Superego, turned out to be the Id of one of the space travelers. Sold to television, *Forbidden Planet* is sometimes titled *Id: The Creature from the Unknown*, a spoiler title that divulges the entire plot.

25. ON THE OFFENSIVE (TWICE): THE PRINCE OF REPRINTS

In case the LAPD missed a word, Embry, the "Prince of Reprints," blew hard and reprinted his most offending articles almost immediately in *The Best and the Worst of Drummer*. In that issue, he also outed readers' complaints when he wrote, page 64: "We were even accused by a couple of readers of repeating ourselves, when the first chapter of *Epilogue* [a "memoir" by Robert Payne aka Embry] was published in our Book Section." (Page 64)

In *Drummer* 100, page 4, new publisher DeBlase vowed not to rerun contents the way Embry famously recycled writing and graphics. "A common complaint about *Drummer* in recent years," DeBlase wrote, "from myself as well as from others, was about the frequent reuse of material." Unlike Embry's passive-aggressive style, DeBlase was not dismissive of readers. He was pro-actively solicitous of feedback from *Drummer* fans. He actually read the "Letters to the Editor" and frequently sought comments in person. In an act of smart marketing seeking to avoid blowback, he published a mail-in form,"The *Drummer* Questionnaire: Twenty Questions for Readers," in *Drummer* 125, pages 97-98.

Through sins of commission and omission against *Drummer* contributors, Embry was a scofflaw regarding reprints that disrespected the rights and intellectual property of individual authors, artists, and photographers. He also misled the readers. For instance, in *Drummer* 41 (December 1980), page 63, Embry and Rowberry pirated my "Astrologic" column from *Drummer* 21 (March 1978), page 30. Not only did the two of them collude in this direct violation of my copyright for which I was not paid, they falsely assigned my byline to "Aristide," and, most deceitfully, set out to cheat the *Drummer* readership by rearranging the line items within my "Astrologic" original 1978 "Aries" so that they could recycle and resell what would appear as if written for 1980 "Sagittarius." In that same *Drummer* 41, pages 43 and 44, they also reprinted without permission two photographs shot by David Sparrow and me doing business together as "David Sparrow."

In *Drummer* 117 (June 1988), page 55, DeBlase wrote a notice alleging that Embry in his *Manifest Reader* was re-doing material formerly published exclusively in *Drummer*.

This marked a new overt battle in the corporate civil war between Embry's Alternate Publishing, Inc., and DeBlase's Desmodus, Inc.

DeBlase thought Embry emotionally unable to let go of *Drummer*. I remember that in *Drummer*'s first few months, Embry exposed his separation issues over his lover who had dumped him in 1975 at the high moment when the first issue of *Drummer* was at the printer. He felt that 1980s *Drummer*, which had outgrown him, also dumped him, and, immediately after he sold it, his separation anxieties re-emerged as seller's remorse. Actually, Embry in his vanity boasted that without him *Drummer* would immediately go out of business. DeBlase tried to keep his distance and forge ahead with his new *Drummer*. He was no fool. But at the point of sale, he had unwittingly insulted Embry, where no offense was meant, when he had asked Embry to sign a non-competition promise not to create, for five years, any new magazine that could impact original-recipe *Drummer*. At least, that is what DeBlase told me during the years he made me his consultant.

In 1998, Embry, the King of Schadenfreude, took a cheap shot at the unfortunate DeBlase who had by then lost *Drummer*. He emblazoned the front cover of his *Drummer* doppelganger, *Manhood Rituals* 2, with the bold challenge: "With the Excitement of the First 100 *Drummer*s by Its Originators."

Sometimes the full moon restores the virginity of the Gypsy's daughter, and sometimes it doesn't.

ONE-HIT WONDER
Units of Measure in John Embry's Virtual *Drummer* Magazines:
Embry Had One Vision
in His Magazine Cartel of Cloned Replicants

If a young reader sat down at a table spread with open copies of any and every old magazine title and issue published by Embry, the reader would not be able to tell one magazine from the other without looking at the exact title on the covers. Layout, graphics, font, paper, photos, drawings, writing, and content are interchangeable from 1975-2003. Embry was a One-Hit Wonder. He purposely confused his later magazines to make them all seem like special issues of his only success, *Drummer*. In 1968 when Andy Warhol wrote his conceptual novel titled simply, *A*, he said he wanted the reader to throw the unbound pages in the air, pick them up, and read them in whatever order came from the shuffle. The toss is the same with Embry's magazines. Each one was cloned in form, content, and style from *Drummer*. Every *Mach*, *Alternate*, *Manifest Reader*, and *Super MR* was a virtual *Drummer*.

"Everything that came after *Drummer*," Jeanne Barney wrote to me, "was his obvious attempt to duplicate the earlier magazine and early success."

Chapter 6

DUTCH TREAT
WHO'S DRIVING *DRUMMER*?

- Post-Homophobic Stress Disorder (PHSD) and Reparations to Gay Folk
- The McCarren Act (1950) Legalizing USA Censorship and American Concentration Camps Has Never Been Repealed
- *Drummer*: "The American Review of Gay Popular Culture" and Other Tag Lines
- Wickie Stamps, the Second Female editor of *Drummer*
- Robert Davolt: The Last Editor of *Drummer*
- Embry's Unsustainable *Drummer*: The Cancer of Two Lovers, an Office Full of Fistfuckers, and One Colostomy
- The *Drummer* Personal Ads Were the "Facebook" of Their Time

> "Sometimes it almost seems as if the universe was designed by the Marquis de Sade."
> —Tennessee Williams, *The Night of the Iguana*

Following almost a year of ailments, John Embry had cancer surgery March 16, 1979. If illness can be caused psychosomatically, or even if it is simply symbolic, was the cancer eating Embry's guts during the Summer-Fall of 1978 and the Winter-Spring of 1979 caused by the LAPD? By that I mean to indict American homophobia as a direct cause of cradle-to-grave gay mental anxiety, physical illness, and Post-Traumatic Stress Disorder. The psychosomatic template around Embry's personal disease foreshadowed the intersection of government denial and medical neglect of the physical suffering and societal tensions around AIDS which was a homophobe's dream disease.

In the free-love 1970s, we were young and callow enough to meet up in the crowded waiting room of the San Francisco Health Department and joke, like Stephen Sondheim's "Gee, Officer Krupke," about penicillin and our social diseases which somehow mystically bonded us. In the uptight 1980s, the joke was on us when homophobic AIDS hysteria reminded us that in 1950 Congress had passed the McCarren Act allowing restrictions of civil liberties and free speech, as well as the rounding up of undesirable Americans for detention in existing federal "concentration" camps that continue to be used for illegal immigrants. That McCarren Act has never been repealed. Its threat continues to smoulder perilously under gay culture.

Because of the centuries of abuse queer people have been forced to endure as children, teens, adults, and seniors, we gay Americans might follow Native Americans and American Blacks and demand an apology and financial reparation from the American government for physical, psychological, and civil rights' damage dating back to the first execution of sexual deviants by American Christians in colonial New England, as reported by Puritan William Bradford in his diary *Of Plymouth Plantation 1642-1650*. The Protestant Christian torture and murder that landed on Plymouth Rock with the Pilgrims on the *Mayflower*, including the beheading by Miles Standish of an Indian Chief two years after the first Thanksgiving, could be the premise for a BDSM sex story in *Drummer*.

> William Bradford ...legally detailed the crime and punishment of a list of sins common among the colonists: bacchanalian drunkenness, witchcraft, homosexual sodomy, and buggery, as in the case of the young Thomas Granger who for "buggering a mare, a cow, two goats, diverse sheep, two calves, and a turkey" was hanged on September 8, 1642, but only after the mare, the cow, the goats, the sheep, the calves, and the turkey were killed before his eyes.... The score at the Salem witch trials of women and men was 144 accused, 54 confessed, and 19 hanged. —Fritscher, *Popular Witchcraft*, University of Wisconsin Press, pages 43-44

Who knows what caused Embry's colon cancer? But if his were a fictional story, it would dramatize possible cause and effect. In reality, the very large-boned man Embry seemed unstoppable except for illness. That twist of his bad luck was an ill wind that blew some good luck. As editor-in-chief, I had to take charge of *Drummer* even as he cycled through months of failing health, diagnosis, surgery, treatment, and recovery. In 1975, only four years earlier, Embry confessed he had been psychologically "traumatized" when his then lover, a blond from whom he was separated, was hospitalized with cancer, and refused, for whatever reason, to see him. The profile of his emotional health appeared in his autobiographical *Epilogue* in *Drummer* 2, page 46; in an *Epilogue* revision in *Drummer* 6, page 15; in *The Best and the Worst of Drummer*, page 64; and in *Drummer* 188, page 23.

Embry wrote about "the Angel of Death," and how "the Big 'C,'" which was how he termed cancer, was "the bogey man" who had come for his lover Don, and how he had "wished I could exchange places with him," and how the last time he saw him "was the day that the first copy of the first issue of *Drummer* was first unleashed on an unsuspecting public....The first *Drummer* came off the press on June 23, 1975, Don's and my second anniversary. The magazine was bound by hand...and delivered with two roses in a gold box to Don's hospital room." (*Drummer* 188, page 23)

Jeanne Barney, who was their go-between at the hospital, revealed to me: "The particular lover was an alcoholic who left John when he got sober. It had nothing to do with his leukemia."

In 1970, Erich Segal's romantic tear-jerker novel and hit movie, *Love Story*, swept through popular culture a dozen years before its archetypal story would be retold as an AIDS movie. Segal's plot featured a young college co-ed dying of cancer in the arms of her boyfriend. In tune with Segal, Embry's romantic telling of his own "love story" differed in what seems a harsh rejection which left him reeling. During the many months when he simultaneously fled LA, fled the LAPD, and fled his unrequited lover, our San Francisco *Drummer* staff had to cope with his bruised psyche.

In health and love, Embry's human anguish, which touched one's heart, was a hidden anxiety that stood like the First Elephant in the Room at our *Drummer* office on Divisadero Street. Illness seized him, and isolated him, years before illness, seizing us all, brought us together. Turning fifty, he was a generation older than we who in the 1960s had marched with protest signs saying, "Don't trust anyone over thirty." Even on the rebound with his second choice, his non-blond lover, Mario Simon, to comfort him, Embry, who said he preferred "Nordic blonds," seemed a lover who carried a torch of "unrequited love" made worse by the fact that the ex-lover, romantically portrayed as doomed, did not die, and continued to live in LA, estranged and out of touch.

I only observed his "love story" from the outside in, but as Embry himself grew privately aware that he too was becoming ill as had his partner, he became, in his public mood swings, increasingly unavailable to *Drummer* for quite some time even before his long ordeal of disability from cancer and stress from court appearances stemming from his arrest at the Slave Auction. On fate's wheel of fortune, I felt no Schadenfreude that his bad year from Summer 1978 to Summer 1979 was the best year I had working for *Drummer*. The staff had dismissed his biting temperament as simply "very LA" until the night in Autumn 1978 when he sat us all down so charmingly, so disarmingly, and, smiling through, revealed what was happening to him, and how he wanted us to carry on whether he lived or died. He said he had confidence in all of us. He shook my hand. I believed him.

When he returned full-time, Al Shapiro and I were driving *Drummer* in a new direction of an American masculinity wider than the simple leather identity of the "Leather Fraternity." Dumping Embry's obsession with Puritan LA cops and local LA bars, Al and I wrote gonzo sex articles about actual guys having real erotic experiences in real sex venues in San Francisco and New York where gay liberation was in full swing. Our switch to a national point of view was noticed by readers and by Embry. We both wrote our New Journalism from insights and experience gained in the erotic life we were living among thousands of leathermen who, the mornings after the nights before, exchanged sexploits over braggadocio brunches at cafes such as the Norse Cove across the street from the Castro Theater. Because I had been one of the founding members of the American Popular Culture Association in 1968, and was one of the speakers at the follow-up American Studies Association conference on October 31, 1969, I was motivated to add an inclusive "tag line" to *Drummer* to brand the our new content and direction on the masthead beginning with *Drummer* 25: "The American Review of Gay Popular Culture."

MILLENNIAL EDITOR WICKIE STAMPS

In the 1990s, against all odds, Wickie Stamps became the "editorial manager" and then the "editorial director" of *Drummer* when what staff remained turned to her for help, and she stepped up to keep *Drummer* on life support from *Drummer* 183 (March 1995) to *Drummer* 208 August 1997. Like every other person who ever worked for *Drummer*, she was caught in a web that was bigger than any one of us. Examining the monthly issues Stamps produced under the most difficult circumstances, I have the greatest empathy and sympathy toward her efforts, and toward her who is so talented. She told me that as a woman, she would not herself have applied for the job, but she stepped up when the staff of five, fearful for their own jobs, asked her to deal with the new publisher Martijn Bakker who, she said, quickly subverted her authority as editor. Among that staff, she was the only person involved in BDSM.

Seeking content, she found the archival filing cabinets were in disarray, and that most of the previous contributors *Drummer* relied on were dead. She could not recruit new writers and photographers because *Drummer* was deep in debt. In a corporate outsourcing move, Bakker hired a designer named Sam Sanchez who, she said, had "minimal if any exposure to the men's leather scene." Nevertheless, this outside consultant was Bakker's choice to pull the final version of each issue together. "Sam had to get almost all of the photo shoots for free from porn companies," Stamps said. He "... did an amazing job getting what he could for free as well as doing a great deal of writing as well as design work. For herself, Stamps underscored, "I had a great deal of responsibility but virtually no influence."

With Stamps backed into a corner, queer historians may note that in *Drummer* 188 (September 1995), she penned a minimalist, and, therefore, revisionist, introduction to "The *Drummer* Twentieth Anniversary Issue." Her editorial set out to track the changing marketing "tag lines" on *Drummer* mastheads, such as "The Mag for Macho Males" and "The American Review of Gay Popular Culture." However, as she told me, she did not have time to dig through all the jumbled in-house archives or the 187 existing issues. Nevertheless, someone on staff might well have taken a quick peek at the nineteen previous *Drummer* anniversary issues to assess what was standard "anniversary" content. Or what was quirky. For instance, in "The Fifth Anniversary Issue," *Drummer* 38 (June 1980), ventriloquist Embry conducted a coy conversation with himself, using bodybuilder Greg Strom as his "interviewer," so he could pen his own personal "parthenogenesis" origin story of *Drummer*, its pre-history, and, to Stamps' point, its tag lines. She, however, counted down the timeline of her tag lines from *Drummer* 187 to *Drummer* 63, bypassing all the original tag lines in issues 1 to 62. This decision made all that earlier marketing work by all the *Drummer* forebears invisible, even as she and her staff soldiered on in an office surrounded by rifled file drawers spilling over with the institutional history of *Drummer*. Robert Davolt explained the irony of this office turmoil when he wrote in notes he gave to me that *Drummer* had "The greatest photo and art collection in SM/leather history (or at least everything that had survived 25 years of looting by former employees) was sitting in boxes—unsorted, unusable and decaying rapidly."

Stamps, never fully titled as "editor," approached a leather-history signature moment for *Drummer* and for herself that evaporated when she produced "The Twentieth Anniversary Issue" which should have been published on time three months earlier in June. The tardiness was not hers. During the nearly three years I was editor-in-chief, I had no control over how Embry managed almost monthly to fail to find funds to pay the printer so that my issues could maintain their schedule. Knowing some of the ancestral history of *Drummer*, Stamps, who was always of good will, was percipient in inviting survivors such as Joseph Bean, John Embry, and me to write our own eyewitness histories of *Drummer* for her anniversary issue.

However, it was disappointing that circumstances caused her to excerpt my bespoke text without consultation. That, I admit, is an editor's professional prerogative. What author and editor always see eye-to-eye? But it was the first time in twenty years that anyone at *Drummer* edited my writing simply to cut costs, and to fit the page, in an issue cluttered with what amounted to "filler." It was an opportunity lost to leather history that fewer than twenty-five of the anniversary issue's eighty-two pages (32 percent) covered *Drummer* history. Even with Bean, Embry, and me attached to the issue, it seemed de rigueur that an editor who was not disabled by the publisher would have also included essential eyewitness histories from two of the several founders of and original contributors to *Drummer*: Jeanne Barney and Larry Townsend.

Judging that decaffeinated anniversary issue, a journalism student grading it might ding Stamps' editorial choices which seem cornered by Bakker as much as Sanchez's advertising choices seem driven by Bakker. In the ratio of the few pages of low-budget editorial content to the dozens of high-income pages of video advertising, what could have been a splendid anniversary issue missed its historical purpose within the leather community. That issue flopped because it gave little to the *Drummer* faithful and never became a popular-culture success and was never coveted as a collectible. Anniversary issues existed to excite readers' continuity of loyalty, and to drum up subscriptions. Had Stamps not been hobbled, and had the good-natured Sanchez any instinct for BDSM design heat, she might have helped sustain *Drummer* by making what could have been a rich and glamorous anniversary issue one for the ages. Historically, that was what Embry tried to do with *Drummer* 50. It was what DeBlase intended when he published *Drummer* 100. It's not as if *Drummer* had no autobiographical tradition in writing about itself in special issues dedicated to preserving its institutional memory.

Stamps worked against the odds to fill pages inexpensively, but was a picture really worth a thousand words? A larger-than-necessary reprint of the famous Robert Mapplethorpe cover of *Drummer* 24 failed to give any editorial mention of the historical importance of *Drummer* to Mapplethorpe or his importance to *Drummer*. The old photos were a slight to monthly subscribers always demanding new porno. Most likely not aware that the graphics assigned to him had been previously published, Sanchez recycled juiceless pictures and reruns of large Bill Ward drawings that ate up the pages, squeezing out seminal *Drummer* photographers such as David Hurles (Old Reliable), Mikal Bales (Zeus), and Lou Thomas (Target), as well as ignoring key artists such as Tom of Finland, Rex, the Hun, and A. Jay (Al

Shapiro). Was it a ringer of gay culture's feminist bias that the reprinted fiction included several pages by Anne Rice who never wrote for *Drummer*? The rest of the writing was banal bits of "filler." Where one page would have been too much, there were five pages of cliched photographs of two porn stars, Rick Bolton, and the atypical *Drummer* model, the boy-chick Scott O'Hara who once was favored by Embry on page and screen but was so unpopular he was lucky he could suck himself off.

The charge "filler" applied also to the wobbly two pages of the "Drum Media" feature, reviewing books and videos, written by the amateurish "Dyrk" who reviewed himself having his own problems with "new media" when he might better have written a conceptual column of the rich history within *Drummer* of reviewing the arts, including the New York Arts special issue *Son of Drummer* featuring Rex and Mapplethorpe, or even the publishing of early performable BDSM leather plays such as George Birimisa's *Pogey Bait* (*Drummer* 12 and 13), David Hurles' *Scott Smith: Heavy Rap with a Solitary Ex-Con* (*Drummer* 21), and my *Corporal in Charge of Taking Care of Captain O'Malley* (*Drummer* 22 and 23). Was it feminist privilege that injected that interesting, but gratuitous, excerpt from Anne Rice's *Beauty's Punishment* into a leathermen's erotic magazine? Why was the polished Rice served up with a sticky non-erotic drawing that, taking up two-thirds of page 36, was repeated exactly full page on page 39? The three unexceptional and limp "Sex Art 4" photos, having no connection to *Drummer* history on pages 40 and 41, show how Bakker's budget squandered the space in this anniversary issue. Where was a collage of the reader-reflective selfie photos that, since 1978, actual *Drummer* readers sent in as "Tough Customers" to inject into the magazine its grass-roots identity, its street cred, and its face? Jeanne Barney, wrote in "The First Anniversary Issue," *Drummer* 7 (June 1976), that "...an Anniversary Issue [should] be initiative," which means that the issue should look to the future as well as to the past. But that mix was off balance in *Drummer* 188 which failed to respond to its rich history of 187 previous issues.

Further editorial space was nibbled up by the scattershot design whose specifications wasted many column inches and pages. In addition, the *Drummer* "Style Guide" must have gone missing because the proofreader did not bother to italicize the word *Drummer* or other titles in most instances. The failure of form and content in this anniversary issue, which is typical of most all the other issues of the 1990s, proved that editing *Drummer* required as much respect, expertise, and professionalism as any straight magazine.

Stamps had the distinction of being the *fin de siecle* managing editor. Driving that rising millennial perspective, she might have looked into the rear-view mirror to animate what she could in the soul of each of her new issues of *Drummer*. She had only to look at issues produced by *Drummer* editors such as Jeanne Barney, Tim Barrus, JimEd Thompson, and Joseph W. Bean, or browse through our 1970s San Francisco issues, 18-30, that helped set the bar for leather publishing during that first decade of gay liberation when we were inventing the vocabulary, and the qualitative criteria, with which we wanted to represent ourselves as we uncloseted our leather culture in American media.

Because editors and owners change, I kept my allegiance true to *Drummer* itself. In the 1990s under the absent third publisher Bakker, I was not paid in cash but in trade. For the last dozen years of the magazine's run, it cost *Drummer* nothing to exchange my writing and photography for a quarter-page display ad for my Palm Drive Video in each issue. When in 1998, Mark Hemry and I met in the *Drummer* office with Davolt, an obviously non-S&M accountant swished in and told me I owed *Drummer* six-hundred Dutch guilders—I mean dollars—for my one little Palm Drive display ad because stories and fiction were worth only sixty dollars. After I politely offered him a new body part, and explained the ancient *Drummer* trade agreements to him, he ran away in his wooden shoes. That ended that conversation. Stamps, no matter what she tried, faced the same European devaluation of her work. During this time of chaos at *Drummer*, I debated why I even bothered to have anything to do with the Dutch *Drummer* where all the power and decisions and taste were far away in Amsterdam.

Nevertheless, Stamps and I continued to work together. She published nineteen newly stylish "frame grab" photographs of Colt model Dave Gold starring in my Palm Drive Video feature *Dave Gold's Gym Workout* as an interior photo spread along with my story "Hustler Bars" in *Drummer* 204 (June 1997). On June 12, 1997, at the suggestion of Stamps' friend, the poet Chris Hewitt, I faxed Stamps an assortment of five of my new and seasoned leather and fetish performance poems which Hewitt liked but whose receipt Stamps never acknowledged: "The Young Turks Dream of Derek Jarman," "Foot Loose" from *Drummer* 29 (May 1979), "The Real Cowboy" from *Man2Man Quarterly*, "Tomorrow on TV Talk: Adults Who Wear Leather," and "Rough Trade: Chico Is the Man" from *Son of Drummer* (September 1978) which had won two poetry awards. In 1998, I gave Stamps four of my color photographs of Palm Drive's Mickey Squires, the Colt model, which I offered for publication in *Drummer* itself, but somehow they jumped into the *Drummer* spin-off magazine *Tough Customers* 12 (1999) where they were shifted from editorial content and turned into a two-page commercial ad selling that magazine.

Did my photos travel from *Drummer* to *Tough Customers* in someone's carry-on luggage? Or was it the accountant's revenge in that underhanded gay way we dismantle each other? Whatever the twist in the case, it seemed forgotten that the "Tough Customers" concept, column, and title were my invention, and legally belonged to me because, as a freelance contributor, I owned the copyright to all my writing and photography in *Drummer* as did Larry Townsend and all the other contributors.

Defense of copyright is a lifelong task that continues after death for the length of the copyright. On page 41, in *The Advocate*, July 16, 1975, the West Coast Larry Townsend began defending his copyright from East Coast publishers printing knock-offs of his writing. In 2008, he died while suing one specific publisher for reprinting his books—and fifty bookstores nationwide, named as co-defendants, for selling those counterfeits. As a widowed elder on a fixed income, he reacted to this alleged abuse of his business and his writing which was his identity. He panicked in his self-defense and created so much havoc among bookstores who had no way to tell an authorized book from a fake, that Deacon Maccubbin, founder of the Lambda Book store, the *Lambda Book Report*, and the Lambda Literary Awards, asked me in an exchange of emails beginning on June 19, 2008, to intervene and calm Townsend down. Maccubbin used the term "scorched-earth lawsuit." On July 2, Townsend finally surrendered and told me, "If you'll tell me which bookstores you have heard from specifically, I'll make sure...[the attorney]...drops them." Eleven days later, Larry fell into a coma July 13, and died July 29.

My column "Tough Customers" was in the same copyright category as my other feature articles. The only "work for hire" that I did as a paid employee was as editor-in-chief, not as a writer and photographer, and even then, Embry fell far short of paying the editing fees owed. In the whole absurdist comedy as *Drummer* died, I kept my silence because none of the new people, innocent of the messy past, really seemed authorized to be in charge of anything. What ancient agreements I had with Embry and DeBlase were unknown, and of no concern, to the third owner and his staff, and that was the core to how "old" *Drummer* business was dismissed by the Dutch *Drummer* that distanced itself from everything Embry and DeBlase had done. My copyright claim to "Tough Customers" would have fallen on deaf ears that had no money to pay me royalties anyway. I chalked it up to experience, and let it go for the love of the game, and love of the Platonic Ideal of *Drummer*.

Stamps, under stress and duress in the madhouse that was the *Drummer* office, accidentally also violated my copyright by requesting my previously published *Drummer* story "Foreskin Prison Blues" and then, without permission, cutting its 5,000 words down to three columns of text (*Drummer* 186, July 1995) while splurging a half-page on my drawing by the artist Skipper that I had commissioned for that story.

MILLENNIAL EDITOR ROBERT DAVOLT

The blond and bearded Robert Davolt, whose life and talents were about much more than *Drummer*, arrived fully formed in San Francisco in 1996. His name first appeared on the masthead of *Drummer* 202 (February 1997) making him the last *Drummer* "operations manager" while Stamps was "editorial director." To his many friends and fans, Davolt was a hale fellow well met who, despite some vagaries, I truly respected even as the death of *Drummer* consumed him. In a sad coincidence, he himself, like Embry, became ill with cancer. Stamps told me, "I believe Robert was pretty challenged by his drinking which affected his professionalism, but boy did he work hard and when we had conflicts, he worked to flesh them out. I appreciated that." Mister Marcus who wrote his leather "gossip column" for thirty-eight years in the *Bay Area Reporter* took his own measure of Davolt at *Drummer* and labeled him in print as "Robert Revolting." In Marcus' obituary for *Drummer*, he wrote that "Martijn Bakker, the Dutchman was the sole killer of *Drummer* and all it stood for." This is the turmoil in which Wickie Stamps was trying to work.

Davolt's "operations manager" title on the masthead of *Drummer* 201 (January 1997) expanded fifteen months later to "publisher and editor"in *Drummer* 209 (April 1998). Between 1998 and 1999, Davolt produced only six issues of the "monthly" *Drummer*, ending when *Drummer* ceased publication with *Drummer* 214 (April 1999), and the business closed on Folsom Fair weekend in September 1999.

On January 6, 2001, Davolt, over lunch with Mark Hemry and me at the Café Flore, personally handed me his "Outline" for his proposed history about the "fall of *Drummer* magazine" which he had, quoting Wagner and straining to be clever, provisionally titled *Götterdämmerung: Twilight of the Odds*. "That title's a mouthful and too obscure," I said, "It's too camp. Make it a high-concept title telling exactly what it is. Sort of what I'm doing on the manuscript I'm writing, *The Rise and Fall of Drummer.* "

Davolt had charmed Embry who fell for his blondness. Embry flattered Davolt in his new publications by listing him as associate editor and by publishing his article, "Guide to Painfully Correct Leather Bar Behavior," in *Super MR*, January 2000, just ninety days after the death of *Drummer*. He figured he could use Davolt to get his hands on even more archival material from the *Drummer* stash of files that he could recycle in his *Super MR* magazine in which he was regularly recycling my writing with my permission from 1970s *Drummer*. Davolt, however, was too bright to be exploited. Seeking my *imprimatur*, Davolt wanted to run his generational eyewitness past my generational eyewitness and collect my endorsement because he vested me, as he had Embry and his credentials, with a certain authority and continuity insofar as I was so often listed on the masthead as a contributing writer, and, more significantly, Embry had told him I had been a paid consultant to DeBlase. Even so, he and Stamps on their masthead misspelled "Fritscher" as "Fristcher" [*sic*]. Nevertheless, "over the cups, the marmalade, the tea" at Café Flore, I wanted to give Davolt what he wanted for his specific passion project while I protected the more inclusive institutional memory of *Drummer*.

From the first issue in 1975 to the last in 1999, civil war raged inside *Drummer*. Stamps, with her evolving titles, was replaced in *Drummer* 209 by Davolt himself who in his notes for his *Drummer* history explained about Stamps:

> As a woman, she felt uncomfortable being the primary moving spirit behind an infamous men's magazine, and she was unconnected to the local Leatherati. [She had no *Drummer* Salon.] She did not have the required commanding personality...nor did she have the sort of obsession that other editors had. Even as editor, she worked only part time.
>
> Few of the employees were on speaking terms with each other.

Davolt, who claimed himself the champion of diversity in *Drummer*, erred. Being a woman had not hurt Stamps. Unwittingly, she was yet one more textbook picture of the kind of well-intentioned, guileless, and inexperienced persons of all genders for whom, during the Great Dying of the 1980s and 1990s, it was a step up the old career ladder to walk into a legendary gay male publication depleted by the suffering and death of staff and contributors.

With respect to many of the other women pro-active for years in leather culture and literature, Davolt's reductive gender-profiling of Stamps revised reality so that leather history was fed his fable that she suffered because of gender issues rather than that she was, as she admitted, not really qualified professionally to handle the editorship nor the office politics. Wickie Stamps would be the first person to admit she was no Jeanne Barney when it came to creating leather culture and leather politics, but her fortitude showed that diversity in leather culture was a general asset and not a problem.

In 1983, I wrote a thought voiced by the cheeky narrator, Magnus Bishop, in *Some Dance to Remember*, pages 180-181:

> [Pat] Califia [before FTM transition] and [Camille] O'Grady...held an almost enshrined place in his Catholic heart. They seemed all the more fully women for having transcended radical feminism with the feminist humanism of their art. They were women who had performed the impossible the way Mary became a Madonna through virgin birth. Now that was the first truly, and maybe world's only, feminist act.

While she was editor, Stamps' issues were so argued about by *Drummer* fans that it seemed timely and camp and punk-like to satirize her troubled tenure with an unforgivable pun when I wrote in a history of *Drummer* for *Checkmate* magazine (issues 19 and 20, May and August 1997) that "*Drummer* had become a wickless stamp of its former self." Stamps, who is no weakling anymore than I am Dorothy Parker, sent me a typed note on *Drummer* letterhead emblazoned with the tag line "America's Original Leather Magazine"—which is an odd choice of self-identity coming from a Dutch-owned magazine. Writing on September 9, 1997, she zinged back: "Jack, Congratulations on your piece in *Checkmate*. Keep up the good work. Sincerely, Wickless Stamps."

If satiric awards were given for the "Worst Issue of *Drummer*," Editorial Director, Wickie Stamps, and Operations Manager, Robert Davolt, might be the unwitting winners for *Drummer* 201. Curious queer historians seeking internal evidence based on "form and content" might compare the arguably "Most Perfect Issue of *Drummer*," *Drummer* 21 (March 1978), with John Embry's reader-rejected *Drummer* 9 (October 1976) and Martijn Bakker's commercial sellout, *Drummer* 201 (January 1997), which are tied for the "Worst Issue of *Drummer*."

Differences of esthetic opinion aside, Wickie Stamps was a good sport, and a valuable eyewitness of what working at *Drummer* was on her watch. Her initial response when I queried her about an interview on Facebook, January 5, 2011: "Ask away. Glad you are documenting *Drummer*." We accomplished our professional accord when she and I conversed frankly by email on January 20, 2011. Her stylized observations are her own subjective point of view and are quoted verbatim, all lower case, minus conventional italics.

WICKIE STAMPS' EYEWITNESS TESTIMONY ABOUT HERSELF, DAVOLT, AND THE DEATH OF *DRUMMER*

FRITSCHER: Wickie, Thank you for switching us from Facebook to personal email. As a gay historian, and as a journalist, as well as the eyewitness founding San Francisco editor-in-chief of *Drummer*, I wish to acknowledge all the other eyewitnesses of *Drummer*, of which you are a very valuable one. In this regard, may I ask you these questions, any one of which you may answer or not any way---or with any variable I don't know about that you feel tells the *Drummer* story during its final collapse.

I don't wish to impose on your time or your generosity in responding. Your answers may be brief sentences--or more, if you like. And you needn't answer all of my suggested questions. Pick what you like and feel you know about. I am most interested in your own point of view on specifics you remember as suitable for history.

Who hired you? And when did you begin to edit *Drummer* (begin and end dates and issue numbers of your tenure). Why did you personally and professionally want the job? Any professional credentials you care to mention? Were you a practitioner of BDSM? Had you published any BDSM fiction or features? At what age did you become editor? How did you feel editing a magazine that was in such transition between owners? Did the office staff feel it was heading toward collapse?

STAMPS: i was already working at drummer handling advertising. frank strona who i knew from gay community news in boston had suggested to the advertising person that he hire me. while working handling advertising, i walked in one day and there was a note on my desk from the then current editor marcus wonacott thanking me for being supportive of him as a writer. marcus had asked my opinion of his writing as i guess martijn had told him he couldn't write (not sure it was martijn but someone in authority). when i read the note i said to other staff "oh, that's nice." they said "you don't understand, the editor came in and cleared out his desk during the night." i was then asked into the front office and met with mark (can't remember his last name). he was the administrator of drummer working directly with martijn (forgive the spelling). mark who knew i was a published writer (although i did not write for drummer) asked me if i would be willing to be the managing editor (i think that was the title). i said yes. and there you have it.

by the time i was hired at drummer, i was deeply involved in the united states' dyke bdsm scene. i'd also written extensively on sm and radical sexuality including a sm column for The Guide to the Gay Northeast. i was both a journalist and a non-fiction writer and extensively published. i knew mark thompson and john preston personally and had written pieces for some of their anthologies.

FRITSCHER: In a feminist era, if a man edited a women's magazine, there would be a certain outcry—even though twenty years before you my pal Jeanne Barney was a great editor-in-chief of *Drummer*. What was your feeling and intellectual take (and/or difficulties) as a female editing a famously male magazine? What might you judge to be your greatest difficulty at *Drummer*? Or your greatest contribution to *Drummer*? Or the best/worst/hardest thing about editing *Drummer*?

STAMPS: i knew that drummer had had female editors before. [Factually, before Stamps, *Drummer* had only one female editor, Jeanne Barney, who was not "editor," but was, in fact, "editor-in-chief" of Los Angeles issues 1 to 11, 1975-76. The only two people ever named "editor-in-chief" were Barney and Fritscher.] most recently albeit briefly pat califia who was the editor before marcus wonacott. [Factually, while Marcus-Jay Wonacott was the editor of *Drummer*, Pat Califia, never the editor of *Drummer*, was billed as an "associate editor" (issues 173-176), and then double-billed with "associate editor" Wendell Ricketts (177-179).] i had been the one that had informed pat of an opening at drummer. personally, i would not have applied for the job because i was a woman. but when mark asked me i knew that drummer was in a lurch. plus as a writer and editor i love text. when i was editor it was in tandem with an outside consultant that martijn hired on sam sanchez. the staff had shrunk from around 11 to about 5. sam was the first outside consultant/designer at drummer. he was a latino gay man who had minimal if any exposure to the men's leather scene. he was a designer and wrote text and basically pulled the final product together. sam and i had many conversations about how to restructure my role or his role but he did not want to be editor. unlike anyone else at the time at drummer i was the only person involved in the sm scene. i saw my role as one of identifying the key photographers, writers, filmmakers and illustrators already involved in drummer and maintaining the magazine's vision. i did not see myself as a figurehead nor setting a new direction. quite honestly, i had very little if any authority as editor. martijn had the final say on everything. i had a great deal of responsibility but virtually no influence. it was a messy situation with lots of vagueness. it seemed that drummer had disconnected from the leather men's scene before i arrived. perhaps it had already run its course. many of the original writers, photographers and illustrators were dead from aids-as was a massive portion of the men's leather scene. the wild abandon including the photos that were shot in bars capturing real sex had ended. the archives at drummer were in complete disarray. the magazine with in deep debt. there was no money to pay for much of anything. sam had to get almost all of the photo shoots for free from porn companies. the internet was exploding perhaps replacing print publishing. sam did an amazing job getting what he could for free as well as doing a great deal of writing as well as design work.

what was most difficult about my working at drummer was the position i was in - one where i had all of the responsibility but none of the authority. i really liked mark, martijn and sam as well as many other men. but it was incredibly stressful to be in an environment where there was so much anger and resentment against martijn by people at drummer as well as the community.

FRITSCHER: Regarding "The 20th Anniversary Issue" of *Drummer*: What was your take on Larry Townsend, John Preston, and Anne Rice in regards to *Drummer*? Did you have any contact with any of them personally?

STAMPS: through my own writing i knew john preston personally and considered him a personal mentor. he had died by the time i became editor of drummer. i met larry via drummer. he stayed in touch with me via cards many years after drummer. anne rice. i did not know her. i negotiated with her agent to re-run some of her work that had previously appeared in drummer.

FRITSCHER: How did Robert Davolt involve you, help you, not help you, or, what are your thoughts on Davolt? Have you read his own history of *Drummer*?

STAMPS: i have not read davolt's history of drummer. although i found robert a very difficult personality to work with and for. i cannot say that i was always at my best. i felt that he was a man who was deeply connected to the united states' men's leather scene—something that had been missing from drummer. we were both close and conflicted. he did his best to work with me. i did my best to work with him. sam who i had been close too became persona non grata at drummer. that ruined our relationship. robert was very devoted to drummer as well as to the men's leather scene. i think robert helped to try and get drummer back on track. i think he was a editor in the old school way—totally devoted to the vision of the magazine and its role in the men's leather scene. i believe robert was pretty challenged by his drinking which affected his professionalism. but boy did he work hard and when we had conflicts, he worked to flesh them out. i appreciated that.

FRITSCHER: What is your main feeling about John Embry at the end of the 1990s? Had you any relationship to him? What is the main thing you remember about Davolt's relationship to Embry?

STAMPS: i was probably more connected to and friendly with john than anyone else at drummer. i can't remember if he called me or vice versa. i'd visit him often in his offices on 18th street. he seemed to wish he still could be involved at drummer. i liked john a lot. in fact after drummer i consulted on i think it was manifest reader. through john, i learned a great deal about the history of drummer. *i introduced robert to john. i think there were conversations between robert and john about somehow involving john back in drummer.* [Italics added.] i think robert liked john perhaps admired him for starting drummer.

FRITSCHER: In the last days of *Drummer*, what happened to the files at *Drummer*? That is, the fiction and article manuscripts, the art work, the photography? Did Davolt give or sell everything to Embry who always wanted to buy *Drummer* back?

STAMPS: i was laid off from drummer and robert continued on. so i wasn't around when it closed and don't know what happened to everything.

FRITSCHER: Is there anything else that you might relate regarding Martijn Bakker or Robert Davolt or Tony Deblase or John Embry, or anyone else, or anything else? Is there any one thing or two things, besides the internet, that you think caused *Drummer* to shut its doors?

STAMPS: no i think i've covered everything.

FRITSCHER: Who took over the editorship when you left? How did you feel about *Drummer* and all the cast of characters when you left? In fact, why did you leave? Were you not paid, etc.?

STAMPS: robert was the last person left at drummer. like my relationship with sam, robert's and my roles was very unclear. he finally became what i think he wanted all along—to be the editor of drummer.

FRITSCHER: In one word, what was it like to edit *Drummer*?

STAMPS: an honor.

Signed: Wickie Stamps, former editor of *Drummer*, author and head of Monstre Sacré, creative coaching and consulting at monstresacre.net

FRITSCHER: Thank you for your consideration of these questions. I appreciate all the input you have as an eyewitness on the history of the last days of *Drummer*.
Cheers, Jack

Fed up with all the shenanigans, Davolt revealed the tone of his association with *Drummer* in his collection of essays in *Painfully Obvious: An Irreverent and Unauthorized Manual for Leather/SM* (2003). The unfortunate title reviewed itself: the book was both painful and obvious social twitter about teacups and leather perhaps best suited to the drag issue of *Drummer* 9. The revealing quote he wrote for his book's back cover said: Davolt "... has earned a *paycheck* [italics added] producing *goods* [italics added] for the leather community." But what about producing art and writing? *Ars gratia artis*? Significantly, Davolt mysteriously made no mention of his connection with *Drummer* on the covers of his book, although he specifically named his associations with other periodicals.

Perhaps he intuited that *Drummer* was played out. By the end of the twentieth century, we leathermen came to realize that a once-specific leather culture of S&M had divided into something even more specific with the advent of kink and fetish categories of BDSM. Perhaps he felt justified that as an editor with no budget he could stuff almost anything into the ninety pages of *Drummer* 210 with its dozens of pages of corporate video ads; dozens of pages of tired and stolen photos credited blithely as "From the *Drummer* archives"; irrelevant "twinkie porn" video reviews; and very little editorial material that was not a reprint dumped in as filler between ads. Once upon a moment, Davolt mentioned that under his aegis *Drummer* could not afford to pay good authors and photographers for their work, even as *Drummer* funded him with travel perks. His observation confirmed my experience. *Drummer* had famously never paid the talent. Yet new material from unsuspecting writers and artists and photographers, ripe for ripoff, continually poured in through the mail slot. Back in the day, DeBlase himself had written a "Letter to the Editor" titled "Raw Deal for US Writers," lamenting the historically poor pay for writing erotica, in *Drummer* 189, page 6.

Davolt may have lacked that certain *je ne sais quoi*, that gumption, and that enterprise which are the defining stuff of editors aggressively developing creative material while stroking the talent in the *Drummer* Salon. Playing at being a romantic bohemian and abandoned artist among the Leatherati, he often projected presumptions about *Drummer* loyalty that were not true. Rescue was, in fact, there for his asking from empathetic writers and artists and photographers, but he did not ask, because he himself so figured *Drummer* was about money, and earning a living off art, that he couldn't fathom that payment was not an issue with seasoned *Drummer* veterans and Salonistas who, almost as a "leather community service," created specifically for *Drummer* because they loved the leather heritage of *Drummer*. Truth be told: even at the end of the 1990s, most writers and photographers with a bucket list would have paid Davolt to have their work published in *Drummer* because it was the *sine qua non* pedigree of "Who's Who in Leather Heritage, Literature, Pop Culture, and Art."

As one of many eternal supporters of *Drummer*, I was pro-active in congratulating Davolt to support him in person, on the phone, and in letters. In 1999, *Drummer* was in an embarrassing nose dive and because Davolt was in a tailspin, I wrote him offering encouragement as well as photos, features, and fiction. The letter was dated March 2, 1999, six months before *Drummer* closed shop.

Robert Davolt
Publisher, Editor, *Drummer*
PO Box 410390
San Francisco CA 94141-0390

Dear Robert,

Of all people, having done once virtually alone for early *Drummer* what you are now accomplishing virtually alone, I can understand your one-man battle to keep the pages hot while fighting censorship inside the gay world and outside in the world of distribution. Keep up the good work.

Enclosed is a new video (very *Drummer*) which I shot: *Party Animal Raw*. The ruff-sex themes are included on the cassette box itself. Several photos are included. If you'd like to write up a paragraph or two about the video, please feel free to use the photos all on one page or over a couple-page layout.

Please credit photos on each page: "Tom Howard, *Party Animal Raw*," © Jack Fritscher/Palm Drive Video.

If you would like some feature articles or fiction from me, or more photos, I'd be glad to do the usual trade for a Palm Drive Video ad which we can supply you.

Also, on your current masthead, it's fine if you want to continue to list my name, because it links you to early *Drummer*. Could you have your copy editor please correct the spelling of my name. Thanks.

Call if you wish to chat.

Regards,
Jack Fritscher (Phone/Fax Numbers)

If Davolt needed material, he should have queried the huge national leather community he claimed to know through his contest-circuit travels and his blogs, but then he could not have held *Drummer* and its Mr. Drummer Contest possessively close to his chest for reasons of blond ambition known only to him.

He did not want to share *Drummer*.

He wanted to be "Mr. Drummer."

With less hubris, with telecommunications, and with less of his own so-called "*Drummer* travel" funded from *Drummer*'s cash so he could party nationwide, Davolt could have evolved and driven *Drummer* from the printed page onto the internet screen featuring text, photos, drawings, social media personals, and videos, and become the biggest hero in *Drummer* history. It was Davolt's millennial chance in the generational change at *Drummer*, and he blew it. So why blame the Dutch? If I was able against all odds to produce *Drummer* under John Embry, Davolt should not have been stopped by the lesser of two evils, Martijn Bakker.

When Stamps met Davolt, their biggest misstep was their imitation of Embry in reprinting old material, and not developing original articles, erotic stories, media reviews, and reader-reflecting photography specifically for the new 1990s *Drummer* audience, whether funded by Bakker or not. All great underground mags—especially in a *fin de siecle* characterized by punchy little "zines"—were pop art created on a shoestring. In the 1970s, we artists who were writers, designers, and photographers created the golden age of *Drummer*, which had begun in 1972 as a trial-balloon zine, produced on a budget of thin air, talent, sex, drugs, and rock 'n' roll.

Even the front cover of *Drummer* 201 was a corporate sell-out. It was a commercial photo from Falcon Video that was nothing more than a corporate ad. Was there a kick-back for such product placement? Traditionally, previous

Drummer covers featuring a film, such as *Sex Tool* or *Born to Raise Hell* or *Pec Stud in Black Rubber,* were sourced not from corporate entities but from grass-roots artists with boutique studios. With no editor funded to acquire and vet genuine leather content, this cover suffered a disconnect in featuring Falcon's model "Max," one of the least authentic actors in 1990s corporate porn.

DRIVING DRUMMER FORWARD: VIDEO PRODUCTION AND THE MILLENNIUM

As editor-in-chief in 1979, I wanted to lift the *Drummer* esthetic from page to screen to harvest some box-office profits that could help fund the magazine. Having shot 8mm films since the 1950s, I pitched a plan to Embry to launch, direct, and shoot an X-rated line of brand-name *Drummer* films in Super-8. *Drummer* contributor David Hurles of Old Reliable had been selling Super-8 sex films since 1974. Embry warmed to my idea, but he could not match it with a believable, equitable, and guaranteed business plan. Once again we agreed to disagree. Three years later in 1982 when consumer video cameras began to be sold, Mark Hemry and I founded Palm Drive Video, and Embry founded his Wings video. Casting and technical problems plagued him as a producer. He soon enough changed his producer's hat for a distributor's cap because he could make more money with less effort selling other videographers' features through his mail-order business located South of Market where he had twice moved the *Drummer* office after my departure from the Divisadero Street office.

The back rooms of that new Natoma Street office became the back lot for his Wings studio where he hired cast and crew for several stereotypical S&M scenarios such as *Slaves for Sale* and *Slaves for Sale II* starring Scott O'Hara, one of the blonds Embry said he preferred in his *Epilogue.* As "director Robert Payne," Embry was certainly no Hitchock filming blonds in peril and most certainly no Warhol filming hot young superstars in his avant garde Factory in Manhattan. Conflating the *Drummer* brand, he stepped on his print-magazine *Drummer* to launch his onscreen "video magazine" by naming it with the exact same title as an earlier special print issue of *Drummer*: *The Best and the Worst of Drummer.* Touting his plastic VHS cassette as a "rare" and "limited-edition" "video magazine," he trumpeted in *Manifest Reader* #17, page 69, "We can only sell 500 of these!" He should have been so lucky. And why only five hundred when video copying costing pennies was an endless resource?

Finding video production a struggle of great technical, legal, and emotional difficulties, Embry saw the wisdom of turning a quicker buck by switching from production to distribution. At Palm Drive Video, I gave him a fifty-percent discount at his newly named "Wings Distributing" where I dealt only with his manager, Frank Hatfield aka *Drummer* advertising director and author, "Frank O'Rourke," the self-professed bank robber and ex-convict, who wrote "Prison Punk" and ran the kind of slippery postal operation that gives mail-order a bad name. Hatfield, who lived in a rental owned by Embry at the Russian River, was attacked there on Canyon One Road by wilding dogs who tore his chest open at the armpit, and he soon after died.

Romancing his erratic video career as Embry/Payne with no irony, Embry wrote about the "Robert Payne Production" of *The Great Slave Video Adventure* in his Wings Catalog inside *Manifest Reader* 17 (1992), page 58. Trying to sound as glamorous as a director from the Hollywood he left behind in Los Angeles, he revealed his daydream and his inexperience when he failed to recognize that no director can simply turn his cast loose any more than a zookeeper might expect a group of monkeys with keyboards to type out *Hamlet*. Ten hours of tape for a sixty-minute feature can create a tangle few editors can cut.

> Many of us have, at one time or another, envisioned being involved in the making of this sort of a video. To those of us in the leather mode, the prospect of putting it together as a director, a producer, a cameraman or maybe especially a performer...is the stuff of which daydreams are made. Robert Payne explores such a dream, then turns his cast loose....The camera rolled through ten hours worth of tape.

By 1990, no magazine could support itself without its own video production company. Tony DeBlase, to save post-quake *Drummer*, teamed up with Mikal Bales' Zeus Studios in LA to star in and create the perfectly titled *USSM*. In 1995, the four-part series documenting gay pop-culture S&M activities ran into trouble with the LAPD, and became immediately censored and unavailable.

As editor-in-chief in the late 1970s, I was pushing *Drummer* forward to the 1980s the way Stamps and Davolt might have pushed it to the Millennium. Besides pitching the idea of film production, I set out to upgrade our leather literary fiction (rooted in my university years teaching journalism and creative writing); and to mix in some leather ritual and spirituality (after the experience gained from a lifetime of Catholic S&M asceticism, and from experiences researching my witchcraft book); and to add practical how-to features (from our communal night games) similar to the articles I had already developed about the Society of Janus (*Drummer* 27, February 1979) and the "Dr. Dick" health column I wrote, beginning in *Drummer* 21, March 1978), from my ongoing interviews with the amiable Dr. Richard Hamilton (1945-1989) who was, with Dr. Earl Baxter, one of the two practicing San Francisco doctors involved with our *Drummer* Salon.

For example, in 1980, Dick Hamilton saved the life of my longtime friend, Hank Diethelm, a post-war immigrant from Germany, who was suffering from an accidental drug overdose that caused him to hallucinate for weeks that he was still a fourteen-year-old member of the Hitler Youth fleeing to the West to escape the Nazis before he was rescued by American troops in Spring 1945. Having dived into the gay American melting pot, Diethelm founded the legendary Brig bar in 1979 on the 1347 Folsom Street site of the earlier No Name bar and the later Powerhouse bar. Like Tom of Finland, Diethelm as a boy was sexually attracted by Nazi style, and sexually terrified and turned on by Nazi cruelty. Tom transposed his fears into drawings, and Diethelm deflected his PTSD paranoia by using S&M games as sensual counterphobic rituals. In May of 1970, the Denver leather priest Jim Kane introduced me to Diethelm who had invited Kane, David Sparrow, and me to crash with him for a month at his 708 Waller Street home. Three days later I shot eyewitness evidence of Hank's concentration camp fantasies in my Super-8 color film of him suspended, naked and spreadeagle upside down, so that "erotic Nazi torture" could jolt his balls to orgasm with the wicked *snap* of a rubber ring triggered by castration pliers. In another bondage scene at his next home at 226 Bemis Street, Hank Diethelm was murdered, and set on fire allegedly by a trick from the Brig, in what may have been an assisted suicide, on April 10, 1983.

TWO ABSENT PUBLISHERS, ANOTHER ELEPHANT IN THE ROOM, AND THE *DRUMMER* WORKERS' REVOLUTION

In sum, I had great empathy with Wickie Stamps and Robert Davolt. Their experience with the absent third *Drummer* publisher was a cracked-mirror of my experience with the first absent publisher.

In the late 1970s, Embry was torn between his joy at the sudden new success of *Drummer* and his patriarchal envy that we younger leathermen who were bringing that success were more avant garde than he with his dated camp humor from the 1950s. In *Manifest Reader* 26, page 53, he looked back at his first four years at *Drummer* and, still challenging the staff who saved him twenty years before, insisted that in 1976 he was the one "feeling avant garde" despite the retrograde fact that he often plagiarized his bylined writing from straight men's pulp adventure magazines like *Argosy*. He forgot that back then, suffering psychosomatically from the homophobia of the LAPD, he was not a well man emotionally or physically. Unlike his arch-rival David Goodstein who would die of a similar bowel cancer in 1985, he was a cancer survivor inconveniently disabled with a colostomy in an office staffed with ironic ass-fuckers and joking fistfuckers who treated his ambiguously once-and/or-future bag like the Second Elephant in the Room.

In recovery during the summer of 1979, Embry returned to the 1730 Divisadero office from his constant round trips to what was left of his support circle of friends and lawyers and backup doctors in LA. He had a new lease on life. He was full of piss and vinegar, roaring with mood swings of pent-up anger over his illness and his endless legal problems with the LAPD. Upon his arrival, we unsuspecting staff stood, grinning like leather footmen, holding what we intended as a surprise gift to welcome him back: the new San Francisco *Drummer*.

Hoping to make him better, we made *Drummer* better. During his ordeal, we, with instinct and impulse and subtlety, had driven the magazine forward from his unsustainable fixation on LA politics, camp humor, frenemy feuds, and mail-order gimmicks to the participatory New Journalism and emerging gender joys of the bold new homomasculine identity and avant garde leather scene. It was what national and international readers in the late 1970s came to expect in editorial content. The *Drummer* personal ads were the Facebook of their time. They reveal everything about the hearts and minds of the readers we reflected monthly. The readers drove *Drummer*. In those "Leather Fraternity" personals, the most frequently chosen words of "search" and "self-identification" were *masculine* and *masculinity*.

Embry was a rich corporate LA businessman who misread our editorial evolution as a workers' revolution. *Drummer* was being created by its hired office staff and by the writers, artists, and photographers who made it, and not by the estranged publisher who paid for it.

He realized he had in his hands the hit he had always wanted.

That good deed did not go unpunished.

AMERICA'S MAG FOR THE MACHO MALE   ISSUE 24

DRUMMER

More pages, more fiction, more original artwork than any other Gay publication

Australia $3/Belgie 180 frs.
Canada $3.50
Danmark 30 Kr. inkl. moms
France 20 NF
Israeli 17 Israeli Pounds
Italy 3000 Lire/Japan 16 v
Nederland 15 Fl.
New Zealand $3
Norge 27 N. kr.
Oesterreich 100 Sch
Schweiz 16 frs.
Sverige 20 kr. inkl. moms
United Kingdon 120 p.

2.95
OUTRAGEOUS!

EX-CONS
'WE ABUSE FAGS'

SEXSTAR RICHARD LOCKE

JOCKS CENTERFOLDOUT

CASTRO BLUES

BONDAGE

SLAVE TRAINING QUARTERS

Cover Portrait by Robert Mapplethorpe

ROBERT MAPPLETHORPE'S *AUTHENTIC* "BIKER-FOR-HIRE" COVERMAN

UNCLASSIFIED

CHAPTER 7

THE *DRUMMER* SALON

ON THE 69TH DAY, GOD CREATED QUEERS AND THE QUEERS REBELLED

- Declaring Homosexuality a Religion Protected by the Constitution
- The Manic-Depressive 1970s: Gay Saints; Gay Civil War; the Printer as Censor
- Blasphemy: The Outer Limit of the Radical *Avant Garde*; *Jesus Christ Superstar*; Kenneth Anger; the Satanic Mapplethorpe; and "Jesus D'Pressed"
- *Man2Man Quarterly*: "Virtual *Drummer*"
- East Coast-West Coast Literary Rivalry: New Yorkers Try to "Manhattanize" San Francisco
- Allegedly: Kramer, Picano, White, and the Violet Quill; Sasha Alyson; Elizabeth Gershman, and Knights Press
- Erotica: The Essence of Gay Literature
- Despite Feminist Fantasy, Anne Rice Never Wrote for *Drummer*

> "Erotic writing begins with one stroke of the pen
> and ends with many strokes of the penis."
> —Jack Fritscher

I confess after eleven years studying for the Catholic priesthood, I have a certain apostolic quality that is outlaw and hard to institutionalize because I think homosexuality is the natural and intuitive Old Religion predating revealed religions such as Druidism, Judaism, Christianity, and Islam. In this *carpe diem* concept lies the liberation of homosexuality through Constitutional freedom of religion. Why not? Joseph Smith did it in the 1820s conjuring up the Mormons with his doctrine of polygamy to justify to his screaming wife why their pretty young maid was his mistress. British witch Gerald Gardner did it in the 1950s declaring in Britain that wicca was in fact the Old Religion thereby ending all the UK laws against witchcraft and the women and gay men who practice it. Patrick Califia, that immortal changeling, mentioned me in one of his books as a "prophet of homomasculinity" which seems, although I am not a prophet of anything, a cool poetic metaphor in an age when gender identity and queer spirit are hot topics in gay theology.

Pioneer leather author William Carney shocked the 1960s when he advanced the idea of spiritual orders of gay men in his epistolary novel *The Real Thing* (1968) whose mystic leather rituals I analyzed in *Popular Witchcraft* (1972). Then, funny enough, I was censored. I was not allowed to mention the charismatic Carney during my editorial run at *Drummer* because John Embry from LA, wary of anything transcendental, had grown wary of the successful and challenging Bill Carney of San Francisco—which, Embry implied, was not a big enough town for the two of them. Just as Embry had damned his Los Angeles rival Larry Townsend with a scathing review of his novel *Chains* in the very first issue of *Drummer*, Embry also blacklisted Carney and his esoteric book, especially after longtime *Drummer* reviewer Ed Franklin had given *The Real Thing* an absolutely glowing review in *Drummer* 7 which made novelist Embry jealous. Characteristic of his Imperial Majesty, Embry famously neglected to read copy we writers gave him, and as editor I took positive advantage of that freedom to shape what I wanted *Drummer* to say. Even so, Embry's pique kept certain authors and a certain mysticism out of *Drummer*. I lamented that. I was a Catholic until history caught up with me and I evolved like a sensible human from the revealed religion of Catholicism to a more natural, intuitive religion free of institutional hierarchy and especially free of terrorizing children with threats of hell. (In August 1989, after Embry sold *Drummer* to Anthony DeBlase, William Carney was finally cited in the pages of *Drummer* 132.)

The Square Root of Embry

John Embry was a stocky, red-faced, belligerent man, a Protestant always looking for a fight. When he was frustrated by not being able to get political traction in Los Angeles from the Slave Auction arrests or any literary credential in San Francisco with his own novels, he took his aggressions out on his friends and associates in the arts in both cities. Hardly any employee, freelance writer, artist, or photographer escaped his jealous meanness in his *Drummer* soap opera of alienated souls. If a *Drummer* reunion were held, there would be enough angry people to fill the Cow Palace.

If one thinks sex is God and God is sex, and sometimes as Tennessee Williams' Blanche DuBois says about sex partners, "Sometimes there's God so quickly," Embry seemed cowed, not only by the LAPD, but by the fundamentalist South San Francisco printer who agreed to feed *Drummer* through his presses on the very "cheap" but only after midnight when no one, including his God, was looking. That right-wing hypocrite Christian printer was San Francisco *Drummer*'s first gratuitous censor. If the printer might balk and cause Embry to have to seek out a more expensive printing service, Embry would self-censor and yank any offending article or photo. To me, this was nothing new, because I remembered that it was their printers' refusal that stopped Leonard and Virginia Woolf's Hogarth Press from publishing James Joyce's *Ulysses*.

In the then new culture war, Embry cowered even on cover photography when various bookstores across the nation refused to sell select issues in communities where the local onward-marching Christian soldiers judged magazines by their covers. When the *Drummer* covers were too gay, they were censored in Wichita, Peoria, and Knob Noster, Missouri. As both editor-in-chief and photographer, the more I coded the cover art to look like 1970s men's pulp adventure magazines, such as the popular *Soldier of Fortune* and *Easy Rider* magazines, they were safe from censors: e.g., my prison cover of *Drummer* 21, the Mapplethorpe cover of *Drummer* 24, and my arm-wrestling cover of *Drummer* 30 whose vivid subtext to the keen eye is fistfucking not arm-wrestling.

That religious censorship of *Drummer* was such bull that just as Embry had started *The Alternate* as rival sibling to his own *Drummer*, I ginned up the *riposte* of *Man2Man Quarterly* as a little magazine so low budget that printing costs were not an issue and could not impact the contents that I purposed to be grittier and more aggressive than Embry would allow in *Drummer*. In late 1979, as I was preparing to resign my job at *Drummer*, I inserted an announcement for *Man2Man* as a "Trojan Horse" advertisement inside *Drummer* 30, page 18, and began publication as "the first 'zine of the 1980s" with Mark Hemry as publisher in January, 1980.

Man2Man was, essentially "Virtual *Drummer*." Embry, the constant plagiarist, knew it, and he immediately stole its title for his existing "Leather Fraternity" personals to add the new tag line: "Man-to-Man Personals." And then, after he sold *Drummer*, he trashed *Man2Man* in his furious "letter to the editor" in *Drummer* 108. Much of my writing in dozens of magazines during the 1980s was very specifically *Drummer* material diverted from *Drummer* and published by an array of LA and NY editors wanting to inject a bit of the *Drummer* cultural mystique into their own gay magazines. Ironically, the notoriety of my exiting *Drummer* identified me even more with *Drummer*, and in a clean way distanced me from Embry.

Much to Embry's chagrin, readers often weren't sure who owned *Drummer*. For more than ten years after I stopped editing *Drummer*, my home phone would ring, and some reader would ask me, "When is the next issue of *Drummer* coming out," or worse, "I sent in my money and you guys screwed up my subscription." In the way that Larry Townsend had to tell his confused mail-order clients that he was not Embry, so did I.

GAY SAINTS ALEISTER CROWLEY, ANDY WARHOL, KENNETH ANGER, ROBERT MAPPLETHORPE; & THE NEW YORK GAY LITERATI

> In reviewing my anthology of *Drummer* writing, *Corporal in Charge of Taking Care of Captain O'Malley and Other Stories*, fiction editor Steven Saylor minced no words in his review in *Drummer* 81 (February 1984). A true-born Texan, he was not afraid to declare that in *Corporal*, "There's enough ghettoized angst to keep the Manhattan literati wired for months." He exposed the polarity between East Coast attitude and West Coast authors. His review held special interest in that his essay was in a sense the first review of *Drummer* itself because *Corporal in Charge* was the first collection in book form of original *Drummer* writing.
>
> Saylor, who went on to become a *New York Times* best-selling author, proved too big for *Drummer*. For twenty issues (68-87), he was Embry's most professional fiction/department editor (1983-85), and, like guest editor Bert Herman (issue 93), he edited only one issue (87), and then immediately quit, writing he was "underpaid" and "disrespected [by Embry] on a daily basis."
> —*Steam* magazine, 2 #1

To Embry, censorship and cost-consciousness meant that religious "blasphemy" was out. That was an odd line in the sand for a purposely provocative publisher who started up his magazine with necrophilia, bestiality, a touch of pedophilia, missing only cannibalism and a couple other topics, like blasphemy, that existed on famous Satanist Aleister Crowley's list of favorite Black Magic things. The Marquis de Sade, the dirty master behind *Drummer*, wrote: "There is a kind of pleasure which comes from sacrilege or the profanation of the objects offered to us for worship." In fact, blasphemy was the outer limit of the radical avant garde which scared Embry who refused in 1978 to publish my 1967 poem, "Jesus D'Pressed," to illustrate a photograph shot by Rimbaud-influenced blasphemer, Mapplethorpe, who was known to say to people, including Embry, "If you don't like these photographs, you're not as avant garde as you think."

Embry dismissed my American pop-culture argument when I pointed out that *The National Lampoon*, months before in June 1977 had queered Malcolm Boyd's book *Are You Running with Me, Jesus?* publishing the article "Are You Cruising with Me, Lord?" Certainly, the *Lampoon* was a suitable measure of changing "community standards." And if it weren't, then the soft-core blasphemy of *Jesus Christ Superstar* was.

The best-selling *Superstar* album was released in 1970, three years before the hit stage musical. Its popular title track, "Jesus Christ Superstar," played incessantly in post-Stonewall gay bars along with Andrew Lloyd Webber's poem about Jesus, "I Don't Know How to Love Him," which couldn't have been a more gay anthem if it had been sung by Judy Garland. The *Superstar* plot was Hollywood S&M, but I couldn't get Embry, the Protestant, to put the stripping or whipping photographs from *Superstar* into *Drummer*. He had no problem with publishing stripping and whipping stills from any other movie, including the race-baiting *Mandingo*, in our monthly "Movie Mayhem" pictorial feature.

In the 1970s, for a gay generation skilled on interpreting the subtext of 1950s-1960s popular culture, the *Superstar* signifiers were absolutely clear that the gay but troubled lovers were Jesus and Judas. They lived rough with bearded workingmen in a hippie commune where Mary Magdalene was the "beard" who sang the other songs that Jesus and Judas should have sung to each other: "Everything's Alright" and "Can We Start Again, Please?"

The gay pop-culture phenomenon of *Superstar* was such that in LA, I witnessed that the outdoor Universal Studios Amphitheater was packed with pre-ironic leather gays cheering the live stage musical, *Jesus Christ Superstar*, with the nearly naked Christ crucified high on a cross with all of LA laid out below in the night-grid of street lights like a dark and weeping Jerusalem. San Francisco gays lined up for the 1973 premiere of the film at the Regency 1 Theater on Van Ness. In those days before VCRs with their *rewind* and *freeze* features, the leather custom was to pay one admission and arrive near the end of one screening to catch the whipping and crucifixion, and then sit through the whole film to watch the whipping and crucifixion again.

What gays won't do in the search for the transcendent erotic experiences that have come to be known as "gay spirituality"! This was before Marxist queers and right-wing Christians attacked the gay village, sucked eros out of Hellenic Christianity, and created a far-left backlash against Christianity within the gay culture of feeling and intellect. Soon enough in the 1980s, gay culture itself, brought to its knees by AIDS, grew virulently anti-Christian with the rise of the radical gender Marxism imported with the politically correct fundamentalism and separatist feminism that tried to whip the disease-stricken gay male culture into politically correct subservience. The Marxist coup in the gay community allowed Christianity to be trashed in a way that Judaism couldn't be, and that Islam, popular with cross-dressing whirling dervishes performing afternoons on carpets in front of the Hibernia Bank at 18th and Castro Street, dared not be.

I'm no Catholic apologist, and I had no problem skewering Christianity in my 1965 novel *What They Did to the Kid: Confessions of an Altar Boy* or satirizing the New Testament in my 1960s activist poetry. My little "Jesus D'Pressed" poem was a double homage: First, to the Catholic Andy Warhol as the publisher of *Interview* magazine as well as for his Velvet Underground with their "shiny boots of leather, whiplash girl child," and, second, to Satanic Magus Kenneth Anger who created the first gay leather-biker-piss-orgy blasphemy film, *Scorpio Rising* (1964). Anger's iconic film marked me forever the night I attended the 1966 Chicago premiere at the Illinois Institute of Technology in the company of pioneer leathermen: Chuck Renslow, Dom Orejudos, Sam Steward, Cliff Raven, Bob Maddox, and a gang from the Gold Coast. In his consistency, Embry, scoffing at the zero degrees of connection and loyalty within the *Drummer* Salon, also refused to allow me to review or feature the leather films and photographs of the magus blasphemer, Kenneth Anger, who was a friend of my friend, Sam Steward. Embry also interdicted my publishing anything Satanic, including the reprint of my juicy 1971 interview of my friend, Anton LaVey, the founding High Priest of the Church of Satan in San Francisco.

Because since 1969, as a literature professor traveling to London, I had become a longtime, and—sometimes intimate—friend with the British leather poet, Thom Gunn, I was well aware that in England in 1976, his friend, the gay poet James Kirkup had seen his publisher prosecuted and fined for blasphemy for printing Kirkup's tender and infamous poem, "The Love That Dares to Speak Its Name." Kirkup wrote of a "still-warm" dead Jesus taken down from the cross by a Roman centurion who strips off his uniform to hold the dead God in his strong arms, "the tip of that great cock, the instrument of our salvation," concluding that Jesus' crucifixion is the same crucifixion all "same-sex lovers suffer, patiently and gladly."

Mapplethorpe and I, both saturated Catholics, matching his photographs to my poem, were reading Rimbaud and Verlaine, and somehow the artful metaphor of blasphemy had become my litmus test for the Protestant literalist Embry. Apropos that, in 1986 with eight dust-grain photogravures, Mapplethorpe illustrated a luxurious bilingual quarto edition of Rimbaud's poems, *A Season in Hell*, whose crimson goatskin cover featured Mapplethorpe's portrait of himself as the horned Devil, Pan. In a less elite version, those beautiful pictures could have democratically graced *Drummer* seven years earlier than the Limited Editions Club press run of one thousand signed copies. But Embry refused, earning Mapplethorpe's haughty disdain.

Embry, never avant garde, grew more conservative after his 1976 arrest and slap-down by the LAPD, after his 1977 exile from LA, and after his 1978-1979 cancer nearly killed him. A child born and raised during the Great Depression, Embry was a tightwad businessman who could squeeze a nickel till the buffalo screamed. Applying some of the profits from *Drummer*, he could have been a champion in that Stonewall decade when the emerging gay press was nothing but magazines—and gay book publishers still had to be invented. Diverting *Drummer* profits away from editorial development and into his personal real estate empire that he began when he moved to San Francisco, he had no fight in his millionaire's heart to push the art-envelope of *Drummer* and risk profiting a penny less. *Drummer* achieved its worldwide editorial identity despite him.

In short, Embry who was a Methodist refused to publish "Jesus D'Pressed" which was, for all its little satirical and sexy silliness, meant to be nothing more than an iconoclastic 1960s pop-art poem about a God who is crucified out of human jealousy because, with his divinely double-jointed back, he can fellate himself. The poem, part of my juvenilia and pertinent in its impertinent time, may or may not travel into any literary canon. However, Embry never said he didn't like the poem. He simply could not bring himself to publish it after his run-ins with the law over various infractions like his bits of blasphemy in the early Los Angeles *Drummer*.

As editor, I wanted the poem to scare him because I enjoyed double-daring him. He was easy to bait and switch. And tricking him was one way to get what needed to be gotten into *Drummer*. If he turned down a manuscript as too extreme, he would feel that he "won," and, blinded by that pyrrhic victory, would then accept another manuscript that would have seemed "far out" if he had not had to pass judgment on the first document. That was one of the ways art director Al Shapiro and I practiced our intricate choreography so we could insert our homomasculine version of *Drummer* inside Embry's camp version of *Drummer*, changing the core magazine from Los Angeles *Drummer* to the San Francisco *Drummer* that became an international best seller. Robert Mapplethorpe, who disliked Embry, told me that our editorial maneuvering around Embry was the same tactic that editors Fred Hughes and Glenn O'Brien used to maneuver their creation of "Andy Warhol's *Interview* Magazine," minus Andy, who was as much a headache at *Interview* as Embry was at *Drummer* where Embry was no Warhol.

A ROOM OF ONE'S OWN:
CAN WHAT IS WHISPERED BE WRITTEN DOWN?

> Sometimes iconoclasm is a good thing.
> Sometimes a memoir is a portrait
> in a fun house mirror.
> Sometimes it pays to investigate
> where truth lies.
> Sometimes it's wise to dare
> to wear one's trousers rolled, and
> to eat a peach,
> because in the empty rooms
> the queers come and go
> speaking of Michael and Angelo.

THE BIAS BETWEEN EAST COAST AND
WEST COAST CULTURE

> The Geography of *Drummer*
> Imagine *Drummer* as a New York magazine?
> It couldn't make it as a Los Angeles magazine.
> San Francisco was its spot.

During the first ten issues of *Drummer*, my friend James Purdy, author of the S&M literary classic, *Eustace Chisholm and the Works* (1967), sent a short story to Jeanne Barney. Like his longtime friend, Sam Steward, the genius Purdy, though lionized by Edith Sitwell and Gore Vidal, was always rather the redheaded stepchild sniffed at by the East Coast literary establishment. As with Sam Steward, I told James Purdy that *Drummer* might be a suitable way to reach his underground fan club—that is, until the day James Purdy telephoned editor Jeanne Barney with the bad news, he said, that his New York agent thought publication in the *outre Drummer* would be a mistake. *Eustace Chisholm*, however, did influence *Drummer* because James Purdy's book, which should be read universally in leather culture, was one of my seminal texts as I was coming out as an erotic and literary writer in the 1960s.

In the synergy of literature, magazines are one thing; book publication is another; and both need each other. In the parallel universes of magazine and books in the literary world of the 1970s, author Felice Picano, two years after *Drummer* debuted, pioneered two tiny and select book businesses: Seahorse Press, 1977, and Gay Presses of New York, 1980, which seemingly created a base for the Violet Quill fraternity to "self-publish" and review one another, beginning with and continuing after the Violet Quill's formal existence (1980-1981) when *Drummer* was riding high. At the same time, New Englander Sasha Alyson, who famously carried a Teddy Bear in the crook of his arm like Sebastian Flyte, entered book publishing when *Drummer* was five years old in 1980. In 1974, when Pop provocateur Andy Warhol had carried a Teddy Bear under his own arm, walking down Fifth Avenue, Bob Colacello in *Holy Terror: Andy Warhol Close Up*, wrote that Andy claimed he was consciously "just putting on airs," and he quit doing it. (Page 174). By 1990, Sasha Alyson seemed, observers gossiped, to be godfathering gay book publishing. At the 1990 national convention of American Booksellers Association (ABA) in Las Vegas, Alyson popped up what seemed like a good idea: a "Gay Publishers' Row." The "row" as in "a line" turned into a "row" as in "a fight."

Enmity arose because, as Elizabeth Gershman (1927-2000), the publisher of Knights Press, alleged, Sasha Alyson requested a thirty-dollar surcharge to the ABA fees to set up a booth in his privileged corral. She refused his blandishments because her small press budget was down to pennies and she thought that Alyson's apartheid gay ghetto row marginalized the gay books she was trying to sell crossover to the mainstream world, including my new West Coast novel *Some Dance to Remember: A Memoir-Novel of San Francisco 1970-1982*. When Gershman set up her Knights Press booth, I was required to be present as "the author" inside her display, and was trapped for three days in the struggle between these two East Coast publishers, Gershman and Alyson. In the tension of all that attitude stalking the aisles, I politely resisted being tarred with the same brush as the fiercely independent Gershman whom I barely knew before the book convention, and knew too well afterwards. There were no saints at that national ABA convention that some years later became the national Book Expo America (BEA). While Gershman was beloved in *The Advocate* in feature articles such as "Betty's Books," she as a straight woman was hardly equipped to fend off the gay parrying and thrusting of her competition. In 1991, Knights Press went out of business which would have probably happened anyway when Gershman's daughter soon after married Teddy Kennedy, Jr., and Gershman became a Kennedy grandmother.

For an objective correlative about gay power struggles, see "Inside the Gay Mafia," a "true confession" credited only "As told to Kevin Blass" in the gay magazine, *Instinct*, November 2002.

Novelist Picano with his Violet Quill peers, and Alyson, were local colorist writers focused on a circle of East Coast gay authors—none of them "leather" and some of them academics—who found, perhaps, tribal solidarity in their own zero degrees of separation, onanistically publishing, promoting, and reviewing one another in the gay vanilla genres they understood. Years later, East Coaster David Bergman wrote the Manhattan *Rashomon* of the Violet Quill aka, in gay trash talk, the campy "Violent Quill" and the "Vile Quill": *The Violet Hour and the Making of Gay Culture* (2004). In his book *My Life as a Pornographer*, erstwhile *Drummer* author John Preston, himself a New Englander, complained bitterly about his playing second fiddle competing with "Ed White [Edmund White who] might have the crowd from the *New York Review of Books*..." See *Drummer* 188, page 20. The Violet Quill was rather like the Violet Crawley of Maggie Smith in *Downton Abbey*, politely exclusive, unlike the *Drummer* Salon which was extremely inclusive. At core, some of this literary clique acted as if they'd all sprung from the elite Radcliffe Publishing Program then at Harvard.

Charles Bukowski and other straight West Coast writers like John Steinbeck had long pointed out the difficulty of a publishing civil war between East Coast publishers as well as reviewers who tend to ignore West Coast writers.

In 1984, Steven Saylor, author of a prodigious series of mystery novels set in the ancient Rome of emperors and vestal virgins and gladiators, was writing for *Drummer* as "Aaron Travis." In *Drummer* 78, he penned a fine book review of *Urban Aboriginals: A Celebration of Leather Sexuality* authored by the professional biochemist and beloved West Coast leatherman Geoff Mains, PhD (1947-1989) for Winston Leyland's Gay Sunshine Press in San Francisco. Saylor's "thumbs-up" critique skirmished like a skilled gladiator. But, in the third last sentence of the last paragraph, the review spun its peplum, stumbled, and surrendered to the whiplash of bicoastal gay combat in which Saylor drew a gratuitous line in the arena sand by allowing an unnamed "New Yorker," made "down-to-earth" perhaps by little more than subletting a rent-controlled bedsit in Queens, to give his anonymous "thumbs-down" dismissal of Mains' progressive and California-inflected biochemistry, psychology, and vocabulary of leather spirituality as Hippie Woo Woo. Saylor thrust the short dagger of his *pugio* in his punch line: "As a down-to-earth New Yorker remarked to me after reading the book, 'You West Coasters are *too* much.'" (Page 91)

In the 180 degrees of separation between gay leather literature and gay vanilla literature, between East Coast and West Coast, I first contacted Michael Denneny at St. Martin's Press in New York about my manuscript for my "San Francisco *Drummer* novel," *Some Dance to Remember,* on November 21, 1984.

On January 16, 1986, I queried Denneny again and he graciously requested my manuscript and replied on August 11, 1986, that the novel "impressed" him, although at the time, as Denneny announced in a shocking revelation years later on the stage at the 1997 Key West Writers Conference, he was primarily pledged to publish young gay authors dying from AIDS. I was forty-seven and AIDS free.

Letters continued to cross in the mail.

Denneny in that August, 1986, generously suggested I contact Felice Picano whom I had already queried three months previously on May 14, 1986. In his human dimension, Picano, whom I perceived seemed often short-sheeted by his more arch Violet Quill peers, had quickly responded on May 21, 1986. That was three months before Denneny's recommendation to contact Picano who very kindly wrote to me:

> I am familiar with your writing. At this time, both my Seahorse line and the Gay Presses of New York imprints...are...for the next two years...currently behind in publishing our titles already under contract. In fact, I'm phasing out Seahorse Press as a separate entity. It has served its purpose, and has begun to seriously interfere with my own writing. Because of this overload, I have to decline even looking at new mss for at least a year. Good luck with your writing and your book. —Cordially, Felice Picano

Publishing a book is notoriously difficult and not for the faint of heart as told by Ellen Brown and John Wiley, Jr. in their book about a world-famous novel's complicated development: *Margaret Mitchell's Gone With the Wind: A Bestseller's Odyssey from Atlanta to Hollywood.* By design, and out of respect for Margaret Mitchell's embrace of her own culture and heritage, I purposely wrote *Some Dance to Remember* as a gay mid-century memetic jazz riff on the O'Hara clan of Miss Scarlett. Her "descendent" is Ryan O'Hara who, shadowing Scarlett in San Francisco, courts his own Rhett (Kick Sorenson) while trying to save his home and to survive the turbulent civil war around gay identity during the 1970s decade which was doomed to be "gone with the virus."

In 1984-1986, few straight book publishers were even vaguely interested in gay material. Gay book publishers, who first set up business in the mid-1980s were uncertain what to do about my 562-page San Francisco book with a frank approach to gay sexuality that was not politically correct and featured a subplot about *Drummer* magazine fictionalized as *Maneuvers* magazine.

The former Catholic priest, Winston Leyland, my publisher at Gay Sunshine Press, offered to publish *Some Dance* in 1984, but wanted to do so in two volumes to cover the costs of such a large book. I rejected that offer because two volumes seemed ludicrous esthetically, and because from my two books he had already published, I judged that his cover designs were stylishly dreadful, and because, when he took a phone call as I sat in his office in his home, he sounded callous as Embry telling the caller that he treated authors with agents differently from authors (like me) without agents.

Himself famous as an editor republishing classic gay literature that had fallen out of copyright, Winston Leyland was, nevertheless, that rare bird: a publisher who actually paid authors the royalties promised. Ultimately, he paid me an honor beyond money when he included my one-act play "Corporal in Charge of Taking Care of Captain O'Malley" in his Lammy-winning anthology of gay literature: *Gay Roots: Twenty Years of Gay Sunshine: An Anthology of Gay History, Sex, Politics, and Culture* (1991).

This inclusion and the Lammy award were indirect endorsements of the literary value of *Drummer*. "Corporal in Charge," first published in *Drummer* issues 22 and 23 (May and July 1978), was the only play included in *Gay Roots*.

On September 4, 1985, Alyson Publications in Boston sent me a form letter saying it was not considering new manuscripts at that present time. Grove Press in New York wrote on September 28, 1985: "I read your book with interest and respect. It's a big book—ambitious, complicated, and professionally done. Good luck."

Meanwhile, on the West Coast, my fellow author friends looked for a subtext to the letters. Were Denneny and Picano and Grove Press being gracious? Was there a Manhattan message? Was the book too California, too San Francisco, too *Drummer*, too leather, too wild, too politically incorrect, and, as an investigation into gay masculinity, or homomasculinity, was it the wrong kind of "gay"?

Even Elizabeth Gershman balked at first. In 1985, when I queried her at Knights Press in Stamford, Connecticut, she rejected the manuscript on February 3, 1986: "It is a bit more erotic than I like to do....You must make a fortune writing about sex, because you do it very well." Two years later in 1988 when former *Drummer* editor Tim Barrus was hired by Gershman, he educated her about the esthetics of gay writing and handed her the very same manuscript which she then re-read. On February 14, 1989, she wrote to me: "I'd fucking kill to publish *Some Dance to Remember*."

My own West Coast *Drummer* editorial policy of dealing inclusively with authors coming out of closets anywhere indicated I would have welcomed any of those gay East Coast writers into the pages of *Drummer*—the way I gladly published Mapplethorpe—if only they had approached San Francisco gay culture the way so many other New Yorkers were shrewd enough to do. Harvey Milk went west to Castro Street to do what he could have never done on Christopher Street. Mapplethorpe flew directly to me at *Drummer* so I could, in his words, "nationalize his Manhattan reputation." Wakefield Poole left Manhattan to shoot films in his studio on the Panhandle of Golden Gate Park where I interviewed him for *Drummer* in my feature "Dirty Poole" and gave sexy coverage of his movie stills inside and on the cover of *Drummer* 27 (February 1979). New York entrepreneur Michael Maletta, the mega-party producer, transplanted himself to the Castro and connected his startup, the San Francisco Creative Power Foundation, to the creative power of *Drummer* publicity while creating "Night Flight" and "Stars," the parties from whose resultant frisson the White Party was invented. These "gypsies, tramps, and thieves," all migrated east-to-west in what San Franciscans dubbed the "Manhattanization of San Francisco." Manhattanization had as much to do with invasive East Coast cultural "attitudes" as it did with the shock of new high rises changing the City's traditional skyline from horizontal to vertical.

After I exited *Drummer* on December 31, 1979, Felice Picano's "Hunter" was published in *Drummer* 39 (August 1980). John Embry, wanting to widen sales to East Coast readers, generously promoted Picano with "name above the title" status. He heralded the short story in the cover copy as "Felice Picano's 'Hunter.'" That seemingly autobiographical story, based on an "author's" summer-seminar experience at an East Coast literary colony, was, for all its genre merits as a mystery, not a particularly *Drummer* story because the sex was vanilla; there was no S&M in psychology or ritual; and two women characters—one suicidal—intruded into the sanctuary of male space that subscribers demanded of stories in *Drummer*. Inside on the *Drummer* masthead, the billing, plugging Picano's literary pedigree, read: "Hunter" by Felice Picano: The best-selling author of *The Lure*, *The Mesmerist*, and *The Eye* weaves a masterful tale of deadly obsessions and suspense."

Proficient at using the flattery that had messed with the heads of Los Angeles writers in particular, Embry gambled that such publication and billing might induce the prolific Picano aka Christopher Hall aka Miss Bea Oblivious into helping fill the on-going serial-fiction section of *Drummer*. That never happened. Not with the canny Picano. But Embry's tactic worked with another East Coast writer, John Preston, who fell for Embry's blandishments, until he didn't.

ANDREW HOLLERAN'S NEW CLOTHES: DUDE CONDESCENDING A STAIRCASE

"Who'd a thunk it? Who'd a thunk that one day back issues of *Drummer* would be displayed in glass cases at a library like this? [The John Hay Library at Brown University]
—Eric Garber aka Andrew Holleran, an East Coast literary establishment author of *Dancer from the Dance*, and co-founder of the Violet Quill, snapping at *Drummer* in "Making Sex Public," *Christopher Street*, Issue 231, November 1995, page 3

By 2016, *Drummer* was included internationally in gay archives as well as in the permanent collections of museums such as the J. Paul Getty Museum in Los Angeles, and the Los Angeles County Museum of Art (LACMA) which displayed *Drummer* in a glass case during the Robert Mapplethorpe exhibit, *The Perfect Medium*.

IS THERE A GAY LITERARY MAFIA? ARE LGBT CORPORATIONS DEPERSONALIZING GAY LITERATURE?

Is there reason to fear for the integrity of young gay writers seeking sanctuary in New York, the fortress of the publishing world? Do they change their voices to fit in? Is that why virtually no Manhattan gay literary "stars" break out of the received puritan paradigm of vanilla gay literature? Is that why they don't or can't write erotica? Because literary agents might balk as did James Purdy's? Because some gay and straight readers need to be willing to stretch to accept gay literature and its patois, even when it is bourgeois vanilla, much less when it is overtly erotic? The New York lack of erotic writing by major authors dims their own starlight.

The East Coast establishment—even among the rival siblings on the Edmund White-Tony Kushner axis of authors like Larry Kramer lionized during the mid-twentieth century—has a right to its own strictures of gravitas and attitude, but perhaps the price of admission is too costly for a nonconforming writer and for what a human gets. Suffering for one's art is one thing; suffocating it, and censoring one's self, to be published at a big straight house is quite another. In the James Ivory film *The City of Your Last Destination*, screenwriter Ruth Prawer Jhabvala, adapting gay author Peter Cameron's book, penned this exchange between characters to caution over-eager authors: "You don't choose literature. Literature chooses you." Hello, New York! Eros calling!

Sensing this pressurized danger in the 1960s when I was living in New York to sample whether I would move there permanently, I figured a human life in letters could be lived, for me, at least, better on the West Coast, and more so in human-sized San Francisco than in skyscraper New York or freeway-scaled Los Angeles.

A New Yorker living in three tiny rooms in a fifth-floor walk-up, as Mapplethorpe did at 24 Bond Street, writes differently and photographs differently than the same writer or photographer living in San Francisco. *What if the beautiful room is empty—in the Castro?* Unlike Manhattan's insular formality, California is the pop-culture platform that comes with a better chance to grow personally with one's art, and actually to own and live in—what Virginia Woolf said was absolutely essential—a room of one's own, in a house of one's own, in a State that is ten years ahead of the rest of American culture.

When Robert Mapplethorpe and I were bi-coastal lovers, I experienced what his New Yorker friends did not know. There was an essential difference between Robert's "being" in San Francisco *versus* how he "had to be" in New York. The psychic cost to him taxed him long before AIDS killed him.

As his career escalated in 1980s Manhattan, he seemed to become put off by New York faces staring back at him through his lens, and turned to shooting flowers and statues. Much of his best leather and S&M photography was shot in San Francisco out of the personalities in and around the *Drummer* Salon to whom I introduced him. Because *Variety* magazine labeled Mapplethorpe as a continuing "Cultural Bogeyman" in its "Culture War Redux" (March 21-27, 2011, page 4), I wonder if one day his safe New York flower prints will ever begin to outweigh his dangerous San Francisco fetish photographs? As Edward Lucie-Smith reminded me, "Robert's calla lily photograph hanging in an Upper East Side dining room gets its frisson from Robert's fisting photograph hanging in the bedroom."

Why wouldn't such frisson apply to writing as well?

We've all read the calla-lily literature penned by writers in the hothouse of New York. On September 10, 2015, *The New York Times Style Magazine* published a feature, "They Made New York," with a kind of "*Sgt. Pepper* cover" group photo of twenty-eight celebrities including Edmund White and Larry Kramer whose faces under the high-concept title rather much italicized their insular regionalism which is a bit different than San Francisco's peninsular regionalism because the San Francisco peninsula, unlike the margins of Manhattan Island, is actually connected to the rest of the continent. So, where is that island clique's erotica? Ed White is six months younger than I, and six years younger than Larry Kramer, but that self-titled *City Boy*, posing with cane in hand, has vaporized out loud that he is the last of his generation. In his *My Lives*, as Ed grows older and more Falstaff-ian, he might regret a certain Midwest Ohio self-censorship that kept his youthful Id from writing a porno masterwork after his soft-core striptease *The Joy of Gay Sex* which he worried, actually worried, would kill his reputation.

Crown, his publisher, took out a full-page ad in *Drummer* 18 (August 1977) to sell that book by the chummy-named "Ed White." White claims he rescued Foucault, but Foucault should have rescued him. Foucault, at least, sexed around at night in the bars and baths of *Drummer* territory on Folsom Street in San Francisco where we took turns sizing him up with our fists confirmed by our glove size. If it was good enough for DeSade and Pasolini, where is White's *120 Days of Sodom*? Why has no editor like New York anthologists Michael Denneny and John Preston ever gathered together a certain best-seller: a collection of erotic fiction written by Edmund White, Tony Kushner, Andrew Holleran, Felice Picano, and even Larry Kramer, the scourge and Scrooge of 1970s free love, as well as the other usual suspects who maybe wish they could unbutton themselves and cut to the radical masturbation heart of what makes gay literature gay: sex. Appreciating the talents of these writers, I hope that hidden novels by some of these cautious men will eventually be published posthumously like E. M. Forster's *Maurice*. Readers also hope that in a kind of "White 2.0" or "Kramer 2.0," some of their existing novels be republished in years to come with the sex passages restored as happened in 2011 with Oscar Wilde's *Portrait of Dorian Gray* (1890) and James Jones' *From Here to Eternity* (1951). Both were republished in unexpurgated editions, with the censored sentences of Wilde inserted, and the four-letter words and gay sex of Jones's original manuscript restored.

There is no begrudging the dandy-in-aspic New York establishment their local color performing within their gay genre, which is like acting in a scripted Hollywood film, such as *Casablanca*, as opposed to the outlaw literary genre, such as *Drummer*, which is akin to "being and becoming" in a passionate, spontaneous indie film that has the audience cuming in their brain and in their pants. Isn't art about interaction? And shouldn't erotic interaction be addressed now and again, especially in gay literature?

Well into his seventies, Edmund White, bragged he had "written some of the strangest pages anyone's ever typed out about sex." He told *The Guardian* newspaper (6 December 2012), that he judged "conventional sex writing" to be variously in his words: "comic," "tacky," "hackneyed," "ludicrous," "stale," "lurid," "bleak," "seedy," and "impossible to visualize."

Was he patronizing the reporter who happened to be female, when he added: "It seems to me that gay sex writing is a major test for the typical reader, who is a middle-aged woman [*sic*]." A middle-aged woman? Was he born on Planet Absurd? He seemed oblivious of the popular culture of the literary canon of gay male magazine writing written by gay men for gay men who, by the millions over the years, read a thousand gay male stories in *Drummer*. Finally, he grandly credited a few "great sex writers," like D. H. Lawrence and Robert Gluck of the New Narrative movement, for "doing what the Russian formalists said was the secret of all good fiction—making the familiar strange...."

At *Drummer*, introducing stories of sadomasochism to the masses, we made the strange familiar. In this reverse-engineering, many of our authors, skilled participants in the "role of the author" within the New Journalism, could artfully thread the helix of the classic "familiar strange" and spin it to the alternative "strange familiar" for the total intellectual seduction and erotic success of sex stories that, like my own eyewitness New Narrative feature articles and fiction in *Drummer*, purposely started in the head and worked their way down.

Perhaps it's time for this cap-a-pie crew of New York seniors to saddle up, pop a Viagra, and pay their erotic dues as responsible gay elders. The older dancer, Margot Fonteyn, was rejuvenated by the wildly sexy younger dancer from the dance, Rudolf Nureyev who extended her career. Perhaps, thus re-juiced, they'll find themselves triumphantly censored in some fabulous obscenity trial ala Mapplethorpe who succeeded in being both epicurean and arousing.

After all, erotica is the fundamental element of beauty that makes gay literature gay. Otherwise, queer writing is just another polite niche genre. If writers cannot pen erotica, and by that I mean literary porn that indeed "starts in the head and works its way down," those un-licentious writers should lose their license.

I know from Professor David Van Leer, author of *The Queening of America*, that there are cum-stained issues of *Drummer* hidden under certain New York authors' beds.

Tell me what you cum to and I'll tell you who you really are.

Provincial New York queens were chronicled extensively in *Some Dance to Remember*, Reel 4, Scene 2; this is but a sample:

> It was a Ton of Attitude. The immigrant Manhattanite A-Group crashed San Francisco, intent on Manhattanizing "The City That Knows How." They hosted huge, super-produced bashes...It was SFO gays *versus* El Lay gays *versus* Manhattan gays. The Great Gay Triangle of three cities turned positively Bermuda.

Besides Scott McKenzie's 1967 invitation to come to San Francisco wearing flowers in your hair, Embry had from *Drummer*'s earliest issues printed full-page open-call invitations to all writers, photographers, and artists: e.g., *Drummer* 2 (August 1975), page 16, and *Drummer* 6 (June 1976), inside back cover.

As editor-in-chief, I threw open the windows of *Drummer* even further and actively queried, chased, and recruited talent in that first gay decade after Stonewall, because I thought liberation freed us to dare to create emerging "gay erotic art" featuring males, objectified as Platonic Ideals, in the same way as "straight art" showcasing females, but without the sexism.

I meant for frank erotic writing to be regarded as a legitimate esthetic on the page the way the photographs of Mapplethorpe and George Dureau and the drawings of Rex and Tom of Finland are framed as legitimate gay art on the walls of galleries and museums.

On February 16, 1978, I personally wrote to the Manhattan artist, Rex, to request five specific drawings to build into my *Son of Drummer* (September 1978): "Bath House," "21 Tongues," "Mad Doctors," "Black Socks," and his "Andrew-Wyeth" drawing, "Jack Off."

In a letter dated February 21, 1978, Rex responded from Manhattan, airing his smouldering resentment of the New York establishment misunderstanding his art:

> Dear Jack: Thank you for your letter of the 16th. I am most grateful for any coverage I might get from your publication, especially at this transitional stage of my career. I'm enclosing the drawings you requested [with Rex's inimitable comments about each]....I would very much like to see your viewpoint about my work, much

as you interpreted the Mineshaft poster [which he had drawn for the coming year, 1978, and I had reviewed in *Drummer* 19 (December 1977), pages 82-83: "The essence of the Mineshaft is found in page after page of Rex's drawings in his limited-edition portfolios *Icons* and *Mannespielen*."]. You'll be more objective about the work and I would definitely want some critical points mentioned.... I've a great many critics.... A paragraph exploring my [New York] detractors would prove most interesting.... Many thanks for your help, Rex

Continuing in *Drummer* 23 (July 1978), I repeatedly published my full-page invitation to writers everywhere to "Submit to *Drummer*, The American Review of Gay Popular Culture." With everyone in the wild 1970s preoccupied with sex, *Drummer* needed fresh, stylish, intelligent, masculine-identified erotica that would gladly have embraced the traditional and *avant-garde* voices of any of the mid-1970s New York gay literati from Larry Kramer, Felice Picano, Edmund White, and all the serious boys including comic Harvey Fierstein getting his "man" on in the fashion of the leather satires: "Gay Deteriorata" (*Drummer* 21, March 1978), "Castro Street Blues" (*Drummer* 24, September 1978), and "Noodles Romanov and the Golden Gloves" (*Drummer* 29, May 1979).

My grass-roots full-page outreach invitation to writers and artists expressed my goal of directing *Drummer* into the New Journalism so popular in the 1960s and 1970s. I wanted to create a masculine gay magazine reflecting the male gender reality of the 1970s, the first decade of gay liberation testing the New Reality, the New Normal, after Stonewall. In other magazines such as *Esquire* and *Rolling Stone*, *Drummer* subscribers were reading New Journalists like Tom Wolfe, George Plimpton, and even Norman Mailer, who chased experience and exposure so as to include the reality of themselves in very credible, eyewitness, first-person narratives, such as Hunter Thompson's book, which would have been very suitable for *Drummer*, *Hells Angels: The Strange and Terrible Saga of the Outlaw Motorcycle Gangs* (1966). In a pop-culture way, I was also invoking the lesson of the surprise hit, the 1971 PBS series, *An American Family: The Loud Family*, which was the first TV reality show. I wanted our loud leather family to reveal its emerging post-Stonewall identity in writing, photography, and art. I wanted to make *Drummer* the autobiographical journal of all of us. Besides, most magazine erotica is just naturally more powerful written in the first person voice of the New Journalism.

> **"SUBMIT TO *DRUMMER*"**
> **PHOTOGRAPHERS, WRITERS, ARTISTS**
>
> Want to go down in history? *Drummer* pays competitive rates for your photos, artwork, first-person articles, and fiction. Your submissions to "*Drummer*, The American Magazine of Gay Popular Culture," are always welcome. Feature articles average 2,000 words up to 4,000. Short stories run around 2,000 words; longer book-length manuscripts are acceptable for serialization. Photography and/or artwork that illustrates your article or story is a definite plus. Always type and double space your manuscript.
>
> *Drummer* especially encourages single photographs as well as photo spreads of up to 20 shots on matter of your choice. We prefer black-and-white prints, but color transparencies are acceptable and are reviewed for cover use.
>
> *Drummer* will take prudent care of your submissions, but cannot be responsible for their loss. (Wise writers retain a Xerox of their materials.) Always [in bold] enclose a stamped self-addressed envelope for prompt return of your unused work
>
> For *Drummer*'s New "Readers' Section" [my startup of "Tough Customers"] *Drummer* pays $10 for each black-and-white photo accepted for publication from our readers. Submit whatever leather, western, uniform, jock, fetish, nude, fantasy, sports, etc. photos you like. For return of unused photos, include a sufficiently stamped self-addressed return envelope.
>
> *Drummer* Pays Competitive Rates on Publication.
>
> Send to *Drummer* editor. —Best Regards, Jack Fritscher

Including my special issue, *Son of Drummer* (September 1978), in which I featured "New York Art," I did everything but send a singing telegram to Manhattan.

What was *Drummer*? Chopped liver?

If *Drummer* were not good enough for their tastes, why weren't they clever enough to seize the opportunity, for themselves and for the gay community, to send in their own improving "better" fiction and features. I would have seriously considered publishing them.

As if in answer to my open invitation, Picano had sent that story, "Hunter," which Embry published, after my exit, in *Drummer* 39 (October 1980). Picano's 1978 poem, "The Deformity Lover," a spin on Tennessee Williams' disability-as-sex-fetish story, "One Arm," was published in *Drummer* 93

(March 1986). In *The Burning Pen: Sex Writers on Sex Writing* (2001), editor M. Christian included fourteen writers, including himself, Pat Califia, Picano, and me. Picano, whom I single out for no reason other than that he was cool enough to seek publication in *Drummer*, seemed willing to be "one of the boys" among the hard corps. In *The Burning Pen*, his auto-bio explanation of his own sex writing went off-topic and was not about the why and how of writing erotica. His accompanying story "Expertise," while about sex, was not sexy. As the editor of *Drummer*, I would have said his story was generically literary, but it was not the distinct genre of gay erotic literature that, like jazz and blues music in service to eros, has the requisite "Music of the Id" quotient required to make one-handed magazine readers hard.

Quintessential erotic literature is an act of aggression that gets readers off. That is a protean task. Most writers in the GLBT "literary world" are incapable of hauling readers' ashes, and therefore are "above" writing gay "erotica" which is as essential to gay popular culture as "blues" and "rap" are to Black culture.

There are all kinds of gay writing, but isn't there something radical and true and authentic in gay writing that so affirms the reader's sexual identity that it causes physical orgasm?

Tim Barrus, the firebrand editor of *Drummer*, and the founder of the LeatherLit Movement (1997) in San Francisco, wrote scornfully about the schism in homosexuality between the East Coast and the West Coast, and between elitist gay writers and popular-culture gay writers. His clever tirade appeared in the same issue in which DeBlase's partner in *Drummer*, Andy Charles, always the wealthy social climber, wrote an apologetic defense of Edmund White whose book, *The Beautiful Room Is Empty*, Barrus had earlier punctured with a bad review. Barrus wrote in *Drummer* 120 (August 1988), page four:

> ...With our art and our message we are involved, here [at *Drummer*], in the process of creating our own cultural [leather, masculine, literary] mythology. Our own heroes. Our own sensibility around who and what matters.
>
> I have often wondered just exactly what it is many of the (tasteful) writers in such gay publications as let's say *Christopher Street* are trying to say. And I have often wondered if any of the "Lavender [Violet] Quill" boys could write anything that might actually get my dick hard. It's somewhat interesting to lay down a gauntlet to them—hey, boys, have

any of you got what it takes to reach out to gay men in such a way as to turn them on and in the process—often—make them think.

Barrus, himself unable to get publication traction because of East Coast prejudices and politically correct dogma, assumed a new literary identity and began writing under the Navajo name "Nasdijj." In 1998, he sent an unsolicited short feature article manuscript titled "The Blood Runs Like a River through My Dreams" to *Esquire* with a note saying, "In the entire history of *Esquire* magazine, you have never once published an American Indian writer." "The Blood Runs" essay was published in the June 1999 issue of *Esquire* and was so famously well written it became a finalist for the National Magazine Award. Nasdijj wrote two more Nasdijj book memoirs after his first one, *The Blood Runs Like Rivers Through My Dreams* (2000), was selected as a "Notable Book of the Year" by *The New York Times*. The other two titles were *The Boy and the Dog Are Sleeping* (2003) and *Geronimo's Bones: A Memoir of My Brother and Me* (2004).

Then in January 2006, investigative journalist Matthew Fleischer published an expose in *LA Weekly* titled "Navahoax" revealing that Barrus was "a middle-aged white male writer of gay pornography" who—as if it were a bad thing—had "for years, ...written gay leather porn and sadomasochistic novels." When the scandal broke, *Esquire* writer Andrew Chaikivsky contacted me for his deeper query into the identity of Tim Barrus whose picture was to be published full page next to the article: "Nasdijj: Seven Years Ago, He Was Born in This Magazine."

For that May 2006 *Esquire* (pages 138-143), Chaikivsky interviewed and then named me in his article as "one of the founding editors of *Drummer*, a now defunct gay leather magazine where Barrus edited and wrote stories in the 1980s." My goal in responding to the empathetic Chaikivsky was to explain Barrus' sense of frustration with publishing as well as his undeniable brilliance in creating identities and channeling other personas, a gift which was traditionally key to many female authors disguised pseudonymously as male, and to many gays who lived double lives to survive and succeed as straight authors. Barrus identifies as straight, but he learned plenty from the problem-solving stress of living inside gay publishing culture where dissembling is an art form almost of the kind perfected by drag queens.

It did not help Barrus that at the same time, media detectives also unmasked the memoir authors JT LeRoy and James Frey who had conned Oprah and her book club. Timothy Patrick Barrus's shapeshifter story should one day be scripted and directed as an independent film examining the creative process of an author desperate to catch a break when all the politically-correct odds seem against him. A good plot point would dramatize how all the eager magazine, newspaper, and book publishers wrote checks and bought travel tickets for "Timothy Nasdijj Barrus" who was what they wanted until they didn't.

Is there satire for parochial New Yorkers whose western horizon was the Hudson River? To us in California, those island queens lived on the cover of the March 29, 1976, *New Yorker*, skewered by Saul Steinberg's classic insight, "A View of the World from 9th Avenue." Is there any irony in Larry Kramer shouting out at the 2011 Tribeca Film Festival: "Our history has been taken away from us by straight historians who have no concept of who we are or will not let us be who we are." Kramer is the dependably embarrassing Manhattanite who dramatizes himself as one of the keepers of the keys of gay literature. Stranded like swish Family Robinson on their island, they ignore the fact that they have little respect for or concept of other gay American voices. Their alpha and omega is New York. http://www.tribecafilm.com/festival/features/film-coverage/Tribeca_Talks_Outrage.html

I cannot help but think of the shameless behavior of the incestuous East Coast gay "literary" crowd, including keynote speaker White and a screaming Kramer, whose snarling hubris destroyed, and closed down, the 15th Annual Key West Literary Seminar in January 1997. But that's another story told in Chapter 17.

In 2006, when the islander Picano moved to the peninsula of San Francisco, he announced with humorous self-satire on September 29:

> When I arranged to do a reading at Books, Inc. this coming Thursday, October 5th on Market and 16th Street several months ago I had no idea I'd be living in San Francisco. But I am. So this is sort of a welcome party for me....I've been promised a possible "roast" [at this reading], although how this is possible with a sweet, kind, gentle, soft spoken soul as I am, I can't imagine.

Picano stayed in San Francisco only a short time before moving to LA. His move was the reverse of Embry who brought his LA attitude to San Francisco where he was never thought of as a San Franciscan, but always as "John Embry from LA." Northern Californians have always stood back in amazement from both New York and LA attitude with their imperial court contempt of anyone who is not them. Five minutes with grandiose LA personalities like my longtime friend Larry Townsend, or John Embry, or *Drummer* writer John Rowberry would define this arch kweeniness whose fumes can overtake a room in seconds. Their hauteur was a contemptible attitude that San Franciscans joked about.

While in LA for the National Book Expo America in May 2008, I asked editor Jeanne Barney, that veteran of the *Drummer* wars, who at that time was on the "no-fault outs" with both her friends Larry Townsend and John Embry (who hated each other), what was the cause of all the LA gay infighting and attitude. She responded to Mark Hemry and me that I was the second person to ask her that in the past two weeks, but she had no answer. At that lunch at Canter's Deli on Fairfax, no one knew Townsend would die two months later, estranged both from Barney as well as from Embry who himself died twenty-six months after Townsend. That left me, and this book, standing in the rubble of their bitter triangle. Regarding the LA "Attitude"—which I initial-capped to signify it as a "character" in *Some Dance to Remember*, someone else suggested that historically there was so little to be won in the homosexual world that gays continue to fight over every possible crumb. So, giving ultimate LA attitude, John Embry responded with a distancing email, cold as a telegram, when I told him Townsend was dying in hospital.

> From: Jack Fritscher
> To: John Embry
> Sent: Wednesday, July 23, 2008 3:33 PM
> Subject: Larry Townsend in ICU
>
> Our friend Larry Townsend remains in ICU. Hopefully, he may rally, but the situation seems very distressed. If you want more info, let me know. If you don't want to know, let me know. May our world of readers and writers keep Larry in our thoughts and give him good energy during the next few hours and days.
> Jack Fritscher
>
> From: supermr
> To: Jack Fritscher
> Sent: Wednesday, July 23, 2008 6:02 PM
> Subject: Larry Townsend in ICU

[Embry responded in ALL CAPS] THANK YOU FOR NOTIFYING ME. ALTHOUGH LARRY'S AND MY RELATIONSHIP IS IN ABOUT THE SAME STATE AS HIS AND JEANNIE'S [Sic]. BE THAT AS IT MAY, I WISH HIM WELL AND WAS VERY DISMAYED AT FRED'S PASSING [Fred Yerkes, Townsend's partner of forty-four years], WHICH I AM SURE WAS VERY HARD ON HIM.
John Embry

I point out this rather unsavory tale of two-timing cities because the need to move *Drummer* from LA to San Francisco was not so much because of the Slave Auction arrests by the LAPD, but was more because the LA founding staff of *Drummer* were a circular firing squad of love and hate. In order to find its center, the young *Drummer* could not survive such bad gay behavior in LA. Luckily, fate, occasioned by the LAPD raid on the Drummer Slave Auction, caused the magazine to flee to San Francisco, not to New York, to continue finding its true identity, purpose, readership, and salon of contributors.

In perspective, back in the 1970s, to literary book mavens sniffy about high culture, gay magazines were a new and untried post-Stonewall invention in gay popular culture. What was this new genre lately sprung up on the West Coast? When *Drummer* debuted (June 1975) in LA, there were only two other considerable large-size slick gay mags on the racks: the newish self-identified *Queen's Quarterly* (1969) in Manhattan; and the prettyboy *Blueboy* (1974) in Miami, founded by *TV Guide* advertising executive, Don Embinder, who was no Embry. Not until July 1976, did Michael Denneny and Charles L. Ortleb found New York's glossy *Christopher Street* magazine.

QQ, *Blueboy*, and *Christopher Street* had sophisticated publishers and a well-paid class of professionals writing, photographing, and designing them for mainstream vanilla gays. One deceptive business quirk at *Queen's Quarterly*, where future *Drummer* art director A. Jay worked, was that to seem "up and running" in order to sell advertising, *QQ* began publishing with issue two; there was no issue number one.

Drummer, a wild orphan of the leather tribe, was run by the poor-man's Bill Sykes, Embry, who, I'm coloring up here, abused *Drummer* as if it were Oliver Twist. He may have known how to pick a pocket or two in his mail-order business, but he knew next to absolutely nothing about people or the finesse of publishing when *Drummer* fell into his lap in 1975 through his machinations (1972-1975) inside the struggling *H.E.L.P./Drummer* political organization. He thought of the writing and photos in *Drummer* as little more than bait luring mail-order customers to buy the dildos, cockrings, and poppers he hawked in the center of the magazine.

Embry's reputation and cheap production values probably made *Drummer* unattractive to some hoity writers. Out of necessity, I tried to make *cheap* seem *attractive* and *underground* and *outlaw* and *exciting* to men who, like New Yorkers Robert Mapplethorpe and Rex, understood the romance of high-toned slumming at nights with bad boys and dangerous men in rundown piers, dark alleys, skid row hotels, sleazy baths, and rough leather bars—which I referenced when I published Rex's "T. S. Eliot 'Prufrock'" drawings of "restless nights in one-night cheap hotels and sawdust restaurants" in *Son of Drummer*.)

Because of my cover feature, "Remembrance of Sleaze Past," in *Drummer* 139 (May 1990), the Manhattan author and Catholic lady Patricia Morrisroe wrote in her *Mapplethorpe* biography, published nearly a year after my San Francisco *Mapplethorpe* memoir, that I was "the king of sleaze." She meant to be insulting, but she, who went on to write a book about her love of shoes, did not understand the inverted and ironic gay-culture definition of the word *sleaze* anymore than she understood the *mise en scene* of Mapplethorpe whose shoes she could not walk in, and seemed neither to understand, or like, in her judgmental book.

Apparently, Morrisroe was unaware that sleaze is a gay "good thing," and that director John Waters is the anointed "King of Sleaze" I am but a reporter reflecting the kind of sensuality that sweaty *Drummer* readers wanted to read about, especially after the advent of HIV that destroyed the baths, the sex clubs, and, in a way, promiscuity itself.

In his *The Golden Age of Promiscuity* (1996), New Yorker Brad Gooch used the word *sleaze* in his description of the music played at the Mineshaft in the Titanic 1970s.

> The music...was trance music...that included Philip Glass, Steve Reich, and many of the other minimalist artists Sean and Annie [Gooch's two characters] had listened to at the Chelsea [Hotel], music that was labeled 'sleaze' by 'disco' adherents. By dawn there would always be full electronic Vangelis chords mixed with Mahler. (Pages 154-155)

Earlier, in search of eyewitness authenticity as to what were the drivers of the "sleaze" that I had written about in *Drummer*, I interviewed Wally Wallace, the manager of the Mineshaft, about the music in the Mineshaft.

He explained in the video shot in San Francisco, May 28, 1995, that, while the famously international sex inside the Mineshaft was sleaze, the masculine-inflected music, designed to discourage women and the New York disco crowd, was way more than sleaze:

> People talk about the sex at the Mineshaft, but sex was not what it was all about. First of all, I had a policy that the music was never so loud that you couldn't hear the person next to you. I made the tapes myself. We played anything in the world, from western to classics. A lot of classics actually. At the beginning, it was electronic variations on classic themes. Ella Fitzgerald. Jazz. We tried to avoid basic disco, references to females, references to "let's dance," things like that. But the music became kind of famous because we didn't follow the mainstream. We had a somewhat older clientele.

For writers as for everyone else, dues must be paid. Six years after Stonewall, *Drummer* was a wonderful entry point for emerging writers keen to write erotica. Is penning porn a rite of passage? Is a gay writer really a gay writer *before* he makes readers cum?

Gay writing begins with one stroke of the pen and ends with many strokes of the penis.

Who has ever jerked off to the usual nominees in the gay East Coast literary follies? Have they paid their homage to Eros?

Perhaps Manhattanites had legitimate fears about approaching *Drummer* after East Coast writer John Preston and New York photographer Robert Mapplethorpe, a friend of Edmund White, reported back to New York warning how Embry had treated them. Or, perhaps, Manhattan gays themselves bought into the on-going anti-leather rants of the shameful Richard Goldstein at the *Village Voice*. In 1979, they certainly hit the summer streets of Greenwich Village protesting the location shoot of the leather film, *Cruising* (1980), directed by William Friedkin whom they still hated for directing Mart Crowley's *verite* transcription of Manhattan queens, *The Boys in the Band*. Perhaps the "professional" writers, who were fellow travelers with the bourgeois white-bread *Advocate*, thought *Drummer*, seemingly filled by passionately authentic "amateur" experts, was too erotic and *outre* when it was meant to be sexy, forward, and "far out."

These bicoastal pop-culture clashes are early examples of the never-ending civil wars in the gay community analyzed in many magazines and dramatized in *Some Dance to Remember*. As an eyewitness observer of gay folk, I have never met anywhere such a contentious group of people in my life. Personally, I was never bullied or abused by anybody until I entered the killing fields of gay culture where verbal abuse and attitude are acceptable behavior, and visions of patricide dance in feminist heads. John Waters' halo slipped when he told *The Advocate* (11/2/2015) what it liked to hear:

> I love radical feminists, even though I sometimes don't agree with them. I don't like women-hating gay men, but I don't mind women that hate men. They have more reason.

Shouldn't gays, always insisting how we demand tolerance from straight society, first tolerate each other and lip-synch to Joel Grey singing about tolerance in *Cabaret* (1972), "Leben und leben lassen/Live and let live."

The unspoken truism about homosexual psychology is that many gay people are "forced" to be "liberal" because—except for the wild card of homosexuality—they are likely as conservative, prejudiced, separatist, sexist, and racist as their pistol-packing relatives pigging out on fast food in Red States.

Drummer was designed to be erotic.

Eros is the heart of gay literature, pornographic or not.

Erotica is not "time out" from literature.

Erotica *is* gay literature.

ANNE RICE: DID SHE EVER WRITE FOR *DRUMMER*?

Once a San Francisco writer, Anne Rice, in her double-jointed literary career as the aka "erotic author, A. N. Roquelaure and/or Anne Rampling," knew eros was literature. At least she did before her late-in-life return to Catholicism which, after writing a Jesus novel, she seemed to renounce a second time. While it's true she wrote *Interview with the Vampire* in the Castro, and it was published in May 1976 when *Drummer* was a year old, a stake needs be driven through the urban legend about Anne Rice and *Drummer*. I was paying attention because years earlier I had written my occult book, the nonfiction *Popular Witchcraft: Straight from the Witch's Mouth,* in the Castro in 1969-1971, for its first publication in 1972 by the Popular Press, an imprint of Bowling Green State University Press.

Drummer published two excerpts from Rice's novel, *Exit to Eden* (1982): "Beauty's Punishment" in *Drummer* 71 (February 1984) and "Beauty's Release" in *Drummer* 83 (March 1985). An "excerpt from the excerpt" of "Beauty's Punishment" was reprinted on pages 36-38 in *Drummer* 188 (September 1995) under the attribution by female editor Wickie Stamps that Rice herself had actually written for *Drummer* and was a representative author, which she was not, despite any mythic revisionism of the unstoppable feminist fantasy that she was.

Arrangements for the first excerpts from her previously written work were seemingly made with her publishers by *Drummer* contributor, John Preston, who was her Manhattan acolyte. The publicity stunt of her insert into *Drummer* was a corporate publisher's marketing attempt to introduce her Roquelaure/Rampling books to leatherfolk.

One might as well name Thoreau as a *Drummer* author because he was quoted each issue on the masthead.

One might as well also name Maya Angelou as a *Drummer* author because her poem "On the Pulse of Morning" was published across two pages of the ill-fated *Drummer* 161. That issue, truth be told, was plagued with plagiarism and copyright problems so serious that most copies were shredded and never distributed. Nowhere did that *Drummer* issue note permission to reprint Angelou any more than did Embry when he failed to get permission to reprint a section from Peter Shaffer's *Equus* (1973) for my horse-fetish issue of *Drummer* 25 (December 1978). Shaffer was not amused.

Beware the mythomania around *Drummer*.

For politically correct reasons of "gender" as well as "commerce," the two excerpts by Rice/Roquelaure happened to be published incidentally in *Drummer*. Unless someone unearths documents or testimony to the contrary, it seems:

1. Anne Rice was never personally or professionally associated with *Drummer*.

2. Anne Rice never wrote for *Drummer*.

3. Anne Rice's connection to *Drummer* was vicarious through her colleague, John Preston, who specialized in collecting individual authors into anthologies which he packaged for publishers.

On October 17, 2006, John Embry told me on the phone:

> Anne Rice? I never had any truck with Anne Rice. I was so disappointed when I finally got one of her books to read. It was *Beauty's Punishment* and it was kind of interesting, but then she did the thing they made the movie of—not *Vampire*. I never did like *Interview with the Vampire*. The one on the island: *Exit to Eden*.

The closed and cultish Preston was cooking Rice for *Drummer*'s hungry pages. In the 1980s plague years as faithful contributors died, Embry sought even quicker free ways to fill those pages, and he hardly cared or noticed what that filler was. In fact, Embry, the convenient amnesiac who "had no truck with Rice," forgot he listed himself on the masthead as both publisher and editor of *Drummer* 71, which first excerpted her, and of *Drummer* 83 featuring her second excerpt. No one can remember everything, but it was his business responsibility to know that A. N. Roquelaure was Anne Rice. He was already growing his Alternate Publishing brand, and planning to sell *Drummer* off. From his first day to his last as publisher, he paid scant attention to what filled *Drummer*.

In the creative vacuum caused by panic over HIV, Preston himself became HIV positive and conscious of his legacy. With his dour vampire looks, he pursued the Eternal Life of Column Inches. In order to service both Rice's publisher, and Embry (who was Preston's *Mr. Benson* publisher), he went wide to score more coverage. He lobbied to get her *Exit to Eden* excerpts in *Drummer*. He repeated his PR tactic when he again published *Exit* excerpts to give both mainstream and female *gravitas* to his anthology, *Flesh and the Word* (1992). The brand name "Anne Rice" sold books, but it never sold *Drummer*. No disrespect, but Anne Rice has rarely been deemed a proper leather author any more than E. L. James who wrote the erotic BDSM romance novel, *Fifty Shades of Gray*.

Preston, driven to quickness by HIV, was noted for hitching his wagon to established stars whose collected reflected glory could make him seem like a literary powerhouse. He ingratiated himself with the sexual underground by packaging several anthologies, like *Flesh and the Word*, with eager and grateful genre authors he courted, including *Drummer* contributors Phil Andros, Larry Townsend, Aaron Travis, and Patrick Califia. They wrote the stories and he put his name on the cover. In late 1978, when Preston queried Embry seeking his own debut in *Drummer*, Embry tasked me to edit Preston's draft of *Mr. Benson* for content, style, and serialization because it was a book-length manuscript whose chapters could be serialized monthly to keep subscribers coming back for more.

Preston is a case in point. *Drummer* was a magazine open to publishing sadomasochistic novels written by storytellers from New York to Timbuktu. While Preston was happy editing other authors, I experienced in 1979 that he had a less than happy attitude that he was being edited at *Drummer* even though he had agreed to the edit. His friend, Lars Eighner, the author of *Travels with Lizbeth*, wrote: "Preston often told (wrote to) me that he needed a lot of editing. I thought he was being modest until I was given the task of editing the Introduction [to Eighner's book *Lavender Blue*], which was the first time I had ever seen his raw copy." —Lars Eighner, "John Preston Goes in Search of an Author's Lost Manuscript," www.DuskPeterson.com July 2, 2011

SUMMARY OF THE URBAN LEGEND:
ANNE RICE AND THE *DRUMMER* SALON

In the twentieth anniversary issue of *Drummer* 188, editor Wickie Stamps created a brouhaha among the surviving diversity of *Drummer* authors, heirs, and Salonistas who were actually associated for twenty years with the magazine. Wickie Stamps committed the editorial faux pas of re-reprinting seven columns, approximately two *Drummer* pages, from *Beauty's Punishment* as if Anne Rice were representative of *Drummer.*

As much as I respect both Stamps and Rice, one must note that Anne Rice's byline as "Anne Rice" never appeared in *Drummer*. Her excerpts were bylined at a distance as "A. N. Roquelaure."

It was only in the "Editor's Note" on page 38 of *Drummer* 188, that Stamps pulled back the curtain and attributed the excerpt to "Ann [sic] Rice." Misspelled. Properly disclosing some alleged commercial deal with Rice's publisher, Plume, Stamps also included a display ad "in trade" for *Beauty's Punishment*, page 12.

The bottom line of my search of the internal evidence inside *Drummer* pages is that, historically, Anne Rice never wrote for *Drummer*, but was excerpted twice, with one of those excerpted selections repeated.

According to lore, when Anne Rice was born into an Irish-Catholic family, her bohemian mother named her Howard Allen O'Brien. She chose to be called *Anne* before she married Stan Rice. In 1985, was she conjuring on the name of the stylish actress Charlotte Rampling, star of the iconic S&M film *The Night Porter* (1974), when she chose to write the adult fiction of *Exit to Eden* as "Anne Rampling"?

In *Drummer*, again, she never appeared under her brand name, "Anne Rice," but only under her S&M pseudonym from which she seemed to keep a certain polite distance. Did she rather much divorce "A. N. Roquelaure" before renouncing vampires themselves upon her return to the Catholic Church in 1998? As a requivering Catholic myself, I can understand Rice's hedging her bets at a certain age. Her book, *Christ the Lord: Out of Egypt* (2005), is told from the viewpoint of the resurrected Jesus, who has trumped Rice's vampires as the True Immortal. Perhaps conflating phony Christianists with legitimate Christianity, in 2009 she apparently returned from Catholicism to the gay fold escorted by her son, author Christopher Rice.

UNDER THE SNAKE SKIN OF HUMANS:
GAY SUNSHINE PRESS, THE CUTTING EDGE, AND ILLNESS

On the West Coast in San Francisco, *Drummer* literature suited the former Catholic priest Winston Leyland, the seminal publisher, who in 1975, the year of *Drummer*'s birth, founded his Gay Sunshine Press which is the "oldest continuously publishing book house" of diverse gay literature and gay popular culture in the United States. His mandarin literary tastes included rough trade. He printed many photographs by Old Reliable in his books. In 1984, he put me under contract and began publishing three books of my leather writing first published and proved by test-marketing in *Drummer*: *Leather Blues: A Novel of Leatherfolk*; *Corporal in Charge of Taking Care of Captain O'Malley and Other Stories*, the first ever collection of *Drummer* stories; and *Stand by Your Man and Other Stories*.

In the 1970s and early 1980s, several West Coast gay authors and playwrights, such as Mason Powell and George Birimisa, judged the marketing rhythms of serial publication in monthly magazines to be a better connection to eager fans than one-time publication of a single book. They turned their hopes to *Drummer* special-edition magazine-sized "books." *Leather Blues* and *Corporal in Charge* (both 1984) were the first two crossover titles bridging from *Drummer* to Gay Sunshine, from Embry's "magazine format books" to Leyland's "trade paperback books."

On August 1, 2002, the E-Newsletter of Calamusbooks.com, Volume II, #38, nailed this centrality of *Drummer* when it identified my professional persona as "the founding San Francisco editor-in-chief of *Drummer* magazine which, in its early issues, back in the late 1970s [Fritscher at *Drummer*: March 1977-December 1979], was a terrific contribution to the erotic literature of gay men—it even featured photos by Robert Mapplethorpe."

While I wanted *Drummer* to be cutting edge, it was a measure of Embry's *je ne sais quoi* that neither of my formative heroes, the *avant-garde* Andy Warhol nor the iconic leather filmmaker, Kenneth Anger, were ever mentioned or duly honored in *Drummer*. In a nasty bit, Warhol's film, *Bad*, was trashed in one snotty column in *Drummer* 15, page 62.

In all good dramas, sex and medical story arcs and unrequited love writhe under the snake skin of humans. During the manic-depressive 1970s when most gay people were fixing their homophobically wounded and newly uncloseted selves with uppers and downers, we were under the discipline to produce *Drummer* one word, one photo, one drawing, one page, one issue at a time, every thirty days, twelve times a year.

During twenty-four years, the monthly *Drummer* averaged an

issue every six weeks. Each deadline was a triumph against all odds. For instance, during my eyewitness tenure as editor-in-chief and as a longtime contributor, I noticed that the huge subtext of gay gender politics—given grass-roots voice in the subscribers' Sex Personals ads—both informed and deformed *Drummer*. Embry, ignoring the GPS directions of his demographic audience, never bothered to develop cues from the juicy Personals ads into reader-reflexive editorial stories and articles that entertained and informed their concerns.

Embry sadly ignored even applying his own experience. He had the fundamentalist fortitude of a cancer survivor who bravely never complained publicly about what he suffered privately, but his near-death experience hardly educated him to rise up and publish anything on gay spirituality, psychology, or health, even when HIV appeared on his watch. *Drummer* never mentioned social diseases until, in the late 1970s, I noticed a rise in illness among leathermen, and persuaded him to publish my column on gay health, "Dr. Dick: *Drummer* Goes to the Doctor," beginning in *Drummer* 21 (March 1978).

He wanted *Drummer* to live in denial of death. He wanted *eros* not *thanatos*.

He slowed down the evolution of gay culture and the evolution of the magazine. He failed to read his readers. Instead of embracing their ideas and concerns, he kept leathermen at a distance with the kind of LA camp that had created his Cycle Sluts cover.

Nevertheless, we staff were all pleased when Embry returned to the office with a grin on his always reddish face. He had a second lease on life. He had beaten death. He came smiling through, but, as he stood akimbo in the doorway, waiting for applause, blocking our progress, I thought: "Uh-oh, he's back, with a head full of those campy 1950s dialog balloons that he can't resist pasting down on sex photos, and that I have to pull off the flats before they go to the printer."

DRUMMER

the leather fraternity

Australia $2.70/Belgie 150 frs
Danmark 24 Kr.inkl.moms
France 16 Nf
Israel 14,00 Israeli Pounds
Italy 2500 Lire/Japan 12 Yen
Nederland 12 Fl.
New Zealand $2.50
Norge 22 N. kr.
Oesterreich 80 Sch
Schweiz 13 frs
Sverige 17 kr.inkl.moms
United Kingdom 100 p.

2.50
outrageous!

BEGINNING A NEW
MOVIE MAYHEM BOOK!
by ALLEN EAGLES

GO TO A **BODY PAINTING** with **VAL MARTIN** and **CLIFF RAVEN**

KING Leather **COMICS**

center foldout POSTER

Cover Photograph by Roy Dean

complete in this issue
MORE FICTION by **PHIL ANDROS** with illustrations by CHUCK ARNET

CHAPTER 8

THE MAFIA:
STRAIGHT AND GAY AND MAYBE NOT

- Editor-in-Chief Tunes Up *Drummer* Issues 19-33, 1977-1980
- From "Old Guard Leather" to the "New Gender of Homomasculinity"
- Sashes to Ashes: The Mr. Drummer Contest and HIV
- *Verite* Style: Making *Drummer* Reflect Self-Identifying Homomasculine Readers
- Embry's Grudges Become His Blacklist That Poisons the Lineage of Leather Descent
- Eyewitnesses Robert Davolt, Rick Leathers, Steven Saylor
- The Mafia: "Guido Lust," Tony Tavarossi, and the Invention of the Leather Bar

---

TV-Gay Thumbnail. *The Ritz*: The Mafia gets tangled up with Manhattan denizens of a gay bathhouse (Think: "Continental Baths plus Bette Midler") in Terrence McNally's hit Broadway sex farce (1975) and cult movie (1977).

Embry never "got" me.
I never "got" him.
He was petulant.
I was impetuous.
We were totally unrequited.
We were destined for each other.

Drummer editor Joseph Bean wrote in his *Drummer* history essay "Nobody Did It Better," published first by the Leather Archives & Museum in its *Leather Times* #1 (2007), that in 1977 I had pulled Embry's fat out of the fire in the drama that was *Drummer*, and to Embry's chagrin, everyone knew it. In a decade where everybody was balling everybody, particularly in the leather culture around *Drummer* at venues on Folsom Street, between

Embry and me there was "minus zero degrees of fuck." In fact, I never sighted Embry in any louche leather lair lower than a bar. He was, *suum cuique*, not a gonzo journalist, not a leatherman, and not a player at the after-hours clubs and baths on Folsom Street, nor at private orgies at the Catacombs, nor homes about town. In 1997, he admitted in *Manifest Reader* 33 (page 5) that he had been a recluse in the 1970s when he recalled the super parties like *Night Flight* and *Stars* which I reported on in *Drummer*. He wrote:

> ...I remember devoting a lifetime avoiding such affairs – It was only reluctantly that I even attended our own [*Drummer*] parties in those days.

Jeanne Barney told me when I asked specifically:

> I always felt that John was a leather poseur, but why? I don't know. To compete with the famous leather star, Larry [Townsend]? To distinguish himself from every other unattractive guy at the bar? Because there were better pickings at the leather bars where hungry bottoms will go with almost anyone who will top them?

Embry's occasional appearance in leather bars was always about business. He swanned about like a Kiwanis Club booster glad-handing bar owners and popper manufacturers to solicit advertising dollars for *Drummer* and *Drummer* "one-offs" like his Spring 1980 magazine, *The Folsom Attitude*, tagged as "A *Drummer* Action Guide to Folsom Street," whose entire editorial content plugged bars, baths, and businesses like a press agent's brochure for sex tourists. Embry, constantly copying other business models, longed to muscle in on the territory of Bob Damron who was the publisher of the *Damon Guide* series of popular travel books as well as the founding owner of several bars including Febe's leather bar at the southwest corner of 11th Street and Folsom. Embry, imitating Damron's travel guide, and wanting to clone the quintessential leather appeal of Febe's, opened up his *Drummer* Key Club on the northwest corner of the same intersection.

Years later after *Drummer* was made even more international by its new Dutch owner, Damron chanced the wisdom of buying a full-page *Drummer* ad touting the company's "travel services since 1964." (*Drummer* 159, December 1992)

Regarding the success among masculine-identified gay men of the grass-roots homomasculinity concept as framed in *Drummer*, the famously queeny *Damron Guide* finally homomasculinized its image when its president Gina Gata, chasing homomasculinity, announced on September 27, 2007,

> When we were looking for a new marketing twist and many of our hundreds of thousands of readers both online and with the guide asked for more a modern and *masculine* [italics added] look, I called my friend John Rutherford of Colt. We've already heard rave reviews from our solid stable of retailers, distributors, and the like on how much they love the new cover with Colt men Carlo Masi and Adam Champ. —*Adult Video News*, AVN.com

Trying for business synergy in 1980, and perhaps trying to triage *Drummer* fatiguing from the money sucked out of it by gouging printers and delinquent distributors, Embry leased the bar and famous swimming pool at 11th and Folsom, across the intersection from Febe's, to open "The *Drummer* Key Club" and his "Studstore." This bar and pool had been the hot-mobbed after-hours sex club, the Covered Wagon, which had an official fire department capacity of 170 people and after midnight rented SRO space to 300-400 men. It had also been Allen Lowery's Leatherneck Bar (*Drummer* 18), Dirty Sally's, the Stables, and the Plunge (*Drummer* 29, page 72). See "Key Club Carpenters," *Drummer* 41 (September 1980). The photo spread features "Robert Payne's" camp dialog balloons as well as photographs by a variety of shutterbugs, including a photo lensed by Sparrow-Fritscher, and credited on page 44 to Sparrow, although we had given no permission to reprint this photo which—to correct Embry's falsehood—was not shot in the *Drummer* Key Club as asserted, but was shot two years before in Embry's former failed startup, The Quarters, in a basement South of Market. See *Drummer* 24 (September 1978) and *Drummer Rides Again* (1979).

One thing I give Embry credit for is that while he owned *Drummer* and Alternate Publishing, he became a house-proud real-estate mogul in San Francisco and at the Russian River. One of my first conversations with Embry in 1977 was our mutual agreement that gays to protect ourselves from greedy landlords, should buy our own homes and studios. Later in life, Jeanne Barney often spoke of Embry bragging on about his adventures as a landlord buying, selling, and managing rental properties for thirty years while he was a publisher. During those three decades, every Christmas, Embry would return to LA to visit his family in Pomona and to lunch at the French Quarter on Santa Monica Boulevard with early *Drummer* pals including Barney, filmmakers Terry LeGrand and Roger Earl, and sometimes Larry Townsend. The stylish and tiny Barney was the only woman at a table of increasingly plump old men whose friendly nostalgia for the good old days could quickly morph into competition, bragging, and attitude. On December 24, 2007, Barney wrote me the day after the latest of the traditional Christmas luncheons:

> Brunch went well. I realize that now [that] I've accepted the fact that I'll never get my $ out of him [Embry], and [that] I don't have to spend much time with him, he's bearable. I do wish, though, that ...[he] would not regale me with stories of costly remodeling and brand-new LG appliances for...apartments.

Drummer was wildly popular in the late 1970s, yet always burdened with mysterious debt. Al Shapiro and I sensed that *Drummer* profits were financing Embry's fast-moving real-estate deals. He was living off the *Drummer* buck. Respecting that his business was his business, we began to protect our own professional interests inside *Drummer* especially after our salaries trickled down so slowly to nothing in 1979 at the Divisadero office. As soon as Al and I quit because of money owed us, the publisher of the "cash-strapped" *Drummer* suddenly produced an instant down-payment and bought a new office on Harriet Street, South of Market in 1980.

If we'd been in synch, Embry and Shapiro and I in the 1980s might have grown *Drummer* progressively transcendent and practical even as the curse of HIV pulled *Drummer* back from being a 1970s sex magazine with *verite* photographs of real players. In January 1980, four things reshaped 1970s *Drummer*:

1) Shapiro and I exited ending what readers, historians, and Embry called the 1970s "Golden Age of *Drummer*";

2) the new Mr. Drummer Contest reshaped editorial content into a kind of leather-runway fanzine;

3) the arrival of corporate video studios paying for their slick professional models to appear in *Drummer* pushed aside real grass-roots photographs of attainable leather tricks, characterized in reader's selfies featured in the monthly "Tough Customers" column; and

4) AIDS changed the sexual lifestyle from liberal to conservative.

The upside of *Drummer* featuring hundreds of pages of leather contestants is that those photos are a happy record of a generation of leathermen snapped as they are bravely carrying on even while being hit with the tsunami of HIV. Some anti-contest readers complained that 1980s *Drummer* had caught "sash rash" from its Mr. Drummer Contest and published too many repetitive pages of leather contestants. However, of those plague years, who can say if the tail wagged the dog? The historical value of those photos is that some of those dear young men during that first desperate decade of AIDS sported big smiles bravely covering the fact they knew they were positive and this was their last chance to be drop-dead gorgeous before they faded away: sashes to ashes.

As a Mr. Drummer Contest judge and as a video director, I fell privy to a certain back-story narrative told on a sad loop. Having shot five or six Palm Drive feature videos of several handsome Mr. Drummer contestants like Larry Perry (Mr. Detour Leather) in *Naked Came the Stranger*, Wes Decker (Mr. Southeast Drummer) in *Sodbuster*, and Rick Conder (Mr. Southwest Drummer) in *Leather Saddle Cowboy Bondage*, I became both eyewitness and, perhaps because of my eleven years of training for the priesthood, a kind of father confessor administering Last Rites. I asked Keith Ardent, star of my *Pec Stud in Black Rubber*, whom I shot for the *Rubberotica* cover and interior photo spread of *Drummer* 118 (July 1988): Why are you doing this? He said: "Your camera makes me immortal. I want to be shot by as many photographers as possible." Leather contests such as International Mr. Leather and its imitator Mr. Drummer were the opposite of the closet. They offered to males born outside the "straight pale" a chance to stand up in public to be cheered as victorious male personalities exhibited as good as and as valid as their straight brothers. To Embry, Mr. Drummer was little more than a publicity stunt staged to exploit the eager models and the ticket-buying leather community in order to provide him free photographs of "his" contestants.

Under Embry and Rowberry from 1980-1986, *Drummer* recycled several of my original fetish themes such as "cigars" and "older men and daddies." Mostly, however, they diluted the essential leatherfolk reality show of 1970s *Drummer* photography. They welcomed slick photos of *faux*-leather porn models provided free by the first-emerging new video companies. The cost-conscious Embry gladly sold his covers and centerfolds to the highest corporate bidder salivating for international product placement of its video stars on a *Drummer* cover. In the 1970s, *Drummer* had feasted on *verite* leather and S&M "movies shot on film" by a select few talents: Fred Halsted, Wakefield Poole, the Gage Brothers, and Roger Earl with Terry LeGrand who produced the controversial Southern California Mr. Drummer Contest in 1991. In 1982, startup video companies, hearing Embry pitch his monthly press run at 42,000 copies, thought *Drummer* could make kosher their *faux*-leather actors zipped into "costume" chaps. Because Embry was neither personally nor erotically into the existential quintessence of leather itself, he never understood his corporate trespass was betraying the authenticity of *Drummer* for readers who were true leather loyalists.

The very word *Drummer* was an endorsement. In 1996, one May midnight in Paris, Mark Hemry and I, searching addresses for #14 along Rue Keller near the Bastille, rang the bell at Keller's bar, and stood waiting in the cold dark. The brusque doorman was a hard-case inquisitor turning away voyeurs on the doorstep. Enforcing Keller's strict fetish dress code, he judged who drank at the bar and who played in the dark back room. Did our big boots and black Levi's cancel our being American? Between his bouncer English and our menu French, before gestures turned to silly pantomime, I said the magic words: "Je suis l'éditeur de *Drummer*." *Drummer* was a powerful international code word. We were immediately swept into the leather heart of the Paris underworld that was Keller's, with its front bar and its infamous back room.

BDSM VIDEO: GAY FILMS, SILENT IN THE 1970S, BECAME "TALKIES" IN THE 1980S

Between 1979 and 1982, the cost of producing gay popular culture on screen dropped one million percent. The silent films—the gay art-porn films of the 1970s—identified by the personal esthetics of their directors such as LeGrand-Earl's *Born to Raise Hell*, Fred Halsted's *Sextool*, Wakefield Poole's *Boys in the Sand*, and Peter Berlin's *That Boy*, disappeared into the "talking pictures" of assembly-line porn videos of the 1980s that turned authentic homosex into a corporate commodity. It was the difference between leather and Naugahyde. It was a revolution. There is a difference between the precise economy of shooting leathermen on film with an involved director's acute personal point of view and the wanton shooting of hours of corporate footage of actors hired to play leathermen.

Film costs a fortune with each frame shot. Video costs pennies. New Orleans photographer George Dureau, Mapplethorpe's mentor, told me that "The camera is a mindless lunatic." The photographer must control the instrument. After the disciplined underground gay films of the Swinging Sixties and the Titanic 1970s, lunatic video rose as just one more piece of the 1980s iceberg. When Embry hopped on the wagon as a video producer, he further distressed the schedule and budget needed to sustain the magazine itself. In-house video-making at *Drummer* was an ill-fated undertaking, too often featuring miscast twinky blond modelles like the human Easter Peep, self-sucker Scott O'Hara. Embry had little talent as producer or director, and did not long sustain his efforts at making his own *Drummer* videos which he had dreamed would make him a fortune in his mail-order business. In truth, the only *Drummer* publisher to produce viable *Drummer*-worthy videos was Tony DeBlase with his wild *USSM* series of BDSM films shot in the 1990s by Mikal Bales, founder of Zeus Studio. Like the Skulls of Akron's intense BDSM dungeon videos of the 1980s (some shot at the Mineshaft), DeBlase's *USSM* series was also censored by government agencies and pulled from circulation.

In the 1970s, as always, the first thing out of the mouth of a customer entering a porn store was, "What's new?" I lay awake at night pondering what could be "new" to *Drummer* readers notorious for trying everything once. In that lay an answer: the young men always know. So I went to them. In the way a music producer goes to underground clubs to listen for new sounds, and a fashion designer hits the streets to see what new look the kids have thought up, I, who, unlike Embry, was both eyewitness and player, went into the streets, the bars, the bruncheries, the baths, the clubs, the playrooms, the prisons, the rodeos, and wrote notes in my journal, bought film for my camera, shot the shit, and brought back *verite* material for *Drummer* from venues like San Quentin (*Drummer* 21) and the Academy Training Center (*Drummer* 145).

Everything I wrote for *Drummer* was grounded in fact rinsed in the conscious erotic rhythms of authentic sex.

PAY UP, OR CALL THE MAFIA

If Christopher Isherwood could say about his stint in Berlin, "I Am a Camera," the same is analogously true about my eyewitness-camera montage of my early leather adventures in Amsterdam, Paris, London, West Berlin, Tokyo, Kyoto, New York, Chicago, Los Angeles, and San Francisco. It was the 1960s and 1970s, and gay men lived on jet planes. On May 1, 1969, I had flown to England on a narrow-bodied Pan Am 707 with three seats on each side of the one aisle. The bone-shaking experience gave me a full understanding of the hysterical camp "conversion" of frightened hooker Sally Mckee (Jan Sterling) tissuing off her whore makeup on a damaged airliner conking out over the Pacific Ocean in *The High and the Mighty* (1954). On my trans-Atlantic flight, I'll never forget how the beautifully dressed young mother, sitting next to me and traveling without her husband, handed me her baby to hold while she rested for a couple hours. She calmed two little boys at once.

In Amsterdam, two weeks later, a newspaper headline announced that the first Jumbo Jet was debuting in LA. This was one month before

Stonewall, and I enjoyed the Busby Berkeley musical-comedy production number in the Associated Press photo of the pilots and stewardesses standing on the wings of the Jumbo Jet. I was staying at the leather S&M Argos Hotel whose foundation was footed in the gay middle ages (1950) when the owners of the building, circumventing police and building codes, turned their living room into the Argos Bar and their bedrooms into a sanctuary hotel of sadomasochism. I had no expense account. I paid my own way. I lived it up to write it down, and poured the cream of sex into my writing and eventually into *Drummer*.

Early on Friday afternoon, August 3, 1979, in the *Drummer* office, with Al Shapiro witnessing what he wanted to find out, John Embry made a fatal mistake that revealed his character and eventually cost him the ownership of *Drummer*.

That afternoon, I asked Embry for my back pay at $400 a month (nearly $4000, a huge total back then), and said if I weren't paid, I'd be giving notice that I was finishing up all my incremental editorial progress toward the autumn issues 31, 32, and 33, which took *Drummer* through December 1979. Because Embry had only recently returned from his bout with cancer, I did not want to exit abruptly, nor did Embry want me to because I specialized in creating trendy leather-culture feature articles not found in his files. After I exited, no one else went on location to write gonzo journalism of rodeos, prisons, and swimming meets. Jeanne Barney told me in 2006 that when she left *Drummer* in 1976, Embry owed her "...$13,000, and Larry Townsend has even computed the interest on that."

If Embry had paid all of us, he might have been able to own his *Drummer* for twenty-four years. Instead, he cut off his nose to spite his face. As an LA businessman, he knew the cost but not the value of paying the workers who were the contributors and the in-house staff. He ruined his own reputation. The talent drain over time cost him his "beloved" *Drummer* in 1986.

Eight years after my exit, in a letter dated August 24, 1987, the still-enraged Embry, who had not been publisher of *Drummer* for a year, lied to the new *Drummer* publisher Tony DeBlase that Fritscher "still owes *Drummer* nine issues as editor-in-chief for which he was paid in full." Funny, he'd never mentioned that before. Among those who died laughing: Mapplethorpe (died 1989) and Sparrow (died 1992) and DeBlase (died 2000). When *Drummer* photographer David Sparrow died, Embry still owed him nearly one thousand dollars from thirteen years earlier. BDSM author Rick Leathers, who worked eleven years in Embry's mail-order office before and after he sold *Drummer*, wrote, "John never advanced a penny to anyone for anything."

Among the living, everybody, including DeBlase and Barney and Townsend, was guffawing at the suggestion that Embry would pay forward anything to anyone when he was so notoriously forever in arrears paying nearly everyone. At least, Embry remembered the amount was for around nine issues at $400 monthly which would be the nearly $4000 I had requested eight years earlier. I would happily delete this paragraph upon seeing the canceled checks.

Al Shapiro was not surprised that our pay was not forthcoming. In quiet protest, he had withheld his A. Jay cartoon strip *Harry Chess* from *Drummer* 29, page 24. He forced Embry—who had little graphic novel, or cartoon strip, backfill on file—to publish the full-page notice on page 24 that "Harry Chess and His Fugg Pals Are on Vacation...But Will Be Back in the Next Issue [if negotiations go well]."

Embry had turned slow-pay into no-pay. He claimed *Drummer* was always totally broke.

At that, I suggested he contact the Mafia.

His face nearly exploded.

I was not really kidding when I offered the advice: "Everyone knows the Mafia runs gay bars and gay publishing. The Mafia ran the Stonewall Inn. Mafia magazines make money. If you need the Mafia to keep *Drummer* going, here's a dime. Call them."

Embry looked at me in shock.

I wasn't Pinocchio needing Geppetto to shout: "Save yourself!"

I wasn't a puppet.

I was a real boy.

BREAKING UP IS HARD TO DO:
CAN A GRUDGE BECOME A BLACKLIST?

The always calm, mild, and non-confrontational Al Shapiro quietly began packing up his art-director supplies, and he and I spent most of the next months exiting together, followed by a long list of talented friends. All during the sixty days of that autumn of 1979, *Drummer* seemed like the Eagles song, "Hotel California" where "you can check in but you can never leave." Or you leave slowly, like "Harry Chess," in bits and pieces the way *Drummer* itself had fled LA in a hundred carloads to move to San Francisco. Gay life was exactly like track after track of the album *Hotel California*: "New Kid in Town," "Life in the Fast Lane," and "Wasted Time." It was the soundtrack of the Titanic 70s, and one of top-ten best-selling albums of the twentieth century. It played continuously in bars and baths and in our heads.

Recorded in late 1976, it was the perfect score for the three dramatic years, 1977-1979, when I was anchored into that leather-self-invention decade as editor-in-chief of *Drummer*. I could not resist honoring the Eagles' insight into the way we were. It was historically essential to quote the lyrics of "Hotel California" for the title of *Some Dance to Remember: A Memoir-Novel of San Francisco 1970-1982*.

Drummer 30 was my last official issue, although I also edited *Drummer* 31, 32, and 33 from which my byline and some of my work were removed.

Drummer 32 was Al Shapiro's last official issue.

In *Drummer* 33, Al Shapiro's name had also been replaced on the masthead, although, for historical accuracy, both his work and mine, as noted, ended inside *Drummer* 33.

A. Jay, who had been art director for *Queen's Quarterly* in the 1960s, immediately went on to his next successful career as art director for the famous "Dirty Frenchman" at Le Salon bookstore on Polk Street.

Real-estate entrepreneur Embry wasted no time launching a grudge against A. Jay who continued to draw his cartoon characters for Le Salon marketing brochures. Ever jealous, Embry immediately claimed ownership to the copyright of *Harry Chess*. A light laughter drifted like fog across the Bay.

In *Drummer* 34, the second issue after A. Jay's exit, Embry tried to make Al disappear the way he had subtracted Jeanne Barney and me after our exits in *Drummer* 11 and *Drummer* 30 respectively. With no shame, Embry, the claim jumper, deleted A. Jay's name from his own bylined cartoon strip when Embry dared publish four pages of Al's signature brainchild, *Harry Chess*. He trumpeted that he had cut a deal with *Queen's Quarterly* who, as Al explained in a threatened lawsuit against Embry, had no ownership over his cartoon strip which he had created, not as a paid worker, but as a freelance contributor, even while he was the *QQ* art director. At the moment of publishing this theft of intellectual property, Embry was liar-liar, pants on fire. Selling his ill-gotten gains to subscribers, he wrote the following big, fat, dialogue balloon, vengefully making no mention of the famous A. Jay, hoping the corporate bravado of his Alternate Publishing could steal away Al's rights so Embry could not only print the cartoon strip in *Drummer* but also exploit *Harry Chess* in its own special book.

> HARRY CHESS. *Drummer* has made arrangements with *QQ* magazine for their complete collection of everybody's ideal American Boy, Harry Chess! It seems like a good idea to begin at the beginning of Harry's exciting history, and so we shall. These

installments, along with the more current ones that *Drummer* has published, will, with any luck, be put together into a book of the Complete Harry Chess...

On March 28, 1980, I wrote a letter to my LA friend Bob Johnson to whom I provided short erotic fiction. He had created a lucrative career packaging porno magazines for George Mavety at Modernismo Publishing in New Jersey:

Dear Bob, Dirt Time: John Embry, according to Al Shapiro (author/creator of *Harry Chess*) is threatening to sue Le Salon for bringing out Al's complete *Harry*. Al has a letter from *Queen's Quarterly* [the original publisher of the first installments of *Harry*] stating that he [Shapiro] remains the owner of the strip, and can produce his own version whenever. Meantime, it seems Embry has bought tearsheets out of old *QQs* and is now running them in *Drummer* as if they are new work, even though the quality of repro is down several notches because of the genesis of the artwork. I recall your telling me how you smelled rats-around-the Embry-o when the Big *D* [*Drummer*] was still aborning in LA. You remember, of course, how Embry stiffed me. Ah, life. I'm glad our interconnections remain clear in this world of seeming cutthroats.

At the end of Al's life, just before AIDS blinded him, he penned for me his last drawing which I cherish to this day, as told in my "Obituary for Al Shapiro," *Drummer* 107 (August 1987).

Drummer 31 was the last *Drummer* issue published at 1730 Divisadero Street. As Al and I were finally ankling the joint, Embry announced that he was moving the office from the rented Divisadero Victorian to his newly purchased building South of Market at 15 Harriet Street whose garage, stuffed with back issues, already housed the boy-lesque *Stars Magazine* and its publisher Glenn Turner who was funded by Reuben Sturman, the "Father of the Adult Industry"—if not the godfather. Were the new digs conjured by an act of gay magic? Had the money come from Mafia investors? Would the move to South of Market cancel financial problems the way his moving from LA had kept *Drummer* one step ahead of the cops, the censors, the printers, and the talent asking for pay?

We had gifted Embry with a new concept of *Drummer* that would endure as the magazine's archetype of identity throughout the rest of the century. We had a hit on our hands. What was the matter with him? As Gertrude

Stein said of William Saroyan, "He cannot stand the weight of being great." With his Blacklist, Embry became the greatest censor of *Drummer*.

CALLING THE NEXT EYEWITNESSES TO THE STAND: ROBERT DAVOLT, STEVEN SAYLOR, RICK LEATHERS

In a 2000 interview at leatherweb.com, Robert Davolt testified to a truism that began with Embry's ownership of *Drummer*:

> Many people in town were pissed off at *Drummer* for various reasons (some of them pretty good reasons)....*Drummer* was 'both revered and reviled....I...was dealing with some past baggage, some hostility, some criticism, and some doubts.

Steven Saylor (Aaron Travis), who after my exit worked as a fiction department editor for Embry under Rowberry, seemed to understand completely the madness Al Shapiro and I had endured. Saylor, regarding his own "take" on Embry's next act at 15 Harriet Street *Drummer*, wrote in Scott O'Hara's magazine, *Steam*:

> Working at Alternate [Publishing aka *Drummer*] was alternately [*sic*] mind-boggling and mind-numbing—we were underpaid, disrespected and overstimulated on a daily basis—and John [Rowberry, Fritscher's successor] was the eye of the hurricane. *Mediating between publisher John Embry and everyone else required extraordinary finesse, coupled with a will of iron.* [Italics added] (*Steam*, Volume 2 #1, Spring 1994, page 101)

Prolific journalist Rick Leathers (aka Mike Leathers aka Dane Leathers) began working at the *Drummer* office for Embry in 1980, and continued off and on for nineteen years in Embry's employ at Alternate Publishing as Embry's assistant and as one of the main contributors to Embry's various magazines with essays such as his homomasculine series, "Leather in the 90s."

Writing January 1, 2006, in his email essay about *Drummer* titled "That Was the Mag That Was," Rick Leathers included history and allegations which were his own that:

> While in a porn store in Little Rock in 1979, I'd picked up an odd mag called *Drummer* that tickled my frenzy. So I packed up and headed for California where the damn thing had been published.

After many adventures in San Diego's Marine shit-chutes, I wandered up to San Francisco and worked in a leather bar, then a leather shop, then for John Embry at *Drummer*. Jack Fritscher had taken Embry's soft-core mag and made it gritty (and saleable), but they had clashed too often, and Fritscher had departed just before I hired on. Embry was a self-defeating wacko with a monumental temper, but he had the cunning and the cash (plus the Mafia contacts) to keep cranking out issues (though always long past the deadlines). Problem was, with Fritscher gone, most of the mags were just that—dead lines, very dead. Embry gave *Drummer* form, but it needed Fritscher to add the content. The big gap was that Embry wanted campy humor, but Fritscher was focused on fleshing out a new word he had added to the English language—*homomasculinity*: the display of manly attributes by men for other men.

Rick Leathers was correct about the content. Because of Embry's Blacklist, I could not offer early 1980s *Drummer* my evolving cycles of ongoing leather articles, gender-identity fiction, and fetish photography. So the substantial lot of my 1980s writing on leather and fetish was published by other editors in the emerging new vanilla magazines that liked to stir in the leather spice of a *Drummer*-style story. When my editor Bob Johnson flamed out on cocaine and died high in his apartment overlooking the Sunset Strip, John Rowberry, fired from *Drummer* by Embry, replaced Johnson at George Mavety's Modernismo Publishing. Duty-bound to package six magazines monthly for the gay-friendly Mavety who three months before the first issue of *Drummer* had founded *Mandate* magazine in March 1975, Rowberry bought around thirty of my virtual *Drummer* stories for Mavety magazines such as *Skin*, *Skinflicks*, *Uncut*, and *Inches*. Mavety, who reputedly fathered a dozen children, also founded dozens of gay magazines including *Playguy* and *Honcho* which Embry envied as his main competition. Mavety's Modernismo broke the embargo of Embry's Blacklist when, beginning in 1980, Johnson and then Rowberry published stories like my six-chapter novelization of the film *J. Brian's Flashbacks* in *Honcho* and my novella *Titanic* in *Uncut*. When Larry Townsend pulled his advice column published in *Drummer* from 1980-1992, he moved it to *Honcho* where it ran until four weeks before his death in 2008. The only thing Mavety and Embry had in common was their pornographer's zeal for turning magazine profits into real estate holdings.

Considering the undertow of Mafia and gay connections, I think of eleven years of tales of the City told me by my longtime best friend, the native San Francisco Italian leather-guru, Tony Tavarossi (*Drummer* 131). He and I were intimate pals from 1970 to his death in 1981 when he was the first "leather star" personality to die of a mysterious illness no one could name. In the 1950s, he worked in Tenderloin drag bars, instinctively absorbing management skills. He soon attracted the attention of a Mafia guido, and even though he could not be "connected" like a "made man" because he was gay, he became a familiar. The mob flew him to New Jersey to assess a leather bar that had sprung up in New York. Like a good *paisan*, Tony flew back to the Tenderloin, and with discreet backing opened the first dedicated leather bar in San Francisco in 1962 (*Drummer* 131). He was twenty-eight and cool. To name his bar, he reversed the spelling of his first name, added a question mark, and dubbed his "mambo Italiano" pub Tony's "YNOT?" aka "Why Not?" In 1961, an undercover cop entrapped Tony in his own bar, and the SFPD closed it down. Such victimization led immediately to the founding of San Francisco's Tavern Guild to protect bar owners and patrons from harassment. Mob support benefitted Tony. His lesson was not lost on me. When I made my joke to Embry about calling the Mafia to fund *Drummer*, did I accidentally hit a sore spot?

Why did he react so explosively?

Was it because he wasn't "connected," or because he was?

His longtime employee and confidante, Frank Hatfield aka *Drummer* author Frank O'Rourke, who ran Embry's mail-order business was a self-confessed ex-con who liked to brag of his long association, twenty years before, with Mafia boss Meyer Lansky in Miami and Havana before Fidel Castro seized Cuba and drove out the mob in 1959.

One must really consider: Was Embry Mafia?

The principle difference between the Mafia and Embry was that the Mafia was *organized* crime.

Glenn Turner, publisher of the chicken magazine *Stars*, who rented part of the Harriet Street *Drummer* building owned by Embry was alleged to be "connected." Turner's rumored racketeer ties may have been inevitable gossip in the modern gay world where tough young Mafia guidos have long been a hot urban sex fetish akin to the pastoral sex fetish of Sicilian teenagers romanticized by 19th and 20th-century gay photographers like Wilhelm von Gloeden and authors like E. M. Forster with his Italianate interests, and Tennessee Williams in *The Rose Tattoo* and *The Roman Spring of Mrs. Stone*. That arty and literary crowd of sex tourists framed the 20th-century concept of Italian hustlers on the down low as smouldering sex objects igniting gay erotic fantasies. In England, Evelyn Waugh's friend, the writer Sir Harold Acton glamorized the lubricious appeal of Sicilian sexuality and the romancing of guidos when he stated that "Taormina is a polite synonym for Sodom." In the 1930s, Italian dictator Benito Mussolini, calling this erotic stereotype of young Italian males "pornography," sent his Fascist police to destroy von Gloeden's glass negatives in much the same way as Senator Jesse Helms tried to destroy the photographs of the most famous leatherman who ever lived, Robert Mapplethorpe.

In the controversial crime drama *Flipping* (1997), a handsome undercover cop falls for the muscular wise guy he meets in a toilet. This very *Drummer* plot builds on dramatic gay-and-Mafia "archetypes" rather than cop-and-gangster "stereotypes." It reveals the psychology of homomasculine love in the male world of back-slapping Mafiosi. The film itself was for a long time unavailable because of a scandal reported to be about its funding and distribution which was a mob-style way of censoring the gay guido storyline.

The Mafia have played an erotic shadow show inside gay culture for more than a century. The Genovese Family owned the Stonewall Inn which was managed by Matty "The Horse" Ianniello who was the Boss of the West Side. He made cash money off "lewd and lascivious" gay behavior and paid off the NYPD for that privilege until cops, not on the take, busted the bar looking for evidence of mob activity. In the perspective of that June 27-28, 1969, raid, gays were, to both the cops and the mob, merely collateral damage—until the patrons seized the moment to strike back against police brutality.

From 1976-1985, the mob ran the legendary Mineshaft bar which, because of the sensational torture-murder of several patrons, figured docudramatically in the leather-guido plot of the gay film, *Cruising*, directed by William Friedkin who said of Ianniello:

> He was a guy I knew.... Virtually every business on the West Side of New York was either owned or partially owned by him or paying him protection. I asked him if I could film in the clubs. I went down there and saw a number of people I knew and they allowed me to film. They had no problems with me filming in there with Al Pacino." ("The Queerty Interview of William Friedkin" by Jeremy Kinser, Queerty.com, June 16, 2015)

In my historical story titled "Stonewall, June 27, 1969, 11 PM," the drag queens brag about Mafia sex inside the Stonewall bar. The quotation is from the *Harrington Gay Men's Fiction Quarterly*, Volume 8, Issue 1:

"This place [the Stonewall Inn] only looks like a gay bar. It's really an eye-talian bar."

Norma Dessun has a secret taste for linguiça sausage which she indulges starting late one night—early last spring—when the lone guido closing the bar, like, leans back against the cash register and unzips his black gabardine slacks which causes Norma's knees to grow so weak she takes the uncut invitation deep down her throat and hums thirty bars of "Come Back to Sorrento."

The guido's shirt hangs open by three buttons. Around his neck, a gold chain rests in the tangle of thick black hair on his pumped chest. Hot enough himself he's made hotter by the thought of the powerful anonymous interests he works for.

It isn't so much that the guido lies and tells Norma he'll tap her head before he cums (in her mouth) that disturbs Norma.

It's more the gun that Norma's fingers feel strapped to the husky guido's right calf that cautions her to barely mention what was for some weeks an unspoken date that always ended ("Mambo Siciliano") with the guido getting off squeezing Norma's cheeks to make sure she swallows his eye-talian ice.

"That's his trip," Norma says. "I tell him, I don't know who you work for, but I know *you*."

In leather fantasy, swarthy Mafiosi are objects of S&M desire. One of the best of my Palm Drive models re-named himself "Donnie Russo," because he wanted to assume the erotic identity of "a guido in a wife-beater tank top" in my videos *Homme Alone* and *Rough Night at the Jockstrap Gym*. The Jersey Shore image he cultivated had long fit into gay culture as a fetish category of muscular Mafiosi in suits with guns and cigars and baseball bats. In the 1990s, as Francis Ford Coppola resurrected his 1970s Oscar-winning franchise with *Godfather III*, I helped Russo resurrect the 1970s gay fascination with Robert DeNiro in a wife-beater playing the sexy young Don Corleone (*Godfather II*,1974) as well as the Sicilian-American boxer, Jake LaMotta (*Raging Bull*, 1980) who threw a fight to gain favor with the Mafia. My erotic documentary photographs of Donnie Russo were published on the cover and inside pages of *Drummer* 170 (December 1993); in the British coffee-table photobook *American Men*, pages 1, 14, 15, and 21 (1995); and on the cover of *Eagle Magazine*, issue 4 (July1996), published by Dave Rhodes, founder of *The Leather Journal*.

In this Mafia helix, I remember quite clearly that in 1981, Mapplethorpe photographed the homosexual crook, Roy Cohn, who as an anti-gay Fascist in the 1950s worked as HUAC pit bull for the hate-filled Republican Senator Joe McCarthy. Through the 1960s, 1970s, and 1980s, the Jewish Cohn worked as a lawyer for the Italian Mafia and the Roman Catholic Church. Tony Kushner dramatized the homophobic queer Cohn, who died of AIDS in 1986, in *Angels in America*.

APPENDIX

The Difference Between the Italian Mafia and the Leather Family

Tony Tavarossi and Chuck Renslow

1

Star Bartender: Tony Tavarossi
by Jack Fritscher
Bay Area Reporter, BARtab, May 2011, page 30

Born to be a bar star in the Mission District (1933-1981), Tony Tavarossi came out at age twelve giving blow jobs under the tables in the curtained booths of the South China Café at 4133 18th Street and Castro, next door to 4127 18th which, sixty-five years later, would become the GLBT Historical Society museum. It was war's end: 1945. San Francisco surged with carousing soldiers and sailors. As a rebellious Catholic boy, Tony relished being a Sagittarius archer hunting masculine wild things. Cruising waterfront bars that would soon be demolished for the new Embarcadero Freeway, teenager Tony became a one-man USO, learning a lesson on his knees about entertaining the troops.

Long before turning 21, he worked bars in the 1950s Tenderloin, instinctively absorbing management skills and attracting the attention of a Mafia guido who squired him in 1961 to fly to New York to see if the rapidly masculinizing "hard" bars might translate to lyrical San Francisco. Not "connected" because he was gay, Tony was nevertheless an Italian with "backing." He reckoned that the new bar concept would travel. Popularly known for his BDSM games, particularly his role in popularizing fisting, his bar ideas were commercial extensions of private sexuality: performance stages where players could both lose and find themselves in backroom gloryholes with slings. So in 1962, age 28, coding his name backwards, he became the "owner" of San Francisco's first dedicated leather bar "Tony's

Why Not?" at 517 Ellis in the Tenderloin. Within six months in 1962, the SFPD closed the Why Not? when Tony himself was entrapped in his own bar. That arrest, contributing to the founding of the Tavern Guild (1962), made him, like Jose Sarria, a popular local personality years before the rebellions at Compton's Cafeteria (1966) and Stonewall (1969).

San Francisco was awakening. North of Market Street, the neon Tenderloin was too policed. South of Market, the dark industrial area looked outlaw. The leather crowd migrated from NoMa to SoMa. In 1962, having promised sex-tourist Chuck Arnett a job during the run of the Why Not?, Tony found him other work when in 1963 the Louisiana-born Arnett returned to San Francisco. Expert at networking, Tony steered him forward to a creative job at the Tool Box. Having apprenticed under leather artist Etienne at Chuck Renslow's Gold Coast bar, Arnett debuted by painting his iconic mural and became the star artist of Folsom Street even as Tony became a star serving on the creative crews of nearly every bar and bath South of Market in the Swinging 1960s and Titanic 1970s.

With other players crashing in the hippie-leather flat over the Stud bar near Febe's, Arnett imported the psychedelic drugs of the Haight-Ashbury to Folsom Street. During the sex wars of gay lib, bartenders often prescribed the recreational medication needed to survive the battles. Dispensing purposed party favors in bars, Chuck and Tony and their friend Jack Haines introduced fisting as a new sport. According to eyewitness bar stories, Tony had been one of the first men fisted in recorded modern times. In fact, he told me that in 1960, two Marines had hung him upside down in a shower in an Oceanside motel and plunged on in through his cherry. By 1963, Jack and Tony were hosting fisting parties at 111 Gilbert Street in a SoMa warehouse where Jack's father cleaned and restored used refrigerators and stoves. By 1974, Tony was tutoring newcomer Steve McEachern who opened his legendary Catacombs fisting palace in May 1975. In 1977, I shot Super-8 films of Tony fisting a bottom tied butt-up in the wooden stocks in room 226 at the Slot. Folsom Street sexuality rode on Tony's fist and forearm. In the free spirit of the times, he liked nothing better than seducing "virgins" into anything they had never done before.

In 1978 when the SFPD asked me as the editor of *Drummer* to take the current crop of police rookies on a "freshman orientation" tour of Folsom Street, I arranged with Tony to give them some sensitivity training at the Slot Hotel. When Tony on the loudspeaker announced as a courtesy that the expected police were in the house, the doors of nearly every room opened fast and wide with exhibitionist leather twosomes and threesomes competing to be outrageous. Halfway through the fifteen-minute tour, one of the young cops swooned and his buddies carried him to the lobby to revive him, but when he came to, he was still in the Slot and Tony was holding a wet cloth to his face, and he fainted again to much laughter.

For eleven years (1970-1981), Tony and I were friends and sex playmates. I adored Tony's allure. At a swarthy 5-5, 130 pounds, uncut, he was a bearded Sicilian Pan without limits. His natural sensuality was rooted in his infancy thanks to his mother who soothed his sweet temperament by rubbing olive oil circles slowly between his cock and his beautiful Italian foreskin. Living in a scrupulously clean apartment with a wild playroom at 288 Central Avenue at Oak Street, he was a bottom specializing in "topping tops to renew them" as long as they at least tried to top his redoubtable rear in return: fist for fist. That bar-culture cover story "saved face" for his tricks and made him the most popular bartender in town. His tip jars overflowed. Apace with Gertrude Stein, his apartment was filled with drawings, paintings, and photographs from the salon of his creative friends, and from his erotic fans. Lou Rudolph, who was famous for sketching men in Folsom bars, often inked Tony on his large archival watercolor pads.

Tony was a sweet, romantic man, unspoiled by American education. At our first meeting in 1970, he frightened me, the teacher, because he was six years older and was far more pagan, street smart, and sexually sophisticated. I was ashamed that I noticed he was from the underclass and I was middle-class. It took nearly six months of watching him as a bartender beloved in public spaces for me to get over my class consciousness and surrender to his Dionysian style of primal sex. Savvy bartenders always know what's new and what's next, and Tony tutored generations of bar workers during his thirty years of active service. His imprint may still be felt.

After four years of playing together and learning each other's transcendental turn-ons, he wrote me a love note which he hand delivered. In all its longing sincerity, the note reads as if he were channeling Chaucer, with his choice spellings and initial capitalizations, from a wilder "medieval" past. Why not toy with some over-thinking of the reincarnation Tony believed in? From 1967 onwards, bar jukeboxes played Procul Harum quoting the "Miller's Tale" in "A Whiter Shade of Pale." And wasn't Harry Bailey, the host in *The Canterbury Tales*, a bartender? No wonder that Edward III rewarded Chaucer "with a gallon of wine daily for the rest of his life."

> Somthing To Think about;
> I would like to have you see me in pain!
> Having you see me, and hereing me in Pain.
> To see the sweet balls Pop all over me, and

to smell the Pain grow in me more, and more.
Mouth should drink from your juice cock, and
see you sit on my mouth as I ake in Pane.
Having my tongue dig in to you
as you show more parts of me to feel you.
Your ass should muffel my crys, and
having me suck on your ass hole and
when my cock sit up and hard,
Your hands and mine will Tuch my sole and
dance on my braine and you will know
that I am a brother of Pain and
you are the giver of Pain. And
in that I will show you my love of you and
Please you if you let me.
—Tony

In 1981, the fabled Barracks baths burned down slamming the Titanic 1970s to symbolic close. Tony had worked at the Barracks and its Red Star Saloon. Collapsing with shingles and shigella, he had been admitted to San Francisco General where I visited him in ICU. Unable to speak, he was alert. Because one Barracks manager had crossed him, I tried cheering him with the karma he loved: "The Barracks burned down yesterday. It's the end of an era." Reaching for pencil and paper, he scrawled, "Good." In the hall, I asked his doctor, "What's wrong with him?" She said, "We don't know. We've never seen a patient so distressed." No one had yet heard of AIDS. Tony Tavarossi died the next day, July 12, 1981. He was loved. His funeral was enormous.

In 2010 when the San Francisco Planning Commission queried me for suggestions about recognizing and protecting the GLBTQ social heritage of South of Market, I recommended that a street might be named to honor Tony Tavarossi who for all the Folsom fun and games was one of those bartenders who are front-line inventors and caretakers of gay society. His name, and the names of the other SoMa friends I nominated, such as Anthony DeBlase, Thom Gunn, Robert Opel, Mister Marcus, Ron Johnson, Robert Mapplethorpe, and Hank Diethelm, were included in the booklet published by the Western SoMa Task Citizens Planning Task Force, *Recognizing, Protecting and Memorializing South of Market LGBTQ Social Heritage Neighborhood Resources*, March 2010.

2

Who's Your Big Daddy?
Chuck Renslow
by Jack Fritscher
Bay Area Reporter, June 9-15, 2011, page 37

Leatherman: The Legend of Chuck Renslow
by Tracy Baim and Owen Keehnen, Prairie Avenue Productions, 300 Illustrations, $24.99

In *Casablanca*, "Sooner or later everybody comes to Rick's." In Chicago, the world comes to Chuck's. Since 1950, Chuck Renslow, now 82, and one of the most famous gay men on the planet, has safely hosted thousands of GLBT visitors at his thirty venues from his legendary Gold Coast bar (1960-88), to his International Mr. Leather Contest (1979), and his prestigious Leather Archives & Museum (1991). For sixty years, Renslow, a politically aggressive Democrat in the Chicago Machine, has been a person of interest to cops, politicians, fans, and frenemies.

Rather than review *Leatherman*, I can best, as a SoMa historian, serve as local tour guide to this bespoke book with its candid backstage drama of leathermen, lesbians, and Mafia wise-guys shaping homoculture two decades before Stonewall. I came out on Renslow's 1950s Kris Studio photography and his Gold Coast where, beginning a ten-year union, I married his handsome bartender, photographer David Sparrow. As eyewitness, I appreciate the authenticity of *Leatherman* into which my two-bits was invited by leather-village griots Owen Keehnen and Tracy Baim.

Renslow's strategic business mind led gays politically into a new age. He saw first what others only saw eventually. As an occult practitioner of magical thinking, he intuited the private necessity of coming out, and the public necessity of founding safe venues to do it. Starting Kris Studio (1953), he first courted homomasculine men by creating butch social destinations which he eventually diversified to all genders: his 2010 IML winner was FTM wheel-charioteer Tyler McCormick. Pioneering locally, he built a nationally sustainable model proving gay-owned businesses key to building community, politics, and social networks. Born a year before Harvey Milk, and politically active twenty years before Milk hit Castro, Chicago-native Renslow evolved an early 1950s heartland leathersex identity that defied city, state, and federal laws.

In 1954, with lifelong muse, Dom Orejudos, the artist "Etienne," he bought Triumph gym, photographed musclemen, created magazines, was busted by the Post Office for mailing obscene material, and helped push toward the Supreme Court decision that frontal nudity could be sent via US mail. Without that 1967 ruling, subscription mailing of 1970s sex-identity publications could not have reached readers, and *Drummer* would never have become San Francisco's longest-running gay magazine.

Synergizing business with art, Renslow's pre-Stonewall Chicago style, driven by his can-do "Renslow Family," helped stimulate San Francisco's 1970s immigrant boom. For instance, Etienne, Renslow's esthetician, painted the Gold Coast walls re-conceptualizing bars as galleries, beginning the Muralist Movement whose "Rushmore Four" included Tom of Finland, *Drummer* art director A. Jay, and SoMa's Chuck Arnett whom Robert Opel and I dubbed *Drummer*'s "Lautrec in Leather." In 1962, Etienne tutored Arnett who, speeding off to San Francisco, painted his avatar mural at the Tool Box. When *Life* magazine pictured that mural, five years before Stonewall, it invited gays nationwide to bring all regional lifestyles to melt in San Francisco's pot.

Within the extended Renslow Family, B.A.R. columnist Mister Marcus regularly alerted western readers to Renslow's Midwestern entertainments from his annual White Party to Castro diva Sylvester singing on Renslow's "K-Y Circuit" stages. As an IML judge for 28 years, Marcus flew to O'Hare with San Francisco entourages, often including Folsom's divine IML emcee Queen Cougar. Always, folks returned to SFO energized in local activism by the annual leather-family reunion that is IML. After winning "Mr. IML 1985," San Francisco's Patrick Toner, using that celebrity, established the AIDS fund-raiser, the Dore Alley Fair. In 1991, Renslow and Anthony DeBlase, the San Francisco publisher of *Drummer*, and creator of the Leather Pride Flag, founded the IML Trust-funded Leather Archives & Museum with Joseph Bean, editor of San Francisco's *Bear* magazine, as executive director.

In 1978, creating SoMa's first gallery, Oscar streaker Robert Opel chose veterans Etienne and A. Jay to launch Fey-Way Studio's opening exhibit featuring emerging talent like Robert Mapplethorpe who told me, when assigning him his first magazine cover (*Drummer* 24), how his own 1970s photography was influenced by the 1950s beefcake of Renslow who was "genius at lighting his models."

Becoming *Drummer* editor, I purposely injected Renslow's masculine, but not separatist, heartland values into the founding of that magazine that helped create the very San Francisco leather culture it reported on. *Drummer* 9 featured the "Gold Coast 15th Anniversary," and, imitating Renslow's first IML, *Drummer* kick-started the Mr. Drummer Contest which soon anchored the Folsom Fair. In 1980, Renslow's business manager Patrick Batt moved to San Francisco, helped Bob Damron found the Eagle bar, and became business manager of *Drummer* during our editorial shift to safe sex.

Forthrightly, *Leatherman* dares dish dirt, such as how the rift between thwarted S&M lovers Renslow and Sam Steward, both filmed separately by Kinsey, caused Steward to move his Chicago tattoo parlor to Oakland (1964), establishing Steward as famous San Francisco author "Phil Andros." And those are just some local GPS links to this entertaining documentary about 20th-century gay American history.

DRUMMER
ISSUE 118

4^{95}

NEW IN DRUMMER
COLOR NUDES

FETISH FEATURE
RUBBER
JACK FRITSCHER
CONFESSIONS OF A RUBBER FREAK

FICTION
PENAL COLONY FLOGGING

AN INDIAN TRUCKER'S REVENGE

Cover Photograph
by Jack Fritscher

CHAPTER 9

STEALING *DRUMMER*
AN ORIGIN STORY OF GAY MAIL-ORDER

- Copyright War: Protecting Writers, Photographers, Artists, and Heirs
- David Begelman: Hollywood Studio "Money Scandal" Impacts San Francisco *Drummer*
- Richard Locke and Daddies: Turning a Man's Age into Erotic Fetish
- Gay Culture: Entrapped by Law and Then by AIDS
- Mail-Order Pioneers Create 20th-Century Gay Popular Culture:
    Bob Mizer, AMG Studio
    Chuck Renslow and Etienne, Kris Studio
    Larry Townsend, LT Publications
    David Hurles, Old Reliable Studio
- Author Daniel Curzon: An Eyewitness to History Testifies about Publisher Embry

> "We were fools to buy *Drummer*."
> —Anthony F. DeBlase, Letter to Jack Fritscher, 1988

Since the advent of the internet, scan-and-post poachers have continually sniffed around the contents of *Drummer* because there is a popular misconception that everything gay is somehow "gay community property."

From *Drummer* 1 to *Drummer* 214, as far as I know about other authors, photographers, and friends whom I published, and certainly I know about myself, *Drummer* bought only one-time First North American print publication rights. It did not buy second reprint rights, and, certainly, not electronic rights that would allow *Drummer* or anyone else, for instance, to scan a page of *Drummer* and post it on the web.

The principle of "fair use" is a minimalist law.

As the owner of Alternate Publishing, Embry wrote specifically in his *Manifest Reader* 11 (1995) about the intellectual property rights he typically purchased while he owned *Drummer*. Interviewing himself twice-over, both as the "Alternate" asking the questions, and as "Embry" providing the answers, he wrote specifically about the magnificent cartoon panels of the British artist, Bill Ward, but he extrapolated to all the rest of the art and writing he rented for *Drummer*:

> This work [Ward's art] was furnished to his publishers on a one-time publication basis, known as First North American Rights, then the originals go back to the artist. In the case of Bill Ward, re-shipping was hazardous because of British censors [vaguely true, but more revelatory of *Drummer* rarely bothering to send originals back to anyone] and the art was retained on file [that is, kept by Embry] on his behalf....[In the call and response of this interview, he here changes voices to interview himself under his own name.] *Manifest*'s publisher John Embry says, "What we have of Bill Ward's art is safely on file here [still with Embry, nine years after he sold *Drummer*]. It is available to him anytime he [at his advanced age and poor health and living in Britain] wishes. That was the arrangement made then, and it remains the same today, identical to virtually every other arrangement we have with any artist."

From Anthony DeBlase, I possess legally signed paperwork of the limited rights I assigned *Drummer*. Bedeviled by debt and censorship, DeBlase wrote, over his partner Anthony (Andy) Charles's signature, on September 4, 1988:

> Enclosed you will find the statement you requested about your manuscript rights and photo rights. Andy and I both thank you for your kind comments about *Drummer*. The political climate [of censorship] continues to hurt us economically, as I'm sure it does you. Your comment about the need to possess a clear statement of rights in case of sale of the mags amuses me. At this point the sale of the mags/business is a "consummation devoutly to be wished" but no one would be fool enough, as we were, to buy it!

As an eyewitness of what I observed at *Drummer*, I can only speculate on some of the financial secrets behind the scenes. Except insofar as I had to deal daily and practically with *Drummer*'s cash-flow problems, I have no ledgers on what Embry or DeBlase or Bakker did personally with the money which was their business. My questions are keen only because dollar bills tortured *Drummer* to die the death of a thousand paper cuts.

There are many stories about *Drummer*, but there is one chapter in *Drummer* history that few know, and it connects *Drummer* to the infamous David Begelman embezzlement scandal at Columbia Pictures that was one of the biggest media stories of the late 1970s. What I write here I write allegedly.

In San Francisco in 1977, Embry imported from his posse of LA cronies a certain "Dick Caudillo" whom he hired as a business manager with the title "Assistant to the Publisher." At the Divisadero office meeting in which Embry introduced "my friend Dick Caudillo who formerly worked at Columbia," the seven of us staffers sniffed because the smell in the room went "off." Caudillo was famously one of Begelman's accountants; and there was nothing funny or flattering about any gay connection to the financial crimes.

In addition, hard on the heels of Embry's LA attitude, Caudillo's LA attitude, the moment he spoke, immediately bombed. I remember on that afternoon I purposely sat by the door, inside Embry's office, on the arm of his red couch. Having been briefed beforehand by Embry whose choice shocked me, I did not want to go further into his office, and I did not want to sit down, and I gave off my own attitude as editor-in-chief. *Piso mojado!* A pissing contest had begun. All we staff of insouciant leathermen cast side-eye glances at each other, smirking at Caudillo, wondering like Mart Crowley in *The Boys in the Band*, "Who is she? Who was she? Who does she hope to be?" Al Shapiro afterwards said, "'Dick Caudillo' sounds like a porn name."

When I told Embry to dump Caudillo fast, he invoked an odd loyalty. He claimed he had met Caudillo for the first time—in jail—the night they were both arrested at the Drummer Slave Auction one year before. Embry, reminiscing at the turn of the 21st-century, wrote about the group of them locked into the same cell.

> Included in my group was Fred Halsted, Terry LeGrand and a couple of his filmmaker associates, along with a newcomer Richard Caudillo, who gave me his business card. It said that he was with Columbia Pictures and I thought it strange at the time that he was handing them out in jail. —*Super MR* #1, (2000), page 36

Caudillo means *leader* in Spanish, but in the office Caudillo's "leadership" was little more than the kind of nagging that square accountants do who do not understand how to work with staff hired to be creative. For the next two months the personally (to all of us) loathsome Caudillo was the fly in the ointment until the night *Drummer* was burgled and the typesetting machine that Marge Anderson had driven up from LA was stolen along with other items necessary to the production of *Drummer*. We were robbed. Our little sanctuary of art and sex had been invaded. Alarmed, I asked Embry, "Have you called the cops?" He said, "No." I asked, "Why not?" He shrugged mysteriously and walked away.

That broke one bond of trust. A publisher should be a protector giving artists and writers and staff safe space to create. In that den of thieves, I was not about to leave my manuscripts and my Fritscher-Sparrow photographs in a desk in a *tres* gay office to which so many temporary boyfriends and momentary slaves and disgruntled employees had keys.

From all that the media has written about Begelman and Caudillo, who was guilty and who was innocent? Was Begelman Mafia? The book *Indecent Exposure: The True Story of Hollywood and Wall Street* written by David McClintick characterizes Caudillo as a bureaucrat, "a stocky man in his early thirties with thinning hair...who rather enjoyed pricking wealthy show-business personalities with little government forms." (Pages 9 and 10) While Caudillo was pricking us *unpaid* mag-business workers with cost-cutting concerns meaningful only to bean counters, my concern was only how the creative side of *Drummer* could continue because so many of our monthly contributors, like Ed Franklin, were beginning to hold their future writing and pictures hostage for want of back pay. Caudillo's boss Begelman had led a long, secret life as a thief who had also tried to shake down stars like Judy Garland until Oscar winner Cliff Robertson called the cops. In the 1960s, Begelman had been Garland's agent at his company Freddie Fields Associates. He was also the suicidal Garland's lover who bandaged her wrists and pushed her out on stage to sing live.

No one can even allege that Caudillo was the thief who burgled *Drummer*; but, Caudillo seemed a nasty moment in time. I found out later that during 1976 he was president of the "ACLU Gay Rights Chapter of Southern California" which, if he were like Embry infiltrating the H.E.L.P. organization, seemed little more than a political maneuver to drum up business contacts. Did he bring out a deeper venality in Embry? From Caudillo's first arrival, the publicity hungry Embry bragged that Caudillo was "a star in a big Hollywood scandal." It was on the nightly news for months. The complicated legal case involving the IRS whipped up a variety of media speculation including the laundering of Mafia money and embezzlement. Who knows the truth of what Caudillo did or did not do before, during, or after *Drummer*, but several books and articles pro and con have investigated the complicated scandal.

When a certain "Informant," supposedly from inside Columbia Pictures, alleged his own eyewitness memory of what he says Caudillo was like as an office manager at the Hollywood studio, he seemed to reveal specifically almost exactly what we witnessed generically at *Drummer* where the staff never knew what was going on with Embry's latest schemes and his shell games around money, travel, and real estate. As reported in the May 10, 1978, *Los Angeles Herald-Examiner*, Bill Dakota, editor of the *Hollywood Star* tabloid, recorded a telephone conversation with an Informant claiming to be an inside eyewitness to Caudillo's alleged financial behavior which— were it to be what happened at *Drummer*—could explain why, with the diversion of professionally laundered cash, *Drummer* never had the money to pay staff or contributors.

Bill Dakota's Informant alleged:

... Further when the Begelman expose started, there were two gentlemen working, at that time, in the accounting department...one Lou Phillips, who is assistant underneath Johnson, that's the head of accounting, and a worker out in the office, I guess controller of the office, Dick Caudillo. I don't know how to spell his name. Dick was apparently the bookkeeper keeping track of all these things and hiding them along with the fact that he was hiding Lou Phillips' house payments in excess of $640, I'm told, a month and his own house payments that ran close to $600, plus Diner['s] Club cards for both men...airline fare. Dick did quite a lot of flying at that time and apparently charged the airline tickets also to the company. Subsequently, when the Begelman thing broke loose, they just quietly asked Dick Caudillo to resign and he went elsewhere for employment [to *Drummer*] and no one has seen him since...Lou Phillips is still there. —http://the-gossip-columnist-31.blogspot.com/ [Posted October 30, 2009]

In Dakota's Informant's testimony lies a joke-y insult that Caudillo resigned and went someplace "elsewhere" to work, and was seen by "no one" in LA since his resignation. What a sensational Hollywood punch line to that joke: Caudillo disappearing at a gay porn rag in San Francisco!

Two days after the burglary at *Drummer*, our typesetting machine miraculously reappeared in the office. Was it that Caudillo and Embry had quarreled, and that Caudillo had demanded, like the rest of us, to be paid his salary? Had he called Embry's bluff and held the typesetting machine hostage? The caustic office gossip was about honor among thieves. Whatever was the truth about who did what to whom, Caudillo was, as far as my eyewitness, never again seen at *Drummer* after the burglary. He may have been Embry's henchman, but he lasted only two issues. His name appeared as "Assistant to the Publisher" on the masthead of *Drummer* 20 (January 1978) and *Drummer* 21 (March 1978).

Caudillo's sudden disappearance caused not a whit of concern. We were San Franciscans. We specialized in fly-by-night people who appeared and disappeared. Ask Oscar Wilde. "It's an odd thing, but anyone who disappears is said to be seen in San Francisco. It must be a delightful city and possess all the attractions of the next world."

Begelman was found shot to death in a Century Plaza Hotel room in LA in 1995.

Paralleling Dakota's Informant, Jeanne Barney, testifying her own eyewitness, told me in an email, November 14, 2006, that Caudillo

> ...sold John Embry a bill of goods about how much he could do for *Drummer*, yada, yada, yada. Some years after I left [*Drummer*], when I was still handling "The Leather Fraternity" and fulfilling magazine subscriptions [in 1978 before Embry trashed her handling of "The Leather Fraternity" in *Drummer* 30], he showed up here with John and told me that they would no longer be providing the magazines [directly to me], that I would have buy them from the distributor. Which I was forced to do in order to fulfill these people's subscriptions; he and John refused to do it. He should rot in hell. With John. Every year when John [Embry with whom she remained lifelong frenemies] and Jerry [Embry's partner] do The Annual Day-After-Christmas Ladies Who Lunch, John says, "The worst thing I ever did was get involved with Dick Caudillo." And I always respond, "No, the worst thing you ever did was letting me go." By the way: a friend and I used to call DC, "Dick Caudildo."

Were *Drummer*'s financial direction and account books handled by "amateurs" like Mickey and Judy putting on a show? During twenty-four years, was there a business plan? Was there ever a professional financial director or a licensed accountant? Were profits reinvested into the magazine? Or into real estate? Was anyone watching the cash register? Was *Drummer* embezzled to death? Were its accounts run like personal checkbooks? Was *Drummer* a cash cow milked dry? Or was it simply a case of Hollywood accounting where no film turns a profit? No matter how big a film's gross, the studio accountants typically figure it nets zero. These financial questions asked about *Drummer* actually fit all kinds of small gayborhood entrepreneurial businesses run by amateurs lacking financial discipline. I saw several gay businesses in 1970s San Francisco snorted *zip* up the noses of their owners who had a taste for drugs and hustlers. As far as I witnessed, Embry did neither drugs nor tobacco, but he was not averse, according to *Drummer* photographer Jim Wigler, to fluffing models like Scott O'Hara during shoots when Wigler allegedly snapped incidental documentary shots of Embry giving the talent a helping hand.

Wigler told me on June 7, 2011, that he began working freelance for Embry shooting stills and video at *Drummer* in 1981, as Embry was trying to start up his own *Drummer* video production company. In 1982, Wigler told Embry he had to exit the madness at *Drummer* or he would take up drinking again. Angry, Embry refused to agree to let Wigler collect unemployment. This was Embry's management countermove against so many of the hundreds of laborers he hired. Wigler insisted on going to an Employment Board hearing. Embry refused, then agreed. Wigler demurred to say exactly why Embry caved, but a detective might suspect the possible existence of fluffing photos that called Embry's bluff.

If Embry snorted *Drummer*, it was to suck it dry of cash for real estate, and to produce the recording career of his unemployed Spanish immigrant lover, Mario Simon, who, seven years after the founding of *Drummer*, was insinuated onto the masthead like a carefully crafted "Trophy Wife." In 2000, Embry admitted in *Super MR* #1, page 36, that Mario had "somewhat of a language problem." As a ringer listed among actual working staff, the aspiring musical-theater actor Mario Simon, listed as "Mario Simone," played the part of "General Manager" from *Drummer* 59 (November 1982 to *Drummer* 66, July 1983), and then "Co-Publisher" from *Drummer* 67 (August 1983) to *Drummer* 98 (June 1986), Embry's last issue. If *Drummer* had been run like a business investing in itself, it might have survived on page, screen, and internet beyond 1999. It was a brand name that could have been a media franchise like the constellation around *The Advocate*.

In *Drummer* 13 (March 1977), Embry kited another facet of what seemed part of his "Robert Ripoff" hustle in "The Leather Fraternity." On the full inside back cover, he trumpeted his own travel deal. "The Leather Fraternity Announces Three Big European Leathermen Tours for Fall 1977." Managed by "Travel Coordinator" Bob Rose, the escorted tours were to be to Amsterdam/Germany for Oktoberfest ($1295), Greece ($1595), and Italy ($1395). The deadline for the "space limited" tours was June 1, 1977, precisely the moment *Drummer* was in absolute turmoil during its escape from LA, and three months after the March moment when the dying LA *Drummer* was dumped into my San Francisco lap.

As the new editor-in-chief, I said nothing about "Robert Ripoff" or the gay travel scheme except crack a joke about *Drummer* readers becoming stranded in Europe. Of course, no one sent in a *sou*. In the zero degrees of gay separation, tour escort Bob Rose was also the handsome Colt model "Dave Gold" whom I later shot for the Palm Drive Video feature *Dave Gold's Gym Workout*. My photographs of Dave Gold appear in *Drummer* 117 and *Drummer* 204.

WHATEVER HAPPENED TO MARGE ANDERSON?

John Embry: Marge Anderson was no stranger to gay journalism. Years ago she helped set up *Data Boy* in Southern California and did all its typesetting, She typeset *Drummer* as well when we were there, then moved up to San Francisco with us. Her only reaction to our purple prose was to tell me once that "typing this stuff makes me horny as hell and, dammit, there is nothing in the building except gay guys," and she would laugh her hearty laugh. Her cooking was legend and we all tried to keep on her good side along about Christmas cookie time when they would deliver the ingredients by the truckload. But Marge really never had any other side than a good one.

Then she moved to Alaska to be near her son and daughter. The news arrived just before our press time that during an operation her great and generous heart finally gave out. The multitude of friends in the gay community will miss her along with her friends at *Drummer*. "—30—," Marge. —*Drummer* 87 (1985), page 3

DEBLASE AND CHARLES ENTRAPPED BY AIDS:
"WE WERE FOOLS TO BUY *DRUMMER*"

I witnessed DeBlase's deep regret at having bought *Drummer* from salesman Embry who, with his keen sixth sense about censorship (tweaked by the LAPD), unloaded *Drummer* on the wealthy "innocents" from the Midwest, DeBlase and Charles: "...fool enough, as we were...."

DeBlase's bitterness was sharpened by the claustrophobia of the times as gay men were entrapped by AIDS. In 1981, the decade exploded with HIV, causing *Drummer* editorial policy to shift to safe sex and community education. When the October 17, 1989 Loma Prieta earthquake stopped the live telecast of the World Series in San Francisco, knocked down the Bay Bridge, and destroyed the *Drummer* office, DeBlase became so personally desperate that in December 1989—years before charity schemes like GoFundMe—I wrote a fund-raising letter requesting kink community support of *Drummer*, "the leather people's magazine," because *Drummer*, to me, was never about who owned it, so much as it was about the institution and force and voice that *Drummer* proved itself to be in the evolution of gay liberation and leather identity. That authentic *Drummer* voice needed rescue. The open letter was to have been signed by a dozen leather luminaries. My full text contained this excerpt:

> We, the writers, artists, photographers, and videographers who supply *Drummer* magazine, ask you to join up in the rescue of a magazine fighting for survival. After the October 1989 earthquake, *Mother Jones* magazine petitioned its readers to help it recover from its severe loss. The *MJ* readers responded nobly. As you may know, the *Drummer* office building was completely destroyed by the quake. This loss was injury on top of insult—the insult being the censorship rampant in the US [by right-wingnut Republican Senator Jesse Helms and the US Senate]. Both events... have forced *Drummer* to its present shape. The earthquake disaster is in recovery.... The censorship battles are still to be fought. If you compare a 1989 *Drummer* to a 1979 *Drummer*, you will see in the 1979 issues what you can no longer see in the 1989/1990 issues. Bookstore owners across the US tremble when religious fundamentalists come into their stores to censor everything from *Catcher in the Rye* to *Drummer*.... First they come for your magazines, then for your VCRs, then for you. If this sounds alarmist, it is. We are sounding the alarm, because we live in alarming times. We are fast sliding into 1950s McCarthyism which can slide into 1930s Fascism, ironically, while, in other countries, walls [the Berlin Wall had just fallen that November 1989] crumble as individual humans reach for freedom of the self.... —Best regards, Jack Fritscher

The draft of the letter sought the signatures of creatives such as Mikal Bales, Rex, the Hun, Domino, Mark I. Chester, Terry LeGrand, Roger Earl, Mister Marcus, Mark Thompson, Pat Califia, Elizabeth Gershman, Brian Dawson, Richard Bulger, Trent Dunphy, Alan Selby, and Judith Tallwing-McCarthy, among others.

This effort, for enervating reasons, gained little momentum. It was the Great Dying of 1984-1994. The devastated leather community had no inclination to aid an ailing commercial business like DeBlase's private corporation, Desmodus, Inc.

Death unhinged the culture, and despite all the help everyone gave everyone, confusion became hysteria. Chuck Arnett, for instance, was one of the greatest artists published in the *Drummer* Salon. He had been a dancer on Broadway and was the founder of the Tool Box bar. He was also the man who introduced the needle to Folsom Street. On the skids, he seemed very like the failing *Drummer* which his brand-name graffiti art so essentially characterized. No one seemed to be there to save him. I remember seeing him very late one night at the Barracks baths where I walked into the empty and steamless "Steam Room" and saw him sitting naked on the upper wooden bench like a skeletal gaunt ghost of Auschwitz tripping his tits off. Arnett died virtually alone and destitute on March 2, 1988. I profiled him in *Drummer* 134 (October 1989) and in Mark Thompson's book, *Leatherfolk: Radical Sex, People, Politics and Practice*. On March 27, 1990, three months after my plea to save *Drummer*, my friend, the *Drummer* Salonista, Bob Brackett wrote:

Dear Jack:

...I have some of Chuck Arnett's ashes in a crystal box along with some dirt sent to me by my ex [from] where we first made love, and some sand I brought back from Egypt from the base of the pyramids. Not something I've told many people.

I remember near the end when Chuck's roommates were letting him die in his own shit and one of his friends called to tell me. I went crazy. But I called in every favor I had to get Chuck out of there and bumped 50 people to get him into Garden-Sullivan [Hospital] the next day. I had doctors ask me how I did it. I don't know and I probably couldn't do it again. It's just that Chuck and I had a strange love affair, had season's tickets to the ballet (talk about "the odd couple") and a very special friendship.

I've never forgotten the couple of times I made it with you. Only to go on to dating David Sparrow [my former partner of ten years] a few times....What movie am I? [quoting a line repeated frequently in *Some Dance to Remember*]
—Bob Brackett

WORKERS' STRUGGLE: CONTRIBUTORS KEEP OWNERSHIP OF THEIR COPYRIGHT

Meanwhile, back at the 1970s copyright war, Embry, during his own ownership of *Drummer* (1975-1986), may have invalidated even the one-time rights he bought when he failed to pay contributors for their material.

My earliest and fiercest conversations with Embry concerned the Copyright Act of 1976 which became effective January 1, 1978, at the very instant I, having been hired in March 1977, was writing sometimes half of each issue of *Drummer*. In the special issue, *Son of Drummer* (September 1978), I wrote seven pieces bylined as "Jack Fritscher" and "Denny Sargent," and printed one page of "Sparrow-Fritscher" photos, plus eight of my own photographs, and nine of Mapplethorpe's whose attorneys protected copyright Embry dared not compromise.

This seemed the time when every stress from Embry's arrest, exile, and cancer rose and converged. He was ever the scofflaw autocrat flipping off the new copyright procedures which recommended that every author's copyright be posted at the end of each article or story. When I signed my writing in *Drummer* 19 to *Drummer* 33 with "© Jack Fritscher," Embry most often stripped it out because, he said, "I don't like the look." I'd have Al Shapiro paste it back in. Embry would strip it out. He thought I was using the law to piss on his territory. "It looks like you're writing the whole damn issue." In fact, there was a moment in time when I had edited half of the *Drummer* issues in existence.

When I asked Sam Steward if I could do an edit-update on his cop-sex story "In a Pig's Ass" for *Drummer* 21 (March 1978), he was aware of the copyright struggle when he wrote on January 9, 1978: Dear Jack, Here 'tis, please use the circled "c" at the end for the copyright." I added it for him as I did for the other contributors.

He then asked me to check to see that Embry wasn't reprinting his stories "Babysitter," *Drummer* 5 (March 1976), and "Many Happy Returns," *Drummer* 8 (September 1976).

"Whyncha [*sic*] check the contents in *The Best and Worst of Drummer* volume [an "extra issue" which Sam hadn't seen] and see if any of [my] Phil Andros [writing] was used?"

As an historian, a writer, a photographer, and especially as a video documentary maker, for years I have dealt with securing permissions from survivor-pioneers or their heirs regarding their intellectual property, in order to protect against any copyright crisis caused by latter-day poachers.

I'm no attorney, but I have tendered legal action against publishers and websites who violate my copyright. I can opine that no past publisher of *Drummer* may legally reprint, or scan-and-post anything from *Drummer* unless that person has bought and paid for second reprint rights or has bought electronic rights—which Embry and DeBlase would not have done, not even bothering to figure that in the future new methods of publication, such as the internet, would be invented.

In truth, beyond a bit of "fair use," *Drummer* may never be legally scanned and re-published. First page to last page, it is a jigsaw puzzle of intellectual property whose copyrights are owned by the creators or their heirs. For instance, to film my documentary *The Domino Video Gallery* showcasing *Drummer* artist Don Merrick/Domino, I had to secure written rights from both Domino's sister and a surviving friend of Domino, my erstwhile pal, John Dagion (aka JD), the pioneering publisher of the long-running zine *TRASH* (founded 1975). I sought the same permissions from Al Shapiro's partner, Dick Kriegmont, for my documentary, *The A. Jay Video Gallery*, as I did for the living *Drummer* artists, Rex and the Hun: *The Rex Video Gallery: Corrupt Beyond Innocence* and *The Hun Video Gallery I: Chain-Gang Gang Bang*, and *The Hun Video Gallery II, Rainy Night in Georgia*.

Because *Drummer* was rarely run as a "real business," but as a "gay business," its legal paperwork seemed either nonexistent, helter-skelter, or a lie in Embry's early and unlikely masthead claims, for instance, that certain words like *Drummer* were trademarked—even though *Drummer* is not the only magazine named *Drummer*.

Trademarks take time, money, and lawyers to establish. It is illegal to print the trademark sign without proper registration with the United States Trademark Office. Perhaps legal documents do exist; that was not my province. My research for internal evidence found no 1970s trademark advisement printed in *Drummer* even up to my last issue, *Drummer* 33. When Embry later began claiming "trademarks" on the masthead page, the real-estate property owner he was began to understand the parallel ownership of intellectual property.

Drummer rarely had a legal eye for the future because it was so pressured to fill each next issue, and because, unlike my regard for the valid totality of *Drummer* culture, it did not value itself or its contributors as legal identities. Failing to secure any reprint rights, the publishers made a huge legal and historical mistake that I repeatedly cautioned the first two publishers about.

It will be seventy years after the last copyright holder dies before *Drummer* contents could possibly fall into public domain. As if the Mapplethorpe Foundation will ever let that happen to Robert's photos in *Drummer*! This is why, in order to make this eyewitness peek into *Drummer* happen at all, I limited my scope mostly to my work, not out of ego, but out of respect for others' copyrights which death has made mostly impossible to trace. To clarify copyright, the bibliography of all my own writing and photography, signed and unsigned, was published online and in the book *Gay San Francisco: Eyewitness Drummer*, pages 679 to 705. Any claim jumpers thinking *Drummer* is community property or that the copyright law is a joke might meditate on this punchline: "While publishers may not be able to find the copyright holder, the copyright holder will always find the publisher."

DRUMMER SUCCESS SURPRISES EMBRY: *BEING* AND BECOMING

How clueless was Embry about the essence of *Drummer*? In *Drummer* 1, Embry, as "Robert Payne," offered for sale through his Alternate mail-order Leather Emporium a set of bed sheets made from Naugahyde (!) which as a faux fabric was anathema, taboo, and camp joke to genuine leather fetishists. Among bar buddies, one line tossed off to dismiss a leather wannabe who was too new or too plastic to "dig the scene" was: "Lips that touch Naugahyde will never touch mine." (See *Naugahyde* as insult: *Drummer* 1, page 9.)

In 2003, Embry, the first publisher of *Drummer*, told Robert Davolt, who in late 1997 became the last editor and nominal publisher of *Drummer*, that he, Embry, "never foresaw the impact that *Drummer* would have. 'It was a big surprise to me....I'm amazed.'"

Knowing Embry, I suspect that his ingenuous "Butterfly McQueen" quote is true. Revising history in *Drummer* 188 (September 1995, page 23), he boldly claimed he invented *Drummer* solo, himself, alone, as an almost "immaculate conception"—his exact words—inside his *Leather Fraternity Newsletter* which was—he did *not* say—cloned out of the early gay-lib H.E.L.P./*Drummer* newspaper and the 1960s magazine *Drum*. Robert Davolt wrote about Embry's wriggling revisionism:

> After [my] extensive conversations with...[Embry, he]...either claims the [Mr Drummer] contest as one of his most brilliant ideas or blames it on staff members [Shapiro and Fritscher], depending on how the conversation is going....Val Martin was picked by the publisher or the staff (depending on who is telling the story...). www.leatheweb.com/histdrum.html, March 11 2002.

Embry was a generation older than I in gay years, particularly in the youth culture of the 1960s-1970s. He was born October 14, 1926, thirteen years before I was born June 20, 1939. When he hired me, I was thirty-seven and he was fifty-one. As an adult who came out in the 1940s-1950s, he struck me as kind of an "LA, Johnny Ray, cocktail-lounge lizard." He was distinctly different from me who as a teenager also came out in the 1950s, not in a bar, but in a nice boys school run by the Pope. There from 1953 to 1963, I survived the tsunami of Vatican II and experienced firsthand the temper tantrums of queeny priests and draggy bishops which prepared me to deal with the mercurial publisher of *Drummer*. My schoolmate for six years at the Pontifical College Josephinum was Bernie Law who grew up to become Bernard Cardinal Law of Boston made famous by his illegal coverups of priest molestations of minors as dramatized in the film *Spotlight* (2015), Oscar winner Best Picture. The Pope disciplined Bernie, that "Prince of the Church," by recalling him to Rome and sentencing him, with no Vatican irony, to a life of powerful luxury in his own palace attached to Basilica di Santa Maria Maggiore.

Embry, before *Drummer*, was a salesman from Winslow, Arizona, and an advertising copywriter wandering in his job searches as far as Hawaii. Insofar as Embry's was the name that floated to the top out of the internecine squabbles among the several possible LA "founders" of *Drummer* who, except for Barney and Townsend, seem lost to history, I give him this salute.

Entrepreneur Embry was, I agree with Jeanne Barney, the "motivated force" who caused *Drummer* to "be" as a business.

In the same way, Barney and I were, along with Al Shapiro and a few early contributors like Robert Opel and Ed Franklin and Fred Halsted, part of the "dedicated force" that caused *Drummer* to "become" a reader-reflexive leather community voice.

BONE-MARROW TRANSPLANT INTO *DRUMMER*:
"WHAT I DID FOR LOVE"

In 1977, I cleaned up Embry's *verboten* content that had caused censorship trouble in LA, and introduced new content, themes, and styles that became ongoing or repeated staples in *Drummer* till the day it closed in 1999. Noting this, *Drummer* editor Joseph W. Bean, who began editing the magazine one hundred issues after the last issue I edited, wrote his own eyewitness in the Leather Archives & Museum newsletter, *Leather Times*, Issue One, 2007:

"What do you want done with the 'Leather Lifestyles' theme you announced for *Drummer* 132?" I asked my boss, *Drummer* publisher Tony DeBlase. "Go all the way with it," he answered, apparently leaving me unsure of what he meant. "You know," he added, "do a Fritscher!" Yes, I knew.... Subject after subject thereafter, the concept kept being "do a Fritscher" on it. Brown leather (*Drummer* 134) fell far short of that goal; leathersex and spirituality (*Drummer* 136) almost made it; bears (*Drummer* 140) got pretty close; spandex (*Drummer* 141) felt like a success. We really "did a Fritscher" on that "kinky softwear" as we called the form-accentuating garments. Edge play (*Drummer* 148) felt even more fully Fritscher-ed... The now infamous "Remembrance of Sleaze Past" issue (*Drummer* 139) has to be the best of that lot and, if I remember correctly that idea either came from Fritscher or DeBlase in conversation with Fritscher [who wrote the feature].

My original-recipe *Drummer* was, by internal example in each issue (19-30), an open invitation to all contributors in that first decade of gay publishing to stand and deliver in terms of evolving leather esthetics, emerging identity concepts, and erotic themes, including:

1) "Gonzo New Journalism" emphasizing true experiences of participatory sex written in a first-person voice: "Leather Christmas" (*Drummer* 19, December 1977); "Prison Blues" (*Drummer* 21, March 1978); "Bondage" (*Drummer* 24, September 1978) which was my personal interview with world-famous New York bondage top, Gary Bratman, eventual mentor to Richard Hunter, the owner of "Mister S Leather Company," San Francisco; and, later, my *piece de resistance* of gonzo journalism reporting real BDSM with real cops, "The Academy" (*Drummer* 145, December 1990).

2) "Homomasculinity" as theme, lifestyle, gender identity, and ancient urge resurrected in a New Age of masculine-identified gay males fetishizing male secondary sex characteristics of leathermen, daddies, and bears through erotic identifiers such as facial and body hair, muscles, baldness, bulk, and deepening voice.

3) "Theme issues" assertively outing closeted fetish materials for the first time into gay publishing: cigars (*Drummer* 22, May 1978); redneck blue-collar men and white trash ex-cons (*Drummer* 23, July 1978); tit play (*Drummer* 30, June 1979); gay sports (*Drummer* 20, January 1978, years before "gay sports" rose up with the first Gay Olympics aka the "Gay Games 1982," whose physique contest Mark Hemry and I videotaped on the stage of the Castro Theater); the first men in kilts photographs (*Drummer* 25,

December 1978); ex-con rough trade (*Drummer* 24, September 1978); brown leather (*Drummer* 134, October 1989, centerfold); and the first writing on bears in *Drummer* (*Drummer* 119, July 1988; and again in *Drummer* 140, June 1990, including shooting the bear cover of that "Special Bear Issue").

4) "Leather *Verite*" turning *Drummer* conceptually into an ongoing "Song of Myself" for leathermen by inviting grass-roots readers to submit selfies to make *Drummer* reflect an image of authentic leather as lived, not by professional leather models, but by the honest multitudes of common men defined in *Leaves of Grass* by Walt Whitman, a friend of Thoreau who gave *Drummer* its name; to ground *Drummer* as "reader reflexive," I initiated my monthly column "Tough Customers" (*Drummer* 25, December 1978) which celebrated personal selfies exhibited in the first decade men dared show their faces.

5) "Daddies: Pivoting 'Age' from Ageism into Erotic Fetish," by writing the first "Daddies" feature, originally titled "In Praise of Older Men"and announced in *Drummer* 24 (September 1978); withholding that article from *Drummer*, I re-titled the essay, "The Daddy Mystique," for publication as the cover feature, *In Touch* #56, June 1981; emphasizing his seniority into the 1970s youth culture, I introduced model Richard Locke, age thirty-seven, specifically as an "older man" (*Drummer* 24, September 1978), and personally secured Locke a contract for his autobiography, *In the Heat of Passion: How to Have Hotter, Safer Sex* (Leyland Publications aka Gay Sunshine Press; Fritscher letter to Winston Leyland, April 29, 1987).

I wanted to uncloset a repulsion-attraction demiurge in gay culture: many gay men, both sissy and butch, remembered or fantasized they were somehow misunderstood or abused by their rugged blue-collar fathers. Sometimes shoved by a patricidal feminism, they fairly or unfairly demonized their straight dads who, despite the glib anti-patriarchal bias of gay culture, were in "gender truth" the very essence of the masculine erotic authority gay men advertised for in *Drummer* personal ads searching for daddies. I wanted to "out" and validate that erotic desire within Freud's and Jung's "Father Complex" so that gay men did not have to go against their personal gender identity as masculine men who unapologetically prefer men masculine. *Drummer* eventually published three special issues of *Drummer Daddies*.

Drummer had a cast of hundreds of talented contributors. Embry, thundering with the autocracy that publishers have over writers, artists, photographers, and subscribers, was like "the old woman who lived in a shoe. She had so many children she didn't know what to do."

Embry mistook original-recipe *Drummer* to be entertainment wrapped as bait on the hook of his money-spinning center-section, the "brochure pages" selling his sex toys mail order, and—in one variation—his "Leather Fraternity" sex ads at twenty-five cents a word. Jeanne Barney, sometimes using "ALL CAPS," alleged to me in an email dated July 1, 2006, what is here quoted exactly, that

> in LA, Embry's alter-ego, Robert Payne, was known as "Robert Ripoff" because of his reputation for NOT delivering on mail-order merchandise. (If you want to know about this practice, please ask.) I handled The "Leather Fraternity" long after I "fled" *Drummer*. There was NO CHARGE for Leather Fraternity ads. Here's how it worked, and here's what John did/did not do: A subscription to the magazine cost $35, which included a FREE Fraternity listing. An interested guy could send in $1 for an application/questionnaire, which he could return with $35. Before I started handling The Fraternity, John would take out the $1 and never send the application. After I started handling The Fraternity, that was not a problem—but a much more serious one arose: the $35 would come in for the subscription—which John would then NOT FULFILL. To me, John would blame whoever in the office was responsible for subscriptions. To the people who'd been cheated out of their $35, John would blame me.

Embry was aware of the awesome LA mail-order business model of Bob Mizer, a pioneer sex revolutionary, who had founded his Athletic Model Guild in 1945, and went on to shoot more than 10,000 models. Mizer had started his Hollywood photography business climbing inside the underpants of young ex-soldiers who at the end of World War II descended on the wild sex party that was LA. Mostly straight trade servicing rich and closeted johns and famous movie stars, they hustled nights in and out of Scotty Bowers's Richfield gas station on Hollywood Boulevard at North Van Ness as lovingly detailed in Bowers' autobiography, *Full Service: My Adventures in Hollywood and the Secret Sex Lives of the Stars*. They earned a few more bucks appearing afternoons in front of Mizer's camera at his AMG Studio in his garage behind his home where he lived with his mother at 1834 West 11th Street, and a few more by "going on location" to trick with select AMG clients who appreciated that Mizer had test-driven them on set.

Mizer with the heart of a long-distance runner sold his AMG photographs and his 3,000 8mm films through his *Physique Pictorial* magazine which he published to great success for forty-five years. In 1972, Embry took a gander at the throngs of young leather-inflected talent descending on LA bars. As a born salesman, he figured to cash in on the mail-order success of both Mizer and Larry Townsend. Embry's imitation of Townsend's leather publishing business ignited the on-again and off-again feud between the two that lasted their entire lives, and was made worse by the mail-order public often confusing one's name with the other. It was a purposeful confusion nurtured by Embry to his own advantage.

"TOP 10" HIT SONG 1955
"Black Denim Trousers and Motorcycle Boots"

The seminal "Black Denim Trousers and Motorcycle Boots" was the first biker song. I remember it and its thrilling teen-identity context clearly. I was sixteen. I bought the black-vinyl 45rpm for 25 cents. I sang along with the lyrics I learned by heart. A week after the release of this single composed by Jerry Lieber and Mike Stoller, and sung by "The Cheers," James Dean, age 24, died in a car crash—the ultimate 1950s Teen Tragedy—fueling in straight and gay popular culture the archetypal romance of biker rebels without a cause that Marlon Brando had ignited in *The Wild One* (1953).

> "He wore black denim trousers and motorcycle boots
> And a black leather jacket with an eagle on the back
> He had a hopped-up 'cycle that took off like a gun
> ... axle grease...underneath his fingernails
> On the muscle of his arm...a red tattoo..."
> © 1955 Lieber and Stoller

With producer-distributor Mizer's tough young studs in mind, seeing the LA bike gangs streaming on the freeways, and noticing the crowds at the LA leather bars, Embry calculated, for cash and not passion, to exploit the innate homoeroticism of straight bikers' appeal to a gay consumer audience. We had all experienced the pop-culture wave of mid-century media, from AMG to Chuck Renslow's Kris Studio Chicago to major Hollywood studios, making homomasculine stars and icons of blue-collar workers, bikers, and cowboys defined by the combustion-engine styles around motorcycles and hot-rod cars: Marlon Brando in *A Streetcar Named Desire* (1951) and *The Wild One* (1953), James Dean in *Rebel Without a Cause* (1955) and *Giant* (1956), Kenneth Anger in *Scorpio Rising* (1964), Dennis Hopper and Peter Fonda in the Swinging Sixties' culture-changing *Easy Rider* (1969), and the ultimate leather biker William Smith in *C C and Company* (1970). This was raw material ready to be served up in a new kind of magazine in which the new ways of being a masculine gay man would destroy the straight stereotype that gay men are sissies. Embry hadn't thought his concept through personally or philosophically, but he knew the marketability of the newly emerging gay masculinity, even as he nervously tried to inject it with 1950s Old School camp humor that did not sit well with 1970s New School *Drummer* subscribers.

He insinuated himself into Townsend's affairs at the *H.E.L.P./Newsletter*, which Townsend edited, when he returned to LA from an advertising venture in Hawaii and volunteered to upgrade the mailer for H.E.L.P., beginning with the first issue of the prototype folio zine *Drummer* in 1971, four years before the landmark founding of glossy *Drummer* in 1975.

Embry's pulp-paper *Drummer* of 1971 was a queeny LA bar rag very like West Hollywood and very unlike its 1975 evolution into a leather magazine for men. Needing a mailing list, he waltzed into H.E.L.P. to get his paws on its member lists so he could jumpstart himself as a mail-order guru writing, publishing, and distributing his own work. Writing as "Robert Payne," Embry proved himself a busy leather "author," often retyping straight fiction he plagiarized from men's adventure magazines, such as *Saga* and *Argosy*, turning the text "gay" as he typed. He sold his magazine-sized "books" along with leathersex toys including "aroma" popper variations on the drug amyl nitrite.

Trial Balloons

Small Folio Chapbook and Tabloid
titled *H.E.L.P./Drummer*
(4.25x5.5 & 8x11)
1971-1973
Sets Stage
for Glossy Full-Size *Drummer*
(8x11)
June 1975

* * * *

H.E.L.P./Drummer, Volume 1 #1: November 19, 1971
H.E.L.P./Drummer, Volume 1 #2: December 10, 1971

H.E.L.P./Drummer, Volume 2 #1: September 15, 1972
H.E.L.P./Drummer, Volume 2 #2: October 15, 1972
H.E.L.P./Drummer, Volume 2 #3: November 15, 1972
H.E.L.P./Drummer, Volume 2 #4: December 15, 1972
H.E.L.P./Drummer, Volume 2 #5: January 15, 1973

Embry, who built his fortune selling over-priced poppers for thirty years, denounced poppers in *Drummer* 98 (1986) solely to spite incoming new *Drummer* publisher DeBlase and to hurt DeBlase's mail-order competition. On October 21, 1991, he enlarged his hypocrisy by condemning poppers in his new *Manifest Reader* magazines at the same time he offered them for sale. Embry was a drug dealer whose concern was not respiratory health. He loved only his mail-order company Alternate Marketing. In an age of AIDS, he mass-mailed a coded snake-oil "drug letter" from 31855 Date Palm Drive, Cathedral City, CA 92234:

Dear Friend,
    As you know, a federal law was passed that prevents the sale of aromas [poppers; variations on the inhalant amyl nitrite]. We cannot break the law and thus no longer carry or sell aromas. We do however have a wonderful new automotive carburetor cleaner [what a euphemism] that you should consider buying. It is priced at $12 per bottle or 3 bottles for $29, post paid. The product carries a full money-back guarantee that will perk up your engine's pistons as any buddy who is used to working on them can show you.....
    We also ask that you allow up to 3 weeks for delivery as this new carburetor cleaner is in limited supply from time to time.
My Best Regards,
Alternate Marketing...
If you order now, we'll send you a free cock ring.

That last line should be on his tombstone.
    Embry profiled his evil-twin "Robert Payne" and his reputation in a full-page ad he wrote for *Manifest Reader* 15 (1991), page 57. As a prose stylist, his advertising copy did no more for him than it did for Mario Simon's disco records in *Drummer* 81 (February 1984).

> When Robert Payne Finally Writes a Book, It's Industrial Strength! Alternate Publishing proudly presents *The Exchange*.
>
> *Robert Payne* [that is, John Embry; italic added] has been at the forefront of the world of leather even before *Drummer* burst on the scene. His stories first delighted the readers of *Drummer,* then *Mach* and *FQ* [*Foreskin Quarterly*], along with the myriad of special projects coming out of that magical publishing era [the 1970s]. When *The Exchange* stories were unleashed on the unsuspecting pages of *Manifest Reader*, the reaction was elctric [sic]! So it was decided to put the rest of *The Exchange* into a book instead. Be sure to read these unforgettable adventures carefully to keep the pages from sticking together. Who else can grab you like that? Enclose this ad with you're [sic] *the Exchange* order and, with any luck, Mr. Payne might autograph your copy for you!
>
> [British artist Bill Ward also drew a cartoon strip titled, *The Exchange*, which can be sampled in *Manifest Reader* 17 (1992), pages 63-65.]

WHAT EMBRY WANTED: GAY MAIL-ORDER, THE FIRST BUSINESS OF GAY LIB; THE ROOTS OF "LEATHER HERITAGE" IN LARRY TOWNSEND'S "THE QUESTIONNAIRE"

After Stonewall, "gay business" began coming out of the closet, and competition among gay startup companies was fierce. The Gay Grail in the Titanic 70s was mail-order, because most homosexuals needing magazines, sex toys, and amyl nitrite "Aroma Room Freshener" lived in Iowa. Historically, the mail-order "business models" that Embry cut his teeth on were classic. Bob Mizer, the Wizard of Mail-Order, who lived the most discreet of dangerous lives, began his Athletic Model Guild studio in 1945 and synergistically sold his photos and films nationwide in his gorgeous mail-order brochure disguised as a magazine, *Physique Pictorial*. Every issue of that handmade *Physique Pictorial* mailed to men living isolated in Iowa was an enlightening and consoling catechism teaching homomasculinity by featuring the palm-driving inspirational thrills of men such as Arnie Payne, Gable Boudreaux, and John Tristram, who was a friend of my 1970s longtime partner, the blond bodybuilder champion, Jim Enger. My eyewitness interview of the private and guarded Bob Mizer, "AMG Duos," was partially published as a "Virtual *Drummer*" feature in *Skin*, Volume 1, Number 5, 1981.

In the 1950s, Chuck Renslow and Dom "Etienne" Orejudos founded Kris Studio in Chicago. They recruited models within the straight authenticity of their Triumph Gym, the very old-school iron pile they purchased on Van Buren Street in the Loop. They introduced a Midwestern crop of butch leather models, like the homomasculine icons, Ron Rector and Mike Bradburn, in their classic magazine, *Mars*, which was the first dedicated *leather* magazine to publish continuously (1963-1967). Renslow, daring to mix sex and politics, wrote an editorial titled "Victory for Censorship!" in *Mars* 21 (September 1966). He analyzed how unconstitutional censorship was impairing the media of gay culture. With *Mars* as a kind of mail-order catalog, Kris Studio sold its image of homomasculinity in photographs and 8mm films, such as *Cabin in the Woods*, *Black Magic*, and *Slave of the Sheik*. Because even the gayest of 1960s gay magazines liked masculine-identified men, Kris Studio's images, particularly of Rector and Bradburn, went wide in other periodicals such as *The Young Physique*, Volume 6 #3, February-March 1965. In 1976, Kris Studio gave its mailing list to my longtime friend Lou Thomas to use to build up his mail order at Target Studio. Thomas had also been, with Jim French, the co-founder of Colt Studio. His Target brand provided many covers and centerfolds to *Drummer*.

Was rivalry the reason Chuck Renslow did not give his mailing list to Embry when the needy *Drummer* was one year old and busted by the LAPD? Or why Renslow's iconic homomasculine Kris photography was never published in *Drummer* even though Etienne's drawings were? Or how Renslow felt when immediately after his first International Mr. Leather (IML) Contest in 1979, Embry "invented" the Mr. Drummer Contest?

As an eyewitness at the 1982 IML, *Drummer* employee Patrick Batt revealed insight into Embry's one-sided feud with Renslow in the biography *Leatherman: The Legend of Chuck Renslow*, page 36.

> I was living in San Francisco, and I was in [traveled to] Chicago that year for the IML Contest because I was working for *Drummer* at the time. Our contestant was Luke Daniel. I didn't think he'd have a chance in hell of winning, because there was some tension at the time between John Embry and Chuck [Renslow]. I don't know what it was about or even if it was legitimate. I think it was a bigger deal to John than to Chuck.....Well, Luke ended up winning, and I was representing *Drummer*...and suddenly had to do all these things. I...got through on the phone to Embry, who was [at his summer home] in the Russian River area, to tell him our contestant had won.

At the very moment Embry was planning the June 1975 LA debut of *Drummer*, his nemesis, San Francisco investment banker David Goodstein, rode into Los Angeles and bought the *LA Advocate: The Newsletter of Personal Rights in Defense and Education (P.R.I.D.E.)* from founders, Dick Michaels and Bill Rand. Goodstein was no friend of leather or masculine gays even though he briefly moved *The Advocate* to the San Francisco industrial suburb of San Mateo before he ferried the LA publication back to LA where its uptight politically-correct Southern California editorial policies belonged.

During his San Mateo experiment, Goodstein hired writer John Preston and columnist Pat Califia who instantly became persons of interest to Embry eager as ever to poach any talent he could from *The Advocate*. It took four years for Embry to reel Preston in by promising to serialize his raw manuscript *Mr. Benson* in *Drummer*. Califia, under timing and terms only he knows—during the lesbian sex wars around his own book *Sapphistry* (1979)—eventually became a 1980s contributor to, and associate editor of, *Drummer*.

When the LAPD busted the Drummer Slave Auction in 1976, Embry, imitating Goodstein, moved his Alternate Publishing, Inc. north to San Francisco, and, when Goodstein quickly returned his headquarters to LA, Embry was left standing stupid in the geographical snipe hunt that Goodstein's own business plan had unwittingly sucked him into. Goodstein was, for Embry, the gold standard of what Embry wanted to be. In November 1977, he even named his *Drummer* spinoff magazine *The Alternate* to crib frisson off *The Advocate*. By accident, *Drummer* found its true home in San Francisco. Without the unique geography, men, and erotic spirit of San Francisco, LA *Drummer* would have died long before its rebirth in issue nineteen, December 1977.

In the mid-1970s, when Embry and Goodstein moved their corporate businesses and their LA attitude north to the more artisanal San Francisco, they were the cold foreshadow of the gentrifying "Dot-com millionaires" that the 95-year-old eyewitness Lawrence Ferlinghetti said, "moved into San Francisco with bags full of cash and no manners." —Lawrence Ferlinghetti, Interview by Jeffrey Brown, PBS, March 24, 2015

In the bars and bistros of 1970s San Francisco, *The Advocate* was little more than an LA rag widely scorned as "fish wrap" whose existence was justified only by its "Pink Section" with its sex classifieds that rivaled capitalist Embry's "Leather Fraternity" personals. In *Drummer* 1, pages 6-8, Embry kited details (with strings attached) of how to join his primary business, "The Leather Fraternity," and receive—almost as an after-thought—a "free subscription to *Drummer*."

In the late 1960s, Larry Townsend was using the United States Postal Service to collect nationwide information profiling leathermen, sex rituals, and fetishes for the book he would publish in 1972, *The Leatherman's Handbook*. Townsend, well qualified with a degree in industrial psychology from UCLA (1957), invented the first market research aimed at leathermen. His questions about S&M scenarios helped men uncloset themselves, and made his book a vivid expose of the core realities of BDSM in the Swinging Sixties decade before Stonewall. Simply called "The Questionnaire," it penetrated gay popular culture very like a chain letter that leather guys redacted, re-typed on carbon paper in their new versions, and circulated by first class mail during the 1960s and early 1970s.

As a pioneer Leather Heritage "liberation" document, it was as important to me—I filled it out and mailed it to him—as it was to Larry Townsend who, if he did not originate "The Questionnaire," perfected it, and circulated it through the underground of leathermen in his demographic inquiry into leather identity. I unraveled some of the DNA of "The Questionnaire" and analyzed it when Larry Townsend asked me to write my Introduction to his *Leatherman's Handbook*, Silver Anniversary Edition (1997). When I was *Drummer* editor-in-chief, I often used the grass-roots demographics of Townsend's "The Questionnaire" as my "tickle file" to develop, produce, and publish formerly subliminal and closeted themes and angles for features, fiction, and photography. "The Questionnaire" was a primordial index for my version of *Drummer*.

In 1969, I added my own list of occult questions to "The Questionnaire," typed my own revised version on mimeograph stencils, and printed twenty-five purple-ink copies. I mailed them to leathermen around the country. Their responses gave insight into how leather rituals sometimes mixed with occult rituals which I reported in my book, *Popular Witchcraft*, page 115, 1972 edition; page 170, 2005 edition:

> In S&M psychodrama I dig the following scenes with related gear and torture. Check your choice.
> Soldiers ( ) Firemen ( ) Cyclists ( ) Sailors ( ) Marines ( ) Airmen ( ) Coast Guard ( ) Nazi SS ( ) Policemen ( ) Inquisition ( ) Witch Trial ( ) Executioners ( ) Black Mass ( ) Cowboys ( ) Witches Sabbath ( ) Leather Types ( ) Doctors ( ) Satanic Coven ( ) Crucifixion ( ) Hot Wax ( )...

On August 22, 1968, leather priest Jim Kane indicated the internal workings of how "The Questionnaire" was a leather folk document built by many, just like *Drummer* itself would be. He wrote to me:

> Jack, boy— ...I just finished my contributions to the sixth and final (for the present) edition of that Questionnaire you may have seen at Ed's [Ed Tarlton, leatherman, Chicago]. An ambivalent friend of mine [a slave], late of LA [where he got his draft from Townsend] and now in Houston, is doing most of the work. Let me know if you're interested, and I'll try to send along a copy in a few weeks. —Cheers, Lord Jim

On September 23, 1968, Jim Kane wrote:

> Midnight, Monday. Jack, boy— ...the other author [one of many claimants] of the Questionnaire was in for four days last week. Found a lone pine standing in the center of a small grove up the hidden valley. Nice scene.... —Lord Jim

On February 2, 1971, with my *Popular Witchcraft* book at the printers, Jim Kane complained about his edit of "The Questionnaire" being ripped off by a gay mail-order company in LA:

> DearJackandave [*sic*; David Sparrow]— ...I've got a grudge against the Inter-House Introduction Service in LA [a forerunner of Embry's "Leather Fraternity" hook-up scheme] because they swiped and degraded the Questionnaire form. —Jim

The chorus of authorial claimants was a group grope in the zero degrees of leather incest. If future *Drummer* columnist, Larry Townsend, did not compose the first edition of "The Questionnaire," he certainly knew its quintessential value for his reader-reflexive book, as I did for *Drummer*.

Obsessed in 1970 with mass-market mail-order, Embry was keenly aware that Townsend was selling his own leather S&M books which he wrote and published as LT Publishing. Embry's twin, "Robert Payne," was also penning fiction to sell via mail-order. What he needed was to invent a magazine to wrap as alluring disguise around his mail-order brochure. Embry and Townsend, both physically huge opera queens, hated each other with the grand passion of frenemy divas who can kill with an air kiss. Larry Townsend told me on October 10, 2006:

John asked me to go into business with him on *Drummer*, but I didn't because I did not want to get involved in the pressures of writing and producing a dated publication that had to come out monthly or else, and I also did not want to be in business with John.

MAIL-ORDER: OLD RELIABLE, BOB MIZER, AND *PHYSIQUE PICTORIAL*

In my "Gay Sports" feature in *Drummer* 20 (January 1978), I first introduced the wrestling photography of my friend David Hurles, the gay mail-order pioneer whom I had met in May 1976 through *Drummer* photographer Jim Stewart who had been my longtime friend since we both lived in Michigan in the 1960s. Jim Stewart roomed with David Sparrow and me at our 25th Street home when he moved to San Francisco in 1975. In our intimacy, I produced his photographs for *Drummer* 14 (April 1977) in my run-up to becoming editor. In that same issue, page 65, was a half-page display ad for Stewart's Keyhole Studio. Two Hurles' boxing photographs appeared on page 70 in *Drummer* 20. Another Hurles' photograph, featuring our friend, the gay-sports trendsetter, John Handley, founder of the New York Wrestling Club, appeared on page 71.

Working with fetish themes, I began my campaign to launch Hurles' important American erotic art into our *Drummer* Salon and into the leather-stream of gay popular culture. I introduced him very aggressively in my lead feature, "Prison Blues," *Drummer* 21 (March 1978), as a gonzo character under his professional name, Old Reliable, who was fictitiously kidnaped and brutalized in Beirut. That porn-mogul character, already in progress in "Prison Blues," prefigured the fictitious character of the pornographer, Solly Blue, loosely based on David Hurles, in *Some Dance to Remember*.

In the same *Drummer* 21, I transcribed, re-wrote with a polished edit, and printed Hurles' oral history interview, "Scott Smith: Heavy Rap with an Ex-Con" with his "Mug Shots" gallery. That edgy monolog and the fourteen Old Reliable photos were two "firsts" in gay publishing history: the authentic first-person voices and the photographs of straight ex-cons forcefully presented as dangerous, irresistible, and available sex partners printed to frighten readers into a masturbation frenzy.

Before I determined to "discover" Old Reliable, who was as Weegee as he was Arbus, and before I set up his debut in *Drummer*, no gay magazine would touch his scary photos, and not even he had thought to turn his recorded Old Reliable audio tapes into writing. David Hurles had been laboring underground since the late 1960s with H. Lynn Womack at Guild

Press, Washington, DC. However, in March 1978 with *Drummer* 21, Old Reliable who had worked at his craft for years became an "overnight" star.

Embry did not want "stars." Heaven help any editor such as Jeanne Barney or me, or any contributor, such as Halsted (who left in a boil) or Mapplethorpe (who left in a rage) or Opel (who left in a hearse), who outshone the publisher or the magazine. The very visible Embry thought he was playing the *invisible starring role*, the "one singular sensation," around whom all of *A Chorus Line* circles. He quickly turned against Old Reliable who had run, since 1971, his own mail-order business selling his own erotic audio tapes and his own one-reel, four-minute Super-8 films to fans of dangerous, hyper-masculine, young American men who were hustlers and ex-cons from Polk Street, Union Square, the Transbay Bus Terminal, the Zee Hotel at 141 Eddy which was the hustler hotel of the Tenderloin, and the Old Crow hustler bar at 926 Market Street.

David approved the true line I wrote to characterize him and his extreme *verite* documentary photography: "Terror Is My Only Hardon." When Rex assembled *Speeding: The Old Reliable Photography of David Hurles* (2005), our mutual friend Trent Dunphy asked me specifically who wrote the terror-hardon line, Hurles or Fritscher, perhaps because Rex figured that sentence as "true north" in the character of Old Reliable and wanted to credit the source properly. In point of fact, my line, quoted at my site from my feature "Call Him Old Reliable" in two publications *Skin* (2 #5, May 1981) and the *California Action Guide* (1 #3, September 1982), apparently rang so essentially true in fact and cadence to John Waters that in his book *Role Models* (2010) his third sentence about Old Reliable was "Danger is the turn-on for Mr. Hurles." The Googling Waters tipped no hat to acknowledge the coincidental source of his paraphrase, perhaps figuring that his softening of *terror* to *danger* and *hardon* to *turn-on* made my original rhetoric somehow his.

Hurles may have begun his career with Dr. Womack, but his muse was Bob Mizer who in 1970 became Hurles' artistic mentor, business model, and friend for whom Hurles wrote a perfect and loving eulogy for *Outcome* magazine, issue 12, in 1992. In 1980, Hurles introduced me to Mizer, and I interviewed him poolside in the backlot of his AMG studio. He gave me his personal tour of his sets and his film-archive building behind the studio which was also his home where he had grown up and where for years every Saturday night he hosted an open house, showing his newest photos and films and introducing his models to guests with checkbooks. Embry, meanwhile, was continuing his Blacklist. So my feature on Mizer, "AMG Duos," a "Virtual *Drummer*" feature, was published in *Skin* 2 #5, May 1981, alongside my article on Hurles. In 2004, Hurles, asking for editorial comments, sent me his final revision of the insightful and tender manuscript of the Introduction he had written for the Janssen book, *Bob Mizer, Athletic Model Guild : American Photography of the Male Nude 1940-1970.*

Hurles made a point in the draft of that Introduction to credit Mizer for directly aiding the careers of a dozen famous gay artists and photographers including Tom of Finland, Harry Bush, Etienne, and Larry Townsend who were all frequent contributors to the sustainment of *Drummer*. He could have added Robert Mapplethorpe, the art student at Pratt, who began his career making collages of Mizer's photographs in *Physique Pictorial* which he bought as a teenager in the dirty bookstores on 42nd Street.

In Washington, DC, Hurles had created a sensation when, during a 1968-1969 obscenity trial involving Guild Press, he testified twice: once as a Guild Press model, and once again as a Guild Press photographer, to demonstrate that posing erotically for a camera did not destroy the sanity or the humanity of the person being photographed. The judge complimented Hurles on the cogency of his testimony as well as for his ability to simultaneously photograph and fellate himself in a series of best-selling pictures.

Embry's personal enmities were destructive to *Drummer* considering how much *avant-garde* edge David Hurles mainlined into middle-brow *Drummer* with his low-class models. Readers loved Old Reliable who gave them dangerous hustlers they would never dare invite into their lovely homes. Small wonder that when I walked out, David, with whom I had bought a house on May 25, 1978, exited with me. We maintained as steadfast friends because we were never lovers. In 1984, when John Rowberry could take no more abuse at *Drummer* and extricated himself for a year from Embry, Rowberry was hired by George Mavety's Modernismo Publications to work on the magazines that Bob Johnson, with my stories and features in all his first issues, had begun publishing in 1979: *Inches, Just Men, Skin,* and *Uncut*. The always conflicted Rowberry set up himself up in a South of Market office not far from the *Drummer* office. To his chagrin, he knew what Hurles and I had done to boost *Drummer*. He enlisted us to help him keep his new job. In the world's weirdest three-way ever, we *Drummer* refugees—writer, photographer, and editor—were perhaps ill-suited to each other, but functional.

Years later, David Hurles gave me a hundred of his letters from jailbirds and clients including Rowberry's 1984 letter to him which was Rowberry's overture to begin his repetitive publishing of Hurles' Old Reliable photos. Rowberry solo, after years of riding Siamese tandem with Embry, revealed something of his own disproportionate judgment. While Embry abhorred

Old Reliable, Rowberry obsessed on Old Reliable. He stuffed his magazines with Hurles' photos and mail-order ads which, of course, made Old Reliable happy, but editorially made Rowberry seem unable to attract other photographers and, especially, other advertisers who resented that they had to pay for the kind of coverage that Hurles received free from Rowberry's obvious insider trading for mail-order ads.

In a completist bibliography covering the early 1980s, I wrote several interview-articles of Mizer and Hurles which I intended for *Drummer*, but which were published instead in various magazines such as *Skin*: "AMG Duos: Who's Who in American Chicken, Veal, and Beef," *Skin* 2 #5, 1981, page 20; "Old Reliable: The Company Dirty Talk Built," *Skin* 2 # 5, 1981, page 30; and "Beauty and Terror: The Art and Trash of Old Reliable," *Skin* 4 #3, 1983, page 10; and "Terror Is My Only Hardon: Old Reliable Speaks," *Man2Man Quarterly*, Issue 8, October 1981, pages 24-32. German publisher Marco Siedelmann reprinted these Old Reliable articles as background introducing my twenty-first century biographical essay, "David Hurles: Rough-Trade Director, Eyewitness Life inside Old Reliable Studio," in the book, *California Dreamin': West Coast Directors and the Golden Age of Forbidden Gay Movies* (2017).

While Hurles and Rowberry and I were otherwise employed filling magazines rivaling Embry, for the twenty-four months of 1984-1986, *Drummer* was dying.

Blackballed by Embry, I was an eyewitness watching from a distance, and listening to the confessions of disgruntled *Drummer* staff, as well as of dissatisfied artists, writers, and photographers, and even of angry subscribers.

Instead of *Schadenfreude*, I put my energies into transferring my *Drummer* vision to other magazines and to my boutique fetish studio, Palm Drive Video.

In terms of timeline, Rowberry, trying to save himself, had deserted the sinking ship of *Drummer* several times. Having left in early 1984, he rejoined Embry in late 1985 until DeBlase, the new buyer of *Drummer*, insisted that Rowberry had to be fired if the magazine were to be purchased. Embry cheerfully sold his "slave" Rowberry downstream in his desperation to unload the magazine that had become the content-impaired victim of Embry's own exclusionary Blacklist.

For his part, when Embry dumped *Drummer* on Tony DeBlase in 1986, he revealed where his heart lay. He sold the magazine, but he did not sell his main business interests in his "Leather Fraternity," in his Alternate Publishing, and in his mail-order company, Alternate/Wings Distributing.

Dropping Names: The Delicious Memoirs of Daniel Curzon
"John Embry"
by Daniel Curzon

"Angry, bitter, and dangerous, with chips on both shoulders, Daniel Curzon is also ferociously honest and very funny. *Dropping Names* is the most enjoyable, gossipy memoir since Gavin Dillard's *In the Flesh*. As Curzon says, 'It's gossip when you're alive; it's literary history when you're dead.'" —Ian Young, *Torso Magazine*

Daniel Curzon, the author of *Dropping Names* (2005) is the author of "the first gay protest novel," *Something You Do in the Dark*, and of the "comedie grotesque novel," *Saving 'Wacko' Jane Austen*, as well as of the non-fiction *The Joy of Atheism*. Before John Embry done him wrong, Curzon's roman a clef, *Among the Carnivores*, received a rave review in the *Drummer* sibling magazine, *The Alternate*, issue 9, 1979. Curzon is a gay *flaneur* whose impassioned eyewitness testimony about his professional experiences with John Embry quite accurately expresses in detail the publisher's high-handed villainy and attitude. From my own experience, I have no reason to doubt anything Curzon states about Embry, and his Blacklist.

Dropping Names
"John Embry"

Daniel Curzon: I was introduced to [John Embry] the publisher of the *Drummer* magazine publishing empire by John Rowberry, his long-suffering editor.

From the beginning I was wary of the man because nobody, but nobody had a good word to say about him (Unflattering memoirs are still coming out!) Embry had somehow managed to capitalize on the S&M scene with coarse fantasies and liberal doses of tit-rings and big cocks and become rich. There was something sinister about this big hulking middle-aged man that made me not want to get to know him better. Unfortunately, I couldn't avoid him. Even a bout of cancer couldn't make most people shed a tear for this caricature of the ruthless entrepreneur.

Even when Embry's empire was centered in L.A. I had bad experiences with him. Jeanne Barney, a straight woman, was the editor of *Drummer* at that time, and since we were sort of friends I sent her a short play, which she intended to use until Embry read it and said his readers would find it too hard to understand.

When Alternate Publishing (the empire) moved to San Francisco,

I began to be a regular contributor to *The Alternate*, which was John Rowberry's means of keeping his sanity in the midst of the daily deluges of S&M sex, which he [like Embry] didn't even engage in himself. Rowberry was able to publish some quality material this way. It likewise allowed him to put up with Embry's temper tantrums, forgetfulness, and financial mismanagement.

I would go to the office often, even did some proofreading to help my spindly budget. Embry had to approve every check, and so sometimes I'd find myself having to wait until a staff member could locate him and get his signature before I could get my money. I would nod hello if I had to, but I didn't want to talk to him any more than I absolutely had to.

His publications were doing well in the late 1970s, and then Embry got too ambitious. He decided to open the *Drummer* Key Club, modeled after the *Playboy* clubs, only for South-of-Market types. Rowberry told me his boss also spent some of the profits on a new house for himself and his lover, cars, the usual. The Key Club was a flop, and money became tighter. The empire moved to humbler quarters.

The staff, with few exceptions, came and went like migratory workers. Once or twice even Rowberry resigned. "What's wrong?" I asked. "That man's a liar, a cheat. I can't work for him any longer." But Rowberry would return. He was the only one who could make the empire function.

I'll have to give Embry credit for something. I did see him doing layout for *Drummer* at times, so he wasn't above dirtying his hands. As a matter of fact, he wasn't above dirtying his soul either.

Even when Alternate Publishing began to publish books, I did not suddenly cotton to John Embry. But I did submit one of mine to Rowberry, *The Y*. It was accepted and we signed a contract, but then the novel lay around the office for a year or more. When I asked Rowberry why it was taking so long to get the galleys, he said he had to wait to get each book published, in some kind of complicated trade with the printer that printed the magazines. Embry wanted the prestige/sales of real books, but he wanted to do the job on the cheap. So my book lay there, changing titles almost daily, as Rowberry and I discussed calling it something else. We finally settled on *Deathsman*.

About this time, poor David Lamble was hired by Embry to run his new newspaper. Lamble worked for a month gathering news stories and features, some from me, only to have Embry bail out at the last minute. He decided to buy the failing *California Voice* from Paul D. Hardman (on the cover of which my lover and I had once appeared, in some other strange publication deal). *California Voice* too disappeared almost at once. Lamble had nothing good at all to say about Embry after working with him, and he usually held his tongue.

I thought I'd been clever in avoiding having to deal with the man directly over quite a number of years, but I was too optimistic. After Rowberry had finally left for good and Steven Saylor (later a writer of junky gladiator porn and formulaic Roman mysteries, in hardcover book form no less) had taken over as a departmental fiction editor, I got a call from Steven after I queried him about the status of my novel. He said he thought I should take back the book because the publishing empire was dawdling with its book line, and, if the book ever did come out, most likely it wouldn't receive any promotion. I sighed, but agreed to withdraw the book. Another publisher had expressed interest in it anyhow. (It never came out.)

Stephen, in a postscript as I was leaving his office with my novel manuscript, said maybe I should send a clarifying note to Embry, telling him I was taking back the book. This I did.

Well, I began to have second thoughts about mentioning the affair to the unreliable Emperor Embry, and I called Steven to tell him to intercept my letter. But it just so happened that Embry was going through the mail and found my letter a few moments before Steven could snatch it to safety.

I thus got a telephone call from the Evil Emperor himself, telling me that his evil empire wanted my novel. Blah, blah, blah! He even admitted he hadn't known that his firm had accepted a book of mine! "But you signed the contract," I informed him. "I did?" he said. "Nobody around here tells me anything!" He went on and on about how his staff kept things from him.

When I mentioned in passing that I had received a $300 advance, he was very interested. Soon he was saying, "Well, if you don't want us to publish your book, you have to return the $300." Now everybody in publishing knows that authors do not have to return an advance on a book the publisher agrees to publish and then keeps beyond the deadline specified in the contract. The Emperor had already exceeded his deadline by a whole year! But he was so intimidating and I didn't have the contract in front of me, so I'm not sure if I even mentioned this to him.

I couldn't believe how belligerent and obnoxious Embry was in that telephone call. I just wanted to get him off my back, so I said possibly I could return the advance. As soon as I hung up, I said to myself, "He'll rot in chains in an S&M Hell before he sees a penny from me, after what I've been through."

A letter from the Emperor followed, threatening me with legal action. I got out my copy of the contract. The asshole hadn't even signed it! So legally he didn't know if I had received an advance or not. In the same letter this charming gentleman said words to this effect [regarding his Blacklist]: "If you don't give back the $300, you'll never again be published in any of the empire's publications and there aren't that many places to publish."

Can you believe this? I couldn't. I decided not to answer the letter. Steven Saylor said I should just wait, since Embry would no doubt forget about it in a week, just as he forgot about most things.

Needless to say, the Evil Empire began to collapse. What else do you expect with a demented emperor running affairs of state? *Drummer* was sold into new hands, and as a consequence the world had to be a better place.

The only way he'll ever get that $300 is to suck it out of my ass. Then again, maybe he'd like that. But I wouldn't give him the satisfaction. © 2005 Daniel Curzon

---

Even though most gay book publishers did not really start up their companies before the mid-1980s, as soon as *Drummer* became fully successful as a brand in 1979, Embry wanted to expand into book publishing. Through magazine editing and serializing, I helped develop John Preston's *Mr. Benson* as a book, but I resisted Embry's blandishments to publish my novel *Leather Blues*, which he had begun to serialize in *Drummer*, because I adamantly refused to sign away any rights to a publisher who would not pay me. Soon after I left *Drummer*, Winston Leyland of Gay Sunshine Press bought my novel and paid properly. Curzon was lucky that he escaped with his manuscript. He was generous to gay and leather history in writing his profile of Embry, and then permitting this reprint of his eyewitness experience.

DRUMMER

AMERICA'S MAG FOR THE MACHO MALE

3^{50} OUTRAGEOUS!

Cover Photograph
by Jack Fritscher and David Sparrow

ANNIVERSARY ISSUE

More pages, more fiction, more original artwork than any other Gay publication

ISSUE 30

CHAPTER 10

THE *DRUMMER* CURSE:
WHY I NEVER BOUGHT *DRUMMER*

- The *Drummer* Curse of Debt, Disease, and Death: What Happened to People Who Owned *Drummer*
- Leather Heritage: Blacklist Lies Revise *Drummer* History
- 3 Roberts: Mapplethorpe, Opel, and Davolt
- John W. Rowberry: Son of Embry, Bane of Barney
- Franken-*Drummer*: Embry Tries to Reanimate the Past in His New Monster of a Magazine: *Super MR*
- *Drummer* Purpose: Normalizing the Leather Fringe of Gay Culture
- Cash and Copyright: Brush Creek Media and *Bear* Magazine
- Cynthia Slater and Frank Sammut: The Catacombs Wedding

In 1978, the ninth of our ten years as lovers, David Sparrow loved me enough to give me this advice about *Drummer*: "Why buy what you already 'own'?" As the domestic spouse I had married, with leather priest Jim Kane officiating, on the rooftop of 2 Charlton Street in New York, he knew intimately my experiences as editor-in-chief. When I hired him as the freelance and official house-photographer for *Drummer*, he became his own eyewitness inside *Drummer*.

Considering my fifty-year career in gay writing, people have asked me a hundred times why I never bought *Drummer*. What was there to buy? Its one-word name was all *Drummer* had to sell. That, and an insatiable deadline that had to be fed every thirty days or the magazine would starve and die. Everything else existed upstairs over a vacant lot. Despite Embry's dodgy masthead claims, I reckoned there were no legally registered trademarks for sale, no filing cabinets spilling over with a backlog of good stories and photos and drawings panting to be published, no legal paperwork identifying what publishing rights, and republishing rights, had been bought from contributors who were mostly pseudonymous and lost to history, no model identification documents or signed releases, and no mail-order business.

Drummer was a brand name, yes, and had momentum, yes, and an ardent fan following, yes; but *Drummer* was made by all three publishers into a suicidal succubus draining cash, time, and talent because it was always run not as a proper business but as a gay business. It was Mickey and Judy putting on an unsustainable show in the barn. The first publisher, Embry, hitched his chapbook *Drummer* to the *H.E.L.P Newsletter* to access its subscriber list in order to sell personal ads, sex toys, and poppers mail-order. My friend from the 1960s, the Chicago psychiatrist Andrew Charles, who had deep pockets and a loaded checkbook, became the second publisher when he established Desmodus, Inc., and bought *Drummer* as a trophy-toy for his lover Anthony DeBlase, who, moving to San Francisco, and throwing his jolly weight around at *Drummer*, became an instant leather celebrity and corporal instructor of eager young leather bottoms worshiping "everything *Drummer*." The eyewitness evidence of this dynamic is in DeBlase's four-feature *USSM* video series starring himself as the epicene "Fledermaus," the San Francisco whipmeister to hot and handsome young men—models from Mikal Bales' Zeus Studio in Los Angeles—who would have been out of his league were he not the publisher of *Drummer*.

Embry and DeBlase, with paradigms of Hugh Hefner dancing in both their heads, figured *Drummer* was a gay *Playboy* with the *Playboy* lifestyle. DeBlase and Charles stuffed their new mansion, south of San Francisco, with designer furniture, and staffed it with a revolving crew of leatherboy butlers and servants waiting on visiting LA leather-porn moguls such as Bales, and BDSM models such as Scott Answer who, like an Edwardian aristocrat changing into proper attire for morning, afternoon, and evening, slipped unironically every hour or so into new West Hollywood fashions made of leather, then rubber, then latex, pushing his didactic LA fetish exhibition at rival San Franciscans, happy with basic black leather. Embry struggled vaingloriously to open his "exclusive *Drummer* Key Club" on Folsom Street where it flopped. Embry also exploited the start-up of the Mr. Drummer Contest to turn the contestants into free models for centerfolds like *Playboy* Bunnies. In the annals and anals of gay liberation, sexual objectification has an enthusiastic and valuable tradition, but only as long as the contestant models are complicit in their pop-culture roles, and thus empower themselves through performances which can enhance their self-esteem, perhaps damaged in their youth by nationalized American homophobia.

However, the Hefner business model was more than about content or contests. *Drummer* needed to follow Hefner's paradigm for *Playboy*, or Larry

Flynt's for *Hustler*, or Andy Warhol's for *Interview*. Warhol had founded *Interview* in 1969, but the magazine did not turn its first profit until 1979, unlike *Drummer* which, although few believed it possible, never turned a 1979 profit. Or so Embry swore when our pay was not forthcoming.

Among all the parties in our *Drummer* Salon, there were two significant dinner parties that, like all things *Drummer*, turned inevitably to discussions about *Drummer* money, and talent not being paid. The first was the February 9, 1978, supper for nine men that Al Shapiro and I hosted at Jim Kane and Ike Barnes' 11 Pink Alley firetrap so that some of my star *Drummer* contributors, Tom of Finland and his lover Veli, and my lover Robert Mapplethorpe, and Sam Steward, and Robert Opel could all meet each other for the first time. These men were all gents and artists and had many pleasant interests in common including being in various degrees of stress about not being paid properly by Embry who was twice as slippery to the Europeans contributing from afar, with no redress but to beg the editor-in-chief to shake the publisher for payment. As editor, I apologized for Embry whom they knew I could not change. Around our pleasant table, the badinage of the hot-blooded artists, all at their peak, revealed that they all were pleased that Al and I had decided not to invite the cold-blooded Embry.

The second essential *Drummer* Salon dinner party was the September 28, 1986, supper for seven guests whom the significant San Francisco art dealers Trent Dunphy and Bob Mainardi invited to their Victorian home to welcome new *Drummer* owners DeBlase and Charles to their table around which sat we survivors of Embry's *Drummer*. In attendance were the three hosts Dunphy and Mainardi and *Drummer* artist Rex, guests of honor Tony DeBlase and Andy Charles, Al Shapiro and his partner Dick Kriegmont, photographer Mark I. Chester, and my spouse Mark Hemry and I.

Between courses at that 1986 power pow-wow, DeBlase unrolled an emotional monolog. Only a couple months into owning *Drummer*, Tony said that he and Andy thought they had purchased *Drummer* free of any encumbrances, until they were immediately besieged by creditors and vendors hoping the new owners would pay them what Embry's *Drummer* still owed them. A bit touchy, DeBlase cracked a nervous joke hoping that none of us would ask him to pay what Embry owed us. They rather appreciated the good humor when I mentioned how one of the last of Embry's editors, Tim Barrus, took his revenge for not being paid properly. Barrus, who—with Joseph Bean—was one of my two favorite *Drummer* editors, had written to me about the chaos in the office that had caused him to quit as Embry's editor and move to Key West a short time before DeBlase rescued *Drummer*. Barrus recalled:

John Embry always sucked. He once made an accounting error against himself and sent me several checks for the same article. Then he saw his error and screamed bloody murder he wanted that money back....He owed me so much I cashed every check. Fuck him.

Buying *Drummer*?

I never bought *Drummer* because it never had a real-world business plan for itself. It never fit the business plan for my life. That's why while editing, writing, and photographing for *Drummer*, I never quit my day job which, after my tenured career teaching journalism, literature, and film at university, was as a corporate marketing professional managing a staff of twenty writers while working at Kaiser Engineers thirty minutes away from the *Drummer* office. Instead of buying *Drummer*, even after David Sparrow and I divorced, Mark Hemry and I created an alternative to *Drummer* in 1979.

With our reader-interactive *Man2Man Quarterly*, we made the point that even intense underground erotic magazines can succeed with a low-budget business plan that does not include the publisher's hand in the till. When *Man2Man* ceased publication in 1982 because desktop publishing did not yet exist to speed our hands-on labor, we moved forward with new media, evolving from page to screen by starting up our Palm Drive Video company featuring *Drummer*-like models and BDSM themes I had introduced to *Drummer* such as cigars, fetish play, and homomasculinity. However, unlike the mail-order bandit Embry who never refunded anyone anything, publisher Mark Hemry calculated how much of a subscription rebate was owed to our thousand *Man2Man* subscribers, and he sent each one a small check. Several men sent thank-you notes saying they had never heard of any gay publisher doing such a thing.

I saw what happened to people who bought *Drummer*. They seemed cursed with debt, dishonesty, disease, and death. *Drummer* itself did not curse them. *Drummer* was merely the medium through which their personal dysfunction and bad business behavior was amplified the way a friend of mine, who helped proofread this manuscript, won eight million dollars in the California lottery and each one of his addiction problems multiplied eight million times. Like Hollywood itself, *Drummer* was a golden opportunity for creative people, and a tempting trap for business people exploiting its resources for money, power, and sex.

Ten years after Embry sold *Drummer* to Anthony DeBlase, and a year after *Drummer* itself ceased publication, Embry continued to stew that

DeBlase's *Drummer* had sometimes taken potshots at him both in and out of *Drummer*. The overweight Embry took glee in DeBlase's nickname "DeBlob." When DeBlase, an obese cigar smoker died young of heart disease on July 21, 2000, Embry, rendering his own fat, cooked up a snotty, minimalist 75-word obituary that DeBlase was out of the picture in his *Super MR* #6, Autumn 2000.

In that sarcastic obituary, the dick-swinging Embry called DeBlase "Mr." instead of "Dr." which would have infuriated the "Anthony F. DeBlase, PhD" on the *Drummer* masthead. Embry further succeeded in disrespecting DeBlase by sidestepping any direct mention of DeBlase as the second publisher of the world-famous *Drummer* who, faced with the social and viral changes of the 1980s, successfully struggled to open *Drummer* to all genders and to safe-sex guide lines.

Instead, he mentioned two of DeBlase's earlier small magazines, *SandMutopia Guardian* and *DungeonMaster*, and then mashed *Drummer* into a roll call with these B-List magazine titles. In Embry's appliqued subtext, he implied that *Drummer* was too much of a footrace for the sprinter DeBlase who bought and, all too quickly, sold the magazine to the Dutch within six years because he couldn't handle *Drummer* for the grand total of eleven years that Embry, the long-distance runner, had owned it. In the bully department, Embry finished up with a gender smackdown which was not cool in a masculine-identified magazine. He insinuated in the connotative spin of his subtext that DeBlase was a sissy "best known" for running up the leather flag on his, well, Betsy Ross sewing machine.

Editorial

We were saddened to hear that Tony DeBlase passed away at 58 in Portland, Oregon. Mr. DeBlase wrote under the name "Fledermaus" and published *SandMutopia Guardian* and *DungeonMaster*. He and Andrew Charles, through their company Desmodus, purchased the *Drummer, FQ [Foreskin Quarterly]*, and *Mach* titles from Alternate publishing in 1986. The Desmodus company was then sold to Rob of Amsterdam in 1992. Mr. DeBlase is perhaps best known as the designer of the leather flag. –John Embry, *Super MR* #6, Autumn 2000

Eight years later, in 2008, in the thirty-first year of my sine-wave relationship with John Embry, I thought someone should tell him at the Russian River that his frenemy Larry Townsend in Los Angeles was unconscious in an Intensive Care Unit. In response to my email, Embry, never one to forgive a grudge, wrote in ALL CAPS.

> From: Jack Fritscher
> To: John Embry
> July 23, 2008 3:33 PM
> Subject: Larry Townsend in ICU
>
> John, Our friend Larry Townsend is in ICU. Hopefully, he may rally, but the situation seems very distressed. If you want more info, please let me know. If you don't want to know, let me know.
> May our world of writers and readers keep Larry in our thoughts and give him good energy during the next few hours and days.
>
> Jack Fritscher

> From: John Embry
> To: Jack Fritscher
> July 23, 2008 6:02 PM
> Subject: Re: Larry Townsend in ICU
>
> [Embry writing in all UPPER CAPS] JACK, THANK YOU FOR NOTIFYING ME. ALTHOUGH LARRY'S AND MY RELATIONSHIP IS IN ABOUT THE SAME STATE AS HIS AND JEANNIE'S [sic]. BE THAT AS IT MAY, I WISH HIM WELL AND WAS VERY DISMAYED AT FRED'S PASSING [Townsend's partner of 38 years] WHICH I AM SURE WAS VERY HARD ON HIM.
>
> John Embry [lower caps]

Larry Townsend died six days later on July 29, 2008. In the gay archives of the dead, the Embry file boxes will forever be in a scholastic gay studies feud with the Townsend file boxes.

Regarding the universally contentious Embry, the writer and frequent *Drummer* author George Birimisa wrote to me on January 29, 2012:

> Jack, I guess you know I have a reputation as a very gay Off-Off Broadway playwright, but over the years, queer men would see my name and say, "You wrote that novel in *Drummer*. The magazine

was an incredible expression of free speech and that is why the LAPD practically tar-and-feathered John Embry to get him to flee LA for San Francisco. Love, George

The *Drummer* curse, from the 1970s through the 1990s, devastated those who owned it or claimed they owned it. Even though Embry had sold *Drummer* in 1986, he suffered seller's remorse. When the young Midwestern blond Robert Davolt showed up in San Francisco to work as proxy for the Dutchman Martijn Bakker who had bought *Drummer* from DeBlase, Embry astutely judged that he could manipulate Davolt in San Francisco against the absentee Bakker in Amsterdam to his own advantage. Portraying himself as *Drummer* Incarnate, Embry cosied up to the ambitious Davolt and turned him into a double-agent who could work for the faraway Dutch owner while feeding Embry private business information which included handing over to Embry whatever manuscripts, art, and photographs were stored in *Drummer*'s treasure-chest of neglected filing cabinets. Proof of collusion lay in the fact that the minute the well-rehearsed Davolt was fired by Bakker, Embry hired him to edit his *Super MR* magazine.

Embry was desperate to create a new "Franken-*Drummer*"magazine by reanimating *Drummer*. Damn the rights, he wanted whatever backlog of material that Davolt smuggled out from *Drummer* to help fill his *Super MR*. Because I was not one of the dead *Drummer* contributors whose grave he could rob, he came directly to me, which pained him dearly, to ask permission to publish in *Super MR* fiction and features that twenty-five years before I had written for *Drummer*. He was intent on returning to our mutual roots. So I consented to his republishing my original 1977 through 1979 writing because I think supporting gay publishing and history is more important than anyone's grudge against anyone. Embry knew I was faithful to the pure idea of *Drummer*, but more, he knew that after nearly thirty years I, with Jeanne Barney, was one of only a few survivors of early *Drummer*, and the only founding author who would have anything to do with him. I'm sure his rosacea face broke into red bloom when, a survivor himself, he had to acknowledge that I was the last living of his original *Drummer* writer-photographers as well as his editor-in-chief who had, during his cancer, steered the concept of *Drummer* to its first national fame. In his "Getting Off" editorial in *Drummer* 83 (March 1985), he had sniped like a dumped lover about our then eight-year-long relationship with spinning animosity:

> We had an editor [Fritscher] some years back who still refers to the time he spent with us as "The Golden Age of *Drummer*." We

remember the good parts of those times, but if there is a Golden Age for this magazine, it would be the here and now, beginning with this issue [*Drummer* 83]....

Even so, while featuring my *Drummer* writing and photographs as headline leads in the first six pages of his first *Super MR* issue (2000), edited by Davolt, he refused to pay me cash for any *Super MR* reprints, offering instead an ongoing trade for advertising space for Palm Drive Video as he first did on that issue's page 57 with a half-page ad for bodybuilder Chris Duffy starring in my feature-length video, *Sunset Bull*.

It was satisfaction enough that he asked me to help him re-constitute what he finally admitted was, as often called by *Drummer* subscribers, the "1970s Golden Age of *Drummer*." In old age, he needed me as he had needed me years before when his dishonesty turned off contributors and cancer kept him absent from *Drummer*. In the long struggle between the corporate publisher and the artist writer, his republishing my work spoke volumes about his grudging admission and approval of our mutual history.

However, spinning around our detente, Robert Davolt, ambitious with a nostalgia for a *Drummer* past he had never personally experienced, became Embry's tool for falsifying the institutional history of *Drummer* which was wider than Embry's ownership. As a social climber, he was seduced that the veteran Embry offered to take him, the new recruit, under his Mephistophelian wings. With the American mole Davolt spying inside Dutch *Drummer*, Embry grew bolder, sponsoring Davolt to write a bespoke history of *Drummer* tailored to the inclusions and exclusions of Embry's famous little Blacklist.

On the San Francisco leather scene in bars and at regional Mr. Drummer contests, the attractively blond and bearded Davolt, who loved to travel nationwide on *Drummer* dollars, was "charming" in the same way that Embry's "charm" disarmed people who did not know him. The young Davolt, reveling in the reflected glory of *Drummer*, and keen on being the next publisher of *Drummer* under Bakker, but under the thumb of Embry, was characteristically way more "Son of Embry" than he ever was "Son of *Drummer*."

In many ways, Davolt's 1990s recruitment to the scene typifies the way some latter-day revisionists have tried to rewind the 1970s by brainwashing the young eager to learn their elders' history and fish stories. Accuracy depends on which elders and which agenda. The 1990s, in particular, was a freaked-out decade because the Great Dying of the 1980s raised everyone's anxiety about the evaporation of gay oral and written history from the 1970s.

Into the void rode Marxist feminist academics of all genders, and vanilla gay institutions with mainstream misconceptions and stereotyped suspicions about outsider leather culture which they were all too happy to codify and label from their politically correct points of view, typically fingering men, in their fundamentalist chapter and verse, as patriarchal oppressors.

Gay history, more oral tradition than written, had always existed sub rosa. With the official invention of Queer Studies and Queer Theory around 1990, it became the "Gay History Business." In earlier days, people had come to San Francisco to feast on sex. After Foucault partied himself to death on fists at the Slot and Barracks baths of Folsom Street in the late 1970s and 1980s, academic carpetbaggers flocked into the City in the Queer 1990s like Hitchcock's *The Birds* to pick the bones of leather history which some of them, in their only S&M gesture, tied down to their preconceived Procrustean beds.

Gay and leather history were new hooks for footloose or forlorn professors needing to score academic tenure or grants, and for university libraries and archives to establish themselves, like churches promising everlasting life, by goading the dying at the height of the AIDS crisis, to donate their estates and their cash. Despite some intellectual abuse, gay history accommodated this expanding of legitimate political, academic, and gender agenda as well as new vocabulary by coopting words like *queer*.

Professional homosexuals and lesbians, especially privileged academics and politically correct protectionists and fundamentalists of every gender, race, religion, and grievance, began announcing "new rules" for telling the past the way they saw it or wanted to slice it. By the early 1990s, they started to rewrite history both by commission and omission. It seemed leatherfolk were to be reeducated in a brave new world where a Marxist type of patricidal feminism, minus irony, tried to retrofit and trump male homosexuality.

The towering babble of voices proved that history is indeed very *Rashomon* in all its points of view leading, hopefully as in a court trial, to the truth about the past from all the reasonable participants within that history.

Revisionism, meaning incorrect "ideological information" rather than the input of new but unknown truth, is wrong. For instance, on the internet at dozens of hate sites is a Blacklist of fifty or so "American Jewish Leaders in the Degenerate Homosexual Movement." Round up the usual suspects of Larry Kramer, Tony Kushner, Allen Ginsberg, Harvey Fierstein, Martin Duberman, Gayle Rubin, Richard Goldstein, and Jack Fritscher named as "the influential Jewish editor who took over *Drummer* in 1977." This is grand ethnic company to keep, but it would be a newsflash to my Irish-Catholic mother and my Austrian-Catholic father. So much for the accuracy of anti-Semitic, homophobic, and politically correct revisionism. So much for Embry, the Cyclops, whose two-dimensional one eye could never see the three-dimensional perspective around *Drummer*.

Herein lies another literary panel for a GLBT writers conference. Analyzing the contributors and the contents of *Drummer*, one notices that except for Al Shapiro there was very little Jewish presence in *Drummer*, which is strange because S&M with its precepts, ritual, justice, and discipline is very Old Testament even with its add-on of the New Testament Crucifixion and Stations of the Cross whose details are iconic S&M in art and eros. I thought the "Interrogation" drawings of Leon Golub (1922-2004) with their parallels to gay S&M drawings by the Nazi-impacted Tom of Finland and Rex would have been an obvious fit in their own art layout or as illustrations for fiction. Embry did not. The Methodist Embry, ever jealous of publisher David Goodstein, borrowed everything and everybody he could from *The Advocate* except its then somewhat Jewish soul which was beyond his cultural understanding.

Although Embry published ads for the gay Nazi party in early *Drummer*, he quickly learned to correct his insensitivities about how far free speech can go. For all that he was, he was no bigot. *Drummer* in contributors and content might have been less Catholic and more Jewish if more writers from the incestuous New York clique of gatekeepers had not stood aloof in a virtual boycott of its pages, warned off, perhaps, by the demagoguery of Richard Goldstein who wrote "S&M: The Dark Side of Gay Liberation," published in the *Village Voice* (July 7, 1975) three weeks after the first issue of *Drummer*.

This is only a casual observation of S&M "Papists," from the Catholic aristocrat DeSade to the Catholic iconographer Mapplethorpe. Perhaps some daring GLBT panel might discuss: Is S&M, which at heart contains deep sentiments of religious ritual and psychology, a Catholic or a Jewish recreational sport?

The following exchange appeared in "Letters to the Editor," *Drummer* 3, page 12:

> Gentlemen, Please cancel my subscription. I do not wish to receive any publication that carries advertising for the "National Socialist League [Nazi]." —Fred, Wyoming

> Dear Fred, While we are certainly in sympathy with your feelings, and while we have no particular empathy with the "National Socialists," we feel that by denying any group the right to a voice, no

matter how we disagree with what they say, we are violating the very freedom we are trying to defend. *Drummer*'s only censorship is that no group attack any other. After all, everyone among us belongs to some minority. Thank you for taking time to let us know how you feel. —Robert Payne [aka John Embry]

BLACKLIST AGENDA: THROUGH A DAVOLT (DARKLY); JOHN ROWBERRY & THE REVOLVING KITCHEN TABLE

Embry's angry Hit List began in LA and grew enormously over time in San Francisco. His Blacklist was a red badge of courage. If you weren't on it, you weren't as avant garde as you thought. As Embry alienated more people in San Francisco, word spread about him and his lover Mario Simon, the two dramasexuals, sitting, as Jeanne Barney wrote, on their weekend deck at the Russian River piously clucking on about everyone who had done 'em wrong.

Immigrants to new cities need orientation. When Davolt moved to San Francisco to work for *Drummer* and found craziness in its office, he himself decided to court Embry who upon meeting him took control of the relationship. Perhaps Davolt wanted advice, but he did not stand a chance. Embry never met an immigrant he couldn't turn into a wage slave, or a sex slave, or a ventriloquist's sock puppet. Fresh from the Heartland of Missouri and Wisconsin, Davolt, who had belonged to the Young Republicans, was too naive to first investigate how San Francisco sexual politics might work against him if he hooked up with a scam artist like Embry whom leatherfolk had long since dismissed as a trickster. In short, his liaison with Embry hurt Davolt's reputation. Nearly every time he would mention that he was the "new editor and publisher" of Dutch *Drummer*, his next words would be about Embry, and all the help Embry was in "reconstituting" the past. Of course, Embry was trying his utmost to rewind *Drummer* history and, with most eyewitnesses dead, make it his own gospel, and he wanted Davolt to be one of his key evangelists. Sadly, Robert Davolt's young life was cut short when he died suddenly from skin cancer on May 16, 2005.

Frankly, I tried not to include Davolt, whom I liked, in the seamy parts of *Drummer* history, but he made himself part of it and what he did is a marker, but not a mark, on his character as an apparatchik keeper of leather history. Davolt may have been mouthing what he believed to be true, but some of the history he'd been told was disinformation. And he was, as he revealed about himself in his memoirs, a self-admitted ambitious man keen on getting ahead in leather publishing.

Blogging on his leatherpage.com, Davolt wrote secondhand comments repeating a mythology that never happened, such as, "The Victorian apartment building on upper Market Street where early [*sic*] *Drummer* editor John Rowberry put together several issues in his kitchen." God is in the details, and as the tiniest "Exhibit A" of Davolt tampering with truths small and large, that phony "kitchen table" image is revisionist history lacking perspective because Rowberry was not an "early *Drummer* editor" insofar as he did not become even "associate editor" of *Drummer* until 1980, and only then after I exited which would have made me an early-early *Drummer* editor, and Jeanne Barney an early-early-early editor. His bump to full-fledged "editor" occurred only with *Drummer* 40 in January 1981, one full year after my departure, and six years after the first issue of *Drummer*.

And that kitchen table? That hands-on image is something either Embry or Davolt Googled and lifted, in their wishful confusion of attribution, from my website where since 1995 I was posting, among other history, local-color details about my own writing of early *Drummer* on my kitchen table in 1977 when *Drummer* was not yet two years old. One truth about John Rowberry is that he was always a pisser marking his territory. No office worker nervous about his competition was ever more jealous of holding down his own desk in the *Drummer* office than Rowberry, or, later, when I worked with him, at his very big office with the giant desk provided him South of Market by the Mavety Corporation. A kitchen table? Not his grand Los Angeles style because he liked to be seen sitting like a media mogul enthroned behind a desk that helped counter the fact that during the 1970s he was referred to at *Drummer* as the "office boy" who could not even make more than a twelve-issue "go" of Embry's pretentious passion project, *The Alternate*, which, pretending to be *The Advocate*, no matter what the two tried, was as disconcerting a flop as the disco career of Embry's lover, Mario Simon.

In the 1970s before computers and keyboards, we all wrote *Drummer* in long hand or on our own manual typewriters. My wordsmithing tool was my first typewriter, a gray 1956 Smith-Corona Portable with forest-green keys which, as a retired totem, has long sat atop a bureau in my bedroom because that non-electric typewriter was amazing: it was a keyboard that did not need a printer. So with strong fingers, we *Drummer* contributors gave our "medieval" copy to our unflappable typesetter, Marge Anderson, who, short, jolly and obese, with her Pall Mall cigarette always dangling from her lip, re-typed every word in *Drummer*. Marge herself could have written an extraordinary eyewitness testimony insofar as she had moved house from her 13940 Oxnard Street apartment in Van Nuys to follow her job with Embry and *Drummer* to San Francisco.

Davolt was also confused as to how many people had in fact been "editor-in-chief." There were only two editors-in-chief. After Jeanne Barney was the "founding Los Angeles editor-in-chief" and I was the "founding San Francisco editor-in-chief," Embry never gave the freedom of that high a title to any editor ever again. In Barney and me, Embry hired functional professionals who often resisted, and then led him, while we both insisted that the contributors be paid for writing, artwork, and photography. After us, he took a cue from his own sadomasochistic publication and sought out subservient staff and editors such as Rowberry.

As David Sparrow, and visitors to our home including Robert Opel, Robert Mapplethorpe, Al Shapiro, Thom Gunn, and even John Embry on truth serum could attest, *Drummer* in the 1970s was mostly written and edited on my kitchen table at my 25th Street Victorian, because, trying to avoid all the office politics and infighting, and keen to keep my own leather voice separate from Embry's camp leather voice, I never kept a formal editorial desk at the *Drummer* Divisadero office. Instead, each day I carried in all my "home work" which included my own original writing for *Drummer* as well as manuscripts and photo sets I edited on my kitchen table for other contributors who sat in my kitchen at that very table, including Robert Mapplethorpe, Oscar Streaker Robert Opel, *Advocate* editor Mark Thompson, and writers John Preston, John Trojanski, Bob Zygarlicki, and Jim Stewart who lived with David Sparrow and me. Each day, I assigned the next phase of production on the manuscripts and art work to various staff including Al Shapiro. Not wanting to lord it over anyone from a tyrannical editor's desk, I spent my in-office time sitting as equally as possible with staff at each of their work stations.

THE 3 ROBERTS: ROBERT MAPPLETHORPE AND ROBERT OPEL, PLUS/MINUS ROBERT DAVOLT

Always I headed back to my safe white-oak kitchen table, which I am using at the moment. It belongs in the Leather Archives & Museum because it became famous for the elbows that leaned on it over the years. That table is itself a minor character in *Some Dance to Remember*. It was at that table that my bicoastal lover Robert Mapplethorpe, who often stayed with me, ate breakfast and talked on the telephone to Patti Smith. It was at that table that Mapplethorpe watched Robert Opel jerk off while I read, at Opel's request, a story he had asked me to write for his new magazine, *Cocksucker*. When Opel shot his load as I finished the reading, Mapplethorpe, watching Opel write me a check of $125, said: "I thought I was the master-hustler of the hard sell." I handed Opel a paper towel and said, "Why can't you be like other publishers and just let me mail it in." I was ever so thankful that I did not have to read my erotic material personally to John Embry.

Before I wrote Shapiro's obituary in *Drummer* 108, Embry never gave any indication that he had ever read anything of mine that he had published in *Drummer*. He thought of me as inches, column inches, faithfully filling *Drummer* against its deadlines. With my training for the Catholic priesthood, I sometimes thought of *Drummer* as a droll parish bulletin sent out nationwide to instruct and thrill reader-subscribers who were only then learning how important it was to uncloset the homomasculine lifestyle in a gay culture whose media image was dominated by drag queens and effeminacy. As a humanist, I had to ask if a political masculinism existed, shouldn't it be equal to feminism?

Regarding Davolt, what college credential or professional training did he have for writing history? He majored in political science at the University of Missouri. He listened to Embry's version of Embry's eleven years at *Drummer* which as a magazine lasted twenty-four years, including the thirteen years when Embry as persona non grata to both the second and third owners was not privy to its internal workings. If Davolt simply double-checked the ongoing masthead of *Drummer* issues, he could have sorted the fact that by the time John Rowberry became editor with *Drummer* 40 (January 1981), the Titanic 1970s were dead as disco, and the "early" (Davolt's word) *Drummer* of wild sex had collapsed into the new normal of safe sex. In my archeology, "early" *Drummer* occurred in LA with Jeanne Barney helming the first eleven issues, and concluded in *Drummer*'s teens with my first fully San Francisco issue, *Drummer* 19 (December 1977).

ROW, ROW, ROWBERRY: OFFICE BOY ON THE MAKE;
SON OF EMBRY, BANE OF BARNEY

If ever a character deserved a "character sketch" it was John W. Rowberry whom I grew to know extremely well and worked with off and on for sixteen years from 1977 to his death in 1993.

Scene 1, Take 1: Beginning after my departure, while following my editorial production of the last issues of the 1970s (31, 32, and 33), *Drummer* found new digs at 15 Harriet Street where, once he moved in, the territorial Rowberry never left his desk to go home to "a kitchen table," for fear his seat would be taken by Embry's next "slave-boy" hire. That "position" of servitude was a running joke in the office. Rowberry, for instance, seemed intimidated when Embry succumbed to the wiles of the self-identified hustler-writer John Preston whom Rowberry saw as competition for his office job. He needn't have feared because Preston had been fired as the editor of *The Advocate* after only ten months in 1975, and his editing reputation was in tatters. In addition, Preston was a writer who himself, according to his friend, the author Lars Eighner, always needed heavy editing which I had to do, in fact, to produce the final copy of his draft manuscript of *Mr. Benson* for serial publication in *Drummer*.

On October 31, 1985, I wrote Rowberry a letter congratulating him on his being hired to edit *Inches* magazine for which I had already written steadily for five years with its founding editor Bob Johnson. For all our attitudinal differences, we never quarreled. I did not rub it in that I had given him a good recommendation at Modernismo Publications which published *Inches* and other vanilla magazines. I also thanked him for his generous help in suggesting his friend, the agent, Bill Whitehead, who might represent the manuscript of my novel *Some Dance to Remember* that I had completed in 1984.

Before Rowberry matured and escaped *Drummer*, he was always Embry's minion. It was something like hero worship. Both were very strange men. Jeanne Barney told me she remembered Rowberry taking Embry's part when Embry trashed her "mercilessly and libelously" in LA after she left *Drummer*.

Rowberry fled *Drummer* before DeBlase bought it from Embry, because DeBlase loathed the trouble-making Rowberry, the co-dependent of Embry, and refused to buy *Drummer* unless Rowberry was fired. Eyewitness DeBlase railed in *Drummer* that Rowberry some years before had accepted three of DeBlase's S&M stories; but when DeBlase wrote to Rowberry asking to be paid for the first story, Rowberry turned petulant, refused payment, and rejected the remaining two stories which DeBlase published months later in Modernismo's *Honcho*, the specific rival of *Drummer*.

It is a suitable storyline for a television sit-com that one of the prime problems in running a gay S&M magazine was dealing with the psychology of employees who were sexual slaves. Seeking abuse, these slave-boy hires were all too eager to work for pennies for a cruel master. Seeking identity, they got hard bragging they worked for an S&M business by day and played S&M games by night. In the unbridled 1970s, I thought Embry abused this dynamic to get cheap obedient labor the way the priest, Jim Kane, used it to rent his Pearl Street apartments to obedient bottoms like my gal-pal, Cynthia Slater, who in the *Drummer* Salon nearly became my sister-in-law while she was dating my straight and hot military-career brother just before she took a fistful of dollars to marry the gay Australian immigrant, Frank

Sammut, at City Hall in 1979, with Catacombs owner Steve McEachern as best man. (Sammut's eyewitness email of January 8, 2012, endnotes this chapter.) Embry seemed absurd and unprofessional exploiting young leathermen's sex needs and neuroses to run his publishing sweat shop. When it came to social justice, no wonder he and I did not see eye to eye.

I was looking for creatives.

He was looking for submissives.

Embry knew how to top Davolt, because he had practiced on Rowberry and Preston and hundreds like them.

Barney, Barrus, Bean, Shapiro, Townsend, and Fritscher no more bowed to Embry and his Blacklist than did Halsted, Hurles, Mapplethorpe, Menerth, and Sparrow.

When the aggrieved Rowberry fled *Drummer* because of DeBlase, he decided to tell Embry a thing or two himself, and thus moved from accomplice to *persona non grata* on Embry's Blacklist. Rowberry followed the exact exit journey I had taken moving from my publisher Embry at Alternate Publishing to my publisher George Mavety at Modernismo. As strange bedfellows, Rowberry and I strategically bonded in a marriage of convenience when he came to work for Modernismo to replace my drug-addled and dysfunctional friend, the editor, Bob Johnson, with whom I had first joined forces creating the premiere issues of Modernismo magazines such as *Skin* on January 4, 1979, with still a year to work as editor-in-chief at *Drummer*. The other magazines Johnson and I started together pre-Rowberry were *Skinflicks* (1980), *Inches* (1980), *Studflix* (1981), and *Just Men* (1982).

Johnson and I exchanged a vast correspondence chronicling the state of gay publishing from 1979-1984. His archived letters are filled with anguish apologizing for spending his money on drugs and not paying his writers, and begging for me to please send him one or two stories for the next issue, because he "really, really, really" would pay up. I stood faithful to him because unlike Embry, Johnson ultimately always paid up. Mark Hemry and I last visited Bob Johnson in his stylish house overlooking the Hollywood Strip during Thanksgiving 1985 to console him after Rowberry's takeover. At that time, glass-top tables were all the rage because their surface made chopping cocaine into lines with razor blades easy. Mark Hemry and I stood back, askance, watching Johnson bent over the table snorting again and again, while outside in the pouring rain the red taillights of traffic slowly headed west out Sunset Boulevard. It was a scene from a movie. One we didn't want to be in. Soon after, the ravaged Bob Johnson, whose real name was not his porn-business name, joined the disappeared.

Johnson had been Mavety's packager, scrambling to fill the hungry monthly magazines, and I had been his writer. Rowberry, who never met Johnson, was as mixed-happy-sad as Rowberry ever got that he and I had inherited each other. Because I had learned ways to handle his passive-aggressive personality, we were both content to work together at long distance. Within his own office, the snappish Rowberry added another disgruntled former *Drummer* employee, Steven Saylor/Aaron Travis, to help fill Johnson's list of magazines. Unlike, my friend, the sweet cocaine-addict Johnson, Rowberry stayed sober, and, unlike Johnson and Embry, paid the talent.

When describing sex writing, Rowberry sent me a handwritten note in summer 1986: "Jack, Remember I *love* [his italics] detailed descriptions of the characters' genitals. —JWR"

Historical Principle: Editor Rowberry in the 1980s focused *Drummer* on genitals. His godfather, Embry, focused on leather contestants. Rowberry and Embry both missed the mirroring essence of what made my 1977-1979 *Drummer* have *verite* appeal in a decade self-fashioning gay-male identity: faces, fetishes, fiction, and features reflecting grass-roots readers.

A *Drummer* reader emailed about my writing: "You differentiate masculinity, sexuality, genitality, and the physical experience of leather and S&M as a constellation of foci that, as now, can, but need not be, joined."

My *Drummer* was not about penis, and not about beauty contests. It was about homomasculinity as a concept of emerging gender identity for men who like men masculine.

I replaced prescriptive LA attitude with descriptive San Francisco latitude.

When it came to sex impacting publishing, Rowberry was no pedophile. But as we worked together on *Studflix*, he so exclusively reviewed videos of blond chickens who were legally eighteen but not looking it, and he was so wrongly prejudiced against the emerging sunami of daddies and bears in magazines and video, that I told him, "If sperm could act, you'd give it a good review."

Nevertheless, Rowberry often published my photographs of grown men, and reviewed my homomasculine Palm Drive Video titles. Wrapping his review text around three of my bodybuilder photographs (pages 12-13), he wrote in *Studflix*, February 1987:

Of special interest at Palm Drive Video are the following bodybuilding features: *Bodybuilder Hunks* which includes rare footage of the first "Gay Games" Physique Contest and a very young Frank Vickers before he ever dropped his trunks for Colt Studios [or for Robert Mapplethorpe]. In *Buckskin Musclemen*, your jaw will drop when you recognize this former triple crown winner, Chuck Sipes (Mr. America, Mr. World, and Mr. Universe).... Fritscher's Palm Drive Video approaches what amounts to public voyeurism with such a casual hand that it comes off as *cinema verite*, documenting the spontaneous everyday thrills and knowing exactly where to look.

In *Inches*, February 1991, Rowberry wrote his own eyewitness insider's review of *Some Dance to Remember* because he figured that the *Leather Man* magazine portrayed in that memoir-novel was *Drummer*. "Rest assured," Rowberry wrote in his positive review, "*Some Dance to Remember* is about real people...." What he meant generally was that he thought I had created more than one fictitious character out of the *Drummer* Salon. What he meant specifically was that he thought my character Solly Blue was based on David Hurles, his new best friend, who was supplying him hundreds of Old Reliable photographs to quick-fill his empty pages.

Overall, Rowberry found *Some Dance* normalizing and therefore familiar in the way University of California professor David Van Leer, who might have been describing my mission in *Drummer* itself, wrote in "Beyond the Margins," *The New Republic*, October 12, 1992:

> Classic gay novels like Gore Vidal's *The City and the Pillar*, Baldwin's *Giovanni's Room*, and more recently Andrew Holleran's *Dancer from the Dance*, Larry Duplechan's *Blackbird*, and Jack Fritscher's *Some Dance to Remember* all introduce readers to settings and psychologies that had not previously been depicted in literature. In so doing, they enlighten straight readers, but they also have a more particular mission for gay readers, which is to reassure them. They tell people who might otherwise have thought themselves abnormal that many share their sexual interests.

Van Leer, the author of *The Queening of America: Gay Culture in Straight Society*, limned a good observation that defined how both *Drummer* and *Some Dance to Remember* introduced stories and psychologies that helped expand the consciousness of gay liberation.

At one brief moment in time, I had edited half of all the *Drummer* magazines in existence. So I took the beating heart of that magazine and transplanted it into the body of my book to give readers a privileged peek into how *Drummer* helped create the very leather culture it reported on. With Embry still helming *Drummer*, I dramatized its reality as a comic parody in the memoir-novel's three fictional leather magazines titled *Maneuvers, Leather Man* and *A Different Drum*. *Some Dance to Remember* was written between 1972-1983, completed in 1984, shopped to publishers through 1988, and published in 1990 through the auspices of *Drummer* editor Tim Barrus at Knights Press.

Queer historians might do well to convene a workshop at some GLBT convention and gather papers for an anthology, or pitch gay television producers, such as Rob Epstein and Jeffrey Friedman, or Randy Barbato and Fenton Bailey, to make a documentary about this "magazine DNA" inside gay popular culture in the first decade of gay liberation after Stonewall, which was fictively dramatized in *Some Dance to Remember*:

> Ryan liked wising off in print. He liked the largeness, the exaggeration, the metaphor that is the essence of all writing.
>
> His *Maneuvers* [magazine] remained erotic entertainment. Each cover promised: "What you're looking for is looking for you." [This was also the tag line of my 1980s zine, *Man2Man*] The magazine gave good head. Solid smut. Sleazy pix. All nasty leather S&M. A new network of personal ads written by readers and answered by phone or mail. Circulation grew. *Maneuver*'s only competition broke into a sweat.
>
> The rival mag, *Leather Man* [*Drummer*], ran middle-of-the-road S&M stories, not-too-dirty photos, and campy copy. Silly cartoon balloons of queenly dialog deflated *Leather Man*'s hardly hot pix of clonish young gay boys wearing leather chaps and chrome armbands available through the mag's 800-number shop. Slender pages of fiction and drawings were a fat-cat publisher's thin come-on to get readers to subscribe to a monthly magazine that was a glorified mail-order catalog to sell leather toys and poppers and his lover's latest disco records. In the first rise of gay magazines, it was fast-buck publishing. For guys not knowing the difference, *Leather Man* passed as the real thing.
>
> "Lips that touch Naugahyde," Ryan said, shaking his head at his competition's latest issue, "shall never touch mine."
>
> The [*Masculinist*] *Manifesto* made masculinism a theory.

Maneuvers made it a fashion. *A Different Drum* reviewed the tempest with sympathetic amusement. *Leather Man* didn't get it at all. Ryan was prick-teasing everyone, even his own kind, and having a wonderful time doing it. —*Some Dance to Remember: A Memoir-Novel of San Francisco 1970-1982*, Reel 3, Scene 3, pages 176-177]

Historically, it is a zero-degrees-of-separation footnote that Terry LeGrand, the West Hollywood producer of the film *Born to Raise Hell*, read *Some Dance* in galley proofs while he and I and Roger Earl and Mark Hemry were shooting a series of six BDSM video features on location in Europe in 1989, the last summer that West Berlin existed. LeGrand, excited by the name of my fictitious magazine, *Leather Man*, decided to begin his own LA magazine titled *Leather Man*, which, in issue 2, on its masthead page, credited *Some Dance to Remember* as the inspiration for LeGrand's title. Soon after, in the way that *Drummer* had moved from LA to San Francisco, LeGrand sold his LA magazine title to Beardog Hoffman, owner of Brush Creek Media in San Francisco, where it was produced by former *Drummer* editor, Joseph W. Bean.

Tweaking the *Leather Man* title in the way that *Drummer* was rechristened *International Drummer* by its Dutch owner, Hoffman added *International Leatherman* to his other Brush Creek magazines such as *Bear*, *Powerplay*, and *Bunkhouse*. As it happened, Brush Creek had cash problems similar to *Drummer*. Like Embry not paying staff workers, contributors, and suppliers, Brush Creek also had default problems that I first noticed when its business office stopped paying some accounts, including my Palm Drive Video company even while I was actively supplying hundreds of cassettes of my bear videos to Brush Creek for its mail-order business. One Sunday at Mass at Saint Sebastian's Church in Sebastopol near the Russian River, I noticed Beardog Hoffman standing next to me in line to receive Communion, and I wanted to ask him what-the-fuck, but out of respect for the sacred venue I did not.

Because of years inside gay publishing, I was hardly surprised when Brush Creek was busted by the United States Internal Revenue Service. In 2002, the IRS padlocked the doors of Brush Creek Media, shut down its magazines, and seized its inventory for back taxes. For historical purposes, I shot a photo of the IRS sign posted on the sealed front door at 367 Ninth Street. Nevertheless, I found no Schadenfreude in the situation because I personally liked and appreciated both Beardog Hoffman and his partner Jack Boujaklian and their efforts to create a gay media empire that so often and so generously published my writing and photographs and sold the video features

I directed and shot. In 2007, a court assigned the ownership of *Bear* Magazine and all the Brush Creek Media copyrights to a creditor of Brush Creek, Butch Media Ltd., and its parent company Bear Omnimedia LLC, Las Vegas.

If only *Drummer* and the rights to it had also been legally negotiated with such clarity through all three publishers, analog *Drummer* might also have been revived like *Bear* in the digital twenty-first century. Instead, the *Drummer* title fell, it seems, by disuse into legal limbo, and all rights to its contents belong, as they always have, to the original creators of its writing, photography, and drawings, or to their estates and heirs; and their intellectual property may not be republished without their permission.

That's why I never bought *Drummer*.

Writing History One Eyewitness at a Time:
Sex, Immigration, the Catacombs, and
the Marriage of Cynthia Slater and Frank Sammut

From: Frank Sammut, Wednesday, December 14, 2011, 12:24 AM
To: Jack Fritscher
Subject: Catacombs

Dear Jack,

My name is Frank Sammut. I lived in San Francisco from 1977 to 1983. I went to the Catacombs for at least 3 of those years. I knew Steve McEachern well. I used to also every Monday for a while clean the Catacombs. Cynthia Slater I married in 1979, this was re helping me to get my green card. I left SF in 1983 back to Australia. Have been living here since. I have had several trips back to SF. I read your write up on the Catacombs and of course it made me very emotional; am I the only one left living from that place and that period. If you can help me track some people down from that period I would so appreciate it. Attached are two photos. I do have others but am rushing to send this after I read your article on line. One of me from the 80's and one as I look now. Thank you and look forward to hear some word from you. —Frank Sammut

* * * *

From: Frank Sammut, Sunday, January 8, 2012, 7:05 PM
To: Jack Fritscher
Subject: Catacombs

Dear Jack,

Happy Twenty 12 to you too mate. Sorry it took me a while to answer, was in Sydney with partner and family for Christmas, then came back home and a day later went out [to the] bush to celebrate the New Year at a friend's property. I have scanned some photos. I have a whole wedding album. The dark skin one of course is me, the fair skin one, with the big mow was my best friend Paul. He used to be door man at the Balcony and Toad Hall, he lived on Market St next to I think a gas station before one turns into Castro.

We met Steve through our then dearest friend, whom I think has left the planet, the black man in the picture, his name was Bob Mahoney. He took us to the Catacombs first, then Steve would call us every week to join in. Bob got sick later. I was in SF round about 1986 maybe and he was not well. He was then living with his partner on Divisadero. Two others in the photos; Mikael Fry and then his partner Paul Sorenson. I think I had heard that they also left us.

I met Cynthia at the Catacombs. We became good friends. She wanted to take my hand and in return she'd do me. I was more of top. The first time I was fisted was at the Handball Express, so taking Cynthia's hand was a relief, small hands. She knew that I was there illegally and wanted to help. We got married. I wanted to buy her a ticket to bring her to Australia for the holidays, and to meet some of the other fellas who used to come to the Catacombs. Later on she opted for cash. Before I left the States, we divorced to have a clean slate. I worked with her in her dungeon on a couple of occasions. I used to also clean her house. The wedding was a civic ceremony with Steve and my then partner as witnesses. The wedding reception was held at dear friend of mine's house down by the water front. We had heaps of friends who were invited to the party. We had a wedding cake and all. In one of the photos you will see Doris Fish and Miss Leading or Tippy. They lived on top of us at 115 Haight Street, corner of Octavia, right behind the church with the round dome and then a revolving cross. Did you know she was married to me?

My doctor, and also a dear friend of mine, was doctor Tom Ainsworth. He was on 18th Street round the corner from Castro in front of that supermarket [Cala]. He later on gave up work and retired. I Googled his house and I have a feeling that he has also gone. His house was up for sale in 2002 under a revocable trust. I cannot find any signs of him. He was a great man. He was the one who in 1981 when I fell sick (sero-converting) said to me: something was really strange with my blood results. Of course they did not know what the hell was going on.

In two days I am doing a long drive 8 hours to Northern New South Wales, where we used to live. I will not have access to computer unless I get my phone to start sending emails out which I will work on the next two days.

I wish you all the best and hope to see you when my partner I come to San Francisco next year.

Frank

A DRUMMER EXCLUSIVE

UPSTAIRS OVER A VACANT LOT... THE CATACOMBS BY JACK FRITSCHER

If you want to know exactly where Tony Bennett left his heart, chances are you'll find it in a footlocker at the handball palace called The Catacombs. Saturday nights, by invitation only, the baaad and the beautiful haul ass into San Francisco's Mission District.

No North Beach neon lights the location.

The Catacombs is dark and underground. Debutantes from Dubuque never find it. Only reputation, referral, and friendsoffriendsoffriends can get you down the Victorian steps, past the cement watchdog, and up to the bell at the Joe-sent-me-door.

After you enter, you can do what you prefer and call it by the best name possible. The Combs is gay, bi, or straight, depending on the night, the guest list, and what you make it. The entrepreneur hosts are so much into "whatever's right" that Werner Erhard, if he were hot enough to wrangle an invitation, would climb the walls, literally, while some topfister opened his ass and raised his consciousness. In that order.

WHERE THE BIG BOYS PLAY

San Francisco is an x-rated bargain – an adult city with a nominal admission over either bridge. Sexually San Francisco enjoys a Golden Age that the rest of the US pretends not to notice.

After all, San Francisco is the place where when you go there, you turn yourself inside out.

The Catacombs is the spot to blow off your socks.

By 4 AM of a Sunday dawning, you can crawl up and out of The Combs on your hands and knees into the fog and know in the future, when your whole life flashes before your dying face, if you've been through The Catacombs, you're in for one hell of a rerun.

Little shots like:
• 40 men variously hanging in leather slings, tied down on restraint tables with their legs raised by shackles, or laid back on waterbeds and mattresses while 40 other men crisco up their fists to start the one finger march to a full fist gliding up the asshole to the elbow.
• A tanned, mustachioed bodybuilder crucified spreadeagle, hanging face toward the heavy beamed cross, while two leatherjeaned dudes flog his shoulders and ass taking time out only for six or seven fists, smallest to largest, to be plugged up his butt.
• A man with a lean blond swimmer's body hanging upsidedown by his paratrooper boots from a pulley hoist, needled through his tits and foreskin, being enthusiastically deepfisted by a 6'4" Texan plungefucking his big paw up to the USMC tattoo on his thick bicep.

This isn't pornofantasy. This is documentary. You don't need fantasy headtrips at The Catacombs. The reality is heavy enough.

And the balance is perfect, sane, and civilized.

S&M at The Combs stands for Sensuality and Mutuality. Nothing happens to any man against his will. Not even a well choreographed "rape" trip. You're safe

DRUMMER
ISSUE 113

4.95

BOOTS
FETISH FEATURE

MEN & BOOTS
by TOM OF FINLAND

SCOTT TUCKER
Interviews
ETIENNE

1/500 Tom ©Tom 1982

CHAPTER 11

RAIDERS OF THE LOST ARCHIVES

THE SECRET PROTOCOLS OF JOHN EMBRY AND ROBERT DAVOLT

- Eyewitness Queen Cougar: Why Mr. Marcus Shamed Robert Davolt
- Starting Tony DeBlase's "Passion Project": "A Leather Timeline" for the Leather Archives & Museum
- Leather History Video Interviews: Founders of the Ambush Bar, the CMC Carnival, and the Jaguar Bookstore
- *Drummer* Editor Joseph W. Bean and *Drummer* Photographer David Sparrow
- Three Crises Change *Drummer*: Slave Auction Arrest (1976), HIV (1982), and the Loma Prieta Earthquake (1989)

"The history business is not the candy business.
It's not always sweet."
—Jack Fritscher

Robert Davolt
Measure of the Man

Robert Davolt so drove himself to distraction with his disdain for Dutch publisher Martijn Bakker that he accidentally helped drive *Drummer* out of business. "Best men are molded out of faults," Shakespeare wrote in *Measure for Measure*, "and, for the most part, become much more the better for being a little bad." Robert Davolt, as controversial professionally as he was beloved personally by so many was that little bit of bad's more kind of better.

ROBERT DAVOLT: BLOND AMBITION AT CAFÉ FLORE

In San Francisco on Market Street, over lunch at Café Flore on January 6, 2001, the blond and bearded Robert Davolt queried the blond and bearded Mark Hemry and me about the possibility of our helping him sketch out his history of *Drummer*.

Something made Davolt seem dubbed like Steve Reeves in *Hercules*. His lips moved, but Embry's voice came out.

I blanched at his request to narrate to him the personal details of my early *Drummer* history, not only because I had already been writing and publishing parts of this very book in print and at my research website for years, but because I figured his not-so-secret agenda was to report back to Embry what progress I was making on my *Drummer* history. Davolt seemed blind-sided by Embry whose ancient *gravitas* he seemed to think gave him the *gravitas* of the long-lost son come home to papa.

Davolt voiced an identification he said was "ironic" that Embry was the first publisher, and he himself was the last. He confused *irony* with *coincidence*. I never really believed he was truly the "publisher" of *Drummer*. It sounded good, but if he were "publisher" under the third owner, publisher Martijn Bakker, the definition had changed from what Embry and DeBlase were.

However, as a university journalism professor and as *Drummer* editor-in-chief, I never discouraged young writers. I promised Davolt enthusiastic support if he wanted to be a fellow surveyor of the narrative arc of *Drummer*. I figured he was as expert an eyewitness of his experience at the end of *Drummer* as I was analytical about mine twenty-some years earlier. History needs all its *Rashomon* points of view.

I knew that Embry was using Davolt to erase my 1970s contributions the same way that Henry Luce made his co-founder of *Time* magazine, Briton Hadden, disappear. I may not have been an LA co-founder of *Drummer*, but I was the founding San Francisco editor-in-chief of *Drummer* who was hired to nurture the *arriviste* Embry. He owned the business of *Drummer*, but he seemed incapable of giving the magazine any resonant human heart, soul, or sensibility. Without mouth-to-mouth intervention in San Francisco, *Drummer* would have smothered to death in its Los Angeles crib and Embry would have struggled on publishing his true passion project, *The Alternate*.

At the Café Flore lunch, Davolt confided his plans and gave me his outline and completed sections of his book titled *GotterDrummerung* [sic] or *The Rise and Fall of Drummer Magazine* which abbreviated "the rise" of the 1970s to focus largely on "the fall" that Davolt himself had experienced during his 1996-1999 involvement with the Dutch owner. He asked specifically for my comments. Similar to my take on early *Drummer*, his take on final *Drummer* was:

> I had landed in the land of lunatics....the tension in the office was so thick that it was impossible to get anything done. The company had serious problems that could not be...tackled by this backbiting, screaming, hysterical rabble.

Overall, Davolt's writing about *Drummer* is more about the economic collapse of greedy queers doing "bad gay business"—like John Embry and, as he alleged, Martijn Bakker—than it is about the esthetics or the erotica of *Drummer*, which, of course, was the essence of *Drummer*.

However long Davolt was conscious he was ill, he sought to share his eyewitness experience with me because he figured that, among others, I would outlive him and could promote his book. He alleged in his 2001 "Outline" to his *Rise and Fall*:

> The real undoing of Desmodus [DeBlase's iteration of *Drummer*] was a December 1997 agreement signed by then General Manager, Greg Byfield. It transferred all the [*Drummer*] trademarks [as purported to exist] to an AKKV, BV, a Dutch holding company.

His expose continued at length with details I don't feel free to disclose. I will note that Davolt, trying to keep *Drummer* afloat, felt more than a little betrayed that he did not know of this two-year-old agreement—allegedly to gut *Drummer* and drain its money—until 1999. Davolt had been kept out of the loop. He felt he had been used as a Dutch puppet with hollow job titles like "publisher" and "promoter" to keep *Drummer* and the Drummer Contest looking alive and legitimate. While that Dutch insult contributed to his suffering in the last days of his life, did he ever realize that Embry was also a famous puppeteer? All puppets have strings, unless there's a hand up their ass.

Davolt never pretended to be an artist, a critic of art, or an erotic writer. He was a talker. A producer. Blogging made him a "journalist." He was a business manager. He appreciated our old-school *Drummer* mystique and was desperate to be identified as part of that mystique. Like John Rowberry, Davolt was exploited by Embry as a virtual and complicit sex-slave hire. Our 1970s origin story and development of *Drummer,* predating him, was beyond his ken and capacity. He knew it. He died with that disappointment.

Davolt had promise, but he arrived with too little too late and fell in with some wrong people. *Drummer* to his mind had existed as a condensed erotic abstraction before he arrived in San Francisco at the scene of the business accident where *Drummer,* having been bled to death, was already a corpse.

Like so many guys who grew up, or came out, after the Golden Age of the 1970s, he was nostalgic for the idyllic sex-past that was legendary. He wanted to make it his. But because it was not his by experience, he figured he'd make it his by inheritance. Trying to graft himself to our origin saga, he made himself believe anything old dogs told him. He wanted to fit into the romantic lust of *Drummer* so he could belong, like a time-traveling sex tourist, to that idyllic erotic history which he missed. Born too late in Washington state, he was a twenty-year-old sailor in the US Navy when *Drummer* was at its peak in 1978-1979. He did not move to San Francisco until 1996 when the dying *Drummer* had been in business for twenty-one years.

In an interesting sociological phenomenon, I have been eyewitness to hundreds of such young men grieving, bittersweet, that they missed the party of the first golden decade after Stonewall. My valentine to them is, of course, my novel of Castro and Folsom, *Some Dance to Remember*, which may be why my shoulder has become one for some to cry on in letters and emails and on telephones. After all, as a gonzo journalist, I press people to tell me their stories. As a father confessor, I was trained professionally by the Vatican to hear confessions. People know the *Drummer* name, but they don't know the *Drummer* story. They think they know what *Drummer* published in 214 issues, but they have no clue what the people who created it went through.

In the Dark Age of the AIDS 1990s, Davolt complimented my salad days as editor-in-chief when he confessed in his "Outline" to his *Rise and Fall* that he needed to perform a resurrection: "I would have to take *Drummer* back to what it was in the 1970s for it to survive." That was music to my ears, because he meant my version of *Drummer*. He made me think of the William Wordsworth poem that gay playwright, William Inge, had re-popularized with his novel and film, *Splendor in the Grass*, in 1961: "Though nothing can bring back the hour of splendor in the grass, of glory in the flower, we will grieve not, rather find strength in what remains behind."

Davolt also committed the fatal flaw of naive young bohemians: he expected to earn his living off art, particularly gay art. He wrote in his "Outline" that he asked *Drummer* for a company van after complaining about his paying for taxis to travel to contests and fund raisers, and that he was embittered that after paying some *Drummer* bills he had "less than $20 a week for food...[while admitting he] was technically homeless" because he lived on a cot inside the *Drummer* office.

I could only shake my head and be thankful that for the nearly three years that I edited *Drummer* by night and on weekends, I also had a "day job," a real career managing the publications and marketing departments at Kaiser Engineers, Inc., in Oakland. Never dependent on *Drummer* for my livelihood, I felt free to experiment and push the gonzo journalism of our editorial content just to see what grass-roots power lay latent in the very concept of *Drummer* as a formative voice in the leather community it was helping create.

Surrounded by the Great Dying during the 1990s, Davolt seemed to me, loving, sympathetic, and understandably a bit panicked by his illnesses during his tour of duty at *Drummer*.

However, had he slowed down from the distractions of his S&M travels, leather contests, and blogs, and had he thoroughly studied back issues of *Drummer*, he could have examined the primary evidence of *Drummer* culture. He could then have put a gyroscope under Embry's spinning oral history, and under his own redesign of the magazine thwarted by the sabotage of Dutch wooden shoes thrown into the machine.

At the Leather Archives & Museum, on whose Board Davolt once sat, the keepers of the "Leather Timeline," who have the patience of monks illuminating manuscripts, also know the benefit from an accurate hands-on turning of the *Drummer* pages in search of the telltale heart of the leather timeline beating within *Drummer*.

GAYLE RUBIN STUDIES *DRUMMER*, A FIRST DRAFT OF LEATHER HISTORY

The Michigan anthropologist, Gayle S. Rubin, PhD, who emerged in her teen years in the 1960s as a feminist in the Midwest, was a woman in the 1980s daring to write San Francisco men's history, the reverse spin of which no man would dare do. Earning her doctorate, she set good academic example in San Francisco. She studied *Drummer*, San Francisco's longest-running LGBT magazine, as a primary source of men's leather history, and she wrote for *Drummer*. Her essay, "The Catacombs: A Temple of the Butthole," appeared in *Drummer* 139 (May 1990), twelve years after I wrote the first feature on the Catacombs with my documentary photographs in *Drummer* 23 (July 1978).

As a fellow academic who also once taught university in Michigan, I was professionally interested in how my leather colleague, as a feminist anthropologist, parsed *Drummer* and our masculine-identified tribe around *Drummer*. Her arrival in San Francisco reminded me of anthropologist Margaret Mead arriving in Papua New Guinea, after which she wrote the 1935 tract, popular with feminists, *Sex and Temperament in Three Primitive Societies*. However, when I sought to read her 1994 dissertation, *The Valley of the Kings: Leathermen in San Francisco, 1960–1990*, the University of Michigan said it was not available. Two friends who were librarians, including Jim Stewart, retired department head of the Social Sciences and History Department at the Chicago Public Library and author of *Folsom Street Blues*, also pursued this intellectual inquiry. Because of the notion that dissertations, including my own *Love and Death in Tennessee Williams* (1967), are written to discover and publish new knowledge, I finally asked directly. She responded on February 1, 2014: "My dissertation isn't available."

Ever professional, she did, however, kindly attach three pdfs of her essays, totaling fifty-six printed pages, all of which I'd read previously in anthology books such as Mark Thompson's *Leatherfolk: Radical Sex, People, Politics, and Practice* (1991). In that volume, her essay on "The Catacombs" followed my essay on Folsom Street artist, "Chuck Arnett," in which I memorialized the iconic founder of the Tool Box bar profiled in *Life* magazine (June 26, 1964). In the endnotes of *Leatherfolk*, she graciously credited *Drummer* and my writing of leather history:

> For further reading on the Catacombs, see Jack Fritscher's knowledgeable and affectionate memoir of the Twenty-First Street Catacombs in *Drummer* 23, 1978. The article is accompanied by [his] priceless photographs of the interior. (Page 140)

Sweet words. No wonder I wanted to read her complete dissertation.

It was for just such a new generation of leatherfolk like Davolt and younger academics like Rubin that, as editor and writer, I consciously shaped *Drummer* editorial policy in the 1970s with an eye to our community future. Having been one of the founding members of the American Popular Culture Association in 1968, I knew that gay popular culture was valuable even as I was "inside the moment" of the Titanic 1970s helping *Drummer* create the very leather culture it reported on.

When I added the tag line, "*Drummer*: The American Review of Gay Popular Culture," it was because I was always, from my childhood diaries and journals during and after World War II, a devoted documentarian conscious of future history. Anticipating the next gay generation, I wrote very explicitly, for instance, in *Drummer* 24 about the Castro Street Fair, "Castro

Blues: Years from Now When You Read This, and You Will Read This, Remember the Way We Were, 1978 Style." In *Son of Drummer* (September 1978), I began my "Target Studio Retrospective" by repeating with a variation: "Years from now when you think of the Seventies, and you will think of the Seventies..."

PEDIGREE OF *DRUMMER* EDITORS: LEATHER HISTORY, INVASION OF THE REVISIONIST AGENDA

Had he paged through *Drummer*, Davolt, upon proper timeline investigation, would have found that, always discounting the "aka" aches and pains of "Robert Payne," the "early" *Drummer* editorial pedigree was simple.

In the immortal opening words of *A Chorus Line*, "Five, six, seven, eight, again!" There were only two "editors-in-chief" of *Drummer*, and that was from June 1975 to December 31, 1979: Jeanne Barney (1-11 + hybrid issues, 11 and 12), and Jack Fritscher (19-30 + hybrid issues, 16, 17, 18, 31, 32, and 33).

Lists, timelines, and bylines need not be complicated affairs. My "Eyewitness *Drummer* Bibliography" of my own writing and photography is a simple list verified in the pages of *Drummer*. However, deciphering pen names and making correct attribution of authorship can pose literary and legal copyright problems. That ambiguity can also lead to speculation and revision of leather history. For instance, *Drummer* 85 (June 1985), the Tenth Anniversary Issue, pages 102-108, published Steven Saylor's "*Drummer* Fiction/Fetish Index" which listed writing by "Denny Sargent," but for some reason did not identify that I was "Denny Sargent."

As a best-selling writer of detective novels set in ancient Rome, Saylor might have found a clue in my special issue, *Son of Drummer* (September 1978), where I published an excerpt from my novel *Leather Blues* under its original title, "I Am Curious (Leather): The Adventures of Denny Sargent." Strangely enough, Saylor himself had reviewed *Leather Blues*, whose main character is named "Denny Sargent," in *Drummer* 81, four issues before his "Index" was published. The opening line is: "Denny Sargent, eighteen, kicked his sheets to the floor." Understandably, Saylor also missed my frequent use of the pen name "David Hurles," a real name used with permission from my longtime friend David Hurles who understood that Embry was fuming that my byline appeared on too many articles and stories. As "David Hurles," I wrote "End Product: The First Taboo," *Drummer* 22 (May 1978), and "High Performance, Or, Sex without a Net," *Drummer* 26 (January 1979), as well as my one-act play "with David Hurles," *Corporal in Charge of Taking Care of Captain O'Malley*, serialized in two issues, *Drummer* 22 (May 1979) and *Drummer* 23 (June 1979). The valiant Saylor, working hard as a literary gladiator years before computer searches existed, did what heavy lifting he could to create the very bibliography *Drummer* needed and its contributors deserved. A complete bibliography for the nearly 25,000 pages of *Drummer* has yet to be written.

Saylor once published his own recall about the grief he got working inside *Drummer*. Was the employee even aware of the employer's stealthy Blacklist agenda? Was his "Index" expurgated by Embry's late-night deleting of his "enemies"? Ever eager to reprint material so he could sell everything even more than twice, Embry tidily illustrated Saylor's *Drummer* 85 "Index" with the very picture from *Drummer* 44 that had introduced "'Blue Light,' A Short Story by Aaron Travis," Saylor's pseudonym.

With *Drummer* 31 in 1980, Embry refused to name John W. Rowberry as "editor-in-chief." Rowberry was a manager without portfolio, until Embry begrudged him the limited title of "assignments editor," which by *Drummer* 40, in 1981, metastasized into "editor." In *Drummer* 49 (1981), Embry, always quick to give staff "masthead titles" instead of salary increases, listed Rowberry as "associate editor." Sorting Rowberry's titles can correct certain leather timelines cloned out of the Leather Archives & Museum's early "Leather Timeline"—before the LA&M began its twenty-first-century fact-checking oversight, and fine-tuning, of that timeline first drafted in chunks by Tony DeBlase and me as announced in *Drummer* 126 (March 1989).

Vetting of Rowberry's pedigree lies in the masthead credits of nine 1980 issues (31 to 39). Only after entering his second year as "assignments editor," did Rowberry, according to DeBlase (in *Drummer* 100), finally achieve the single-word title of "editor" in *Drummer* 40 during the sixth, nearly seventh year, of middle *Drummer*. I was editor-in-chief of 1970s "Divisadero Street" *Drummer*. Rowberry was editor of 1980s "Harriet Street" *Drummer* which became AIDS *Drummer*. Rowberry mainly plugged leather contest photos and video reviews. He was a lone wolf from LA and never part of the San Francisco *Drummer* Salon of serious writing and erotic art during the orgy of the Titanic 1970s.

Critical thinkers should be careful of any free-range revisionist's foreshortened perspectives written years after the facts. Revisionists should also be wary that for far into the future there will always exist one more "last" eyewitness of *Drummer* history, just as there is always one more "last" eyewitness of the Holocaust to keep facts sorted properly.

DeBlase thought these distinctions important enough to hire me in 1988 to startup what would be my continuing leather-history column, "Rear-View

Mirror." It was his intent to incubate and grow leather history in *Drummer*. In that pre-Google decade, using the reach, resources, and friends of *Drummer* was the in-house way he and I started to gather up, rough out, and construct the foundation of his late-1980s concept of that "Leather Timeline" for his passion project, the Leather Archives & Museum, which he would co-found with Chuck Renslow in 1991 in DeBlase's native Chicago.

The founding of the LA&M, like the founding of *Drummer*, took several people and several years to create itself, finally completing its six-year origin story with the appointment of *Drummer* editor Joseph W. Bean as executive director in 1997. Bean, in his words, said he arrived to "legitimize" and "professionalize" the infant LA&M. I had the same two goals when Embry hired me to edit the infant *Drummer* when it was eighteen months old. From the first, I positioned *Drummer* to be a first draft of leather history. On the masthead of *Drummer* 23 (July 1978), I lead with my tag line of intent, subtitling *Drummer* as the "American Review of Gay Popular Culture."

Writing journalism before the internet, I put my leather-research boots on the ground to support DeBlase by gathering first-hand eyewitness historical information. In 1988, accompanied by the leather poet Ron Johnson, I shot hours of videotaped interviews of iconic San Francisco leather pioneers such as

- California Motor Club (CMC) founder (1960), Linn Kiefer;
- Ambush bar founder (1970), Kerry Bowman;
- African-American Folsom Street leatherman, Al Smith; and
- Jaguar Bookstore founder (1971), Ron Ernst, who originated the first printed Hanky Code (1972) with Alan Selby (Mr. S.) for their 18th and Castro store, Leather and Things.

Given the technology of the 1980s, the "Leather Timeline" lifted off to a good start, but has, since the introduction of fact-checking on the internet in 1995, proved that, even with the best contributors, every timeline will always be a work in progress, open to corrections and additions as more leatherfolk and researchers participate and bring in new eyewitness line items.

WRITER DEBLASE, WANTING TO BE PUBLISHED, BOUGHT *DRUMMER*

Looking at the internal evidence of leather history inside *Drummer* 17 (July 1977), I know that DeBlase as his pseudonym "Fledermaus" had sent a "Letter to the Editor" (Embry) asking to be published as a fiction writer (page 7). This was nine years before DeBlase bought *Drummer* from Embry.

Even as DeBlase, listing his leather-tribe credentials, was trying to enter the *Drummer* Salon, global leather culture had not yet heard of "Fledermaus." Nevertheless, what imp of the perverse in Embry caused him to misspell DeBlase's pseudonym?

> FLENDERMAUS [sic] WRITES.
>
> Dear Sir: I have been writing Gay S&M fiction under the pseudonym of Flendermaus [sic] for several years now. Most of my work has been published by Larry Townsend in his Treasury series. RFM has also published some of my work under the pen name, Pipistrelle. I am a charter subscriber to *Drummer* [Note his connecting himself to *Drummer*'s roots in his goal to become part of the *Drummer* fraternity, the *Drummer* Salon] and have enjoyed seeing the magazine grow. I would like to be included among the authors who have their work featured. —Tony, Illinois

Three years later, DeBlase wrote me a letter from Chicago dated April 20, 1980, answering my *Drummer* display ad for "Writer's Aid" (*Drummer* 25, page 94, and *Drummer* 26, page 86) through which I counseled emerging erotic authors, and auditioned new writing for *Drummer*.

> GAY WRITERS! *Sold any lately?* Pro-writer/editor/agent thoroughly critiques your poetry, fiction, articles, scripts! Erotic or straight. Novice writers also welcome. Send self-addressed stamped envelope for *very* reasonable rates and totally professional advice: WRITER'S AID, 4436 25th Street, San Francisco CA 94114 [my home address at the time].

Some of my "students," like DeBlase and John Preston, became famous personalities; other writers, still living, I will protect till they're dead.

By *Drummer* 98, DeBlase, a ball of fire, had bought his way into *Drummer* from Embry, a burnt-out case.

GRAVE ROBBERS STEAL THE "TREASURE HOUSE" OF *DRUMMER*

Years after that, the health-impaired Davolt strove to spark off the flinty Embry his own heritage heat as a leatherman. In Embry, Davolt found his Darth Vader: "Luke, I am your father." The two men might have achieved a certain higher nobility if they had spent their last years returning all the photographs and original art that belonged to the creators and copyright holders. None of that intellectual property was given to *Drummer* to keep. It disappeared into what garbage can, what leather closet, what university archive, or what eBay auction?

As a back-story of evidence, in January, 2006, Bijou Video in Chicago advertised at its site that it was selling back issues of *Drummer* in a way that would have seemed to violate copyright. When I alerted Larry Townsend he alerted Jeanne Barney who alerted John Embry who wrote a well-distributed email dated January 9, 2006.

Embry stated that he had bought the *Drummer* archives from Robert Davolt. He stated this, significantly, only *after* Davolt's death: "While in charge, Davolt sold the files, the inventory, and the office lease to us."

Had Davolt ginned up the claim that he had somehow gained ownership of the *Drummer* files and was permitted to sell them? He tried to fix his lie into history. Talking through his hat and up his sleeve, he told historian, Dusk Peterson, some untrue tales that did not belong at Peterson's truetales. org. The skeptical Peterson, leading off with the telling words, "considered himself," wrote of Davolt:

> Davolt considered himself to be the guardian of *Drummer*'s legacy. He was the man who claimed rights over the publication (though another claimant existed) [A major point; who was the other claimant? Publisher/owners Embry or DeBlase or Bakker?], and who kept what he called the "mortal remains" of *Drummer*: the magazine's existing records.

Perhaps Davolt held the *Drummer* papers and artwork hostage because he could not wrest his wages or ownership control of the magazine itself from the Dutch. Whatever transpired around *Drummer* in *fin de siecle* San Francisco was a continent and an ocean away from Amsterdam. As Davolt admitted in interviews, he was desperate for money for his personal expenses, for publishing *Drummer*, and for producing the Mr. Drummer Contest. About his ownership, he might have lied to Embry who, for once, could have been repeating the lie as a "truth" he'd been told. When Davolt asked me for donations of my books and videos, I sent some to support him, and asked him to return all my photographs still stuck in *Drummer* filing cabinets.

Did Davolt ever have the right or the authorization to sell art work and photographs he did not own? With so many *Drummer* contributors dead from AIDS, who knew what former lover or what straight niece inherited the copyright to the intellectual property? Was Embry like some rich art collector buying artifacts smuggled out of a lost civilization by a dying grave-robber who had tucked the loot into his carry-on luggage? Is this situation akin to twenty-first-century dealers selling art confiscated during the Holocaust?

Everything proven and alleged on this subject can be corrected if these phantom intellectual property deals claimed by Embry and Davolt are ever made transparent by a paper trail. Even so, it cannot be emphasized enough in a digital world of piracy and plagiarism, that the photographs, drawings, and manuscripts are the intellectual property of their creators and their heirs.

In *Super MR* #7 (2001), Embry made an astonishing claim on page 37: "When *Super MR* acquired the original *Drummer* archives, we really didn't realize what a *treasure house* [italics added] we had."

I am really curious (leather)!

Embry's little braggadocio needs a paper trail.

In *Drummer* 137 (February 1990), page 5, managing editor Joseph W. Bean addressed *Drummer*'s "enormous archive of erotic" treasures. He began the 1990s setting an ethical standard Davolt might have followed in the late-1990s, of pro-actively seeking to identify and return original material.

> Missing in Action: Over the years, *Drummer* has collected an enormous archive of erotic artwork and photography. Unfortunately, some of the best items...have no identification.....So from time to time, we will be running some of these unidentifiable masterpieces in this feature, "Missing in Action." If the artwork is yours, we want to hear from you. Or, if you know who the artist is [in this age of plague]....

In a June 1997 interview, Joseph Bean told me some information that contradicted Embry and Davolt's smoke screen that former *Drummer* owners and staff had discarded all the artwork and photographs. For the most part, neither had destroyed originals, even though they were often too busy to systematically store them. While I was editor-in-chief, I chastised Embry for disrespecting and tossing original art work, photos, and manuscripts into a jammed closet to the left of art director Al Shapiro's drafting table. Bean also confirmed Embry's mercenary statement that after *Drummer* closed in 1999, he bought its "treasure house" of art and photographs.

JOSEPH BEAN AND DAVID SPARROW, *DRUMMER* PHOTOGRAPHER

The institutional memory of *Drummer* was short and often amnesiac because, during twenty-four years and three owners, a thousand people, often using subversive outlaw identities, and paid under the table, worked for or contributed to its creation. Bean revealed this in-house shortfall when he reported that DeBlase did not know who the famous "Sparrow" was, even though I had twice introduced DeBlase to my former lover, David Sparrow, who was for years listed by his full name on the masthead page under "Photographers." Insisting on burying my bylines, Embry credited our "Sparrow-Fritscher Photography" reductively as "Sparrow Photography" which should have impressed the name even more on DeBlase who was quite canny. Did DeBlase who died in 2000 suffer memory loss? How did DeBlase fail to remember that before Andy Charles became his lover, Andy was great, good, and intimate friends with David Sparrow and me back in Chicago in 1969.

Perhaps DeBlase's eye was not on that "Sparrow," my Sparrow. Perhaps DeBlase confused my "Sparrow" with the "Sparrow" who was the iconic leather author Sam Steward also known as the tattoo artist, "Phil Sparrow." Perhaps DeBlase threw his hands up in frustration in an office full of pseudonyms that were further muddled by the de-selections of Embry's Blacklist. Bean made me even more aware of this identity confusion, and of the loss of hundreds of my photographs in June 1997.

> Bean:.... I have to go backwards for just a split second. The photographer, "Sparrow," David Sparrow.
> Fritscher: Yes?
> Bean: [who had suddenly connected my mention of David Sparrow to another Sparrow] Sparrow! His identity is an important [intellectual property] issue because there are in the *Drummer* archives dozens or maybe hundreds of photos just marked "Sparrow." When I was editor there, I didn't know who that "Sparrow" was and Tony DeBlase didn't either. We didn't know if the "Sparrow" photos had been used or not. [A dozen issues of *Drummer* numbered in and above issues 19 to 33 contain hundreds of our "Sparrow" interior photographs and cover shots, nearly all identified explicitly with our byline.]
> Fritscher: Those are my photos as well. So that's where they are? OK. I get it.
> Bean: When I left, there were a lot of photos there.
> Fritscher: Those aren't just Sparrow photographs. Those photographs were hi-jacked. and those photographs are mine as well, just for a fact. That's very interesting.

Bean: Perhaps you just take a stab at getting them back then. When I left *Drummer*, Tony DeBlase had sorted all of the photography that existed in the whole Desmodus building by the first letter of the last name or pseudonym of the photographer. *There was enough "Sparrow" photography there that it had its own drawer.* [Italics added] So it was like "S" and then "Satyr" and then "Sparrow" and then "T." I don't know if they still have that system, but if they do, there's a whole drawer full of Sparrow photographs there.

Fritscher: Where is the drawer?

Bean: At *Drummer* [At that moment, in the hands of Davolt].

Fritscher: OK, I'll check there. Mark [Hemry] and I were just discussing this recently, the mysterious disappearance of all this stuff belonging to David and me, because so much has disappeared with people dying and...the same thing happened with Robert Mapplethorpe. Stuff disappears. Nobody has ever seen his scatology photographs. Where did those go?

Bean: I have heard of them before.

Fritscher: Or Mapplethorpe's "Nazi" photographs. I've seen them, even have copies of some. David Sparrow... How can I put this? As I told you, for ten years, the exact same time I was editor-in-chief of *Drummer*, David was my lover. We moved together to San Francisco from the Midwest where I had put him through college—somewhat against his will. He was a particular somebody [whom I loved and whom] I supported—into whose unemployed hands I put a camera that I purchased, loaded with film stock that I purchased, and took on shoots I set up and cast with models where I'd say, "OK, now I'll shoot this angle, you shoot that...." [My freckled and redheaded David Sparrow was born hard-scrabble in Evansville, Indiana, in 1946; he had the great beauty of the Celtic gene bank as well as its addiction disorders, and a poor boy's lust for bright and shiny things in pawnshop windows that stopped him in his tracks on our sex-trips from Manhattan to LA to San Francisco. More than liking photography itself, he liked cameras as expensive objects; but he was never really all that interested in actually taking pictures because film, and the development of film, cost even more money. In the upwardly mobile way that I forced him to go to university, and again paid for it, I cajoled him into fronting, and being, my *Drummer* photographer, and paid for it, because he was frequently jobless, and acting in my stead even the few times I made him shoot alone; and, for that service, I expected Embry to pay me back by paying Sparrow who put it in our marital household account.] The "Sparrow" credit line was another invention of that time when I was writing nearly everything in *Drummer* to front some of it with Sparrow's name to satisfy Embry who thought my name was in too many bylines in each issue. [In our longtime marriage, David and I drew up our own binding agreements about our money and our mutual businesses, including his permission for me to write about him from inside our intimacy and privacy. After our divorce, he stopped shooting and was never published again.]

Bean: I don't know what's there at *Drummer* now, of course—what Sparrow photographs. I've been gone six years.

Fritscher: Has it been that long? I've always thought of you as the soldier-editor. In the leather world, you moved from front to front, fighting battle after battle, war after war, and have never yet yourself became a casualty.

Bean: [Laughs] Last night, Gayle Rubin asked me, what's next, and I told her that I thought my next move would be to Chicago to work on the Leather Archives & Museum, because it really needs to get legitimized, to get professionalized....

PARVENU DAVOLT TWICE DECEIVED

I don't want to blame the parvenu Davolt, a holy innocent who should have known better, but his caving into Embry and the Dutch "pirates" was no noble way to end *Drummer*. There was no respect in it for the thousands of working writers, photographers, and artists who created *Drummer*. In his "Outline," Davolt revealed the debris in the *Drummer* office when he arrived:

> The physical condition of the office was another story: piles of paper...mice in the filing cabinets. A splendid little patio in the back was overgrown with weeds that were encroaching on the office windows. The greatest photo and art collection in SM/leather history, or at least everything that had survived 25 years of looting by former owners and employees, was sitting in boxes—unsorted, unusable, and decaying rapidly.

Davolt was rather elitist underestimating *Drummer* readers. He asked Mark Hemry and me at the Café Flore about what he had written in his "Outline":

> Do you think references to Wagner and Shakespeare are too highfalutin'? Where should I be aiming this manuscript? Ex-*Drummer* readers? Gay history junkies? Should I write a complete, definitive history of *Drummer* from beginning to end, or as primarily a story about the end with the earlier stuff as background.

Besides advising him to drop the unreadable bi-lingual tongue-twisting pun in his title, *GotterDrummerung*, I told him what I told my university writing students for years: "Write what you know."

After I wrote to Davolt telling him I would meet him for lunch to discuss his book, he emailed his set purpose on Wednesday, January 3, 2001,

> Re: Happy New Year Yes Lunch:
> I have never quite known how to "do" lunch. Eat lunch, yes. Drink lunch, occasionally. But "doing lunch" always seems to be slightly obscene. Foreplay to a food fight?
> How about Saturday? Name the place and may I suggest some time post-lunch-rush, say 1300?
> I could hardly think of such a project without you. I will take what I can get and impose on you until you wish me into the cornfield. Let's start with the outline and something of a mission plan/priority list. With your permission I will send it ahead for your perusal.[Instead, he handed his feasibility "Outline" over during the lunch.] I would be fascinated to hear how you would approach this if you were me.
> Thanks so much!
> Robert

After our lunch, he emailed on January 20, 2001:

> Jack,
> Thank you for the two books! [*Some Dance to Remember* and *Mapplethorpe: Assault with a Deadly Camera*]. I am honored that you also inscribed them for me. It took UPS a week to actually deliver them, but the result was well worth bullying their customer rep!

It was good to sit and talk—in addition to the enlightenment, it was a warm and enjoyable conversation. I hope you felt the same and we can continue some of the topics some time in the future. I hope that you and Mark might be able to stop by the house if time permits next trip into the City.

It is my goal to have a manuscript ready by May at the latest. To accomplish that, I am trying to keep to a schedule of producing at least two chapters a week, which would seem to be doable wrapped around the job search and other projects. Focusing on a more personal memoir [as was suggested to him at the table] will reduce the range of the required research, but it will make editing a little more of a problem.

Once again, thank you for the meeting and the books.
Best Regards,
Robert

In his book, *Painfully Obvious, An Irreverent and Unauthorized Manual for Leather S/M* (2003), Robert Davolt graciously included me in his list of writers he thanked for help and encouragement. Mark Hemry and I had indeed given him both, but to what avail? Instead of a courtier's curtsy, Davolt might better have returned my photographs and manuscripts from the early *Drummer* as well as those I sent to the editors during the last seven years of double Dutch *Drummer*. It was also painfully obvious that Davolt's book needed proof-reading just to keep up with Google's search accuracy available since 1999. He missed the "S" in *Fritscher* which, in leather culture, no bottom "M" should ever do. From the earliest *Drummer* issues, the "Letters to the Editor" continually complained about *Drummer* not fact-checking, as well as about blunders in proofing, spelling, and punctuation. As early as *Drummer* 6 regarding *Drummer* 4, a reader wrote: "Your editors don't care." More like the publishers did not care. Especially after the Titanic earthquake, October 17, 1989.

Three *Drummer* Crises:
Slave Auction Arrest (1976), HIV (1982),
Loma Prieta Earthquake (1989)

The Loma Prieta earthquake did to 1980s *Drummer* in the 1990s what AIDS did to 1970s *Drummer* in the 1980s.

The shaking *Drummer* building at 285 Shipley Street, its second South of Market office, became instantly unsafe. Publisher DeBlase heard the news while touring Europe, panicked, and flew home from Heathrow. Editor Joseph Bean soldiered on. What last vestiges of the unbridled lust and personal sex joys of 1970s *Drummer* had not been destroyed by AIDS were finished by the earthquake. Once again, as in its desperate 1977 move from LA to San Francisco, *Drummer* needed to be reinvented to fit the times. So, in search of safer sex that we could promote as the hot new normal in S&M, I convinced Deblase—post-earthquake—to send me to Missouri on an undercover assignment at Chip Weichelt's Training Center Academy to report back about sex-free, man-to-man physical discipline adventures with five straight cops and Marines in the *Drummer* cover story, "The Academy: Incarceration for Pleasure," *Drummer* 145 (December 1990).

Chip Weichelt posted his Academy advertisement offering authentic reality in dozens of *Drummer* issues that mostly offered only fantasy. It was the dawn of a new kind of S&M at *Drummer* when a man offered a toll-free number that could change fantasy into reality. Weichelt turned the magical thinking of masturbators into an authentic experience that was sex-free, but—in every other S&M fetish way—erotic. This new authenticity did not survive Deblase's sale to the Dutch who preferred to publish free pictures from slick sex videos ground out at corporate video companies that had not the personal soul of early *Drummer* film favorites directed by actual leathermen: Fred Halsted's *Sextool*, Roger Earl's *Born to Raise Hell*, and the Gage Brothers *Kansas City Trucking Co.*

THE ACADEMY

The Academy, a full-time staffed prison facility, continues to offer men with a serious interest a unique alternative service. The Academy can design and implement each detail of your experience in various environments and scenarios for weekend or week-long sessions. Special situations such as public arrest, hostage, and other complex programs are executed in realistic correctional or military atmosphere. Cell confinement, immobilization, isolation, interrogation, sensory control and endurance situations are all offered in safe, sane, discreet, and monitored environment. All Academy programs are administered by professionally trained military, corrections and law personnel. A brochure or videotape is now available. Reservation and deposit require (deposit and/or video may be charged by credit card). References provided after commitment.

Contact: The Academy, PO Box [deleted], Washington MO 63090. 1-800-deleted. NOTE: The Academy cannot offer sexual situations as part of its programs.

WHEN QUEERS COLLIDE: MR. MARCUS AND MR. DAVOLT

At www.leatherweb.com/histdrum, Davolt, who had been denounced by Mr. Marcus, the beloved leather columnist for the *Bay Area Reporter*, admitted, in the name of business and raising funds for charity, that he had lied, or prevaricated, or at least covered up the truth about what was really going on financially with *Drummer* and the Mr. Drummer Contest:

> ...to keep up appearances...and the confidence...of contestants, sponsors, customers and suppliers long enough to fix what was wrong...We put on our game faces. The immediate past is not something anyone currently involved with the *Drummer* names is eager to talk about.

Davolt's "immediate past" was where the last of the archive treasures disappeared. His admitting to his bit of a hustle put me on guard from my previous support of the Mr. Drummer Contest for which, over time, I had been a judge as well as a sponsor-patron offering prizes to the winners. In 1979, Embry and Al Shapiro and I, sitting trio behind closed doors in our office, handpicked the first Mr. Drummer ourselves. Later, as part of leather panels, I helped judge Mr. Drummer 1988, September, 24, 1988, and Mr. Northern California *Drummer* 1990, April 28, 1990. As the owner and film director of the leather and fetish studio, Palm Drive Video, I was listed in the program for the "Mr. Drummer 1989 Contest List of Prizes" as the first video artist to create a cash prize of a $500 video contract to the runners-up, and to the winners of regional Mr. Drummer Contests. Some of the winners I filmed were Wes Decker in *Leather Discipline Duo: Punch and Boots*, Larry Perry in *Naked Came the Stranger*, and Southwest Mr. Drummer, Rick Conder, in *Leather Saddle Cowboy Bondage*.

On June 18, 2001, Davolt wrote:

> I am writing for a favor (naturlich) [*sic*]. I enjoyed your books (*Some Dance to Remember* and *Mapplethorpe: Assault*). I was wondering if you would do me the honor of sending a signed volume to be used as a raffle prize at my birthday party (a fund raiser for the AEF Breast Cancer Emergency Fund) on Wednesday, 27 June at Daddy's Bar.

The late Mister Marcus Hernandez, who was for thirty-eight years the principal eyewitness and news reporter of good, bad, and ugly leather behavior on Folsom Street, loathed Davolt's dishonesties privately and in print. Marcus dubbed him "Robert Revolting." Eyewitness Queen Cougar, the beloved emcee of nationwide leather contests, was Marcus' longtime friend and caretaker. She nurtured him in his last illnesses and became the keeper of his archive. She wrote to me on January 18, 2012 clarifying:

> Marcus's beef with Robert Davolt was that he felt Davolt was weak and not a worthy leader. They [in their long feud] really only made up in print because of pressure from the BAR [*Bay Area Reporter*] management—putting pressure on Marcus to not keep the flame going with Davolt, as Davolt had come to them asking for Marcus's head on a platter....Yes, he did try to have Marcus fired....[He wanted to take over Marcus' job as the BAR leather columnist. After Marcus' death, the BAR leather column eventually went to Race Bannon.] Bob Ross had no intention of firing Marcus, but they did want to maintain a reasonable truce between Marcus & Davolt not wanting a lawsuit to be mounted....Marcus knew Davolt was playing games with the [*Drummer*] money... he was very savvy about who in the community did that kind of thing ... and it disgusted him. He knew the community was being damaged by all the rip-off artists.... He was very concerned about preserving our history, and, despite the dishy aspect of his work, he truly wanted the best at all times for the community as a whole. He was not afraid to dish out punishment in print to those who it was clear had committed serious infractions against their club or organization. He often chose to let "sleeping dogs lie " regarding one scandal or another, because he was getting older and felt it was sometimes like swimming upstream to get [leather] people to realize the truth about their so-called [leather] "icons."...He hated how people didn't have any balls when it came to exposing and dealing with the rip-offs and bad-asses of our community. [Marcus had]...an interesting story of the night at the San Francisco Eagle when they [Martijn Bakker who sold rights to the Mr. Drummer Contest to Mike Zuhl] unceremoniously snatched *Drummer* out of Davolt's hands [freeing Zuhl to create his ongoing and omnisexual DNA "Drummer North America" leather contests]

As a survivor of the AIDS crisis, I want to know what survivors of the Holocaust want to know about their families' art treasures. Where are my missing photographs? The missing Mapplethorpe photographs? The missing Etienne drawings? The missing Bill Ward cartoon panels? The missing Tom of Finland sketches? The missing work of countless others?

That physical loss is similar to the missing credit lines in Davolt's 1990s *Drummer* which regularly failed to credit by copyright or by name photographers such as Lou Thomas of Target Studio whose work graced so many homomasculine covers and centerfolds of early *Drummer*. In its last falling down days at the height of the AIDS epidemic, the last generation of *Drummer* editors and staff had the misguided *chutzpah*, without permission, to publish and republish living, dying, and dead artists' photographs and drawings with the one lazy and dismissive credit line: "From the *Drummer* Archives."

Drummer was indeed a first draft of leather history.

So *Drummer* had a duty.

But the leather Rorschach that was *Drummer* lost its roar.

Drummer was dying.

How sublime and elegiac its twenty last issues could have been if editorial staff had only bothered to research the twenty-four years of purloined art to identify it with clear provenance, historic captions, or obituaries honoring the artists and photographers, living and dead, one last time before epic *Drummer* died with the century's end.

Drummer 148 Centerfold "Slap Happy" by Jack Fritscher

DRUMMER

FOLLOW US TO WHERE THE ACTION IS!

VOLUME 1 / NUMBER 1

PIERCE
PAGE 17

PIX
PAGE 16

**Drummer Trial Balloon
Vol 1 No 1
November 19, 1971
Predated Glossy Full-sized
Drummer No 1, June 1975**

GODSPELL
SEE CALENDAR PAGE

CHAPTER 12

DRUMMER ROOTS IN THE SWINGING SIXTIES: CREATING AN EYEWITNESS LEATHER TIMELINE

The Cultural Revolution of 1968
Ignites Stonewall Rebellion (June 1969)
and the Golden Age of Leather (1970-1982)

- The Prague Spring 1968: Student Protests against Vietnam War Sweep World
- 1968 Shootings: Martin Luther King Jr. (April 4); Andy Warhol (June 3); Robert Kennedy (June 5)
- Feminist Separatist Valerie Solanas Shoots Warhol and Leatherman Mario Amaya; Reaction to Solanas's "Society for Cutting Up Men" and Her *SCUM Manifesto* Brings Masculine-Identified Men Out of the Closet, and Ignites "Gay Civil War" over Gender(s), Introducing Concept of "Homomasculinity"
- August 1968: Chicago Police Riot at Democratic Convention: Citizens Fight Brutal Cops, Igniting the Fuse on the Stonewall Rebellion Ten Months Later
- John Embry Trashes DeBlase's "Leather Timeline" and DeBlase's Pet Project: the Leather Archives & Museum, Chicago
- Guide to Photographs of Some Staff in *Drummer*

Allen Ginsberg's "Gay Succession"
or, "69 Degrees of Gay Separation"

Walt Whitman Slept with Edward Carpenter.
Edward Carpenter Slept with Gavin Arthur.
Gavin Arthur Slept with Dean Moriarty.
Dean Moriarty Slept with Allen Ginsberg.

Allen Ginsberg Slept with Thom Gunn.
Thom Gunn Slept with Jack Fritscher.
Jack Fritscher Slept with Robert Mapplethorpe.
Robert Mapplethorpe Slept with...

To keep this oral history transparent, I must fold open my "Lap Map to Leather Heritage," and disclose my own whereabouts within the GPS of this "Eyewitness Leather Timeline" showing how American civil rights culture, Stonewall, and leather liberation built up to *Drummer*.

Many years before there was a John Embry or a *Drummer*, from 1968-1975, I carried on an S&M affair with my longtime friend, Lou Thomas, who photographed me with a 42nd Street hustler for Target Studio (1968), and published my writing in his *Target* magazine as late as *Target 3*, Winter, 1982. Leather priest Jim Kane, who was a fan of my manuscript *I Am Curious (Leather)*, introduced me to Lou who had publishing experience in New York. He started Colt Studio with Jim French before launching his own Target Studio. Lou, who was thirty-five, and I, who was twenty-nine, began corresponding in the early autumn of 1968, with Lou's letter to me, dated September 20, 1968, discussing *I Am Curious (Leather)*, and scheduling our first sex meeting at his studio in New York, which I confirmed in a letter dated September 22, 1968. Because October in Manhattan is unspeakably beautiful, I had long made a habit to fly in for the Fall.

That year, Lou Thomas and I met and played together for the first of many times on Thursday, October 20, the night of the day I arrived at JFK on a flight made memorable when, circling low over the towers of Manhattan, the captain came on the intercom and announced to us psychedelic jet-setters that Jackie Kennedy had just married Aristotle Onassis. Everyone gasped in shock. The captain added that the flight crew would be serving complimentary champagne.

In the American soap opera that was the Swinging Sixties, Jacqueline Bouvier Kennedy reinvented herself as "Jackie O" less than five years after Jack Kennedy's assassination in Dallas (November 22, 1963), nine months after the assassination of Martin Luther King, Jr. (April 4, 1968), and less than four months after Bobby Kennedy's assassination in Los Angeles (June 5, 1968). The iconic Jackie Kennedy Onassis was escorted by gay men not only to Studio 54 but also to the leather bar, the Anvil. The gay urban legend of "Jackie at the Anvil" was confirmed by her escort, Jerry Torre, in *The New Yorker*, March 6, 2006, page 30.

Earlier, during that thrilling revolutionary Spring season of worldwide student revolution, with the Vietnam war at fever pitch, on June 3, 1968, two days before Bobby Kennedy was shot, Andy Warhol and my friend, leather player, museum curator, and art critic, Mario Amaya, were shot by Valerie Solanas, founder of SCUM, the "Society for Cutting Up Men."

Solanas was the author of the very real *SCUM Manifesto*. That gave my protagonist "Ryan O'Hara" in *Some Dance to Remember* the impetus to pen the fictitious *Masculinist Manifesto* which, as written in that book, was his character's opinion and not the opinion of the author who wrote all the characters. (Amaya died June 29, 1986; Warhol died February 22, 1987; Solanas died April 26, 1988.)

Jim Kane, who had introduced me to Mario Amaya, wrote on June 21, 1971:

> Dear Jack— ...While playing with Mario [in an S&M scene], I noticed two dime-sized scars beside his spine.... "Oh, those are my souvenirs from the shooting at Andy Warhol's." He says that the scene [at the time of the shooting] was so bad [traumatic] that he and Andy shy away from each other...seems the jerks at the hospital didn't know who Andy was and were going to let him bleed to death until Mario started raising absolute hell about "one of America's greatest contemporary artists, etc." That Warhol is alive may be Mario's (fault) [*sic*]... —l&k, jhk [Love and kisses, James H. Kane]

CHICAGO POLICE RIOT (1968)
INSPIRES STONEWALL RIOT (1969)

During August 26-29, 1968, not far from Chuck Renslow's Gold Coast bar, the Chicago Police rioted with Gestapo tactics for four bloody days at the Democratic National Convention, attacking with batons our huge anti-war crowd chanting to the television cameras, "The whole world is watching." Having been a social worker on the South Side of Chicago in 1962 and 1963, and a recent doctoral graduate from Loyola University (1967), I gladly marched back into the streets because we gay folk knew in our hearts that every protest for black civil rights and international peace was an archetype of our own struggle for gay human rights and cultural peace. Those four days of televised police brutality beating protestors in the streets, and roughing up TV reporters like Dan Rather of CBS inside the convention hall, shocked the nation on television in much the same way as had the television coverage of the vicious police brutality against five-hundred civil rights marchers on the Edmund Pettus Bridge in Selma, Alabama, on Bloody Sunday, March 7, 1965, a watershed moment so important to gay rights that I mentioned it on the opening page of *Some Dance to Remember*.

In this particular battle in the culture war, however, the main difference was that while Bloody Sunday made the American public a bit more liberal, the Chicago Police Riot turned Americans so conservative that in reaction they elected Richard Nixon as the next president beginning January 20, 1969, six months before Stonewall.

Increasing the degree of difficulty in gay liberation, the uptight Richard Nixon regency (1969-1974) book-ended the 1970s which ended with the advent of the vile Ronald Reagan regency (1981-1989). From Nixon and Stonewall (1969) to Reagan and AIDS (1981), that first decade of modern gay lib, found its only brief relief in Jimmy Carter's timid presidency (1977-1981) which emboldened fundamentalist Florida Orange Juice queen, pop singer Anita Bryant, to use her Christian celebrity to light the fuse nationwide on the homophobic culture war against gay human rights in her "Save the Children Campaign" (1977).

Fleeing the Chicago cops with crowds of fellow demonstrators, including Abbie Hoffman and Tom Hayden, we retreated from the violence downtown in the Chicago Loop to Lincoln Park where I remember my excitement seeing film director, Haskell Wexler, catching in his camera the bullhorn blasts and running fury of the excited crowds of college students, psychedelic hippies, and activist Yippies. As a university professor teaching film, I respected Wexler for his lensing of gay playwright Edward Albee's 1966 play-into-film, *Who's Afraid of Virginia Woolf?*, for which he won the Academy Award for best cinematography; and for his shooting of *In the Heat of the Night* (1967 Oscar winner Best Picture) in which he invented a revolutionary lighting scheme that finally allowed Hollywood studios to color-balance African-American skin tones properly so that movies about blacks no longer needed to be shot, as said back then, only in black and white.

In Lincoln Park, Chicagoan Wexler, acting on his premonition that there would be trouble at the Convention, dumped his tripod and used a shoulder-mounted camera that allowed him, his crew, and his actors to move virtually unnoticed through the surging crowd who all became his cast of thousands. He wanted precisely such eyewitness realism for the climax of his film, *Medium Cool* (1969) which contains the famous reality-check line yelled by one of his crew screaming in the midst of the ricocheting riot about the violence: "Look out, Haskell. It's real!" After Stonewall, Wexler's roving eyewitness *cinema verite* style quickly became the gonzo gay style for the first Gay Pride parades shot on Super-8 film, years before video cameras arrived in late 1981.

When Abbie Hoffman and six other radicals were arrested for inciting a riot at the Convention, the whole country followed the trial of "The Chicago Seven" which ran, parallel with the rising post-Stonewall effect, from September 1969 to February 1970. As detailed in *Gay San Francisco: Eyewitness Drummer*, I responded with an essay titled "The Chicago Seven: Art, Politics, and Revolution" for my monthly column in *Dateline Colorado* (March 1970), the diocesan newspaper edited by my intimate friend, the Catholic priest and leatherman, Jim Kane. Seventy days later, only eleven months after the police attack at Stonewall, as the 1960s revolution entered 1970s liberation, the National Guard fired their army rifles into a student anti-war demonstration at Kent State University, killing four and wounding nine.

I mention this background to suggest a revolutionary context for what soon would emerge as *Drummer*: That wild 1968 was a formative year because our youth culture of open-mindedness, sex, protest, drugs, and freedom inspired the 1969 uprising at Stonewall and the 1970s Golden Age of Leather.

Wanting to play in the international sex and revolution scene, I took off for Europe, May 1, 1969, International Workers Day, and the Celtic feast of Beltane.

Six weeks later, drag queens fueled by bootstrap feminism, outed their "don't-fuck-with-me selves" at Stonewall. Leathermen also acted up in those running battles those hot nights around Stonewall, declaring their own "don't-fuck-with-me masculine identity" to be valid.

In the leather bars of the 1960s and 1970s, it was as if a "new gender" for men was emerging within the gay culture previously dominated by sissy archetypes that, while legitimate in themselves, needed diversifying. As drag queens needed to out their identity to be their type of feminine, so did masculine-identified gay men need to come out of the closet for their own right to identify as their kind of masculine.

This was the gender polarity as the 1960s became the 1970s. I referenced this exciting tension in my effeminate fiction, "Stonewall, June 27, 11 PM, 1969," the lead story in *Harrington Gay Men's Literary Quarterly*, Volume 8, Issue 1, 2007, edited by Thomas Lawrence Long, Ph.D., with the theme, "Nature Is a Continual Drag Show." The story was also published in the Stonewall Rebellion fortieth-anniversary anthology, *Stonewall: Stories of Gay Liberation*.

While the famous Kinsey Scale accepts the entire range of all heterosexual and homosexual identities, why do some feminist gay males for their own reasons despise masculinity, even in themselves, which seems to others a gender self-hatred more primordial than hating oneself for being gay?

Hatred of masculinity causes hatred of the symbols and metaphors of masculinity, such as leather.

Some fundamentalist, conservative, and Marxist gays in their feminism, and others in their separatist masculinism, have turned against the tradition of liberated humanism in homosexuality. Their solipsistic agenda of jaded dismissal can be crushing to genuine human identity. Their radical gender politics becomes their total identity. Their politically correct rhetoric has become entrenched social bigotry not just in their heterophobia against straight men, but also their homophobia against masculine-identified gay men whom they exclude, vilify, and bully with their sad, discriminatory, separatist epithet, *cisgender*, and wrongly blame as scapegoats—born this way—for the mistakes of straight men. Reducing a man to his dick is as sick, vulgar, and immoral as reducing a woman to her parts.

The *Drummer* I edited and wrote in San Francisco strove to echo Walt Whitman singing words celebrating homomasculine men without trashing other genders. In modern gay history, *Drummer* was the first mass-media magazine to report empathetically on gay male behavior and desires. This was true in the editorial copy of fiction and feature articles, as well as in the grass-roots voices in the personals ads where "men seeking men" statistically used the word *masculine* more than any other word. In *Drummer*, leather pilgrims sought the holy grail of a masculinity that straights denied them, and a homomasculinity that politically correct gays trashed as oppressive.

In the leatherpage.com interview (2000) when Robert Davolt claimed he wanted to focus his late 1990s *Drummer* on gender diversity rather than on leathermen, he was a revisionist revising his own leather history. He defied *Drummer* columnist, Guy Baldwin, who bravely championed the premise that erotica is not politically correct nor inclusive. Growing desperate to be "beloved" in the GLBT community, Davolt bragged he was doing something "diverse" even if the buzzword meant internally betraying the *Drummer* demographic who paid his salary. When he wrote he intended "radical changes within the magazine and within the contest" at www.leatherweb.com/hitdrum.htm, he ignited yet another battle in the gay civil war over gender.

That civil war, first fictionalized in *Some Dance to Remember: A Memoir-Novel of San Francisco 1970-1982*, has been fought inside leather-heritage groups as varied as Chuck Renslow's International Mr. Leather Contest (which was won in an historic first by female-to-male transman Tyler McCormick in 2010); as well as Peter Fiske's The 15 Association; Harold Cox's Delta Run; and Inferno's annual raucous caucus.

Et tu, Davolt?
Trying to be all things to all men, he wrote:

> The judging panel [for Mr. Drummer] is another radical change. *Drummer* was the first international contest to include a leather woman as judge. In 1997, I invited the first transgendered leatherman to judge an international men's contest. When you think about it, few men have to face and wrestle with issues of gender and masculinity... [He was wrong. *Most* gay men, from boyhood, have to fight for their masculinity to escape the heterosexual "bully box" which dismisses all gays as "sissies who want to be women." Outing gay masculine identity was, of course, one of the essential purposes driving *Drummer*.]...to the extent that female and transgendered members of our community have, so I welcomed their opinion on the panel along with a majority of leathermen. I was refocusing *Drummer* as a men's magazine for leathermen [*sic!*], but this was one opportunity to include the rest of our community and actually sharpen that focus.

Davolt in his dashed-off internet writing-style miss-wrote what he clarified elsewhere. He lacked the finesse of Mark Thompson who, ten years before, had gathered all genders together in his anthology inclusively titled, *Leatherfolk: Radical Sex, People, Politics, and Practice* (1990).

He also lacked the business sense of Embry who, instead of diluting the sexual identity of *Drummer* as did Davolt, would have jumped at the chance to clone yet another sibling magazine, perhaps titled *Leatherwoman* or *Leathergender* or even *Leatherfolk*. In fact, if Davolt had done his homework by studying the contents of all the issues of *Drummer*, he would have discovered that—while he was still a teenage undergraduate at the University of Missouri—Tony Deblase bought *Drummer* and immediately invited leatherfolk of all genders into the pages of *Drummer* during his six-year ownership from 1986 to 1992.

To me as a *Drummer* editor, and as a person who sat next to Davolt more than once listening to him talk in private and in public about his messianic mission, his last sentence more accurately reflects his intent when edited this way:

> I was refocusing *Drummer* from being a men's magazine for leathermen, and this was one opportunity to include the rest of the community of leatherfolk and change *Drummer*'s focus.

Fatefully, before it had a politically correct forced sex-change, *Drummer* was dead on its feet, if not buried.

Like any corporate publisher responding to the special-interest markets of emerging genders, Davolt said what he needed to say to keep up the subscriptions, and fluff the good will of the leather community which, like the pool of *Drummer* talent and readers, had been shrinking with the AIDS deaths of men, and growing with the gender diversities of feminist subscribers. Who can blame him for pushing his own agenda? Time was never on his side. Not only did skin cancer cut his talented life short, he was late for the 1970s party he idolized when he finally arrived in San Francisco in 1996 when the twenty-one-year-old *Drummer* had only three more years to live.

During all that terminal turmoil around *Drummer*, he was a good guy, with his own good intentions, who crafted his legacy by writing his own obituary as was often the custom during AIDS. (Reported by Joe Gallagher, leatherpage.com, retrieved http://truetales.org/writings/peterson0506davolttributes.htm)

Contextually, in 1972, when Davolt was fourteen, three years before the founding of *Drummer*, Charles Aznavour captured the "gender despair" of queer lives before gay liberation with his existential chanson, "Comme ils disent" ("What Makes a Man a Man"), a narrative short-story sung by an Old School drag queen who has seen every fit of gender, and goes home alone singing the lyric, "I change my sex [gender] before their eyes."

Aznavour might well have written that movie-like song for his longtime friend, Liza Minnelli, who that year won the Academy Award for *Cabaret*, and went on to sing "Comme ils disent" to adoring fans at the Palais Des Congrés in Paris during the academic rise of queer theory around gender in 1992.

In 1975, as the first issue of *Drummer* hit the stands, that 1970s fascination with the new "out" masculinity was one of the many identity themes that made writers James Kirkwood and Nicholas Dante's *A Chorus Line* the gay Broadway hit of the decade:

> Paul: I always knew I was gay, but that didn't bother me. What bothered me was that I didn't know how to be a boy. See...what I was... trying to find out who I was and how to be a man. You know, there are a lot of people in this world who don't know how to be men.

Who knew that issues of gender and homomasculinity were stirred into Broadway musical comedy? Or into a leather magazine that was more than pornographic?

In my analysis, *Drummer* was the first gay magazine to drop gay "youth" and "prettiness"—and *Queen's Quarterly* attitude—and head toward the fresh "de-forming" queer edge where "leather" breaks the forms of "gay being" and "gay thinking" with its progressive ritual, discipline, and metaphor. This "de-forming" leatherphobia has long caused the queenstream to disrespect and fear the cultural sensitivities of the leatherstream. That's my sixty-year impression from reading, editing, and writing for gay media where the rather paranoid agenda of trashing masculinity is as shamefully common as gay media's page after page of screaming heterophobia.

Valerie Solanas' *SCUM Manifesto* and her gunshots, fired into the leather-friendly Warhol and the leatherman Amaya, caused me in my journal notes to draft the kind of "Masculinist Manifesto" inherent in my every issue of *Drummer* 19-33 and in my contributions post-Embry. It also figured in the fictive subplot of gay civil wars over gender fascism among all genders as dramatized in *Some Dance to Remember*.

Truly, it is disrespectful to see Lou Thomas's homomasculine Target Studio photos reprinted anonymously and labeled "From the *Drummer* Archives" as if those four words canceled his ownership of his own intellectual property by some overriding gay eminent domain. What that means is the editors and publisher in the End Days of 1990s *Drummer* failed professionally in their responsibility to assign credit and copyright, and to return materials. Their appropriations certainly exceeded "fair use."

At our 1730 Divisadero Street office, the *Drummer* closets upstairs in that old Victorian where I worked were jammed floor to ceiling with art work and photos. When I asked Embry about hiring someone part-time to mail back the original goods to contributors, he used a couple phrases like "no return postage" and "no return addresses."

Where did all that treasure trove go with Embry's move to Harriet Street, and every move of office thereafter?

Ending up with mice and Davolt?

And then sold privately, secretly, to Embry?

EMBRY'S GRUDGE AGAINST DEBLASE AND DEBLASE'S LEATHER ARCHIVES & MUSEUM

In the 1990s, Embry often scorned the Leather Archives & Museum because he hated any competition in collecting the art objects and ephemera of leather history for which he figured he had first dibs by right of his one-time ownership of *Drummer*. He was always jealous of the older, wiser entrepreneur Chuck Renslow who, with his pioneer magazines, bars, and museum, outsmarted him at every turn.

Making matters worse, Embry's nemesis, Deblase, named Renslow as the spearhead founder of the LA&M in his open letter to the leather community, "The Leather Archives & Museum" (*Drummer* 157 (August 1992) page 32. A second official announcement of the establishment of the Leather Archives & Museum appeared in *Drummer* 159 (December 1992), page 24 with the headline: "Leather Community Announces Establishment of Leather Archives & Museum."

The LA&M was seed-funded by Chuck Renslow's International Mr. Leather organization whose money-making IML Contest rivaled Embry's unintentionally non-profit Mr. Drummer Contest. Was Embry bewitched, bothered, and begrudging? Was he suddenly seeing competition for the spoils? Was his fantasy of hoarding a leather archive of endlessly republishable free art and writing suddenly impeded? Ultimately, Deblase outfoxed Embry. Despite Embry's entitled tactics, the LA&M created its own gravitas as an organized, professional repository of gay leather heritage. Always trashing his Blacklist enemies, Embry revealed his own private land grab of the estate treasures of quick and dead leatherfolks. He was a ventriloquist who put words into the mouth of the great British artist Bill Ward, who was no puppet, when he outrageously tried to anger subscribers into protesting Deblase starting up the "leather archives" in his *Manifest Reader* 26, page 98:

> We asked Bill Ward to come up with something above and beyond for this issue. Bill is currently desperately trying to get fifteen years of his artwork originals back from the Desmodus group [owned by Deblase] which has appropriated them *to start its leather archives* [italics added] and has refused to release the originals even for publication of his *The World of Bill Ward*. Losing fifteen years of his work is quite a blow.... We wish the very best to Bill, who is hampered in his retrieval efforts by residing far away in England. Bill Ward asks that comments on his behalf be directed directly to Andrew Charles/Anthony DeBlase dba "Leather Archives," 8948 S. W. Barbour Blvd, Portland OR 97219.

Behind Embry's attack lies the fact that his own Alternate Publishing had published the first book of Ward's homomasculine drawings in the large-format magazine, *Drummer Presents the Erotic Art of Bill Ward*. Embry's seventy-page edition mysteriously had no masthead, no publishing information, no date, and no copyright notices to protect Ward; but it did have a self-promotion ad for *Drummer* mail order. Based on internal evidence in that mail-order form, page 70, I can date this *Bill Ward* first edition as 1979, after my *Son of Drummer* (September 1978) which the ad pictured for sale, and before Embry's move of office in mid-1980 from Divisadero Street which is listed as the address for the *Drummer* mail order.

In what was a campaign of disinformation done with fun-house mirrors, Embry wrote about himself in the third person using doublespeak in *Manifest Reader* 27 (1995), page 79. His special "news" box interview is datelined as if reported from "London":

> British artist Bill Ward admits to a couple of problems. His former publisher [DeBlase and Charles] won't turn loose of his popular comic strip, *Drum*, a feature in [Embry's] *Drummer* magazine since 1978. And his new/old book publisher [Embry's Alternate Publishing] has signed an agreement to republish much of it in a third [large, magazine-like format] book, *The Fantastic Art of Bill Ward*, but [Embry] can't because someone else [Deblase-Charles] has physical possession of the originals. Ward...regularly shipped his originals to *Drummer*'s originators, [Embry himself at] Alternate Publishing. When Andrew Charles and Anthony DeBlase, dba Desmodus, Inc., purchased the *Drummer* title, they were given access to the Ward work. Now, both Desmodus and *Drummer* have been sold to new owners, ROB of Amsterdam, who also can't shake the 450 *Drum* and *Beau* panels loose from Messers. Charles and DeBlase.... At the time Desmodus, Inc. was sold to Martin [*sic*] Bakker of Robb [*sic*] of Amsterdam, Charles and DeBlase allegedly removed the originals and took the entire collection with them.

As eyewitness editor-in-chief of *Drummer*, I can swear again that in the 1970s at 1730 Divisadero, Embry did indeed keep a closet, just to the left of Al Shapiro's drafting table, and that closet was a "trash heap" of discarded artwork, including dozens of three-by-four-foot cardstock boards, all original "Bill Wards," each pasted up by Bill Ward himself with page after page of his erotic cartoon art for his continuing feature, *Drum*. Over the years, as people pass on, two of those panels have come into my possession. Historically, the majority of Bill Ward's work that was not sent to *Drummer* was saved, upon his death, from a shed in England by his friend Guy Burch who wrote to me about the difficulties of saving Ward's art work as well as finding the copyright owners for other deceased gay artists on November 10, 2013. Burch's scholarly essay on Bill Ward, AIDS, and copyright can be read at http://www.guyburch.co.uk/?p=2662.

Editors's Note:

ROGUES' GALLERY:
Photos of Some Editors and Publishers in *Drummer*
and a Gay Defense of Sowing Wild Oats

As a sidebar, here's a brief list of photographs of the pioneer cast of characters who created *Drummer*: An LA photo of John Rowberry appeared with his poem, "White Death," in *Drummer* 5, page 36. There is another leather-cult photograph of Rowberry crawling up stair steps wearing a dog collar at the end of a leash. It was given to Fritscher in 1983 by Al Shapiro, and was published in Fritscher's Gay *San Francisco: Eyewitness Drummer* (2008).

There are two great photos of Jeanne Barney: Robert Opel's shot in *Drummer* 9, page 7; and in a mini-dress at the Hawks' 1976 Leather Sabbat where Rob Clayton photographed her receiving the Hawks Humanitarian of the Year Award in *Drummer* 11, page 25.

Gene Weber took the photo of a just-becoming-editor Fritscher that appeared in *Drummer* 17, July 1977, page 11 top, along with, in the same issue, Weber photos of Society of Janus leather priest, Jim Kane, with Ike Barnes, page 9. Weber also pictured Fritscher in his scuba photos of fisting underwater in *Drummer* 20, page 17, and *Drummer* 25, page 91. A second photo, a set piece shot by David Sparrow, shows Fritscher in a jockstrap at the CMC Carnival in *Drummer* 20, page 76, because editor-in-chief Fritscher, pressed by the necessity of invention, anticipated on location how his CMC photo layout should look in the next issue, and acted out what other leather players were still reticent to do in public on camera at that time. This *ad hoc* "improvisation on location" is similar to the photos of Fritscher, after the model did not show, in "Bondage" in *Drummer* 24, pages 17, 18, 20. A photograph of Fritscher appeared in Embry's Tenth Anniversary Issue, *Drummer* 85, page 85, with Fritscher's text, "Smut Is Where You Find It," page 86.

Fritscher published one of B. Moritz's several photographs of the naked streaker Robert Opel confronting LAPD Chief Ed Davis in the Harvey Milk obituary issue of *Drummer* 26 in January 1979. The Moritz photo appeared previously with a second, even more dramatic, Moritz photo of Opel's lovely body striding though the crowd toward Chief Davis in Fred Halsted's *Package* 6, pages 22-23, January 1977. LAPD Police Chief Ed Davis also appeared in *Drummer* 6, page 13.

In a casual photo, Embry appears with his face turned ninety degrees away from the camera in *Drummer* 25, December 1978, page 91. "Why did he turn?" Fritscher asked. "Was it his 1950s reflex of self-defense against being photographed at a gay event? Was it the LAPD arrest? Why did we publish his faceless photo?"

Fritscher added: "In a priceless photo true to their characters, DeBlase and Charles pose with my sex-playmate, 'Mr. Drummer 1987, Mark Alexander,' in *Drummer* 108 (September 1987), page 52. DeBlase also appears with whip, wearing maharaja jodhpurs, in *Drummer* 142, page 69."

Regarding critical thinking about composing gay history, including his own personal kiss-and-tell revelations such as in this list, Fritscher observed: "Too often when authors writing memoir books, or talking in video documentaries speak of history, they cover their asses and take out personal policies of slut-shaming insurance so they don't incriminate themselves with youthful indiscretions. They feign a pearl-clutching distance between the false 'purity' of their miss-remembered historical selves and their eyewitness memory of, and participation in, operatic, legendary sex that they sniff was, well, tawdry; or, my dear, the cause of AIDS; or never happened—at least to them. They never sowed the wild oats all young men must? That's the mendacity Tennessee Williams condemned in his drama about the closet, *Cat on a Hot Tin Roof*. That's the lie that talking heads tell when they deny their own history and shove the true sexual past of their youth into the closet where conservative, angry, old gay men go to rant and die. When reading such writing, or watching such video documentaries, people who are critical thinkers might assess how history is being distorted by the agenda of some fact-changing puritan looking in the rear-view mirror. When watching or reading any documentary about the gay past, including even Joseph F. Lovett's interesting documentary video, *Gay Sex in the Seventies* (2005), or Larry Kramer's cherry-picking documentary novel, *The American People* (2015), the viewer or reader cannot help but judge that some documentaries on screen and page are less devoted to honest first-person history than to the second-hand pleasures of voyeurism.

"That censorious denial within 'politically corrected' attitude is the basis of most of history's wrong-minded appraisals about the life and work of Robert Mapplethorpe. I lived the roller-coaster reality of 1970s sex with that bold boy, and with the wild staff and wilder subscribers of *Drummer*, and I was honest about how wild we were in the HBO documentary, *Mapplethorpe: Look at the Pictures* (2016). I am not into any conservative kind of senior citizen's denial of the most fun we homosexuals ever had. Why shrink from our own history? Why not embrace the true sexual exploits of our youth the way we love the pop music of our teenage past. I sing with the sainted bisexual Edith Piaf, 'Non, Je ne regrette rien (I regret nothing).' In my eyewitness experience of the ongoing sex salon around *Drummer*, my *menage a trois* dates of 'dinner and dancing' with the likes of Colt Studio star Mark Alexander (*Drummer* 108 cover model) and his bodybuilder partner, Peter Morrison (Colt model "Joe Falco"), at their home in Venice Beach were not shameful. Those two, like all the others, were worth kissing. They were worth telling. They were indeed some dance to remember."

In his *History of Our Leather-S/M Fetish Sub-Culture and Communities,* leather historian David Stein, a founder of Gay Male S/M Activists (GMSMA), adroitly sussed out that the unabashed salon around *Drummer* was a hyper-active hive of esthetic, social, and sexual connections: "Fritscher, one of the great *Drummer* editors, seems to have been everywhere and done everyone during the 'good old days' of leather."

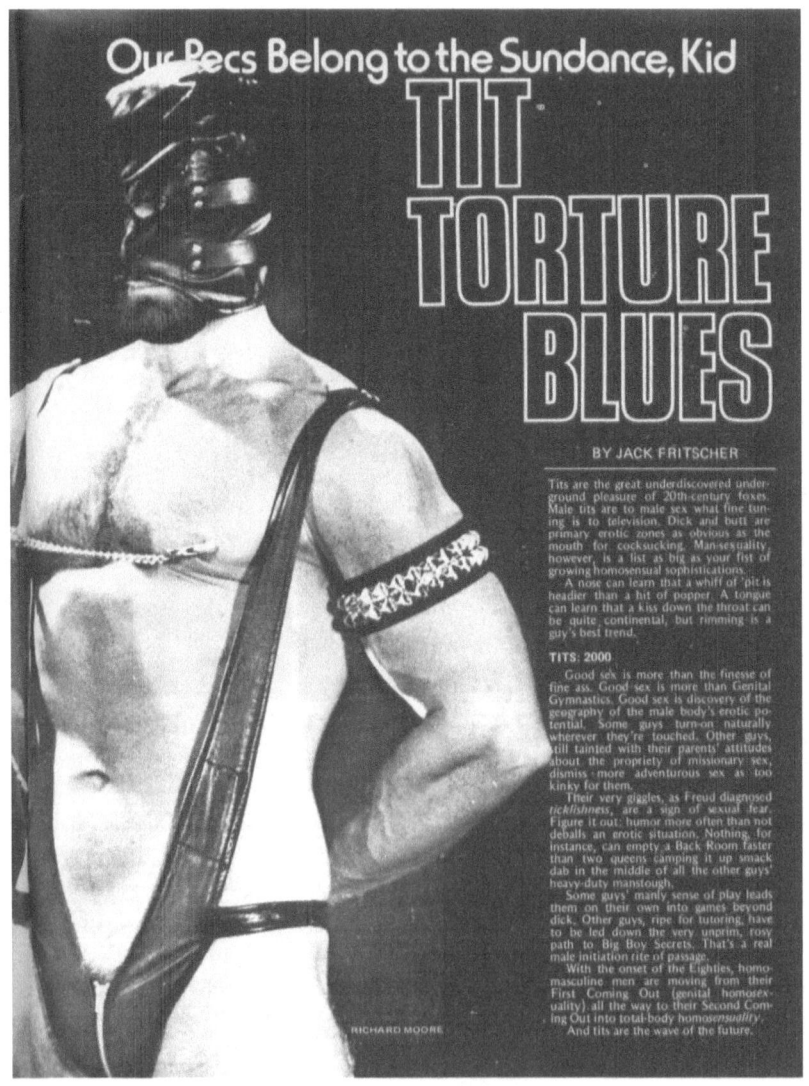

CHAPTER 13

ANNUS MIRABILIS 1979
(THE WONDERFUL YEAR 1979)

My *Drummer* Desk Calendar
Personal Annotations and Bibliography
My 1979 Life Editing *Drummer* in Real Time

- 1978-1979 Eyewitness *Drummer* Timeline: Fulsome Details of Folsom Street
- 2 Guns: Harvey Milk Assassination (27 November 1978) plus Robert Opel Murder (July 8, 1979) Both Impact *Drummer*; Fritscher Turns Down Job as Deputy Sheriff of San Francisco
- Fritscher Desk Calendar: Editing *Drummer*; Dating Robert Mapplethorpe and Introducing His Photography into Leather Culture; Colt Models Chuck Romanski and Dan Pace; Bodybuilder Champ Jim Enger; the Artist Domino; Meeting Mark Hemry at Harvey Milk's Birthday Party, and Outing Gay Cowboys with Randy Shilts
- December 31, 1979: Fritscher Exits *Drummer* having edited *Drummer* issues from 18 to 33

> "A career in the arts can make anyone crazy..."
> —Christopher Bram, *Eminent Outlaws: The Gay Writers Who Changed America*

My *Wonderful Year*, my action-packed *Annus Mirabilis*, was 1979. I had the good fortune to be the young editor-in-chief of the hottest gay magazine on the planet. Everyone was having carefree, simultaneous, and epic polyamorous affairs. Besides romancing the troops on the streets and at the baths, I was having fun playing at being Joe Orton's "Mr. Sloane," entertaining my intimate significant others: Robert Mapplethorpe, Jim Enger, David Sparrow, Tony Tavarossi, and Mark Hemry.

My "Annotated 1978-1979 *Drummer* Eyewitness Timeline" grew from my editorial desk calendar. In 1979, San Francisco and *Drummer* were both freaking out over assassination, riot, murder, lust, cancer, hysteria, cash, and creativity. As editor-in-chief, I exited *Drummer* officially as New Year's Eve, 1979, flipped into the 1980s with its transformative threesome of Ronald Reagan, the VCR, and AIDS.

Because timelines are *Roshomon* and inevitably repeat narrative text, some items in this fact-checked rear-view mirror offer different provident angles on calendar and character. For all the bliss of writing, the creating of a *Drummer* issue took a prodigious amount of work. During the wild 1970s with all the sex and fun and love affairs we all enjoyed, I kept focus, and edited solo fifteen issues of *Drummer* (18 to 33), more than anyone else at that time, and contributed 147 pieces of writing and 266 photographs (including covers and centerfolds) before the end of 1979. During this splendid time, I had edited more than half of the *Drummer* issues in existence. As my desk calendar changed to the new decade, I continued contributing much more writing and many more photographs to many issues of *Drummer* after the second publisher, Anthony Deblase, ended first publisher John Embry's Blacklist in 1986.

Each issue of *Drummer* averaged about 100 large-format pages which, folded, would equal a 400-page trade paperback book. I edited exactly 942 pages of *Drummer*, issues 18 to 33, or the equivalent of a 3,778-page book. When I withdrew my editing, writing, and photography during late 1979 because I wanted to be paid for all this work, Embry was forced to shorten each issue by the nearly twenty percent I had contributed "free" each issue. "Minus me minus my paycheck," he had to pare my beefy 96-page average issue down to a slim 80 pages in *Drummer* 28 and *Drummer* 29. In 2010, he died, one of the one percent, having never paid me—one of the ninety-nine percent of unpaid *Drummer* contributors—for this work completed thirty years before. Never one to make the huge mistake of trying to live off gay art and writing, I have always had a university teaching job or a corporate writing job in the real world, even during the very years I worked for *Drummer*. Nevertheless, money was never the point. This 1979 log, growing out of the context of 1978 and into the swim of 1980, covers that year's *Drummer* issues 23 to 33.

MY *DRUMMER* DESK CALENDAR
SOME TIMELINE ANNOTATIONS
April 1978 - October 1980

John Embry's health problems caused a pivotal change in his physical and psychological demeanor in mid-to-late 1978 even as the quiet onset of his unseeable colon cancer took its toll before being diagnosed and treated with surgery on March 16, 1979. Autocratic as a publisher before his surgery, and then dodging death, he felt so entitled to "live life large" that during his long recuperation, he became so increasingly difficult to work with that the staff was glad he was mostly AWOL from the office for five whole months during Spring and Summer.

When he finally returned to work, he sputtered and fumed with faint praise because his ego was somehow wounded to find that *Drummer* had become new and improved with an inflected editorial change, and a huge rise in subscriptions during the long production time he was out of the picture. No good deed goes unpunished. He was jealous of his own staff who had protected his business and erotic interests and changed *Drummer* from a local LA publication into a San Francisco magazine with international appeal. He had a literal "gut reaction" reflected in his rhetoric in his writing. He combined metaphors of bondage and illness. He revealed his own physical and psychological state, as well as inadvertently his bad behavior, only six months after his colon cancer surgery on his knotted-up guts. Safely disembodied in the hollow voice of his alter-ego 'Robert Payne," Embry editorialized, preaching without irony, about psychosomatic illness and karma in the "In Passing" column in *Drummer Rides Again* (November 1979). In his exact words:

> Being "all tied up"...can refer to various parts of the body and psyche. A stomach "all tied up" in knots can denote nervousness, apprehension, or just indigestion. Being "tied up" can keep one from dinner, or coming to the phone, or missing an appointment [or showing up at the *Drummer* office]. But the being "tied up" we are dealing with at this moment, Gentle Reader, is an internal constipation [*sic*] that all of us suffer from....We get what we give. And usually deserve what we get. Next time you are "all tied up," let it be literally, not emotionally. (Page 62)

Peddling this advice to others, Embry explained how and why his treatment of the *Drummer* staff and the business had escalated so hysterically. His cancer may have been caused by the homophobia of the LAPD. Under tremendous stress from the 1976 Drummer Slave Auction arrests that led to years of court dates and costs, he was forced to flee LA, the city he loved, and to set up shop in San Francisco where he tried to "tie up" us *Drummer* workers and make us his whipping boys. Over Embry's eleven years of "Plantation Boss" behavior, hundreds were hired, and hundreds quit. Is it at all revelatory that his personal favorite movie covered multiple times in *Drummer* was the plantation and slavery pot-boiler *Mandingo*. His favorite author was Kyle Onstott who, mixing race, slavery, and S&M, had written both the novel *Mandingo* and its sequel—titled what else?—*Drum*.

September 1978: Publication of *Drummer* 24, the famous Mapplethorpe cover. Embry was turned on by the fresh "takes" of Robert Mapplethorpe's work. In an envious plagiarism, he tried to restage and shoot Mapplethorpe-like photos to fill future issues without having to pay royalties. Jealous, he took to a fatuous denouncing of Mapplethorpe who had, during Halloween 1977, arrived very sweetly at the *Drummer* office to introduce himself to me on his enterprising trip to San Francisco. The start of his trip on "Saturday, October 16, 1977" was documented by petite British author and resident of the Chelsea Hotel, Victor Bokris, in his book, *Beat Punks* (1998). Bokris also wrote *Patti Smith: An Unauthorized Biography* (1999). Embry was miffed at the personal Mapplethorpe-Fritscher bicostal affair which lasted passionately—nearly the whole time I edited *Drummer*—from October 1977 to its sweet evaporation over health-and-hygiene issues during spring 1980. Robert, the New Yorker, was frequently sick intestinally and I, the San Franciscan, was not, and I had to back away to protect my health.

Footnote #1: Inside the Timeline
Mapplethorpe, the Mainstream, and *Drummer*

Here, inside this timeline, it is appropriate to show how influential *Drummer* was, and how *Drummer*, properly written and properly edited, could transcend itself with a readership far sleeker than critics might guess, and certainly smarter and more sophisticated than scoffers thought it to be.

The zero-degrees model to illustrate this is Robert Mapplethorpe, and how he was featured in *Drummer* in the years from 1978, when I introduced him, to 1989 when I wrote his obituary..

Drummer connected me by one degree of separation to Patricia Morrisroe as informant for her biography, *Mapplethorpe* (1995). My own insider gay-*verite* book, in progress since 1978, *Mapplethorpe: Assault with a Deadly Camera*, was published in 1994, the year before Ms. Morrisroe's outsider book. While doing interviews and writing her book, she may have suffered, I alleged, a "gay panic" attack about the rough subject matter of homomasculine culture ranging across racism, promiscuity, drugs, S&M, and dirty sex. Or, at least, so it seemed to me as I reviewed the internal evidence of her attitude and voice in her "straight" biography of the gay artist. Seventeen years later, critic Christopher Bram in *Eminent Outlaws* thoroughly documented the "gay panic" typical of the mid-century New York literary establishment who trashed gay artists such as Tennessee Williams, Gore Vidal, James Baldwin, and Christopher Isherwood. Critic Richard Labonte wrote at his site, Books to Watch Out For (btwof.com), "Of the two biographies of Mapplethorpe, Fritscher's was the first and is still the best."

After Mapplethorpe died, March 9, 1989, I championed him in *Drummer* where Paul Taylor, an understanding *New York Times* art critic, noticed my "*Pentimento* for Mapplethorpe," *Drummer* 133 (September 1989). Taylor wrote the following letter dated October 11, 1989:

> Dear Mr. Fritscher, I am a former friend of Robert Mapplethorpe and an art critic (*New York Times* and various magazines), and I was pleased and interested to read your article about Robert in *Drummer*. In fact, I have brought it to the attention of Patricia Morrisroe, a journalist for *New York* magazine (with no special credentials regarding art) who is writing a biography of our friend for Random House publishers. I hope she will be in touch with you if she hasn't already. ---Yours sincerely, Paul Taylor.

A week before I received Taylor's letter, Patricia Morrisroe, straight and Catholic, contacted me for an interview for her book funded by Random House. With both of us recording, I talked to her on the telephone for nearly five hours. Days later, on October 10, 1989, she wrote me a thank-you note from her Riverside Drive address in Manhattan. Quoted briefly from her copyrighted letter, she was very sweet: "Dear Jack. Thanks so much...even though I've interviewed over 120 people at this point, I haven't spoken to anyone who is as articulate on the subject of Mapplethorpe as you are. Your piece [in *Drummer*] was really well-written." Noting she was having a "hard time" building a timeline for Robert because he kept no notes, she inquired about his letters to me, saying she would appreciate my help, and she signed off: "Thanks for the help you've already given me. Best, Patricia Morrisroe."

FOUR POINTS: *DRUMMER* AND MAPPLETHORPE

1. My "*Pentimento*: Mapplethorpe" article was the apogee of *Drummer* magazine assaying a political *cause celebre*.

2. In the midst of the culture war over art and homosexuality in America, the 1989 "Pentimento" rose like a flare over the memory of the sinking Titanic 1970s.

3. Its publication in *Drummer* 133 (September 1989) completed the eleven-year "circle of life" I had begun by reporting on Mapplethorpe in *Drummer* 24 and *Son of Drummer* (both September 1978).

4. On May 9, 1990, Mark Thompson, who was collecting authors for his landmark anthology, *Leatherfolk: Radical Sex, People, Politics, and Practice*, wrote:

> Dear Jack, Thank you for the...[article] on Robert Mapplethorpe. I sat down and read the essay last night and was completely overwhelmed by the power and the beautiful writing of the piece. You've caught something extremely important. So, a thought occurs: What would you think about including the "Arnett" [an article I'd written on artist, Chuck Arnett, in *Drummer* 134 (October 1989)] and "Mapplethorpe" pieces together, back to back, in the leather anthology? Both are very personal pieces about two important artists, from different decades and coasts, yet who had immense influence over the culture of the time. Furthermore, each man liberated the leather image, advanced its meaning, each in his own particular way....Having both pieces of your articles together would also express an historical continuity as well....
> —Warmly, Mark Thompson

If Embry had still owned *Drummer* in 1989 his Blacklist would not, in my opinion, have allowed any obituary of his nemesis Mapplethorpe to darken the pages of *Drummer*, much less one written by me, his "rogue" editor. The consequence of Embry's "embryonic 180 degrees of separation from the evolving soul of *Drummer*" would have segregated *Drummer* into a marginal ghetto of sex fantasies, with one less connection to the real world of erotic art and politics.

When Embry's hired gun of a book critic, John F. Karr, reviewed *Leatherfolk* in *Manifest Reader* 16 (1992), page 88, Karr extended himself into liking the book of essays even though he could not resist one flick of his vanilla wrist: "At times this collection makes S/M sound like a civic duty." Nevertheless he listed ten of the twenty-five contributors, mostly *Drummer* authors, by name: John Preston, Pat Califia, Scott Tucker, Jack Fritscher, Sam Steward, Dorothy Allison, Arnie Kantrowitz, Joseph Bean, Geoff Mains, and Mark Thompson.

In the same *Manifest Reader* 16, Karr seemed to hew to Embry's Blacklist agenda in his review of the 1992 Lammy Award Winner, *Gay Roots: Twenty Years of Gay Sunshine, An Anthology of Gay History, Sex, Politics & Culture*, edited by Winston Leyland. Karr correctly mentioned some contributors such as Jean Genet, the Malcolms Boyd and McDonald, Walt Whitman, and Yukio Mishima. However, journalist Karr failed to anchor the local-color "hook" of his review in the glories of Embry's salad days as the publisher of *Drummer* insofar as the only gay drama included in *Gay Roots* was also the only selection that was published originally in *Drummer*: *Corporal in Charge of Taking Care of Captain O'Malley*. As editor-in-chief, I had written and published that erotic play in *Drummer* 21 and *Drummer* 22. *Corporal in Charge* was, as well, the title of one of my anthologies of my fiction that had appeared originally in *Drummer*. In fact, *Corporal in Charge and Other Stories* was the first book collection of *Drummer* writing.

If Karr had connected *Drummer* to the Lambda Literary Award winner *Gay Roots*, Embry could have basked in the credit of having been the publisher who debuted that drama made canonical by inclusion in *Gay Roots*. In the Grudge Match that was his publishing life in San Francisco, Embry never really understood the esthetic, intellectual, and spiritual gestalt and power of *Drummer* which he thought of as a little more than a campy leather magazine using sex pictures to sell dildos through his main business: mail-order.

The whole of *Drummer* was greater than the sum of its parts. Or, in Kurt Koffka's phrase, "The whole is other than the sum of its parts." That "whole," which readers loved, eluded Embry, but was understood by *Drummer* columnists such as Guy Baldwin and Larry Townsend, editors Tim Barrus and Joseph W. Bean, and publisher Anthony DeBlase.

HOW THE *DRUMMER* SALON REPRODUCED

November 1977: In the erotic mosh pit of the 1977 CMC Carnival, I met bodybuilder Dan Dufort from LA. In *Drummer* (May 1978), on pages 8 and 14, I published two of my photos of Dufort for "Cigar Blues."

On August 25, 1978, Dufort played matchmaker at his home at 7560 Willoughby, Los Angeles. He introduced me to his friend, the blond LA bodybuilder, Jim Enger, who, like Mapplethorpe, had asked specifically to meet the editor of *Drummer*. During the torrid thirty-one-month Enger-Fritscher affair, the professional instantly became personal. And the personal became public. In gay popular culture, the coupling of the famous bodybuilder and the editor of *Drummer* grabbed the attention of muscle-queens and leathermen. Enger was so much better looking than almost anybody that wags figured that to have bagged the beauty I must have been hung huge or been the best S&M top on the planet. Actually, we were a Vulcan Mind Meld of transcendent mutuality, muscle-sex, and homomasculinity. Well-managed affairs in the free-love 1970s tended to be non-possessive, and my liaison with Enger ran parallel to my affair with Mapplethorpe so I was able to bring them together for a creative photo session. What happens in sex shapes the world. Both Enger and Mapplethorpe helped me shape the homomasculine look of *Drummer*.

In my special *Drummer* issue, *Son of Drummer* (September 1978), pages 6 and 7, I published a drawing of Dan Dufort by Los Angeles artist Ralph Richter. When Dufort introduced me to Richter at Richter's LA apartment, I was admiring Richter's framed work hanging on the wall when, astonished, I saw that one of the drawings was of me, taken, Richter said, from my face and pose in one of Walt Jebe's photographs for *Whipcrack* magazine (1970). The moment of discovery was so hilarious that Richter immediately gifted me with his pencil drawing.

On August 15, 1986, Dufort became the second-place winner of the Physique Contest at Gay Games II, San Francisco. A year later, Dufort starred in my video feature of his fetish, *Gut Punchers* (1987). Historically, it is the first video on gut punching which quickly became its own pop-culture genre. Two more of my photographs of Dufort appeared in *Drummer* 115 (April 1988), page 40. These same photographs were published by author Brian Pronger in his book, the *Drummer*-influenced *The Arena of Masculinity: Sports, Homosexuality, and the Meaning of Sex* (1990). *Drummer* anticipated Pronger by twelve years with my "Gay Jock Sports" feature article in *Drummer* 20 (January 1978).

Footnote #2: Inside the Timeline:
Colt Models, the Platonic Ideal, and *Drummer*

Jim Enger was a masculine-identified uniform man—a man's man, in the best sense, who was also a blond bodybuilder champion. Viewed as a kind of Platonic Ideal, Enger became for me Emerson's "representative man" incarnating the homomasculine identity emerging in *Drummer*. Enger was virtually the quintessential Mr. Drummer.

Outside of *Drummer*, I spun our real-time meeting in Dufort's apartment into my fictitious fantasy with no personal connection to Enger other than basic muscle-sex choreography in *Some Dance to Remember,* Reel 1, Scene 10. Two muscle-sex scenes from *Some Dance* were excerpted pre-book publication in *Drummer* 124 (December 1988) with a review of the book by Paul Martin in *Drummer* 141 (August 1990).

Four months later at Christmas, 1978, Enger moved into my San Francisco home, ending his domestic relationship, but not his friendship, with Colt model, Clint Lockner. These men were objective correlative of the kind of homomasculine beauty in my life in the 1970s. Clint Lockner was Chuck Romanski. One man: two hot names. Both sounded porno. In real life, Charles (Chuck) Romanski was the LAPD police officer who shocked the LAPD by appearing in photographs and films shot by Rip Colt aka Jim French for Colt Studio. The thirty-five-year-old Romanski had served in both the Army and Marine Corps and at the time of the shoot had been an LAPD officer for eight years.

The handsome Romanski took gay popular culture by storm in magazine photographs and in the Super-8 Colt films we worshipers projected on the roll-down silent screens hanging in our bedrooms before the invention of the VCR. Rip Colt created the entire issue of *Colt Men* 7 (1980) to showcase Chuck on the cover and in the contents: including gun, nightstick, and boot fetish photos that became templates for Mapplethorpe who from the 1960s had cruised 42nd Street dirty book stalls to study leather photography in magazines for inspiration. In the zero degrees of *Colt Men* 7, Romanski interacted on several pages with Colt model Mickey Squires who was also my Palm Drive Video model. Colt/French also shot Enger privately.

Looking up from my bed of roses, I figured *Drummer* had come full circle from the LAPD "Slave Auction" arrest in 1976 to the retired LAPD officer and Colt icon, Romanski, in 1978.

Enger and Romanski were such an archetypal muscle-uniform "power couple" in 1970s LA that Tom of Finland, attracted by their high-profile beauty which seemed born out of his own homomasculine Platonic Ideal, insisted on drawing them together in uniform. Tom's Enger-Romanski drawing was very popular, appearing on the cover and on page 47 of *Olympus,* A Colt Studio Publication (1982); inside *Drummer* 79 (December 1984), page 10; in the book, *Tom of Finland,* Taschen, 1992, page 62; and on the cover of the German translation of the Samuel Steward aka Phil Andros novel *The Boys in Blue, Bullenhochzeit* (1994).

I arranged for another *Drummer* artist, Domino (Don Merrick), to draw Jim Enger in our bedroom on March 26, 1979, and for Mapplethorpe to photograph Enger in a condo near Twin Peaks on March 25, 1980. (See my *Domino Video Gallery,* Palm Drive Video, as well as the "Interview with Domino" by Shapiro and Fritscher in

Drummer 29, May 1979). Domino and Mapplethorpe, both gritty New Yorkers walking on the wild side, were drawn to Enger's blond California brightness. Their dark East Coast interpretations of Enger's universal appeal were contrapuntal and useful because Enger, so publicly in bloom in 1970s California, was more in the sun-kissed tradition favored by straight and gay photographers besotted with him in San Francisco and LA. A star on the straight physique contest circuit where he was often invited as the Guest Poser, Enger was simultaneously the most ogled and desired man on the streets of San Francisco and in the beach-and-gym cliques in LA where on Sunday afternoons at a certain steroid doctor's Hollywood Hills palazzo the bodybuilders stood on one side of the pool and the checkbooks stood on the other.

One Sunday, walking south with Enger on Castro Street in front of the Spaghetti Factory restaurant, I watched as Rudolf Nureyev and his party walked north toward us. As we passed, Enger, as always, kept the custody of his eyes straight ahead. I, however, couldn't resist turning around to glimpse Nureyev from the rear, and what I saw was Rudy turning around, in slow full 360-degree pivot, to take one more look at Enger which he confirmed with a direct look, a big grin, and a thumbs-up to me! Then Rudy sailed on to the north, and Enger and I to the south leaving no ripple. As for my own artistic interpretation, Enger, as symbol, influenced my various homomasculine articles such as "Fucking with Authentic Men" (*Drummer* 24).

Enger, who honestly enjoyed exhibiting himself in public, never allowed his photographs to be published in *Drummer* or any other gay venues. When I arranged for Robert Mapplethorpe to photograph Enger in the unforgettable star-feud shoot on March 25, 1980, Enger, as it turned out, would not sign a release as he had not for Jim French at Colt. He was a physique celebrity, and, not unreasonably, he wanted to approve the photographs that he felt we were co-creating with Robert. But Mapplethorpe, always wily and thinking ahead, had shot several frames of Enger's torso pictured from the neck down. One of those headless torso shots of Enger was produced by Mapplethorpe as a color greeting card sold in museum gift shops; and it was reproduced by Tony Deblase with my Mapplethorpe obituary in *Drummer* 133 (September 1989), page 14. Earlier in 1979, a Castro photographer, one of the street paparazzi who loved Enger, had snapped the two of us, Enger and me, hooked together at the hip, and holding court "in our spot," leaning against the sunny west wall of Donuts and Things, one Sunday afternoon at 18th and Castro. Every weekend the sidewalks were jammed with thousands of cruising immigrants and sex tourists strolling in concentric circles in a kind of gay *paseo* around the intersection. When that photo was turned into a postcard sold at shops on Castro, Enger politely confronted our appropriation by the photographer, but, of course, we were a public couple lensed in public. So we were fair game. Nevertheless, Enger charmed the photographer into withdrawing the card.

I photographed Enger dozens of sessions in stills and color Super-8 films, at home, alone in popular gyms after midnight, at his physique contests, and most beautifully out on the rugged rocky top of Corona Heights overlooking all of San Francisco and Castro in particular. (Corona Heights is romanticized as the gay Wuthering Heights in *Some Dance to Remember*, Reel 5, Scene 13.) Enger, as a public personality on the streets and on the bodybuilding stages, where his abs had a terrific ripple effect, gladly supported and appeared on the cover of my first issue of *Man2Man Quarterly* (January 1980), as well as in the article that I wrote about him, "Jim Enger: On the Way Up," in the straight physique magazine, *Dan Lurie's Muscle Training Illustrated*, Number 80, December 1979; also in *Iron Man*, July 1979, page 42.

I must clarify to anyone inserting autobiography into my fiction, that the character of Kick Sorenson in *Some Dance to Remember*, even as excerpted in *Drummer* 124, pages 20-25, and "Bodybuilding" (*Drummer* 124, pages 7-9), is not based on Enger. Although beautiful, he did not have what Sam Steward wrote in *Chapters from an Autobiography*, "the disease of beauty, which in its progression rots the soul and destroys the will." Enger's playful *modus operandi* was nothing like the diseased beauty of Kick Sorenson. However, our experience together in competitive bodybuilding allowed him to win trophies and me to write the insider psycho-erotic observations made in *Some Dance*. In *Les Liaisons Dangereuse* and *La Ronde* around *Drummer*, I always tried, as a gentleman in the sexually liberated 1970s, to make my fictitious writing be dynamically fueled by real-life sex, and to remain friends with the many lovers and tricks who inspired that writing, and to whom I remain forever grateful.

For instance, in remaining friends with Lockner/Romanski, I wrote on August 12, 1979, while I was editor-in-chief of *Drummer*, a feature article reviewing Romanski's leathersex-uniform act with Dan Pace (legally, Daniel Pacella) who, as a Zeus Studio model, was the centerfold of my *Drummer* 27 (February 1979). That summer, "Lockner and Pace" toured, performing for one-hand-clapping audiences in sold-out porn theaters nationwide, beginning in Alex de Renzy's Screening Room theater at 220 Jones Street in San Francisco. Because I was exiting *Drummer*, Embry dropped my review, "In These Last Days of the American Empire: Dan Pace & Clint Lockner Together." It was quickly published as part of my

"Virtual *Drummer*" collection in the premiere issue of *Skinflicks*, Volume 1, Number 1, January 1980.

In November 1979, Daniel D. Pacella, who had also starred in the Gage Brothers' *LA Tool and Die*, wrote from his Orange Drive address in LA:

> Jack, A thousand thanks from Chuck and me for your... review. We loved it. We enjoyed it. We even got off on it....We were glad you wrote about our effort as more than just a sex show....Sorry to hear there's so much trouble at *Drummer*, but use the photos included with the review wherever you get this published....We look forward to sharing once again with you a joint and a jug of wine.
> —Dan & Chuck

With aching nostalgia for the 1970s, I recall, like Chaucer's vigorous Wife of Bath joyously counting her grand slams, that while I was editing *Drummer*,

- the Enger-Fritscher affair ran (September 1978-January 1981) parallel with
- the Mapplethorpe-Fritscher affair (Halloween 1977-Spring 1980) which ran parallax to
- the Sparrow-Fritscher gay marriage (1969-1979) running in step with
- the Tavarossi-Fritscher affair (1971-1981), and coincidental with
- the Hemry-Fritscher union beginning May 22, 1979, and continuing to the present.

Like all of us in that Titanic decade, I lived the 1970s to the hilt, but I did have some limits.

When the drop-dead handsome Romanski, who had the biggest cock in porn, but not as big as Enger's, wined and dined and courted me, and played the piano (which he did beautifully), I politely declined his gorgeous advances because it seemed incestuous to ball my hairy blond lover's ex who seemed overly curious about what he had heard my conjure-energy was like sexually. My refusal in the free love of the 1970s was probably foolish, because Enger joked, "You don't know what you missed."

Maybe I do: Chuck Romanski died of AIDS June 17, 1993.

During that same summer, in August, 1993, I saw Dan Dufort for the last time when the hills around LA were on fire, and security for the visiting Nelson Mandela had slowed all traffic to a crawl. He was desperate: his mother had died some months before, and his lover and *Gut Punchers* co-star, "Gino Deddino," had recently died from an overdose. Dan had come home to find his lover's dead body moved around the apartment by "roommates" who stole what few belongings the two had not squandered in trade for drugs. Deeply depressed, Dan was soon fired as "hairdresser for the wigs" in the LA road show of *Phantom of the Opera*. He was a long way from his stardom at the Gay Games II when I had videotaped him posing fully oiled and nearly naked at high noon on the steps of City Hall while tourists walked around him staring and applauding. When I last kissed Dan goodbye, the gaunt physique winner was working part-time as a night porter at a West Hollywood motel and living in an abandoned store front, literally one step up from the sidewalk, at 1057 N. Curson and Hollywood Blvd. With no family, and no one to notify, my sweet buddy sadly, simply disappeared...

April 24, 1978 (Monday): The maniacal Zodiac Killer sent his twenty-first letter to the media warning San Francisco he was back to serial killing which affected gay safety and attitudes in bars whose doors opened to the lurking dark of cruisy streets South of Market. Several leathermen, such as my friend Tom Gloster, exited Folsom Street bars and were never seen alive again. At the same time, my friend, Larry Hunt, who posed famously in lace-up boots for Mapplethorpe, left an LA bar and disappeared until his jawbone was found in Griffith Park two years later.

July 1978: Publication of *Drummer* 23. As editor-in-chief, I gathered and shaped the content of the 96-page issue, contributing twelve pieces of my own writing and twelve of my photographs. My writing included "Gay Pop Culture in *Drummer*," "The Catacombs," the poem "Redneck Biker," "Astrologic," Act Two of my play *Corporal in Charge of Taking Care of Captain O'Malley*, "Target Men: Target Studio," and "Reviewing Straight Magazines," as well as the start up of ongoing publication for my humor column "Tough Shit."

August 25, 1978 (Friday): On this date, my life changed forever, and I began actively inserting a personally experienced "Platonic Ideal of Homomasculinity " into *Drummer*. Having flown PSA to Hollywood-Burbank, I met Jim Enger through Dan Dufort who thought we, his two friends, were meant for each other. The Enger-Fritscher affair began immediately that day in August 1978 and lasted until January 1981, through almost the entirety of my editing *Drummer*.

Autumn 1978: Panic over the Zodiac Killer became specific as another serial killer stalked gay men on Folsom Street until bartender David Likens, not the Zodiac Killer, was charged with the alleged mutilation murder of three men, including my friend Tom Gloster. Separately abducted, the gay men's bodies were discovered along roadsides north of the Golden Gate Bridge. See February 6, 1979, entry below. See also the sibling to *Drummer*, *The Alternate* 8 (January 1979), as well as my editorial, "Cruising: The Most Dangerous Game in the Whole Wide World," in *Drummer* 29 (May 1979). Eros and death in specific relation to Tom Gloster is narrated in *Some Dance to Remember*, Reel 4, Scene 2.

September 1978: Publication of *Drummer* 24, "The Mapplethorpe Cover." While editing the 94-page issue, I contributed nine pieces of my writing and forty-nine of my photographs. Among the features I wrote were: "Authentic Men," "Bondage Interview," "Castro Street Blues," "Part One, In Hot Blood: Ex-Cons: We Abuse Fags," "The Quarters," "Farewell to Larry's Bar," and "Tough Shit." The coup for the million-dollar cover of *Drummer* 24 was that I was able to give the not-yet-famous Robert Mapplethorpe his first magazine cover.

September 15, 1978 (Friday): Publication of *Son of Drummer*, a special *Drummer* publication. For my 64-page *Son of Drummer*, I edited what I thought of as my "New York Art" issue. Featuring my first writing about Robert Mapplethorpe, which was his first coverage in the gay press, I contributed eight pieces of my writing and forty-three of my photographs. Among my features were: the illustrated "Robert Mapplethorpe Gallery (Censored)," "Arab Death," "Turkish Delight (Wrestling)," "The New York Artist Rex Revisited," the poem "Chico Is the Man," and the serialized first chapter of my novel *I Am Curious (Leather)* aka *Leather Blues*. My photographic essays were "Ass-Sets," "Filmstrips: Candle Power," and "Filmstrips: Rude Rubbers."

November 18, 1978 (Saturday): While Embry's onset pains of cancer upset happiness at *Drummer*, San Francisco, suffering its own urban nervous breakdown, was a tumult of political upheaval and danger. People's Temple guru Jim Jones, active in city government since 1971 and supported by Harvey Milk and George Moscone, shocked San Franciscans and the world with the mass suicide of nearly 1,000 people in Jonestown, Guyana, the largest death toll of American civilians in a single disaster before 9/11. Also killed by Jones on their fact-finding expedition were five of his political visitors, including San Francisco Democratic Congressman Leo Ryan. Jackie Speier, Ryan's congressional staff person, was shot five times and left bleeding on the tarmac for twenty-two hours. The gay-ally Speier later became California state senator. The People's Temple on Geary Boulevard was only a few blocks around the corner from the *Drummer* office on Divisadero.

November 28, 1978 (Tuesday): Ten days after the Jonestown Massacre, Supervisor Harvey Milk and Mayor George Moscone were assassinated by Golden Gloves boxer Dan White who was not a fan of the People's Temple or of gays. (For details, see "Dan White" in *Some Dance to Remember*, Reel 1, Scene 16, and Reel 3, Scene 1.) Assassination made Dianne Feinstein mayor. My lover, *Drummer* photographer David Sparrow, was in City Hall at the time of the shootings and witnessed the two bodies being wheeled out. As editor, I regretted that the SFPD had confiscated his film from his camera the way the LAPD had confiscated all the *Drummer* photographs shot at the Slave Auction two years earlier. At the moment of the murders, the latest issue of *Drummer* was almost out the door to the printer. Despite the tragedy, I had always wanted to shout, "Stop the presses!" I told Embry I needed a couple hours to write a new last-page editorial eulogy for *Drummer* 26 (January 1979): "Harvey Milk and Gay Courage."

December 1978: Mapplethorpe and I, loving New York nightlife, commiserated that Studio 54 was being raided eighteen months after opening April 26, 1977. Mafia lawyer Roy Cohn was the attorney for Studio 54 owners, Steve Rubell and Ian Schrager. The ever-shrewd Mapplethorpe photographed all three gay men in separate portraits.

December 1978: Publication of *Drummer* 25, "The Christmas Issue." Editing this entire 104-page issue celebrating the holidays, I contributed seventeen pieces of writing and thirty-four photographs, including the 35mm color cover shot of Mike Glassman, the future Colt Model "Ed Dinakos"—who took direction nicely—with a big smile on his face, and a rimmy tip of tongue provocatively extended. Among my features and fiction were "Sleep in Heavenly Peace," "Afraid You're Not Butch Enough," "Looking for Mr. Drummer," "*Drummer* Gift Guide," "Astrologic," "Fetishes: Horses," "Horsemaster: Come to the Stable," "Part 2, In Hot Blood: Ex-Cons: We Abuse Fags," film review of *The Norsemen*, "Scottish Games: Men in Kilts," "Dr. Dick: Amoebiasis, Your Ass Is Falling Out," and the debut, the first installment, of my ongoing column "Tough Customers."

December 8 and 9, 1978 (Friday and Saturday): Enger and I traveled to Oceanside, California, where he, standing at 5-7, stuffed his sculpted 178 pounds into a two-ounce posing brief cantilevered with his best nine inches. He won "First Place" and "Best Poser" trophies at this, the first, physique contest he entered, the AAU Junior Mr. Ironman contest, judged by bodybuilder Rod Koontz, and produced by Roger Metz. The handsome AMG model and bodybuilder John Tristram, an LA friend of Enger's, asked me how I felt during the loud cheering Enger received in the hall full of Marines from Camp Pendleton. "I feel," I said, "like Jack Kennedy who quipped about himself: 'I'm the man who accompanied Jacqueline Kennedy to Paris.'"

January 1979: Publication of *Drummer* 26. Having edited the 96-page issue, I contributed eleven pieces of my writing and twenty-eight of my photographs. Among the major features I wrote were: "Grand National Rodeo Blues," "High Performance: Sex without a Net," "Astrologic," "The Battered Lex Barker," "CMC Carnival," "Tough Customers," "Tough Shit," and, as a tribute obituary, "Harvey Milk and Gay Courage."

January 13, 1979 (Saturday): Jim Enger and I drove his maroon Corvette to the Mr. West Coast physique contest in San Jose where Enger won "Second Place" and the "Best Legs" trophy. I shot Super-8 film and 35mm color transparencies.

January 16, 1979 (Tuesday): Jim Enger and I joined gay film director Wakefield Poole and New York television producer Helen Whitney for supper to discuss Whitney's San Francisco pre-production casting for her upcoming documentary *Homosexuals* which finally aired nationally on *ABC Closeup* (1982). The Oscar-nominated Whitney liked Enger's look, because, I think, of his homomasculinity and wanted us to appear as a couple in her footage. In *Some Dance to Remember*, I based the character of the television producer "January Guggenheim" on the attractive Helen Whitney, a Woodrow Wilson scholar, who, of course, was nothing like the fictional January who made the fictional TV documentary, *The New Homosexuals*.

January 18, 1979 (Thursday): Arrival in San Francisco of New Yorkers Elliot Siegal and his lover "John." I had cast my frequent New York sex partner Elliot to be photographed by Mapplethorpe for the cover of *Drummer* 24 (September 1978), and Mapplethorpe then shot Elliot and John together for several other of his photographs in his book *Ten by Ten* (1988). On this date, Siegal, who was the manager of the St. Mark's Baths in Greenwich Village, came to San Francisco, from his apartment at 58 Charles Street, to play S&M games with friends I set him up with in the *Drummer* Salon through Sunday, January 28.

January 27, 1979 (Saturday): Jim Enger and I drove again, this time by popular request, from my home in San Francisco to Oceanside, South of Los Angeles, where he was the featured guest poser for, again, an auditorium full of Marines. Even though in 1980 "our song" was Olivia Newton-John's "Magic," we had choreographed his posing routine to "The Love Theme from *Superman*." We both got off on the hot fact, with no irony, of a hall full of straight and closeted Marines cheering on a masculine gay man wearing only a suntan-brown pair of nylon posing briefs and a big cock ring.

February 1979: Publication of *Drummer* 27. While editing the 94-page issue, I contributed ten pieces of writing and four of my photographs. Among the features I wrote were: "Basic Plumbing Unplugged," "Dirty Poole: Interview with Film Director Wakefield Poole," "S&M: The Last Taboo, The Society of Janus," film reviews of *Movie Movie* and *Superman*, "Tough Customers," and "Tough Shit."

February 6, 1979 (Tuesday): Jim Enger's father died unexpectedly. Embry's *Drummer* venture, The Quarters, located in the half-basement of an old building South of Market, was broken into by us "leather vigilantes" forming our own gay search party for missing leatherman Tom Gloster. A week later, his bound body was discovered shot to death in notoriously redneck Tehama County, north of San Francisco, and his memorial service was February 17, 1979. I wrote about him in my editorial in *Drummer* 29 (May 1979), and again in *Some Dance to Remember*.

February 9, 1979 (Friday): Lab work and chest x-ray with San Francisco society doctor Fred Hudson for my cough. Doctor Hudson gave me gamma globulin shots every six weeks throughout the 1970s as protection, he said, against nightly exposure to disease. Was he the reason I never contracted HIV?

February 20, 1979 (Tuesday): Lunch with *Drummer* circulation manager Bill Cushing and some of the *Drummer* Salon including Al Shapiro and Frank Hatfield who billed himself as a former bank robber and ex-con who served time at San Quentin. Hatfield ran Embry's mail-order business for years and, under the name "Frank O'Rourke," frequently wrote his own *Drummer* fiction, including his serial "Prison Punk." In the 1990s, while working Embry's mail-order at one of Embry's Russian River properties in Rio Nido, he was savagely attacked on a forested street by a stray dog, and, coincidentally, soon after died.

February 23, 1979 (Friday): Writing freelance outside *Drummer*, I wrote the article, "Jim Enger: On the Way Up," for Roger Metz, owner of the Ironman Gym in Oceanside; the article was published in *Dan Lurie's Muscle Training Illustrated*, issue 80 (December 1979). Unlike Embry, Dan Lurie paid me the going freelance rate of fifteen bucks.

February 26, 1979 (Monday): Ending our ten-year marriage, David Sparrow and I slept together one last time on the eve of his receiving a cash award from a lingering court case. Money and food always made David Sparrow amorous, and I knew how to twist his tits into an ecstasy he bottomed to even when we love-hated each other and continued to fuck after our divorce.

March 1979: Trouble in the Bubble. No *Drummer* issue released because of Embry's illness and censorship problems with the printer. The staff continued working daily to prepare upcoming issues.

March 3, 1979: The "First Anniversary" exhibit and party for Fey-Way Studio was its first and last anniversary. The pioneer gallery was founded and owned by *Drummer* writer and photographer, Robert Opel, showcasing leather S&M artists and photographers, bringing egos of art and leather personalities to a boil South of Market: Mapplethorpe, Rex, the Hun, A. Jay, Jim Stewart, Lionel Biron, Lou Rudolph, Larry Hunt, Tom Hinde, Robert Opel, and the un-billed artist and drug addict Chuck Arnett who, I reported in *Drummer* 133 (September 1989), "introduced the needle to Folsom Street." Arnett's invitation for the "Christmas Fix" party at "Fey-Way, Midnight, December 30, 1978," featured a drawing of a Santa injecting his forearm with a hypodermic whose previous tracks spell out *NOEL*. My eyewitness intuition from the 1970s is that the sharing of needles, more than unsafe sex, was what wiped out the speed-driven A-List leather players—both the disco bunnies shooting up at Probe and Trocadero, as well as the muscle guys injecting steroids, the most popular and secret drug used by gays in the 1970s when, without pecs, you were dead.

March 5, 1979 (Monday): Diary entry - "I can't handle the situation at *Drummer* anymore." Spent two hours last night on a *Drummer* photo shoot.

March 6, 1979 (Tuesday): I spent several hours this day and dozens of other days editing chapters from *Mister Benson* (as originally titled inside *Drummer* before shortened to *Mr. Benson*) for its East Coast author John Preston who, dangling his ten-chapter novel for serialization, had hustled Embry into publishing him in *Drummer*.

March 8, 1979 (Thursday): Jim Enger flew into Santa Rosa airport in a small plane to surprise me at my home in Sonoma County. "Omigod! He can fly!" said David Sparrow who was visiting me trying to fend off the man he thought was his competition. Nevertheless, I spent several hours working on the *Drummer* swim meet photographs David and I shot, including sitting down to write the poem "Wet Stough" to caption the photos for *Drummer* 28 (April 1979). On this date, outside the Gay Ghetto, but reflecting my professional design and production involvement with *Drummer*, I won two first-place awards in two categories from the Bay Area Society of Technical Communicators for brochures I wrote and produced during my concurrent day job as Manager of Publications at Kaiser Engineers in Oakland.

March 13, 1979 (Tuesday): *Drummer* publisher John Embry told me he had cancer. His growing "dis-ease" the last few months now had a name. What turmoil. "It's a full moon tonight." As editor-in-chief faced with producing *Drummer* without the publisher, I sat down and outlined the next three issues of *Drummer.*, continuing its metamorphosis in style and content. I wrote: "Embry might die. Will *Drummer*?"

March 14, 1979 (Wednesday): Embry checked into the hospital for surgery. The new issue of *Drummer* appeared—six weeks late: *Drummer* 27 (February 1979).

March 16, 1979 (Friday): Embry had cancer surgery.

March 17, 1979 (Saturday, Saint Patrick's Day): David Sparrow and I officially divorce. Having met in Chuck Renslow's Gold Coast Bar, July 4, 1969, and having been married in Manhattan by S&M priest, Jim Kane, on May 7, 1972, we formally and amicably ended our ten-year domestic affair, but continued to share our home, and to photograph together for *Drummer*. David took possession of our cameras. I took possession of our negatives and transparencies and their copyright. David, knowing the risks of living with an author, signed a contract that freed me to write about him in fiction and nonfiction. And I thanked him for assigning me his share of our copyright by forgiving the sizeable financial debt to me he had run up during the previous ten years.

March 19, 1979 (Monday): As editor-in-chief of *Drummer*, and standing in for publisher Embry in hospital, I met with author John Preston for three hours at the second-floor restaurant bar called "Caracole" on the northwest corner of Market Street and Noe Street across from Café Flore. Calling himself "Jack Preston," Preston looked at my edited pages of the first chapters of his raw manuscript for his novel *Mr. Benson* which Embry had bought unfinished because he loved serializing stories to fill future hungry issues. He also had a lech for getting into Preston's pants.

Preston was a good enough writer that he didn't have to flirt or put out. He did, however, require heavy editing. During my *Drummer* time with him, when he was young and sorely stressed out with anxiety having just been fired as editor by *The Advocate*, he was a bit touchy about anyone, not just me, editing his draft manuscripts, even though the publisher had made it a condition for publication. (I was six years older than Preston, and when we met, I had already logged twenty years of magazine editing experience.) Later in his career, as he burned transparent with HIV, he owned up to his friend and sometime editor, Lars Eighner, the author of *Travels with Lizbeth*, that he knew he had always required a great deal of editing.

During the previous months as Embry's health deteriorated, Embry was desperate to secure for *Drummer* serialized material that was easy to produce. With his haunted vampyr eyes, Preston behaved as if he might have been on some kind of drug, or was it his masochistic attitude that made him an eerie and scary young man. "So you're the star of *Drummer*," he snapped. I joked back: "Yeah, I guess I've become identified as the *Drummer* 'Jack.' How about you using your real name, John." He, with competition from Rowberry, had little or no chance of Embry ever hiring him as editor of *Drummer*, but he had envious Iago's sharp elbows. Still creating his porn identity, he was billing himself in *Drummer* bylines as both "Jack Preston" and "Jack Prescott." At Embry's order, I had edited every chapter of *Mr. Benson*, whether Preston gave attitude or not, so that it could be published. Editors don't fear writers as much as writers fear editors. It was the first and last time I ever met with the young Preston which was more than *Drummer* staff usually met with most authors who most often mailed in their writing from distant zip codes.

March 20, 1979 (Tuesday): With Embry ill, I heard that my pal Ron Clute, who led a romantic double-life with a career in the Financial District and as a bartender at the Leatherneck and at the Black and Blue, had been killed by the drug PCP. Surrounded by our real life in the 1970s, I assessed some of the dangers of euphoric gay life and wrote my editorial "The Most Dangerous Game in the Whole Wide World" for *Drummer* 29 (May 1979), page 6. A photograph by Jim Stewart illustrated the obituary for Ron Clute, page 56. At the same time, health issues also figured into my 1979 story "Caro Ricardo" aka "Caro Roberto" which was a fictional telling of difficulties I was witnessing in the style of "dirty gay sex" as practiced by many leathermen like Mapplethorpe. Eventually Robert and I split amicably because of my "Irish hypochondria." I like things clean. A year earlier, in *Drummer* 21 (March 1978), well aware of the shocking gay men's health crisis, I had inaugurated my cautionary column "Dr. Dick, *Drummer* Goes to the Doctor" with the essay "PCP: Short Cut to Suicide," p. 77. I wrote my monthly columns based on my telephone interviews with Dr. Richard Hamilton.

March 21, 1979 (Wednesday): I visited Embry in hospital and brought him a goldfish in a small bowl for an amusement. Later at my house, the 180-pound David Sparrow (divorced a total of four days, and high) entered and threw the 150-pound me to the floor, throwing water on my manuscripts, shouting about my not being able to make Embry pay him, as well as about my affairs with Enger and Mapplethorpe.

March 24, 1979 (Saturday): Enger and I, with others from the *Drummer* Salon, attended the opening for the artist Domino hosted by Robert Opel and Camille O'Grady at Fey-Way Studio.

March 26, 1979 (Monday): I set up my bedroom so that Jim Enger, who had posed for Tom of Finland, could pose seated on a chair for the artist Domino during the afternoon to create a drawing that became iconic Domino.

April 1979: Publication of *Drummer* 28. Editing the 80-page issue, I contributed six pieces of writing and ten of my photographs. Among my features were the poem "Wet Stough," "Bare-Ass Wrestling," the review of *The Deer Hunter*, "Tough Customers," and "Tough Shit."

April 8, 1979 (Thursday): On the phone, I talked to Embry who was feeling better. He told me details of his colostomy which he hoped was temporary.

April 13, 1979 (Friday): After I pleaded with my pal Al Schaaf at San Francisco Municipal Railway, he gave the perpetually unemployed David Sparrow a job as an analyst so he could finally move out of my 25th Street home. If David had not had a college degree, Al said he could not have hired him. I was flat out pleased that after I had motivated David in 1969 by telling him that education was essential if we were to have a middle-class life together, and, after I paid his four years of tuition at Western Michigan University, he actually graduated so he could take care of himself.

April 17, 1979 (Tuesday, 7:30 PM): As a journalist for *Drummer*, I interviewed poet Camille O'Grady with Robert Opel at Fey-Way Studio beginning at 7:30 PM. My audiotape was Opel's last interview, and the photos, shot by David Sparrow and me, were among the last of Opel and O'Grady pictured together before Opel's assassination, July 7, 1979.

April 20, 1979 (Friday): Jim Enger and I drove his Corvette to Salinas. We took a room at a Quality Inn where I shaved the upholstery of his hairy blond chest, torso, arms, and legs for the Mr. Western California physique contest.

April 21, 1979 (Saturday): Jim Enger and I drove into Carmel for the 9 AM check-in for Mr. Western California. The senior division morning pre-judging alone took nearly three hours. At the evening contest, Enger won "First Place" as "Mr. Western California" as well as three more trophies for "Best Abs," "Best Legs," and "Most Muscular." The four trophies were so many and so tall that they hardly fit into the Corvette. Documenting Enger live on stage performing for the audience, I shot three roles of 35mm transparencies and black-and-white stills, one of which Enger later chose as his favorite photograph: full face in a side "double-arm shot," both arms extended to his right, his eagle-eye piercing straight into my camera over the blond brush of his moustache. The photograph is extremely intimate considering that I shot it from forty feet away with a telephoto lens. It would have made a wonderful *Drummer* cover or centerfold. Later, in May, 1980, I had fun with that vigorous Enger photo when I made bold to enter it with its hot, burning, masculine appeal into a very staid "employee photo show" exhibited in the lobby of the very Republican Kaiser Engineers. The punch line to my joke? It won "Best in Show"!

April 28, 1979 (Saturday): Jim Enger and I drove to Oceanside where Enger won first place in the Mr. Physique USA contest. After sleeping all night at a Marine-friendly motel in Oceanside, on Sunday we walked shirtless and in shorts on the strand while in San Francisco David Sparrow began his final move out of my house.

April 30, 1979 (Monday): Jim Enger and I traveled on to the Muscle Beach outdoor iron pit in Venice, and then to the Nichols Canyon Road home he built with Chuck Romanski, the Colt model Clint Lockner, who greeted us with his new lover, the model and bodybuilder, Dan Pace about whom I wrote several times for pictorials in *Drummer*. "Dreams do come true," I wrote in my *Journal*. " Me with three bodybuilders shot by Colt." Discretion draws the shades.

May 1979: Publication of *Drummer* 29. While editing the 80-page issue, I contributed nine pieces of my writing and three of my photographs, and published "Chapter One" of my edit and serialization of John Preston's *Mr. Benson*. Among the features I wrote were "Cruising: The Most Dangerous Game," "Drawings by Domino," the poem "Foot Loose," "Noodles Romanoff and the Golden Gloves," "On Target: The New American Masculinity," "Tough Customers," and "Tough Shit."

May 7, 1979 (Monday): David Sparrow and I dined out for supper to celebrate his thirty-third birthday, and despite our divorce had each other for dessert. Our sex was always hot, but his drug and alcohol addictions got in the way of any kind of sustainable domestic life.

May 12, 1979 (Saturday): On Castro Street, a riot broke out, caused by tensions in the on-going trial of assassin Dan White.

May 16, 1979 (Wednesday): David Sparrow invited me to lunch. "Don't you ever," he said, "speak to me again." And he waved before me the settlement he received that morning in his court case ending the matter of his motorcycle accident: $3,186.00. He told me I could keep all our camera equipment (which I had bought) and shove it. Yeah. Yeah. Yeah. That evening I kept my dinner date with the gay author and photographer John Trojanski whom I had hired on my writing staff at Kaiser Engineers and whom I convinced to write several articles for *Drummer* including "The Whip Creaming of Cincinnati" because we both had Catholic seminary experience in common.

May 20, 1979 (Sunday): I shot 35mm photos of Val Martin and Bob Hyslop for my upcoming *Drummer* 31 (September 1979) on location at Ed

Linotti's ancient barn on Pleasant Hill Road outside Sebastopol in Sonoma County.

May 21, 1979 (Monday): Mixing business with pleasure, I spent the afternoon balling with a man named Kurt Baron playing with his rack, hoists, and sling as a fun preparation to use his dungeon for a *Drummer* photo shoot. At twilight the White Night Riot erupted. Ten years after the Stonewall rebellion in New York, angry gays attacked San Francisco City Hall, and set twelve SFPD squad cars on fire protesting assassin Dan White's light sentence based on his junk-food "Twinkie Defense." In retaliation, the SFPD charged into the heart of the Castro clubbing their way down Castro Street, and beating gay and straight patrons inside the Elephant Walk bar at 18th and Castro. See my "Tough Shit" entry "Bloody 'Marys' at Elephant Walk" in *Drummer* 30 (June 1979), page 72. On May 23, 2005, *The New Yorker*, page 38, named 18th and Castro "perhaps the gayest address in the world." Once again, the East Coast failed to understand the West Coast with too little too late. Even before 1990, 18th and Castro had turned into the postmodern, dirty, ugly debris field of the colorful "Titanic 1970s." By Saint Valentine's night, February 14, 2007, 18th and Castro had become its own private Bangkok diversified with attractive bar-hopping young Asian sex tourists trailing laughter and cologne and cigarette smoke, and with homeless Caucasian beggars—some of them ghosts of the "70s Past"—the last of an extinct species crying out its bird call for "Spare Change."

"To me this part of the city always seemed joyful/but now is just horror and nothing more." —Pier Paolo Pasolini, "The Search for a Home," *Roman Poems*

When did the changing Castro neighborhood become the Fourth World? The Fourth World is the entropy that comes after the fall of the First World, the Second World, and the Third World.

May 22, 1979 (Tuesday): The 6 PM Castro Street party, originally announced to celebrate the birthday of Harvey Milk—then dead for six months, turned into a peaceful protest against the SFPD. Under the marquee of the Castro Theater, I, age 39, met Mark Hemry, 29, for the first time. In the year 2000, after twenty-one years together, we two marriage activists were joined in a civil union in Vermont. In 2003, we married in Canada. In 2004, we married on the grand staircase of San Francisco City Hall on Valentine's weekend during Mayor Gavin Newsom's "Winter of Love" named after San Francisco's legendary 1967 "Summer of Love." On June 20, 2008, we were one of the 18,000 couples married legally in California before

Proposition 8 halted gay marriage until the State Supreme Court approved marriage equality within the state on June 26, 2013.

May 31, 1979 (Thursday): Our *Drummer* office was raided by the post-riot and still angry San Francisco Police Department: cops stopped in, messed us about, and left. It was frightening. With Embry gone, I was in charge. No one was arrested. I told the SFPD right away that I was the editor-in-chief and, desperately seeking some fraternal bond with them, I freaked and mentioned that I had placed at number 11 on the San Francisco Deputy Sheriff Civil Service exam—to which they said *Hmmph*! So I personally felt empathy with what John Embry and Jeanne Barney had felt when the LAPD harassed them during the difficult first year of *Drummer* (1975-1976) when cop arrests nearly killed *Drummer* in its crib. It led me to empathy as well for all the anti-gay stress they suffered during the three years (1976-1979) of attorney meetings and court hearings in LA which continued to bedevil Embry, and distract him from the work at hand.

June 1979: Publication of *Drummer* 30, "The Fourth Anniversary Issue." While editing the contents of the entire 96-page issue, I contributed eight pieces of my writing as well as the arm-wrestling (coded: fisting) "Cover Photograph of Val Martin and Bob Hyslop," and published "Chapter Two" of my edit and serialization of John Preston's *Mr. Benson*. Among the features I wrote were: "Tit Torture Blues," "Meditations on Photographer Arthur Tress," "Zeus Men in Bondage: Introducing a New Studio," "The Brothel Hotel," "Tough Customers," and "Tough Shit."

June 2, 1979 (Saturday): *Drummer* art director Al Shapiro and his partner Dick Kriegmont hosted a water sports party at their apartment for the *Drummer* Salon—and fifty other *Drummer* subscribers and fans.

June 4, 1979 (Monday): My single calendar entry copied off the toilet wall of the Without Reservation restaurant on Castro: "Madness takes its toll because sanity has lost its appeal."

June 6, 1979 (Wednesday): David Sparrow stopped by my house and asked me for a loan so he could buy a new motorcycle. While we were arguing, he slapped me flat across the face. I fell to the floor. Shocked. I had only seen that in movies. Amazed, I wrote: "I never believed you couldn't see it coming. That's it. Nobody hits me."

June 20, 1979 (Wednesday): I turned forty. *Drummer* turned four.

June 24, 1979 (Sunday): Fifty feet west of 18th Street on Castro Street, Jim Enger and I were cruised by Paul Gerrior and his lover, Craig Caswell, whom we cruised back. Ten minutes later, our foursome was at my home. (The handsome actor Paul Gerrior was the original Colt model Ledermeister. I had been lusting after him since 1968.) I saved the sweaty designer sheets from that Sunday afternoon, and will always treasure those souvenirs, still archived, with their long shelf life.

June 25, 1979 (Monday): "*Drummer*: The Fourth Anniversary Issue." *Drummer* was golden, hot, and *haute* because it was created out of our ten-year reality of liberated, joyous sex performed as a high-wire act without a net. Trying to keep his enemies close, David Sparrow propositioned Jim Enger who put him off by saying "Not now."

Footnote #3: Inside the Timeline
Ledermeister: Homomasculine Archetype
of the Leather Archetribe

Here is an eyewitness-participant "oral history" told in the present tense. It is mentioned because it is typical of the erotic spontaneous combustion available to all in the Titanic 1970s. A chance meeting on one of those cruisy, mobbed summer Sunday afternoons (June 24, 1979) at 18th and Castro throws Enger and me together into an epic four-way at my home with legendary sex icon, Ledermeister, the 1960s Colt super-model, who was walking with his own friend, Craig Caswell. Enger, who caused traffic to rear-end on Castro, and who stopped the legendary Ledermeister in his tracks, stalled the guests in the living room while I excused myself to take Ledermeister's framed photo down from the bedroom wall. The homomasculine fantasy Enger and I had wished for had arrived in the gorgeous flesh.

Here the curtain discreetly draws, but the beige designer sheets, like a *madeleine* from Proust, have been saved as holy relics which to this day have never been washed. Those sheets are among my souvenirs with a lock of David Sparrow's strawberry-roan hair, a small chunk of cement from the Berlin Wall, a fragment of bone from the leg of Saint Isidore, the suntan-brown posing briefs of Jim Enger, a tiny Titian, the key to Mapplethorpe's 24 Bond Street loft, my personal ticket and program treasured since August 7, 1961, when Ethel Merman opened in *Gypsy* at the Curran Theater in San Francisco...all the photographs and papers that fill my archives.

I dance to remember and to think.

This is done because my friend, Sam Steward had tutored me early on with his good example. Sam had saved pubic hair he had stealthily clipped from Valentino while blowing him, potpourri from roses in Gertrude Stein's garden, Alice Toklas's hand-written hash-brownie recipe, a ceramic rose chipped off Oscar Wilde's tomb in Pere-Lachaise, sailors' caps, and police patches which I helped him collect.

To remember, when we are old, and to think, Sam wrote,

> We need all the inner resources, or at the very least a treasury of memory to sustain us. Since our emotional lives are fragmented, we should have a vast stock of tangible things to invest our love in: mementos, memorabilia, photographs, an old blue cloak..., a water glass his lips had touched, anything which can stimulate us, can make us remember. (*Chapters from an Autobiography*, page 141.)

July 1979: No *Drummer* issue released because of Embry's illness and censorship problems with the printer. With my staff working daily, Al Shapiro and I used this months-long hiatus to re-conceptualize *Drummer* even more by bringing up from the sexual underground never-before-published homomasculine S&M themes for future issues. Separately and together, Al and I set out actively seeking new angles on the new sex styles, and recruiting new BDSM writers, artists, and photographers who had not yet dared come out of the 1960s closet enough to be published and publicized in 1970s *Drummer*.

July 7, 1979 (Saturday): Art, Civil Rights, and Murder. Almost exactly ten years after Stonewall (June 27-28, 1969), late in the evening of July 7, 1979, Robert Opel was shot to death in his Fey-Way Studio gallery. His partner Camille O'Grady, unharmed physically, survived, and disappeared underground in the City and then in LA. Urban legend whispered that Opel had been set up by the SFPD, because of his anti-cop performance art, "The Shooting of Dan White by Gay Justice," which, with a handgun he had borrowed from *Drummer* photographer Jim Stewart, he had acted out "live in Civic Center Plaza" at the Gay Parade on June 24 before he was murdered thirteen days later.

July 24, 1979 (Tuesday): Seeing *Drummer* in hysterical turmoil, and figuring *Drummer* could go out of business, I did not want our exciting new gay publishing world to lose its foothold because of Embry's malfeasance. On this date I filed a "Fictitious Business Name Statement" with the County Clerk, San Francisco, for my alternative to *Drummer* which I named *Man2Man Quarterly*. I followed the example of *Drummer* art director Al Shapiro who had filed his own "Fictitious Business" statement for his "Powerhouse Productions" on May 25, 1978. On November 28, 1979: Al Shapiro's name appeared on the masthead of *Man2Man* as the hyphenated "man-aging editor."

July 25, 1979 (Monday): Before and after lunch with Leonard Matlovich, I spent most of day talking to Golden Gate Distributors because *Drummer*, with its "porn" content in the new and escalating right-wing culture war started by Anita Bryant, could not find a cheap, liberal printer for the next issue. Making occasional deals with Bay Area printers of religious magazines eager for a quick buck, Embry often got *Drummer* printed after midnight by Christian hypocrites whose presses were otherwise silent from dusk to dawn.

August 1979: No *Drummer* issue released because of Embry's absence and censorship problems with the printer. With lead-times slipping, Al Shapiro and I continued our talent search for contirbutors while planning the contents and layout of the next two or three issues refining the new grass-roots point-of-view of *Drummer*.

August 3, 1979 (Friday): I asked Embry to pay me nearly $4000 in back pay and fees. I also asked him to pay my former lover, David Sparrow, $2000 for the photographs David and I shot partnered together as "Sparrow Photography" on film stock I had purchased and processed with my cash, not *Drummer* cash. When Embry exploded about the money and his illness and the difficulties with printers and censors as well as with the LA judge and lawyers still screwing him over the Slave Auction, I gave him notice that he could pay me and David, or I would be leaving *Drummer*, effective on or before December 31. I would no longer be his editor-in-chief. I would no longer contribute my writing and photography. I did not want to strand an ailing man or mess up *Drummer*. So I gave him ample lead time to prepare for my exit. In the next weeks, I gave him all my edited materials and, because I was a cockeyed optimist, some of my future writing and photos to be published up through *Drummer* 33, which was to be my last issue created as editor-in-chief. During the stretch from August to Christmas 1979 and to the finish of *Drummer* 33, I was in and out of the office—when Embry was absent—in order to make a smooth transition.

I didn't care so much about the ailing shyster Embry as I did about the ailing innocent *Drummer*.

At the same time, Embry was cherry-picking my incoming editorial work, articles and photos, and removing some of my bylines—which only became known when the issues finally appeared on the news stands. Immediately after my conversation asking Embry to pay or else, Mark Hemry and I drove to Reno to photograph the Gay Rodeo which, suddenly, I had decided I was no longer covering for *Drummer* as I had originally planned.

August 5, 1979 (Sunday): Outing "gay cowboys" twenty years before *Brokeback Mountain*, Randy Shilts and I, as reporter and photographer, covered the Gay Rodeo in Reno, with Mark Hemry assisting me on our first publishing venture together, even as he gambled life and limb, and our future matrimonial bliss, as a bull-rider. The Associated Press (AP Wire Service) published Shilts' article and my several "gay cowboy" photographs nationwide in newspapers on August 6, 1979. The Shilts-Fritscher piece was the first introduction into mainstream media culture of the concept of "gay cowboys."

Footnote #4: Inside the Timeline:
Randy Shilts, Reno Rodeo, Queering the Cowboy Myth

On August 7, 1979 (Tuesday), the day after the AP coverage of the Reno Gay Rodeo, Dave Wilson, the working cowboy I photographed, was fired from his ranch job. When he signed his photo release, I asked him if he was sure about coming out so publicly. He said he was willing to risk that ride. He was handsome and blond, and his sunny open face can be seen smiling in the *San Francisco Chronicle*, August 6, first section, page 3, column 1.

Because of the tensions within *Drummer*, I withheld my gay rodeo photos from Embry. His distemper was *Drummer*'s loss because Dave Wilson would have been one of the hottest *Drummer* covers ever.

I saved all my Reno cowboy photos for my coffee-table photo book, *American Men*, and for the cover of the fiction anthology, *Rainbow County and Other Stories*, as well as the zero-degrees cover of the British edition of the novel, *Narrow Rooms*, by my friend James Purdy who was also the close friend of *Drummer* author, Sam Steward.

Six months previously, in *Drummer* 26 (January 1979), intent on "queering the cowboy myth," and on co-opting the sex-appeal of the world-famous Marlboro Man, I had written "Grand National Rodeo Blues: Comes a Horseman." It was the first gay feature article panting about straight cowboys *Drummer* wished were gay, including cowboy *paparazzi* photos shot by Fritscher-Sparrow at the Grand National Rodeo, inside the Cow Palace, San Francisco, Halloween weekend, 1978.

August 6, 1979 (Monday): In a letter addressed to Al Shapiro at *Drummer*, the scatalogical graffiti artist Martin of Holland (died 2011) wrote of international rumors about the murder of Robert Opel:

"Martin Van De Logt
P. O. Box 66g
2501 CR Den Haag/Holland

Dear Allen, Thanks for your letter. It was sad to hear about Robert Opel's death. A few days earlier, I heard another version of the shooting. They said it involved the Mafia.... —Martin"

August 23, 1979 (Thursday): Mark Hemry and I began going out socially as a couple, seeing Patty Lupone and Mandy Patinkin appearing in *Evita* previewing at the Orpheum Theater before heading to Broadway. Embry's thirty-something lover, the immigrant from Spain, Mario Simon aka "Mrs *Drummer*," whose bejeweled hand was always in the *Drummer* cashbox and our paychecks, was, according to Embry, a disco singer "famous in Spain," but not in the Bay Area despite the *Drummer* money Embry spent producing 45-rpm records sold through *Drummer*, because, Embry told discomusic. com on May 20, 2010, "of Mario's heavy accent." Mario was hardly competition for his San Francisco contemporary, Sylvester James, the African-American "Queen of Disco" (1947-1988) who was a popular recording star, and an iconic member of the Cockettes,

Embry referenced his conflicted feelings for Mario in his editorial in *Drummer Rides Again*: "The rare great love affairs of my life have been with guys who were not my type. The ones who were my type (Roberts: Redford, Conrad, and Mitchum) turned out frequently," said Robert Payne, "to be hardly worth knowing."

While Embry paid many of the staff on the cheap under the table, he paid Mario as if he were staff, so that, in one gesture of monkey business, Mario could show an income and earn social security while at the same time the pair of them could take home more pay from *Drummer*. It was their business and their cash, but it caused resentment, and a bit of scandal, among both the actual workers whose pay was so famously small, and the contributors who were so frequently unpaid. Besides the cash, Mario got credit where credit was not due. Even though English was his second language, and even though he was not a writer, nor a photographer, nor an artist, nor even interested in any business other than his career, Embry began crediting him as "General Manager" (issues 58-66) and as "Co-Publisher" (issues 67-98, their last issue before the sale to Anthony DeBlase).

The ambitious Mario spurned San Francisco because, living "La Dolce Evita (Loca)," he figured LA was better for his music career. He was one of the main reasons that Embry, who was also permanently angry about them both being "deported" out of LA, never quite adjusted to living in San Francisco where they both ended up because of their *Drummer* publishing venture which had found its first, best, and only success in San Francisco, and because of their real estate holdings which they had bought during their, to them, endless exile in the Bay Area. Neither one of them was able to make it in LA, or even back to LA.

Frequently absent from *Drummer*, but never missed, Mario took extended trips to LA well into 1990 when he appeared in Oxnard, fifty-six miles from stardom in Hollywood, in a local production of *Evita*. Swimming laps in his cologne, he was typecast with no irony as the sleazy Lothario "Magaldi," the over-the-top tango singer who gives Evita her first "leg up" singing "On This Night of a Thousand Stars." The *Los Angeles Times* wrote, July 19, 1990: "As the first rung on Evita's ladder to the top, nightclub singer and romantic idol Augustin Magaldi, [Mario] Simon is a pompous, vain popinjay—sort of a Wayne Newton of the pampas." For someone who was always acting, Mario Simon (1942-1993) just couldn't act.

August 30, 1979 (Thursday): I drove to Berkeley to visit Sam Steward in his home and to drive him to lunch at his favorite blue-collar steam-table cafeteria several blocks away.

September 1979: Publication of *Drummer* 31. While managing the work of incoming writers, artists, and photographers for this and future issues, I edited the contents of this 88-page issue to which I contributed eight pieces of my writing as well as forty of my photographs, and published

"Chapter Three" of my edit and serialization of John Preston's *Mr. Benson*. Among the features I wrote were: "An Interview with Martin of Holland," co-written with Al Shapiro; the first feature article ever written about IML, "The First International IML Contest"; "Spit, Sweat, and Piss Centerfold with Val Martin and Bob Hyslop"; "The Macho Images of Photographer Tony Plewik"; "Men's Bar Scene: Pure Trash"; "Tough Customers"; and "Tough Shit." Because I was exiting *Drummer*, publisher Embry, returning to the office, removed my name as editor-in-chief on this issue, and credited the editing to his pseudonym, "Robert Payne."

Summer-Fall 1979: A debate, which greatly affected me and my attitudes toward the evolution of *Drummer*, raged in the mainstream press and vanilla gay magazines about the controversial and changing nature of both S&M as a legitimate practice, and masculinity as a legitimate gender. It also raged in the streets, where during summer 1979, New York vanilla gays, without seeing a single finished frame, picketed with prejudice the leather-themed S&M thriller, *Cruising*, being shot by William (*The Boys in the Band*) Friedkin on location on Greenwich Village streets around the piers, the trucks, and the Mineshaft. Six years later, on February 22, 1985, a high-profile S&M murder shocked Manhattan when the male fashion model Eigil Vesti was killed in a torture slaying that touched the Mineshaft and the New York Hellfire Club. The rumors that Mapplethorpe was involved were false and typical of even gay popular culture's fear of his visionary art. For details, check elsewhere within *Gay San Francisco: Eyewitness Drummer*. Also see *Drummer* 126 (March 1988), page 53, for the Bruce Marcus article, "The Crispo Case, Consent, and S&M Reality," and the David France book, *Bag of Toys: Sex, Scandal, and the Death Mask Murder*, 1992.

October 1979: Publication of *Drummer* 32. Continuing to work on *Drummer* from my home more than in the Divisadero Street office, in order to keep moving forward creatively and responsibly on new issues while Embry and I kept our distance from each other, I edited the contents of this 88-page issue to which I contributed five pieces of my writing, and published "Chapter Four" of my edit and serialization of John Preston's *Mr. Benson*. Among the titles I wrote: "A Confidential *Drummer* Dossier," "The Men: From the Writing of Robert Opel," "Conrap," "Tough Customers," and "Tough Shit." As he had first done in *Drummer* 31, Embry deleted my name as editor-in-chief on this issue, and credited the editing to "Robert Payne." In a kind of vengeance for my leaving him after my changing *Drummer* to "new leather" with overt gender themes that he had little feel for, he also deleted my credit lines on my articles, but he failed to notice I outfoxed him by coding my "A Confidential *Drummer* Dossier" with my birth-date numbers published at the top of the feature.

October 3, 1979 (Wednesday): I sent Robert Mapplethorpe a draft manuscript for the book of entertainment we planned to do together: his photos, my text—most of it from *Drummer.* Our proposed title was *Rimshots: Inside the Fetish Factor.* Originally conceived to be excerpted in text and photos in *Drummer,* it went unpublished, but can be synthesized insofar as it was very like a combination of the anthology, *Corporal in Charge and Other [Drummer] Stories,* fore-shortened, with fifty Mapplethorpe leather and S&M photos. Our original manuscript became part of the permanent Mapplethorpe Archive at the Getty Research Institute in Los Angeles.

November 1979: *Drummer 33*—meant to be the November issue—was stopped because Embry, without my active input recruiting contributors and without my offering my own writing as "filler" he had come to rely on, did not have enough finished material in his files to fill it. Instead, November's stalled issue merged into what materials he had for the December issue which, in combination, became the Christmas issue, *Drummer* 33. Faking it as Embry was, he was at the same time also trying to turn a fast buck by creating another special extra issue, insisting on ending 1979 with both a Christmas issue of *Drummer* as well as the special extra issue which I had titled *Drummer Rides Again* as a follow-up to my special extra issue *Son of Drummer* (September 1978). Deleting my completed and intended feature articles and fiction, Embry replaced my texts in *Drummer Rides Again* with the easy in-fill of drawings and photographs, many reprinted from earlier *Drummer* issues. What literary value and heat *Drummer Rides Again* had in text came from stories by T. R. Witomski, G. B. Misa (George Birimisa), and John Preston masked as "Jack Prescott." What graphic bump it had came with the centerfold art by Bill Ward and the drawings by Cavelo, plus five photos by Mikal Bales for Zeus Studio captioned by my text with the byline removed, and with seventeen of my photos on six pages (pp. 45, 52-56) credited by Embry not to me but to the more "anonymous" Sparrow Photography run by David Sparrow and me. Embry's bootleg reprint of Mapplethorpe's photograph of a tied cock and balls to illustrate his "In Passing" editorial did not, needless to say, make Robert and his attorney happy.

November 6, 1979 (Tuesday): With the 1970s ending, I was actively considering how *Drummer* should develop in the 1980s. What imaginative forces might we draw in for the second decade of post-Stonewall liberation? Always auditioning new people for possible articles for *Drummer*, I took professional time to have supper with an apparently rich man who alleged his name was "Dick Biezevelt" at the Café du Nord on Market Street. "Biezevelt" was an idealistic fifty-something gentleman who, dismayed by the new gay hippie leather culture, wanted to institute a kind of Old School gentleman's military culture based on the stiff Prussian model predating Nazism that would train young gay men on Castro and Folsom to behave like proper gentlemen. Having seen Embry's ads for Nazis, men with such right-wing "esthetics" often courted me because I was editor of the megaphone that was *Drummer*. "Biezevelt" gave me an envelope full of copious notes about psychological discipline and physical training. However, I was soon to exit *Drummer*, and did not write an article about him and his uniform fantasies around hazing young men into being polite to older gents.

The newly liberated 1970s was very much a world of closets and mirrors and alias sex identities. In fact-checking the past to connect the dots of who was actually who, I searched for the man known to me as "Dick Biezevelt" of Marin. I found he may possibly have been a *doppelganger* for Nicolass "Nick" Biezeveld, the Marin inventor (1926-1997). This aka "Nick Bieseveld," forced to live in drag as a teenage girl in the Haag in order to escape being drafted into Hitler's army in Nazi-occupied Holland, came to America and in 1962 invented the first call-screening device for telephones. "Nick's" online obituary mentioned specifically that his experience during wartime caused him to "have a special place in his heart for the Marines that would last his entire life." If "Dick Biezevelt" was not "Nick Biezeveld," apologies to them both, but I know how gay identities peel themselves to amazing transparencies. Coincidence or not, GLBT history is all the better for adding in "drag" inventor, Nicolaas Biezeveld, who, living with a taste for USMC discipline, most likely read *Drummer*.

November 12, 1979 (Friday Night): At the Barracks Baths, I met with leather-players Peter Fiske, Dan Folkers, and a man named "Mike." Illustrating how I experienced real night games and bath sex, and then wrote the S&M athletics up as erotic New Journalism "reality reporting" for *Drummer*, I took the very *Drummer*-like ritual of that Barracks night, and whipped it up into a "true experiences" article for *Drummer*, even though Embry continued to refuse payment for grass-roots reportage he himself could never ever have written because he never went out to play night sports. My ability to experience what the readers were actually experiencing and then to report that sexual reality back in *Drummer* to reflect readers' actual lives was my basic concept that changed *Drummer* from Embry's static LA "Stand and Model (S&M)" rag into a dynamic reader-reflexive jerk-off magazine where the wild sex that men were actually inflicting on each other started in the head and worked its way down in hot column inches. Instead, that sacred scene of sexual purification and discipline through bondage and whipping at the Barracks fit appropriately into one of the historical reportage scenarios in *Some Dance to Remember*, Reel 2, Scene 11.

November 20, 1979 (Tuesday): Jim Enger and I attended the victory dinner for Dianne Feinstein who a week earlier was elected mayor of San Francisco on her own merits having become mayor by a bullet a year earlier. The Sunday before, I had stood on the northwest corner of 18th and Castro, in front of the Star Pharmacy, holding up a big blue "Feinstein for Mayor" poster, because not all gays liked her.

November 28, 1979 (Wednesday): *Drummer* art director Al Shapiro (A. Jay) and I designed the letterhead and masthead for the new magazine I intended to publish with Mark Hemry, *Man2Man Quarterly*. A. Jay, who was also ankling his way fast out of *Drummer* because of money and copyright issues about his cartoon strips, was listed on the *Man2Man* masthead beginning with the first issue which featured a gray impressionist photograph of Jim Enger on the cover.

December 1979: Special Extra Issue, *Drummer Rides Again*. Having edited the entirety of this special issue, I watched the tempest-tossed Embry gut it. In order not to list me as editor, he went against all journalism principles and dropped everyone's masthead credits, just as he had in the first issues of *Drummer*. In one line buried at the bottom of the credits page, he named "Robert Payne" as editor. In addition, cutting and pasting, he changed our long-planned features and fiction and substituted whatever was in the *Drummer* "archives." Ultimately, my contributions surviving in the 64-page issue were one piece of writing and seventeen photographs, plus the production work behind the entire issue. The article was "Bound and Gagged: Zeus Studios"; and my "Sparrow Photography" images were shot at Embry's "Quarters," his failed attempt to start a commercial playroom in a basement South of Market to rival the 21st Street Catacombs. I also edited and produced the two graphic features Embry included about the LA artist Cavelo and the San Francisco photographer Rink.

December 1979: Publication of *Drummer* 33, Holiday Issue. Two months before I finally waltzed out the door of *Drummer* on New Year's Eve 1979, I edited the first draft of the entire contents of this 88-page issue which I had planned as our "Great Big Finish for the 1970s." While grooming contributors, I also penned nearly a dozen pieces of writing which were reduced by Embry to five pieces of writing and two photographs, including "Chapter Five" of my edit and serialization of John Preston's ten-chapter *Mr. Benson*. My little written bits that Embry did not delete were "The *Drummer* Christmas Gift Guide," and the two columns I had invented which he came to rely on: "Tough Customers," and "Tough Shit." On the masthead, Embry credited "Robert Payne," as editor. I was the last of only two "editors-in-chief" of *Drummer*. After Jeanne Barney and me, everyone else was simply "editor."

December 4, 1979 (Tuesday): For "the *Drummer* novel," *Some Dance to Remember*, written in my journals during the 1970s, I invoked the romanticism of *Wuthering Heights* with my "Corona Heights" scene of transcendental masturbation on the rocky mountain outcropping that overlooks the Castro: Reel 5, Scene 13. Part of character Ryan O'Hara's "Garden of Gethsemane" anguish reflected my sadness at having to part ways with a magazine I loved owned by a publisher I found impossible. Also, that December 1979, after the shocking trial of Dan White, everyone was feeling instant nostalgia for the decade that had surprised everyone with its wild-child sex, drugs, and rock and roll. With only days till New Year's Eve, the glorious 1970s were about to be lost in the *auld lang syne*. That December was worrisome. It was mere days before the unknown new decade of the 1980s. It was eleven months before the election of Ronald Reagan as president. And too many guys were getting sick and heading back home where they came from never to be heard of again. It was less than eighteen months before anyone read the headline of "Gay Cancer."

The Titanic 1970s: 1970-1982
From the Harakiri of Yukio Mishima
to the Folsom Fire at the Barracks Bath
and the Advent of AIDS

The 1970s actually lasted until 1981. The Leather Decade that began with the famous harakiri of S&M leather-muscle author Yukio Mishima on November 25, 1970, ended with the Folsom Fire when the legendary Barracks baths burned down on July 10, 1981. And the dying began. The charred ruins of the Barracks, which I described in *Some Dance to Remember*, were erotically interpreted in a photograph by Mark I. Chester in *Drummer* 137, February 1990, page 17. Hit with hard luck, Chester, burned out of his apartment next to the Barracks, was burned out a second time on February 2, 1991; the fund-raiser for him was reported in *Drummer* 147, March 1991, page 61.) When artist Chester published his handsome photo book, *Diary of a Thought Criminal*, he sweetly inscribed on the title page, "For Jack, Who knows me longer than almost anyone else in San Francisco, Mark I. Chester, 9/20/96."

Two days after the Barracks fire, leather pioneer, Tony Tavarossi, died of unknown causes in the ICU of San Francisco General Hospital. He was my longtime friend. I kissed him goodbye. "What's the matter with him?" I had asked the ICU doctor two days before. "We don't know," she said, "We've never seen a patient so distressed." (See details of the Folsom Fire and the burning of the Barracks and the death of Tony Tavarossi in *Some Dance to Remember*, Reel 4, Scene 3 and Scene 4.)

December 13, 1979 (Thursday): For the second of three times, I waived my option to become a San Francisco deputy sheriff. I also telephoned Don Embinder, the Florida publisher of *Blueboy*, to discuss his bid for my services. Embinder and *Blueboy* were mutual enemies with Embry and *Drummer*. I figured I might as well sleep with the enemy as long as he had a magazine and a checkbook. But Florida? At that time the raging home of Anita Bryant?

August-December 1979: The end of 1979 was a perfect storm in purgatory. During my last five months with Embry, as if coping with a family feuding and divorcing, Al Shapiro and I managed to create the contents and design layouts of *Drummer* 30-33.

After the July murder of our *Drummer* contributor and friend, Robert Opel, hysteria and high anxiety began to destroy the salon around *Drummer*. With Embry's slow and fractious "fits and starts" of re-entry, things fell apart. Born recalcitrant, the LA publisher could not get up to speed with the pace of the new consciousness we had created in the new San Francisco iteration of *Drummer*. He'd come into the office by night, and, playing a leather Penelope, he'd undo the editorial work we had done by day. Like children caught in a divorce, junior staff fled his unpredictable autocracy, and resigned, mostly unpaid, because, as editor, I had no control over Embry's purse strings.

Besides the specific grief Embry caused, there was a kind of generic and existential "gay grief" that impeded working conditions and deadlines. If within seven months, gay activists Milk and Opel could be shot to death, was the gay press the next target of some bullet or ballot? Or could we expect yet another raid on our *Drummer* office by the SFPD who on May 21, 1979, charged down Castro Street, pounding the pavement with their billy clubs, pumping themselves up before invading the Elephant Walk Bar, at the ground-zero "rainbow corner" of 18th and Castro, where they blocked the doors and beat the patrons crawling under tables and scrambling for safety into the small toilet crammed with nearly twenty terrified gay men and lesbians, all of an age old enough to remember primal fears of pre-Stonewall violence being resurrected as they were being attacked in the new culture war spearheaded by onward-marching Christian soldiers led by Anita Bryant.

Once again sex and death combined. It was open season on gays. It was suddenly the wrong autumn for Embry to come barging in on the offensive after his spring and summer absence dealing with his own cancer.

December 31, 1979: After a Sisyphean two years and ten months (March 1977 to December 1979), I resigned officially as founding San Francisco editor-in-chief of *Drummer*, and continued on for years in my day job as manager of my staff of a dozen writers at Kaiser Engineers, Inc.

February 9, 1980 (Saturday): Five weeks after exiting *Drummer*, I was hired for two jobs by straight publisher Michael Redman. He asked me to write "lesbian-themed" fiction for the straight male readers of his *San Francisco Pleasure Guide*, and to be the founding editor of his new gay tabloid venture, the *California Action Guide*, whose first monthly issue appeared July, 1982, featuring the debut of a dozen feature articles I had written originally for, but never published in, Embry's *Drummer*. My "lesbian" fiction, played for fun, followed the tradition of pop-culture camp in Andy Warhol's underground films like *Chelsea Girls* (1966), Russ Meyer's movie of Roger Ebert's *Beyond the Valley of the Dolls* (1970), and Wakefield Poole's *The Bible* which I featured on the cover of *Drummer* 27 (February 1979). Ebert, the international film critic, was an ardent devotee of Meyer's raunchy comedies, and he gave—at that time in our new sex revolution— a certain cachet to the pop art of "sexploitation writing" as practiced in Warhol's *Interview*, *Drummer*, and in my *San Francisco Pleasure Guide* stories with my titillating news stand titles like: "Nurses Who Play Doctor," "Fit to Be Tied," "Goddess Worship Love Temples," and "Pussy Pussy Bang Bang." As penance, I later wrote a proper, and well-reviewed, lesbian literary novel, *The Geography of Women: A Romantic Comedy*.

March 25, 1980 (Tuesday): Trying to connect brilliant talents, I arranged a photo shoot between my two lovers, Robert Mapplethorpe and Jim Enger. One was the star photographer and the other was the star bodybuilder. As I guided the two, who separately were wonderful, through the shoot in a rented condo on Diamond Heights Boulevard, they both began to simmer silently—one against the other—with gay attitude. But, by God, by cooing, and by soothing, I did with them what I couldn't do with Embry. I made sure, despite egos, that we produced the drop-dead gorgeous pictures I had insisted we try to make. Both men, geniuses of the camera and body sculpture, managed to be polite and civil, although at the end of the session, Enger, a knowledgeable trophy-winning Best Poser, did a Southern aw-shucks stall on signing his release until after he could see the proof sheets. Mapplethorpe, ever "cool," did not press the issue because he knew his camera was full of wonderful trophy shots of an artist who was an extraordinary bodybuilder. He figured his printed photos would eventually seduce the esthetically minded Enger into signing.

Despite the dust-up, that same evening, our on-rolling *Drummer* Salon of Enger and Mapplethorpe joined Mapplethorpe's friend and model, the bodybuilder Lisa Lyon for supper at Without Reservation on Castro. Later, at 7:30, Mapplethorpe, Enger, Lisa Lyon, and I swanned in together to appear at Edward Brooks DeCelle's Lawson-DeCelle Gallery, 3237, Sacramento Street, where photographs of the entourage were shot by noted San Francisco paparazzo Rink. The famous Lawson-DeCelle photograph of the four of us, standing with photographer Greg Day (Enger's college roommate) was published in my book *Mapplethorpe: Assault with a Deadly Camera* (1994). The back cover of the same book featured a two-shot of Mapplethorpe and me, also lensed that night by Rink who was known for capturing spontaneous historical moments.

One of Mapplethorpe's torso-only shots of Enger from that afternoon on Diamond Heights was published in *Drummer* 133 (September 1989), page 14, to illustrate my feature obituary of Robert, "Pentimento for Robert Mapplethorpe: Fetishes, Faces, and Flowers of Evil."

March 27, 1980 (Thursday): My friend, Jim Singleton, the African-American psychiatric nurse at Langley-Porter Hospital, and member of the *Drummer* Salon, died of a lingering and mysterious illness. His funeral was Monday, March 31. A gay funeral was something new. Singleton's funeral, whose ritual we rather much invented out of whole cloth, was attended by friends Hank Diethelm, owner of the Brig bar; Peter Fiske of the 15 Association; Castro Street entrepreneur George Benedict; and a hundred other leathermen. I first wrote about the shock of "gay death" in my editorial, "Cruising: The Most Dangerous Game in the Whole Wide World," in *Drummer* 29 (May 1979), two years before the advent of AIDS.

April 3, 1980 (Thursday): I cooked an oven supper at my home for Jim Enger, Robert Mapplethorpe, and Mark Hemry all sitting at my white oak kitchen table. Eenie, Meenie, Miney, Mo.

April 8, 1980 (Tuesday:) Supper with Robert Mapplethorpe at Hamburger Mary's on Folsom Street; then to the Ambush bar on Harrison where Robert, to whom fetish was everything, instantly felt uncomfortable wearing his cool New York leather in a laid-back flannel-shirt bar. He asked me to drive him to my home where he could change into one of my shirts and jean jackets, and adjust his sex vibe, before we headed back to the Ambush where we hung out that evening with poet Thom Gunn and the artist Lou Rudolph who often sat in the Ambush, like Otto Dix in the Weimar cabarets of Berlin, sketching the customers.

April 29, 1980 (Tuesday): At his home at 36 Camp Street, I met with male-madam and film producer J. Brian, who procured hustlers for Rock Hudson, to collaborate on his screenplay *J. Brian's Flashbacks*, as well as to write a novelization of his film for publication as a serial in three issues of *Honcho* (April, May, June, 1982) and six issues of the *California Action Guide* (June-December 1982).

May 27, 1980 (Tuesday): Jim Enger thanked me for letting him read an excerpt from the manuscript in progress of *Some Dance to Remember*.

May 28, 1980 (Wednesday): Robert Mapplethorpe called me to please ask Jim Enger about using Enger's name on one of the headless torso photographs.

June 1, 1980 (Sunday): After a year as lovers, Mark Hemry moved into my home on 25th Street.

June 10, 1980 (Tuesday): I received word that my model and playmate Leonard Sylvestri died, allegedly, of hepatitis about three weeks earlier. A well-built man with a beard, Sylvestri was one of the San Franciscans whose photographs I published in *Drummer* to ground it in a reality of local, handsome, muscular men. His Italian surname translated suitably to *wild*.

October 1, 1980: Nine months after my exiting *Drummer*, Mark Hemry and I, as publisher and editor, released the first issue of *Man2Man Quarterly*, which, as our "Virtual *Drummer*," featured a cover photograph of Jim Enger who, in January 1981, without signing a release for a single "perfect moment" frame of the Mapplethorpe shoot, moved out of San Francisco.

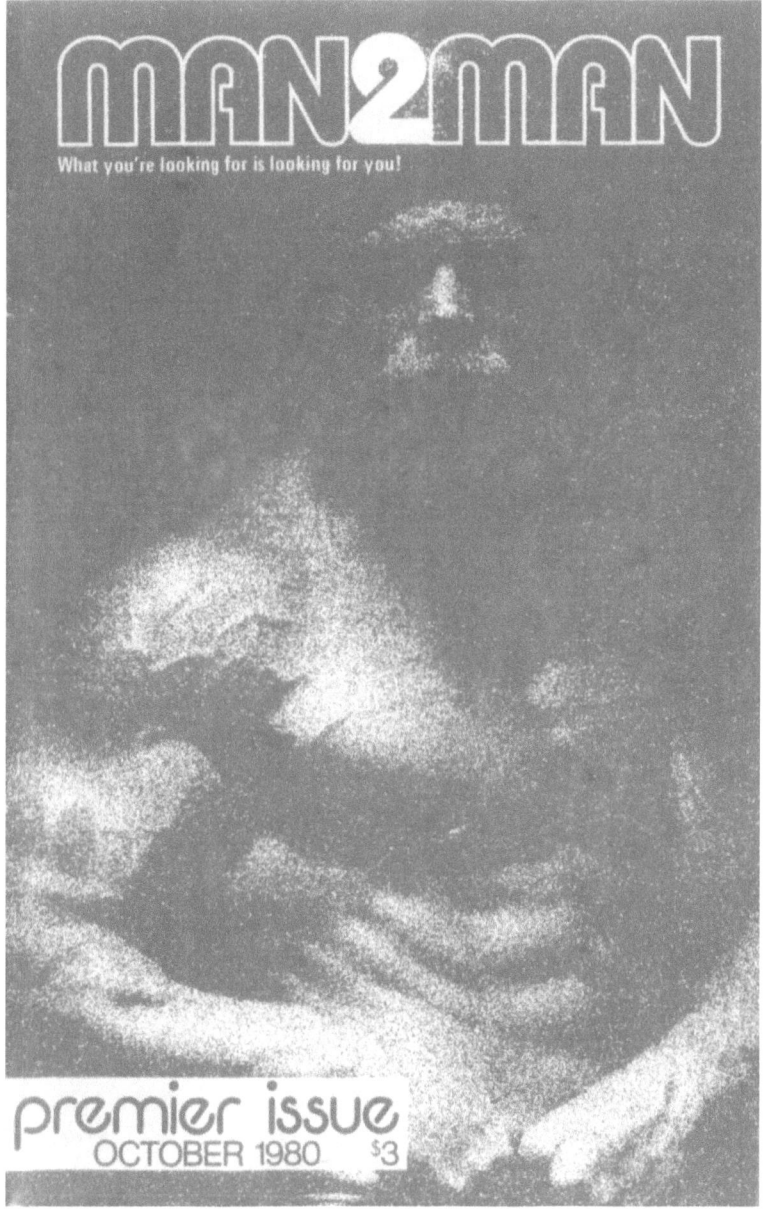

SPECIAL BEAR ISSUE

DRUMMER

ISSUE 140 / $5.95

The Sociology Of The URBAN BEAR

NEW BEAR FICTION BY
Jack Michaels
Michael Agreve

DRUMMERMAN JIM CVITANICH
Founder Of Men Behind Bars

LEATHER HISTORY NEWS
By Cavelo

Cover Photograph by Jack Fritscher

A SPECIAL PULL-OUT SECTION:
1990 LEATHER EVENTS CALENDAR

DISTRIBUTION TO MINORS PROHIBITED

CHAPTER 14

BACK STAB!
The Back-Stage *Drummer* Musical

- *Drummer* Editors Joseph W. Bean, John W. Rowberry, Robert Davolt
- Slave Boys, Wannabes, and the GLBT Historical Society
- The Dutch Connection: Who Killed *Drummer*?
- Eyewitness Mister Marcus

"*Drummer* catered to the awakening diversity of gay taste, and popularized fetishes that had never been outed before *Drummer* came along and helped create the very culture it reported on." —Jack Fritscher, "Being Obscene: A Panel of Pornographers," Featuring Susie Bright, Tom Bianchi, Tee Corinne, Jack Fritscher, Robert Davolt, and Willie Walker, Presented by the San Francisco GLBT Historical Society, GLBT Center Rainbow Room, September 27, 2002

* * * *

On October 9, 2003, Joseph W. Bean, who edited *Drummer* for Anthony DeBlase from 1989 to 1992, wrote me an email explaining how he handed over all contents of his own last three issues of *Drummer* to the new Dutch owner, Martijn Bakker. Bean's experience was exactly the same as mine with John Embry during Autumn 1979 when I also saw my final four strong issues as editor turned into insipid hybrids by Embry himself, with his churlish Los Angeles amanuensis John Rowberry standing behind the curtains like Eve Harrington with a knife. In addition, both Bean and I, without credit on the masthead, had both edited issues of *Drummer* earlier than the issue on which we first were listed as editor. Joseph Bean wrote:

> Jack, To answer your question about *Drummer*:
> I started working for *Drummer* months earlier [than it seems in the paper trail on the masthead credits], filling in because Peter Lackey was unable to do his job and Paul Martin (Heltsley) for all

his energy was not really familiar with the publishing business. So, it's hard to say which issues would be the first I actually edited since that was a creeping reality. But, starting with *Drummer* 132 [August 1989] (where I am not yet credited), I was working on everything in the magazine. I began to be officially credited as editor with *Drummer* 133 [Fritscher's "Mapplethorpe" issue, September 1989] as "Assistant Editor" along with Paul. Then as "Managing Editor" in *Drummer* 134, October 1989. At *Drummer* 50, September 1991, the credit changed from "Managing Editor" to "Editor," but nothing in my job description changed. Then, with *Drummer* 159, December 1992, was the last in which I was credited as editor. [Martijn Bakker purchased *Drummer* in September 1992 and changed its name to *International Drummer*.] For the next several months, contracts, contacts and even editing from my tenure [as editor] were used in the [Bakker version of the] magazine (along with my writing), but I was outta there. Issues #159 through #161 were a mixture of things I prepared before I left and things that were done after I was gone. So, my tenure was very short, starting in reality around March 1989 and ending officially in December 1992....

Eyewitness Jeanne Barney, the founding Los Angeles editor-in-chief of *Drummer* for one year (1975-1976), said the same hybrid mix and flow happened to her editorial work when she left Embry after *Drummer* 11, December 1976. She also testified that John Rowberry, Embry's default puppet, twisted the hybrid issues and militated to trash her in *Drummer*.

Facts are facts, and even if history turns out to be all *Rashomon*, the clock and calendar are absolute.

For literary detectives and historians, all the internal evidence necessary to substantiate these points of fact and opinion about who drove *Drummer* lie in the pages of *Drummer* itself.

Embry's high-handed autocracy was why so many independent artists and writers broke off with him. Even while owing money to the *Drummer* talent, Embry made working conditions worse. He stood foursquare against the moral and legal issues of us workers asking that our intellectual property of writing and illustrations and photographs needed to be branded with the copyright symbol for each of us creators. None of us was under contract. We were all freelance. We all owned our individual pieces of *Drummer* content. When he did pay, Embry never bought rights beyond one-time publication while he liked to think that he owned everything ever published in *Drummer*. His constant reprinting of *Drummer* contents angered the creators and contributors, and pissed off the subscribers who did not like buying the same thing twice. Jeanne Barney recalled that in Los Angeles Embry was tagged as "Robert Ripoff, the Prince of Reprints."

DECONSTRUCTING JOHN ROWBERRY, REFUGEE FROM LA: 1978-1979

Regarding John W. Rowberry during March 1977 and December 31, 1979, I must report that he did not work for *Drummer* when I was editor. When I first heard his name, he was working as the night porter at a motel in West Hollywood until, in one of his fits of mood, he suddenly chased after Embry, moving to San Francisco, where he talked Embry into hiring him to edit *The Alternate*. Rowberry was second choice, after my friend David Hurles first took the job of editing that magazine which Embry always really wanted instead of *Drummer*. *The Alternate* was supposed to be the rival of the political *Advocate*, and was supposed to make Embry as relevant as his competitor, *Advocate* publisher David Goodstein.

To Embry, *Drummer* was a bastard child sired out of Larry Townsend's *H.E.L.P. Newsletter*. The wild child *Drummer* found success not in politics but in erotica which, Embry judged, did not lead to the gay mainstream respectability that reassured big corporate advertising agencies fearful that their product placement might land next to ads for dildos or poppers. Hurles who was a genius photographer and entrepreneur could not, on top of his own agoraphobia, handle Embry's volatile business style. He retreated to his SOMA studio apartment at the exact moment that Rowberry roared into San Francisco seeking employment from Embry.

Bonded by their magazine work and roots in LA, Embry and Rowberry convinced each other that in tandem exile they might make *The Alternate* happen in San Francisco—the way Al Shapiro and I had made *Drummer* happen in San Francisco. Having published the first six issues of *Drummer* in LA, Embry had changed the business name from "Drummer Publishing" to "Alternate Publishing" in *Drummer* 7 (July 1976). It was not a good counterintuitive move to subordinate the brilliant brand name of *Drummer* to a backup magazine titled purposely to equate it to, or confuse it with, *The Advocate*.

When Rowberry waltzed into our *Drummer* office, he tried casting the spell of his LA attitude that, like his *padrone* Embry's, didn't play in San Francisco. Both Embry and Rowberry were, at heart, petulant LA queens, and neither ever was one of the boys among the leather players. Embry thought San Francisco was little more than Los Angeles' ugly stepsister. The leather staff of *Drummer*, ourselves all newish immigrants to San Francisco, with some attitude of our own, kissed the entitled Rowberry off as the "office boy," as a "page boy" to the self-consciously "royal" Embry who, dreaming for himself the memes of the divine right of queens, bragged about "all the years of my [his] *reign*" [italics added] at *Drummer* in his *Manifest Reader* 30 (1996), page 82.

Back in LA in 1976, Rowberry's first writing for Embry was his snuff poem, "White Death," in *Drummer* 5. In a truism of publishing, most freelance poetry in magazines is "filler" designed in to finish a page of other material. In its first LA issues when *Drummer* was new, and its filing cabinets were empty, and no one was sure that "leather" would in fact be the core *Drummer* identity, Embry was so desperate to fill empty pages that he published writing, new to him, that was sometimes as off-topic as the drag cover of *Drummer* 9. Or, worse, he would plagiarize entire feature articles from straight men's magazines such as *Argosy*. With Rowberry's poem, Embry flouted the laws against snuff pornography existing in the homophobic city of the LAPD where the groundbreaking S&M film *Born to Raise Hell* (1974) could not even be screened. Embry, of course, further endangered the very LA existence of *Drummer* when he featured that forbidden sex film on the cover of the infant *Drummer* 3.

Breaking the straight community's taboo against "snuff sex" pornography presaged the offensiveness the LAPD found in the feature article, "The Great S/M Murder Mystery," which Rowberry—with former *Advocate* employee, Rue Dyllon aka Larry Reh—had co-authored as a freelancer for *Dateline*, a magazine that Embry considered his rival. When *Dateline* imploded after one issue, Embry crowed victory, and with quick Schadenfreude serialized the Rowberry-Dyllon piece, edited heavily by editor-in-chief Jeanne Barney, in *Drummer* 9 through *Drummer* 11. In publishing Rowberry-Dyllon, Embry, who had hated *Dateline*, took up dancing on his competitor's grave with harsh words in *Drummer* 9, page 72, and *Drummer* 10, page 76. Barney was fierce in reminding me how much editing Rowberry's writing always required.

Years later, Embry also spit on the fresh grave of my successful *Man2Man Quarterly* which publisher, Mark Hemry, and I had shuttered because as our subscriptions increased, the personal sex ads grew increasingly unsafe and dirty in the psychological denial of the first years of AIDS (1981-1982). As an eyewitness, journalist John Calendo wrote a gloriously perfervid review of *Man2Man* in *In Touch for Men,* Number 58, August 1981, quoted below as a finale to this chapter. For the same health concerns, my longtime friend and *doppelganger*, Sam Steward, as verified by Joseph Bean in *Drummer* 153 (March 1992), had retired his "Phil Andros" character from his books so as not to encourage unsafe sex. Embry, who was so instantly envious of *Man2Man* that he immediately began tagging the *Drummer* "Personals" ads as "Man to Man," nearly died when Mark Hemry and I ended *Man2Man* by doing an unheard-of thing in lesbigay publishing: we calculated the amount remaining in each subscription and sent out complete refund checks to all subscribers. Jim Stewart (M. J. Stewart-Addison), owner of Fetters in London wrote on March 19, 1982:

> Dear Jack,...Sorry to hear *Man2Man* has come to an end. It will certainly become a Collectors Item. Congratulations on keeping up the standard and the output so consistently. Please thank Mark Hemry for the very "together" letter which reached me last week. I'm sure readers of *Man2Man* will appreciate the refund and be amazed that in gay publishing a magazine has ended on such a businesslike level. All my very good wishes. Congratulations on 8 issues of *M2M*. —Jim

ROWBERRY & I: SURVIVING EMBRY

In recalling Rowberry, I wish to take nothing away from his true contributions to *Drummer*, because, as I did with Lou Thomas and Al Shapiro and Bob Johnson, Rowberry and I both later worked cordially enough together, in separate locations, away from *Drummer* and from Embry. We both worked as freelancers in San Francisco producing several new magazines for George Mavety at Modernismo Publications: I as a writer beginning in 1979, and Rowberry, years later, as a fulltime packager beginning in 1986 when he was fired from *Drummer*, continuing up to his death in 1993.

To fill Mavety's magazines, Rowberry bought maybe thirty erotic stories and articles from me. In fact, on June 14, 1988, Rowberry, whose South of Market office was 1156 Howard Street, paid me a check for $500 so he could buy one-time rights to my 1987 novella, *Titanic: The Untold Tale of Gay Passengers and Crew*, for his *Uncut* Magazine, September 1988. That was more than twice what Embry had paid me ten years before for a month of editing *Drummer*. Our running joke was that we were two of the hundreds of escapees from "The Embry Experience" which was worse than David Goodstein's emasculating self-help program, the risible *"Advocate* Experience" spun gaily out of Werner Erhard's EST that caused the *Advocate* to turn even more politically correct.

San Franciscans held so much contempt for *The Advocate* in the 1970s that almost as soon as Goodstein chose to move his editorial and his "pink pages" sex-personals office to San Francisco, he realized that the City had too ironic and hip an attitude toward his bourgeois Southern California rag, and that he had better quickly return to the gay fundamentalism of LA with its Werner Erhard philosophy, its WeHo lingua franca, and its Hollywood veneers. Embry, who had been forced to move *Drummer* from LA to San Francisco, rejoiced that his archenemy had "retreated" the way that his early publishing competition at H.E.L.P. and *Dateline* had disappeared. Still feuding in 1979, the triumphalist Embry, whose publishing tentacles always remained deep in LA, could not resist printing a satiric screed, full of Los Angeles vitriol, trashing Goodstein and "The Advocate Experience" in the cover feature, "The Thing That Ate the *Advocate*," written in LA by alleged former *Advocate* employee, Dean Gengle, for *Alternate*, issue 9, edited by Rowberry who listed on the masthead his old pal, Rue Dyllon, as Los Angeles correspondent, and Embry's Slave Auction attorney, Al Gordon, as Los Angeles legal counsel.

ROBERT DAVOLT AND MISTER MARCUS

At the end of the twentieth century, in the thirty-year swirl around *Drummer* history, Embry, no longer owning *Drummer*, embraced Robert Davolt like a new John Rowberry. As a smiling ventriloquist whose lips rarely moved, Embry always needed a talking sock puppet in which to shove his fist of sticky fingers. He liked the fact that Davolt had managed to be hired by the third publisher of *Drummer*, Martijn Bakker, conveniently out of the picture in Amsterdam. He figured that Davolt, thus embedded, could be hired as a double-agent—working inside *Drummer*, while spying on *Drummer*, and stealing from its library of original photographs, drawings, and manuscripts that Embry coveted as if it were his own private heritage. Davolt's character as a reliable historian—that is, as a mouthpiece for Embry and a spokesman for *Drummer*—must be judged on how Embry and Davolt colluded. Davolt, who was much loved in the bars, exuded blond bonhomie. Behind the public face, he had the blond ambition of a social climber arriving late after the main party was over. When Embry met Davolt, the 1970s party was long gone, *Drummer* was dying and dead, and the pair bonded like two geezers at one of those historical re-enactments of a past gone with the wind.

Truman Capote would have recognized Davolt and his glomming on to Embry. In *Answered Prayers*, Capote wrote:

Ann realized something that only the cleverest social climbers ever do. If you want to ride swiftly and safely from the depths to the surface, the surest way is to single out a shark and attach yourself to it like a pilot fish. This is as true in Keokuk, where one massages, say, the local Mrs. Ford Dealer, as it is in Detroit, where you may as well try for Mrs. Ford herself.

Davolt worked industriously to install his name and stabilize his reputation within leather culture using *Drummer* as a baited hook and, I think, for his part, preying upon the ancient Embry in a way opposite to that in which Davolt tried to destroy and usurp the venerable leather columnist, Mister Marcus, whose job Davolt coveted at the *Bay Area Reporter*. Because Davolt tried to start a feud, Mister Marcus dubbed him in print as "Robert Revolting."

Davolt, so went the story in San Francisco, had the nerve to query the publisher of the *BAR* to fire its star columnist, Mister Marcus, so Davolt could replace him. Leather Elder Mister Marcus Hernandez began his leather column in the *BAR* in 1971-1972 when Davolt was in grammar school. After eighteen years of not being in *Drummer* where he belonged, "Marcus the Merciless" began a regular column, "Leather Bulletin Board," in the newly Dutch-owned *Drummer* 170, December 1993. That same issue featured my photographs of Donnie Russo on the cover as well in the centerfold where my eight-page photo-plus-essay feature, "Russomania," had been skillfully laid out by art director, Brendan Ward.

Ten days after Davolt died, Mister Marcus, ever the gent, noting their huge "personal and professional differences," wrote a very carefully considered elegy: "Honorable in Words and Deeds." He complimented Davolt, but defined him as "stormy." Tim Brough, author of *Sgt. Vengles' Revenge*, reviewed Davolt at Amazon.com as "a crank, but my kind of crank."

When Davolt and I were invited to a seminar, "Being Obscene?: A Panel of Pornographers," we were scheduled to appear with Susie Bright, Tom Bianchi, Tee Corinne, and Willie Walker. The San Francisco GLBT Historical Society brochure announced:

> Jack Fritscher, Ph. D., founding SF editor-in-chief, will open the tale of *Drummer*, the landmark gay male leather magazine, and Robert Davolt, its last editor and publisher, will close it. Together, they will highlight how this magazine not only gave birth to a whole panoply of alternative erotic images and publications, but also *how the magazine became the center of a whole cultural phenomenon*. Fritscher is a

noted author and historian and Davolt is a respected leather historian. [Italics added to show the GLBT Historical Society judgment that *Drummer* was more than a magazine. Was Embry, who lived in San Francisco, asked to appear, or did he refuse, or did he simply not respond to an invitation?]

Mark Hemry videotaped the event in the GLBT Center Rainbow Room on September 27, 2002. During the audience Q&A, I turned sideways to Davolt and joked: "I may be the first San Francisco editor of *Drummer* and you may be the last, Robert, but I'll never be the one to say you killed it."

For the whodunit of who finally killed *Drummer*, Robert Davolt was the keeper of that scandal—and I have the notes which he gave me to quote. *Drummer* was killed by more than just the internet which unplugged the life support on most gay magazines by the year 2000. Mister Marcus, writing as San Francisco's "Leather-Heritage Journalist of Record," made great public note that the *Drummer* brand and the *Drummer* contest were collapsing through the long-term neglect on the part of the Dutch owner, Martijn Bakker.

In the *Bay Area Reporter*, October 2, 1997, Mister Marcus, reporting on the previous Saturday's International Mr. Drummer Contest, wrote:

> Kyle Brandon, the departing Mr. Drummer, in his farewell speech, thanked everyone who was instrumental in making his year traveling with the *Drummer* title a memorable one. He even chided *Drummer* publisher Martijn Bakker for his inattention—all year—to his marketing icon [the IMD winner-traveling spokesman]. The same complaint [from previous departing winners of Mr. Drummer] seems to come up every year, but it always falls on deaf ears! But this is the first time it [the outing of this non-support] was delivered in front of a *Drummer* contest audience, so *maybe* the "message" came through loud and clear. We can only hope!

Davolt, who was Embry's understudy, continued to antagonize the leather feud with *The Advocate* which had disguised its famous Pink Section "Sex Classifieds" inside its spin-off magazine, *Unzipped*. A very anti-*Drummer* slam slipped into *Unzipped*, January 6, 1998, page 11, when gossip-queen Jack Francis in his column, "Secrets of the Porn Stars," reviewed Leather Week in San Francisco and trashed the Mr. Drummer Contest:

Thursday night I went carousing with Cole Tucker to —huh?— two auctions. The first was a pre-Drummer Contest function where the contestants had baskets of "goodies" to be auctioned off [how typically *Drummer*] to help defray their pageant expenses. You can imagine the contents...which included a spray bottle of 100% W. C. Urine. And I somehow got Kyle Brandon to tell the owner of *Drummer* magazine how snotty his people had been to me when I tried to mooch press credentials to their little contest....

Could I make these Machiavellian plots up? These kinds of shenanigans are the reasons that my eyewitness memoir-novel *Some Dance to Remember* has so many characters and plot lines. I didn't shag 13,000 soul-mates and eat 4,000 brunches at the Norse Cove on Castro in the Titanic 1970s without hearing every story in the effing village. As God is my eyewitness, I fucked Mapplethorpe who licked my eyeball with his tongue because he wanted me to be *his* eyewitness. "I want to be," he commissioned me, "a story told in beds around the world." And so, analogously, did others, behaving and misbehaving, standing in front of me, the journalist reporter. Immediately after *Some Dance to Remember* was published in 1990, a few leatherfolk asked me why I hadn't included them in the story as I had so many others. Considering the requests for walk-ons, I could have sold space for personality placement in that memoir with sentences such as: "When the fire engines arrived at the flaming Barracks bath, the headlights swept across the faces of_____." (Fill in the first and last names of any Tom, Dick, and Harry.)

* * * *

In 1979 when Mark Hemry and I began *Man2Man Quarterly*, times had changed during that first decade of gay liberation after Stonewall. Whereas *Drummer* had been founded in puritan LA in 1975, *Man2Man* was a 1980s San Francisco magazine that set out to go farther into wild sex than *Drummer* dared. *Drummer* was a large-format slick magazine dependent on advertisers and censorious news stands. Our low-budget *Man2Man* was the first zine of the 1980s and, as our passionate hobby, depended on no one but us two. It lasted two years because our little magazine was all hand-typed on typewriters, pasted down with wax, and hand-stapled and hand-mailed in those last years before personal computers. Its very success made it too much work for us with our own real careers.

In addition, the classified ads, despite what we could do, became increasingly dirty at the very moment when AIDS first changed sex to safe sex. It was this same dirty sea change that had caused me earlier to break off sex with my bicoastal lover Robert Mapplethorpe who was into dirty Manhattan sex typified by the Mineshaft. Never a puritan, I loved both Mapplethorpe and the Mineshaft. Nevertheless I knew I had to be a hygiene freak from the day I came out of the closet. So while art in magazines may play at being dirty, in real life, edgy sleaze is a whole other issue.

I wrote nearly every word in *Man2Man* as I had done with much of the text in the issues of *Drummer* which I edited. Truth be told, I wrote fifty percent of the first sex classifieds in *M2M* because each to me was like an exciting dirty little sex poem. I wanted each classified ad to be the same experience as going into one different movie booth after another at a dirty book store. Once the readers picked up on the rhetorical tone and style I was showing them by example, they found permission to push open their own versions of lust which is what I wanted when I first seeded the classifieds. However, I had no intention of unleashing every lurid fantasy in a classified format that suggested that these little entries were real. I meant them as jerk-off fantasies no one need try. I figured if they masturbated to risky sex acts at home, it would acquit their urges to go out and do them with others. The Id is mightier than the Superego. It was odd how fast simple sex in gay liberation turned dirty. Other magazines took notice.

In Touch for Men, titillating its own readers with the cheap thrills it could not resist in our *Man2Man*, pretended LA "shock" at San Francisco sex, and reviewed *M2M* in the August 1981 *In Touch* #58 that also published my short story about David Hurles, "B-Movie on Castro Street."

* * * *

PEOPLE HELPING PEOPLE
Man2Man Magazine
Vivid, Interactive Mag for Readers by Jack Fritscher

by John Calendo,
In Touch for Men #58, August 1981

What a nice world it would be if people did as these two do [referencing a 1960s photo of two British lads kitted up in rubber and necking with mud]. What they're doing exactly is, of course, up for grabs. You know, putting out a gay magazine is tough. You have to keep abreast of all the latest developments in gay sex. But even we have trouble following the many twists and turns coming out of San Francisco.

Take this picture, for instance. It comes from a wild sex journal called *Man2Man* (PO Box 6052, San Francisco CA 94101; $3) which lists its contents with one, very apt word: INTENSE. Edited and mostly written by Jack Fritscher, former editor of *Drummer* and author of our fiction this month ("B-Movie on Castro Street"), the 52-page booklet's most intense part is its bizarro classifieds, which take up one-third of the publication—rather vividly. While the rank majority of the ads can most effectively be described as "101 Things You Can Do On A Rainy Day With Your Best Friend's Feces," certain classifieds take us far beyond that, proving for all those fuddy-duddies who are still into blood-sex and raping Hell's Angels that such pastimes are—let's face it—simply not the *dernier cri* of kink.

Here then is an update: a few of our favorite *Man2Man* personals.

"BALLOON FUCK: Hot WM, 34, seeks bright butch stud to blow up huge balloon to bursting while I suck/fuck/jerk you off."

"L.A. ANIMAL FREAK: Wants muscular owners of stallions, Great Danes and Weimaraners. Photo of you and pets gets immediate reply."

"STALLED VEHICLES: Into cigar smokers in the driver's seat of stalled cars. Firebirds and Camaros are real auto-fetish treats!"

"NAVY SUBMARINE OFFICER: Wants to exchange his black nylon socks and garters for yours."

"HARMLESS PSYCHOPATHS: And weird far-out men wanted for everything including MC's, piss, scat, sweat, kidnaping, cannibalism and anything a gay Charlie Manson might think about. No nuts."

"EUNUCHS: I want to join you!! Who out there can castrate me skillfully?"

"SMEGMA WANTED: Drugs O K Y"

"IT'S SHOW TIME: Dog slave needs to be trained (punished), groomed (shaved), shown (bondage) and rewarded (fucked). Long show sessions desired. Can reciprocate for right puppy."

"SECLUDED PROPERTY SOUGHT: For outdoors scenes and target shooting. Those interested in holding tin cans, reply also!"

"FIELD PHONE BALL WORK: WM, 35, seeks CBA torture, especially having his weighted, separated balls tightly wrapped with barbed wire and worked over with adjustable field phone with Brazilian parrot's perch."

"PARAMEDIC SOUGHT: Am mansex adventurer in search of following scenario: smearing of the muscular scat-donor with a pint of my own blood, drawn paramedically before scene. With the Top glowing bright, glistening red, his muscles would be visually more spectacular than ever."

And last but not least our very, very favorite:

"MONEY FUCK: Fuck in a bed full of money. We'll go out together and ask hot straight guys (construction/truckers/cops) if they can change a ten-spot with bills from their wallets riding tight against their butts, and with coins heated in their pockets hanging in next to their warm dicks. You can move in close on a straight guy when he figures he's doing a man a favor; you can watch the intensity of his face close-up while his big hands count out the change; you can touch his hands as he lays the bills on you. We'll head home with our mouths full of man-collected coins. Spit cash into each other's mouths. Suck cock. Shove rolls of dimes/quarters/halves/and silver dollars up each other's ass. You haven't shit till you've shit dinero. Let's jerk off worshiping the money. Money is the only power. Money is the root of all evil. Let's put our money where our mouths are. Let's put our cash on the sheets and celebrate male greed, power, lust, and the comfort of the almighty dollar. This is a very honest trip. You bring a couple of hundred to match mine. All cash returned at end of night when we hose off the grease together. No foreign currency and definitely no Susan B's!"

Man2Man has got to be the best roller-coaster ride in the West. It's not for everybody--OBVIOUSLY. Still it is definitely worth every penny of the three dollars it costs. But just remember: no Susan B's!

CHAPTER 15

REQUIRED READING

Gender Identity in *Drummer*
A (Descriptive) Masculine Alternative
to the (Prescriptive) Sissy Stereotype
The Gender War and Homomasculinity

- Apartheid and Segregation: Politically Correct LGBT Terrorists Kill Gay Liberation
- Are there Leather "Nazis"? Richard Goldstein, "S&M: The Dark Side of Gay Liberation," *Village Voice*, July 7, 1975
- Homomasculinity: Philip Nobile, "The Meaning of Gay: An Interview with Dr. C. A. Tripp," *New York Magazine*, June 25, 1979: "50% of all young boys eroticize male attributes....90% of homosexuals show no effeminacy."
- Robert Mapplethorpe, Urvashi Vaid, and a Gender Fight for *The Advocate* cover, "Person of the Year"
- Gender Satire: The Red Queen Arthur Evans versus *Drummer*

"Gay men are guardians of the masculine impulse. To have anonymous sex in a dark alleyway is to pay homage to the dream of male freedom. The unknown stranger is a wandering pagan god. The altar, as in pre-history, is anywhere you kneel."
—Camille Paglia, *Sex, Art, and Culture: Essays*,
"Homosexuality at the Fin de Siecle," p. 25, Vintage, 1992

During the Titanic 1970s before the iceberg of HIV, I kept on my home desk a copy of the shocking anti-leather feature article that gay journalist, Richard Goldstein, wrote for the *Village Voice*, July 7, 1975, when *Drummer*, first published June 20, was only seventeen days old.

I was acutely aware of the gay vanilla villains trashing leatherfolk in the separatist gender war of butch and femme. In fact, to bridge the empathy gap between genders, I wrote a reflexive novel on that very theme: *Some Dance to Remember: A Memoir-Novel of San Francisco 1970-1982*. At *Drummer*, there was a vivid consciousness that the onward marching bourgeois enemies of leather culture were dangerous propagandists ranging from the *Village Voice* to the anti-leather *Advocate*. Most villainously, the enemy, pathologizing leather behavior, was most often not straight. It was our Enemy Within. With the rise of separatist feminism—not humanist feminism—into the community of genuine same-sex homosexuality rolled the Trojan Horse of politically correct and prescriptive gay "terrorists" using masculine-identified gay men for target practice.

Their prejudicial presumption was that masculine gay men are somehow simply an intramural bully version of the intermural straight male oppressors who frightened them in high school, and, therefore, deserve to be marginalized in LGBT culture. Ain't it a wonderful life? Every time gays disrespect each other another gay is burnt at the stake.

In the Voodoo Politics of gay apartheid, any and all gender separatists who think themselves superior activists are in truth hardly more than reactionaries whose separatism is the ugly social crime of segregation within the already divisively sorted alphabet soup of the LGBT community.

Masculinity, in short, was suspect—as if a good man was hard to find. In general, masculine gay men, having suffered as gay boys, embrace not the worst of straight male stereotypes, but the best of the Jungian male archetype balanced off the best of the Jungian female archetype. Homomasculinity for gay men, like homofemininity for lesbians, aims at the quintessential purity at the heart of the two gender norms that bookend the diversity of all other genders on the Kinsey scale. Noting such pecking order, the psychotherapist leatherman Guy Baldwin wrote in his "Ties That Bind" column in *Drummer* 127: "Social rules say that straight is better than gay. The rules also say that vanilla is better than kinky. So there is hiding. And a part of us is cut off from ourselves."

Richard Goldstein, who had not yet heard of *Drummer*, titled his leather smear-campaign manifesto, "S&M: The Dark Side of Gay Liberation." While his essay was interesting for his eyewitness reporting on the New York leather scene that I loved, his vanilla prejudices and Manhattitude spoiled his testimony. Trolling our bars to sample our culture, was he an immature sex tourist? Unsophisticated? Kidding? Was he dog-paddling in his own pool of "morality"? Was he swamped by the sudden popularity of S&M in liberated females, fashion, and films favored by leather players? Had he been unable to handle esthetically, intellectually, and morally the 1970s new wave of women directors featuring Nazi brutality and sexuality as in Liliana Cavani's darkly romantic psychological film, *The Night Porter* (1974)? Or Lina Wertmueller's dark *Seven Beauties* (1975)? Or even in Don Edmonds' pop-cult classic, *Ilsa: She Wolf of the SS* (1974) that played to eager leather fans for two solid years at the Strand movie theater on Market Street? What was Goldstein really on about when, after he went slumming in gay bars like the Eagle, he condescendingly slandered gay S&M sex, art, and leather uniforms, by connecting our erotic disciplines to Nazi punishments?

His only insight into our folkways was a truth we all know, and one that was not original with Goldstein because it came out of the mouth of an unidentified leatherman he interviewed: "Sadism, if you really want to call it that, is really forcing someone to do what he is already eager to do. It has the same kind of feeling as a flood of tears in a movie—it's a dramatic experience."

He abridged the 1970s rise of "gay liberation for all" when he, as an aggressive gay separatist, trashed the ritual and emotional validity and personal choice of S&M, fisting, piss, and scat; hanky and key codes of *left* and *right*; leather-heritage bars like Keller's, the Anvil, the Spike, and the Eagle's Nest (the actual name of the bar that guys called "The Eagle"); leather-heritage stores like the Pleasure Chest and the Marquis de Suede; bike clubs like the Praetorians, Empire City, Wheels, Trash, and CYA (Up Your Ass); straight leather folk heroes like performance artist, Chris Burden, and leather sculptor, Nancy Grossman; and artists like Tom of Finland (Eons Gallery, *Drummer* 13), and especially my longtime crony and sometime collaborator, the *Drummer* artist, Rex, whom Goldstein labels a "Naziphile" for his book *Mannespeilen* (Les Pirates Associes, Paris, 1986). On page 41, *Mannespielen* featured the Rex drawing for the cover of my book, *Leather Blues: A Novel of Leatherfolk* (1984).

In his insular Manhattan trashing of our international leather art, Goldstein, had he rounded out his research, would have been confounded in his gay theory by the moxie and sophistication of one of the first and finest sources of mid-twentieth-century S&M photography, the iconic British discipline studio, Studio Royale, established in the early 1950s, and beloved by Tom of Finland (mentioned by Goldstein), and Tom's friend, Alan Selby, founder of "Mr. S" leather fetish clothing. In Royale's erotic catalog of esthetic images of S&M, each single-frame tableau was as perfect a moment as any "Perfect Moment" shot by Mapplethorpe. Partly printed on marvelously opaque onionskin paper, those pages, in the 1960s, arrived at my American home in plain envelopes from 110 Denbigh St., (near the bed-sit of Quentin Crisp), London S.W.1. Royale's "story board" series of approximately fifteen frames each, featuring non-nude casts of ordinary guys with natural bodies and the authentic look of underpaid squaddies and bonafide guardsmen posing "gay for pay." Making a fetish of non-nude manliness, its mix of uniform kit with corporal punishment hugely influenced my homomasculine concept of natural-born leathermen practicing S&M in *Drummer*.

Goldstein's article was a valuable warning to me because he was the first East Coast enemy of the leather life my friends and I and Michel Foucault and the artist Rex, whom he ridiculed, were happily leading in San Francisco. Can you imagine what it was like to fist Foucault on Folsom Street? Goldstein's politically-correct 1975 article created prejudice, and played to the prejudice of, Manhattan vanillarinas suspicious of leather culture, leather art, and leatherfolk. And, ultimately, against *Drummer*. By the end of the 1970s, prescriptively petulant New York gays, who had not even read the script of William Friedkin's *Cruising*, demonstrated in the streets to stop the acclaimed director of *The Boys in the Band* from shooting his new leather-themed film on location in the Meatpacking District.

It was not just New Yorkers. Worldwide, the straight and gay bourgeoisie agreed intellectually and esthetically on their mutual distrust of the S&M jamboree they could not separate from real-life sex abuse, mental illness, and low-class violence. To each other about leatherfolk they said, "NOCD. Not our class, darling." A few years later, San Francisco *Focus* Magazine (November 1985) railed against leatherfolk and prematurely announced "The Death of Leather." *Focus* was the magazine of the politically correct San Francisco PBS television station, KQED, which was also responsible for the wretched anti-male and discriminatory documentary, *The Castro* (1997). Its seemingly politically correct producer-writer-director and propagandist, David L. Stein, deleted virtually any representation of the formative male presence in the roots of Castro Street which was effectively created in the 1970s by gay men, such as Harvey Milk, as a destination for any and all sex refugees still coming out in their own time across the country. He might better have tacked a specific feminist subtitle to his generic title which, by itself, *The Castro*, promised conceptually way more inclusion than he delivered in terms of representing the decades, genders, and populations he selected.

Because of the army of leather haters, including the self-named "Red Queen" of Castro, Arthur Evans, who made the biggest mistake of his intellectual life identifying leather with patriarchy (See *Drummer* 134, October 1989), I was thankful for the following magazines which I kept on file to guide my version of *Drummer* magazine.

Decades before search engines such as Google existed, especially during the first decade of gay liberation in the 1970s, writers doing research had to collect their own leather pop-culture archive of hard copies of authoritative publications for the kind of topics, themes, and fact-checking suitable for emerging gay journalism, gay studies, and GLBT archives.

SOME EYEWITNESS REFERENCE DOCUMENTS
FOR THE 1970S:
SOME "GLBT REQUIRED READING"

• *Look* magazine (January 10, 1967)) in its Special Issue, "The American Man," published Jack Star's gay history, "The Sad 'Gay' Life of the Homosexual," with a photograph by Douglas Jones, featuring a close-up face of a leatherman wearing a leather cap decorated with bike run pins reading "Badger Flats 1966"and "Recon Annual Run May 7." As a note of my own archeology into our lost civilization, as well as a measure of how GLBT culture often fails to dig for its roots, this mention of this particular issue of *Look* is fairly much the first mention ever (that I know of) in any GLBT coverage of gay history. This seemed also the case of the once-and-oft forgotten feature, "Homosexuality in America," *Life* magazine, June 26, 1964, which, after I first referenced it in *Drummer* in my feature obituary, "Artist Chuck Arnett," *Drummer* 134 (October 1989), has since been cited endlessly as a commonplace fact, which, of course, is the reward for us pre-internet writers unearthing lost treasure for future researchers in what has become the gay history business.

• *Harper's* (July 1975), the same month as Goldstein published his screed, and the first month that the first issue of *Drummer* was on the newsstands, featured the cover story "Masculinity: Wraparound Presents 60 Points of View." Perhaps this article was *Harper's* penance for its hateful September, 1970, cover story, "Homo/Hetero: The Struggle for Sexual Identity," written by Joseph Epstein, a straight anti-pop-culturist, who declared two months after Stonewall, "If I had the power to do so, I would wish homosexuality off the face of this earth."

• *Time* (September 8, 1975), two months after Goldstein and three months after *Drummer* 1, published the famously patriotic cover of Leonard Matlovich, "I Am a Homosexual: The Gay Drive for Acceptance." The good-hearted HIV-positive Matlovich, cannibalized by fund-raising carnivores in the gay community demanding his time and money and publicity, was driven to an early grave at age forty-five in 1988.

• *Muscle Builder/Power* (December/January 1976) published an editorial by Armand Tanny, "The Male: An Endangered Species." The well-reasoned humanist Tanny argued for male emancipation from stereotypes in this popular international men's health magazine published by Joe Weider who was Arnold Schwarzenegger's Dr. Frankenstein. Indirectly connected to homomasculinity in *Drummer*, the magazine's lead article featured bodybuilder Bob Birdsong who also made gay S&M erotic films in the 1960s and early 1970s with other bodybuilders such as Ken Sprague who was the Colt model "Dakota" and an early owner of Gold's Gym. Dakota also made bisexual and gay homomasculine films with bodybuilder Jim Cassidy who was so frequently his co-star in gay movies that they were known in sniffy camp bars as the "Nelson Eddy and Jeannette McDonald of gay porn." The bodybuilder Roger Callard, pictured by Tanny, appeared in nonsexual roles in several gay films. In the 1960s and 1970s, I bought many of the these 8mm and Super-8mm black-and-white and color films that influenced me greatly in fashioning the male archetypes of *Drummer* even while at that time we were all guessing which bodybuilders led double lives in gay cinema. Some of Weider's bodybuilders also made nude solo films for the crisply brilliant Film Associates company which, as Chuck Renslow's very homomasculine Kris Studio had been in the 1950s and 1960s, was the go-to studio to buy muscle films cast straighter than those shot by the openly gay Athletic Model Guild and Colt Studio.

• *High Times* (August 1976) published Glenn O'Brien's positive feature on the leather-culture explosion, "Piss, Leather, and Western Civilization." For review comment, see early *Drummer* columnist Fred Halsted's perfervid and quite surreal "Editorial," *Package* 5 (December 1976) in which Halsted, whose ancestral roots were in the Caucasus, waxed on about the mystic qualities of piss, mushrooms, Aryan culture, and ritualistic spiritualism in leather sex, in terms of Joey Yale, Kenneth Anger, William Burroughs, and himself as a leather guru.

• *Psychology Today* (January 1977) published a special issue, "Masculinity," based by diverse reporters on the responses of 28,000 readers of *Psychology Today* twisting in the wind blowing around concepts of liberated men, macho, and androgyny.

• *Time* (April 13, 1979) published on its cover a pair each of male and female hands with the huge headline, "How Gay Is Gay? Homosexuality in America." Having been accused that my *Drummer* was "not gay enough," I wrote editorials for *Drummer* 25 and 26 about "Fucking with Authentic Men." As if in confirmation of this endless sussing out of "measuring" homosexuality, photographer Mark I. Chester wrote in *Drummer* 138, pages 24-25, that his work was judged "too explicitly gay."

• *Blueboy* (October 1979) publisher Don Embinder, adding a consideration of leather into the vanilla *Blueboy*, featured Ian Young, whom I have long respected, writing his consideration, "What Is this Thing called S&M?" To his credit, John Embry in his publisher's column in *Drummer* 9 (October 1979) took *Blueboy* publisher Don Embinder to task for misrepresenting leather and S&M in that issue.

• *The Advocate* 238 (December 1979) showcased Pat (Patrick) Califia authoring "A Secret Side of Lesbian Sexuality" which connected to *Drummer* through Samois, the Society of Janus, and the Catacombs. I had already published the Samois hanky code in *Drummer* 31 (September 1979).

• *New York Magazine* (June 25, 1979) published Philip Nobile's exhilarating cover story, "The Meaning of Gay: an Interview with Dr. C. A. Tripp" just as homomasculinity exploded to the surface in *Drummer*. Author Tripp, who finished the recently deceased Kinsey's work in *The Homosexual Matrix* stood four-square against born-again homophobes. Dripping with credentials, Nobile reinforced my archetype of homomasculinity in *Drummer* when he wrote this essential statement in *New York Magazine*, page 37:

> 50 percent of all [straight and gay] young boys eroticize male attributes...90 percent of homosexuals show no effeminacy...furthermore, a great many people involved in homosexuality are the opposite of what the layman would expect, meaning that they are macho males of the truck driver-cowboy-lumberjack variety....*Those he-man types place great emphasis on maleness and male values—and thus have an extraordinary tendency to eroticize male attributes, which is, after all, what most male homosexuality is all about.* [Italics added.]

Continuing to write for *Drummer* over the years, I also kept:

• *The Advocate* 472 (May 12, 1987) made unusual amends with leather culture in the feature essay by Scott Tucker, "Raw Hide: The Mystery and Power of Leather," pages 40-49. In the evolution of BDSM in gay popular culture, butch covers that were once singular to *Drummer* began to appear on one or two covers of *The Advocate* in the first decade of the twenty-first century. However, after leather photographer Robert Mapplethorpe died, I had to browbeat *The Advocate* into putting that most world-famous of gay men and gay leathermen on the cover as their "Person of the Year" as 1990, the very high-profile year of the Mapplethorpe scandal, was turning into 1991 when the issue on the stands was *The Advocate*, December 18, 1990.

According to then *Advocate* editor Mark Thompson, my pressure ignited an internal fight at *The Advocate* which, in the end was a fight I won for Robert. Even so, queens being what we are, the cover photo which was published was, of course, not Robert in the characteristic personal leather he wore and was famed for photographing, but him in an experimental self-portrait wearing women's makeup as a male-effacing masque. Having more or less embarrassed *The Advocate* into doing the right thing by the kind of artistic genius that gay culture is not likely to see again soon, I was hardly surprised that the magazine so patently begrudged putting a famously dead world-class gay leatherman on its coveted annual cover.

Perhaps to save face, or to find the balance, in the gender war, *The Advocate* finally decided to divide the real estate of its cover in half so it could also picture the famously alive Indian-American lesbian, Urvashi Vaid, as yet a second "Person of the Year" in a kind of politically correct timeshare of two worthy persons titled "Woman and Man of the Year" with Vaid pictured on the left and Mapplethorpe on the right. It may very well be the only year that *The Advocate*'s "Person of the Year" ended in a tie, much like the 1969 Academy Awards when Katherine Hepburn and Barbra Streisand tied for Best Actress in *The Lion in Winter* and *Funny Girl*.

Before I had contacted *The Advocate* nominating Mapplethorpe, I think the magazine may have already decided to name Vaid solo as its "Person of the Year." She was freshly partnered with feminist comedienne and in-house *Advocate* columnist Kate Clinton; and, at that moment, Vaid's media profile was beginning to rise because she had just been named executive director of the National Gay and Lesbian Task Force; and finally, because the persons on the *Advocate* phones seemed rather disconcerted that I was upsetting their in-house plans for the cover with this outsider intervention which eventually "shamed" them into doing the equitable thing even if, like the mother in Kings 3:16-28, they defied King Solomon's wisdom and divided their baby in half. I apologized for my urgency with them, and I argued that 1990 would really, really, really be the last year that the recently deceased Mapplethorpe could reasonably be honored as a person of the year.

• *Manifest Reader* 17 (1992), Embry's post-*Drummer* magazine, headlined by Dane/Mike/Rick Leathers, in the essay, "A New Mazeway for Homomasculine Men," pages 33-39. The ascetic worshiper of bulls, Rick Leathers authored more than twenty-five homomasculine stories and articles for Embry in *Drummer*, *Mach*, and *Manifest Reader*. See the useful bibliography in *Manifest Reader* 30 (1996), pages 62-63.

• *The New Republic* (June 13, 1994) published Bruce Bawer's "The Stonewall Myth" in a special and important American Booksellers Association issue that addressed gay linguistics, politics, and masculinity. Another "myth" about Stonewall is that the riots were populated en masse like Woodstock which happened two months later with thousands of participants: every author who claimed to be in New York in June 1969, including the mandarin Edmund White, has written himself into the narrative of that night that he "just happened to witness" like Woody Allen's time-traveling protagonist in *Zelig*.

Truth be told, "Stonewall" as a concept did not really penetrate the national gay culture—outside New York—as a popular metaphor until the early mid-1970s when Manhattan writers, in assumptions of artistic powers, alchemized their local event into a convenient watershed symbol of national gay resistance as if Stonewall were, indeed, "a shot heard round the world" like the one in Emerson's "Concord Hymn" that started our Revolutionary War, or the shot that killed Archduke Ferdinand in 1914 starting World War I. Having just returned that June, 1969, from Europe on Pan Am, I was not in New York during the Stonewall rebellion. Visiting that week in Chicago, I remember only one bit of news exactly: the radio said Judy Garland was dead. Joining those New York writers, my own gesture to enhancing this archetribe symbol was my story, "Stonewall: June 27, 1969, 11 PM," published in *Harrington Gay Men's Fiction Quarterly* (Volume 8, Issue 1, 2006) and in the anthology *Stonewall Stories of Gay Liberation* (2008).

In defense of homomasculinity and *Drummer*, and the 1970s quest for defining new genders and old, I rest my case.

1976, October 9: Wally Wallace begins managing the "Temple Bar of Masculinity," the Mine Shaft [written as two words on his opening night invitation, but more commonly spelled Mineshaft] at 836 Washington Street, New York, which I wrote about in *Drummer* 19 (December 1977).

1976: Alexander Shulgin stimulates leather culture when he unearths a lost 1912 chemistry formula to introduce one of 1970 leather culture's most popular drugs, MDMA, with its gentle psychedelic and stimulant effects; not to be confused with popular and speedy MDA (Mapplethorpe's favorite drug), innocent little MDMA soon becomes famous as Ecstasy.

---

* * * *

EXHIBIT A

From *Drummer* 25 (December 1978)

THE GAY CIVIL WAR OVER GENDER:
An Introduction to a *Drummer* Editorial

"ARE YOU BUTCH ENOUGH?"

Drummer Presents
Some "Found" Prose
from the Red Queen, Arthur Evans
by Jack Fritscher

I wrote this editorial, as a case in point, noticing Arthur Evans in September, 1978, and published it in *Drummer* 25 (December 1978), to help sort out the new Gay Civil War over Gender in the Titanic 1970s. For all its entertainment value, *Drummer* was a timely test-bed for purposeful versions and visions of the gay-liberation dream unfolding.

Some gender activists misunderstand homomasculinity as if it were a Fascist principle and not what it is, a gender identity innate to those born that way. When I coined the term *homomasculinity* in 1977, I meant not masculinity as a power tool of male privilege or male entitlement, but rather a masculinity whose identity was rooted in traditionally masculine goodness in the Latin sense of *virtue*, which comes from the Latin word *vir*, meaning *man*, causing *virtue* to be "the quality of a man." That was the quintessence I sought to define in my coinage.

I published this satirical piece written by the self-crowned "Red Queen, Arthur Evans," who was an evangelical gender missionary come from the island of Manhattan to convert the peninsula of San Francisco whose butch gays he rejected as much as they rejected him. Even so, he had a genuine political authenticity rather like the authenticity of political analysis of unfolding gender ambiguities made by University of California Professor David Van Leer in his benchmark book of the pop-culture period between World War II and Stonewall, *The Queening of America: Gay Culture in a Straight Society*.

In the gay civil wars of the 1970s, with some apostolic gender crusaders trying to gentrify other genders, I respected Arthur Evans' representing one kind—his Faerie Circle kind—of "authentic" queening and queering. In *Drummer*, I chose to give his "red"—did he mean

Marxist-Communist?—gender voice free exposure. At that time, I had already opened *Drummer* up, in my "Leather Christmas" feature in *Drummer* 19 (December 1977), to the first mentions of authentic female leather players such as Cynthia Slater, co-founder of the Society of Janus and author of first-person feminist S&M fiction like "Discovery" in *Drummer* 125. I also published one of the first press-releases from Samois, the first lesbian S&M group, founded by the transman Patrick Califia and the feminist Gayle Rubin in 1978. Samois disbanded in 1983 allegedly because of infighting, somewhat like *Drummer* itself. Those intramural spats reflected the very essence of the passions and politics being parsed about fixed and fluid gender identity in the leather community.

I openly tub-thumped an emergent defining theme of a populist homo-masculine "authenticity" which actually did exist among *Drummer* readers as revealed in our confessional Leather Fraternity personals ads where *masculinity* and *masculine* were the two most repeated words. Homomasculine identity was the key ingredient leading to *Drummer*'s success because no one had anticipated, or affirmed, the unexpected news that masculine-identified gay men had to come out of the closet just like all the other gay identities.

By "authenticity" I meant something as authentic as a Platonic Ideal: a gay man in a police uniform, for instance, with his fetish act together and his head together, may be more "authentic" than an actual, credentialed, straight cop in uniform, because the gay man has the feeling and soul to plunge to the heart of, and understand and act out the quintessence of "copness" which the cop may not understand because to him his job's just a paycheck.

By "authenticity" I mean the heart of the archetypal best that males do, not the stereotypical worst. Perhaps that should be repeated for the blind-and-deaf politically correct fundamentalists. In her essay, "The Fiction Writer and His Country," Flannery O"Connor, the great Catholic novelist of the American South, wrote: "To the hard of hearing you shout, and for the almost-blind you draw large and startling figures." Latter-day critics should not misread *Drummer*, which they are only perceiving in their rear-view mirror, when we, back then, were looking forward through the windshield of *Drummer* which was about on-coming, large, and startling archetypes, not stereotypes.

I was coincidentally predisposed to a sibling kinship with my peer, Arthur Evans, who was diametrically opposite *Drummer*. Early on, we both were graduate students majoring in philosophy, and working toward our doctorates: Evans at Columbia University, and I at Loyola University,

Chicago. Evans' dissertation was not approved for, he said, anti-gay reasons, and he withdrew from his doctoral program where his radical and polarizing political stances made him somewhat of a pesky persona non grata. My own dissertation, *Love and Death in Tennessee Williams*, about ritual, race, and gender, was published in 1967 when I received my doctorate. From the early 1960s, Evans and I led parallel lives as activists in black civil rights, the peace movement, and then as gay activists theorizing on the nature of homosexuality. Evans was one of the founders of the Gay Activists Alliance, 1969. Representing gay inclusion, I was one of the founders of the American Popular Culture Association, 1968.

Inside our lateral lives, Evans was helping invent the "Radical Gay Faerie Movement" and working toward writing his nonfiction book, based on his doctoral work, *Critique of Patriarchal Reason*, while I was championing masculine-identified queers in *Drummer* and writing my reflexive fiction book *Some Dance to Remember* which, while dramatizing the immense disaster of masculinist patriarchy, eschews both "bully patriarchy" (masculinism) and "bully matriarchy" (feminism) for something grander—humanism–which was also perhaps Evans' goal. In some ways, *Patriarchal Reason* and *Some Dance to Remember* are complementary reading.

In the mid-1970s while Evans was working with the faerie magazine *Fag Rag*, I was editing and writing the leathery *Drummer*. Both gender magazines might be studied together as might our two books in which we both wrote about magic and wicca, ritual and culture, and sex and gender identity. At the same time as I published him in *Drummer* 25, Evans published his *Witchcraft and the Gay Counterculture*. His *Witchcraft* book immediately caught my attention, coming, in 1978, six years after Bowling Green University Press published my own occult history book, *Popular Witchcraft: Straight from the Witch's Mouth* (1972).

No scholar has yet written a cohesive literary analysis of the gay books written during the pioneering 1970s, particularly those written outside the literary bunker of New York. These books, as art objects floating to the surface after the Titanic 1970s hit the iceberg of HIV, are particularly valuable, because like *Drummer* itself, they are intellectual and esthetic time capsules, authentically in and of the time when gay culture first came queening, queering, butching, and bitching out of the closet. They show modern gay culture self-consciously inventing itself. These pioneering books' texts are not inauthentic revisionist or condescending peeks looking back at the 1970s. They were written during the 1970s. In such a literary and historical project lies, perhaps, for next-generation scholars a grant, or a doctoral dissertation of value.

People mouth the word *Stonewall* like a magic pebble on their tongue, but the invocation of Stonewall and who threw the first brick is meaningless if analysts, critics, and historians dismiss the 1970s decade of post-Stonewall literature and culture as ten years of gay juvenilia based on gay bacchanalia when that decade was, in fact, an important stratum in the long history of gay archeology.

If the Stonewall standard of measurement is legitimate, then serious scholars cannot pretend—like righteous sex bigots who hate the 1970s for "causing AIDS"—that worthwhile gay culture and gay literature only began after the advent of HIV in 1982, or when actual gay book publishers first started up in the mid-1980s. In American literary evolution within mass media, gay magazines were the first voice of gay culture for more than twenty years before GLBT book publishing began in earnest.

As a young university professor experiencing sexually, and esthetically, the rise of modern gay civilization during the revolutionary 1960s, I traveled across the globe to visit other cradles of queer civilization and culture. I had been taught the principles of cultural relativity by my mother who grew up as an amateur archeologist digging for ancient arrowheads, clay pots, and river pearls in her birthplace of Kampsville, Illinois. That village is wedged between the converging Illinois and Mississippi rivers on the delta which archeologists term "the Nile of North America" because it is the site of twelve Native American civilizations dating back to 7000 BC. She taught me, born only fifty miles away, that the information—in those ancient burial mounds' archeology—was not just about linear dates but was also about relative and cultural behavior. One type of arrowhead, like one type of gay magazine or book, may follow another in time, but what do their comparison and contrast tell about causality and the identity of the makers? *Drummer*, with its 214 issues streaming for twenty-four years to millions of readers, may very well be the Nile Delta of Gay Leather Culture.

In the dolmans of Ireland, the catacombs of Paris, and the ruins of Rome, I have seen stonewalls of early civilizations as telling as the archeological debris left standing in San Francisco on the site at 4th Street and Harrison where the artist Chuck Arnett's seminal Tool Box bar once stood, or in New Orleans at 141 Chartres Street where the Upstairs Lounge stood until set afire by an arsonist in a blaze that killed thirty-two patrons, or in Greenwich Village at 53 Christopher Street where the Stonewall Inn itself remains as a kind of gay Parthenon. Stonewall is one of the more important surviving snow globes of modern gay history.

Reading our Stonewall decade's tectonic feminism, masculinism, and humanism should be no less valued and valuable. A person ignores his own roots at his own risk. One of the faults of critical thinking within politically correct attitude is its fundamentalist inability to understand its own agenda as sexist apartheid and not as the true fair play of diversity.

This back-story introducing the "Red Queen" is a sketch of that gadfly some call a saint. Evans was typical of the diverse chorus I aimed to reflect in *Drummer* which I wanted open wide to all gay voices so *Drummer* could serve the times it helped create even as it reported on them. Because *Drummer* needed reflexive material, I gladly peeled the Red Queen's "protest poster" off a telephone pole during the Castro Street Fair and published it in *Drummer*. The archeology of this "found" poster shows how the effete New Yorker Evans, who admitted losing his sex drive, poked fun—what he called "satire"—at the masculine clothing and athletic sex styles of very earnest young gay men on Castro and Folsom which he misdiagnosed as butch costuming, guilt-driven S&M punishment sex, and a pecking order not unlike high school bullying.

He held an entitled sense of the primacy of his own fluid gender identity, causing more needless trouble in the uncivil "gay civil wars." So many were those petulant fights, I have often wondered why academic queer-culture theorists have never yet dared call the strife in the 1970s gay community a "civil war." In 1982, I applied the words "civil war" in this way for the first time. For the very focused back cover of the Lambda Literary Finalist *Some Dance to Remember*, I wrote copy referencing my avatar James Joyce introducing his Stephen Dedalus to the world in *A Portrait of the Artist as a Young Man*. It offered readers a quick orientation into the *who, what, where,* and *when* of the book. Because we are all film fans, I designed the copy to read like a movie poster in a theater lobby:

> The Cosmos. The Solar System. The Earth.
> North America. California. San Francisco.
> 18th and Castro. South of Market.
>
> The Golden Age 1970-1982
>
> A Drop-dead Blond Bodybuilder
> A Madcap Gonzo Writer
> An Erotic Video Mogul
> A Penthouse Full of Hustlers
> A Famous Cabaret Chanteuse Fatale
> A Hollywood Bitch TV Producer
> A Vietnam Veteran

An Epic Liberation Movement
A Civil War Between Women and Men and Men
A Time of Sex, Drugs, and Rock 'n' Roll.
A Murder
A City
A Plague
A Lost Civilization
A Love Story

The operative line here is, of course: "A Civil War Between Women and Men..." and then the purposeful bada–boom break in rhythm: "...and Men." Between women and men, it was still the same old battle of the sexes. The battle between men and men was something new, and that new spin of "men versus men" was locked in a civil war to define and control the new gay word, *lifestyle*. This civil war included the very nasty bitch fight between two gay corporations: Liberation Publications (*The Advocate*) and Alternate Publishing (*Drummer*) which created a gay apartheid of artists, writers, and photographers that exists to this day.

The two corporations' rivalry to control and own gay culture divided gay culture and its artists and readers. Their rivalry, represented by John Embry's Blacklist and David Goodstein's villainous exclusionism, destroyed the very unitive notion of Stonewall. The two businesses caused rifts in gay American culture that may take generations to heal. The fighting publishers divided contributors by demanding fierce loyalty: if you work for him, you'll never eat lunch in this town again.

Running a gay profile on the so-called graduates of "The Advocate Experience," I offer that Goodstein's "Advocate Experience," mixed with Marxist-Leninist politics from New York and Berkeley, helped create the Fascistic monster-machine of the politically correct. *Drummer* wanted tie-you-up and tie-you-down erotica. *The Advocate* wanted to sway your, uh, un-chic feelings about déclassé S&M. *Drummer* offered alpha-dog, aggro-lit celebrating rough sex with working-class bravado. *The Advocate* was soignee sweater "essays" ranging from timid to outright negative about S&M preferences.

Let some seasoned scholar or some young graduate student, with a grant, decipher this civil war between corporate publishers seeking control of the "official" gay lifestyle. This apartheid in gay arts and culture, fought out in real time between *The Advocate* and *Drummer*, deserves its own book studied out of research and internal evidence in both magazines, as well as from discussion panels at gay literary conferences and queer studies seminars.

Drummer, like leather culture itself, stayed below the radar, never acceptable to bourgeois homosexuality. This corporate apartheid of talent, from artists to writers to photographers continues to this day in a literary circle jerk that remains a constant conversation running in the background about concerns of fair play and the literary canon of gay publishing. The East Coast literary establishment, famous for books reviewed by *The Advocate*, often "wins" Lammy Awards from the East-Coast-originated Lambda Literary Foundation corporately sponsored by the Los Angeles *Advocate* which owned frequent award winner, Alyson Books, from 1995-2008.

Drummer is symbolic of the West Coast literary establishment of "erotica" which the Lammy Awards, founded in 1989, did not recognize, according to iconic book reviewer Richard Labonte, as a "literary award" category until a dozen years later, as if the previous century of GLBT literary erotica was embarrassing. One needs to follow the DNA of the incest in literature, gay and straight, to see who's fucking, publishing, reviewing, awarding whom and who's jerking each other off. I can be an eyewitness analyst and historian of literary texts, but someone more objective needs to see why back in the 1970s, the Red Queen Arthur Evans, who after founding the Gay Activists Alliance and forming the Faerie Circle, took such a dislike to *Drummer* and to *The Advocate* where he soon enough sold out and became a contributor.

I introduced Evans "Butch Enough" poster with a thumbnail about the mysterious Red Queen in 1978. His glossary: " Zombie Works" is the gym the "Muscle Works"; "All-American Clone" is the popular clothing store, "All-American Boy," which was at that time considered both a sexy and political thing to be; the "Avocado Experience" is the expensive "Advocate Experience" that *Advocate* publisher "David Goodsteal" (David Goodstein) pushed on all *Advocate* employees to increase their "sensitivity," which, of course, turned into "political correctness." "The Advocate Experience" was a joke in San Francisco from the first day any of us heard about it.

As a result of the rivalry between Embry and Goodstein, the middle-class *Advocate* for years mostly hated leather and manliness and Mapplethorpe, rather much continuing Richard Goldstein's nasty East Coast take on leather, "S&M: The Dark Side of Gay Liberation," in *The Village Voice*, July 7, 1975.

That *Village Voice* essay, published when *Drummer* was less than a month old, shows how misunderstood S&M was in New York by Goldstein, about the same time as S&M was being misunderstood in Los Angeles by Goodstein.

THE EDITORIAL

The editorial was written in September, 1978, and published in *Drummer* 25, December 1978.

GETTING OFF
Bitch bites butch, and vice versa...

BUTCH ENOUGH?
Drummer Presents Some "Found" Prose
from the Red Queen, Arthur Evans
by Jack Fritscher

Drummer, The Magazine of Gay Popular Culture, has tracked "The Red Queen" [Arthur Evans] in his/her rapier-like dissection of gay rip-off stereotyping. *Drummer* strives to be the authentic chronicle of gay fantasies, realities, attitudes, fads, postures, and politics. We wanted to send this letter from Mecca out to the national and international gay community of men. Whoever is the writer of this anonymous insight, incite-fully pasted up on Castro walls and lamp-posts in the dead of night, deservedly wins our "Golden Drumsticks Award—even if *Drummer* turns out to be next on the (s)hit list! Remember: Just because a guy is gay doesn't mean you can trust him like a brother.

The crusading New York effeminist Evans wrote about homomasculine life in San Francisco.

AFRAID YOU'RE NOT BUTCH ENOUGH?
by Arthur Evans

Those who join now will get a free enrollment in the HUNGRY PROJECT, a humanitarian program designed to eliminate world hunger by the year 7,000. The HUNGRY PROJECT is based on the brilliant insight that mass starvation is not caused by the greed of the rich but by fuzzy thinking among the poor. As a member of the HUNGRY PROJECT, all you have to do is sign a statement saying you're opposed to hunger. That's it! Elegantly simple! You get to take a strong moral stand and keep all your middle-class privileges.

Worried that the "soft" half of your personality might be showing through? Then join the ZOMBIE WORKS! [The Muscle Works Gym] With our scientifically designed devices, you can make your body look just like a 1950s stereotype of the butch straight male. These wonderful machines were designed by government scientists in Germany during the 1930s. They'll make you look straighter than the straights!

After just a few weeks at the ZOMBIE WORKS, you'll look just like everyone else on Castro Street. No more anxiety over being an individual! Now you'll blend in and look like you came from the same mould as everybody else. Only $250 a month (or $200 a month if you work out before 5 AM).

Once you get your ZOMBIE body, you'll want to complete your image with a new wardrobe from the ALL-AMERICAN CLONE [All-American Boy clothes shop on Castro]. Here you can get a wide assortment of Alligator Shirts specially preserved in formaldehyde since the 1950s and tailored with that tasteful David Eisenhower look.

In addition, you can get blue jeans in six different hues of blue, as well as a fine collection of vinyl visors (in white, red, or green, to match your mood).

This week only, the CLONE is featuring Hong-Kong-Made Naugahyde baseball caps at a special reduced rate of only $45.00 each. When you shop at the ALL-AMERICAN CLONE, you never have to worry about being a big hit on Castro Street. We know that conformity makes sex appeal.

With your ZOMBIE body and CLONE clothes, all that remains is to build up your middle-class values. For this, we offer "The AVOCADO EXPERIENCE," ["The Advocate Experience"], a marathon six-day encounter-group bonanza sponsored by David Goodsteal, [David Goodstein] , the multi-millionaire publisher of The AVOCADO newspaper [*The Advocate*]. Through 108 uninterrupted hours of intense mutual sharing (at only $650 a head!), you'll learn that whatever happens to you in life is solely your own responsibility and nobody else's. —The Red Queen

* * * *

TWO CAN PLAY THIS GAME

I think the reason Evans' eyewitness essay caught my eyewitness response was that during 1978, before I published him in the December issue, we were both, for all our differences, somewhat on the same satirical page. Earlier that year, I had written two *Drummer* satires of "life" on Castro Street and Folsom Street. One was based on the poem *Desiderata* and titled "Gay Deteriorata," *Drummer* 21, March 1978, page 38. The second was "Castro Street Blues 1978,"*Drummer* 24, September 1978.

Satyr Satire...

CASTRO STREET BLUES 1978:
or, Even Blue Boys Get the Cows

Years from now when you read this—
and you will read this—remember
The Way We Were (1978 Style)

In SFO, gay guys talk about sex, gyms, and real estate. They worry about being hot, too hot, or not hot enough. They fly so often they call cities by airline baggage initials. They hate LAX "attitude." They call the West Hollywood boys up for a visit: LAXlanders. They love NYC and want to fly to JFK for some Manhattan "energy." They wish SFO weren't quite such a laid-back fishing village.

Yet gays have the same love affair as straights with SFO. Paradise is the place where when you go there, you get to be yourself. SFO has a grand tradition of tolerance for offbeat characters whose best creation is themselves.

TRUCK SLUTS

On SFO weekends, little Algonquin Clubs brunch at Mena's Norse Cove across from the Castro Theater. They dish the macho boys in the Ford pick-ups jockeying down to the intersection of Sodom and Gomorrah at 18th and Castro. They watch the Harleys, Kawasakis, and Mo-Peds park side by side in front of Toad Hall. Vehicles are an extension of gay sexlife. You are what you drive. Bored by Castro? Cruise over to Polk. Revolted by Polk? Head down to Folsom. Tired of Folsom? Try Land's End.

HOT

Hot is as hot does in SFO. Scratch the word *hot* from gay chatter and stop the conversation. *Hot* is the ultimate review of anything. Roller skating Tuesday nights in South SFO once was *hot*. Currently, every Saturday midnight it's *hot* to light candles on cue at the Strand's ritual *Rocky Horror Picture Show*. *Architectural Digest* on an art-deco table is *hot*. So is the straight outlaw biker magazine *Easy Riders*. So is Disco. So is Crisco.

Only God Herself knows what next will be *hot*.

TWINK CITY

Gays in SFO prefer costumes to clothes. Twinkies live in the Castro. Twinkies are no older than 24 and no taller than 5 foot 6. They sport cropped black moustaches and short black hair often with a gratuitous long lock left at the nape of the neck. They have hairy little muscular bodies of death.

Only a clone could figure the source of the breed.

Twinkies wear too-small Lacoste alligator shirts and size 28-28 pressed jeans. They tuck red hankies meaninglessly in their rear pockets. They prefer thick-soled hiking boots to gain an inch or two in height. With no visible means of support they are whisked away like Dorothy and Toto in Corvettes to Diamond Heights, in Jaguars to Marin, and by PSA to Palm Springs.

FOLSOM TUCKERS

Leathermen hang out South of Market. Their bearded faces have the character that comes from surviving one's own roaring twenties. They admit to no more than "mid-thirties." They corset themselves in tight leather, western, or uniform gear. Unlike the Twinkies, Leathermen own several units of escalating real estate. By night they are rugged, because by day they are disciplined professionals who fill your teeth, bank your money, and draw up your last will and testament. A hanky in a right-hand leather pocket means the tucker is a catcher. In the left, at best he'll negotiate who will pitch. Leathermen prefer cycles and Jeeps, but only as second vehicles. Leathermen look fine in the acid-red light of bars and baths on Folsom. At 2 AM in the back of a fluorescent MUNI bus, they look like mackerel.

GYM TRICKS

In SFO, no one who is anyone lives alone. Gays have roommates to handle press releases. Roommates blab to friends what hot tricks you were up to the night before. In LAX, chandeliers are for show. In SFO chandeliers are for swinging from. You can buy designer track lights at "Work Wonders" (which should be the name of a gym, but isn't).

Bodies are, after all, what this is all about.

A guy gets in shape by pumping iron M-W-F at the Pump Room. Some work up a sweat at the Y with its game-set-and-match-making of dollies in Levi's. More re-fined types pop their niacin, and get their cardiovascular flush riding their naughty Nautilus exercise machines sidesaddle. Steroids to build muscular bulk are the street drug favored by jocks. At the hustlers' corner of Sutter and Polk, ten Arnold Schwarzeneggers loiter under a lighting shop sign that says, "Any object made into a lamp."

THAT'S ENTERTAINMENT?

Spectacular parties in SFO are not thrown. They're produced. Everybody is a star. Disco systems are flown in for the night from NYC. Fountains splash. Light shows flash. Grapes cascade. Rome declines. Aerialists perform above oiled wrestlers. Stud-mouse Mr. America types pose like 200 pounds of dynamite that won't go off.

SFO doesn't measure gay Saturday Night Fever with an oral thermometer.

Start dancing at Alfie's on Market, move on to the I-Beam on Haight, and cruise out at Trocadero Transfer, South of Market. Collapse at dawn in the tubs on Folsom. Civilizations are judged by their plumbing. The SFO gay subculture bathes in elegant whirlpool grottos and Fellini Memorial steam rooms.

The hallways at the baths are the real gay parade.

NATURALLY GAY

American boys are not raised to be gay. Mom never takes her son aside the way she does her daughter and says, "Look, kid, you're going to be gay. Lose some weight." Gay kids have to figure it out themselves. SFO is full of theories. "Would Anita understand," a gay priest confides at the Elephant Walk, "that God calls certain people to a gay vocation? Homosexuality is a religion." Down the bar, twin Latino gay brothers smirk and say they were born again, yeah, born again for Salsa. Outside the Star Pharmacy, an ancient peg-legged newsboy cackles out the single raw word, "*Chronicle!*"

Precisely because of the newspaper headlines from the dark interior of the American continent, gays bring their hearts and other parts to SFO.

THE STREET WHERE YOU LIVE

Sunday afternoons male belly dancers perform for coin-tossing crowds in front of the Hibernia Bank [at the south-east corner of 18th and Castro, aka "Hibernia Beach"]. A blond boy with punk-chopped hair recently mimicked the belly-boys' boogie. He wrapped himself in a swirl of bedspreads and garter belts. He twirled like a laundromat dryer exploding. The crowd threw pennies at him as hard as they could. He retreated to play toreador with the traffic.

Buses often drive picture-taking tourists through the Castro. Gay photographers snap back through the bus windows at the Iowans dressed in their polyester Protestant Anita-wear. Cameras are the guns of our time. SFO supervisor Harvey Milk's Castro Camera develops the film.

STAR PHARMACY

A man leans against the Star Pharmacy. He played a bit part in *Close Encounters of the Third Kind*. He saw ACT's *Travesties* twice. He jots notes for the very, very wonderful screen comedy he is writing about a macho type who freaks out at 18th and Castro. Movie mad scenes fascinate gay men. In his script, his jock hero blocks traffic by locking himself inside his truck in the center of the intersection. He rubs Oil of Olay all over his face, screaming in three languages how moist he is. A crowd gathers on this very Castro spot where a baby was born on an 8 Market/Ferry bus, attended to by a dozen gay waiters. Restaurants again carry white towels to the intersection. The man jots more notes.

The Star Pharmacy is closed on Sundays. Just when you need aspirin, where is the Star's Jackie, the Sweetheart of the Castro? In SFO, gay refrigerators carry gay staples in their gay freezers: ice cubes, brownies, and poppers.

DOWN HERE ON A VISIT [Reference to Christopher Isherwood's 1962 novel *Down There on a Visit*]

In SFO, believe it or not, some gays are native to the City. One third-generation gay man centers himself against the gay immigrant madness. He shuns motorcycle christenings, tricycle races, bedraggled empresses, and full-moon bar promo parties. He owns no albums by Donna Summer. He meditates. He refuses to do to himself gay illnesses with [hepatitis] symptoms like an RCA Colortrak TV commercial: "My eyes are yellow, my urine's brown, my shit is white." In SFO, love is always chance-y. But better a positive visit to the clinic than never to have loved at all.

OUTER SPACE

"Maybe we gays are a religion," he says. "More likely, the difference between straight and gay is simple. Straight people are the real earthlings. Gay people are just dropped down on this planet for a visit. That's why we seem alien.

Another difference is straight people don't stand you up for dinner."

He looks down at his vintage Earth Shoes.

"With all this religion and politics, I don't know how long we can hang around on Castro singing some gay national anthem like 'Over the Rainbow.' Gay surveillance squads on Folsom? Gay deputy sheriffs? Bryant? Briggs? Shit! I can't wait till we all fly back to Alpha Centauri."

Just like the last reel of *Rocky Horror Picture Show*.

Meanwhile, in SFO, without pecs you're dead.

DRUMMER

ISSUE 139/$5.95

Remembrance Of SLEAZE
Past...And Present And Future
By Jack Fritscher

REXLAND
All New Art By Rex

THE CATACOMB
A History By G. Rubin

USSM/ONE
A Flogging Odyssey

MR. DRUMMER 1990—91
The Search Begins

Cover Photograph by Jim Wigler

DISTRIBUTION TO MINORS PROHIBITED

DANNY BECK
Mr. East Canada Drummer

CHAPTER 16

DRUMMER: FIRST VICTIM OF THE CULTURE WAR

THE SLAVE AUCTION SPRING OF 1976

The Final Word Published in *Drummer* Ended with .com

- Born (Again) to Raise Hell: End-Time Christians vs. Satanic *Drummer*
- *The Advocate* Prejudice Against Leather Culture and Gay Masculine Identity
- Leather Contests: International Mr. Leather (IML) Begets Mr. Drummer
- Leather Immigrant: Val Martin, First "Mr. Drummer"
- John Embry's Lover from Spain, Mario Simon: "Evita" as "Mrs. Drummer"
- Photographer Lionel Biron: Social Justice, Gay Liberation, and *The Advocate*
- *Drummer* Stars: JimEd Thompson, Chris Burns, Scott O'Hara

John Embry was incorrigible. He wouldn't have changed if we had put a horsehead in his bed. Nevertheless, Godfather Embry, out in the La-La-Land of LA in 1975, should have paid smarter attention to the enemies and allies who were out there doing what amounted to a practicum in the hateful queer theory practiced by religious fundamentalists. Embry's shady behavior set *Drummer* up as one of the first victims of the culture-war uprisings by 1970s Christian conservatives like Ed Davis, Anita Bryant, John Briggs, Pat Robertson, and Jerry Falwell who created his Moral Majority mix of church and state in 1979.

Had he gathered his political wits, Embry could have done leather culture a service by rebutting the anti-leather Richard Goldstein at the *Village Voice*, and, in so doing, he might have decided to turn the seventeen-day-old *Drummer* off its own suicidal course of forbidden topics in issues 2, 3, and

4 that alerted the LAPD that gay men in leather were up to something new and wicked. However, in all of *Drummer*, I found only one passing reference to Goldstein's "S&M: The Dark Side of Gay Liberation" in a "Letter to the Editor," titled "Hanky Panky," *Drummer* 10, page 4, proving Embry knew about the article and thought it a joke.

> An article on S&M in New York's *Village Voice* the summer of 1975 started the current fad [pennies tied into color-coded hankies so they'd swing fetchingly from your butt at the disco], and they're still laughing about it back in the [*Village Voice*] press room.

In a slight historical correction, the writer of the letter was wrong: the hanky code, with and without pennies, existed for many years coast to coast before Goldstein mentioned it. Proof lies in *Drummer* 1, published before the Goldstein piece, in which editor-in-chief, Jeanne Barney, discussed what I called, deep back in the 1960s when the fad began, the "semaphore of hankies." The point is that Goldstein's vanilla rant required instant refutation by leatherfolk as much as did the rants of the faith-based Fascists rising on the religious right.

Embry may have missed out fingering Goldstein, but he was on the money tagging 1) the LAPD; 2) the anti-leather, and politically correct tabloid, *The Advocate*; 3) the rising Orange-Juice queen, Anita Bryant, who taught the Religious Right its anti-gay tactics continuing into the 21st century; and 4) the grotesque Southern California congressman, John Briggs, who powered up United States Senator Jesse Helms. In 1989, homophobe Helms, funded by his own tobacco state's taxes and Political Action Committees, condemned the premier photographer of leather culture, Robert Mapplethorpe, and dismantled funding of the National Endowment for the Arts in the early 1990s.

However, Embry's purpose for *Drummer* soon revealed itself as business not politics. After he was burned by the lesson taught him by the LAPD Slave Auction bust, he retreated to his "basic default identity" as a mail-order sex-toy salesman named "Robert Payne." For all his process-analysis fiction about S&M written by Payne aka Embry, he seemed not to comprehend the message of the decade's most popular straight book among leathermen, *Zen and the Art of Motorcycle Maintenance* (1974), except insofar as he knew the price of the poppers he sold, but not the value of the pages he sold. He never understood the Zen and the Art of *Drummer* Maintenance.

Embry had not conceived of *Drummer* as a cultural or literary or political force. He founded the magazine with its sex stories and photos as attractive fishwrap around his centerfold mail-order catalogue where he made his real money selling over-priced cock rings, tit clamps, dildos, and poppers retail to subscribers closeted in small American towns. In fact, Embry named his business venture "Alternate Publishing" because his first love was not *Drummer,* but rather his first-intended magazine named *The Alternate* which he founded specifically to compete with *The Advocate.* However, *The Alternate* was more Baby June than Gypsy Rose Lee and it never took off.

Embry was not one of the late-night players at the baths on Folsom where *Drummer* staff and readers were power-fisting Foucault into a higher consciousness just to shut him up and make him scream, "Merde!" Foucault was fifty-four and French, Embry was forty-nine and bourgeois, and I was thirty-six and hustling sex when *Drummer* debuted in San Francisco where Foucault during his tenure in Berkeley had long been a player on Folsom Street.

BORN (AGAIN) TO RAISE HELL: END-TIME ABOMINATION

Also, at the very moment in March, 1977, when Embry was propositioning me to become editor of *Drummer,* I had to consider who Embry was and what political and legal mistakes he may have committed, because a new Christian Fundamentalist book, *The Homosexual Revolution: End-Time Abomination,* written in 1977 by D. A. Noebel, was fanning the flames around the stake at which the onward-marching Christian soldiers like Anita Bryant and John Briggs wanted to burn the kind of sinners who would publish a cultural occasion of sin such as *Drummer.*

What's the difference between dancing around a May Pole and burning at the stake?

Very specifically aware of the "Satanic" *Drummer,* Noebel wrote:

> On April 14, 1976, gay community leaders complained about the arrest of 40 persons in what police called a sado-masochistic slave market [the Drummer Slave Auction]. Captain Jack Wilson said the building in which the auction took place was equipped with dungeons and cell blocks. In the dungeons were all forms of chains and articles of restraint. Mark IV Club [4424 Melrose] was maintained by a group calling itself "the Leather Fraternity" [the name of Embry's mail-order club which he owned separately from *Drummer*] as a private club for homosexuals and sado-masochism cultists.

Who provokes cops? Embry was not Thoreau using passive resistance against taxes. He caused his own trouble baiting the LAPD by advertising a "Slave Auction" to Ed Davis who was of an age alarmed by the perils of the words "white slavery." In the early twentieth century, the urban legend of "white slavery" was a pop-culture term of sexual, and often racial, panic regarding young white women forced into prostitution by nonwhite men, usually Asians xenophobically color-coordinated as the "yellow peril." (See the camp film, *Thoroughly Modern Millie*, 1967.) At that time, genuine awareness of international sex trafficking was forty years in the future. In addition, Embry turned his private charity function—limited at first to his "Leather Fraternity" members—into an event open to any of the paying public seeking cheap thrills. Without irony, the LAPD charged Embry with breaking a post-Civil War law forbidding slavery.

Embry made himself the Marie Antoinette of gay publishing.

And the gendarmes knew exactly what to do.

PENIS ENVY: HOW INTERNATIONAL MR. LEATHER (IML) BEGAT THE MR. DRUMMER CONTEST

In the following scenario I was an eyewitness because I was the one being recruited to start the first Mr. Drummer Contest. In 1979, Dom Orejudos and Chuck Renslow in Chicago invented their International Mr. Leather Contest out of their previous experiences producing sanctioned AAU physique contests out of their Triumph Gym where they showcased straight bodybuilders for discreet gay audiences. On a sunny afternoon in 1964, I attended one of their contests on the quiet basketball floor of the Lawson YMCA where a half-dozen straight musclemen—likely graduates from Kris Studio—took one step up onto a large wooden box to pose, up close, under a light clipped onto the basketball hoop, moving gracefully in the silence, no music, so that the ten men in the audience, each sitting solo and aloof, in the twenty metal folding chairs might applaud. It was too intimate for me to uncloset myself by filming with my Super-8 camera. Because the contest was so simply produced, it was almost hands-on hot, just as was the new IML, perfectly produced, fifteen years later.

Embry wanted his own huge "production number" to compete with Renslow whom he envied for entering the leather scene in 1950, twenty-five years before the first issue of *Drummer*. He came into my office and told me he wanted me to begin producing a "Mr. Drummer Contest." As if speaking one of his dialog balloons in a *Drummer* cartoon strip, he said something like: "Lots of guys posing for free. Lots of photos." Monthly magazines salivate for fresh material. Filling *Drummer* each month was a huge task, even when Embry plagiarized articles from straight men's adventure magazines. Filling it with original material was even bigger. And that was my job.

He wanted me to produce and manage the first Mr. Drummer Contest, because I was editor-in-chief and he knew from my resume that I had years of experience producing events and the then-popular "happenings" at universities, museums, and in the Folsom Street leather bar, the No Name. Its manager, my longtime pal, the redheaded poet, Ron Johnson (1935-1998), also helped me schedule and videotape oral histories for my *Drummer* column, "Rear-View Mirror." Johnson, a friend and peer of Thom Gunn on Folsom Street, authored many books including *To Do as Adam Did: The Collected Poems of Ronald Johnson*, 2000.

Ron Johnson, with his partner, Mario Pirami, founded the Rainbow Motorcycle Club in 1972. The club's home bar was then the No Name. The RMC, whose especially wild biker membership was by invitation only and more exclusive than the Catacombs, continues to exist rapaciously and below the average gay radar in the second decade of the twenty-first century. In his February 12, 1992, letter to all the RMC, Ron Johnson documented the tradition of Folsom Street performance-art happenings in the early 1970s before commercial leather contests replaced them:

Dudes—
This year marks the 20th anniversary of the club, and it's high time to throw a bash. Our Christmas party was so fine we've got to really rise (or stoop) to the occasion—no?
....One of the things that made the Xmas party such a great success was Lurch as Santa on a beer-shell throne, greeting one and all, and we need again to come up with something so extraordinarily sleazy and daring they'll all talk about it after. Not many now remember the first anniversary RMC party [1973] where Jack Fritscher was the Entertainment Committee. He brought in [to the No Name] three stand-up cages with live, sexy slaves inside. Spotlights! Crowd focus! Promiscuous flagellation! Frenzy! [Plus his live-action cast, three slide projectors, and two Super-8 projectors of his transparencies and leather films]....Where can we go from there?
At the Lone Star [bar], of course...
—Ron Johnson

I recoiled from Embry's rip-off proposal. I did not want to steal thunder from Orejudos and Renslow, two artist-entrepreneurs I had known in my formative leather years in Chicago where my masculine-identified "leather roots" had come out sexually, esthetically, and philosophically in the late 1950s and early 1960s. In 1990, the contentious Embry proved my instincts were correct when he summed up twenty years of his subtle enmity against Renslow on the inside back cover of *Manifest Reader* 12: "The Mr. Drummer Contests have always been more exciting than the International Mr. Leather shows."

In fact, Embry from Arizona, Hawaii, LA, and other push-pins on the map, had no idea that as a gay-leather "medium" I was channeling and evolving the Chicago homomasculinist leather-art scene of Orejudos-Renslow into San Francisco *Drummer*. Embry also did not know of the sexual reach of Orejudos-Renslow who kindly supplied *Drummer* contributor, Sam Steward, with hustlers. As he became a man of a certain age, Steward, profiled in Justin Spring's *Secret Historian*, revealed in *Chapters from an Autobiography* (page 119):

> I went into the land where Everyman must eventually go, that of the older human being...romantic encounters...were vanishing.... No question: one had to begin to purchase, or do without—and here again the Chicago studio [Kris] which had [previously] pimped for me helped me enormously. They sent me many young men....

I advised Embry not to start a Mr. Drummer Contest because it would sap the company's time, energy, and money. (In the year 2000 at leatherweb.com, Robert Davolt revealed that the Mr. Drummer Contest "lost money for at least fifteen out of eighteen years.") I predicted to Embry that the tail would wag the dog. I reminded him every issue of *Drummer* was notoriously behind schedule because of his misguided budgets. The Fourth Anniversary Issue coming up was only *Drummer* 30 which, if published monthly, should have been *Drummer* 48. I told him that for me writing and editing *Drummer* meant everything in political and erotic terms of masculine-identified gay identity. I saw *Drummer* as the wave of the future which I was keenly aware of positioning because I had been one of the founding members of the American Popular Culture Association (1968), and had militated, before Stonewall, for the PCA to include gay popular culture in university curricula.

I told him *no*.

Nobody told John Embry *no* and got away with it.

That look on that "Publisher Dearest" face!

Like the LAPD, I could not be bent to his purposes.

Previous lack of payment of my wages already had me considering leaving *Drummer*, but his never-ending imperial LA attitude was not attractive in laid-back San Francisco where no one wanted to be Embry's slave. He made a big mistake in his pathetic fallacy. He figured because *Drummer* was about BDSM, he was master of a staff of slaves. As a result, the average length of employment inside the *Drummer* office in the late 1970s was six minutes to six months. When I got my pal David Hurles/Old Reliable hired in to edit *The Alternate*, he lasted ten days before the twisted tag team of John Embry and John Rowberry, both up from LA, drove him out the door with their shenanigans.

As it turned out in the leather timeline, I wrote the leather world's first article on the first IML in *Drummer* (*Drummer* 31, September 1979). This IML article was also the first appearance in print of my high-concept coinage, *homomasculinity*, which I applied to IML.

Embry printed my article because my friend Dom Orejudos/Etienne of IML had sent to me, care of *Drummer*, a dozen free photographs of the sexy contestants. My enunciated title, "The Envelope, Pleez," was my little sneer at the idea of male beauty contests in general. Nevertheless, I celebrated IML with a bit of philosophy about masculine-identified leather as well as with ironic lines such as "...the hottest twelve contestants this side of the Apostles."

The feature article was reprinted in the book, *International Mr. Leather: 25 Years of Champions*, compiled by Joseph W. Bean for IML, Inc. and the Leather Archives & Museum, Chicago (2004).

(In 1989, it was not *Drummer*, but the magazine *FirstHand Events*, produced by publisher Jackie Lewis, that became the "official magazine of IML." See *Drummer* 128 [May 1989], page 86.)

In a zero-degrees-of-separation letter from Boulder, Colorado, October 12, 1988, Dom Orejudos expressed his interest in my translating his drawings from page to screen in the leather-heritage "Video Gallery" artist series I was shooting at Palm Drive Video featuring his peers Rex, A. Jay, Domino, Skipper, and the Hun.

Dom Orejudos wrote:

> Hi Jack:...Yes, let's follow through on discussing the possibility of an Etienne video gallery by you at Palm Drive. I've had some ideas in that area (video) for some time now, and I'm sure we could come up with something interesting. I enjoyed visiting with you during

the Mr. Drummer Contest weekend [We were both judges]...I'll look forward to seeing you again....Sincerely, Dom

His last years of illness kept Dom from going forward with the project. Without producing a video of his art, and before the futurism of the internet, he died September 24, 1991. The Leather Archives & Museum, however, had been founded principally to preserve his work.

In 1981, as if the debt-ridden Mr. Drummer Contest were not drain enough, Embry began awarding the sash-rash title, "Mr. Manifest," thankfully without a contest, through his new *Manifest Reader*. In point of fact, his concept "Mr. Manifest" was more a direct imitation of my invention of "Tough Customers" in *Drummer*, because "Mr. Manifest" contestants were asked to submit photos of themselves for free publication. In 1989, he was still plugging his faux "contest" in a full-page advertisement in his "Virtual *Drummer*," *Manifest Reader* 9, page 53.

In the end, International Mr. Leather (IML) had the last word and the last laugh.

The last ad on the last back cover of the last issue of *Drummer* 214 (April 1999) was for the "1999 IML Contest."

And the last word of that ad was the last word printed in *Drummer*: .com.

A TALE OF 2 IMMIGRANTS: VAL MARTIN (MR. DRUMMER) & MARIO SIMON ("MRS. DRUMMER")

Val Martin, as no one has yet analyzed, was swept up as an immigrant pawn in all this. For Embry, Val Martin was the incarnate alter-ego of *Drummer*. Not only was he the star of both *Sextool* and *Born to Raise Hell* in 1975, he was the avatar leatherman whose face and torso graced the covers and centerfolds of several pre-Slave Auction issues in 1975, including issues 2, 3, and 8. For the LAPD, Val Martin was a trophy arrest. He was the figurehead Chief Ed Davis wanted to mount on his wall. He wanted to put the fear of God into all the macho fags in leather bars he couldn't bust fast enough. The LAPD, as did we all, found Val Martin to be "a person of interest."

Val Martin was a world-class stud exuding mystery, romantic risk, and Latin machismo. He was the other side of the American existentialist hard man, the blond WASP, Fred Halsted who had directed him in *Sextool*. The deep, dark secret of his real name, Jeanne Barney, told me was "Vallot Martinelli" which sounded Italian, although he was born in Colombia, South America. He claimed to have been a New York City cop. He had wanted to join the LAPD, but disliked the homophobia.

Drummer artist Olaf Odegaard explained in his 1984 eyewitness profile of Val Martin in *Connection*:

> The door to Val Martin's apartment in Hollywood was open... the master had never before given an interview.... Val grew up on a farm in Brazil [*sic*]. He had 18 sisters and no brothers. He has been married and has two children. An American citizen, he has been in this country for 18 years. He speaks Portuguese, Italian, Spanish, and English. A Cancer, he studied medicine for four years and has worked as a farmer, a handyman, a construction worker, a horse trainer [shades of almost all the Village People]. He spent three years in the army and worked as a police officer in New York City.... One entire wall [of the apartment] contains representations of Val by numerous artists and sculptors.

In LA, Val Martin was a business partner with my pal, Dick Saunders, owner of the throbbing Probe disco chronicled in director Paul Schrader's Richard Gere film, *American Gigolo* (1980).

In the zero degrees of publishing around Val Martin and *Drummer*, Dick Saunders was the editor and publisher of *Probers*, the newsletter of Probe disco from December 1980-September 1983, and he told me he knows the identity of the burglar-arsonist who got away with setting Probe ablaze on September 21, 1981. Fifteen years earlier, as the homomasculine world began mobilizing toward leather and western gear, thus anticipating in 1965 the 1975 DNA of *Drummer*, Saunders wrote and published the LA tabloid, *Frontier Bulletin Gazette*, from January 1965-October 1969, which Embry read while dreaming up *Drummer*. In our zero-degrees *Drummer* Salon during the late 1970s-1980s, Saunders and I shared for two years—without knowing it—an extremely handsome sex-bomb body-builder lover who hustled each of us on identical rides until the day we compared notes, and it dawned on us, that "his guy" and "my guy" were one guy whom we immediately dumped and sent running for cover back to the Redneck Riviera where he came from.

Val Martin was thirty-six when arrested at the Slave Auction. Born three weeks after me on July 16, 1939, he died at forty-five on April 13,

1985, as inscribed in Jeanne Barney's *Rolodex of the Dead*. She wrote me on September 25, 2006:

> When I talked to Val for our piece on bestiality, he was quite forthcoming and said that he'd had no problem screwing poultry or livestock, but that he couldn't make it with a dog because, he said, "They have such bad breath." [That's] absolutely [Barney quipped] one of THE best lines of all time.

Val Martin was, in 180-degree sense, the photogenic and masculine version of Embry's own longtime Latin lover, Mario Simon, who was an immigrant from Spain to LA, and built chunky like Embry. When Mario Simon arrived as a human hatbox with the *Drummer* luggage in San Francisco, Embry announced Mario as "a singer who is famous in Spain for his best-selling disco recordings." Al Shapiro considered working the following line into his satirical *Harry Chess*: "I'm 'famous in Spain' like Jerry Lewis is 'beloved in France.'" Jeanne Barney remembered that Larry Townsend openly jibed Embry by saying, "Give my regards to that 'Puerto Rican.'" And Embry would reply, "The 'Puerto Rican' says hello."

Embry himself revealed in *Manifest Reader* 26 (January 1996) that even when they lived in LA, Mario was not suited for the business of Alternate Publishing's enterprises. Mario shouldered a chip of an attitude about Embry's moving them to San Francisco because show biz is in LA. Mario Simon as Embry's life partner had a right to a certain status and dignity. But, I must confess, the irreverent 1970s staff at Divisadero *Drummer*, thought him a condescending LA attitude queen who had arrived in San Francisco on a *vaporetto* of his own imagining.

One camp image clung to him: being arrested in a splash of sangria at the Slave Auction. Embry later verified the basis of the running joke in *Super MR* #5, page 35: For the event, "Mario...prepared gallons of real Spanish sangria, with red wine and fresh fruit."

Rarely did Mario show up at our office, but when he did appear, he entered the room voice first, swathed in clouds of Hai Karate cologne, dragging his mink. Channeling the iconic 1940s film star, Maria Felix, who was the Mexican Marilyn Monroe, Mario exuded an attitude of petulant entitlement, even though during my editorship he had nothing to do with *Drummer* except parade through the office carrying his Capezio shoulderbag stuffed with his Toto-like Cairn Terrier named "Mac" whom Embry flew in from Spain. His English was a new and second language, and so not very useful to an American magazine needing a proofreader.

In the summer of 1978, *Evita* opened at the Orpheum in San Francisco before its premiere on Broadway. If Mario had stood in front of the *Evita* poster, he would have disappeared. Later in 1990, type-casting struck, and he appeared, where he always longed to be, in Southern California on stage in Oxnard in a "Music Theater of Ventura County" production of *Evita*. He played Magaldi, the over-the-top tango singer who gives Evita her first leg up singing "On This Night of a Thousand Stars."

Embry once told me, without any sense of irony, that Mario wooed him and won him on their second date by taking out a guitar and singing "Feelings."

You just can't make this stuff up!

(See *Manifest Reader* 26, January 1996, page 52.)

"Mario Simon," as spelled in his obituary (March 5, 1942-December 12, 1993), was also known as "Mario Simone." Long after I exited, Embry listed "Mario Simone" on the masthead of *Drummer* 57 (October 1982) as "General Manager" which was optimistic—and, one figures, tax-deductible, with insurance coverage. Benefits were never offered to us workers. *Drummer* 60 (January 1983) featured a quarter-page "house" ad of Mario wearing a leather vest and disco headband; the text read simply: "Leather Disco, Valverde, 14, Madrid 13, Spain." In 1985, the full inside-back cover of *Drummer* 81 (February 1984) blatted perhaps the worst advertising copy in history with Embry's flat-footed prose pushing singer "Mario Simon's hot new song done by a better singer than one hears in pop music these days. It is exciting."

Produced by Embry's Wings Distributing, Mario's "Drummerman" was backed with "Be My Clown"—insert joke here—and was available on cassette through mail-order for $7.95. *Drummer*'s Tenth Anniversary Party was also the finals of the Mr. Drummer Contest 1985 at the Japan Center Theater. Reporting that event in *Drummer* 85 (December 1985), pages 8 and 10, Embry's "Social Notes" published a Robert Pruzan photo of Mario Simon, noting: "Mario Simon belts out...the show-stopper 'Drummerman'... his Wings recording over the huge theater sound system. It was electrifying."

Eyewitness Jeanne Barney assessed the Embry-Simon vortex that twisted the psychology of both the LA and San Francisco offices where Mario Simon treated all the staff including Barney, Shapiro, Rowberry, and me, like dirt. "Mario," she said, "was only into the psychological sadism that he could inflict on others. He would leave John home alone while he went out dancing with the other Latinas." In that email dated September 24, 2006, Jeanne Barney recalled:

Mario Simon was an arrogant, pretentious queen. I never liked him, but tolerated him for John's sake; and Mario was not shy about exhibiting his fierce jealousy of me and my longstanding relationship with John. Consider the contrast: John's Own True Love, about/for whom he was/is writing *Epilogue*, was fair but not blond. His successor was dark-haired, but had a similar name: hmmmm, Dr. Freud. (Number 1 was Don Briggs and Number 2 was Don Britt.) I think that John took up with Mario because Mario was the only person who would have him. When Don Briggs got sober at AA, he left John. Don Britt, who was also an alcoholic, left John for Vince Lumbleau, a local realtor—and a REALLY HEAVY TOP, as opposed to John. The only types John really didn't like were milk-skinned redheads [which may explain Embry's dismissive attitude to my milky-red lover, David Sparrow who worked freelance as a *Drummer* photographer]. Otherwise, I think his main criterion was that they were breathing.

At the northwest corner of 11th Street and Folsom, photographer Jim Stewart managed the *Drummer* bar and swimming pool which had been Allan Lowery's Leatherneck bar and became Embry and Simon's "The Plunge." Stewart whom I had met in 1974 when he was manager of a popular movie theater, and responsible for all of its receipts, was an eyewitness of what it was like doing business with Embry and Simon at *Drummer*, and how hard it was to be paid. Rumors alleged that *Drummer* funds were often deposited in Mario Simon's name and that Mario Simon, perhaps behind even Embry's back, had secret accounts whose total, according to Rick Leathers, who managed the office for Embry for eleven years, went allegedly to Mario's relatives in Spain. Jim Stewart wrote to me on September 21, 2007:

Dear Jack,
 Working for John and Mario at the bar was a trip. Their heads didn't really seem to be into running a bar/swim club. Their ideas seemed to fit more into Southern California than San Francisco, South of Market. For instance the leather shop had one mannequin to display leather harnesses, etc. It was a surfer boy. I convinced John to let me trade it in for two male mannequins that looked more like they belonged in a San Francisco leather bar. John would sometimes call meetings of the bar staff for suggestions. However, he was very reluctant to follow through on any of them.

Either the two of them had no head for finance or they were working very close to the bone or both. I used to walk the previous night's cash receipts, complete with register tapes, paid bills, etc., over to *Drummer* offices on—was it Natoma?—in a bank bag. John would either say, "Just put it down over there," or, "Just give it to Mario." In either case I never saw anybody ever count it to verify what was what. It sure was not like I had been taught by the scrupulous Butterfield Theater Chain when I managed the Campus Theater in Kalamazoo. One must remember that when I worked for John and Mario in 1980-1981, these were the days before banks had widespread computer use and instant deposit.

When payday rolled around, Mario would take the cash and deposit it in a branch bank way out in the Avenues [out by the ocean far from South of Market] just before John would write the paychecks. If you took your paycheck to the main branch downtown, the record of the deposit would not have been received and the account would be underfunded to cash the paychecks. If you waited a day or two, and all paychecks were cashed, someone usually came up short. John would apologize and sometimes cash it himself, or tell you to go back to the bank again as Mario had just made another deposit. What a way to run a business. Well, Max Morales and I finally figured out what was happening. We'd try to predict Mario's moves and would get on Max's BMW motorcycle and go over to the branch bank in the Avenues to cash our checks. An added bonus of going to the bank in the Avenues—there was a great butcher shop just across the street from the bank—much better than anything I could get at the Dented Can grocery South of Market.

Let me know if I can help you with anything else with your book endeavor. Since I have seriously started writing, I realize how much work is really involved.
—Jim Stewart

Meanwhile, back in 1976, Val Martin on the cover of *Drummer* was a "Wanted Poster" to LAPD Chief Ed Davis.

Drummer became a brand name by hiring Val Martin who had the Universal Appeal of his face, his body, his name, his genial personality, his porn-film celebrity from Fred Halsted's *Sextool*, Terry LeGrand and Roger Earl's *Born to Raise Hell*, and his public appearances at popular leather venues where crowds cheered his charisma.

Val Martin was *Drummer*.

After a three-way conversation including Embry, Al Shapiro, and me, we three alone agreed unanimously that Val Martin was the logical hot guy to be the first Mr. Drummer at the CMC Carnival, November 1979.

We *appointed* Val Martin to the title.

Two years later, contestants *competed* for the title.

The drum iconography of being a "Drummerman" began in 1977 with a series of publicity photos shot with no contest in mind. In these centerfold photos in *The Best and the Worst of Drummer*, pages 40-41, each nude model is shot with a large marching drum posed over his genitals. The 360-degree-sides of the drum are cleverly pasted with covers of early *Drummer*. The caption reads:

> There have been many "Drummers" [guys carrying a drum] since the magazine first took shape. When *Drummer* was a newspaper years ago, a drummer [nude and posed like the aggressive drummer in the American Revolution painting of three men carrying flag, fife, and drum] by [photographer] Pat Rocco graced its editorial page. Much more recently [for photographer Hy Chase], sex superstar Jack Wrangler posed, wearing nothing but a drum. Ken [a model shot by Dave Sands] grabbed up the drum at the Pleasure Chest in our [First] Anniversary Issue. Chuck Quinlan, winner of "Mr. Groovey Guy" and "Mr. CMC Carnival" [shot by Rob Clayton] posed for us as well. [All the models happened to be white.] Then Mr. USA [who happened to be African-American and unidentified] posed for us during a session with [British actor and photographer] Roy Dean [1925-2002, who was much published in LA *Drummer*, including his cover of Val Martin body-painted by Cliff Raven for *Drummer* 8 (September 1976)].

Val Martin's image branded *Drummer* visually in the 1970s.

I adored Val Martin's homomasculine sexiness personally and professionally. He was a sweet man, and very hot and sensual at pot parties and orgies at his apartment near Folsom Street. As a photographer, I lensed him on several occasions, including the Fritscher-Sparrow coded fisting photograph of him and his partner, Bob Hyslop, on the cover of *Drummer* 30. On May 20, 1979, I also shot 35 photos of the Martin-Hyslop duo for the black-and-white "Spit" centerfold of *Drummer* 31 in which Embry published my work, but credited the photos to David Sparrow who was not even present at the Sonoma County shoot north of the Golden Gate Bridge. Without permission, Embry reprinted one of my photos of Val Martin in *Drummer Rides Again* (1979), page 45, and again spitefully credited "David Sparrow." Long after Embry departed *Drummer*, I shot a second "Spit" photo series, featuring Palm Drive models Goliath and Thrasher, for the color centerfold of *Drummer* 148 (April 1991) which Tony DeBlase, after selling *Drummer*, also published as the cover of his *DungeonMaster* 47 (January 1994). Building that *Drummer* 148 issue on the "rough sex" idea I had suggested when he asked me for a theme, DeBlase featured my *Drummer* story "USMC Slap Captain" and reviews of two of my roughest videos, *Slap Happy* and *Rough Night at the Jockstrap Gym*.

Four years before Val was "Mr. Drummer," he was the first "Mr. Leather" chosen at the Hawks' Leather Sabbat, Halloween 1975, at Troopers' Auditorium, Los Angeles.

That event was emceed by another immigrant, my longtime friend, Peter Bromilow (1933-1994). We met as playmates through Jim Kane in 1969. He was a strapping tall leatherman and British stage actor who had played in many films, including the role of the butch knight, Sir Sagramore, in the film, *Camelot* (1967). A friend of the film's star, Vanessa Redgrave, Bromilow came to Hollywood to shoot the musical at Warner Brothers in Burbank, and he never left. He appeared in many films including David Lynch's *Wild at Heart* (1992). He often visited me in San Francisco and we loved to hang out midday at a little lunch-and-beer-bar with outdoor tables, sitting among the returning fishermen on the sunny boat docks in China Basin, south of South of Market before its charm gave way to urban developers. Peter's wicked wit made him a popular LA leather personality and event emcee. In his Hollywood apartment where we smoked cigars, drank wine, and had sex, he had hung a poster-size framed photo of his very longtime friends, Vanessa Redgrave and Glenda Jackson, both in period-drag costume for their film, *Mary Queen of Scots* (1971). The duo had signed it: "Dear Peter, From two Queens to an even bigger Queen! —Vanessa and Glenda."

The LAPD vice squad, connecting circumstantial dots, drew a target on Val Martin's back. His face had been on the back cover of *Drummer* 2 and on the front cover of *Drummer* 3 which reported his leather coronation by the Hawks motorcycle club. *Drummer* 3 also condemned the LAPD for raiding the fundraiser at the Black Pipe bar. Val did not work for *Drummer*. He had nothing to do with *Drummer* editorial policy and he had done nothing illegal, but the LAPD had a price on his head because he was the "recruiting poster" for the kind of new masculine queers that the cops saw walking out of the bars—and into the pages of *Drummer* which recruited even more butch faggots into the new leather bars that mystified the cops, who thought they owned masculinity.

These "threatening" homomasculine gays were not the usual femme and drag stereotypes that homophobes love to hate because if they can define us as "men wanting to be women," then they can abuse us the way they abuse women.

FRED HALSTED, THE SLAVE AUCTION, AND *THE ADVOCATE*

When the LAPD arrested forty-two people at the Drummer Slave Auction at the Mark IV Health Club, only four were formally charged: Val Martin, John Embry, Jeanne Barney, and Douglas Holliday, an accountant not directly connected to *Drummer*. Fred Halsted, as an auctioneer with Val Martin, was also arrested and thrown into the same holding tank as Embry.

That was a *Drummer* reader's fantasy: to be locked by angry cops into a cell with the S&M sex beast, Fred Halsted.

Whereas Embry seemed traumatized in his raging anti-LAPD editorials, the more cerebral Halsted, who belonged to the Libertarian Party, wrote a coherent narrative of the arrest, of the wild media coverage, and of the gay community aftermath. In his editorial in *Package* 2 (September 1976), Halsted rousted and roasted *The Advocate* 189 (May 5, 1976) and *The Advocate* 190 (May 19, 1976) for what he perceived as its non-supportive, shameful, bourgeois, anti-leather stance virtually siding with the LAPD. Halsted accused publisher David Goodstein and *The Advocate* of using "Gestapo-like" pressure to make the wild gay leather community conform to the pretentious bourgeois standards of *The Advocate*.

No wonder the cash-sniffing Embry hated the corporate-scented *The Advocate*. He disliked its anti-leather policy, but, worse, he envied David Goodstein for every penny *The Advocate* earned. Embry's successor as publisher, Anthony DeBlase, continued his own sparring in the ongoing feud with *The Advocate* over its anti-leather and anti-male policies. In *Drummer* 126 (March 1989), page 4, DeBlase wrote an impassioned editorial against *The Advocate* for publishing its latest anti-leather propaganda, "Of Inhuman Bondage: Why I Left the World of Sadomasochism," penned by a "Jake Drummond" whose very pornstar-sounding byline name also *sounded* like a queen's backhand swipe at the *Drummer* name itself.

GOODSTEIN'S ATTITUDE, ANXIETY, AND ANDROPHOBIA

When the cover of *The Advocate* 185, March 10, 1976, featured the coming out of football star, Dave Kopay, publisher David Goodstein wrote a very naked editorial about his own queasy reaction to Kopay's homomasculinity. His essay was an anxious queen's Manifesto of Masculine Ickiness published exactly one month before the April 10, 1976, Slave Auction raid for which *The Advocate* blamed the victims.

In his attitude, Los Angeles' David Goodstein at *The Advocate* was a pair with New York's Richard Goldstein at the *Village Voice*. Forgetting Stonewall, both demanded politically correct gay behavior. Goodstein's public statements exposed the 1970s toxic climate of anti-male and anti-leather prejudice among the dominant and privileged queen culture promoted by *The Advocate* which presumed its own evangelical and fundamentalist queer self was review-proof.

A reductive banner carried in the 1977 Gay Parade in San Francisco exposed the androphobia of the gender war's insensitivity in ignorantly and cruelly lumping gay white males in with straight white males: "No more power to white male supremacists straight or gay." Of course. But *Drummer* in the 1970s was not about the supremacy of anyone's race or gender; its humanist goal was to declare that masculine-identified gay men were equal to feminine-identified gay men, to separatist lesbians, and to everyone riding the sliding scales of gender.

In this same Slave Auction Spring of 1976, iconic photographer Lionel Biron wrote his eyewitness essay, "*The Advocate*: Capitalist Manifesto," exposing Goodstein's own separatist and divisive quotes published in his "Invitational Letter" for his "*Advocate* Invitational Conference" which he chaired at the Chicago Hyatt Regency Hotel on March 27, 1976. In *Gay Sunshine* magazine, Biron revealed the kind of gay conformity that the assimilationist Goodstein wished to enforce.

> To celebrate his first anniversary as publisher of *The Advocate*, David Goodstein wrote a controversial article on the Gay Liberation Movement in his "Opening Space" column in the January 14th [1976] issue of that paper. In the wake of the article, George Whitmore, editor of *The Advocate* Humanities/Literature section, resigned. Dave Aiken, David Brill, Arnie Kantrowitz, Vito Russo and Allen Young, all regular contributors to *The Advocate*, joined Whitmore in criticizing Goodstein's column in a letter to the editor published in the February 11th issue. The New York Gay Activists Alliance [G.A.A.] also responded to the column in the statement, "In Defense of the Gay Liberation Movement: An Open Letter to David Goodstein and *The Advocate*," adopted at its January 22nd

general meeting....[because Goodstein had written such divisive diktats as] "We must find ways to keep the emotionally disturbed members of our community [e.g.: sadomasochists] out of center stage roles and on the counseling couches where they belong....[And]... Most gay organizations are nearly always insolvent and dominated by people [e.g.: Embry at H.E.L.P.] who took them over from more responsible persons [Larry Townsend] through hysterical attacks on their integrity. These are the spokespeople whom our majority shuns....[And]....The most obvious examples of this new pride are the many new, well-lighted, expensively decorated bars and clubs [advertising in *The Advocate*] that are rapidly replacing the dingy toilets of old [e.g.: leather community bars featured in *Drummer*]."

Goodstein's article was not idle rhetoric. His remarks provide the firm ideological base from which he intends to operate as a self-declared "practicing capitalist" [*Advocate* No. 156]. Anyone who would doubt this, should take note of the invitational letter sent by Goodstein to a select "group of like-minded people," [*sic*] and announcing "The 1976 *Advocate* Invitational Conference."…. [In addition] Goodstein's "Opening Space" column is nothing less than a "Gay Capitalist Manifesto."

Gay Sunshine, No. 24, [in its article "*The Advocate*: A Turn to the Right?"] reported how Goodstein, after purchasing *The Advocate* in the fall of 1974, shifted "the basic editorial position from dead center to somewhere between conservative and reactionary." During the past year, *The Advocate* has been transformed into a show place of white, middle-class gay America. Features on travel, fashion, and entertainment suggest an affluent, carefree lifestyle in which *gay* means little more than fun and chic. Editorial statements, lashing out at the Gay Liberation Movement [and at leather culture], have promoted a myopic gay politics whose sole end is the passage of gay civil rights legislation, as if all will be well with gay America once anti-gay discrimination laws are enacted. Consequently, news items dealing with gay liberation spokespeople and organizations have been tailored, or censored, to conform with this editorial policy.

—Excerpt from Lionel Biron, *Gay Sunshine*, No. 28, Spring 1976

Even though Goodstein felt compelled to present Dave Kopay in *The Advocate* cover story (March 10, 1976), what comes through in his editorial is Goodstein's inability to be existentially inclusive of the range of masculinity in his vision of the gay 1976 world dominated by rich sweater queens skilled at exclusion. Perhaps proof lies in the subtext of Goodstein's editorial through analysis of some of his precisely felt sentences, quoted for analytic rebuttal below, wherein he codified internal evidence of antimale bias in *The Advocate*. Was he abused by athletes in high school? Was "David Badstein," as he was often pegged, stuck in a high-school panic as he struggled with the reality of the adult sportsman Dave Kopay?

Goodstein flailed emotionally even as he was trying to manipulate Kopay's butch image to his own ends in the civil war over gender-identification in the new gay culture that he was trying desperately to control and commodify through his corporation. He knew the power of the press belongs to him who owns one. He intended to influence generations of queens to come.

David—not Dave—Goodstein sang the following aria about Dave—not David—Kopay:

> ...Dave [Kopay] spent three days with us. He was an unsettling and disturbing presence. We concluded the discomfort we felt was healthful to our consciousness ...His effect on us was different from his effect on them [the professional sports establishment]—almost the opposite, in fact. His directness and delight in the virtues of "manliness" and athletics are as unusual [inside *The Advocate* bubble] to our jaded [*sic*] movement psyches as Matlovich's defense of his presence in Vietnam. [Even as Goodstein inched forward around Kopay in LA, the Olympic athlete, Dr. Tom Waddell, in San Francisco ran ahead and invented the Gay Olympics aka Gay Games that would change the athletic image of homosexuality.] We had to learn to handle a [homomasculine] point of view different from the conventional gay movement wisdom [said the conventional publisher in a decade of riotous social change].
>
> Once we got used to Dave's restlessness, and our own [Were Dave and David both uneasy in the gender war?], we concluded that he personifies, in a slightly exaggerated [*sic*] way, the emerging gay mover and shaker. [Goodstein, always a cheerleader for the "exaggerated ways" of drag and effeminacy, was wary of what he perceived as a competing "exaggerationist" male profile over at *Drummer*.] He is different from the people [Goodstein is self-referential] who heretofore have moved gay liberation forward....
>
> To many, the athlete is a turn-on [*Drummer*]; to others a turn-off [*The Advocate*]. I confess that I belong to the latter group [but, of course!]; I have always preferred admiring jocks from afar [rather

than seducing them as at *Drummer*] to the smell of the gymnasium up close [which "smell" *Drummer* was selling monthly as a fetish of "jockstrap culture" evidenced in the "Gay Sports" issue of *Drummer* 20, January 1978]. Jocks get what they want in our culture. [A jealous fantasy?] They are the favored few in most American schools. We alleged intellectuals [Goodstein's self identity] resent [note the angry word] the power of brawn [worshiped at *Drummer*]. Kopay brought back many painful memories of growing up. [Or of not growing up.]

...He is used to taking what he wants. [Cue Blanche DuBois! "Oh, Mister Man!"]

Dave Kopay intends to change society's perception of gay men. [This was also the mission of *Drummer*.] His own perceptions, I forecast, will not only unsettle the straight community [who dismiss gay men as effeminate], but a great many gay people [wary of the rise of homomasculinity] as well....

Enjoy *The Advocate*!
—D. B. Goodstein

In a victory for *Drummer*, forty years after this 1976 feature, the pop culture world of kink finally overwhelmed *The Advocate* which surrendered its anti-leather tradition in its breathy feature, "30 Kinky Terms Every Gay Man Needs to Know." Ignoring forty years of *Drummer* roots, boots, and brutes that helped create the 21st century of Kink.com and *Fifty Shades of Gray*, *The Advocate* published thirty designer photos visualizing leather basics such as the hanky code, flogging, fisting, nipple torture, water sports, safe words, S&M, and CBT illustrated with a witty photo of an egg squeezed between the jaws of a machinist's metal vise.

If gay life was a giant ballroom (and it kind of is), kinky leathermen have been lingering [more like *crusading*] in the back, in the shadows, for generations. But thanks to the internet and porn giants like San Francisco-based Kink.com, fetish play has stepped onto the main floor over the *last decade*....[This] will help you navigate Scruff profiles.... *The Advocate*, February 12, 2016

HALSTED, THOMPSON, BURNS, AND O'HARA

Fred Halsted published his Slave Auction feature, "Slaves," in the first issue of his magazine, *Package* (July 1976), and he editorialized further against

The Advocate in *Package* 2. On his masthead, Halsted listed *Drummer* contributor, Bob Opel, as photographer, and, as his production manager, JimEd Thompson, who in 1988 died in the saddle while he was the associate editor of *Drummer*. In a valedictory, as a famous leatherman in a famous leather couple, Thompson (1946-1988), with his lover, porn star Chris Burns (1958-1995), appeared in a two-shot on the cover of *Drummer* 120 (August 1988) which published JimEd Thompson's obituary.

In the zero degrees of very cool *Drummer* contributors who did not outlive *Drummer*, I had met and played with JimEd Thompson in LA in 1971 when he began publishing his bondage magazine, *Action Male*. His later lover, Chris Burns, who was one of my Palm Drive models, was a sweet and athletic madman hustler. In fact, the short blond Scottish-American pornstar, Burns, was often confused with another player in the salon around *Drummer*, the short blond Irish-American pornstar, Scott O'Hara (1961-1998), who singlehandedly and very foolishly "squealed" and alerted cops nationwide with his accurately detailed list of the addresses of America's cruisiest truck stops and toilets in his magazine, *Steam*. That's another story confirming the idiocy of two very indiscreet publishers who got their readers arrested: "Embry and O'Hara, Who Adored Each Other, Together Again!"

I was connected to *Steam* insofar as *Drummer* salonista Scott O'Hara bought one-time rights to several of my photographs of Donnie Russo to print on the cover of the rate cards O'Hara mailed to advertisers. Blonder than an Easter Peep, the twinkie-punk O'Hara's claim to fame was his penis which had won a gay-bar award as the biggest in San Francisco. As a demanding bottom, he had been photographed for both print and videos at *Drummer*, and a photograph of him by Mark I. Chester appeared in *Drummer* 137, page 18. The last time O'Hara and I chatted was by chance when we were suddenly thrown together shuffling along in the crowd heading into Marines Memorial Auditorium to hear Gore Vidal speak in conversation about his new book *Palimpsest* in 1995.

With the blond pornstars Burns and O'Hara, a certain twinkie freakshow circled *Drummer* which preferred hard leather boys to creamy twinks. Chris Burns had a voracious butthole famous for hoovering up what wasn't nailed down. Scott O'Hara was a one-trick pony famous for sucking himself off. In 1987, David Hurles, reconnecting to the *Drummer* mystique where I had launched his career as Old Reliable Studio in *Drummer* 21 (March 1978), hired Chris Burns for a shoot. From my archives, I noted that on November 2, 1987, David Hurles wrote about Burns in his *Unpublished and Confidential Journal of Old Reliable Hustler Videos* which he typed on blue paper and bound with a red plastic comb:

Burn is the correct word. I don't know why I ever wanted him, with the baggage he had to carry, enveloper of fire-hydrants and small vehicles, lover dead of you know what! But I not only paid him about $250 PLUS air fare, but he partied the night before, gave me the bum's rush to get done, was hung-over, did not follow directions, had no personality, did not get a good erection...and no one bought his pix. Older than God.

A month later on December 5, 1987, I wanted to see if I could fire up in the black-belt karate instructor, Burns, the burn that had eluded Hurles. I shot him on location in his San Francisco karate studio at 317 10th Street, next door to Stompers Boots, for the Palm Drive video, *Karate Kock Warrior*. Looking through my viewfinder, I saw what Erich von Stroheim saw in Norma Desmond descending the staircase in *Sunset Boulevard*: the protoplasm of a living ghost. He was a sweet man, but his sex appeal had died. His videos for both Old Reliable and Palm Drive sold, literally, zero copies. He had starred in over a hundred videos, and his career was dead of overexposure. In 1994, the power bottom Chris Burns, made mystical as a martyr by illness and drugs, begged me in a recorded conversation to videotape the elaborate S&M suicide he fantasized for himself as his *Götterdämmerung* way to seize control of his death.

I declined.

CHAPTER 17

WHEN QUEERS COLLIDE
HOW GAY CIVIL WARS KILLED
OUR STONEWALL MOMENT

- Leather Historians: Critical Thinking and Fact-Checking *Drummer*, the First Draft of Leather History
- Independent Authors and Corporate Gay Publishers
- Wild Tim Barrus: From Editor of *Drummer* Magazine to Author at *Esquire* Magazine
- MGM Star Ann Miller, Publisher Elizabeth Gershman, and the Kennedy Family
- Edmund White and Larry Kramer Thrown Out of the Key West Writers Conference
- Embry Shames Jeanne Barney, the Founding Los Angeles Editor-in-Chief of *Drummer*
- *Mach* Magazine: *Mach* Is Short for Machiavelli

Suddenly in the 1970s we were in the brave new world of corporate gay publishing. That peculiar kind of indentured servitude is not why young authors get into writing, but the age-old business model was there, a kind of necessary evil, constricting the free spirit of being gay, and exploiting the passion of writers burning to be published.

Immediately after Stonewall, gay liberation became a commodity coopted and commercialized by corporate businesses intent on selling our voices, our art, and our identity as product from *Drummer* and *The Advocate* to the startup in the mid-1980s of gay book publishers who were no more saintly than straight publishers.

A gay book publisher is a member of the 1% who buys the work of authors who are the 99% to whom he or she pays only 7-10% of the cover price. A gay magazine publisher, buying rights, pays far less than any minimum wage.

All writers from Joe Anonymous to Edmund White to Larry Townsend, and publishers from Winston Leyland to Sasha Alyson to David Goodstein to John Embry, had to learn how to make their gay business work within the straight business model.

Gay culture in the 1970s had a fast and steep learning curve as profit replaced innocence with the drama, intrigues, jealousies, and ambitions around cash, competition, and assimilation. Segregated for so long from the straight world, we thought our gay world was somehow superior, but as soon as given the chance, we sold out our Eden, and all hell broke loose.

The gay media business was born.

* * * *

John Embry was never transparent or accountable. His public life, at least his thirty stentorian years in leather publishing to which I was both an eyewitness and accomplice (1975-2009), was one long grudge match of "Embry VS The World." Masking his jealousies masking his greed, Embry filled the few published sections of his autobiography, *Epilogue*, with his own remembered agenda. His selected memories are as validly *Rashomon* as anyone's. His papers and memoir stand open to anthropologists, critical thinkers, and ironic comedians as a forensic dig of internal evidence of his pugnacious mindset in the pages of *Drummer* and his other magazines.

As a gay mail-order salesman, John Embry was the Willy Loman of gay publishing. Both men were drummers peddling their wares. I think attention must be paid to whatever baggage the cunning Embry left behind in any of his polemical periodicals, manuscripts, and archives. Any bits of his memoir, *Epilogue*, must be evaluated critically and fact-checked historically as must mine and other Folsom Street historians such as the photographer-memoirist Jim Stewart and feminist-Marxist anthropologist Gayle Rubin. The huckster had tales to tell and he was never afraid to rant loudly in print about cops, competitors, and staff. When proved to be true, or revealed as false, his then adjusted recall may help reveal an even more objective story of *Drummer* which as a cultural force was bigger than any of us who created it.

As documented by letter and by email after 2001, I offered several times to interview Embry about his "take" on *Drummer*, but he always declined because, I think, as a publisher he knew investigative journalists pursue facts, nuance, and accountability. Nevertheless, despite the blood under our bridge, my former employer asked me four times if I were interested in copy-editing his long-gestating manuscript of *Epilogue*. Like him, I demurred. I always answered: "Not now. Maybe later. When my own writing is completed." As editor, I did not want to repair his manuscript the way I had to shine up most of the manuscripts submitted to me at *Drummer*, including

John Preston's raw first draft of *Mr. Benson*. Oftentimes, authors "hate" editors who do what editors must. Instead of Embry paying me to edit his manuscript, I paid him a substantial amount for reprint rights for two selections from *Epilogue* to use as evidence, inclusive from his point of view, in my logging of *Drummer* history. That was rich: me paying him after him not paying me for my work in *Drummer*.

By 1998, Embry was not only trying to collect his own memoirs, he was also trying to reconstitute his own greatest hits of 1970s classic *Drummer* in his new *Manifest Reader* magazines. So he asked me for permission to reprint several of my articles and stories from that free-love "Golden Age of *Drummer*, 1977-1980," which was a different *Drummer* from the safe-sex *Drummer* (1980s-1990s) circumscribed by AIDS, political correctness, and leather contests. That golden run of *Drummer* (issues 19-30) was also very different from the *Drummer* (issues 1-18) that had fled LA, bullied, and beaten almost out of business by the LAPD.

If Embry and his erstwhile LA founding fellows of *Drummer* had not quarreled among themselves, if they hadn't given each other the attitude of feuding bit players at a Hollywood studio, if they hadn't alienated their peers contributing to *Drummer*, if they hadn't caused most of their own LAPD troubles, they might have launched *Drummer* into an earlier, higher, better, brighter orbit in that first decade of gay liberation after Stonewall.

Instead, Embry estranged his collaborators like Jeanne Barney and Fred Halsted and Larry Townsend, dumped *Drummer* in the LA political toilet, and fled to San Francisco. The convenient irony was that the reputation of *Drummer* as a "fugitive outlaw" fit into sexual outlawry of Folsom Street culture, but the tempestuous mail-order mogul Embry could not shed his attitudinal LA roots. He remained in laidback San Francisco what he had been in quarrelsome LA. San Francisco in the 1970s was still very much a 1960s Haight-Ashbury love commune evolving into the new concept of gay community. The smack talk that Embry and his peers in LA cocktail bars applauded as campy blood-sport infighting was a lifestyle choice of words and attitude not liked by men on Folsom and Castro streets.

From the 1960s, up until Larry Townsend and John Embry died (2008 and 2010), Embry's feuding and fussing LA *Drummer* Salon famously fought like cats and dogs. Their tiffs made for legendary gossip and giggles. Perhaps fancying their coterie as an LA Algonquin Club, they were wits halfway between Theater of the Absurd and Theater of Cruelty. And then they'd all go out to lunch. Again. Always at the French Quarter Restaurant at 7985 Santa Monica Boulevard in West Hollywood where San Franciscans Mark Hemry and I were invited several times to join the LA pals who were that day deigning to speak to each other. Always bitching about the parking, they went into that coffee shop to see and be seen.

With its overwrought-iron decor of main-floor plaza dining and surrounding balconies straight out of *A Streetcar Named Desire*, the French Quarter was a surging tide pool of cruising talent. So many colorful WeHo characters from the gyms, bars, and streets swam around its dining tables and sex boutiques, no one ever cared about the food because the people-watching was worth the cost, carbs, and calories. Fascinating to me among the many sex-toy and greeting-card boutiques surrounding the dining plaza was the office front of a doctor whose one-stop specialty was prescribing steroids, the most closeted drug in gay culture.

Even as AIDS arrived in the 1980s, up in the Hollywood Hills, on Sunday afternoons around a certain doctor's swimming pool, the steroids stood posing on one side of the sparkling blue water and the checkbooks stood shopping on the other. In 1992, another LA doctor, whose deleted name I remember musclemen invoking with reverence in serious gyms even in San Francisco, pleaded guilty to one count of receiving illegal steroids, with more than twenty charges against him dropped.

The crisis between the two lovers in my *Some Dance to Remember*, star-crossed because one was a bodybuilder from LA and one was a writer from San Francisco, was caused by steroids' devastating roid-rage effect on the personality.

My experience in getting that *Drummer* novel published revealed that magazine publisher John Embry was no worse and no better than the many book publishers who exploit authors whom, for all their original work, they pay so little. Few authors dare write exposes about publishers for fear of never being published again. Whistle-blowers rarely win.

Analogously, my problems were nothing compared to the travails of the underestimated American author Margaret Mitchell who created one of the world's great gay icons in Scarlett O'Hara. Mitchell's Scarlett is the sine-qua-non archetype of Tennessee Williams' Blanche DuBois, as well as of my protagonist Ryan O'Hara, the magazine editor, in *Some Dance to Remember*. *Gone with the Wind* informs *Some Dance*, which transports Mitchell's Civil War "romance" dynamic to the civil war over sex, race, and gender on Castro and Folsom streets. Ryan is several times referred to as "Miss Scarlett." In my gay spin, Ryan (Scarlett) turns the tables on his lover Kick (Rhett), and, tossing Kick out for bad behavior, declares the equivalent of: "This time, Rhett Butler, you get out! I don't give a damn." So for several reasons, I found fascinating an eye-opening book chronicling the epic struggles between author and publisher in Ellen F. Brown and John Wiley's cautionary tale,

Margaret Mitchell's Gone With the Wind: A Bestseller's Odyssey from Atlanta to Hollywood (2011). It was, in fact, Margaret Mitchell's lifelong crusade, waged internationally, that helped change international copyright law to protect authors against publishers.

In an eyewitness *Drummer* "open letter" written August 24, 1994, former *Drummer* editor, Tim Barrus lacerated Embry for failing to live up to a publisher's responsibilities. Barrus was the founder of the 1990s San Francisco literary movement "LeatherLit" which published Geoff Mains' *Urban Aboriginals*. Gay studies scholar Claude Summers' writing about the legendary Barrus in *The Gay and Lesbian Literary Heritage* noted: "Some of the best pornographic fiction to come out of the leatherman tradition is by Tim Barrus." In the zero degrees of separation, I must disclose that after Barrus exited *Drummer*, he began working at Knights Press, Stamford, Connecticut. There in early 1989 he advised LeatherLit publisher, Elizabeth Gershman, to acquire my *Some Dance to Remember: A Memoir-Novel of San Francisco 1970-1982*, which Tony DeBlase, recognizing *Some Dance* as "a *Drummer* novel," had excerpted as "cover fiction" for *Drummer* 124 (December 1988). That specific *Drummer* connection (1988) helped launch that book (1990) the way that my feature obituary for Robert Mapplethorpe in *Drummer* 133 (September 1989) led to another book contract for *Mapplethorpe: Assault with a Deadly Camera* (1994). Previously, in 1984, twenty pieces of my fiction and features from *Drummer* compelled Winston Leyland of Gay Sunshine Press to publish my anthology *Corporal in Charge of Taking Care of Captain O'Malley and Other Stories* which was the first collection of leather fiction and drama from *Drummer*.

The serial novel *Mr. Benson* that John Preston wrote under the pseudonym "Jack Prescott" in 1979 for *Drummer* also jumped to book form under the name "John Preston" four years later in 1983. In 1978, Embry had decided to move into book publishing with my *Drummer* serial novel, *Leather Blues*, written in 1969 and published in a limited edition in 1972. I wanted a written contract detailing rights and royalties, but I declined even that because Embry's failure to pay me my full monthly salary told me his contracts were not worth the paper they were written on. That did not stop the presumptuous Embry from announcing in *Son of Drummer* his publication of *Leather Blues* as a forthcoming "*Drummer* novel."

How *Mr. Benson* became a book was another story. Preston admitted it was the first fiction he ever wrote and that he wrote it "as a laugh." He told me he thought it was a comedy. When Embry took it seriously and I serialized it to *Drummer* specifications, Preston pressed on. Banking on Embry's low-grade lust for him, Preston was, like Sondheim's sloe-eyed vamp in

Follies, as provocative as he needed to be to have this serial become his first published book. When he arrived, hiding behind the mask of one of his seven or so pen names, he seemed depressed and bitter after having been fired as editor of *The Advocate*. He was not the first dumped *Advocate* employee to head straight for *Drummer*. He followed in the footsteps of other *Advocate* refugees such as first *Drummer* editor-in-chief Jeanne Barney and early columnist Aristede Laurent. The East Coast Preston of 1979 imitated the East Coast Mapplethorpe of 1977. Just as the virtually unknown Robert, seeking leather fame, arrived at my desk at *Drummer* with his portfolio and his hat in hand, Preston needed the power of *Drummer* to help rebuild his self-esteem and to kick-start his sadomasochistic writing career. So he ran the gauntlet to climb between the covers at Embry's Alternate Publishing.

A man's reach should exceed his grasp, but Preston's ambition exceeded his erotic talent. In the mid-1980s he became an intriguing editor of books who opportunely found social power in anthologizing authors grateful to be published at the height of the AIDS crisis, but he hadn't the gift of editing magazines.

Having lost face when he lost his position at *The Advocate*, he never became what he was desperate to become in the early 1980s: the editor of *Drummer* magazine.

His own nemesis, the ruthless John Rowberry, who became editor after my exit, kept his foot on Preston's neck.

Drummer had a palpable power and magic. When its contents were managed synergistically, the magazine was a rich source for growing features and fiction into books because book publishers found a certain trial-balloon confidence in the pre-sold "pitch" made by such magazine publication to an eager core audience of fans reading the 42,000 copies of *Drummer* published monthly in the late 1970s.

Knights Press also grew out of *Drummer* in terms of staff, authors, and books. Even *Advocate* journalist Craig Rowland took note, writing a perky feature about its founder Elizabeth Gershman titled "Betty's Books" in issue 517, January 3, 1989, page 56. A year later, Elizabeth published *Some Dance to Remember* on St. Valentine's Day, February 14, 1990. With Knights Press' three printings, that first edition sold over forty thousand copies and was a Lambda Literary Award finalist as best book, "Gay Men's Small Press" category, the third year of the Lammy competition. It placed as a Finalist in that contest, staged by the East Coast bookstore Lambda Rising, when three of its four fellow Finalists were books published by the Boston corporation, Alyson Publications, which was bought by *The Advocate* in 1995. While *Some Dance* finished tied with Robert Chesley's *Hard Plays/Stiff Parts*

(Alamo Square), it was surrounded by Stuart Timmons' *The Trouble with Harry Hay* (Alyson) and Kate Dyer's *Gays In Uniform* (Alyson). The winner was Michael Willhoite's controversial thirty-page children's book *Daddy's Roommate* (Alyson). Unfortunately, Knights Press, while quarreling with Sasha Alyson and Tim Barrus, suddenly went out of business for reasons ranging from gay heterophobia against Elizabeth Gershman to money to marriage.

In the scenario at the American Booksellers Association (ABA) convention in Las Vegas, 1990, Elizabeth Gershman told Mark Hemry and me that Sasha Alyson, allegedly, was "leaning on" her who opined to us that Sasha Alyson was gouging her for "gay protection money." I respect Alyson's gaystream reputation as a genius of corporate business and a social saint who spent his later years teaching literacy in Laos. So I am recounting only one encounter with him, perhaps atypical, which no doubt has several *Rashomon* points of view: Sasha's, Elizabeth's, Mark's, and mine. This incident shows no more than the colorful workings of raw capitalism courting art to turn it into profitable product. My testimony based on what I observed is mixed with allegations told me by other eyewitnesses. The Sasha Alyson of that time and place, Elizabeth alleged, asked for money from her, but she indignantly refused to pay to join his exclusive "LGBT Book Aisle" at the ABA. She figured Alyson resented her small press as competition outside his control. She claimed she told him in private to go to hell when she perceived he became sniffy—so she alleged—that a straight businesswoman was publishing gay books independently from the gay mainstream, and was refusing to take direction from him. So she said.

In my Impressionist memory from that time where I was already observantly writing this memoir of gay history, I can recall the drama of recriminations, allegations, and confusions. Sasha Alyson seemed colorful—from his gender-ambiguous moniker to his childlike Teddy Bear, apparently referencing Lord Sebastian Flyte in *Brideshead Revisited*. Perhaps to disarm authors suspicious of corporate publishers, he carried that Teddy Bear, which Flyte had named "Aloysius," in the crook of his arm. The Valley Girl saying of the day was, "Gag me with a spoon." The sick Ick of that stuffed Teddy signaled Alyson a bit precious at the height of the 1980s-1990s gender war that attacked fair-minded gay masculine identity of the kind I asserted in *Drummer* and dramatized in *Some Dance*. If East Coast publisher Alyson had known that West Coast publisher Richard Bulger had four years earlier already reinvented the Teddy Bear as a homomasculine mascot when he founded *Bear* magazine, he might have tossed his tiny Teddy in the toilet.

Shades of publisher Embry, Alyson, who had taken quondam *Drummer* author John Preston into his publishing house, pulled me aside for a tete-a-tete lecture. Hectoring me to join his book row, he seemed intent on turning me against Elizabeth who did not want her product, my book, to be in what she called Alyson's ghetto-side aisle. "Gay Alley, Son" was the joke. Not wanting to be marginalized in Alyson's gated community, Elizabeth had paid for Knights Press to host its own booth out on the wide-open floor with other mainstream, new age, and feminist small presses. As a result, Sasha Alyson—whom I met only that once—seemed a participant in the stealth feuds of the kind favored by Embry, as well as the kinds started in the 1980s by the self-anointed New York literary establishment against West Coast writers such as Larry Townsend, and even John Rechy and Armistead Maupin who both eventually got a nod because of their mainstream popularity (fans) and sales (cash) which earned a begrudged inclusion in the gay canon guarded by a three-faced Cerberus of two-faced Manhattan literary mandarins.

Some of those most famous gay authors, seven years later in January 1997, were chased off the stage of the San Carlos Institute at the annual Key West Writers Conference, "Literature in the Age of AIDS," because of the outrageous behavior of the screaming Larry Kramer, and other panelists being too sexually graphic, and others trashing fellow panelists, including the straight writer Ann Beattie for her not writing more about AIDS. The Key West president of the Conference, fed up, ran up on stage and—cutting entitled and rude queens down to size—told everyone on that stage and in the audience to get out. "The conference is over."

No matter how dramatic the spoiled tantrums of even the "greatest" gay writers, respect cannot be demanded. Ask Tennessee Williams, Truman Capote, and James Baldwin. To straight people, gay authors, from porn novelists to Pulitzer winners, are little more than genre writers penning guilty pleasures like romance novelists, sci-fi cult authors, or formula mystery hacks. Our segregation from mainstream American literature is perhaps one cause of the bitter intramural civil war among status-conscious gay American writers and publishers who work their anger out bullying each other.

That scandalous January afternoon in Key West all of us invited to leave, guilty or not, included alpha authors and agents such as Michael Bronski, David Leavitt, Jewelle Gomez, and Michael Denneny who made way to the exits while an even-tempered Tony Kushner surveyed the embarrassing exodus.

Standing in the fourth row where we had been sitting, Mark Hemry and I were loving the slapstick Commedia dell'Arte of witnessing high-button queens thwacked with pig bladders. Suddenly we saw the stunned and sweating keynote speaker Edmund White, who is younger than I, wobble down the stage steps toward the empty seats around us. He was having the vapors, flushed, feigning, and fanning himself as melodramatically as a Southern Belle with his manuscript pages.

"Is it hot in here?" He gasped, sweating calories. "Has someone used up all the oxygen?"

We took the pudgy pink hand he fluttered at us, as if we were groupies, so we could lean into a close-up shot of him playing the Great Man. We reassured him. An hour later at a very private garden party under whispering palms, White's pit crew had re-inflated his ego, and enthroned him in a white rattan chaise from which he reigned imperiously, staring into mid-distance, making fanning gestures tinier than the Queen Mum waving from a golden landau. My better angels kept me from telling Eddie what Robert Mapplethorpe and Elizabeth Gershman thought of him.

In 1989, a year before the ABA, Elizabeth Gershman confessed to me—who had advised her to be careful about rivalries—that she had written a friendly letter to White requesting his generosity in throwing a bit of support to her fledgling Knights Press by writing a pre-publication quote for a couple of books including *Some Dance*. He begged off in a one-sentence postcard. Hurt by what she called condescension, she was in no mood to deal with another "gay godfather" like Alyson whom she alleged was blackballing Knights Press the way the literary Mafia refused to deal with her or her books. The one exception was Boston culture critic Michael Bronski who, contradicting White, supported her books like my *Some Dance* with perceptive and positive reviews.

Michael Bronski wrote in *The Guide*, Boston, July 1990:

> Jack Fritscher's mammoth chronicle of Castro Street, *Some Dance to Remember*, is, at heart, an historical epic: a tale of heroes struggling against not only one another, but fate and history as well. That his protagonists are leathermen, musclemen, and pornographers whose battles are against hate, repression, and AIDS only heightens the book's sweeping epic stature. Like the huge, hyper-masculine stone figure that graces Fritscher's cover, the characters loom large both on the page and in their own lives. At the center of *Some Dance to Remember* is the romance of Ryan O'Hara, topman/porn-scribbler/erotic philosopher/ex-seminarian, and Kick Sorenson, a blond bodybuilder who gets higher on pumping up than on any of the drugs he and Ryan take to enhance their musclesex. Focusing on

Ryan and Kick allows Fritscher to tell his real story which is the rise and decline—not really the fall—of the golden age of Castro and Folsom Street 1970-1982. There are scores of minor characters, hundreds of episodes, thousands of historical details and a plot that makes *Gone With The Wind* seem like a short story.

Some Dance to Remember is a great ambitious work and a rarity in modern fiction: a novel of ideas. (In fact, it has so many ideas that, at times, even its author seems overwhelmed by them.) Fritscher is concerned not only about telling the truth of gay men's lives—how we lived and loved, struggled and survived—but in examining in the psychological and philosophical underpinnings of those lives—the intricate interplay of self-expression and self-destruction, of sexual autonomy and erotic dependency. But more importantly, he has recreated more than a decade of gay history—its sights, smells, nerves, and guts. If *Some Dance to Remember* both astonishes and bewilders, seduces and frightens us (often at the same time) it is because Fritscher has captured, with intelligence and love, the way we live, both then and now.

Alyson's attitude made him seem very like Embry with his Blacklist. Alyson perhaps disliked the challenge presented by the strong-willed Elizabeth long before he met me, and, even while he was evangelizing me for our fifteen minutes together, I said nothing to him that was divisive or offensive. I had respect for what I knew about his decade of pioneering work as founder of Alyson Press, but in our conversation I could tell he knew nothing of my thirty years in publishing, my dozen years in teaching writing at university, my five already published books (two gay, three straight), and my three years editing *Drummer*. I had just turned fifty years old. I was an old hand. He could not top me as he might his usual desperate young authors who would do anything to get published. As a gay business mogul recruiting talent, he had not done his homework.

He did, however, presume I had some control over financiers Elizabeth Gershman and her husband who were both connected, not to the Mafia, so much as they were to the power of the Kennedy family. Within a year, their daughter married Teddy Kennedy, Jr. Having grandchildren surnamed Kennedy stationed them higher in the family, Elizabeth bragged, than other in-laws whose Kennedy grandchildren carried surnames other than Kennedy, such as Shriver, or, worse, Schwarzenegger.

It was amusing at the ABA to eyewitness Sasha Alyson take on the very gay-friendly Gershmans whose business goal, more niche than his, was to keep gay male-identified literature from the margins of genre, niche, and ghetto. Frankly, I did not want my fourth book populating Alyson's gay aisle because *Some Dance to Remember*, with its comic relief of straight characters, was a San Francisco book as much as it was a gay book. I liked Elizabeth's maneuver to present my literature equally with straight books out on the main floor. Fans of gender-fucking, if not scholars of gender studies, may assay that Elizabeth and I seemed to be doing the liberated crossover thing for the "gay male gender" in an age when galloping feminist separatists and politically correct fundamentalists were highjacking gay publishing with no compunction about punishing masculine gay men for the perceived wrongs that straight males had done them in high school.

Additionally, our Knights Press booth had a video monitor screening a twenty-minute loop of Folsom Fair footage that Mark Hemry and I had shot, edited, and produced to present *Some Dance* while, behind the images, I read from passages from the book in a voice-over. Ours was a forward-thinking display that one-upped Alyson's sideshow that had no mixed media. Indeed, if the Knights Press booth had not been out on the main floor, publishers from the straight Hastings House in New York would never have stopped by to chat, and, finding out about my relationship to the recently deceased Robert Mapplethorpe, and seeing my obituary for him in *Drummer*, would never have offered me a contract to write my pop-culture memoir *Mapplethorpe: Assault with a Deadly Camera*. The fact of an uppity West Coast author writing about a Manhattan photographer (presumably the property of Big Apple authors) chuffed the East Coast circle-jerk of New York writers blurbing, reviewing, and rewarding each other with literary prizes. Social class structure may be muted in the United States, but class and gender and race bullying is the soul of gay culture, and gay publishing is its high-school locker room.

In 1995, nine years after Embry sold *Drummer* to Anthony DeBlase, Alyson sold his Alyson Publications to Liberation Publications, owner of the man-hating *Advocate*. It was a perfect fit of queens who deserved each other. The merger proved John Embry correct in his disdain for the politically correct *Advocate* chauvinists. With the power of its press propaganda, it was David Goodstein's *Advocate* with his Werner Erhard est-driven "*Advocate* Experience" that eroded the social cohesion that had existed for a moment in the 1970s among all the genders of being gay. To me, it seemed a tragedy that we had lost our Stonewall Moment. The divisive cultural Marxism of the effeminist-dominated media, proclaiming multi-cultural diversity, was neither universal nor intramural. It was not meant for men self-identified as masculine. The effeminati culture defining themselves as victims, rejected masculine identity as the oppressive "other." *Drummer* by comparison grew its core readership by planting the gay pride flag of homomasculinity—even while evolving to include all the genders of leatherfolk. *Drummer* began with a female editor, Jeanne Barney, and ended with a female editor, Wickie Stamps.

Among the Las Vegas slot machines, a parallel drama unfolded on the floor of the ABA mobbed with thousands of book buyers. Elizabeth's husband, Jim Gershman, was already angry at what looked like Sasha Alyson's scheme. It was gay insult to straight injury when a Knights Press writer, T. R. Witomski, a *Drummer* author, and a friend of Tim Barrus and me, walked up unannounced to the Knights Press booth and launched his ambush attack on the Gershmans. One of those "radical" guys from New Jersey who think that "causing a scene" is essential to rebellious homohood, Witomski was a tall man who towered over the crowd. Wound up, he began screaming at the top of his lungs about his contract and the royalties he was owed for his book *Kvetch*. Erotic filmmaker Witomski had no bourgeois boundaries when shooting his surreal BDSM sex features with mud, raw eggs, and Daiquiri douches for his cophrophagic Katsam Video Company that made John Waters' *Pink Flamingos* seem like Disney. He certainly had no boundaries in his performance art that afternoon. He hated the Gershmans.

Terminal with AIDS, he went mad ranting at the Knights Press booth with thousands of conventioneers milling around us. His heterophobic gay tantrum, denouncing the gay-straight alliance attempted by Knights Press, embarrassed Mark Hemry and me. We were two guys, partners, happy with my new novel and high on our author gig, standing at the booth chatting with the legendary Hollywood actress, Ann Miller, MGM's star dancer, who had stopped by out of curiosity, asking, "What kind of dancing is *Some Dance* about?" She was one of the big celebrities at the ABA publicizing her own forthcoming New Age book *Tapping into the Force*. Dear Annie, all eyelashes, red lipstick, and sleeked black hair. She was the 1940s star with the legs my father adored. Standing with us, obviously mortified, watching Witomski explode, she took the hands of both Mark and me and said, "Darlings, don't be embarrassed. I see this all the time." And with an air kiss to each of us, she and her publicist walked on.

Within months, Knights Press closed its business because Elizabeth Gershman—who could blame her?—turned her attention from the politics and stress of gay publishing to her daughter who was marrying Teddy Kennedy, Jr. For his part, Tim Barrus never forgave Elizabeth for killing her infant company that Barrus had worked so hard to establish. For my part, I can't forget that Gershman exited owing me $12,000.

Tim Barrus, endearing for writing outrageous letters, sent me and others reams of open-letter correspondence about the injustices done him by the Gershmans and about the state of gay publishing. In his writing, the former *Drummer* editor accused Elizabeth of sexual harassment while he worked at Knights Press. His frankness as an author writing honestly about publishers Gershman and Embry could seem absurdist and preposterous, but only to the inexperienced. I believed him about both persons.

In fact, even though she was a dozen years older than I, Elizabeth did, swear to God, come on to me the last night of the ABA. Her husband had left Vegas, and Mark had flown back to his career in San Francisco in the afternoon, leaving me alone with Elizabeth in the two-bedroom condo we four had shared for the convention. That evening in a kind of French farce of slamming doors, Elizabeth treated me like I was straight. Shocked, because I adored her as a person, I told her, "Very funny, I'm gay. I'm a virgin. With women, I'm a virgin." That only made the sexual tension worse. I wasn't going to lose my cherry to a granny. Trying to joke my way back to friendship, I said, "Are you trying to seduce me, Mrs. Robinson?" Finally, I, a fifty-year-old gay man, retreated to my bedroom, and closed the door which she opened, and which I closed, several times, until I pushed a chest of drawers against the door to keep her out. It was hilarious. In the morning, over coffee and croissants, we were all smiles as if the farce had never happened.

I took Elizabeth's ardor as a compliment, but her pursuit I found to be a disrespectful challenge of my essential homosexual identity as well as a dismissal of my then ten-year monogamous marriage to Mark. In chasing gay men, some straight women act out the magical thinking of a certain female hubris that they can change gay men. Such feminist "gay reparative therapy" is as presumptuous as Jane Austen's first two sentences of *Pride and Prejudice* that press men into a stereotype.

"It is a truth," Austen wrote, "universally acknowledged, that a single man in possession of a good fortune must be in want of a wife. However little known the [straight or gay] feelings or views of such a man may be on his first entering a neighbourhood, this truth is so well fixed in the minds of the surrounding families, that he is considered as the rightful property of some one or other of *their daughters*." [italics added]

Or, if Jane had ever traveled farther than thirty miles from her home, where life was gay, *their sons*.

The retort to Austen's predatory sexism of owning men as "rightful property" is that the women hunting these men are gold-diggers. But that, even muttered sotto voce, is a heresy that dare not speak its name.

T. R. Witomski, the director of *Barber College* and *Mess*, gave up the ghost in 1992, but provocateur Tim Barrus never let up on their mutual nemesis, John Embry, who, later as publisher of *Manifest Reader*, remained to Barrus the same villain who had screwed up thirty years of gay publishing in *Drummer*.

The shape-shifting Barrus whom I helped journalist Andrew Chaikivsky profile in his feature, "Nasdijj," in *Esquire*, May 2006, was never one to let those who screw him escape. Retorting Barrus, John Embry in *Manifest Reader* 17 (1992), played coy with Barrus's reputation which he tried to destroy when he published a feature by the pseudonymous Vee Kay (sloppily billed as "Kay Vee" on the contents page). The exercise in scorn was titled "Portrait of a Wild Thing: Interview with Tim Barrus, the Enfant Terrible of Gay Publishing," pages 41-46.

At that moment, *Drummer* and its identity had once again been tossed in the air like a dog toy because the innately American magazine, spun out of the quintessence of the Marlboro Man cowboy, had just been sold on May 19, 1992, to its third publisher, the Dutch businessman Martijn Bakker whose corporate ownership in Holland plus his amateur editors in San Francisco finally killed everything that was grass-roots leathersex in *Drummer*. Over seven agonizing years, Bakker drained *Drummer* of its American sex appeal and identity, and stuffed it with sex photos from corporate video companies aping real leather action until he ceased publication with issue 214 in 1999. Embry danced on *Drummer*'s grave, eulogizing 1970s *Drummer* (issues one to thirty) as the Golden Age of *Drummer*. Vee Kay's sarcastic interview, "Portrait of a Wild Thing," was calculated to justify Embry's onward-marching Blacklist. Plowing through Roget's *Thesaurus* to damn Barrus with faint praise, Embry/Vee Kay's poison pen set about spinning the truth about the delightfully controversial Barrus into insults and lies that only made Barrus more colorful. Vee Kay wrote:

> This was an almost impossible interview to get. Tracking Tim Barrus down takes the skills of a detective...this most elusive and difficult of writers. Getting Barrus to sit down long enough to verbally organize his thoughts...takes the skills of a psychiatrist and a travel agent. Contrary to current literary opinion, Tim Barrus is neither crazy or institutionalized. He is volcanic, lucid, vehement, arrogant, seductive, childish, vulnerable, serious, unforgiving, and one of the most impassioned writers of words alive. There is perhaps no other writer quite like Tim Barrus in the small, idiosyncratic world of gay publishing. Barrus is disliked in the inner circles of

gay publishing like no other writer past present, gay or straight or in-between.

Embry insured that Vee Kay's interview skewered Barrus with phrases such as:

> ...foam at the mouth...bossy, bitchy, and markedly bizarre... hardly an editor or a publisher who hasn't been pissed off royally...a talent for enraging his public, his critics, his friends, his ex-friends (which are numerous), his ex-lovers (which are numerous), and his ex-wives (which are numerous)...insanely charging up twenty paths in twenty different directions....In 1988, Barrus became (for a time) the Associate Editor of *Drummer* magazine (which had published his fiction more extensively than any other publication, the first Barrus piece in *Drummer* being titled "Oh, Shit." A year later, Knights Press published *Genocide: The Anthology*, truly a sci-fi nightmare if ever there was one. Barrus left *Drummer* to become a consulting editor at Knights Press where he worked on such book projects as Robert Patrick's *Temple Slave*, Jack Fritscher's *Some Dance to Remember*, and Jeff [incorrect spelling of "Geoff"] Mains' last book *Gentle Warriors*. Barrus' brainchild LeatherLit, a proposed line of above-average books that would be aimed at the leather community (a market Barrus feels has been totally ignored) never got off the ground....Barrus left Knights Press in a turmoil of lawsuits, mega-angst, and literary barbs that flew between other writers in publications from one coast [East] to the other [West].

Vee Kay's very aggressive first questions to Barrus were about his hair style (his trademark Mohawk) and his age: "Your writing makes you sound older than you are." The third question was: "You are frequently charged with being psychotic and homophobic." Instead of punching Vee Kay and ending the interview, Barrus, wiley as a fox, managed to overpower Vee Kay and capture what he wanted: column inches in his arch-rival Embry's rag.

Undeterred by invective, Barrus revealed his own eyewitness "take" on the quality of 1970s *Drummer* when I was the editor-in-chief. He then went on to trash what *Drummer* became under Embry and Anthony DeBlase during both the politically correct revolution of the 1980s and the AIDS quake that sucked the eros out of homosexuality. His insider's literary opinion about *Drummer* history is valuable and accurate—and directed to Edmund White and his kind.

People ask me what my favorite short story is—one that I wrote; published in what else? *Drummer*. It's called "A Measure of Waste."... Pornography has become [1992] very demure. Almost ladylike....I hear gay men talk about bonding constantly. Blah, blah, blah—words. Bullshit in the wind...the more you talk about it the less it happens. Pornography used to be a way I could create alternative realities versus the realities that are imposed upon us....

In the beginning [late 1970s], *Drummer* had an edge. A real serious bite. It was about ideas and those ideas had to do with sexual images that had not really been put out there before. [Editor's note: Fritscher's "Cigar Blues" in *Drummer* 22, May 1978, was the first erotic article on cigars in the gay press and it was that feature that popularized the now evergreen homomasculine cigar style for daddies, musclemen, and bears.] *Drummer* wasn't slick. And no one else was doing what those folks were doing. It was extremely creative. It was magic. [Editor's note: During this period when Barrus wrote the word *Fritscher*, Embry with his Blacklist, creating synonyms, replacing *Fritscher* with *folks*, would most often quite obviously edit out Fritscher's name from *Manifest Reader* and his other magazines.] Some people [Fritscher, Shapiro, Sparrow, Mapplethorpe] got burned in the process because it was a process of fire and brimstone. But *Drummer* had an identity. Today it's fat. It's old. [Two swipes at the weight and age of both past publisher Embry (age 66) and then current publisher DeBlase (age 50).] It has become a how-to manual [a change brought about by DeBlase because of politically correct demands for safe sex even in the art of fantasy BDSM fiction] and does not reach down into the imagination—the brain—which is an organ...that is bigger than your dick. *Drummer* should mess with your imagination. It used to. I used to jerk off and have normal, heterosexual, everyday fantasies [Barrus identified as straight] and then something from fucking, goddam *Drummer* would creep up on me and my dick and invade the whole orgasmic process. Which is why I loved *Drummer*.

The old [1970s] *Drummer* was not safe. *Drummer* was not sane. And sometimes *Drummer* was not about consensuality. It was not about how to tie a knot around someone's balls. It was about the tension and the sweat and the relationship that existed between the knot and the knotted and the balls and the room and the smell and the richness and the humanity and the absolute, far-reaching joy to be found in absolute, far-reaching submission and the absolute, quiet satisfaction that comes from having learned real dominance. *Drummer* was redefining who we were with words, photographs, with ideas, with images, with metaphors, with flesh and blood. NONE OF IT had been done before. It was truly an exciting, alive, vibrant, flawed place.....I may not be gay but I understand how privileged I was to be published in the company of those men. It actually hurts to read the magazine today. [1980-1990s] *Drummer* takes no risks. And yet it whines constantly that the forces of repression...are everywhere....It no longer has that snarly fuck-you attitude. It's tired. It bitches....It reads like a clubby newsletter. A rich boys' clique. [The second *Drummer* owners DeBlase and Andrew Charles were, like real-estate mogul Embry with his mink-dragging Mario Simon, ostentatiously rich.] It is no longer unique. It has become like the rest of gay sex...totally meaningless....*Drummer* was starting to make me throw up when I read it and I was the one [as editor!] responsible for what was being published....There I was a whore and an editor. I was giving them what they wanted and it was all my fault. Blame the editors. [For the bad, and credit them for the good] Which is why so much of gay publishing is so fucking colorless and impotent. Gay publishing should be more like rock-and-roll and less like Edmund Fucking White.

Two years later, in August 1994, Barrus, exercising his right to rebut Embry's lies, excoriated Embry in another "open letter" addressed to "Dear John." The gorgeously shameless Barrus mailed multiple copies of this letter, tossing pages from the open cockpit of his biplane strafing Gay Metropolis. Never embarrassed even by Barrus, Embry, who sucked up free column inches anywhere he could to fill his pages, published most of Barrus' open letter in his column, "Roses and Brickbats from All Over," in *Manifest Reader* (October 1994), pages 5 and 15. Embry liked getting a rise out of Barrus whom he provoked, as he had also manhandled Jeanne Barney, in order to inject controversy and gossip into his magazines. He had severely trashed, slandered, and shamed Barney as early as *Drummer* 30 (June 1979). As editor-in-chief of that issue, I was an eyewitness to the war. It's not my opinion about Embry attacking allies. It's fact. Embry liked the vigor of fighting in print.

Embry Blacklists Jeanne Barney in Print
Drummer 30 (June 1979)

Affecting the legalese patois written by people who are not lawyers, Embry revealed his snide LA attitude, sexism, heterophobia, jealousy, and revisionism about the woman who was his valued Los Angeles editor-in-chief who stood together with him founding and filling the first eleven issues of *Drummer* (1975-1976) until she quit because of the growing notoriety of Embry's business practices and his failure to pay her salary. His libelous sarcasm turned his heroine "Jeanne" into his villain "Mrs. Barney." At Embry's *Drummer*, no worker was safe from the Blacklist.

* * * *

NOTICE! Mrs. Jeanne Chelsey Barney, aka "Barney" and "J. Barney" is representing herself as the owner of the LEATHER FRATERNITY [started by Embry] and is operating out of a mail box drop in La Crescenta, California. She has solicited memberships in this "Fraternity," promising subscriptions to DRUMMER magazine as part of its benefits. Later, after being cut off by DRUMMER and two of its distributors for nonpayment, she is substituting a multilithed "Newsletter," promised monthly and containing offers of merchandise in the "FRATERNITY's" name, membership pitches and solicitation of contributions as well as scurrilous attacks on ALTERNATE PUBLISHING [the actual name of Embry's business running *Drummer*] and its people.

Notice is hereby given that THE LEATHER FRATERNITY is a fully protected name since 1973 and has no connection whatever with Mrs. Barney's effort. THE LEATHER FRATERNITY does not sell merchandise, nor does it accept nor solicit donations. It does not publish names of members as Mrs. Barney has unfortunately done.

Mrs. Barney is offering remnants of her unpaid-for DRUMMER inventory at inflated prices and offering subscriptions to DRUMMER at $3.50 per issue. DRUMMER has no subscription agents and cannot honor any such obligation. Up until December 31, 1978, DRUMMER made good the FRATERNITY membership subscriptions that had been sold in DRUMMER's name via Mrs. Barney. Henceforth any monies sent to Mrs. Barney cannot be the responsibility of ALTERNATE PUBLISHING. We would appreciate being notified of any checks to DRUMMER or ALTERNATE PUBLISHING endorsed and negotiated by anyone other than this company. —*Drummer* 30, June 1979, page 38.

Tim Barrus, the author of the books, *Mineshaft*, *Genocide*, and *The Boy and the Dog Are Sleeping*, wrote to Embry in 1994:

> ...What, *moi* engage in sarcasm?...It's too bad we [Embry and Barrus] never connected....Together we could have given the publishing *status quo* a run for its money. But no. Such heresy gives you, the gay bitch queen, hives. We could have done some truly innovative things together....At least when you created *Drummer* you were hands on with it (some of it had to have been created on your kitchen table)....I wonder how someone in your position could have gone through the outstanding minds and the talents you have known (and used) without really knowing the people (and the talents) that were necessary to support the many projects you have created. Names like John Preston, T. R. Witomski..., Steven Saylor, even Rowberry (you never really knew Rowberry or you would have exploited him far more effectively than you did). *Sometimes I wonder if you even once...had an inkling as to the talent...assembled.... I would note...over the years how you were surrounding yourself with more and more really meager talents. You seemed far more comfortable with this than the times when you found yourself surrounded (besieged?) by powerhouses....* [Italics added] For a long time you were cutting edge. But now you are content to be history....Which leads me to think that your association with rebels in all of this was an accident and not something you consciously set out to put together....While the more itchy talents (such as Fritscher) went their own (often odd) way, it might amuse you to know that Robert Mapplethorpe and I (while in the middle of our torrid New York affair) [Mapplethorpe never mentioned to me any affair with Barrus, but then Robert kept all his friends separate —JF] used to discuss you for hours and wonder, really what the hell you were like....You were everything from Machiavelli to Maria Callas....I would suggest that you stick to selling real estate [that phrase, *real estate*, crops up in the testimony of several eyewitnesses who knew that *Drummer* profits financed Embry's property empire] and get out of gay publishing.

Embry, equally sarcastic, responded in the same *Manifest Reader* (October 1994, pages 5 and 15):

> Mr. Barrus desperately wants to be disliked, that is his shtick. We find him amusing, even likeable, if annoying, sometimes. However,

with such a small present-day staff, and the abundance of calamities that have befallen us recently there has been little time to...communicate with our contributors the way we would like.....We felt we should [publish this letter]. It is certainly not to ridicule Mr. Barrus, whose abilities we often admire.

In his own patronizing and dismissive words in this quote, Embry gave evidence of his emotional problems that ruined him as a businessman.

He always seemed attracted and repulsed by Barrus and by most other contributors in the village it took to create an issue of *Drummer*. He was attracted because he needed writers, artists, and photographers to fill his magazine. He was repulsed because they made creative demands and argued to be paid. Mostly, he was jealous that many of his contributors were more gifted than he, the publisher, whom they made look good. He wanted to be "Mr. Drummer," but he wasn't loved. He wanted to be one of us boys in the *Drummer* Salon creating the magazine, but even as publisher, he managed to cause his own ostracization.

So he played a tiny thumb-and-forefinger violin, singing his sad story as a publisher-saint, beset with calamity, who can't keep up with "correspondence"—which meant "payment"—to his contributors. The cynical Embry lied when he wrote that he did not wish to "ridicule" Barrus who topped his Blacklist.

Embry's sadist heart liked ridiculing people. His masochist heart loved being ridiculed. He got a cheap thrill publishing readers' letters bitching about him and the trickster way he did business. By issue eleven, Barney said, he had earned the nickname "Robert Ripoff" in publishing and mail order.

On December 11, 2008, Tim Barrus wrote to me:

> John Embry always sucked. He made an accounting error once and sent me several checks for the same article. Then he saw his error and screamed blood he wanted his money back. I was in Key West at that time. I cashed every check. Fuck him.

Embry, as a business man, had a loud stentorian voice in print. The power of the press belongs to him who has one, and Embry had platforms. From the early 1970s to his death in 2010, he owned nearly a dozen magazines such as *Mach, The Alternate, Manifest Reader,* and *Super MR*. He was miles wide, but only an inch deep.

When he asked me in 1978 to help him create *Mach* as a *Drummer* sibling, was I the only one who thought *Mach* was short for *Machiavelli*?

Drummer, however, could have thrived better as an only child who did not have to support other magazines. In the 1970s, *Drummer* was so strong a brand name that it helped create the very leather culture it reported on.

After that powerful Golden Age of sexual entertainment, Embry used his later magazines as power tools to settle scores, revise history, and romance his own legend.

Too often his thirty-years of prevarications and mistakes are quoted by legitimate journalists, historians, and anthropologists as if they are true.

Critical thinking is required. Fact-checking is necessary. Turn to the texts inside *Drummer* and other Embry publications for internal evidence to examine his character and agenda, including his plagiarisms, feuds, and ads for pedophiles and the Nazi party.

Embry's tallish tales only survive *postmortem* when his revisionism is made "true" simply by being repeated by incurious bloggers and ingenuous researchers and innocent historians who, not knowing the *dybbuk* they are dancing with, fail to realize they are "accessories after the fact" in resurrecting and perpetuating Embry's crime of injecting his disinformation into the leatherstream.

Even DeBlase, who loathed Embry, could be tricked.

Immediately after paying Embry thousands of dollars to buy *Drummer*, DeBlase tried to write up a fair-handed *Drummer* history in the landmark *Drummer* 100. But minus critical thinking about, and fact-checking of, Embry's slanted innuendo and lies published in previous issues of *Drummer*, he fell into the booby trap Embry had set, and reprocessed and reprinted some of Embry's bombast chapter and verse.

Unfortunately, his uncritical repetition of Embry's fibs and falsehoods damaged his editorial in *Drummer* 100, as well as some of the informational entries DeBlase later made in the first uncorrected draft of his ambitious "Leather Timeline" which the fact-checkers at the Leather Archives & Museum in Chicago will spend years correcting.

DeBlase was not shy about pegging Embry as a shady character who had defrauded him by lying about hidden financial liabilities when he bought *Drummer*. Intellectually, DeBlase with his doctorate might have safeguarded himself better. He was an eyewitness who knew from his own experience that after he bought *Drummer*, Embry made a hobby of trashing DeBlase and *Drummer* while constantly revising the real history of the magazine's talent base.

Embry was an unreliable and often unknowledgeable keeper of the institutional memories of *Drummer* which he owned for only eleven of its twenty-four years. For the other thirteen years at *Drummer*, "Embry" was a dirty word.

Nevertheless, the Age of AIDS made him feel safe rewriting *Drummer* institutional "group history" into his personal hagiography. He figured few would bother to rebut him because most of his eyewitnesses were dead.

CHAPTER 18

VENOM NEVER DIES
The *Drummer* Blacklist

Summary Evidence
Suitable for a Cross Examination

- Unknown to GLBT Readers, Wicked Grudges Poison the Well of Gay Culture with Publishers of Books, Magazines, Newspapers, Archives, and Websites
- Feuding, Fussing, and Fighting: Robert Mapplethorpe, Larry Townsend, John Rowberry, John Preston, *Mr. Benson*, Frank Hatfield, Rick Leathers, Jim French, Colt Studio
- Embry vs. the LAPD, David Goodstein, *The Advocate*, LA Publishing Peers, Other Gay Magazines, His Own Talent Pool of Writers and Artists, as Well as *Drummer* Publisher #2, Anthony F. DeBlase, and *Drummer* Publisher #3, Martijn Bakker
- Embry's Final Grudge: Against *Drummer* Itself

"Don't throw your past away. You might need it some rainy day."
—Peter Allen, *The Boy from Oz*

In the twentieth century, few people took time to take notes on the gay past while it was the speeding present they paid scant attention to from the 1960s to 1999. Recalling that *Rashomon* past which I chronicled beginning in my mid-century journals, I am no innocent naif amazed at the politics, skullduggery, and dirty laundry in gay publishing, literature, or any other gay or straight pecking group. I am an academically trained arts and popular culture analyst who, having climbed up from my father's traveling-salesman household, has had several careers inside groups way more dynamic, powerful, and byzantine than gay publishing.

Starting out at seventeen as an editorial assistant in the snake pit of the Catholic press, I survived religion (eleven years in the Catholic Seminary), academia (graduate school plus ten years of tenured university-level teaching of literature, writing, and film), corporate business (eight years writing and managing writers for Kaiser Engineers, Inc.), and government (two years of working as a writer with the San Francisco Municipal Railway).

Subjective insider experience must always be verified objectively through internal evidence, such as found in the pages of *Drummer*. As a survivor of the twentieth century, I am an artist who is a writer who lived inside *Drummer*. If, by default, AIDS deaths made me a motivated keeper of the institutional memory of *Drummer*, then great is my responsibility to the dead for presenting true internal evidence in writing this New Journalism remembrance of things past.

HOW THE EMBRY BLACKLIST WORKED

For the last quarter of the twentieth century, and until he died in 2010, John Embry nursed grudges. Jeanne Barney in 2006 painted a cosy, but lonely, picture recalling that partners John Embry and Mario Simon frequently whiled away the hours sitting on the front porch of one of their homes at the Russian River, going over and over the Blacklist of people they imagined had "done 'em wrong."

1. AGAINST POLICE CHIEF ED DAVIS & THE LAPD

From his early 1970s start in publishing, John Embry wanted to be a player in gay liberation politics. His personality, however, subtracted what gravitas he might have exerted as a publisher. He was strategically unwise using *Drummer*, a dedicated sex magazine, as if it were an anti-establishment political tract. Well into the 1970s, conventional gay wisdom counseled keeping politics out of newly emerging sex publications to protect the magazines from the revenge of powerful politicians who used the sex as the excuse for government censorship when it was really the politics they sought to silence. Embry was born a hard man with that kind of entitled male hubris that usually destroys guys who think they are tough.

Wanting a high-profile adversary, he tried to bait and provoke the most powerful lawman in LA, Police Chief Ed Davis, whom he variously satirized through the years as "Crazy Ed" (*Drummer* 9, page 4), and, again, through the century, showing venom never dies, twenty-four years later in his *Super MR #5*, 2000); as a "liar" (*Drummer* 7, page 68: "Chief Davis lied..."); pictured in an unflattering photo (*Drummer* 6, page 14); and fiercely parodied as a bit of a "pedophile S&M crusader" (*Drummer* 14, page 82). In *Drummer*

6, page 14, Embry blasted: "The reason the Democratic Convention is not being held in Los Angeles is the instability of its chief of police."

Editor-in-chief Jeanne Barney poked jokes at the arresting officers, who nicked her at the Slave Auction, because their names were "Peters," "Bare," and "Gaily" (*Drummer* 9, page 4). Robert Opel satirized one "E. Davis" endorsing Opel's porno mag, *Finger* (*Drummer* 9, page 43); Opel frightened the LAPD Vice Squad's morality enforcement by stirring up the urban legend that there was, based on the reputations of Fred Halsted (*Sextool*) as well as Roger Earl and Terry Legrand (*Born to Raise Hell*), a hidden "underground gay movie network" in LA shooting porn-sex movies in gay theaters after closing time (*Drummer* 3, page 11); wanting to get a rise out of Davis, Embry showcased both those leather S&M films on the first covers of *Drummer*.

2. AGAINST LAWYER/PUBLISHER DAVID GOODSTEIN & *THE ADVOCATE*

Beginning with a hardon for *The Advocate*, and its publisher, David Goodstein who had bought it for $300,000, the insolvent Embry retaliated in his first feature after his arrest by Ed Davis in "*Drummer* Goes to a Slave Auction," *Drummer* 6, pages 12-14: "the...*Advocate* was even more inaccurate [about the Slave Auction arrest], loading its columns with attacks on Southern California Gay leaders and the Leather Community."

Embry continued in *Drummer* 9, page 43, insulting Goodstein in a taunting display ad. Blacklisted by *The Advocate*, Embry created his own Blacklist as a response:

• Primarily because *The Advocate* 189 (May 5, 1976) had trashed leather culture in Judy Willmore's "The Great Slave Market Bust," an article that gave Embry no empathy in its cherry-picking of lurid quotes from the prejudicial police report; nor did Goodstein's "Trader Dick" editorial column, "D. A. Claims Four Slaves Were Pandering," and its companion piece, "To 'Free the Slaves' L. A. Plays Itself. Again," both in *The Advocate* 190, (May 19, 1976).

• Secondly because *The Advocate*, taking vengeful fun fucking with Embry, reported on the Slave Auction without once mentioning the commercial word *Drummer*; that omission of identity deprived Embry of the free publicity and empathy he craved from other gaystream media, such as the offbeat *Advocate* competitor, *Gay Times* #43, in its sympathetic cover story written and photographed by Robert Leighton, who had been present at the event: "Free the Slaves: Full Coverage of the L. A. 'Slave Auction' Raid and Its Aftermath."

- Thirdly because the word in LA was that the bad PR around the nasty counter-culture of leather and its Slave Auction arrests—fanned by the conservative *Advocate*—hurt *The Advocate*'s mission of social engineering its scrubbed image of gay politics and the gay male demographic who were interested in fashion, hot clubs, celebrities, and sex; but that sex, because it was unscrubbed and a money-maker, Goodstein tucked away inside *The Advocate* as the special "Pink Section" of personal ads titled "Trader Dick." *The Advocate* was bourgeois and *Drummer* was bohemian. Knowing that *The Advocate* was based on politics, I made certain as editor that San Francisco *Drummer* was, like San Francisco itself, based on pleasure. Both *The Advocate* and *Drummer* helped create the very cultures they reported on. In fact, in San Francisco, the joke was that local Castronauts and Folsomaniacs threw away *The Advocate* and kept "Trader Dick" as a guide to the men and escorts offering free sex or hustler sex.

Confirming this Embry-Goodstein feud, *Drummer* editor Joseph W. Bean, a longtime insider eyewitness of leather culture, penned a wonderfully sardonic history about the Slave Auction, "L. A. Police Free Gay Slaves in 1976" in *Leather Times: News from the Leather Archives & Museum*, Spring, 2005. Bean wrote:

> I have personally met at least 75 of the forty (40) men arrested, just as we have all heard from hundreds of the several dozen people involved in the Stonewall Riots. Oh, well, this is a case that is pretty well documented, even if many of the facts published by *Drummer* [i.e.: Embry] are (let's call it somewhat) inaccurate, and those published by nationally known news dailies are a shallow gloss, and even *The Advocate*'s coverage fails as good journalism. The truth can be sorted out, and should be, and might make someone rich as a movie script or Broadway play.

"Goodstein maintained," Jeanne Barney told me, "that the typical *Advocate* reader drove a foreign car, owned a house in the Hollywood Hills, and ordered his booze by brand in bars. Which prompted me [Barney] to ask, in print, 'That's swell; but what about the rest of us?'"

In Gus Van Sant's film *Milk*, screenwriter Dustin Lance Black who won an Academy Award for balancing historical drama and accuracy portrayed the elitist Goodstein as a righteous snob who so misunderstood real gay people that he opposed Harvey Milk's populist politics. In truth, the only thing Goodstein liked about Harvey Milk was his assassination because the living Milk's mere existence and election were Goodstein's waking nightmare of radicals in the streets. Goodstein, who was an easily enraged short pudge, and a self-shaming and self-described "troll" twisted with scoliosis and cursed with a high voice, was a member of the pretentious 1% of gays intent on re-educating the 99% of gays—on political correctness and proper behavior—in his tabloid paper and in his gay version of "est," his cultish human-potential re-education program all *Advocate* employees had to endure. Needing no help from Embry or *Drummer* to be made a mockery, Goodstein's hyper-gay version of the controversial Werner Erhard's New Age gimmick made Goodstein and *"The Advocate* Experience" the laughing stock of San Francisco in the late 1970s even as San Francisco writers Randy Shilts and Armistead Maupin attended the opening session at the Jack Tar Hotel.

Whatever his dogmatic etiquette to control his *Advocate* staff, Goodstein, to his credit, was a bit more effective than the politically inept Embry. In 1975, while the Women's Caucus challenged Goodstein for dedicating the majority of *The Advocate* to gay men's news and sex ads instead of women's issues, he was one of the gay-image makers who helped pass the California Consensual Sex Act legislation (1974) which Morris Kight and Jeanne Cordova of the National Gay Task Force dismissed as a waste; he also helped found the Gay Rights National Lobby (1976) and the Human Rights Commission (HRC, 1980). Goodstein's money, and the cachet of the Rembrandt he exhibited in his dining room, made him socially and politically influential, but he was nevertheless revengefully banished from the White House in 1977 when the National Gay Task Force meeting with Midge Constanza, public liaison assistant to President Carter, blacklisted him. That put the Task Force on Goodstein's own Blacklist. Embry spent his cash not on politics, but on real estate and his three years of endless legal fees stemming from the Slave Auction. As each magazine self-fashioned itself, *The Advocate* was for assimilation of middle-class queens into polite society and *Drummer* was about independent, rougher, outlaw homomasculinity. Shadow-dancing Goodstein by "plagiarizing" *The Advocate* name for his own wannabe political magazine, *The Alternate*, Embry felt impelled to march into the escalating gay civil war over gender.

In the first issue of *Drummer*, on page 1, on the matter of sexual identity of masculine-identified gays *versus* queens, Embry, even though he was often campy, shot off what might be called "The First *Drummer* Masculinist Manifesto" by introducing newcomer *Drummer* to LA as a champion of masculinity *versus* the giddiness of magazines like *The Advocate*. Because Tony Deblase mentioned in *Drummer* 100 that I put emerging gay masculinity ahead of leather identity, and because writer Patrick Califia once defined me in one of his articles as "an apostle of homomasculinity," I should acknowledge that at that time I took my populist cue for tub-thumping masculinity in my issues of *Drummer* because the evolution of men identifying as masculine was part of the roots of *Drummer* itself. Historically, *Drummer* writers Toby Bailey and Bernie Prock, proclaimed the triumphant debut of the new masculinity of leather culture in their *Drummer* column, "The Leather Journal," in which they collected the best concepts of their previous columns in *Drummer* 6 (May 1976): "Masculinity and Masochism," "The Masculine Fetishist," "Men Who Go to Leather Bars," "Clothes and the Leatherman," and "Ageism." As Joseph W. Bean noted in his history, *International Mr. Leather: 25 Years of Champions* (2004), I summed up this new breed of gay masculinity by coining the word *homomasculinity* in *Drummer* 31 (September 1979), pages 22-24.

Embry's on-going feud with Goodstein encouraged *Drummer* columnists to take gratuitous Blacklist swipes at anyone in anyway associated with *The Advocate*. One of his reviewers, Ed Menerth aka Ed Franklin aka Scott Masters, gratuitously trashed photographer Crawford Barton's exquisite coffee-table book, *Beautiful Men* (*Drummer* 12, page 15; and *Drummer* 13, page 30), because my pal Barton's publisher was Liberation Publications, the umbrella over Goodstein's *Advocate* empire which also bought Sasha Alyson's Alyson Publications. The hurt to 1970s *Drummer* was that the stellar San Francisco photographer, Barton, whom I thought a lovely man, subtracted himself from helping Embry's *Drummer* in San Francisco, even as Barton, whom I interviewed on tape, helped me create my book, *Mapplethorpe: Assault with a Deadly Camera*.

Ed Menerth was the LA reviewer who, disgusted at being an unpaid Embry apparatchik, finally untied the bondage of his puppet strings and exited the pages of *Drummer*. I was an eyewitness because Ed Menerth, who was a vocal coach, called me at least once a month crying me a river to get Embry to pay up or he would withhold his review columns as well as his serialized stories written as "Scott Masters."

Jeanne Barney told me that Menerth, "the prolific writer was always paid during my tenure as editor-in-chief, more often than not out of my own pocket."

Frustrated with no pay and no return of his manuscripts, he soon quit *Drummer* cold. In an end run around Embry, Ed Menerth, as his own eyewitness, wrote to me, not at *Drummer*, but at my home address on January 21, 1979. That date is important because it gave me a model for my own exit for the same reasons at the end of 1979. Menerth said:

Dear Jack: Now that my long-time association with *Drummer* is "officially" terminated would you kindly return any material of mine that has not been used.... If Embry has published [these latest pieces], I am certainly unaware of it. Just wanted to add that I think you are doing a spectacular job with the magazine, giving it tone and thrust it so badly needed. Keep up the good work. —Ed Menerth

Embry hurt *Drummer*. Defections like Menerth's and columnist Halsted's caused me to begin to write even more features to fill those holes left by disgruntled columnists in a golden age of sex when most would-be writers, artists, and photographers preferred getting laid, or, in Halsted's case, chose to start his own magazine, *Package*, to rival *Drummer* by picking up specific coverage of the LA leather scene after Embry fled West Hollywood for San Francisco. Some of Menerth's on-file writing may have appeared in *Drummer* in 1979, but Menerth, who had been part of early LA *Drummer*, had exited, as noted, a year before I ankled out of *Drummer* December 31, 1979.

When, with *Drummer* 12, Embry in 1976-77 had to flee LA, he simply mimicked publisher David Goodstein's destination. Goodstein, who had settled in San Francisco in 1971, had moved *The Advocate* north out of LA after he bought it in 1974 from *Advocate* founders, Dick Michaels and Bill Rand who in 1967 had started up publishing 500 copies of letter-sized pages in the samizdat style. When the tabloid, *The Advocate*, set up shop at 1730 Amphlett, Suite 225, San Mateo, minutes south of San Francisco, future *Drummer* hire Pat (Patrick) Califia was its San Francisco editor; Mark Thompson was its associate editor; and John Preston, for eleven months, its general editor—before he was fired and became a contributor to *Drummer*. While Embry had been driven out of LA by the LAPD, Goodstein was driven out by gay activists who could all too easily demonstrate outside the doors of *The Advocate* in LA, but would never ever go to San Mateo to protest anything.

Over time, Thompson matured into the most leather-savvy of non-leather journalists at the leather-lorn *Advocate*. We met in 1978 when he, investigating the mystic side of leather, came to my 25th Street home to interview me both as the author of *Popular Witchcraft* (1972) and as the editor-in-chief of *Drummer*. We sat at my kitchen table for what, I think, turned out to be for him, as a young investigative reporter, a slightly shocking conversation about the wild carnality that was frankly happening in the fast-evolving San Francisco leather scene. The gentle Thompson, familiar with sexuality gentler than leather and coprophagy, was a writer-photographer of gay spiritualities in his books *Gay Spirit: Myth and Meaning* and *The Fire in Moonlight: Stories from the Radical Faeries*. Unafraid of opening himself up with the exciting 1970s, he eventually authored a couple of stories in *Drummer*, shot glorious photos of Robert Mapplethorpe, wrote perceptive articles about Folsom Street (*The Advocate* 346, July 8, 1982), and astutely collected and edited the anthology, *Leatherfolk: Radical Sex, People, Politics, and Practice*, which he somehow managed to get published by Alyson Press in 1990.

Suddenly, in the beat-down of the Embry-Goodstein Punch-and-Judy show, Goodstein moved *The Advocate* back to LA because he could; and Embry couldn't. He was trapped in San Francisco, in exile from his home base in LA, because the LAPD was salivating to harass him.

Was it karma that caused Embry to be the victim of his own "unrequited envy"? By his acts he seemed always in competition with Goodstein, but Goodstein and *The Advocate* sadistically ignored Embry and *Drummer*—which, every queen knows, is the best way to cut someone dead.

For his part, Embry never saw a former *Advocate* employee or associate whom he didn't hire or feature: Jeanne Barney, Pat Califia, John Preston, John Rowberry, Aristede Laurent, and others, including LA's Durk Dehner, who was mentored by Goodstein into starting up the Tom of Finland Foundation. Embry published Dehner as "Durk Parker" in the centerfold of *Drummer* 15 (May 1977) in remarkably sultry photos shot by Lou Thomas of Target Studio. Most of these talents had been let go one way or another by Goodstein who did not like "neurotic" (his word) and left-leaning (disobedient) editors and staff.

To his credit, gay peacemaker Mark Thompson, made individual repair of this publishing-war damage in his grass-roots anthology, *Leatherfolk*. Thompson reprinted writing from *Drummer* such as my essay on Chuck Arnett (*Drummer* 133, September 1989). He also considered reprinting my "*Pentimento* for Robert Mapplethorpe" (also *Drummer* 133), but I chose to reserve it as the anchor chapter for my own book about Robert.

In my *Rashomon*, I watched Embry's unrequited hate of *The Advocate* impact *Drummer* as he diverted cash, content, and energy from *Drummer* into *The Alternate*.

Unlike Larry Townsend who commanded his confused clients to keep his mail-order identity separate from Embry's, attorney Goodstein didn't even bother to sue over the possible confusion of brand names. Embry was a claim-jumper and his bait-and-switch tactic was straight out of the play book of the notorious Countrywide Publications which, in New York in the 1960s, devised look-alike publications to confuse readers into buying its magazines. For instance, in title and layout and "feel," Countrywide's *National Mirror* imitated the *National Enquirer*. As Robert Stone recalled in *The New Yorker*, October 16, 2006, page 130: "The lord of this empire of the ersatz was a man we called Fast Myron...who had many such replicant....[and] ringer schlock magazines whose names were bogus household words....'If Myron wanted to make a magazine like *Harper's*, he would call it *Shmarpers*.'"

At the same moment Embry established the first of his own "MR" brand magazines, a new gay rival came into existence, *Mr.: A Magazine of Men*, published in San Diego. On its masthead was printed: "*Mr.* is a registered trademark of Dawn Media." Embry's *Manifest Reader* published its first quarterly issue in December 1986. *Mr.* was first published in January 1987. Soon after, Embry began printing a great big graphic "MR" on each cover of *Manifest Reader*, imitating his competition again, as he had done with *The Advocate* and *Man2Man*. In all this publishing incest calculated to lure subscribers, Donald Hauck, the publisher of *Mr.*, affected a 1970s *Drummer* "look" in his design for his *Mr.* which, besides the *Drummer*-esque cover, type face, and page layout, featured the photographs of *Drummer* discovery David Hurles in *Mr.* 24 (1989).

When Embry asked me in 1978 to also edit *The Alternate*, I suggested he hire my friend, photographer Hurles, owner of Old Reliable Studio, as editor. The charming Hurles, who was no screamer, lasted four days before he went yowling into the streets to escape the snake pit of Embry's office. Because nature abhors a vacuum, Embry scanned the room where the office boy/cleaner was literally running the vacuum over the wood floor. Rowberry was Embry's understudy for anything and everything. That's how he became editor of the little orphan *Alternate*. That *Advocate*-clone was floated on the unpaid salaries and fees owed to staff, writers, photographers, and artists, and was funded, Embry years later admitted in print, by the profits of *Drummer*.

I went deep into creating the essential *Drummer*-ness of being *Drummer*. I was a leatherman. Embry went wide into generic publishing. He was a business man. I wanted *Drummer* to have its own pop philosophy the way Hugh Hefner nurtured his *Playboy* philosophy. Embry liked my work. He never threatened to fire me. In 1978, he even asked me to start up a third magazine he wanted to title *Macho*. In the way the word *Alternate* sounded like *Advocate,* he wanted his *Macho* to beat up *Honcho* which had premiered its first edition in New York.

Macho was "designed," he wrote in *Manifest Reader* 26, page 54, "to take some of the wind out of Modernismo's new *Honcho* sails."

If taking on Goodstein in LA was a gay cat fight, messing with straight Italian guys in Jersey might have meant a horse head in the bed.

His foolishness aside, I told him, bold-faced told him, that he could not dub his mag, *Macho*, because there was already a straight magazine named *Macho* located in South San Francisco. I had worked with *Macho* before Embry fled LA. I knew the "straight macho" *Macho* publisher would sue to protect his intellectual property.

This, history might note, is how Embry and I settled on the shortened title, *Mach*.

I also warned him that grinding out the third-banana, *Mach*, would mystify and confuse the *Drummer* faithful who were upset enough to write hundreds of letters that *Drummer* was always late.

Mach was Embry's own "Virtual *Drummer*" the way *Man2Man* was mine.

Mach Quarterly appeared in January 1980. *Man2Man Quarterly* arrived in October 1980. The internal evidence of Embry's editorial incest is within the first issue of *Mach*. Embry "revisited" (his word) the photos from *Born to Raise Hell* that he had published five years before in *Drummer* 3. *Mach* contributors and design layout were interchangeable with *Drummer*.

In a shell game to distance the two San Francisco magazines, he listed a single blind address for *Mach* that made it seem produced in LA: *Mach*, 7985 Santa Monica Blvd, Box 219, West Hollywood CA 90046 (page 62).

In *Drummer* 85, Embry proved the point when he confessed on page 4 of the *Drummer* Tenth Anniversary Issue that "we are even considering including the contents of *Mach* within the pages of *Drummer*."

After Embry sold *Mach* to DeBlase, I photographed two covers: *Mach* 20 (April 1990) and *Mach* 29 (July 1993).

3. AGAINST HIS FOUNDING PEERS AT
DATELINE NEWS MAGAZINE

In LA in November 1976, *Dateline News Magazine*, published by Dennis Lind, edited by *Drummer* editor Jeanne Barney, and backed by Embry, folded after one issue. Was it money? Was it politics? Was it Embry's sabotage of the partnership of several personalities, such as his frenemy Barney, trying to establish their own ideas of gay publishing in LA? Was it a mirror of Embry's feud with Goodstein? The minute after *Dateline* tanked, Embry danced on its grave. He revealed what had always been his secret plan: to kill any and all *Drummer* competition. Were his erstwhile business partners at *Dateline* surprised when he announced that, in less than sixty days, dumping them, he would publish the first issue of his own news magazine, *The Alternate*, January 1977, and "magnanimously" take on the remaining subscriptions to *Dateline*? In *Drummer* 9, page 72, Embry wrote two paragraphs titled "*Dateline*'s Death":

> We will try to make some arrangements to fulfill *Dateline*'s subscription obligation in our launching of what we should have done in the first place, our own national NewsMagazine [*sic*]...It will be called *The Alternate*, and it will be all ours [Embry's].

He added in *Drummer* 10, page 76: "*Dateline*...was to have been *our* [italics added] publication..."

In *Drummer* 6, page 4, before the death of *Dateline*, the editor's column in *Drummer* had been titled "Date Line" which Jeanne Barney renamed "Getting Off."

Answering my questions about the news magazine, *Dateline*, Jeanne Barney wrote me on September 23, 2006:

> The main reason *Dateline: The NewsMagazine of Gay America* collapsed are these: 1) I had sole editorial responsibility for it, in addition to *Drummer*; 2) Given that the first issue had been put together during and immediately after The Great Slave Auction of '76, I was stretched even thinner; and 3) *By the time we were supposed to be putting together the second issue, I'd already had it up to here with Embry and, indeed, was in the process of leaving.* [italics added] John was gleeful over the demise of *Dateline*, I rather imagine it was because he could blame it on my "desertion" and what he viewed as disloyalty.

Embry was expert at absorbing small magazines. In 1971 in Los Angeles, Embry, who had been an advertising salesman hustling column inches in Hawaii, had a brainstorm. He figured if he published his own magazine, he could keep the ad revenue to himself. All he had to create was just enough editorial content to wrap as an attractant around the heart of his mail-order brochure which was where the real money was. To have a credible periodical with ad space to sell, he devised a free zine-sized gay bar magazine, a trial balloon, which he dubbed *Drummer*, in imitation (again) of the 1960s S&M magazine *Drum*, published in Pennsylvania by Clark Polak, with art direction by Al Shapiro whom Embry soon hired as art director for *Drummer*. His "proto *Drummer*," however, was not S&M. It was a queeny bar rag filled with camp, gossip, recipes, and ads for toupees, gay paperhanging, and the self-satirizing BlaBla Café. Those topics were already covered by the then infant *Advocate* whose advertising Embry coveted in an age when gay businesses, forbidden to advertise in the telephone Yellow Pages, turned to the gay press.

Eager to dig up an existing gay sales base, political or sexual, with its own members' mailing list, Embry approached the founding president of the Hollywood Hills Democratic Club, Larry Townsend, and his struggling "Homophile Effort for Legal Protection" organization, of which Townsend was also president. H.E.L.P. provided assistance to gays entrapped by the LAPD who would soon entrap Embry.

Townsend was editor of the twelve-page *H.E.L.P. Newsletter* and he, speaking as a novelist, told me how he always hated the burden of publishing a new issue every thirty days. Sensing an opportunity, Embry swore fealty to Townsend and his two organizations. He offered to assist H.E.L.P. publish its newsletter which he, as the new editor, quickly combined with what he had called in his first "proto *Drummer*" editorial "our brave little *Drummer*." Even though he published the Townsend short story, "The Loner," in a badly pasted layout in the first issue of his "proto *Drummer*," his next moves constituted a hostile takeover of H.E.L.P.

Townsend's *H.E.L.P. Newsletter* became Embry's *H.E.L.P./Drummer* which in June 1975, dumping H.E.L.P., became large-format *Drummer* with its own "Issue One." A legend was born. The games began.

4. AGAINST HIS FOUNDING PEERS AT *DRUMMER*

At the beginning, *Drummer* was a Petri dish of creative, intellectual, and financial cultures. At the LAPD police station after the Slave Auction, Embry admitted in *Super MR #5* (2000), page 37, that he openly walked up to the man who owned the Stud bar and kissed him in some gesture of leather fraternity even though "the Stud's owner and I had been to court over an advertising bill and, when I won, he had ceased to speak to me." Was it a Judas kiss to endanger or embarrass the man in front of "twenty uniformed police" dripping with the homophobia of the raid? The ingrate Embry stirred up the deadly nightshade of his Blacklist when in *Drummer* (June 1979) he attacked the most important woman who had ever helped him, Jeanne Barney who, four years earlier, while still working for *The Advocate*, had come to hold his hand and to edit the first issues of *Drummer* (1-11).

As eyewitness editor-in-chief, I was embarrassed when Embry drew up his "bill of divorcement" from Barney. His attack was thrust on my full attention in the last complete issue which was not gutted of my editing, "The Fourth Anniversary Issue," *Drummer* 30, page 38. Thinking of Hester Prynne forcibly marked with an "A," I asked Embry not to print his harsh notice against the first editor-in-chief of *Drummer*. With the divine right of publishers, he ruled what he would rue, and immediately, he revealed his moral character.

His private hit list came out of his closet as his Blacklist.

His lesson to editors, writers, artists, and photographers was, "Don't cross me." Nevertheless, his public denunciation of Barney poisoned the Kool-Aid at *Drummer*. Unlike Rowberry and his 1980s peers who thought of *Drummer* as a "job" interchangeable with other gay jobs, we dedicated and committed 1970s staff were not drinking it.

What no one knew in the 1970s was how Embry's over-eager 1980s hand-puppets in his full and part-time employ, like John Rowberry and Scott O'Hara and John Preston, would take his divisive grudges and his Blacklist poison out into the nationwide gay publishing business the way the mythic "Patient Zero" spread AIDS, causing a 1980s second generation to blackball each other without knowing how the hate started.

Illustrating a kind of inherent abuse in S&M practice where ritual is sometimes confused with reality, Embry was like the leather priest Jim Kane, the property investor who rented his Pearl Street apartments to indentured masochists like Cynthia Slater happy to accept their slumdog units as no more than what they deserved from a leather top.

Embry exploited this card-carrying S&M "slave" concept to control and program some of his hired bottoms with his attitude, grudges, and untruths that they, in turn, dined off of as gossipy former *Drummer* employees spreading his Blacklist wherever they worked during the 1980s and 1990s. What happened at *Drummer* did not stay at *Drummer*.

Rowberry kept his own version of Embry's Blacklist. When Rowberry became editor after my exit, the first thing he did, without Embry's knowledge, was blacklist Larry Townsend who had finally consented to write his "Dear Larry" monthly advice column in *Drummer*. Two weeks before Townsend died, he told me in a recorded conversation that Rowberry fired him out of revenge. In 1979, when Embry had asked me to produce the first Mr. Drummer Contest, I told him producing *Drummer* was hard enough. I suggested that "Rowberry can manage the beauty pageant," which the always-derivative Embry, was producing in imitation of Chuck Renslow's International Mr. Leather Contest in Chicago. Putting Rowberry in charge of Mr. Drummer 1980, Embry invited Larry Townsend up from LA to be a contest judge in San Francisco.

Larry said, "Rowberry's contributions to that contest were minimal. Mostly, he ran around with a clipboard, feeling up the contestants backstage at the Trocadero Transfer. I told Jeanne Barney what an embarrassing joke Rowberry had been, and," Larry alleged, "Jeanne told Rowberry what I said."

For years, Rowberry and Barney had been on-again-and-off-again friends, as were the sparring Hepburn-and-Tracy duo of Barney and Townsend, and the bickering trio of Embry-Barney-and-Townsend. Jeanne Barney told me that Rowberry, whom she often openly denounced with delight, had at one time in LA been close enough to give her a Miro as a gift.

However, after the 1980 Mr. Drummer Contest, when, according to Townsend, Barney told Rowberry that Townsend had poked fun at Rowberry, saying "Rowberry was a like sex-starved secretary with a clipboard," Rowberry jumped to blackball Townsend from *Drummer*.

After a few months, when Embry, who rarely read *Drummer*, noticed that Townsend's column was missing, he called Townsend and asked why. Twenty-eight years later, Townsend told me, "When Embry asked me to return to *Drummer*, I informed him I would if I never had to deal with Rowberry again."

Rowberry's reputation was known among contestants, writers, artists, and photographers. When Embry started his Mr. Manifest Contest, he tried to reframe the "sexual harassment" of leather contestants as a funny brouhaha and wrote in *Manifest Reader* 12, page 29: "Very little backstage grab-assing." In Chicago in 1985, as a pre-condition to buying *Drummer* from Embry in 1986, Tony DeBlase and Andy Charles insisted that before they would pay a dime or sign a piece of paper, Embry had to fire Rowberry. It took five minutes.

Very "LA," Embry was a diva mogul who acted like he was head of a Hollywood studio. If staff did not do what he wanted, and if a contributor demanded payment for services, he'd thunder some equivalent of "You'll never eat lunch in this town again."

Just before that, in 1978 and in 1979, when I told Embry I wanted to be paid, or I'd quit, he asked me not to, sweet-talking me for a couple weeks with promises of payments and book publishing rewards. Embry was never stupid. He liked how I wrote hundreds of column inches to fill his rag and he figured my personal pals in the *Drummer* Salon might also stop contributing. When I again asked to be paid, he floated a little "threat" that he would drop my novel, *I Am Curious (Leather)*, which he had announced in *Son of Drummer*, September 1978, as "a forthcoming *Drummer* novel from Alternate Publishing." Some threat: a year had passed since that promise.

Shortly after I exited, Embry told me that he was replacing *I Am Curious (Leather)* aka *Leather Blues* with John Preston's *Mr. Benson*, a nice-enough novella that I had personally edited for serialization which I began publishing in *Drummer* 29 (May 1979). Trying to pit Preston and me against each other, he was playing both ends against the middle. That is precisely how he grew his divisive Blacklist. That bit of intimidation forced the East Coast Preston, who was motivated by the lust all young writers have to be published, to be co-opted on the West Coast. Preston arrived at *Drummer* with his *Benson* draft but no job. After four years as a sex hustler, he claimed he found it difficult to sell his wares—that had sold in LA—to San Franciscans swimming laps in more free sex than the world had ever seen.

To make his novice career move seductively into Embry's *Drummer* Plantation, Preston knew that to get what he wanted he had to choose sides on the Blacklist to rescue his lifebuoy, *Mr. Benson*. According to *Out for Good* (p. 247), it was well known that Goodstein had taught Preston to be the enforcer of the Blacklist of writers at *The Advocate*. Preston, who had "curtly" blacklisted dozens of faithful *Advocate* writers, including the famous activist Arthur Evans, knew this divisive credential would appeal to the tempestuous Embry who envied all things Goodstein. Like most first-time novelists, Preston was desperate. He truly feared for his *Mr. Benson* because in 1979 there was no other existing publisher for it but Embry, and that manuscript was in bondage because Embry had so many puppet strings attached. Preston did not want his novel dropped as mine had been. Soon after Preston submitted and swore fealty, puppeteer Embry, sharpening his Blacklist words to a stiletto, went on to advertise the magazine-sized "book" *Mr. Benson* with the code words "original and unedited." That phrase was his cheeky swipe at my serial editing of *Benson* which readers liked in terms of the story. Embry's "book" edition was neither "original" or "unedited." In fact, all of Preston's writing required editing. Preston's friend, author Lars Eighner, wrote in "John Preston Goes in Search of an Author's Lost Manuscript," in www.DuskPeterson.com:

> Preston was always heavily edited [e.g.: *Mr Benson*].... Preston's stuff, which would have been perfectly clear told at a campfire, needed major surgery—often at the paragraph level—to put into print. Preston was very well aware of this, which is why he admired writers so much. Preston often told (wrote to) me that he needed a lot of editing. I thought he was being modest...until I was given the task of editing...his raw copy.

In truth, the magazine-sized "book" edition of *Mr. Benson* was no longer "original or unedited" because the manuscript had become a concordance of re-writes that was too mixed to be restored to Preston's original draft. Protesting a bit too much, Embry wrote that "...the trade paperback edition has been completely revised [the operative eyewitness word that verifies my contention] by the author, with a revealing new epilogue from Mr. Benson himself."

The phrase "Mr. Benson" thus became for awhile yet another pseudonymous mask for Preston himself—as if he *were* Mr. Benson. Embry shoehorned him into a fictitious identity for marketing purposes, selling t-shirts saying "Looking for Mr. Benson" and "One of Mr. Benson's Boys." Fiction is not autobiography. In fact, Preston was a novice, if not ersatz, leatherman who like all hustlers could mime whatever the paying customer wanted for sex or for publishing. He knew how to strike an S&M ("Stand & Model") pose. He merchandised himself as the *Drummer* photographer "Yank," and as the "Dark Lord" on the cover of his *Tales from the Dark Lord*, published by the aptly named Masquerade Books. He was no more "Mr. Benson" than he was the "Dark Lord" than he was "Franny" in his best novella *Franny, The Queen of Provincetown*.

Like Embry who gestured at being a leatherman for publishing purposes, Preston seemed rather much a vanilla opportunist hooking himself up to the new leather literature which, more than gay literature itself, was hungry to recruit new writers. He calculated in the 1970s decade of very few gay magazines, after he was ejected as editor of *The Advocate*, that he might make a name for himself by hanging his bespoke leather manuscript on the S&M band wagon that was *Drummer*. Recycling his *Benson* idea with little regard for feminist politics, psychology or esthetics, he even contemplated a novel titled *Ms. Benson*, and under the pen name "James Prince" wrote a cliche-ridden spanking-and-fetish story about a heterosexual dominant mistress for *Penthouse Variations* titled "Ms. Benson's Chauffeur."

Conflicted about male S&M, Preston was no famous leather player in San Francisco. In search of a gateway into newly emerging gay magazine culture, he seemed rather much a "leather sex tourist" from the world of *The Advocate*. A lone ranger, he estranged himself from the wide-open fraternity of the *Drummer* Salon that even the elitist Robert Mapplethorpe liked. Even though we were polar peers in our professional relationship as author and editor, I must be morally honest about my eyewitness analysis of Preston because he died so young that he, like Mapplethorpe, never had a chance to mature fully into what his youth may have promised.

Born before him, I have lived nearly thirty more years than he whom Fate shortchanged; but, even with that empathetic perspective, I cannot ignore the *Drummer* history of my memories, my impressions, and my critical thinking about him at that time in that place in the "Preston Origin Story" where he bottomed to Embry's publishing power. To gain the balance of others' perspectives about Preston, the book that is essential is the admirably elegiac 1995 anthology edited by Laura Antoniou, *Looking for Mr. Preston: A Celebration of the Author's Life - Interviews, Essays, and Personal Reminiscences of John Preston* with eulogies by twenty-seven literary friends including Antoniou, Larry Townsend, Sasha Alyson, Owen Keehnen, Andrew Holleran, Celia Tan, Carol A. Queen, Jesse Monteagudo, *Drummer* model Scott O'Hara, and 1990s *Drummer* editor Wickie Stamps. Conspicuous by his absence among the keening eyewitnesses was Preston's Henry Higgins: John Embry.

As Cleve Jones, an intimate of Harvey Milk, finally said to the friends, fans, and idolaters of Milk, "He was not a genius and not a saint." Among some fans, Preston's premature death (age 49) elevated him to a certain cult status. But he died older than the Romantic poets Bryon (age 36), Shelley (age 29), and Keats (age 25), and passed about the same age as Mapplethorpe (age 42) and Milk (age 48). His being swept away in the epic drama of AIDS is a great tragedy, but that fact should not sway or coerce the subsequent history of facts and opinions about any public author's life, personality, or oeuvre.

In 1989, no one gave Robert Mapplethorpe a Viking hero's funeral, a memorial anthology claiming his legacy, or even a culture-war break. Instead, one hundred days after he died of AIDS, right-wing politicians, fundamentalist preachers, and vanilla gays trashed him personally and professionally in the biggest art scandal of the late twentieth century that saw him denounced on the floor of the United States Senate. That Preston died was a terrible loss; but how he lived his petulant life at *Drummer* and in gay publishing is a legitimate and essential measure of the man's actions, at least during the turbulent 1970s. While every canonization requires a Devil's Advocate, Preston, needing one, has not yet had one. As an eyewitness writing memoir, I am not judging him so much as I am holding him up to the same transparency to which I held my controversial Robert in my feature obituary, "Pentimento for Robert Mapplethorpe," *Drummer* 133 (September 1989), which grew into my book about Mapplethorpe.

> "Like Republicans constantly imagining what Ronald Reagan would do or say about the issue of the day, City Hall folks seem to

be channeling the late Supervisor Harvey Milk an awful lot....One of Milk's old friends is tired of all the, shall we say, "got Milk?" talk. The other day in the Castro we ran into Cleve Jones, an old Milk comrade and founder of the AIDS Memorial Quilt project, and asked him why everybody is trying to claim Milk. He said many members of Milk's community died in the AIDS epidemic of the 1980s and '90s and took their firsthand knowledge of the supervisor with them....a generation of gay men was pretty much wiped out and we lost a generation of stories....[Milk] was a normal guy in most respects," Jones said. "He was not a genius and not a saint." —Heather Knight and Rachel Gordon, "Milk's Old Friend Tired of Claims to Legacy," *San Francisco Gate*, Gay Pride Sunday, June 24, 2012

Befriended by Anne Rice who cloaked herself as A. N. Roquelaure, and also wrote about S&M without being a known player, Preston figured that in the way Rice, and I, had a double career writing "literature" and "S&M literature," so might he. Constructing a public-relations dark image with his *vampyr* eyes, sunken cheeks, and sullen personality, he cultivated in the 1980s a commercial air of mystery to pull power to himself by editing collections of grateful writers. Social networking was his magic. His real literary distinction lay in his anthologies. He knew how to make people feel grateful to him during the great hysteria of AIDS dying. He was not far from the A-List Satanic aspects of Rimbaud, Verlaine, and Mapplethorpe. Yet he was no Lestat. As if he were impersonating Rice's characters, he tried to be bad, dangerous, and edgy. As a showman, he fueled his own *artiste maudit* cult by identifying himself with his own "Dark Lord." The tag line on his cover for *Tales from the Dark Lord* tub-thumped the word *erotic* twice to build his audience: "The Master of Gay Erotic Literature Presents an Incendiary Collection of Erotic Stories That Explore the Full Spectrum of Gay Sexuality."

That advertising blurb was a challenging power-grab. Iconoclast Preston wanted to usurp what the iconic Larry Townsend was famous for all his life: "The Master of Gay Erotic Literature." Preston, learning that Townsend was on the Blacklist, might have felt it was a career move to try to steal Townsend's literary stardom. I knew Larry Townsend for years, and I witnessed Preston's attempted coup. Townsend was not amused until Preston, realizing he might have gone too far, rolled over, and courted him. The dying younger author made an offer of endorsement that the older author could not refuse. Preston penned the introduction to the new edition of

Townsend's 1972 classic, *The Leatherman's Handbook*, that was published in February 1994, two months before Preston died on April 28.

Years later in 2003, Townsend sat in his home office on Sunset Plaza Drive and asked me to write a new introduction for *The Leatherman's Handbook: Silver Anniversary Edition* (2004). On his wall, I could not help but notice a framed black-and-white head shot of Preston, humbly signed to Townsend with a flattering message. When I agreed to write the essay that became "Leather Dolce Vita, Pop Culture, and the Prime of Mr. Larry Townsend," I suggested to Townsend that he should keep the leather history scholarship about his book in one place, and include Preston's earlier introduction along with mine, which he did.

According to Edmund Miller in *The Gay and Lesbian Literary Heritage*, Preston, in his soft approach to hard leather psychology, sentimentalized real-life S&M into the "S&M-Lite" of *Mr. Benson* in the very unsentimental hardcore *Drummer*. He adopted, Miller continued, the faux-shocked, faux-appalled, and stand-offish "had-I-but-known tone of [mystery novelist] Mary Roberts Rinehart." With this literary gimmick to explain himself to the New York literati he hoped would accept him, he disingenuously distanced himself from his own novella as if such "low-grade" writing about sadomasochism would damage the "real" literary reputation he craved. This attitude was one more motive for his downplaying, in his East Coast circuit, the genre of leather literature which he nevertheless, as a businessman, continued to mine for a couple more leather novels. Had he but known that *Mr. Benson*, the book he dismissively wrote "for a laugh," would crown his literary legacy.

I always thought the original manuscript of *Mr. Benson* as handed to me for serialization in late 1978 needed the authenticity of Preston's very own revising and editing, and it made sense that Preston and Embry eventually thought so as well. Even though Preston may not have liked it made public that the editor-in-chief of *Drummer* had edited *Mr. Benson*, as far as I know, beyond his general scowling at our editorial meeting, my changes and suggestions were never objected to by the heat-seeking Preston.

If pages of Preston's typewritten manuscript exist, along with all the other writers' and artists' missing *Drummer* primary work among someone's souvenirs, it would be interesting to compare his first-draft "book chapters" to the final-draft "magazine chapters" I serialized in *Drummer*. Whipping his first and only draft into shape, I did nothing to subvert his authorship or his voice. Although I left all the *Benson* original pages with Embry, who probably threw them into our office closet piled deep with the discarded makings of previous issues, I have since found in my possession only one surviving and archived original chapter hand-typed by Preston: the last chapter of *Mr. Benson*.

Back in the day, it was thought that to control Preston as a former *Advocate* employee and as an East Coast legman and reporter for West Coast *Drummer*, Embry "Higgins" teased more work out of his "Eliza" by holding *Mr. Benson* hostage, delaying its publication as an actual trade paperback book for more than thirty-six months to keep Preston dancing to his tune while Embry blamed the delay on printers. Embry may have thought he was playing sadist to Preston's playing masochist. In human terms, he seemed he was just being cruel to Preston, with his unnecessarily protracted tease delaying publication of that book version of *Mr. Benson* for those nearly four years (1983). Embry cited censorship problems with the printer, but, if those claims about the printer were true, those delays were caused by his, and Preston's, absolute insistence on explicit illustrations and not by Preston's tame text.

Lou Weingarden (1943-1989), the owner of Stompers in Greenwich Village, told Robert Mapplethorpe and me that Preston himself, fighting with Lou's lover Bill Burke, caused another delay when Burke aka the artist Brick took his enmity out on the tempestuous Preston and withdrew the drawings he had made specifically for *Mr. Benson*. Founded at the end of the 1970s, Stompers was a boot-fetish emporium and gay art gallery. Like Robert Opel's Fey-Way Gallery around the *Drummer* Salon in San Francisco, it was also a hive of talented Manhattan personalities and extrapolated gossip.

In the real world, as opposed to the *Drummer* publishing microcosm, author Preston would have demanded that Embry's magazine illustrations, which were not necessary for a book, be dropped as were the drawings yanked by Brick. But during this first decade after Stonewall, gay literature was the domain of magazine publishers. Preston had no existing gay book publishers to turn to until the mid to late 1980s. Nor did I, till signed by Gay Sunshine Press who in 1983 bought my novel, *I Am Curious (Leather)* aka *Leather Blues*, as well as my short fiction for my leather anthology *Corporal in Charge and Other Stories* which was the first book collection of *Drummer* fiction. That caused Embry to add Gay Sunshine publisher, Winston Leyland, to his Blacklist.

Within leather-heritage literature, John H. Embry should be remembered as a prolific publisher of homomasculine S&M books, but not in the small "trade paperback" size. Having written his *The Care and Training of the Male Slave* in the late 1960s, Embry excelled in the 1970s "gay book genre" of large-format "magazine-size books" sold at magazine prices. He advertised his "Alternate Book Series" to his mail-order list as "Complete

Books in Magazine Format Lavishly Illustrated. $9.95 Each." His bibliography of gay fiction included a hundred titles, many of them authored by Embry as "Robert Payne" as well as by dozens of other genre writers: *Mr. Benson* by John Preston, *Slaves of the Empire* by Aaron Travis, *Captain Morgan* by Frank O'Rourke, *Cort: Imperial Warrior Slave* by Frank Albright, *The Brig* by Mason Powell, and several volumes of *Care and Training of the Male Slave* by Robert Payne. He also published magazine-format books showcasing photographers such as Rick Castro and artists such as the old master, Bill Ward, and the new master, Teddy of Paris.

What Embry did vilifying Jeanne Barney in *Drummer* 30 was an over-the-top archetype of what kinds of subtle defamation happened to everyone on the Blacklist that was viral and contagious. In publishing John F. Karr's review of Felice Picano's *Like People in History* in *Manifest Reader* 26 (1995), Embry revealed his West Coast bias against the so-called literary establishment on the East Coast who seemed mostly too good to write for his magazines from *Drummer* to *Super MR*. It wasn't so much the bad review as it was the snarky personal attack on Picano whom Embry sabotaged after he had published his short story "The Deformity Lover" in *Drummer* 93 (August 1986). When the East Coast writers read Karr's review, it would have been natural for them to dismiss with extreme prejudice any writer ever involved with Embry's many magazines, fueling yet another round of gay civil war.

> Felice Picano...has been self-consciously literary, as if he had to live up to the reputations of his fellow members of the writing group known as The Violet Quill. Indeed, in the shadow of Edmund White, Andrew Holleran, and even the over-rated Robert Ferro, Picano has been rather shrill about his participation in the group. His 1989 memoir, *Men Who Loved Me*, and especially his brand new *Like People in History*...are stilted with literary pretension, clogged with commas.
>
> Picano's characters...are neither likeable nor anti-heroes.... Further, Picano's gay badinage is neither new nor witty, and his opera fanatics are rote and uninformed...the author never lets passion breathe.... (*Manifest Reader* 26, pages 92-93)

Finally, on this point, even while I was one among many blacklisted, it is only honest that I be the first to blow the whistle on myself for objective, critical reasons regarding some things I have written about Embry. In the back-lot movie musical of *Drummer*, I once had motives as strong as Fred Halsted's or Jeanne Barney's or Larry Townsend's or Robert Mapplethorpe's or Robert Opel's to trash John Embry. He did, by my measure, all of us wrong. Did he cause actual professional harm that cost us all money for which damages and reparation could be sought? No one can prove that intuition any more than Dick Saunders in 2006 "knew," but could not prove, who it was who burgled Probe disco in LA and set it ablaze in 1981.

Was there glee in Embry's trying to contaminate us through his Leather Mafia puppets? Some of the brainwashed who drank his Godfather Kool-Aid continued to do his bidding. They perpetuated his Blacklist even post-*Drummer* when they went out for coffee or a symposium; or, worse, when they—as accomplices after the fact, or as infected victims of Embry's disinformation—carried his defamations to work as "background noise" at book and magazine publishers other than *Drummer*.

Preston, Rowberry, and the rest of Embry's chain-gang staff of "leatherboys" might have recalled the puppet Pinocchio: "To become a real boy, you must be brave, truthful, and unselfish." The first line in *Some Dance to Remember* is a warning about the dangers of living with only a gay heart: "In the end, he could not deny his human heart." In all my writing—in my constant theme of surviving in a fallen and lost gay Eden, there exists an archetypal, lubricious, viral, and disingenuous queer snake just as dangerous as the serpent that curls around straight hearts and minds.

An x-ray of Embry's Blacklist revisionism can be read in *Manifest Reader* 22 (1994) where he lied, and I select that word purposely, in his obituary for John Rowberry who died December 4, 1993. Embry's eulogy was propaganda and lies of both omission and commission. Methodist Embry broke the Protestant Ninth Commandment when he bore false witness that my "Tough Customers" was a "Rowberry concept." He also lied in *Manifest Reader* 26, January 1996, when he wrote that John Rowberry had been "editor-in-chief." In truth, there were only two editors-in-chief of *Drummer*: Jeanne Barney and I. Barney told me that she, not claimant Embry, invented the "Getting Off" title for the *Drummer* editorial column, and "Dear Sir" for "Letters to the Editor." Thirty years on, she remained adamant about Embry stealing her history of her origination of her own concept titles for columns inside *Drummer*.

When I invented my column, "Tough Customers," for *Drummer* 25 (December 1978), I did it alone. In *Drummer* 188 (September 1995), page 23, and in *Manifest Reader* 26 (January 1996), page 47, Embry claimed the creation of *Drummer* was his solo act: "It was," he wrote, "a solitary, if not immaculate, conception." He had no problem staking his claim, nor should the other founders of *Drummer* because it took a village to create its evolving identity, content, and aura.

Embry was the founding publisher. Barney was the founding Los Angeles editor-in-chief. Al Shapiro was the founding San Francisco art director, and I was the founding San Francisco editor-in-chief.

Rowberry's pecker tracks were nowhere on my work. Rowberry's name was nowhere on my *Drummer* mastheads, not even as a contributor. In fact, it was only with my last fully edited *Drummer* 30 that Rowberry's name appeared on the San Francisco *Drummer* masthead. Even then he was listed—and this is precisely accurate—not as part of *Drummer*, but as editor of *The Alternate*. While I was editor-in-chief of *Drummer* issues 19-30 (plus hybrid issues 18, 30, 31, 32, and *Son of Drummer*), Rowberry was sitting off by himself in a small office, very *mondo depresso*, very withdrawn, chewing chocolates and spying on how I managed my *Drummer* staff. He was working on *The Alternate,* and as "assistant editor" on *Mach,* had absolutely nothing to do with how I conceptualized the gestalt in my essentialist run of *Drummer.*

Rowberry water-skied in my wake: my own original feature on Pasolini and *Salo* (*Drummer* 20, January 1978) was followed a year later by Rowberry's feature on *Salo* (*Alternate* 8, January 1979). With his gift for lip-synching leather themes, Rowberry was John Embry, Jr. He was not a "Son of *Drummer.*" Like Preston, he was not even a friend of *Drummer.* He was a "Son of Embry."

Edmund Miller writing in *The Gay and Lesbian Literary Heritage* pegged John Rowberry with a profile in an obituary summary of his talent which gives objective correlative to my eyewitness testimony: "John Rowberry (1948-1993) who has since [*sic*] become a critic and bibliographer of gay video porn, is perhaps less important as a storyteller in his own right than for encouraging writers like [Aaron] Travis [Steven Saylor] and [John] Preston when he [Rowberry] was editor of *Drummer.*"

In fact, Rowberry was never Preston's mentor for *Mr. Benson.* As noted, long before Rowberry became editor, I had accepted, edited, and serialized the entire manuscript of *Mr. Benson,* and had published five of its ten chapters eighteen months before Rowberry followed me with the full title of "editor." The *Drummer* masthead shows that Rowberry succeeded me only as "Associate Editor" (January 1980) and did not succeed me as "Editor" until thirteen months after my exit when his job description was bumped up with *Drummer* 40 (January 1981). Even that title was a discount Rowberry fumed about because he wanted to be editor-in-chief.

Miller concluded with an insight into Rowberry's dissonance: "Though he [Rowberry] certainly plunges into all the mythic themes [the way he tried to plunge into the esthetics and erotics of *Drummer*], the vision is always a little off." (Page 263)

Rowberry and I never had one single conversation about my *Drummer*. Nor one cup of coffee. It may sound terrible to latter-day leather discussion groups, but in the sexual class-and-caste system of the 1950s-1970s, tops like me and bottoms like him rarely spoke. Even if not overtly invoked, leather ritual behavior affected daily life and attitude. It *was* an S&M magazine after all.

When Rowberry, with empty drawers, approached me to help fill his *Alternate* pages, I explained I was identified with *Drummer* and *Drummer* only; to write for the *Alternate* would take time from *Drummer* and would confuse readers about the separation of the two magazines.

Truth be told, this was the real-life S&M pecking order and the leather culture custom at the time when I was editor-in-chief. The new-hire slave-boy, Rowberry, queeny and snotty with LA attitude, was dismissed as, we all joked, "the office boy." He was a closet chicken hawk, and no leather player on Folsom Street. Within minutes of my exiting *Drummer*, Rowberry cozied up to the kindly art director Al Shapiro who was himself exiting because of cash and copyright issues with Embry. Rowberry sought some quick mentoring and gave Al a signed black-and-white photograph shot by Richard Fontaine that is a "signature" and characteristic picture satirizing Rowberry. In the overhead shot, looking down, he is outdoors, naked, with a long rope noosed around his neck, and he is crawling up cement stairs nude on his hands and knees, which is pretty much what he did to become editor of *Drummer* by attrition. Rowberry inscribed the photo: "Thanks, Al, for making it all possible....JWR." Having helped Rowberry whom he did not want to work with, Shapiro shrugged, gave the photo to me as a joke, quit *Drummer*, and took employment as art director for the risque book and video publisher, the Dirty Frenchman, at Le Salon, 1118 Polk Street.

Fifteen years later, Tony DeBlase and Joseph W. Bean, editor 1989-1993, both correctly credited the naming and invention of the "Tough Customers" column to "Fritscher" in *Drummer* 188 (September 1995), the 20th Anniversary Issue. Joseph Bean specified: "The first generation of *Drummer* offspring are the spinoff publications created by the publisher and staff... *Tough Customers*...started as pages devised by Jack Fritscher, and became a new publication when Paul Martin and I hatched the [separate magazine] idea years later [in 1990]."

In *Drummer* 143 (October 1990), pages 18-22, I purposely re-staked my intellectual claim to my "Tough Customers" concept in the feature article I wrote for Mikal Bales and Zeus Studio titled, "Radical Nipples: Photography by Zeus Studios and a Few Other Tough Customers."

My "Tough Customers" had import as the first self-fashioning identity column of leather masculinity filled by the readers. With the dawn of video on the horizon, I had planned to develop my "Tough Customers" concept into a line of *Drummer* videos. Considering the media mentoring I did aiding the startup of the video businesses of Old Reliable (1981), of Chip Weichelt's Academy Training Center (1989), and of Beardog Hoffman's Brush Creek Media (1995), I could have made Embry a million dollars in video that would have supported *Drummer* forever. Instead, I started my own company, Palm Drive Video in 1982.

"Tough Customers" as a high-concept was also "borrowed" for the tag line inside an ad for the wannabe *Drummer* leather bar in Houston called "The Drum" (*Drummer* 65, page 78).

Embry was still spewing in 1995, zinging in little digs in his *Manifest Reader* 26, page 54, in which he, Saint Embry, protesting too much how very conscious he was of writing true history in *Drummer*, misspelled my last name. I mention that only because it was a small thing indicative of his larger dismissiveness, and an index of his pettiness. *Fritscher* is no harder an ethnic name to spell than John *Embry* or Mark *Hemry* or Sam *Steward* or Jim *Stewart* or Robert *Mapplethorpe* or Robert *Opel* if one is paying attention. He could have practiced writing my name on those checks he never paid me. This über-publisher's accidental-on-purpose blunder was a monkey-wrench tossed to deflect research accuracy regarding the "true history" he claimed to value. It was as if he knew Google was coming. To a debutante of Embry's generation raised on the manners of Emily Post, misspelling a name is a major social *faux pas* because one always spells given and surnames exactly as spelled by the person named.

Pronunciation follows similarly. For instance, it insults the memory of Robert Mapplethorpe when someone chats me up about "Mmm-*Apple*-thorpe," and I, without any particular inflection of accusation, reply with Robert's own pronunciation, "May-pole-thorpe," and the questioner continues to say "Mmm-*Apple*-thorpe."

In that same *Manifest Reader* 26 in which Embry claimed he was feeling like gay avatar "Scarlett O'Hara," (page 49), his politically correct feminist reviewer John F. Karr took a swipe at my "*Drummer* novel," *Some Dance to Remember: A Memoir-Novel of San Francisco 1970-1982*. In the course of damning Felice Picano's *Like People in History* (page 92), Karr griped that the publishers of both books and some reviewers, had touted each as "the gay *Gone with the Wind*." In fact, before Karr reviewed my novel, David Perry in *The Advocate* called *Some Dance* the "gay *Gone with the Wind*." Karr slammed his review shut with: "I only finished the book [*Like People* because my editor [Embry] told me I had to in order to review it."

Such hand-jive gives some measure of the longevity and reach of the Embry grudge system and Blacklist. Six years after *Some Dance* was published and won a Finalist Lambda Award, Karr lumped Picano and me together: "This isn't the first time we've seen 'The gay *Gone with the Wind*' bandied about on a dust jacket."

Margaret Mitchell's novel, and the movie that played repeatedly at the Castro Theater in the 1970s, was a paradigm of gay survival. In an age of AIDS, I wanted to make that connection. In *Some Dance to Remember*, the protagonist's name is specifically Ryan O'Hara and his nickname is "Scarlett O'Hara." The "American Civil War" and the "Burning of Atlanta" prefigure the "gay civil war over gender" as well as the "burning of the Barracks on Folsom Street" at the same moment that GRID/HIV/AIDS and the VCR changed gay culture in 1981.

Despite Karr's politically correct *a priori* feminist principles that estranged him intellectually from considerations of homomasculinity, he was nevertheless an insightful arts critic whom I liked personally. As a principal reviewer for the *Bay Area Reporter* in San Francisco, he penned generous reviews of my books and videos, and particularly my magazine work, for which any writer would always remain grateful.

> Jack Fritscher is an anarchist of gay sexual prose, the man who invented the South of Market prose style (as well as its magazines, which have never been the same without him). In anthologizing his work from the dozen magazines in which it originally appeared, under the title *Corporal in Charge of Taking Care of Captain O'Malley and Other Stories*, Gay Sunshine Press has done Fritscher's fans and his initiates a favor, and also thrown down a gauntlet (black leather, of course) to other writers. Fritscher's writing is a cold slap in the face, an awakening to words and the expression of sexuality that never loses its sting....His sex is decidedly unsafe, most at home with spit and slaps, piss and dirty rectums. It is aggressive, abusive, extreme, and at times (I have to say it), politically incorrect....Fritscher has roamed the furthest corners of sexuality, and can lead you on head trips unequaled by any other gay writer I know of. You may resist, as I did, some of the aggression, machismo, and sexual practices, only to be won over by Fritscher's prose....Fritscher is a knee in the groin. —John F. Karr, *Bay Area Reporter*, June 27, 1985

When I investigated emerging homomasculine queer theory in the fiction of *Some Dance to Remember*, his feminist bias overcame his esthetic analysis of the text he rejected as too "butch" in his review "*Some Dance to Remember*: The Rise and Fall of Butch," *Bay Area Reporter*, April 12, 1990. Why did Embry hire a male feminist to review books and videos for the masculine-identified readers of his *MR* magazines? May masculinists write for feminist publications? *The Harvard Gay and Lesbian Review* told me, literally, it did not know how to review my novel *The Geography of Women: A Romantic Comedy* (1998) because it was a story about women written by a man. Goodbye to Henrik Ibsen's Hedda and Nora! So long to Tennessee Williams' Amanda, Blanche, Stella, Maggie, Serafina, Violet Venable, Alexandra Del Lago, and Mrs. Stone! Gore Vidal claimed, "There is no actress on earth who will not testify that Williams created the best women characters in the modern theatre." That *Gay and Lesbian Review* sexism from the 1990s seems a subject for another GLBT literary panel. Karr was a prolific journalist. So Embry paid little heed to Karr's politics because the disciplined Karr could meet deadlines with column inches to fill his hungry magazines.

Surviving my thirty years with Embry, I moved on professionally, like others on the Blacklist. I absorbed Embry's enmity, sucked it up, got a hard-on watching him self-destruct, and let my work speak for itself.

Following Larry Townsend's contentious, and temporary, 1980s "peace accord" with Embry in order to get free publicity for his LT Publications in *Drummer*, I sent Embry a kiss-and-make-up letter on August 25, 1989, ten years after our breakup, and one year before his rental Karr tried to run me down. I saw no reason to exclude Embry from my work in 1990s *Drummer* and I wanted to include him in the pages of this book which was already several years into production.

Mr. John Embry
PO Box [number deleted]
Forestville CA 95436
August 25, 1989

Dear John,

So much time has passed since we have seen each other and talked that the statute of limitations must have run out on whatever, as they say in Hollywood, creative differences colored our past in the highly charged '70s. Playing in *The Rose*, Bette Midler says to her audience:

"I forgive you. Will you forgive me?" If hatchets need burying, let's do it. If there is no hatchet, then let's put our heads together.

My proposal to you is as professional as personal. *Drummer* has asked me to write a continuing column on the history of international leather called "Rear-View Mirror." [See *Drummer* 125, February 1989, page 82, for the DeBlase announcement of Fritscher anchoring "Rear-View Mirror."] I mentioned to Tony, who had also thought of you and heartily agreed, that the time had come to document the history of your conception and invention of *Drummer*. (The LA stuff, Jeanne Barney et al., Ed Davis, your exodus to SF, etc.). However, we'd like to consider a broader interview that is you telling your story for journalistic and gay popular history from even before *Drummer*; then including *Drummer*; finally progressing to your new and current projects and publications.

If this very professional approach pleases you, we can do the interview in person, on videotape, so that your story and your image can exist for gay archives present and future; or we can do it over the telephone as we chat and record your history.

In the issue of *Drummer* due out around September 20, I have an article on Robert Mapplethorpe. I recently was on the interviewee end of a five-hour recorded phone call from Manhattan, as Robert had given a list of friends to the journalist Patricia Morrisroe (who has a major Random House book contract and has interviewed RM's family). It turns out Ms. Morrisroe said that I am the only one on that particular list from the '70s who has survived....Because the A-word has so decimated our ranks, and because you and Al Shapiro and I happened more than one gay generation ago, it's important that you tell your story before others start telling it. As I recall, we had a basic human respect for each other, more than a little professional respect, and some creative fun. (I'll never forget your always trying to put dialog balloons on photo spreads and me always trying to pull them off, and both of us getting our way alternating issues.)

Besides, to tidy things up, it would be nice to collaborate once again. When you arrived in SF, you had a new mag that needed a voice; I had a voice and needed a mag. Ours is almost a boy-meets-boy comedy. You didn't give me my start in publishing, but you certainly gave me a free-handed and free-spirited opening that with you and Al Shapiro (who truly became my intimate friend who drew his last drawing for me) turned *Drummer* into a gay popular culture publishing phenomenon. I like to remember those days in the best of lights, because when they were good, they were very good, and because these days, almost ten years into the plague, with so much death all around us, anyone a person knew "then" has become valuable not only as a link to our personal and gay-group past, but as a survivor who can tell the whole new generation who has come out in the last ten years all the different versions of the way we once were in the golden days when we were Inventing It All.

Please write or call. We live so close to each other here in the country. We can meet for coffee or we can set up a date for the interview, or you can say, what I hope you won't say, thanks, but no thanks. The point is for us survivors to get your story, who you are, where you came from, how you invented an institution, and where you are and are going.

Of course, best regards to Mario, who, if he likes, is most heartily welcome to be part of the interview, because he too has been a part of this whole scenario which has gotten bigger than any one of us.

Sincerely,
Jack Fritscher
cc. Anthony F. DeBlase

Embry, who never buried a hatchet, never responded to my 1989 letter. Perhaps he declined because of his undying disdain for Tony DeBlase. Nine years later in early 1998, he himself phoned me for the first time in twenty years. He was finally a one-man band. In our leather Bloomsbury, he had achieved Virginia Woolf's dream: He had a room of his own, "five-hundred pounds a year," and a computer. He wasn't so much a solo act as he was abandoned by everyone "who done him wrong." As I had brushed up on graphic design for *Drummer* at UC Berkeley, he had learned PageMaker at Santa Rosa Junior College. He proposed to trade some of my photos and stories on disc, not for pay, but for free ad space for my Palm Drive Video. He was designing and building pages for his new magazine venture, the "MR" brand magazines, *Manifest Reader, Manhood Rituals*, and *Super MR* which combined *Manifest Reader* and *Manhood Rituals*.

Neither of us gentlemen made any mention of our past other than to agree that the 1970s had been "the Golden Age of *Drummer*." When *Drummer* changed owners in 1986, DeBlase had Embry sign a non-competition clause. When the limit expired in the 1990s, Embry jumped back in business. As I had done in the 1980s with both *Man2Man* and the *California Action Guide*, Embry followed suit and created yet another "Virtual *Drummer*": his own *Manifest Reader* series.

In the third act of his life, waxing nostalgic for those classic issues of 1970s *Drummer*, he decided to revive those glory-days. In his 1990s resurrection, in *Manhood Rituals* 2, he editorialized on the inside front cover:

But talk about de javu [sic]! Our *Drummer* business manager Jerry Lasley [who arrived and disappeared in the 1980s through the revolving door that was *Drummer*] has reappeared to again do what he did so well....It would have been something to have had Marge [aka Marj as the lady signed her name], our lady typesetter pounding out the copy, cigarette hanging out of her smiling mouth. And A. Jay, our art director, and Jeannie [sic] Barney and/or John Rowberry editing. We even received a photographic offering from former editor Jack Fritscher of what he claims Robert Payne *should* look like. Out of that long ago, there were writers and artists and photographers whose contributions made magic.

The cover-quality photo I had sent him was of my Palm Drive Video model, Chris Duffy aka Bull Stanton. My little joke was that after all these years a photograph of the fictional "Robert Payne" ought to have aged a bit into a guy at least thirty-something and hot. Making no mention of *The Portrait of Dorian Gray*, I offered a sexy pseudonymous face to fit the pseudonymous "Robert Payne" to whom the unimaginative Embry had never tried over thirty years to give a signature "face" that identifies a brand. As it happened, Embry fell for the photo of Chris Duffy, but not to front "Robert Payne."

In *Manhood Rituals* 3 (1999), page 2, he wrote:

We have been pouring though the first 100 issues of *Drummer*, not so much to lift, or re-live, but to check what to seek out, what worked and what to avoid duplicating. It is not a simple task but one pleasantly filled with powerful memories of other times and people and circumstances.

We even looked up our third issue of *Drummer* which might have been no great shakes by today's publishing standards but, considering there was no one else doing it, issue #3 wasn't so bad.

Embry's claim-jumping ego and his revisionist history, declaring "no one else was doing it," conveniently denied all the pioneer magazines that existed around the startup of *Drummer* twenty-five years earlier in 1975. *Drummer* was no immaculate conception born in a vacuum. *Drummer* had gay pop-culture roots. In truth, Clark Polak's *Drum* (1964-1967) had been "doing it" with a circulation of 10,000; *Queen's Quarterly* (1969-c. 1980) was "doing it"; *Blueboy* (1974-2007) was "doing it"; so was *After Dark* (1968-1982). Their publishing standards in form and content were professional. In fact, only six issues after *Drummer* 3, Embry acknowledged the superiority of the competition in *Drummer* 9, page 72, writing about *Blueboy*:

> This publication, out of Miami, has made great strides in circulation, appearance, and national acceptance....Its pages are lush with color, arty as hell, and they have come as close as anyone to the oft aimed at ideal of a "gay *Playboy*."....It even has some "straight" advertisers.

In March 1977, when Embry offered me the San Francisco job of editor-in-chief, I almost turned him down. His LA version of *Drummer* was inferior in form and content to the competing magazines he envied. He himself was a train wreck of psychological and legal troubles from the Slave Auction bust. Nevertheless, I took his offer as a challenge because I saw I might actualize the potential of *Drummer* among the hundreds of leathermen I knew well enough to reflect them and their interests. Two cards that I didn't know were in the hand Embry dealt me were the "wild deuce" of his cancer, and the "Joker" of his obstructionist personality.

To resurrect some of "his" 1970s greatest hits from *Drummer*, he asked to reprint my "Cigar Blues" and "Prison Blues." Although Embry had never put my byline on the cover of *Drummer*, he surprised me with cover billing when he actually printed my name for "Cigar Blues" on *Manhood Rituals* 3 (1999). In *Super MR* #5 (2000), he republished my "Gay Deteriorata" from *Drummer* 21 (March 1978). Was Embry being passive-aggressive? Whereas in *Drummer*, Al Shapiro had designed my *Desiderata* satire as a full-page hippie poster, Embry buried the text on the masthead, reduced it to an eye chart of around eight-point type with my name bylined in maybe a four-point. In the same *Super MR* #5, he reproduced two Sparrow-Fritscher photos of Mike Glassman aka "Ed Dinakos" on pages 6 and 82, crediting them insufficiently to my former lover "David Sparrow" who had died of AIDS in 1992. He also published a half-page photo ad, page 57, for my Palm Drive Video feature *Sunset Bull*. When he serialized "Prison Blues" which he re-titled "Confessions of a Jailhouse Tour Junkie," he listed the title of the feature itself on the covers of both *Super MR* #6 (2000) and *Super MR* #7 (2001).

In 1975, as the forty-something Embry had relied on stills from the 1970s movie, *Born to Raise Hell*, the seventy-something Embry wanted to publish my photos of Duffy who starred in my 1994 feature, *Sunset Bull*.

Embry famously lacked graphic courage and edge for his covers. Most of the eleven-year gallery of covers he chose for his *Drummer* were not so hot, often predictable, and repetitious. Perhaps with censors, printers, distributors, retail sales, and photographer and model fees driving him, he selected, at his worst, generic torsos, or, at his best, pleasant Mr. Drummer contestants who posed for free. Very few of his covers leapt off the page. He had erred on his campy "Cycle Sluts" cover (*Drummer* 9). He had trashed the "Authentic Biker-for-Hire" Mapplethorpe cover (*Drummer* 24). Yet he was on the phone, not exactly hat in hand, but drumming up "my "writing and photography to recreate "his" nostalgia. In *Super MR* #5 (2000), page 6, Embry recanted his strange grudge against the 1978 Mapplethorpe cover when he reprinted that cover with the caption: "Robert Mapplethorpe's first cover anywhere was on...*Drummer* 24 due to the efforts of then-editor Jack Fritscher."

The Chris Duffy Story:
Mr. America, Chris Duffy, in *Sunset Bull(evard)*

Embry was lured by Chris Duffy's universal appeal. Duffy had "It." My cover photos of Duffy had appeared on several magazines rivaling Embry's on the news stands: *Thrust* (November 1996), *International Leatherman* (March 1997), and *Bear* 62 (September 2000). My photos of Chris Duffy also appeared in the coffee-table photo book, *American Men* (London, 1994), and on the cover of the second American edition of *Corporal in Charge of Taking Care of Captain O'Malley* (2000).

Embry, however, had a wicked backhand. Was it spite or stupidity? He squandered the pictures of the international bodybuilding champion Chris Duffy who was passionately followed by legions of fans. He published him not on the glossy cover in color, but six times on interior pages in black and white in *Manhood Rituals* 2 (1998), page 32 (as a particularly bad "inkblot"); and twice inside *Manhood Rituals* 3 (1999), pages 27 and 35—with an additional photo credited to "David Sparrow" which he must have found buried in the *Drummer* files he claimed he "bought" from Robert Davolt; and twice in *Super MR* 6 (2000) on page 16 as well as on page 76 in a Palm Drive Video ad I took in trade; and in *Super MR* 7 (2001), page 42, as part of his Wings Mail Order Catalog.

His spiraling downgrade of the spectacular Mr. America Chris Duffy, fresh off his own ESPN bodybuilding show, was an esthetic and marketing blunder. Duffy's face and body sold thousands of magazines and videos. Once again, Embry made a graphic design mistake. On cheap rag paper, his inkblot presentation of Chris Duffy lacked the punch of a glossy color cover showcasing Duffy's "universal appeal."

Embry lost synergy. A Chris Duffy color cover would have bumped up sales of his magazine as well as my video, *Sunset Bull*, being sold by his own mail-order company, Alternate and Wings Distributing.

Distance, rather than dinner and dancing, defined Embry and me. Through his attitude-free employees, my pals, Rick Leathers and Frank Hatfield, he made a couple more overtures about writing and video. Frank Hatfield aka the *Drummer* author, Frank O'Rourke, was also his own mail-order company as Hatfield House producing and selling S&M audiotapes, and as XYZ Enterprises selling video from a Guerneville P. O. Box at the Russian River.

Frank Hatfield told me that he had worked internationally as a diplomat-spy. It was as if he wanted me to take him for a double-agent reporting to both Embry and me. He colorfully claimed he was a convicted gay bank robber, "an international bank robber," whom I interviewed on tape. He told me he was connected to the Mafia and had celebrated New Year's Eve with Meyer Lansky in Havana the night before Castro took over Cuba on January 1, 1959. One-upping every prison fantasy in San Francisco, he had done time, he said, at San Quentin before becoming advertising director, beginning in *Drummer* 54 (June 1982).

When Embry sold *Drummer*, Hatfield moved north of the Golden Gate Bridge with him. On the split-personalities masthead of *Manifest Reader*, featuring John H. Embry as publisher and Robert Payne as editor, Hatfield was listed as "Associate Editor Frank O'Rourke" and as "Frank Hatfield, Distribution." He was also manager of Embry's Wings Distributing and Alternate mail order, running the book-and-video business out of Canyon One Road under the redwoods in Rio Nido, one village east of Guerneville, where he lived in a house owned by Embry who was his landlord. Alternate Publishing had a P. O. Box one village to the south in Forestville. Their mass-mailer of brochures and magazines was located one more village to the south in Sebastopol. The "Buffalo Enterprises" bulk-mailing service Embry chose happened to be the mailer, and a friend, I had used since 1985 for my Palm Drive Video brochures. I hoped this zero degrees of separation was not a cosmic force field dooming us to be locked together as old souls forever.

Frank Hatfield facilitated Wings' distribution of the features I was directing for my Palm Drive Video. He sold hundreds of my videocassettes for Embry. Soon enough, payments due fell in arrears exactly as had the payment of salaries and fees due at *Drummer*. In no causal order, Hatfield trying his best to conduct daily business, was attacked and bitten severely under the armpit at the Russian River by a large dog that tried, he said, to eat him. He died soon after. Or maybe he joined the disappeared. Perhaps his name wasn't Frank Hatfield.

During those years, only once did Embry and I physically see each other.

In March 1996, Rick Leathers, who had begun working with Embry as early as *Drummer* 56 (August 1982), invited Mark Hemry and me to a reception Embry was hosting upstairs at his 18th and Castro Alternate Publishing office, the Wings Galleria. In the zero degrees, my friend, the Hun, who was a frequent artist in *Drummer*, had discovered a protégé in "Teddy of Paris." In 1994, the Hun had produced an attractive run of sixteen Teddy prints titled *Commando Three*. The severe leather-discipline drawings immediately inspired Embry into debuting the magazine-format book of Teddy drawings, *Magnifique* (1996). Two months later in May, Mark Hemry and I visited Teddy in Paris where our two documentary videos of New Orleans photographer, George Dureau, were inducted into the permanent collection of the Maison Europeenne de la Photographie. Dureau's work was featured in "Maimed Beauty," *Drummer* 93 (1986), pages 8 through 11.

At the Wings Galleria, Embry had not changed much physically, and his temperament was jolly enough, but, for all the *bonhomie*, a personal gulf yawned between us. Trading on nostalgia, we yet once again bonded professionally through the next years.

On June 20, 2000, Mark Hemry sent Embry the discs he had requested for my original-recipe *Drummer* articles such as "Prison Blues," as well as newer pieces such as "Horsemaster," "Wait Till Your Father Gets Home," and "RoughNight@Sodom.cum" (*cum* is correct), and a half-page ad for PalmDriveVideo.com. Embry and I were growing old separately together, and *Drummer* was our adult child who had died a year earlier in September 1999. I remember that death date specifically because *Drummer* and I had shared June 20 as a birthday. In 2000, I turned sixty-one, and Embry turned seventy-four, and *Drummer*, if it had survived the twentieth century, would have turned twenty-five.

Embry, sticking strictly to my 1970s writing, republished "Cigar Blues" (from *Drummer* 22, May 1978) with six of my Palm Drive Video photographs in *Manhood Rituals* #3; and "Prison Blues" (from *Drummer* 21, March, 1978) in *Super MR* #6 (2000). Inside Mark Hemry's package, I enfolded a handwritten personal note that I tried to conceive without irony:

Dear John Embry,

Congratulations on the 25th anniversary of *Drummer*. You created a legend with that magazine, and I am proud I was part of your dream. Thanks for making me your first and only San Francisco editor-in-chief. In many minds, we are inextricably bound together. *Wunderbar*!

Yours as always,
Jack Fritscher

Finally, on the subject of the Blacklist that traveled poisonously cross-country with Embry's apparatchik John Preston, I must add the "fair play" which historical novelist, Steven Saylor as Aaron Travis on Embry's payroll, gave me in his *Drummer* reviews of my books, such as *Corporal in Charge of Taking Care of Captain O'Malley* and *Leather Blues* in *Drummer* 81 (February 1985). Travis was also the creative "associate editor" of fiction to "editor" Rowberry; so he stood in proximity to my work published at the same time by Rowberry in East Coast magazines published by George Mavety, such as *Inches* and *Studflix: The Gay Video Magazine*. Saylor/Travis, while he adroitly pioneered the first partial *Drummer* "Fiction/Fetish Index," even with its alleged Blacklist "omissions," seemed to have escaped the Embry experience at *Drummer* with his spirit in tact, although he wrote in former *Drummer* model Scott O'Hara's *Steam* magazine (Volume 2, Number 1, 1994), that working at Embry's 1980s *Drummer* "was mind-boggling and mind-numbing—we were underpaid, disrespected and over-stimulated on a daily basis...."

However, in Saylor's obituary for Rowberry in *Steam* (Spring 1994), he miss-spoke when he wrote that Rowberry "created all the MMG [Mavety Media Group] magazines virtually by himself." Saylor ducked and covered with the word *virtually*. His adverb and verb choices should be carefully examined, because history is in this way revised. Saylor meant that as a packager for Mavety Media Group, Rowberry filled the existing magazines as a solo editor by collecting the talent together between the covers. In my meetings with Rowberry in his MMG office South of Market, he was alone, but he had plenty of technical, financial, and corporate backup from the "Italians" in New Jersey. Rowberry did not start up, nor did he invent, the magazines, *Just Men*, *Inches*, *Skin*, *Skinflicks*, and *Studflix* which, my stream of archived letters prove, I had helped Bob Johnson create and start during 1979-1981, years before Rowberry came on board.

Rowberry may have launched *Foreskin Quarterly* (1985)—with photographs I had obtained from my friend, German art-scatologist Gerhard Pohl—as well as *Uncut* (1987), but both magazines were commercial applications of the sincere and passionate writing of Joe Tiffenbach and Bud Berkeley in their *Uncircumcised Society of America (USA) Newsletter* and their book *Foreskin* (1983). Tiffenbach, whose name was Lou Alton, was the photographer who shot the cover of my *Drummer* 20 (January 1978), as well as the photos for my article, "Arab Death," which I bylined as "Denny Sargent," my protagonist in *I Am Curious (Leather)* in my *Son of Drummer* (September 1978). Those Tiffenbach photos of a nude young man rolling on wheels in the sand had been shot on assignment earlier in 1975 in Palm Springs. Having paid Tiffenbach for the shoot, Embry insisted that I reuse the three-year-old images for *Drummer* 20 because he wanted to squeeze his money's worth from the generic photos that in sunny concept and vanilla content really had nothing specific to do with leather or with *Drummer*.

The "Prince of Reprints" Embry ordered me to re-write "Arab Death" from pages he had torn out of some men's adventure magazine from the 1950s. The source was something like *Argosy*, one of those mags with an American air pilot tied spreadeagle with a busty Nazi wench poised to torture him. In fact, many of the longer written features in Embry's LA *Drummer*, such as the "Great Sadists in History" series, especially when signed by "Robert Payne," were re-writes plagiarized out of 1940s and 1950s men's pulp-adventure magazines and history books that were popular when he was a teenage masturbator. Some examples of Embry/Payne's "found" articles printed as "filler" in *Drummer* 14 were "The Third Degree" and "The Foreign Legion"; and, in *Drummer* 15, "Devil's Island" and "The Greek Way." At that time, my analysis of this theft of uninspired and stolen stories indicated that *Drummer* needed all the mouth-to-mouth resuscitation original writers could give to make it breathe fresh on its own as a gay men's adventure magazine. With that in mind, and to meet our monthly deadlines, I began writing my own original bespoke stories and features.

Decoding Rowberry personally and professionally in his magazine and video writing, I witnessed that Rowberry, who never met a twinkie chicken he didn't like, was deeply disturbed, even emotionally disturbed, by mature hairy men and facial hair. From 1984-1996, I sported a very full, long, and red-black Walt-Whitman beard down below my pecs. Rowberry once demanded of me: "Why? Why? What's it mean? What's it for?" I responded: "To wrap around cocks." He never asked again. His myopia for twenty-one-year-olds who looked fourteen, made him shortsighted as a journalist and a reviewer of gay culture. He did not get the emerging concept and mature needs of the homomasculine population making an erotic virtue of its own ageing by glamorizing male secondary sex characteristics the way I had begun in *Drummer* with my theme "In Praise of Older Men" and with my features about Daddies that six years later evolved into the new bear mystique.

At age 45, John W. Rowberry died as an adolescence-obsessed LA queen whose horizon, limiting to gay psychology, was "Youth" itself. He completely missed the gay pop-culture phenomenon of bears that publishing guru Richard Bulger glamorized in *Bear* magazine (1987) and that I then folded back into *Drummer* 119 (July 1988) along with the new gay-applied term, "mountainman," as a category with "biker," "cop," "cowboy," and "daddy." The 1980s bear concept of butch, rugged, and hairy men grew out of 1970s homomasculinity in *Drummer*. Insofar as Rowberry did not "get" bear masculinity, did he also not understand leather masculinity in the issues of *Drummer* he edited before he was fired by Embry? He was so personally distant from the *Drummer* mystique that his introductory biography to his personal papers catalogued at the Young Research Library for Special Collections at UCLA significantly listed all the magazines he worked for, but made no mention of his stint at *Drummer* which he never really valued.

Unlike all the real-world talent who rebuffed John Embry, slave-boy John Rowberry, like sex-hustler John Preston before him, sold his soul to Alternate Publishing in order to be published. Rowberry virtually moved bag and baggage into Embry's "Hotel California"—that particular ring of gay hell where, if you check in, you can never leave. *Drummer* exacted a huge toll on Rowberry. His business identity destroyed his personal identity. In the world's worst tutorial, Embry's tactics became Rowberry's values. Because women are born to teach men irony, Jeanne Barney drew back the curtain when she observed the following damage:

> As for Rowberry's lover, the art collector, Charles "Bob" Musgrave, well, he basked, not entirely by choice in Rowberry's light. There was room for only one star in that family, and that was John Rowberry himself.

Charles Musgrave, an artist and a so-called "known art collector," was a person of interest, if not a suspect, in the detective case Robert Davolt later raised about "the missing art at *Drummer*." Musgrave, with his own degrees of easy access to the wealth of art piled around Rowberry's feet, was also listed as a contributor, for instance, in the Embry-Rowberry *Manifest* (without the word *Reader*) 11, April 1983. An example of Musgrave's talent was printed as a book review column in *Drummer* 41 (September 1980), page 67. Musgrave is so smug about airing his own superiority to the books he chose to review that he unwittingly deconstructed Rowberry's editing skills and judgement. First: None of the three books fit the interests of *Drummer* readers and should not have been reviewed at all. Second: If the books were as bad as Musgrave said, there was no reason to review them other than to let Musgrave and Rowberry vent their inner kveens. Their tea-for-two salon around *Drummer* was way different from my international salon around *Drummer*. Years later, a photograph shot by Musgrave was dug up from the archives to illustrate Guy Baldwin's "Ties That Bind" in *Drummer* 131 (July 1989), page 13.

Before Embry and I, in our third act, matured into "working together" again—at arm's length, the following 1979 "Notice," repeated here from an earlier chapter, but with additional annotations, is typical of how Embry waxed his moustache and twirled his cape as he pinned a "Scarlet Letter" on Jeanne Barney who claimed in 2006 that Embry still owed her thousands of dollars, plus interest.

What was Embry's mystique? His ability at fascination? In spite of everything, Barney remained on-again-off-again friends with Embry for thirty-five years until he died in 2010. Like Embry, Larry Townsend ran equally hot and cold, from estranged to ambiguous, with his frenemies from 1970 to his death in 2008, when he was on the outs with both Embry and Barney. I myself was bewitched, bothered, and bewildered by Embry from 1977 to years beyond his passing.

If this shrill "Notice," a kind of slut-shaming of Jeanne Barney, was how Embry spoke in public, imagine what rage he roared in his unguarded voice to his staff and to his contributors, in person and in private letters and emails. Quoted exactly, the Blacklist vendetta that follows was Embry's anti-Barney rant. As editor-in-chief, I told him I did not want his personal harangue in my issue, *Drummer* 30, page 38, which was nineteen issues and three years after Jeanne Barney quit Embry. What is the length of a grudge?

NOTICE: Mrs. Jeanne Chelsey Barney, aka "Barney" and "J. Barney" [Note his hissing high dudgeon about her aliases as opposed to his. And his paternalistic dismissal of her as a heterosexual "Mrs."] is representing herself as the owner of the LEATHER FRATERNITY and is operating out of a mail drop box in La Crescenta, California. [As if a PO Box is somehow proof of crime in a magazine full of postal box addresses.] She has solicited memberships in this "Fraternity," promising subscriptions to *Drummer* magazine as part of its benefits. Later, after being cut off by *Drummer* and two of its distributors for nonpayment, she is substituting a multilithed "Newsletter," promised monthly and containing offers of merchandise in the "Fraternity's" name, membership pitches and solicitation of contributions as well as scurrilous attacks on ALTERNATE PUBLISHING and its people. Notice is hereby given that THE LEATHER FRATERNITY is a fully protected name since 1973 [Again, this claim of the specific word *protected* which he may have chosen because it is illegal to say something is trademarked when in fact it is not] and has no connection whatever with Mrs. Barney's effort.....It does not publish names of members... as Mrs. Barney has done. Mrs. Barney is offering remnants of her unpaid-for [with Embry, it's always about the money] *Drummer* inventory at inflated prices....We would appreciate being notified of any checks to *Drummer* or ALTERNATE PUBLISHING endorsed...by anyone other than this company [spinning a charge of embezzlement Barney never did].

When I asked Jeanne Barney in 2006 about this slam in 1979, she wrote: "Oh, for Christ's sake! There are so many inaccuracies in his rant as to be laughable!"

5. AGAINST OTHER GAY MAGAZINES: LITERARY FEUDS

Is it good business for feuding publishers to trash other magazines to gin up publicity and controversy? Embry took potshots gratuitously attacking magazines such as *Blueboy* (*Drummer* 9), *In Touch, Honcho,* and *Man2Man Quarterly.* For instance, the minute after *Man2Man* first hit the stands, claim-jumper Embry added this new tag line to *Drummer*: "More Man-to-Man Personals Than Any Other Magazine." He also added it to his *Manifest Reader.* The phrase "man-to-man" was a commonplace of American language. My father often said it to me. But it had not been mentioned in connection with post-Stonewall homosexuality, and, except for my announcement in *Drummer* 30 (June 1979, page 18) about the arrival of a new magazine, it was likely never written in *Drummer* before the first publication of *Man2Man*. (By 1982, Mark Hemry had bought MAN2MAN as the vanity license plate for our red Ford F-100 truck used in so many photo and video shoots, including the cover of *Drummer* 140, June 1990.)

Imitation may be the sincerest form of flattery, but, with his light-fingered co-optation of my coinage, I figured Embry gave envious evidence he would have liked to have included my *avant-garde* concept of *Man2Man* as a feature inside *Drummer* exactly as he had my concept of "Tough Customers." Had he paid me for editing *Drummer*, it is conceivable that my *Man2Man Quarterly* would have appeared within his empire of *Drummer* magazines along with *Tough Customers*, *Mach*, and *The Alternate*. When Anthony DeBlase published the landmark *Drummer* 100 (October 1986), he introduced the "Dear Sir" personal classifieds as "Hot Man-To-Man Contact for a Cool 50-Cents Per Word."

Let me play the American pop-culture scholar I became with my analyses of gay popular culture in the 1960s, and continued to be in *Drummer* which I subtitled on the masthead of *Drummer* 23 (July 1978) and in my editorial: "The American Review of Gay Popular Culture." With that, I was planting a flag for a declaration of gay independence, an assertive vision of the new direction and new character of a *Drummer* that reflected its grass-roots readers and how we lived in the emerging gay pop culture of that first liberated decade after Stonewall.

Editorial written May, 1978; published in *Drummer* 23 (July 1978):

GETTING OFF

Drummer expands to bring you the same filth,
but now disguised with socially redeeming scholarly significance...

Drummer: The American Review
of Gay Popular Culture
by Jack Fritscher

All right! So where's *Drummer* get the leather balls to assume, yeah, assume to track, report, and chronicle what's happening in the masculine world of gay men? How legit can a rag get without losing its j/o quality? Pretty g . d. legit and pretty hard-assed. No other mag sticks it into the gay subculture the way *Drummer* sticks it for you. No other gay mag touches the same raw nerve of what goes on in a wide cross-section of gay heads after midnight, after the lights go down low. *Drummer* dares to reassure you that even with the extremes that you fantasize about in your most secret heart of hards: you are not alone.

GAY POP CULTURE: A REFLECTION OF YOU, NARCISSUS

Drummer is no plastic fantasy. Every issue increasingly reflects what our readers want as they send us more of what and where they're coming from: photos they snap, stories and articles they write, artwork they draw. *Drummer* exists by popular demand. Readers need their *Drummer* fix. We can't come out fast enough. IF DRUMMER DIDN'T EXIST, WE'D HAVE TO BE INVENTED. *Drummer*'s lucky enough to be a distinct medium for a genuine level of popular consciousness in the gay community. *Drummer* assures guys it's okay not to be locked into a 21-year-old all-American boy image, because our readers (you) are not boys. You're adult men.

EVEN BLUEBOYS GET THE COWS

You prefer hard sex the way you prefer men. You're not afraid of your rich fantasy life. You're not afraid of actualizing your fantasies. You've begun to notice that some gay periodicals, like *Blueboy*, are little more than soft-focus clones from erotic-photo mail-order catalogs. *Drummer* has always had a different, harder beat. *Drummer* isn't *Vogue* in butch drag. *Drummer* is increasingly a voice of a now less-closeted part of gay society. *Drummer* is a forum for men who enjoy authentic S&M Sensuality and Mutuality.

We want to touch the way you really are "after dark." When you've gone beyond the pretty-baby stage, you want articles, interviews, and fiction that stroke your head. We're not the last word on gay pop culture; but we're the first, and we're working to be the best. We dare to publish attitudes others repress. First, because you want our point of view which we picked up from you. Second, because certain subjects need to be printed to give full dimension to the genuinely alternate ways of being an adult, masculine, gay man in this country at this time.

DRUMMER IS AGGRESSIVE

Just you mention *Drummer* in a roomful of guys. You'll get a heavy feedback of attitude. They either love us or hate us. They either understand us (meaning themselves) or they refuse to understand us (again, meaning themselves). Some of them have every issue from Number One. Some of them wouldn't let *Drummer* sully their art-deco coffee tables. But lots of them interestingly enough, are closet *Drummer* boys: they keep their secret copy of our latest issue hidden handily under the bed next to the grease, the poppers, and the clothes pins.

YOU ARE OUR VOICE: YOU "OUT" THE *POPULAR* IN POP CULTURE

> *Drummer* is a duo-purpose magazine. As we slowly evolve, we want to get your head off as much as we've always gotten your, uh, other head off. In short, *Drummer* has the balls to assume to report, rehash, and reshuffle at a certain expressive level of gay pop culture, because you keep buying and demanding this certain stuff, issue after issue. You keep telling us what you want to see and read. We go beyond "models"—hot as they are. We prefer to reflect more authentic, real-life men. You ask for the same in our articles and fiction. It's you after all, who put the *popular* in pop culture. Your very special, adult, masculine voice gives *Drummer* its very definite responsibility, purpose, and direction.

Considering how Embry himself alarmed the LAPD with risky topics of necrophilia, bestiality, coprophagia, blood, and slavery, it is odd that in *Drummer* 9, page 72, he faulted *Blueboy* (September 1976) for its special leather feature, "S&M 1976." When Embry called the feature a "campy bomb" that "can set off" the "homophobic police," he spoke from experience because he was still clipping newspaper articles about his own Slave Auction "bomb" out of the *LA Times*, the *LA Herald-Examiner*, *The National Enquirer*, *The Sentinel*, and the *San Francisco Chronicle* whose Charles McCabe in his column, "Himself," headlined satirically: "Crimes Against Nature (2)."

> In the zero degrees of San Francisco journalism, when the Irish-American columnist Charles McCabe was found dead from a fall in his Telegraph Hill apartment on May 1, 1983, his daughter needing someone to quickly board up the door the paramedics had kicked down, contacted my friend, the carpenter John Turngren, who needed my truck to transport sheets of plywood. With awe and respect, he and I found ourselves standing alone on the edge of the bloody carpet, hammers in hand, amidst the books, typewriter, clothes, and coffee cups of the popular journalist and activist who had opposed the Manhattanization of San Francisco in the late 1950s when he and his fellow columnist Herb Caen successfully crusaded to block construction of a US Steel Tower, near the Embarcadero YMCA, that would have risen eighty feet taller than the West Tower of the Bay Bridge.

John Embry attacked Don Embinder, the publisher of *Blueboy*, for what he himself had done tenfold. In attacking his rival publisher, Embry gave the first and only glimmer that in his heart of hearts he knew he himself had set off Chief Ed Davis and brought the LAPD down on his own head. He was already diverting the accusation that followed him all the years since.

Embry alone nearly destroyed *Drummer* on Saturday night, April 10, 1976.

Deep down, was this man, who never admitted to shame, covering his guilt through the subterfuge of attacking *Blueboy*?

Less deep down, he was competing in a marketing turf war with *Blueboy* by trying to destroy Embinder's reputation.

That was the bully Embry's core technique for his Blacklist: To destroy the reputation of anyone who resisted him.

It is gut-busting hilarious to read Embry's *Drummer* 9 editorial desperately ridiculing *Blueboy*, founded in 1974, a year before issue one of *Drummer*, for venturing

> ...into an area it was completely unqualified for...the result is disastrous. Four pages of a suicide in a bathtub, with the blood going down the drain. A simulated (we assume) corpse may be somebody's idea of S&M [said Embry, the indignant publisher of the "Fetish: Necrophilia" feature in *Drummer* 4 and the "White Death" snuff poem in *Drummer* 5], but it isn't ours. There are glittering razor blades slicing nipples [raged the publisher who soon after printed Mapplethorpe's photo of a cut-and-bloodied cock and balls tied to a bondage board in *Son of Drummer*]....There are interesting shots of somebody's dungeon entitled "Black Room" [said the publisher who printed photos of his own *Drummer* dungeon and Fritscher photos of the Catacombs].... The feature article on "S&M 1976" is written by a woman who starts off admitting she knew nothing about the subject [complained the sensitive publisher whose founding Los Angeles editor-in-chief was the woman Jeanne Barney]....We have no intention of starting a rhubarb with *Blueboy* [said the publisher who owned a rhubarb patch].... A campy bomb like this [said the publisher famous for pasting camp cartoon balloons on serious S&M photographs].... May we respectfully [said the man who disrespected the writers, artists, and photographers who suggested topics to him] suggest topics to *Blueboy* other than this one. *Drummer* promises to steer clear of seascapes, travelogues, fashion shows [said the founding Barnum of the Mr. Drummer Contest] and the avant garde [said

the anti-*avant-garde* publisher who would soon work with Opel, Mapplethorpe, and Fritscher].

Seven years later, Embry, the Sisyphus, continued rolling his grudge uphill in the April 1983 issue of *Manifest [Reader]* 11, when he wrote on page 5, his "Publisher's Page":

> Things We Never Knew Department. We received the promo pictured at left [a display ad from *Torso* magazine touting, "How did *Torso* become the #1 gay magazine in only 5 issues?"]...which asks a question we would *love* to hear answered. *Torso* is the combined effort of former *Blueboy* publisher Don Embinder and [George Mavety's publishing group] Modernismo (*Mandate, Honcho,* and *Playguy*). But perhaps you didn't realize it was the #1 gay magazine either. We certainly didn't—and don't.

In Embry's unending shell game, he had the gall to print a full page ad in *Drummer* 14 selling—via his own mail-order company—the very issue of *Blueboy* he had condemned in *Drummer* 9. The ad trumpeted what Embry wanted for *Drummer*: the buzz of censorship and scandal that promotes sales. About *Blueboy*, Embry wrote: "Banned in Canada and Belgium. Now a Collector's Item! Only 500 Copies Left!"

6. AGAINST HIS TALENT POOL OF WRITERS & ARTISTS

Here I can only allege how famous *Drummer* contributors felt fall-out from the Blacklist, because the living, even my lovers and friends on this *Drummer* Salon list, may have other versions than my *Rashomon* recall: Larry Townsend, Tom of Finland (who was Blacklisted over money and never got a *Drummer* cover from Embry), David Sparrow, Robert Mapplethorpe, Al Shapiro, John Rechy (*Drummer* 16, *Drummer* 17, page 90), Crawford Barton, Fred Halsted, David Hurles (Old Reliable), Sam Steward (Phil Andros), Jim Kane, Ike Barnes, Ed Franklin, Rex, and Colt Studio co-founders, Jim French and Lou Thomas.

In *Drummer* 9 (Halloween 1976), Embry ran a half-page ad for the "Colt 1977 Calendar." Because of that issue's misdirected "Cycle Sluts" cover, Colt withdrew advertising for *Drummer* 10, and re-appeared no more than once again in the centerfold featuring Colt's Manfred Speer in trade for a Colt Studio ad in *Drummer* 19. Rumor abounded that something caused Jim French to refuse any further association of Colt with *Drummer*. Or was it with Embry? It is worth some scholar's essay in queer studies to opine why, like Tom of Finland, the iconic Colt Studio went missing for years from *Drummer*? What a perfect twenty-four-year marriage of homomasculinity and leather that could have been. Perhaps Colt was too sunny and too LA, and *Drummer* too dungeon-dark and too San Francisco, to be a match the way Lou Thomas' sweaty Target Studio in New York, spun out of the original Colt Studio, was just right for a dozen *Drummer* covers and centerfolds.

In later and less outlaw incarnations, Colt, like the Tom of Finland Foundation, launched a clothing line of leather fashions. Imagine if back in the day, mail-order retailer Embry, who sold *Drummer* t-shirts, had designed his own label of *Drummer* jeans, jackets, and boots, suitable, of course, for the fashion-week runway at the Mr. Drummer Contest and at the International Mr. Leather Contest. A man need only sniff his armpit to figure how a *Drummer* cologne in the 1970s might have been distinct from the scent introduced by the Tom of Finland Foundation in 2008: "Etat Libre d'Orange, 'Tom of Finland,' Eau de Parfum Spray, 50ml, $90, free shipping." While Embry had advertised his mail-order amyl nitrite poppers as potent "aromas" and fragrant "room odorizers" enhancing wild sex, Tom of Finland separated its Parfum from the "stank" of sex with the assurance that it was "...not a pornographic scent. Nor is it shocking."

My longtime associate, Robert Mainardi, editor of the handsome Gmunder book, *Jim French: The Creator of Colt Studio* (2011), mentioned to me the possibility that French perhaps refused to allow Colt photos in *Drummer* because French, taking a page from David Goodstein's *The Advocate*, did not want his noble Olympian photographs sharing a page with ignoble dildo ads. Such ostracism is a part of a possible answer because French's Colt photos and display ads appeared in dozens of other gay magazines and papers, all rivals of Embry when he was his most contentious in the late 1970s and early 1980s, including *The Advocate*, *Blueboy*, *Honcho*, *Mandate*, *Numbers*, and *Stallion*. They all featured erotic toy ads of one kind or another, so was there some personality conflict, or creative difference, that flared up between the tempestuous French and the tempestuous Embry shortly after French moved Colt Studio to LA's San Fernando Valley in 1974? French's former New York partner in Colt, Lou Thomas was happy to have his Target Studio photos published on the covers and centerfolds of *Drummer* in return for the free ads Embry gave in trade. In 1989, when Thomas died, however, he bequeathed his 1970s Target Studio photos not to *Drummer*, but to his pioneer inspiration, Chuck Renslow, founding photographer of 1950s Kris Studio and of the Leather Archives & Museum in Chicago.

In the zero degrees of separation, Embry did not calculate the intimacies and alliances of the shared pasts in the *Drummer* Salon such as I had with Lou Thomas, Robert Mapplethorpe, Sam Steward, David Sparrow, Jim Kane, Jim Stewart, and Al Shapiro who had been pals with Jim French from the time in the 1960s when Shapiro and French both lived in Brooklyn Heights off Joralemon Street in a building so gay its camp name was "KY Flats."

Pissing off both Mapplethorpe and me, Embry's "Inner Brutus" stabbed the two of us. On my own initiative, after Robert had flown from New York to show me his portfolio, I had produced, cast, designed, and personally paid for the Mapplethorpe cover shoot which Robert, unlike other *Drummer* photographers begging to be published "for free," would not do unless he was, in fact, paid. Embry sniped with intent to control and hurt the feelings of both Robert and me with a statement that was not true: "That Mapplethorpe cover was the worst selling issue we ever had."

Embry further angered Mapplethorpe when Embry, suffering a huge case of "Penis Envy," tried to shoot his own photograph to recreate Mapplethorpe's crucified-dick picture which I had published in 1978's *Son of Drummer*, page 16. In his first *Drummer* after my exit, Embry published his own graceless imitation of a Mapplethorpe picture: *Drummer* 31, page 73. For that bit of loose plagiarism, my Satanic Robert pledged to put a joke-y curse on Embry. Instead, Robert claimed he had his attorney send a letter threatening suit for violation of copyright, which, if true, would have made jealous Embry even angrier at me, the zealous editor, who was always pushing him to publish every contributor's copyright in line with the new Copyright Law of 1976 that went into effect January 1, 1978, at the height of the Golden Age of *Drummer*. Was it obstinacy that in the special issue, *Drummer Rides Again* (1979), scofflaw Embry reprinted Mapplethorpe's crucified-dick photograph, with no credit line and no copyright, to illustrate his own "Robert Payne" column on page 62? Was it accidentally on purpose that Embry toyed with the intellectual property of Robert Mapplethorpe in Robert Payne's *The Care and Training of the Male Slave II*?

Embry, republishing Jim Stewart's photos from *Drummer* 16 (June 1977) in *The Care and Training II* magazine, credited Stewart's photo on page 28 to Mapplethorpe who was militant that his photographs not be confused with any other leather photographer. Stewart himself received no credit for all his photos used as illustrations. In fact, the whole photo spread in *Care and Training II*, was so loosely credited that the only byline was for one photo by LA leatherman Dave Sands. Embry's layout seemed purposed to give the readers the "large" impression that virtually all the photos on pages 25 to 27 were by rising star Mapplethorpe. Furthering this grand illusion, Embry also published an authentic Mapplethorpe photo without permission at the end of this photo layout. By its key position, the photo with its accurate credit line, seemed to suggest to the casual reader that the entire photo feature was indeed by Mapplethorpe.

In his vendetta to disrespect Mapplethorpe, Embry, on the last page of *Drummer* 32, did an "end run" calling his theft "fair use." Because I was no longer editor-in-chief, I could no longer stop him. So the trickster published a "picture within a picture," skirting the intellectual property laws. The clever photo by Efren Ramirez showed the back of my friend, Ike Barnes, standing in uniform at the 80 Langton Street gallery (March 21, 1978), and looking at a wall hung with two Mapplethorpe photographs. Embry had directed the talented photo-journalist Ramirez, a frequent *Drummer* photographer, to aim his camera so the focal interest was not Barnes's back, but the exhibited full-frontal "Bloody Penis" photograph by Robert that Embry was forbidden to publish or imitate.

7. AGAINST *DRUMMER* PUBLISHER #2: ANTHONY DEBLASE & HIS CORPORATION, DESMODUS, INC.

Was it separation anxiety? Was it a control issue? Within the first year after selling *Drummer*, Embry, like an obsessive parent who cannot let go, trashed DeBlase and Desmodus, Inc. The occasion was the obituary I'd written in *Drummer* 107 (August 1987) for Al Shapiro who had died May 30, 1987.

At the height of the AIDS emergency, none of us, including publisher Tony Deblase, was taking gratuitous swipes at Embry so much as trying, in the face of tragic deaths, to write satirical comedy about the institutional life of *Drummer* during the three crazy years of the 1970s sex farce when Shapiro had worked as art director with me under Embry from March 1977 to February 1980.

The Embry-DeBlase publishing feud was between them, but Embry was ready to take on any comment about himself in Deblase's *Drummer*, even while he continued to advertise—in trade as part of his terms of sale— his *Manifest Reader* in two-page spreads in *Drummer*.

In *Drummer* 117 (June 1988), page 85, leather pioneer and reviewer Thor Stockman tore the "shameless" publisher and editors of *Manifest Reader* into tiny bits for reprinting stories printed earlier in *Drummer* to which they no longer owned any rights.

Similar comments also appeared in *Drummer* 145 (December 1990). While Embry railed against me, he railed also against Deblase's "almost monthly slurs" about Embry that had nothing to do with me, and everything to do with the public disdain around his reputation among staff, contributors, and subscribers. During that period, my work appeared only in *Drummer* 100 and *Drummer* 107. Hardly monthly. After the first nine issues (98-107) created by DeBlase, Embry exploded. He penned a "Letter to the Editor" slashing *Drummer* for what he felt was bias against himself.

Big mistake.

DeBlase was an S&M sadist top who thought it great sport to let bottoms torture themselves, and to let windbag Embry make fun of Embry. So he published 98% of Embry's letter dated August 18, 1987, and sent me a photocopy of the entire 100% excerpted here.

> Gentlemen: It would probably be best left ignored, but your almost monthly slurs and innuendoes regarding *Drummer*'s past management must be addressed. This past issue (#107) was too much even for me to laughingly pass off as *I cried all the way to the bank*. [Italics added.] In the guise of an "In Memoriam" piece on the passing of Al Shapiro, one-time editor [in chief] of *Drummer*, Jack Fritscher, whipped up a self-serving vendetta [said the inventor of his own vendetta, the *Drummer* Blacklist] that you have published without question or even editing [DeBlase and editor JimEd Thompson vetted my satirical essay, and judged it legally true and accurate for publication]....

The following final sentence—2% in Embry's original letter—was deleted by DeBlase from publication in *Drummer* because DeBlase knew it was false. Did DeBlase's deletion make Embry angry all over again? While he was crying all the way to the bank?

> ...In compensating Jack Fritscher for the article, please be advised that he still owes *Drummer* nine issues [not true] as editor for which he was paid in full [not true; Embry, who famously defaulted on his payments after publication, never paid anyone in advance; nor did he ever even suggest he had cancelled checks to prove such an advance]. —John H. Embry

In truth, much careful editorial and design discussion went into the heavy-duty collaborative tailoring of that DeBlase-Fritscher-Jameo Saunders-JimEd Thompson production of the A. Jay obituary in *Drummer* 107. In the specifics of content and style, we four were honoring one of our own beloved dead, Al Shapiro, who was the founding San Francisco art director of *Drummer*, as well as the creator of his own monthly cartoon-strip satire, *Harry Chess*, which he had begun in the 1960s in *Queen's Quarterly* and continued in the 1970s in *Drummer*. Besides the vetting of the essay by associate editor JimEd Thompson, my rhetorical style had its satire enhanced by the virtuoso art director, Jameo Saunders, who designed the comic-strip layout with so much brilliant whimsy on seven pages that it looked as if the recently deceased *Drummer* art director Al Shapiro himself had come back from the dead for a laugh.

In short, DeBlase, having bought *Drummer* from Embry only a year before, delighted in publishing the feature obituary on A. Jay as a tonal rebuttal to the kind of jealous gossip Embry was spreading about Deblase and the new *Drummer*. From personal experience, Deblase was an eyewitness of how Embry treated himself and others, and Deblase, with *Drummer* as his platform, felt no fear in being one of the first leathermen to come out of the closet of leather history and dare condemn the contrary Embry in print. *Drummer* had long been Embry's smart bomb, and DeBlase hoisted him on his own petard.

8. A GRUDGE AGAINST *DRUMMER* ITSELF: EMBRY'S SELLER'S REMORSE

In the "Grudges Never End Department," John Embry never missed a chance to praise *Drummer* and to bury *Drummer*.

In *Super MR* #7 (January 2001), he published two notices. The first was a five-page editorial concerning his recent health which recalled the crisis of his cancer that had so impacted my iteration of 1970s *Drummer*. The second notice, like a Mardi Gras call-and-response song, published inside the echo chamber of his *Super MR*, was Embry responding to an "anonymous" "Letter to the Editor" which he had also written. In it, he ranted as if Dutchman Martijn Bakker, the third publisher of *Drummer*, had somehow done something wrong in keeping up with the twenty-first century by selling twentieth-century *Drummer* to American leather businessman Mike Zuhl who produced leather shows like his DNA: Drummer North America Contest, and had announced plans for building an online *Drummer*.

In his page five editorial, Embry wrote:

> A funny thing happened to me on my way to the International Mr. Drummer Contest in Florida. All dressed up in cowskin [to him leather was "camp"], armed with carry-on cases, heading to the

airport, I ran down the stairs, missed several and ended up into [sic] the next landing.

I spent the contest weekend and the past weeks recuperating from a broken hip.... Now, months later, I'm still not completely functional, but at least I'm mobile.

...The healing process takes a lot of energy, leaving little for the creative process. [This was precisely my point when his 1978 cancer made him AWOL from *Drummer*, leaving Al Shapiro and me space, time, and energy to creatively grow *Drummer* from an LA magazine to a San Francisco magazine.]

Now the holidays have come and gone, and it is time to get our act together.....you should see the changes in size and content. We have merged with Terrance Hawke to become Alternate Hawke Publishing.... It's a big step for someone still on a couch....Thanks for your patience —John H. Embry

Flat on his back on his couch, Embry, at age 74, continuing to think feuds and controversy incite publicity, decided he would print a general press release from Jake Staley who was representing himself as the new editor of a new generation of *Drummer* Online under Mike Zuhl who soon after founded his spin-off leather-contest organization, Drummer North America, with its clever acronym, DNA.

Embry had not owned *Drummer* for fifteen years, but after he sold it in 1986, he increasingly suffered the world's worst case of seller's remorse.

Characteristically, in his trashing of twenty-first century *Drummer*, ventriloquist Embry tooled his words through his *Super MR* editor Robert Davolt, who was also the terminal editor of San Francisco *Drummer*.

In the end, in this *Super MR* #7 (January 2001), Embry revealed his heart. He bore a grudge against *Drummer* itself. With an introductory sentence, Embry, in league with Robert Davolt, re-published Jake Staley's press release in "Letters to the Editor" (page 6-7):

DIFFERENT *DRUMMER*

This letter [written by the new editor of the new *Drummer* Online who was accusing Embry of lying about *Drummer*] *was forwarded to us by one of our readers...*[Embry's italics]

Jake Staley: *Drummer* – Still Hot, and still America's leading Leather Magazine. We have been reading recently in the leather press, surprisingly numerous but false reports [including Embry's] of *Drummer*'s passing. Our favorite European hard sex magazine [title not mentioned] (which, sadly, has not shown up since June) editorialized earlier this year over "the late *Drummer*," and the current issue [of *Super MR*] from a well-known American publisher [the unnamed John Embry] who moons wistfully over the *Drummer* years as if it were past and shows up only in old copies of former issues. Gentlemen, it is not so.

Anyone who actually believes that *Drummer* is dead, is simply not paying attention to what we are doing. In the year 2000, *Drummer* looked seriously at where it had been and has started with exciting boldness in a new direction, but with a familiar purpose—to deliver the timeless message of *Drummer*, using different and contemporary ways of delivering that message.

Drummer Online brings *Drummer* magazine to the internet and, thus, to a wider community of leathermen than ever before. In addition, *Drummer* has just put on the most smashingly successful International Mr. Drummer and Drummerboy Contest ever. Professionally produced this year by Mike Zuhl and Drummer Contests International, Inc., this too, is the new sound of *Drummer*, with a familiar ring to it—hot men, hot leather, hot sex, with completely fresh energy. The Contest brought us sixteen of the hottest new Mr. Drummer and Drummerboy titleholders you could want to see. And you will see them in the coming months.

Drummer is now, as it always has been, necessary to leathermen and to the life of the leather community, wherever that community happens to be.

Jake Staley, Editor
[*Drummer* Online]

Embry responded to Jake Staley in his signature *Embry über alles* fashion by writing his own "Letter to the Editor" in his own magazine. He hid his authorship by signing it with the name of "Robert Davolt" who had been the nominal last editor of *Drummer* when it closed in 1999.

Editor: We are paying very careful attention. It is *Drummer* that lately seems always to be looking the other direction while the world passes it by.

This is an amazing piece of work [Staley's press release], considering about the only thing vaguely "American" about this new *Drummer* is their eagerness to take U.S. dollars. The new debut online *Drummer*, based in Amsterdam, consists of exactly four "pages"—more than half of which was taken up with this letter.

New direction? In fact, *Drummer* [which Embry did not own in the 1990s] has been trying to launch a successful website since 1996, with dismal results. The U.S. operations of *Drummer* were discontinued last year and the name "rented" out to a Pittsburgh organization [Zuhl], turning the fund-raising Mr. Drummer Contest into a for-profit venture. [Coincidentally, Embry himself had caused the Drummer Slave Auction bust by changing its purpose from a private fund-raiser for the community to a for-profit event for himself, and on those essential changes, the LAPD based its justification for the raid that cost thousands of taxpayer dollars.]

When the magazine ceased publication, employees, advertisers and subscribers were left dangling in the wind. In this letter the "new" *Drummer* clearly takes direct credit for that decisiton [*sic*]. *It was* Super MR *who, as a goodwill gesture, offered* Drummer *subscribers and advertisers a credit equal to their unfulfilled subscriptions and advertising.* [Wrote trickster Embry! Italics added.] It may be difficult to seize the legacy and at the same time dodge the responsibility.

Whatever Zen sort of moving-to-the-next-plane-of-existence spin you put on it, *Drummer*, as we knew it, is plainly gone. It is particularly embarrassing [*sic*] to Alternate Publishing who originated the title 25 years ago, [that] the name is now just an empty trademark. In this case, with limited apologies to both Mark Twain and Mr. Staley, rumored signs of life (or certainly of any continued credibility) are greatly exaggerated.

—[Signed] Robert Davolt

CHAPTER 19

VIRTUAL *DRUMMER*

How *Drummer* Influenced Other Magazines and Publishers

- Some Virtual *Drummer* Magazines: *Man2Man Quarterly*, *California Action Guide* (San Francisco), Patrick Califia's *Newsleather*, Tony DeBlase's *DungeonMaster*, Harold Cox's *Checkmate*
- *Drumb and Drumber*: Fritscher's Satiric, Special "*Mad Magazine*" Issue of *Drummer* (Issue 138)
- Desperate DeBlase Dumps *Drummer* on Dutchman and Davolt

Among such company as the best *Drummer* owners, Dr. DeBlase and Dr. Charles, did I ever really care that this Dr. Fritscher was on that Mr. Embry's Famous Little Blacklist? Did Hester Prynne not love her Pearl the way I loved *Drummer*, and did she not turn the vicious shame of her Scarlet Letter, Embry's Blacklist, into a red badge of courage and honor?

Anyone who worked with John Embry quickly learned to demand payment for their work and to defend their copyrights and reputations. Knowing I needed an exit strategy even before I finished editing *Drummer* 30, the same Anniversary Issue in which Embry cruelly trashed Jeanne Barney, I slipped into the pages of *Drummer* my own "declaration of independence." I'd had enough of office politics and delayed pay days, but not enough of the *Drummer* material I loved, and which I wanted to raise to a more far-out "edginess" without being ripped off financially, and without being abused in that gay sort of way that has no verbal definition.

Planning to publish an alternative *Drummer*, a "Virtual *Drummer*," I wrote my declaration in *Drummer* 30, page 18:

> MAN2MAN QUARTERLY. Tits, Pits, Fists, Hard2Find Fetish Trips. Your sensual ad free with 1 yr. Sub. $5 check. *MAN2MAN QUARTERLY*, 115 Haight, Suite 2, San Francisco 94102. Must state over 21.

Man2Man's Haight Street address was the apartment of my longtime ally from the 1970s, Old Reliable David Hurles, who also divorced himself from *Drummer* and contributed dozens of photographs for covers and centerfolds in *Man2Man*. Many of those shots were so erotic, esthetic, and popular upon their first publication in *Man2Man* that the artist Rex reprinted many of them in his photo book, *Speeding: The Old Reliable Photography of David Hurles* (2005). In fact, Rex's cover for *Speeding* was the same photograph I had published twenty-four years earlier on the back cover of *Man2Man* 6, the first *Man2Man* Anniversary Issue, 1981.

In the comparative timelines of Origin Stories, in 1977, Al Shapiro and I shut *Drummer* down for a four-month hiatus to create San Francisco *Drummer* out of LA *Drummer*. In 1979-1980, while I was editing *Drummer*, it took Mark Hemry and me four months to create *Man2Man Quarterly*. The phrase *man-to-man* was never used by Embry in *Drummer* until after *Man2Man* debuted.

The first issue of *Man2Man*, with blond bodybuilding champion Jim Enger on the cover, hit the bookstores, was a mail-order hit, and was denounced, and imitated, by a pissed-off Embry who almost immediately added this tag line to his "Leather Fraternity": "More Man-to-Man Personals Than Any Other Magazine." In fact, in the June immediately after the January 1980 debut of the first promotional copy of *Man2Man*, Embry published his own first "*Drummer* Super Publication," the "Virtual *Drummer*," *Malebox*, for the 1980 International Mr. Leather (IML) Contest in Chicago. Because I put my lover, Jim Enger, on the premiere cover of *Man2Man*, Embry—in some kind of very personal slap-down feud—put Colt model Clint Lockner, Enger's former lover and my good friend, on the cover of *Malebox* which trumpeted across Lockner's thighs: "More Man-To-Man Malebox Personal Classifieds Than Ever Before!" As sampled in later *Drummer*, such as *Drummer* 60, Embry continued to hawk his classifieds as "Drumbeats: Hot Man-to-Man Contact for a Cool 35¢ a Word!"

When I exited *Drummer*, Embry did not ask, nor did I offer to sign a non-competition agreement; and there was little I could do to stop him from reheating my ideas, or from repeating my themes in his 1980s *Drummer* that I had originated in my 1970s *Drummer*, most especially "cigars" and "daddies" which both, so inviting once reported on, turned into lifestyle fetishes on their own strength.

Years later, he was still cracking on about *Man2Man* in his letter to *Drummer* 108, because *Man2Man*'s code of ethics was quite the gentlemanly opposite of Embry's infamous "Robert Rip-off" character. When publisher Mark Hemry and I closed down *Man2Man* due to the new no-fluid-exchange behavior around AIDS as well as due to the typing-and-layout workload required before computers, we shocked Embry, the mail-order king. Mark Hemry wrote a check to each of our subscribers personally refunding whatever amount remained on his or her *Man2Man* subscription.

What an upside there was to the wild popularity of our very high-concept title of *Man2Man* in 1980. It prompted Embry and queerstream culture to focus, really focus, for the first time outside *Drummer* on gay men as men, on gay men who liked men masculine, on masculinity, and on homomasculinity. The only downside was a bit of static from some female-identified gay men, but not from women. At that time, there still existed the gay liberation unity of the 1970s before Marxist separatists broke that accord into the politically correct 1980s civil war over gender that continued as homomasculine men remained effectively excluded from gay culture in publications such as *The Advocate*.

To Embry's undying chagrin, one of the first fans of *Man2Man* was Anthony DeBlase who had in Chicago, 1979, begun publishing his *DungeonMaster* magazine, as his own "Virtual *Drummer*," to compete with *Drummer*. DeBlase had written a letter to that effect to me, the editor of *Man2Man*, on August 24, 1980.

Sixteen years later, on December 26, 1996, DeBlase, already morbidly ill with congestive heart failure, sent another note (handwritten in red ink) to Mark Hemry and me. He specifically requested a complete "leather heritage" set of *Man2Man* for Chuck Renslow's Leather Archives & Museum in Chicago. With that beatifying letter from DeBlase, the little grass-roots *Man2Man* entered the canon of gay magazine culture.

Other early fans and subscribers of *Man2Man* included generational pioneers such as Thom Gunn, Larry Townsend, Arnie Kantrowitz, Robert Mapplethorpe, Elliott Siegel, A. Jay aka Al Shapiro, Alan Bennett, Wakefield Poole, Jim Kane, Mark I. Chester, Domino aka Don Merrick, Artie Haber, Charles Herschberg, Ed Menerth, David Lewis and Peter Fiske of the 15 Association, Steve McEachern of the Catacombs, Jim Olander of *DungeonMaster*, Don Morrison and Frank Olson of the Anvil Bar in New York, Lou Thomas of Colt and Target studios, David Stein of GMSMA, and Patrick Califia.

Thom Gunn told *The Sentinel* newspaper in San Francisco of his love for the underground genre of dirty little zines like *Man2Man* when he said: "Personally, I have been far more influenced by the wit and style of *The Manhattan Review of Unnatural Acts* than I have been by the tiresome campiness of Ronald Firbank, who is usually taken as one of the chief exemplars of the...gay sensibility." (Quote found in Boyd MacDonald's peerless *Straight to Hell: The Manhattan Review of Unnatural Acts*, Number 44, page 7, c. 1978.) Gunn was also a fan and supporter of our quirky and underground boutique studio Palm Drive Video.

David Stein represented the "Gay Men's S&M Association" in New York. In a letter dated October 30, 1983, he requested permission to reprint two of my articles from *Man2Man #7* in the *GMSMA Newsletter* and for the magazine *Christopher Street*. My features were "Why Bondage?" and "Other Hands, Other Intentions: 48-Hour Bondage Trip." This was another leather-heritage endorsement of *Man2Man*, because GMSMA had never approached *Drummer* for reprints.

By June, 1984, Pat/Patrick Califia, publishing her-then-his *Newsleather* out of Richmond Hill, NY, requested a complete run of all the *Man2Man* issues (particularly issue 8) for the Califia leather-heritage archives.

In a very long letter, dated June 20, 1984, my forty-fifth birthday and *Drummer*'s ninth, Califia, perhaps sensing how I had been battered at *Drummer*, kindly wrote soothing words that show a writer's empathetic "take" on what Embry lost in the 1980s after I divorced him. In 1984, Califia pre-figured DeBlase's 1996 nomination of *Man2Man* to the canon of gay magazine literature in this excerpt:

> Dear Jack: I was very excited receiving the package of *Man2Man*, and also the envelope full of your newspaper [*California Action Guide*]. You are one of the finest gay porn writers around (I hope the word "porn" does not offend you.) I think you write a "dirty-talking" story better than anybody else I know, somehow managing (while using all our favorite four-letter words) to transcend the cliches of the genre. In every single publication you've produced, there's something that hits me right between the eyes....It's pretty clear to me that *Man2Man* was wildly successful...*Drummer* has sold out, sort of a "Mr. Colt in Bondage"....I hope I can finish up my book manuscript of short stories, *Macho Sluts*.... This may sound silly to you, but I'd like you to know that if it wasn't for your work, I'd feel impoverished. There were a lot of times when I felt hopeless about managing to establish a life as a sexually active sadist that a Jack Fritscher story renewed my optimism. —Pat

DRUMB AND DRUMBER: A SPECIAL *DRUMMER* ISSUE; 1989 EARTHQUAKE DESTROYS *DRUMMER* OFFICE

How tempting it was to fantasize publishing a photo of Embry's face, morphed with *Mad* magazine's mascot, Alfred E. Newman, on the cover of the special "extra issue" of *Drummer* titled *Drumb and Drumber*.

In the way I created my *Son of Drummer* (1978), I spun the concept for a new "extra" issue off the pop phrase, "dumb and dumber," which four years later in 1994 Jim Carrey also did for his movie *Dumb and Dumber*. In March 1989, I pitched my spoof to DeBlase as the *Drumb and Drumber 1990 Annual*. He busted his gut laughing at the pun, and we began our slow take-off to production.

DeBlase was an authentic leatherman who, while creating his own iteration of *Drummer*, also created and designed the Leather Pride Flag which he introduced at the International Mr. Leather Contest in Chicago in May 1989. Displayed since as an instant tradition at thousands of leather events, the flag, as DeBlase described it, "is composed of nine horizontal stripes of equal width. From the top and from the bottom, the stripes alternate black and royal blue. The central stripe is white. In the upper left quadrant of the flag is a large red heart. I will leave it to the viewer to interpret the colors and symbol." DeBlase truly loved *Drummer*. When I asked him over coffee about the exact symbolism of his design concept, he said, "The red heart stands specifically for the leatherfolk who love *Drummer*."

Months later, in October, while DeBlase and Charles were vacationing in England, the Loma Prieta earthquake changed all the plans in Desmodus's South of Market Street office. The building at 285 Shipley was destroyed and there was no earthquake insurance. To fundamentalist religionists it was the right-hand of God knocking down the left-wing walls of Sodom in San Francisco. To DeBlase and Charles, it was the straw that broke the camel's back.

October 17, 1989, was a watershed moment in *Drummer* history.

Psychologically, the 1989 Loma Prieta earthquake collapsed DeBlase's umbrella over Desmodus Publishing in the way the LAPD Slave Auction arrest in 1976 had broken Embry who was undone a second time when AIDS in 1984 changed nearly everything in his business model, including the contents of *Drummer*, forcing him to put *Drummer* up for sale.

The morning after the earthquake, October 18, DeBlase telephoned from London saying he and Andy Charles had re-booked their first-class return flight to San Francisco. He immediately stopped the press on all his Desmodus magazines: *Drummer*, *Mach*, *Foreskin Quarterly*, *Sandmutopia Guardian*, and *DungeonMaster*. In the prescient last issue before the earthquake, *Drummer* 132 (August 1989), page 6, a depressed DeBlase, already down at heel from the ongoing financial bleeding of *Drummer*, had felt it necessary to write an editorial defending—to a complaining reader—his proportion of editorial copy to commercial advertising, concluding, "I wish we were making 'mucho bucks.'"

In *Drummer* 135 (December 1989), page 38, the desperate DeBlase began begging for contributions for *Drummer* via the "Desmodus Earthquake Relief Fund." *Drummer* may have been the Leather Bible of the leather community, but very few fans were interested in bailing out his personal business, and he was forced to sell. Nevertheless, in 1993, the ever-enterprising DeBlase, having sold *Drummer*, and having founded the Leather Archives & Museum with Chuck Renslow, risked re-starting his discontinued magazine, *Checkmate*, which he had begun years before in Chicago before he bought *Drummer*. This time his publishing efforts at documenting leather history on the fly were supported by the distinguished leather elders Harold Cox and Bob Reite, founders of the *DungeonMaster Newsletter*, and the annual Delta Run leather weekend hosted by the Delta Brotherhood International. DeBlase and Cox dubbed their new hybrid magazine with the awkwardly blended title: *Checkmate (Incorporating DungeonMaster)*. *Drummer* 160, page 23.

Drummer nearly died in the 1989 earthquake. Its main life support was its new hire, Joseph W. Bean, who, at the moment of the quake, was at work on only his second issue as managing editor of *Drummer*. As eyewitness, I met with Joseph Bean standing in the collapsed bricks South of Market, and watched him soldier on like a medic triaging the bits and pieces of *Drummer* most likely to survive for whatever new issues we could salvage.

Still dedicated to producing *Drumb and Drumber*, I figured a little gallows humor might help release the tension around both the earthquake and AIDS. Turning disaster into a laugh that keeps a person calm enough to carry on, I proposed that the earthquake might inspire, among other features, a satirical two-page cartoon strip of the kind that Al Shapiro created for *Queens Quarterly* and continued in *Drummer*, and that Mort Drucker created to make *Mad* magazine wildly popular. *The National Lampoon* had a comic-strip hit with *Queen Kong* (May 1977) satirizing both that film and the hateful Arnold Schwarzenegger in *Better Homes and Closets*.

Like Max Bialystock in *The Producers* (1968), I envisioned the group of us creating *Drummer*'s own version of *Springtime for Hitler* as a farcical send-up lampooning, with lyrics and photos, the leather history and in-house shenanigans of all us *Drummer* publishers, editors, and contributors trying to survive the roof falling on our heads. The camp reference would be that like singer Jeannette McDonald in *San Francisco*, the 1936 movie about the 1906 quake, Tony and Andy and Joseph and I, in caricature, would stand in the rubble to sing the survivalist title song "San Francisco." I would have titled the strip "Trouble in the Rubble." We needed *Drumb and Drumber*. *Drummer* needed to lighten up.

Years later in June 1997, Joseph Bean told me in interview that he, rather like the young and unformed Los Angeles *Drummer*, had spent his early coming-out years cruising Ventura, California, "almost in drag..., the sweaters, the teased hair and make-up, the fingernails." What comic relief to have known that tidbit about him back in 1989-1990. Our dear departed art director Al Shapiro would have rejoiced in drawing a sexy cartoon of the butch, bearded Bean as Judy Garland spoofing the camp Jeannette McDonald.

> Judy Garland: I never will forget..(long pause)...Jeannette McDonald [Joseph W. Bean]....how that brave Jeannette [Joseph] just stood there in the ruins and sang, a-a-and sang: San Francisco, open your Golden Gate.

Judy was belting out a fundamental gay meme, teaching how Jeannette (Joseph), like all the gay men Judy sang to, just had to keep on keeping on come what may.

Why couldn't the *Drumb and Drumber* cartoon strip also spin out a caricature of John Embry exiting the bank where he bragged he had been laughing, with fistfuls of money, because he had unloaded *Drummer* on the "fools who bought it." My satire was meant as a true homage to *Drummer* editor Joseph W. Bean who can dine out on his own "Trouble in the Rubble" stories forever.

Besides the ruin of the *Drummer* office itself, DeBlase's second brick-and-mortar business, the brand new retail shop, SandMutopia Supply Co., was destroyed. Disaster and debt crushed the plan of any separate "extra" issue of *Drumb and Drumber*. So, for *Drummer* 138 (March 1990), Bean and DeBlase incorporated my downsized *Drumber* parody into one of those stunts where a magazine flipped upside down and backwards has a "new front cover" on its back cover.

During the production melee in the ravaged ruins of the *Drummer* office, someone changed my original spelling design of *Drumb and Drumber* to the asymmetrical *Drumb and Dummer*. The pun referenced the zippy style of previous special issue titles: *The Best and the Worst of Drummer*, *Son of Drummer*, and *Drummer Rides Again*. In the stressed office, someone thought it amusing to write "Cover Photo by Bob Maple Thorp." At least, he emphasized the proper pronunciation of Mapplethorpe who had just died.

Drummer 140, eight months after the quake, was a watershed issue (June 1990). As participant and inside survivor of the *Drummer* experience, I shot the cover of that *Drummer* 140 and several interior photographs.

More importantly, I witnessed up close the anguish of DeBlase who had, without irony, asked if Mark Hemry and I wanted to buy *Drummer*, or buy into *Drummer*, or fold *Drummer* into Palm Drive Video, or...

And we said: "Tony, is that any way to treat your friends?"

DeBlase confessed he was hoping the Mafia would come bail him out as it had so many other gay magazines that were his competition. He had arrived at the same corporate conclusion that I had in the late 1970s when I told Embry, whose long post-cancer recovery nearly bankrupted the magazine, that maybe we should approach the Mafia about underwriting *Drummer*. DeBlase ended his public "For Sale" announcement with a code—that was not a joke—spinning the tag line from *The Godfather*. He really did hope that some handsome Mafioso would make him an offer he could not refuse. Indicating the dollar value he put on the abstract social media value that was *Drummer*, the desperate DeBlase wrote:

DRUMMER IS FOR SALE

Own a Piece of the Drum...Or the Whole Damned Orchestra!

Problems stemming from the October 1989 earthquake are compounding, and Desmodus, Inc. is experiencing severe cash flow problems. We are taking many cost-cutting steps, but are in need of capital to continue producing magazines on schedule.

A loan of several thousand dollars could buy you a piece of a particular issue. A hundred thousand dollars could buy a partnership in the company. Or, for a few times that, you could own the nation's premier Leather magazine, as well as *Mach, Foreskin Quarterly*, the Mr. Drummer Contest, many associated names and titles, a huge reserve of back issues and a spectacular photo library.

DungeonMaster and the SandMutopia Supply Co. [his core businesses] are not for sale, unless, of course, someone makes an offer I cannot refuse.

Interested? Write me at PO Box 11314, San Francisco, CA 94101, or phone (415)252-1195. —Anthony F. DeBlase

Right there in *Drummer* 140, page 5, DeBlase acknowledged the accumulated treasure trove of "a spectacular photo library" which belonged to the photographers and was not really his or *Drummer*'s to sell. It was that "treasure trove" of photos and drawings and original manuscripts and letters that mysteriously disappeared in the 1990s, after Martijn Bakker bought it from DeBlase, and while Robert Davolt was its so-called "editor and publisher" who was dedicated to the pillaging of all things *Drummer* to fatten Embry's files.

In *Drummer* 141, page 8, DeBlase waffled and prevaricated, saying he was "no longer actively seeking a buyer." But he was. In *Drummer* 150, he ran a full-page ad again announcing *"Drummer* for Sale," page 4. In order to unload *Drummer*, he had to change his tune so that the magazine seemed valuable and successful even while he and Andy Charles in private were nervously plotting to dump *Drummer* and escape to Oregon.

In the end, is it wrong to put the "creative differences" of "gay business" (*Drummer*'s business) all on Embry? Publishing *Drummer* was hell for him too, even though his cash and censorship problems were mostly of his own making, whereas DeBlase was undone by the combined punches of the VCR and HIV. Embry's gay publishing competitors, gay advertisers, straight printers, and venal distributors who drove him to distraction were in their own ways guilty of a kind of jealousy, envy, and greed that also shaped *Drummer*. They were all businessmen salivating to make money off the work of writers, artists, and photographers, paid or not.

As a main eyewitness of Embry and of my editorship of *Drummer*, Rick Leathers, author of "A New Mazeway for Homomasculine Men" (*Manifest Reader* 17, 1992), wrote me a New Year's greeting, January 6, 2006. Leathers was one of Embry's most favored and most published writers. The allegations and information are solely his eyewitness testimony:

> ...I worked for Embry and Andy Charles and Tony de'Blob [DeBlase] off-n-on over 19 years. I watched as *Drummer* became a parody of a self-parody. "Your" [Fritscher's] *Drummer* died on the vine when you departed because you had the message and Embry only had the medium. John [Embry] only wanted to publish goofy photos with cutesy-poo dialog balloons for funzies. And suck the pee-pees of blondboyz). His whole approach came from his early imprinting of Judy and Mickey cleaning out the old barn so they could put on a show.
>
> Embry never got over the LA cops' raid on that silly "Slave Auction." He showed me part of his autobiography once. It's a pathetic tale of how EVERYBODY [*sic*] betrayed his vision and refused to build his dreams to his brilliant expectations. He calls it *Epilogues* [*sic*]. Though I'm not big on book burning, I do hope

they toss it on his funeral pyre. "Robert Payne" has spent his entire life wallowing in self-pity. And when Mario died, all business sense went with him. Embry's net worth is only about [amount omitted by JF] (mostly in shabby real estate). Mario's relatives [he alleged] came from Spain and ripped John off for most of the money Mario had stashed away. When Frank Hatfield died [after being mauled by a dog], John grabbed what little Frank had. The whole Embry bio is tacky and pointless.

Embry wasn't the biggest prick in gay publishing.

All professions are the same.

Katharine Hepburn, who played her part in *Some Dance to Remember* (Reel 6, Scene 3), said about acting: "Most people in this profession are pigs."

Cue the villains and violins.

One survives publishing the way one survives the circular firing squad of gay culture: sheer discipline.

My heart was tender in those days before I was hardened by Embry and the cruelty of the gay world which is no more cruel than other worlds; yet it was the gay world that was most cruel to me when my heart was tender.

But, like Joseph and Judy and Jeannette in the ruins, I was never defeated, and if I were, I'd never admit it.

All my writing is the story of that.

In my writing, most of the characters in my stories end as couples.

So do Embry and I couple: although antithetically.

I must confess that I enjoy a tad of *Schadenfreude* that in the pitched battle which Embry waged so jealously against David Goodstein, Goodstein won.

Embry must have cringed when on page 89 in *Drummer* 145 (December 1990), *The Advocate* paid for a full-page display ad with an order blank to subscribe to "*The Advocate*...the most influential gay and lesbian publication in the world!"

Drummer ended bankrupt.

PlanetOut.com announced purchase of *The Advocate* for $31.1 million dollars in November 2005.

So much for laughing all the way to the bank.

Appendix 1

A Quick Who's Who in *Drummer*

Drummer
Timeline & Cast of Characters
(The Evolution of Leather)

- Name Game: Who's Who and Not Who
- Key Timeline: 14 Turning Points of *Drummer*
- 3 Publishers
- 2 Editors-in-Chief, Some Other Editors, and an Art Director

A List of Frequently Confused Names
Sorted for Convenience

- Mark Hemry, editor of this series of books, *Gay San Francisco: Eyewitness Drummer*
- John Henry Embry, first publisher of *Drummer*
- Don Embinder, publisher of *Blueboy* magazine
- Jim Enger, bodybuilder icon 1970s, Fritscher companion
- Kenneth Anger, magus and leather filmmaker, *Scorpio Rising*
- John Rowberry, editor (never editor-in-chief) beginning in *Drummer* 40 through 86
- Robert Opel, Academy Award streaker, Fey-Way Gallery founder, and murdered *Drummer* photographer and writer
- Robert Mapplethorpe, photographer, Fritscher companion
- Sam Steward aka Phil Andros aka Phil Sparrow, legendary forebear of gay male writing and leather culture: intimate of Gertrude Stein and Alice B. Toklas, Chuck Renslow, Dom Orejudos, and Fritscher
- Jim Stewart, photographer, Fritscher housemate, early SoMa insider
- David Andrew Sparrow, Fritscher domestic partner (1969-1979; gay marriage by Catholic priest Jim Kane in Manhattan, May 7, 1972); his name bylines *Drummer* photography shot by Sparrow-Fritscher together

Hemry is not Embry; there is no "Mark Hembry." Robert Mapplethorpe is not Robert Opel; there is no "Robert Opelthorpe."

THE EVOLUTION OF LEATHER

BEGINNING AND ENDING THE LEATHER DECADE: THE 1970s

- September 30, 1970: The Presidential Commission on Obscenity and Pornography releases its 646-page report recommending that all sexually explicit movies, books, and magazines should be legalized
- November 25, 1970: The Leather Decade of the 1970s begins with the harakiri of Yukio Mishima, writer and soldier, who eroticised leather, uniforms, bodybuilding, edge play, and homomasculinity
- July 10, 1981: The Leather Decade ends with the burning of the Barracks Baths and Tony Tavarossi's July 12 death from a mystery disease at San Francisco General Hospital

---

DRUMMER KEY TIMELINE: 14 TURNING POINTS
WHEN, WHERE, AND WHY WHO AND WHAT CHANGED

1. June 20, 1975. *Drummer* 1 premieres edited by Jeanne Barney and published by John Embry

2. April 10, 1976. Great "Slave Auction" raid and arrests by gay-bashing LAPD in tactical "Operation Emancipation" run by Police Chief Ed Davis, 65 officers, one helicopter, one bus, and 40 victims

3. December 1976. Editor-in-chief Jeanne Barney exits original-concept LA *Drummer* after completing *Drummer* 11 and parts of 12 and 13

4. February-October 1977. *Drummer* makes desultory move from LA to San Francisco; *Drummer* 12 (February 1977) is first hybrid issue with both LA and San Francisco addresses on masthead

5. March 1977. Embry hires Allen J. Shapiro (A. Jay) as art director and Jack Fritscher as editor-in-chief to change LA *Drummer* into San Francisco

Drummer; beginning after *Drummer* 18 (August 1977), which Fritscher ghost-edited, *Drummer* takes four-month publishing hiatus, absent from the news stands and starting up again when Fritscher debuts his first issue, *Drummer* 19 (December 1977); the most representative, intense, archetypal, and perfect issue of *Drummer* in writing and graphic content is *Drummer* 21 (March 1978); Fritscher edits *Drummer* for three years: 32 months; Shapiro designs *Drummer* for 34 months

6. Winter 1978-Spring 1979. During Embry's cancer surgery and absence, Shapiro and Fritscher further remodel and refresh *Drummer*; Fritscher refashions leather as the focal point of a broader masculine-identified magazine reflecting its readers' actual gender identity in the personal ads where *masculine* and *masculinity* are the most repeated keywords; Anthony DeBlase acknowledges: "Embry was the main person responsible for...allowing it [*Drummer* while he was absent] to be modified [by Shapiro and Fritscher]." (*Drummer* 188, September 1995, page 19)

> For a year, a fog of depression and paranoia hangs over San Francisco and *Drummer*, both freaked out by the double-whammy of the Jonestown Massacre on November 18, 1978, and the assassination of Milk and Moscone on November 27, 1978. The mass suicide by Kool-Aid of 900 persons, mostly San Franciscans, at the People's Temple in Guyana was committed by former San Francisco Housing Board member, Jim Jones, who earlier had been arrested for masturbating and hitting on an undercover LAPD officer in the men's room of the West Lake Theater in LA; Jones was instrumental in electing Mayor Moscone to office. Jones and Moscone died nine days apart.

7. June 1979. Embry reveals his "Blacklist" in *Drummer* 30 attacking Jeanne Barney; the shadow list begins with Police Chief Ed Davis and continues with anyone uncontrollable by Embry who does not seem to like being held accountable by eyewitnesses

8. July 8, 1979. The assassin-like murder of *Drummer* writer and photographer Robert Opel in his South of Market Fey-Way Gallery follows Jonestown and Milk-Moscone killings by six months, and causes a new kind of gay hysteria in bars, baths, bistros, and the *Drummer* office

9. August to December 31, 1979. Shapiro and Fritscher exit together taking the *Drummer* salon of talent such as Robert Mapplethorpe, thus ending what Embry and others term the "classic 1970s *Drummer*"; Fritscher is the second and last editor-in-chief of *Drummer*; thirteen months after Fritscher exits, John Rowberry becomes editor with *Drummer* 40 (January 1981) to *Drummer* 86 (January 1986)

10. 1982. "HIV and VCR." Virus and video change everything in editorial content of writing and photography; under Embry-Rowberry, *Drummer* becomes a leathery *People* magazine, featuring porn stars and Mr. *Drummer* leather-contest models

11. August 22, 1986. Embry sells *Drummer* to Anthony F. DeBlase and Andrew Charles, Desmodus Inc., whose first issue is *Drummer* 99; DeBlase and Charles take victory lap in special issue *Drummer* 100; Fritscher says, "DeBlase bought *Drummer* to save it from Embry." DeBlase and Embry greet each other in *Drummer* 98 and immediately begin civil war in their various publications: *Manifest Reader*, *Drummer* 107, *Drummer* 120.

- AIDS-era owner DeBlase acts up: increasing with each issue from *Drummer* 100, with *Drummer* 150—e.g.: "Dykes for Madonna!"—being one of the worst of the nagging, preachy, camp issues, DeBlase mistakenly devotes even more pages to congenial leather contestants and, worse, he turns *Drummer* from jerkoff erotica into a whiney self-help examination of conscience over leather identity, gender, sobriety, and "how-to" articles in the magazine that had succeeded in the 1970s because its premise was based on the presumption that the readers, in fact, already knew "how to."
- In their feud, salesman Embry must have cackled as the increasingly papal DeBlase murders his own business by encouraging his staff to publish didactic articles preaching to the politically correct leather choir. Subscriptions and sales of *Drummer* plummet.
- Once famous for writing about fisting with a punch, *Drummer* becomes irrelevant outside San Francisco-NY-and-LA to national readers wanting erotica rather than gay politics and leather mysticism. Rendered impotent, the erotic magazine is going out of business, and DeBlase is seeking an exit strategy when, like a lucky *deus ex machina* (for DeBlase), the earth shakes.

12. October 17, 1989. Loma Prieta earthquake destroys *Drummer* offices giving DeBlase an excuse to offer the floundering *Drummer* for sale in *Drummer* 140 (June 1990) with a more desperate full-page pitch, "*Drummer* Is for Sale," in *Drummer* 150 (September 1991), page 4

13. September 1992. Dutch businessman Martijn Bakker buys *Drummer* and, beginning with *Drummer* 159, mistakenly Europeanizes *Drummer* whose secret of success is that it is a quintessentially American magazine of gay and leather popular culture; Bakker re-titles *Drummer* as *International Drummer*

14. 1996. Internet arrives and causes slow death of 20th-century gay magazines; *Drummer* 214 is the final issue (April 1999); Bakker officially closes the *Drummer* business on September 30, 1999

EYEWITNESS: *DRUMMER* TIMELINE & SCORE CARD
3 OWNER/PUBLISHERS + 1 CONTRIBUTOR

1. John Henry Embry, Publisher: 11 years, 1975-1986, issues 1-98
"Much of the 116 issues that followed the first 100 didn't have all that much to recommend it [sic]." —John Embry

2. Anthony DeBlase and Andrew Charles, AIDS-era Publishers: 6 years, 1986-1992, issues 99-158
"We were fools to buy *Drummer*." —Andrew Charles

3. Martijn Bakker, Publisher: 6 years, 1992-1999, issues 159-214
"The Dutchman was the sole killer of *Drummer* and all it stood for." —Mister Marcus

4. Jack Fritscher, Contributor: 17 years, 1977-1995; founding San Francisco editor-in-chief, March 1977-December 31, 1979; *Drummer*'s most frequent contributor in 65 issues, often with several contributions to each issue; only editor to shoot *Drummer* covers
"*Drummer* was a home, and a home run." —Jack Fritscher

> "Jack Fritscher is...the man who invented the South of Market prose style as well as its magazines which have never been the same without him."
> —John F. Karr, *Bay Area Reporter*, June 27, 1985

3 SAN FRANCISCO VERSIONS OF *DRUMMER* SORTED BY 3 OFFICE ADDRESSES

1. "California Street *Drummer*" *Drummer* 12 - *Drummer* 18: 311 California Street (Embry's first office in the prestigious Robert Dollar Building), San Francisco, on masthead.

2. "Divisadero Street *Drummer*" *Drummer* 19 - *Drummer* 31: 1730 Divisadero Street (a down-at-heel Victorian), San Francisco, on masthead; "Divisadero *Drummer*" is the *Drummer* edited by Jack Fritscher (14-17, plus ghost-editor of *Drummer* 18, *Drummer* 31, 32, and 33).

3. "Harriet Street *Drummer*" *Drummer* 32- following: 15 Harriet Street (a dump over a garage), San Francisco, on masthead; later, offices at 960 Folsom Street followed by Natoma Street and Shipley Street.

"EDITOR-IN-CHIEF" TITLE FOR BARNEY AND FRITSCHER ONLY

1. Jeanne Barney: *Drummer* 1 - *Drummer* 11 + hybrid issues *Drummer* 12, *Drummer* 13; outspoken founding LA editor-in-chief of *Drummer* (1975), and columnist, "Smoke from Jeannie's Lamp"; editor of *Dateline: The NewsMagazine of Gay America* (1976); Leather Awards Humanitarian of the Year (1976); the only woman arrested by the LAPD at the *Drummer* "Slave Auction" and main contact for follow-up print and television news coverage; eyewitness to *Drummer* history through association since 1973 with founding publisher John Embry and to leather history since 1972 through Larry Townsend.

2. Jack Fritscher: *Drummer* 19 - *Drummer* 30, *Son of Drummer*, + hybrid issues *Drummer* 14-18 and *Drummer* 31-33; Fritscher and Shapiro re-fashion *Drummer* while covering publisher Embry's long absences as he seemed to fall ill in 1978 and during his Spring 1979 cancer surgery and recuperation. See Embry's "thank you note" in "Getting Off," *Drummer* 30, 4th Anniversary Issue, June 1979. Anthony DeBlase in *Drummer* 100: "With *Drummer* 19 Jack Fritscher came upon the scene [where he had been producing behind the scenes since *Drummer* 14, ghost-editing *Drummer* 18]. Under Jack's direction SM per se became less prominent, and rough and raunchy sexuality often written by Jack himself became the main theme."

SOME OTHER "EDITORS" & "ASSIGNMENT EDITORS"

1. "Robert Payne" aka John Embry. Following Fritscher's 1970s identity-driven *Drummer* exploring the new "gender" of gay masculinity with its many foci, Embry reductively focused *Drummer* on the leather-pageant contest, Mr. *Drummer*.

2. John W. Rowberry. Following Fritscher, Rowberry was never "editor-in-chief" of *Drummer*; Rowberry had arrived from LA looking for work after quitting as the night porter at the Ramada Inn on Santa Monica Boulevard in WeHo; Rowberry was listed as "assignment editor" from *Drummer* 31 through *Drummer* 39, and finally — thirteen months after Fritscher's exit — as "editor" beginning in *Drummer* 40. Changing *Drummer* from Fritscher's 1970s reader-reflexive *verite* magazine of masculine culture, Rowberry reductively focused *Drummer* on genitality, on Mr. *Drummer* leather contests, and on video stars. After Rowberry exited *Drummer*, Embry turned on him and wrote in *Manifest Reader* (1997), page 79, that Rowberry was "no authority on the type of action" that Embry's readers preferred. Some years after Rowberry's death on December 4, 1993, founding Los Angeles editor-in-chief Jeanne Barney wrote: "I found Rowberry to be a good writer (when I edited him), but based on his editorial skills in magazines where he had sole editorial responsibilities, well, to be frank, he sucked."

3. Tim Barrus. Provocative associate editor for only five issues, with publisher Anthony DeBlase, wrote his first fiery editorial in *Drummer* 117 (June 1988), page 4; earlier his fiction had appeared in Embry's *Drummer* 67, 72, and 77. He also appeared unnamed in a photograph with and by Mark I. Chester in *Drummer* 138, page 24. In *Drummer* 122 (October 1988), a presidential election year, publisher DeBlase noted on page 4:

> Barrus Resigns. I regret having to announce that Tim Barrus has resigned as Associate Editor. I was quite pleased with many of the improvements he had made in the magazine and with many of his plans for the future. However, he became quite concerned about Justice Department persecution of publishers of erotica and decided to sever his relationship with Desmodus Inc.

4. Joseph W. Bean. Editor (*Drummer* 133 - *Drummer* 158 + hybrid issues *Drummer* 159 - *Drummer* 161) with editorial coordinator Marcus-Jay Wonacott; in the process of exiting, Bean's name does not appear on the

masthead of ill-fated *Drummer* 161 (March 1993) which was allegedly mostly shredded and not distributed because of legal action over *Drummer*'s copyright violation of the World Wrestling Federation word, *Wrestlemania*; Bean, however, aids DeBlase's exit and maintains continuity through the sale of *Drummer* to Martijn Bakker; Bean was the "earthquake editor" who kept *Drummer* alive in 1989-1990; see Bean's "The Day the Earth Did Not Stand Still" in *Drummer* 135 (December 1989).

5. Robert Davolt. Operations manager, 1997, under Dutch publisher Martijn Bakker who hired him as an American manager with *Drummer* 209; Davolt titled himself both "editor" and "publisher"; in those straw positions, he managed to produce a total of only six issues of the "monthly" *Drummer* between April 1998 and April 1999 when *Drummer* went out of business with *Drummer* 214. Davolt became an accomplice in the killing of *Drummer*, the magazine, by spending all his energy on Mr. *Drummer*, the contest, where he could indulge his weakness for playing the social lion on his coast-to-coast grand tours producing the contest. Traveling on an expense account wrung from the struggling magazine, Davolt reduced *Drummer* to nothing more than the Mr. *Drummer* contest and video ads.

FOUNDING SAN FRANCISCO ART DIRECTOR

Al Shapiro aka A. Jay: *Drummer* 17 - *Drummer* 32; publisher Anthony DeBlase in *Drummer* 100 (October 1986) wrote that Fritscher's discovery "David Hurles' Old Reliable photos and A. Jay's drawings characterized this era....and A. Jay's illustrations for stories and ads had exactly the right look for Jack Fritscher's version of *Drummer*."

DRUMMER TRIVIA

- *Drummer* 1 and *Drummer* 2 were "closet" issues, with no names on masthead
- *Drummer* 4 - *Drummer* 12: no Thoreau "marching quote" on masthead

What rollicking fun...to reopen old friendships and even some ancient hostilities of that golden age. To be a by-stander to those vibrant talents and hear again those voices.... Can you imagine the pleasure in being able to put one's arms around some of those people, just like you maybe should have done back then when they

were still around and available?
—John Embry, *Manifest Reader* 33 (1997), page 5

Ten years earlier, in *Drummer* 107 (August 1987), page 91, running through *Drummer* 116 (May 1988), page 82, John Embry, having sold his megaphone that was *Drummer*, placed a classified ad seeking what I term "eyewitness *Drummer* participants" from the 1970s for a book he was pitching for his Alternate Publishing. At the height of the AIDS plague, he knew of my completed book *Some Dance to Remember: A Memoir-Novel of San Francisco 1970-1982*. Even though Embry's "eyewitness" book never happened, his instincts were correct. His *Drummer* "Wanted" ad paralleled my own years of preservation and reconstruction of the Golden Age of Leather in *Some Dance to Remember* (written during 1970-1984) and *Mapplethorpe: Assault with a Deadly Camera* (written during 1979-1993).

WANTED
THE GOLDEN AGE OF FOLSOM

We are looking for input into a collection of the phenomena that was South of Market. The men, the experiences, the fact and the fiction, the legends and the graphics. Tell us your memories of those years for the most important leather volume ever. To be published by Alternate Publishing [John Embry], PO Box 42009. San Francisco, CA 94142-2009. Artists, Photographers, Writers may call (707) 869-0945 for more details.

"*DRUMMER* PAID THE BILLS" FOR ITS POOR SIBLINGS

In his latter-day magazine *Super MR* 5 (2000), page 39, publisher Embry, at the sundown of his publishing career, finally confessed in print what *Drummer*'s army of unpaid and underpaid writers, artists, photographers, and staff without benefits always suspected.

Drummer was a cash cow milked to support sibling magazines owned by Embry, to prop up his annual Mr. *Drummer* contests, and to float his assorted ventures in mail order and—it was alleged—personal real estate.

In the nearly three years that I was editor-in-chief, *Drummer* had, according to Embry, a press run of 42,000 copies. A million people had bought and read some issue of 1970s *Drummer* by the end of my editorship with *Drummer* 33, December 31, 1979.

I did the math; I asked to be paid; I exited, mostly unpaid, to begin the 1980s afresh.

If only the income from *Drummer* had been spent on properly paying the talented gayfolk who created it.

If only the profit had been used to upgrade the production of *Drummer* by printing it on better paper that didn't feel like rag stock soaking up the photographs like inkblots.

History will not look kindly on the corners cut at *Drummer*.

Embry finally admitted with some transparency in *Super MR* (2000) page 39:

> *Drummer*'s steady growth made it possible for much experimentation, including [other magazines like] *Alternate, Mach, FQ* [*Foreskin Quarterly*], *Manifest*, and all the annuals [e.g.: *Son of Drummer*] that followed. None of our publishing lost money, some made more than others, of course. But it was *Drummer* that paid the bills and gave us the opportunity to increase and expand.

Fritscher created themes to anchor and develop the following 21 issues of *Drummer* and it was the first time each theme was published in *Drummer*

- *Drummer* 20 (January 1978): Gay Sports
- *Drummer* 21 (March 1978): Prison
- *Drummer* 22 (May 1978): Cigars
- *Drummer* 23 (July 1978): Underground Sex: Gay Pop Culture—The Catacombs
- *Drummer* 24 (September 1978): Authenticity, Mapplethorpe, and Bondage
- *Son of Drummer* (September 1978): New York Art—Rex and Mapplethorpe
- *Drummer* 25 (December 1978: Leather Identity—Homomasculinity
- *Drummer* 26 (January 1979): Cowboys and Performance Art
- *Drummer* 27 (February 1979): Gay Film and the Society of Janus
- *Drummer* 28 (April 1979): Gyms and Prisons
- *Drummer* 29 (May 1979): Dangerous Sex, Boxing, and Blue-Collar Men

- *Drummer* 30 (June 1979): Nipples and Arthur Tress Photography
- *Drummer* 31 (September 1979): Spit and Other Erotic Bodily Functions
- *Drummer* 118 (July 1988): Rubber (Keith Ardent)
- *Drummer* 119 (also dated July 1988): Bears
- *Drummer* 124 (December 1988): Bodybuilders and "the *Drummer* Novel," *Some Dance to Remember: A Memoir-Novel of San Francisco 1970-1982*
- *Drummer* 133 (September 1989): Mapplethorpe and Censorship
- *Drummer* 134 (October 1989): Brown Leather
- *Drummer* 138 (March 1990): Satirical Upside-Down Earthquake Issue of *Drummer* titled *"Dummer": A Unique Drummer Semi-Publication*
- *Drummer* 139 (*May 1990): Remembrance of Sleaze Past in the Titanic 1970s
- *Drummer* 170 (December 1993): Russomania—Shooting Porn

INTERNATIONAL DRUMMER

ISSUE 170

$5.95

PHOTOS, PHOTOS AND MORE PHOTOS

RUSSO MANIA...
A glimpse into this guy. Photos & Interview by Jack Fritscher

"THE GOOD DOCTOR PART 2"

"DANGERS"

Cover Photograph by Jack Fritscher

DISTRIBUTION TO MINORS PROHIBITED

Appendix 2

Jack Fritscher's
Drummer Magazine Timeline Bibliography

The Writing and Photography of Jack Fritscher
An Accounting of Publication and Copyright

Collected and Edited by Mark Hemry

Drummer Issues covered in this Timeline Index:
14, 15, 16, 17, 18, 19, 20, 21, 22, 23, 24, 25, 26, 27, 28, 29, 30, 31, 32, 33, 41, 81, 85, 100, 107, 115, 116, 117, 118, 119, 121, 123, 124, 126, 127, 128, 129, 130, 131, 133, 134, 135, 136, 137, 138, 139, 140, 141, 143, 144, 145, 147, 148, 155, 157, 159, 169, 170, 186, 188, 204

Drummer Special Issues covered in this Timeline Index:
Son of Drummer
Drummer Rides Again
Mr. Drummer Contest Program 1990

Drummer - Desmodus Sibling Magazine Issues covered in this Timeline Index :
Drummer Tough Customers 1, 12
Mach 20, 22, 25, 29 (35, 38)
Foreskin Quarterly 12
DungeonMaster 47

DRUMMER 14, April 1977
Jack Fritscher's first writing in *Drummer*
1 Piece of Writing by Jack Fritscher
1 Photographic Essay Produced by Fritscher
- "Men South of Market," pp. 39-46, captions for centerfold photo essay
- Centerfold Photographic Essay by Jim Stewart, pp. 39-46, produced by Fritscher

DRUMMER 15, May 1977
3 Pieces of Writing by Fritscher as Staff Ghostwriter-editor; A. Jay draws cover as Guest Artist
- "Stunning Omission," letter to the editor, p. 6
- "Cock Casting," pp. 20-21, feature
- "Durk Parker," aka Durk Dehner, p. 39-46, centerfold text produced and written by Fritscher

DRUMMER 16, June 1977
Second Anniversary Issue
2 Pieces of Writing by Fritscher and Produced by Fritscher
- "Tom Hinde Folio: Drawings 1977," pp. 39-46, feature written by Thom Hinde with Jack Fritscher, produced by Fritscher
- "Johnny Gets His Hair Cut," pp. 66-68; photo essay produced by Fritscher

***DRUMMER* 17, July 1977**
1 Feature Article with Photographs Produced by Fritscher
- "Famous Dungeons of San Francisco," pp. 8-11, feature produced by Fritscher including photos by Gene Weber (picturing Fritscher) and text by Joe Cook

***DRUMMER* 18, August 1977**
Masthead: Ghost-editor-in-chief Fritscher is not credited
Last issue of *Drummer* (4-month hiatus) until December 1977
1 Piece of Writing by Fritscher
2 Feature Articles with Photographs Produced by Fritscher
First issue of *Drummer* with byline by Jack Fritscher
- "Body Casting," pp. 66-69, feature article with photographs by Gene Weber produced by Fritscher
- "The Leatherneck," pp. 82-84, feature article written by and photo essay produced by Fritscher
  [Editor's Note: August 1977 – December 1977: Publisher John Embry, Editor-in-chief Fritscher, and Art Director Al Shapiro put *Drummer* on 4-month hiatus to reinvent the LA magazine into a San Francisco magazine]

***DRUMMER* 19, December 1977**
Masthead: Jack Fritscher, editor-in-chief
7 Pieces of Writing by Fritscher
- "Contents Page," one liners
- "Leather Christmas," pp. 8-10, cover feature article
- "Gifting," pp. 20-21, holiday photo feature
- "Astrologic" (Capricorn), p. 26, satire
- "*El Paso Wrecking Corp*: The Gage Brothers," pp. 62-64, film review
- "Steve Reeves' Screen Test," pp. 66-68, feature essay and captions
- "*Star Trick* Artist Dom Orejudos Is Etienne!," pp. 71-74, art review
- "Mineshaft," pp. 82-83, cover feature article

***DRUMMER* 20, January 1978**
Masthead: Jack Fritscher, editor-in-chief
Theme for *Drummer* 20 Created by Fritscher: Gay Sports
10 Pieces of Writing by Fritscher
1 Photograph (Interior Editorial) by Fritscher solo
18 Photographs (Interior Editorial) by Fritscher and Sparrow dba "Photos by Sparrow"
- "Contents Page," one liners
- "Crimes Against Nature," p. 6, editorial review
- 1 Photograph (Interior Editorial): "Jockstrap Chest with *Sports Illustrated* Magazine," p. 10, by Fritscher solo
- "Gay Jock Sports: Wrestling, Boxing, Rollerballing, Soaring, Scuba, Bodybuilding, Dune Bodies, Films," cover lead feature article, pp. 8-17 and 70-71 and 83-84
- "Dune Body," p. 16, poem
- "Gifting," pp. 20-22, feature article
- "Pissing in the Wind: The Mineshaft," pp. 22-24 and 83, feature article
- "Astrologic" (Aquarius), p. 30, satire
- 1 Photograph (Interior Editorial): "David Wycoff, Soldier," p. 39, by Fritscher and Sparrow dba "Sparrow Photography"
- "*Salo*: A Review of Pasolini, Toward an Understanding of *Salo*" pp. 66-67, feature review
- "*Gay Source: A Catalog for Men*," p. 72, book review by Fritscher and Bob Zygarlicki
- "CMC Carnival 1977," pp. 74-77, feature
- 17 Photographs (Interior Editorial): "CMC Carnival 1977," pp. 74-77, by Fritscher and Sparrow dba "Photos by Sparrow"

- "Night Flight: New Year's Eve Party 1977," p. 88-89, feature

DRUMMER 21, March 1978
Masthead: Jack Fritscher, editor-in-chief
The Most Perfectly Representative Issue of *Drummer*
Theme for *Drummer* 21 Created by Fritscher: Prison
9 Pieces of Writing by Fritscher
1 Photograph (Front Cover Portrait): "John Trowbridge as Ex-Con," designed and cast by Fritscher, and photographed by David Sparrow and Jack Fritscher dba "David Sparrow"
2 Photographs (Interior Editorial) by Fritscher solo
4 Photographs (Interior Editorial) by Fritscher and Sparrow dba "Photos by Sparrow"
1 Story ("In a Pig's Ass" by Phil Andros) edited and produced by Fritscher

- 1 Photograph (Front Cover Portrait): "John Trowbridge as Ex-Con," designed and cast by Fritscher, and photographed by David Sparrow and Jack Fritscher dba "David Sparrow"
- "Contents Page," one liners
- "Defending Your Attitude," editorial, p. 6
- "Prison Blues: Confessions of a Prison-Tour Junkie," pp. 8-11 and 70-73; cover lead feature
- 4 Photographs (Interior Editorial): "Prisoners," pp. 8-11, by Fritscher and Sparrow aka "Photos by Sparrow"
- 1 Photograph (Interior Editorial): "RCMP Mountie in Boots and Sweater," p. 27, by Fritscher solo
- "Scott Smith: Heavy Rap with a Solitary Ex-Con," feature interview, written by David Hurles and Fritscher
- "Astrologic" (Aries), p. 30, satire
- "In a Pig's Ass," short fiction by Phil Andros aka Sam Steward, edited and produced by Fritscher
- "Gay Deteriorata," p. 38, satire of "Desiderata"
- "Pumping Roger: Acts, Facts, and Fantasy, A Night at the Nob Hill Theater," pp. 45-46 and 68, feature
- 1 Photograph (Interior Editorial): "Bear on Toilet," p. 71, by Fritscher solo
- "Punk Funk: You Read This, You Deserve It," pp. 74-76, feature, with additional reporting by M. Board
- "Dr. Dick, *Drummer* Goes to the Doctor, PCP: Short Cut to Suicide," p. 77, column, written by Fritscher based on interview with Dr. Richard Hamilton, M. D.

DRUMMER 22, May 1978
Masthead: Jack Fritscher, editor-in-chief
Theme for *Drummer* 22 Created by Fritscher: Cigars
11 Pieces of Writing by Fritscher
2 Photographs (Interior Editorial) by Fritscher solo
1 Interview ("Tom of Finland" by Robert Opel) Produced by Fritscher

- "Contents Page," one liners
- "Attitude Begets Attitude," p. 6, editorial
- "Cigar Blues," pp. 8-12, feature, illustrated with 5 photographs from Fritscher's 1960-1970s collection but not shot by Fritscher
- 1 Photograph (Interior Editorial): "Cigar Smoker USMC," p. 8, by Fritscher solo
- 1 Photograph (Interior Editorial): "Cigar Smoker Dan Dufort," p. 14, by Fritscher solo
- "Firebomber: Cigar Sarge," p. 15, fiction
- "USMC: Strip-Shaving the Raw Recruit," pp. 20-21, feature
- "Astrologic" (Taurus), p. 30, satire
- "Corporal in Charge of Taking Care of Captain O'Malley, Part 1," pp. 32-35, erotic drama

- "*Sebastiane*," pp. 66-67, film review of Derek Jarman
- "*End Product: The First Taboo*," p. 69, book review; Fritscher pseudonym as "David Hurles"
- "Arena Slave Auction," pp. 73-77, feature
- "Tom of Finland Interview," by Robert Opel, pp. 90-91, produced by Fritscher
- "Club San Francisco, Ritch Street," pp. 92-93, feature

DRUMMER 23, July 1978
Third Anniversary Issue
Masthead: Jack Fritscher, editor-in-chief
Theme for *Drummer* 23 Created by Fritscher: Underground Sex: Gay Pop-Culture — The Catacombs
12 Pieces of Writing by Fritscher
12 Photographs (Interior Editorial) by Fritscher solo aka "Larry Olson"
Fritscher adds tag line: "*Drummer*: The American Review of Gay Popular Culture"
- "Contents Page," one liners
- "Gay Pop Culture in *Drummer*," p. 6, editorial
- "The Catacombs: Upstairs over a Vacant Lot," pp. 8-11, feature essay
- 12 Photographs (Interior Editorial): "The Catacombs," pp. 8-11, photographs by Fritscher solo aka "Larry Olson"
- "Redneck Biker," pp. 16-18, poem
- "Astrologic" (Leo), p. 31, satire, limerick
- "Corporal in Charge of Taking Care of Captain O'Malley, Part 2," pp. 32-35 and 73, erotic drama
- "Target Men," p. 45, captions
- "Golden Drumsticks Awards," p. 74, awards column invented this issue by Fritscher
- "Reviewing Straight Magazines: Some Babes in the Woods," pp. 78-79, captions, short essay
- "Tough Shit," p. 84, debut of feature column Fritscher created, collected, and produced for ongoing issues through *Drummer* 30.
- "How I Spent My Summer Vacation, or, Pigging It in New York," pp. 87-88, feature essay by Al Shapiro (A. Jay) with Fritscher
- "Submit to *Drummer*," p. 94, letter soliciting talent

DRUMMER 24, September 1978
Masthead: Jack Fritscher, editor-in-chief
Theme for *Drummer* 24 Created by Fritscher: Authenticity, Mapplethorpe, and Bondage
9 Pieces of Writing by Fritscher
2 Photographs (Interior Editorial) by Fritscher solo
47 Photographs (Interior Editorial) by Fritscher and Sparrow dba "Photos by David Sparrow"
1 Photograph (Front Cover Portrait) by Robert Mapplethorpe, designed, cast, and produced by Fritscher
1 Photograph (Front Cover Portrait) "The Mapplethorpe Cover: Biker for Hire," photograph by Robert Mapplethorpe; commissioned, designed, cast, and produced by Fritscher
- "Contents Page," one liners
- "Let Us Now Praise Fucking with Authentic Men," p. 8 and 72-73, editorial
- "Bondage: Blest Be the Tie That Binds," pp. 16-23 and 76, feature essay
- 13 Photographs (Interior Editorial): "Bondage," pp. 16-23, photographs by Fritscher and Sparrow dba "Photos by David Sparrow"
- "Castro Street Blues: 1978 Style," pp. 32-36, feature satire
- 11 Photographs (Interior Editorial): "Castro Street Fair 1978," pp. 34-36, photographs by Fritscher and Sparrow dba "Photos by David Sparrow"
- "In Hot Blood: Ex-Cons-We Abuse Fags, Part 1," pp. 37-44, feature interview, created by David Hurles and Fritscher

- "Jocks: Holtz and Ed Wiley," pp. 46-52, centerfold, text by Fritscher; see Holtz shot by Fritscher solo on cover of *Rainbow County and Other Stories*
- 3 Photographs (Interior Editorial): "Richard Locke," p. 38, by Fritscher and Sparrow dba "Photos by David Sparrow"
- "Tough Shit," p. 83, feature column created, collected, and produced by Fritscher
- "The Quarters: Slave Training," pp. 10-15, 70-71, essay
- 20 Photographs (Interior Editorial): "The Quarters," pp 10-15, 70-71, photographs by Fritscher and Sparrow dba "From the Desk of the D.I. Photos by David Sparrow"
- 1 Photograph (Interior Editorial): "David Sparrow in Bondage with Collar," p. 76, by Fritscher solo
- 1 Photograph (Interior Editorial): "Skip Navarette in Bondage," p. 76, by Fritscher solo
- "Men's Bar Scene: A Farewell to Larry's," p. 88, essay
- "Gay Writers/Writer's Aid," p. 86, notice of Fritscher tutorial for erotic authors

SON OF DRUMMER, September 1978, A *Drummer* Special Issue, Published Same Month as *Drummer* 24
Jack Fritscher, editor-in-chief
Theme for *Son of Drummer* Created by Fritscher: New York Art—Mapplethorpe and Rex
8 Pieces of Writing by Fritscher
8 Photographs (Interior Editorial) by Fritscher solo
35 Photographs (Interior Editorial) by Fritscher and Sparrow dba "Sparrow Photography"
  [Editor's Note: Fritscher wrote nearly the entirety of this special issue.]
- "Contents Page," one liners
- "Arab Death," pp. 8-11, feature; Fritscher bylined by pseudonym, "Denny Sargent," the protagonist in his 1969 novel *I Am Curious (Leather)* aka *Leather Blues* serialized in this issue
- "The Robert Mapplethorpe Gallery (Censored)," pp. 14-17, feature
- "Target Studio Retrospective," pp. 22-25, captions
- "Turkish Delight: Macho Wrestling with Leather, Oil, and Heavy Sweat," pp. 28-30, essay
- 35 Photographs (Interior Editorial): "Ass-Sets," p. 31, by Fritscher and Sparrow dba "Sparrow Photography"
- 4 Photographs (Interior Editorial): "Filmstrips: Candle Power," p. 34, by Fritscher solo
- 4 Photographs (Interior Editorial): "Filmstrips: Rude Rubbers," p. 35, by Fritscher solo
- "*I Am Curious (Leather)*: The Adventures of Denny Sargent," pp. 41-47, excerpt of Fritscher's 1969 novel *Leather Blues*
- "Rex Revisited," p. 48-51, feature essay
- "Chico Is the Man," pp. 52-54, poem

DRUMMER 25, December 1978
Masthead: Jack Fritscher, editor-in-chief
Theme for *Drummer* 25 Created by Fritscher: Leather Identity—Homomasculinity
17 Pieces of Writing by Fritscher
1 Photograph (Front Cover Portrait) "Ed Dinakos," by Fritscher and Sparrow dba "Staff Photographer David Sparrow"
33 Photographs (Interior Editorial) for Centerfold and Interior Photographs by Fritscher and Sparrow dba "Staff Photographer David Sparrow"
- 1 Photograph (Front Cover Portrait) "Ed Dinakos," by Fritscher and Sparrow dba "Staff Photographer David Sparrow"
- "Contents Page," one liners
- 1 Photograph (Interior Editorial): "Torso," contents page, by Fritscher and Sparrow dba "David Sparrow"
- "Afraid You're Not Butch Enough?" p. 6, editorial
- "*Drummer* Gift Guide," pp. 17-21, captions

- "Astrologic" (Scorpio), p. 22, satire
- "Drumbeats, Yule Recipe: Bat," p. 30, satiric essay
- "Gay Pop Culture Series: Fetishes, *Equus* (A One-Horse Open Sleigh)," pp. 31-39, review
- "Horsemaster: Come to the Stable," p. 40, fiction
- "In Hot Blood: Ex-Cons-We Abuse Fags, Part 2," pp. 37-44, feature interview, created by David Hurles and Fritscher
- "Big Mike (Ed Dinakos)," p. 49, centerfold captions
- 7 Photographs (Interior Editorial): "Big Mike Dinakos," p. 49, by Fritscher and Sparrow dba "Staff Photographer David Sparrow"
- "We're Looking for Mr. *Drummer*," p. 68, promotional text
- 2 Photographs (Interior Editorial): "Looking for Mr. *Drummer*," p. 68, by Fritscher and Sparrow dba "David Sparrow"
- "*The Norseman*," p. 70, film review
- "Tough Shit," p. 73, feature column created, collected, and produced by Fritscher
- "Tough Customers," p. 75, first appearance of feature column invented, collected, and produced by Fritscher through *Drummer* 33; this column continued for twenty years
- "Dr. Dick, *Drummer* Goes to the Doctor, Amoebiasis: Your Ass Is Falling Out," p. 80, feature, based on interview with Dr. Richard Hamilton, M. D.
- "*Drummer* Goes to Its Own Party," pp. 88-91, feature
- 15 Photographs (Interior Editorial): "*Drummer* Goes to Its Own Party," pp. 88-91, by Fritscher and Sparrow dba "David Sparrow"
- "Scottish Games: Men in Kilts," pp. 92-93, feature
- 8 Photographs (Interior Editorial): "Men in Kilts," pp. 92-93, by Fritscher and Sparrow dba "Photos by David Sparrow"
- "Sleep in Heavenly Peace," p. 102, fiction

DRUMMER 26, JANUARY 1979
Masthead: Jack Fritscher, editor-in-chief
Theme for *Drummer* 26 Created by Fritscher: Cowboys and Performance Art
11 Pieces of Writing by Fritscher
6 Photographs (Interior Editorial) by Fritscher solo
22 Photographs (Interior Editorial) by Fritscher and Sparrow dba "David Sparrow"
- "Contents Page," one liners
- "Grand National Rodeo Blues: Comes a Horseman, Cowboys and Mounties," pp. 8-17, feature
- 8 Photographs (Interior Editorial): Cowboys, pp. 10, 12-14, 16, by Fritscher and Sparrow dba "Photo Essay by David Sparrow"
- 6 Photographs (Interior Editorial): RCMP Mounties, pp. 11, 14-17, by Fritscher solo
- "High Performance: Or, Sex without a Net," pp. 18-22, review, by Fritscher using pseudonym of "David Hurles" with permission of Hurles
- 1 Photograph (Interior Editorial): "Mike (Ed Dinakos) with Blond and Ball Gag," p. 21, by Fritscher and Sparrow dba "David Sparrow"
- "Astrologic" (Sagittarius), pp. 30-31, satire
- "The Battered Lex Barker," pp. 32-36, feature article and captions
- "*Midnight Express*," pp. 68-69, review, in collaboration with John Trojanski
- "Tough Shit," p. 70, feature column created, collected, and written by Fritscher
- "Tough Customers," p. 76, feature column created, collected, and edited by Fritscher
- "CMC Carnival 1978: Seaman's Semen's End," pp. 82-85, feature
- 13 Photographs (Interior Editorial): "CMC Carnival 1978," pp. 82-85, by Fritscher and Sparrow dba "David Sparrow"
- "Gay Writers/Writer's Aid," p. 86, notice of Fritscher tutorial for erotic authors
- "Harvey Milk and Gay Courage: In Passing," p. 96, essay

DRUMMER 27, February 1979
Masthead: Jack Fritscher, editor-in-chief
Theme for *Drummer* 27 Created by Fritscher: Gay Film and The Society of Janus
10 Pieces of Writing by Fritscher
4 Photographs (Interior Editorial) by Fritscher and Sparrow dba "Sparrow Photography" and "Photos by David Sparrow"
- "Contents Page," one liners
- 1 Photograph (Interior Editorial): Letters to the Editor, p. 7, by Fritscher and Sparrow dba "Sparrow Photography"
- "Basic Plumbing Unplugged: LA Plays Hard with Itself," pp. 8-13, lead feature, by Fritscher with additional reporting by Terry Sabreur
- "Dirty Poole: Everything You Fantasized about Wakefield Poole," pp. 14-22, cover feature interview
- 3 Photographs (Interior Editorial): "Wakefield Poole," p. 15, by Fritscher and Sparrow dba "Photos by David Sparrow"
- "S&M: The Last Taboo, The Janus Society," pp. 32-36, feature essay, by Fritscher with additional reporting by "Eric Van Meter"
- "*Movie Movie*," pp. 61, film review
- "*Superman*," pp. 61-62, film review
- "Golden Drumsticks Awards: The Pet Gloryhole," p. 64, awards column created and written by Fritscher
- "Tough Shit," p. 70, feature column collected and written by Fritscher
- "Tough Customers," p. 76-77, feature column created, collected, and edited by Fritscher
- "Men's Bar Scene: *Drummer* Goes to Boots," pp. 82-84, essay

DRUMMER 28, April 1979
Masthead: Jack Fritscher, editor-in-chief
Theme for *Drummer* 28 Created by Fritscher: Gyms and Prisons
6 Pieces of Writing by Fritscher
10 Photographs (Interior Editorial) by Fritscher and Sparrow dba "David Sparrow Photography"
- "Contents Page," one liners
- "Wet Stough," pp. 14-17, poem for "Swim Meet" photographs
- 10 Photographs (Interior Editorial): "Swim Meet," pp. 13-14, by Fritscher and Sparrow dba "David Sparrow Photography"
- "Bare-Ass Wrestling," p. 41, centerfold poem, caption
- "*The Deer Hunter*," pp. 53-54, movie review
- "Tough Shit," p. 62, feature column created, collected, and written by Fritscher
- "Tough Customers," pp. 64-65, feature column created, collected, and edited by Fritscher

DRUMMER 29, May 1979
Masthead: Jack Fritscher, editor-in-chief
Theme for *Drummer* 29 Created by Fritscher: Dangerous Sex, Boxing, and Blue-Collar Men
9 Pieces of Writing by Fritscher
3 Photographs (Interior Editorial) by Fritscher and Sparrow dba "Sparrow Photography"
1 Story (*Mr. Benson* by John Preston) edited, serialized, and produced by Fritscher
- "Contents Page," one liners
- "The Most Dangerous Game in the Whole Wide World," p. 6, editorial
- "Drawings by Domino," p. 9-11, essay in two parts, "Domino/Summer of 1978" and "An Artist's Statement," written by Fritscher with Al Shapiro from Shapiro-Fritscher interview
- "Foot Loose," p. 13, poem
- "Noodles Romanov and the Golden Gloves," pp. 14-17, feature article
- 3 Photographs (Interior Editorial): "Golden Gloves," pp. 14, 16-17, by Fritscher and

Sparrow dba "Sparrow Photography"
- *Mr. Benson*, pp. 18-23, Part One of a novel written by John Preston; edited, serialized, and produced by Fritscher
- "On Target: The New American Masculinity," pp. 37, centerfold copy
- "Tough Shit," p. 62, feature column created, collected, and written by Fritscher
- "Tough Customers," p. 62, feature column created, collected, and edited by Fritscher
- "Gay Writers/Writer's Aid," p. 72, notice for Fritscher tutorial for erotic authors

DRUMMER 30, June 1979
Fourth Anniversary Issue
Masthead: Jack Fritscher, editor-in-chief, and contributing writer
Copyright on masthead is incorrectly marked as "1978"
Theme for *Drummer* 30 Created by Fritscher: Nipples and Arthur Tress Photography
8 Pieces of Writing by Fritscher
1 Photograph (Front Cover Portrait) by Fritscher and Sparrow dba "David Sparrow Photography"
1 Story (*Mr. Benson* by John Preston) edited, serialized, and produced by Fritscher
- 1 Photograph (Front Cover Portrait): "Val Martin and Bob Hyslop," by Fritscher and Sparrow dba "David Sparrow Photography"
- "Contents Page," one liners
- "Tit Torture Blues," pp. 10-18, feature article
- "Meditations on Arthur Tress," pp. 22-25, four poems for four Tress photographs: "Code 1: Gifts of Nature," "Code 2: Black Boy," "Code 3: Sebastiane," and "Code 4: Confession de Kafka Caca"
- *Mr. Benson*, pp. 26-31, Part Two of a novel written by John Preston; edited, serialized, and produced by Fritscher
- "Zeus Men In Bondage: Introducing a New Studio," p. 48, centerfold copy, produced and written by Fritscher
- "The Brothel Hotel," pp. 63-64, feature review
- "Tough Shit," p. 72, feature column created, collected, and produced by Fritscher included two original essays by Fritscher, "Bloody 'Marys' at Elephant Walk" and "How Relaxed Can Straights Get?"
- "Tough Customers," p. 74-75, feature column created, collected, and edited by Fritscher

DRUMMER 31, September 1979
Masthead: Fritscher, who edited *Drummer* 31, is not credited; Embry removed Fritscher credit line on masthead, but kept some Fritscher bylines; credit was assigned to "Robert Payne" aka publisher John Embry.
The 1970s *Drummer* salon exited with Fritscher on December 31, 1979
Theme for *Drummer* 31 Created by Fritscher: Spit and Other Erotic Bodily Functions
8 Pieces of Writing by Fritscher
40 Photographs (Interior Editorial) for Centerfold by Fritscher (Solo) credited wrongly by Embry to "Sparrow Photography"
1 Story (*Mr. Benson* by John Preston) edited, serialized, and produced by Fritscher
- "Contents Page," one liners
- "Martin of Holland Interview," pp. 18-19, feature interview, written by Al Shapiro (A. Jay) and Fritscher; Fritscher byline deleted by Embry
- "The First International Mr. Leather (IML)," pp. 20-24, feature
- 40 Photographs (Interior Editorial, Centerfold): "Spit, Sweat, and Piss with Val Martin and Bob Hyslop," pp. 41-48, shot by Fritscher solo——with byline changed by Embry to "Sparrow Photography"
- *Mr. Benson*, pp. 25-29, Part Three of a novel written by John Preston; edited, serialized, and produced by Fritscher
- "Tough Shit," p. 64, feature column created, collected, and produced by Fritscher
- "Tough Customers," pp. 66-67, feature column created, collected, and edited by

Jack Fritscher   Appendix 2   515

Fritscher
- "The Macho Images of Tony Plewik: A *Drummer* Do-er's Profile," pp. 68-70, essay
- "Men's Bar Scene: Pure Trash," pp. 74-75, essay
- "In Passing, Robert Opel: His Last High Performance, His Murder," p. 86, essay, collage from original reporting by Maitland Zane, *San Francisco Chronicle*

DRUMMER 32, October 1979
Masthead: Fritscher, who edited *Drummer* 32, was not credited; credit was assigned to "Robert Payne" aka publisher John Embry; Embry removed Fritscher's credit line on masthead, leaving only the coded byline signature, "20 June 1979," Fritscher's day and month of birth, p. 19.
5 Pieces of Writing by Fritscher
1 Story (*Mr. Benson* by John Preston) edited, serialized, and produced by Fritscher
- "A Confidential *DRUMMER* Dossier," pp. 19-21, byline coded with Fritscher birth date
- *Mr. Benson*, pp. 22-27, Part Four of a novel written by John Preston; edited, serialized, and produced by Fritscher
- "The Men by Robert Opel," pp. 28-29, writing by Robert Opel researched, collected, and produced by Fritscher
- "Tough Shit," p. 66, feature column created, collected, and produced by Fritscher
- "Tough Customers," pp. 68-69, feature column created, collected, and edited by Fritscher
- "Conrap," p. 71, debut of column created, collected, and edited by Fritscher with reporting by David Hurles (Old Reliable)
- "Tough Tales," pp. 72-73, 76, debut of column created, collected, and edited by Fritscher

DRUMMER RIDES AGAIN, December 1979, A *Drummer* Special Issue, published same month as *Drummer* 33
Title of Special Issue Created by Fritscher
No masthead listed; masthead deleted because of arguments over byline representation; issue initially edited and produced by Fritscher; subsequent changes and deletions in content by "Robert Payne" with credit for editing by "Robert Payne" buried at bottom of contents page, p. 3
1 Piece of Writing by Fritscher
1 Photograph (Interior Editorial) by Fritscher solo
13 Photographs (Interior Editorial) by Fritscher and Sparrow dba "David Sparrow Photography"
2 Graphic Features (Cavelo Art; Rink Photography) Produced by Fritscher
- "Bound and Gagged: Zeus Studio." text for photo feature
- "Cavelo's Men," pp. 24-27, produced by Fritscher; new text by "Robert Payne"
- 1 Photograph (Interior Editorial): "Val Martin," p. 44, by Fritscher solo (wrongly credited to "Photo by David Sparrow")
- "A Very Private Orgy: Photos by Rink," pp. 50-52, produced by Fritscher; Fritscher text replaced with text by "Robert Payne"
- 13 Photographs (Interior Editorial): "The Quarters: How I Spent My Summer Vacation," pp. 45, 53-56, by Fritscher and Sparrow dba "David Sparrow Photography"

DRUMMER 33, December 1979
Masthead: Fritscher performed basic edit on *Drummer* 33 which was credited to "Robert Payne"; Embry completed removal of Fritscher byline and deleted two feature articles by Fritscher and five photographs by Fritscher and Sparrow
5 Pieces of Writing by Fritscher
1 Photograph (Interior Editorial) by Fritscher and Sparrow dba "David Sparrow"
1 Story (*Mr. Benson* by John Preston) edited, serialized, and produced by Fritscher
1 Photograph (Interior Editorial), contents page, by Fritscher and Sparrow dba "David Sparrow"
- 1 Photograph (Interior Editorial): "Ed Dinakos Hood and Harness," p. 19, by Fritscher and Sparrow dba "David Sparrow"
- "*Drummer* Gift Guide," pp. 19-23, captions

- *Mr. Benson*, pp. 24-29, Part Five of a novel written by John Preston; edited, serialized, and produced by Fritscher; beginning with Part Six, Embry absorbed the Fritscher edit and serialization through the ten parts of *Mr. Benson*
- "Tough Shit," p. 66, feature column created, collected, and produced by Fritscher
- "Tough Customers," pp. 68-69, feature column created, collected, and edited by Fritscher
- "Conrap," p. 71, column created, collected, and edited by Fritscher with reporting by David Hurles (Old Reliable)
- "Tough Tales," pp. 72-73, 76, debut of column created, collected, and edited by Fritscher

DRUMMER 41, December 1980
1 Piece of Writing by Fritscher (Fritscher's "Astrologic" Pirated and Reprinted without Copyright Permission and Falsely Bylined as "Aristide")
2 Photographs (Interior Editorial) by Fritscher and Sparrow dba "David Sparrow"
- "Astrologic" (Sagittarius), p. 63, written by Fritscher and pirated in a reprint by publisher Embry and editor John W. Rowberry without permission from Fritscher's copyright column "Astrologic" in *Drummer* 21 (March 1978), p. 30; Embry and Rowberry colluded in this direct violation of Fritscher's copyright; falsely assigning the byline to "Aristide," it seems they set out to deceive the readership by rearranging the order of the months in Fritscher's original in order to recycle and resell the column.
- 2 Photographs (Interior Editorial) from "The Quarters," p. 43 (inset in "Key Club Carpenters"), and p. 44, by Fritscher and Sparrow dba "David Sparrow"; both reprinted without permission.

DRUMMER 81, February 1984
1 Editorial Mention: 2 Books Reviews
- Editorial Mention: Book Review, "Drummedia Books: Men Who Say Yo," p. 81, review written by Aaron Travis (Steven Saylor) of two books collecting Fritscher's fiction first serialized or published in *Drummer*: the novel *Leather Blues* and *Corporal in Charge of Taking Care of Captain O'Malley and Other Stories* which was the first collection of *Drummer* stories published outside of *Drummer*.

DRUMMER 85, December 1985
10th Anniversary Issue
1 Piece of Writing by Fritscher
- "Smut Is Where You Find It—Erotic Writers: What They Read to Turn on," p. 86, personal essay

DRUMMER 100, October 1986
Special 100th Issue
1 Piece of Writing by Fritscher (cover lead feature)
   [Editor's Note: In 1986, Anthony F. DeBlase and Andrew Charles, Desmodus Inc., purchased *Drummer* from publisher John Embry]
- "The Lords of Leather," pp. 30-35, short fiction, featured on cover

DRUMMER 107, August 1987
2 Pieces of Writing by Fritscher
- "The Artist, A. Jay: Al Shapiro—The Passing of One of *Drummer*'s First Daddies," pp. 34-40, feature obituary
- "Obituary Sidebar: Shapiro," p. 40, book dedication of *Stand by Your Man and Other Stories*

DRUMMER 115, April 1988
1 Piece of Writing by Fritscher
2 Photographs (Interior Editorial) by Fritscher dba "Palm Drive Video"
- "Fetish Feature," p. 26, schedule of themes created by Fritscher for upcoming issues 116-121
- 2 Photographs (Interior Editorial) for Video Review: "Palm Drive Models Dan Dufort and Gino Deddino," p. 40; plus mention on pp. 26 and 40

DRUMMER 116 (incorrectly marked on masthead as issue 114), May 1988
Masthead: Jack Fritscher, Contributing Writer; Fritscher dba Palm Drive Video, Photography
1 Piece of Writing by Fritscher
2 Photographs (Interior Editorial) by Fritscher dba "Palm Drive Video"
4 Photographs (Interior Advertising) by Fritscher dba "Palm Drive Video"
- "Fetish Feature," p. 40, schedule of themes created by Fritscher for upcoming issues 118-121
- 1 Photograph (Interior Editorial): "Palm Drive Model John Muir in Uniform and Underwear," p. 48, from Fritscher video, *A Man's Man*, by Fritscher dba "Palm Drive Video"
- 2 Photographs (Interior Editorial): "In Passing: Washday at Palm Drive Video, Hanging Out to Dry" p. 98, by Fritscher dba "Palm Drive Video" from the video *Vigilante*
- 4 Photographs (Interior Advertising): "Sonny Butts, Dave Gold, Jason Steele, and Bruno," p. 39, by Fritscher dba "Palm Drive Video," display ad, one-sixth page; this is the first display ad for Palm Drive Video to be published in *Drummer*—four years after the founding of Palm Drive Video (1984)

DRUMMER 117, June 1988
Masthead: Jack Fritscher, Writer, Frequent Contributors; Palm Drive Video, Photography, Frequent Contributors
1 Piece of Writing by Fritscher
2 Photographs (Interior Editorial) by Fritscher solo
4 Photographs (Interior Advertising) by Fritscher dba "Palm Drive Video"
1 Piece of Writing (Advertising) by Fritscher dba "Palm Drive Video"
- "Fetish Feature," p. 41, schedule of themes created by Fritscher for upcoming issues 118-122
- 2 Photographs (Interior Editorial): "Video Daddies: Dave Gold," p. 45, by Fritscher
- 4 Photographs (Interior Advertising): "Sonny Butts, Dave Gold, Jason Steele, and Bruno," p. 17, by Fritscher dba "Palm Drive Video," display ad, one-sixth page
- "New S&M Fetish Videos," p. 86, classified ad copy by Fritscher for Palm Drive Video

DRUMMER 118, July 1988 (*Drummer* 118 and *Drummer* 119 were both dated July 1988)
Masthead: Jack Fritscher, Writer, Frequent Contributors; Palm Drive Video, Photography, Frequent Contributors
Theme for *Drummer* 118 Created by Fritscher: Rubber (Keith Ardent)
2 Pieces of Writing (including Lead Feature Article) by Fritscher
1 Photograph (Front Cover Portrait) by Fritscher dba "Palm Drive Video"
9 Photographs (Interior Editorial) by Fritscher dba "Palm Drive Video"
2 Photographs (Interior Editorial, Inside Back Cover) by Fritscher dba "Palm Drive Video"
7 Photographs (Interior Advertising) by Fritscher dba "Palm Drive Video"
1 Piece of Writing (Advertising) by Fritscher dba "Palm Drive Video"
- 1 Photograph (Front Cover Portrait): "Palm Drive Model Keith Ardent" by Fritscher dba "Palm Drive Video"; plus mention, p. 4, with Fritscher misspelled as "Fritcher"
- 9 Photographs (Interior Editorial): Keith Ardent in "Pec Stud in Black Rubber," pp. 2, 3, 11-18, 32, by Fritscher dba "Palm Drive Video"
- "Nine-Inch Pec Stud in Black Rubber," p. 14, photo caption

- "Rubberotica: Confessions of a Rubber Freak," pp. 28-32, lead feature article
- 7 Photographs (Interior Advertising) by Fritscher: "Palm Drive Models Sonny Butts, Dave Gold, Jason Steele, Bruno, Keith Ardent, Mike Welder, Redneck Cowboy," p. 80, by Fritscher dba "Palm Drive Video," display ad, half-page
- "New S&M Fetish Videos," p. 82, classified ad copy by Fritscher for Palm Drive Video
- 2 Photographs (Interior Editorial, Inside Back Cover): "Grizzly Action" and "Beards, Bears, and Barbarous Butts" by Fritscher dba "Palm Drive Video"

DRUMMER 119, July 1988 (*Drummer* 118 and *Drummer* 119 were both dated July 1988)
Masthead: Jack Fritscher, Writer, Frequent Contributors; Palm Drive Video, Photography, Frequent Contributors
Theme for *Drummer* 119 Created by Fritscher: Bears
1 Piece of Writing (Lead Feature Article) by Fritscher
21 Photographs (Interior Editorial) by Fritscher
7 Photographs (Interior Advertising) by Fritscher dba "Palm Drive Video"
1 Piece of Writing (Advertising) by Fritscher dba "Palm Drive Video"
1 Editorial Mention: Letter to the Editor

- Editorial Mention: "Fritscher/Palm Drive Video's *Mud Pillow Fight*," letter to the editor, p. 5
- "Fetish Feature," p. 19, schedule of themes created by Fritscher for upcoming issues 120-123
- "Bears! How to Hunt Buckskin Leather Mountain Men and Live Among the Bears," pp. 22-26, cover feature article, first Bear article in *Drummer*
- 21 Photographs (Interior Editorial): "Palm Drive Models John Muir, Jack Husky, and Mr. America Chuck Sipes with Mountain Men" pp. 2, 3, 18, 22-26, by Fritscher dba "Palm Drive Video"; Fritscher photo, page 18, is "Daddy's Beerbelly in Bondage"; on pages 22-26, Fritscher photos are numbered as 1-7, 9, 11-13, 15, 17-20; Fritscher photo inside front cover is "Big Bruno" in white cowboy hat, with three more photos on page 3, "Long Hair, Long Beard," "Jack Husky with Hammer," and "Mountain Man Black Hat"
- 7 Photographs (Interior Advertising): "Palm Drive Models Sonny Butts, Dave Gold, Jason Steele, Bruno, Keith Ardent, Mike Welder, Redneck Cowboy," p. 68, by Fritscher dba "Palm Drive Video," display ad, half-page
- "New S&M Fetish Videos," p. 76, classified ad copy by Fritscher for Palm Drive Video

DRUMMER 121, September 1988
Masthead: Jack Fritscher, Writer, Frequent Contributors; Palm Drive Video, Photography, Frequent Contributors
1 Photograph (Interior Editorial) by Fritscher dba "Palm Drive Video"
2 Editorial Mentions: 1 Video Review and 1 Book Review of Fritscher work
1 Piece of Writing (Advertising) by Fritscher dba "Palm Drive Video"

- 1 Photograph (Interior Editorial): "Palm Drive Model Jason Steele," p. 97, shot by Fritscher, illustrating Ken Kissoff's video and book reviews of Fritscher's Palm Drive Video feature *Tit Animal* and Fritscher's fiction anthology book *Stand by Your Man and Other Stories*
- Editorial Mention: Video Review of Fritscher's *Tit Animal*
- Editorial Mention: Book Review of Fritscher's *Stand by Your Man and Other Stories*
- "New S&M Fetish Videos," p. 80, classified ad copy by Fritscher for Palm Drive Video

DRUMMER 123, September 1988
Masthead: Jack Fritscher, Writer, Frequent Contributors; Palm Drive Video, Photography, Frequent Contributors
1 Piece of Writing (Lead Feature Article) by Fritscher
22 Photographs (Interior Editorial, including Inside Front Cover) by Fritscher dba "Palm Drive Video"

7 Photographs (Interior Advertising) by Fritscher dba "Palm Drive Video"
1 Piece of Writing (Advertising) by Fritscher dba "Palm Drive Video"
1 Editorial Mention
- 1 Photograph (Inside Front Cover): "Solo Sex: Cheesiest Uncut Cowboy in West Texas," p. 2, by Fritscher dba "Palm Drive Video"
- Editorial Mention: "Leather Pride Weekend," p. 7, listing of Fritscher as a judge of the 1988 Mr. *Drummer* Contest
- "Solo Sex, A Man's Guide," pp. 34-41, cover feature article
- 20 Photographs (Interior Editorial), "Solo Sex": 8 photographs, pp. 34 and 35; 1 photograph, top p. 36; 4 photographs, pp. 38-39; 6 photographs, p. 40; 1 photograph, bottom, p. 41, by Fritscher dba "Palm Drive Video"
- 7 Photographs (Interior Advertising), "Palm Drive Models Sonny Butts, Dave Gold, Jason Steele, Bruno, Keith Ardent, Mike Welder, Redneck Cowboy," p. 54, by Fritscher dba "Palm Drive Video," display ad, half-page
- "New S&M Fetish Videos," p. 81, classified ad copy by Fritscher for Palm Drive Video

DRUMMER 124, December 1988
Masthead: Jack Fritscher, Writer, Frequent Contributors; Palm Drive Video, Photography, Frequent Contributors
Theme for *Drummer* 124 Created by Fritscher: Bodybuilders and "the *Drummer* Novel," *Some Dance to Remember: A Memoir-Novel of San Francisco 1970-1982*
2 Pieces of Writing (Lead Feature Article and Book Excerpt) by Fritscher
5 Photographs (Interior Editorial) by Fritscher dba "Palm Drive Video"
2 Photographs (Interior Advertising) by Fritscher dba "Palm Drive Video"
2 Pieces of Writing (Advertising) by Fritscher dba "Palm Drive Video"
- "Bodybuilding: How to Judge It Inside and Out: A Sensual Critic's Eye View," pp. 7-9, lead feature
- 4 Photographs (Interior Editorial): "Bodybuilding: How to Judge It: Palm Drive Models Dick Black, Sonny Butts, and Anonymous Bodybuilder Contestant," pp. 16-17
- "*Some Dance to Remember,* Excerpts from the New Novel, *Drummer*'s Sneak Preview of a Literary Event," pp. 20-25, "The *Drummer* novel" about *Drummer*
- 1 Photograph (Interior Editorial): "Handsome, Bald Bodybuilder," p. 35, photograph by Fritscher illustrates review of a documentary video by Fritscher titled *Police Olympics Bodybuilding*
- 2 Photographs (Interior Advertising): "Handsome Bald Bodybuilder and Professional Bodybuilder Mike Sable," p. 53, Palm Drive Video display ad, half-page
- "New S&M Fetish Videos" and "Cop Jock Videos," p. 80, classified ad copy by Fritscher for Palm Drive Video

DRUMMER 126, March 1989
Masthead: Jack Fritscher, Writer, Frequent Contributors; Palm Drive Video, Photography, Frequent Contributors
1 Piece of Writing by Fritscher
1 Photograph (Interior Editorial, Inside Back Cover) by Fritscher dba "Palm Drive Video"
7 Photographs (Interior Advertising) by Fritscher dba "Palm Drive Video"
2 Pieces of Writing (Advertising) by Fritscher dba "Palm Drive Video"
2 Editorial Mentions
- "Rear-View Mirror #1: Home Is the Sailor! Home from the Sea!"; pp. 8-9, debut of Fritscher's GLBT leather history column
- 7 Photographs (Interior Advertising): "Palm Drive Models Sonny Butts, Dave Gold, Jason Steele, Bruno, Keith Ardent, Mike Welder, Redneck Cowboy," p. 87, by Fritscher dba "Palm Drive Video," display ad, half-page
- "New S&M Fetish Videos," and "Cop Jock Videos," p. 95, classified ad copy by Fritscher for Palm Drive Video

- Editorial Mention in "Tough Customers" of Palm Drive Video, p. 98
- 1 Photograph (Interior Editorial, Inside Back Cover): "Palm Drive Model J. D. Slater," p. 99
- Editorial Mention of Fritscher fiction "The Shadow Soldiers" and Fritscher photo for "J. D. Slater Is 'Dirt,'" p. 99

DRUMMER 127, April 1989
Masthead: Jack Fritscher, Writer, Frequent Contributors; Palm Drive Video, Photography, Frequent Contributors
3 Pieces of Writing (Short Fiction, History Essay, and Poem) by Fritscher
4 Photographs (Interior Editorial) by Fritscher dba "Jack Fritscher's Palm Drive Video"
7 Photographs (Interior Advertising) by Fritscher dba "Palm Drive Video"
2 Pieces of Writing (Advertising) by Fritscher dba "Palm Drive Video"
- "Rear-View Mirror #2: Bars and Bikes," pp. 15 and 97, GLBT leather history essay
- "J. D. Slater Is 'Dirt,'" pp. 16-17, poem
- 4 Photographs (Interior Editorial): "Palm Drive Model J. D. Slater," pp. 16-17, by Fritscher dba "Jack Fritscher's Palm Drive Video"
- "Shadow Soldiers," pp. 23-35, short fiction; with four drawings by Skipper produced by Fritscher; Skipper drawings © 1989 and 2007 Jack Fritscher
- 7 Photographs (Interior Advertising): "Palm Drive Models Sonny Butts, Dave Gold, Jason Steele, Bruno, Keith Ardent, Mike Welder, Redneck Cowboy," p. 85, by Fritscher dba "Palm Drive Video." display ad, half-page
- "New S&M Fetish Videos," and "Cop Jock Videos," p. 93, classified ad copy by Fritscher for Palm Drive Video

DRUMMER 128, May 1989
Masthead: Jack Fritscher, Writer, Frequent Contributors; Palm Drive Video, Photography, Frequent Contributors
7 Photographs (Interior Advertising) by Fritscher dba "Palm Drive Video"
2 Pieces of Writing (Advertising) by Fritscher dba "Palm Drive Video"
[Editor's Note: *Drummer* 128 contains a "Letter to the Editor," p. 5, re Fritscher's "Solo Sex" feature in *Drummer* 123. The editorial by Anthony F. DeBlase states that the success of *Drummer* is owed precisely to its showcasing of "real," that is, actual men, the readers, which as a concept was created and inaugurated in the 70s in the column "Tough Customers" by then editor-in-chief Fritscher. On p. 4, DeBlase also acknowledges that Fritscher's "Tough Customers" concept "is obviously one of the, if not the, most popular feature in *Drummer*."]
- 7 Photographs (Interior Advertising): "Palm Drive Models Sonny Butts, Dave Gold, Jason Steele, Bruno, Keith Ardent, Mike Welder, Redneck Cowboy," p. 65, by Fritscher dba "Palm Drive Video," display ad, half-page
- "New S&M Fetish Videos," and "Cop Jock Videos," p. 70, classified ad copy by Fritscher for Palm Drive Video

DRUMMER 129, June 1989
Masthead: Jack Fritscher, Featured Contributors; Palm Drive Video, Photography, Frequent Contributors
1 Piece of Writing by Fritscher
7 Photographs (Interior Advertising) by Fritscher dba "Palm Drive Video"
2 Pieces of Writing (Advertising) by Fritscher dba "Palm Drive Video"
- "Rear-View Mirror #3: Leather's Founding Daddies," pp. 33-34, GLBT leather history essay
- 7 Photographs (Interior Advertising): "Palm Drive Models Sonny Butts, Dave Gold, Jason Steele, Bruno, Keith Ardent, Mike Welder, Redneck Cowboy," p. 67, by Fritscher dba "Palm Drive Video," display ad, half-page "New S&M Fetish Videos," and "Cop

Jock Videos," p. 72, classified ad copy by Fritscher for Palm Drive Video

DRUMMER 130, July 1989 (*Drummer* 130 and *Drummer* 131 were both dated July 1989)
Masthead: Jack Fritscher, Featured Contributors; Palm Drive Video, Photography, Frequent Contributors
1 Feature (Cirby Art) Produced by Fritscher
7 Photographs (Interior Advertising) by Fritscher dba "Palm Drive Video"
2 Pieces of Writing (Advertising) by Fritscher dba "Palm Drive Video"
1 Editorial Mention
- Editorial Mention: "Eroticizing Vietnam" in "Male Call" of Fritscher fiction, "The Shadow Soldiers," *Drummer* 127, pp. 5-6
- "Cirby: The Erotic Artist," pp. 21-23, art feature produced by Fritscher collaborating with Cirby on a Palm Drive Video; Cirby was himself a Palm Drive Video model photographed by Fritscher
- 7 Photographs (Interior Advertising): "Palm Drive Models Sonny Butts, Dave Gold, Jason Steele, Bruno, Keith Ardent, Mike Welder, Redneck Cowboy," p. 83, by Fritscher dba "Palm Drive Video," display ad, half-page "New S&M Fetish Videos," and "Cop Jock Videos," p. 90, classified ad copy by Fritscher for Palm Drive Video

DRUMMER 131, July 1989 (*Drummer* 130 and *Drummer* 131 were both dated July 1989)
Masthead: Jack Fritscher, Writer, Featured Contributors; Palm Drive Video, Photography, Frequent Contributors
2 Pieces of Writing by Fritscher
7 Photographs (Interior Advertising) by Fritscher dba "Palm Drive Video"
2 Pieces of Writing (Advertising) by Fritscher dba "Palm Drive Video"
- "Rear-View Mirror #4: Inventing the Leather Bar (Tony Tavarossi)," pp. 22-23, GLBT leather history essay
- "You're History!" p. 23, Fritscher asks readers to send in their own "Rear-View Mirror" histories to the series he produced
- 7 Photographs (Interior Advertising): "Palm Drive Models Sonny Butts, Dave Gold, Jason Steele, Bruno, Keith Ardent, Mike Welder, Redneck Cowboy," p. 83, by Fritscher dba "Palm Drive Video," display ad, half-page "New S&M Fetish Videos," and "Cop Jock Videos," p. 90, classified ad copy by Fritscher for Palm Drive Video

DRUMMER 133, September 1989
Masthead: Jack Fritscher, Writer, Featured Contributors; Palm Drive Video, Photography, Frequent Contributors
Theme for *Drummer* 133 Created by Fritscher: Mapplethorpe and Censorship
1 Piece of Writing (Cover Lead Feature) by Fritscher
1 Photograph (Interior Editorial, Inside Back Cover) by Fritscher dba "Palm Drive Video"
2 Pieces of Writing (Advertising) by Fritscher dba "Palm Drive Video"
6 Editorial Mentions
- Editorial Mention (Front Cover Copy): "Jack Fritscher on Robert Mapplethorpe: Intelligent People Making Intelligent Sex"
- Editorial Mention: by Anthony DeBlase of Mapplethorpe and Fritscher, p. 4
- Editorial Mention: by Paul Martin of Fritscher and drug use in *Some Dance to Remember*, p. 6
- Editorial Mention: by Paul Martin of extreme S&M in Fritscher's fiction, "The Shadow Soldiers," p. 7
- "Pentimento for Robert Mapplethorpe: Fetishes, Faces, and Flowers of Evil," pp. 8-15, cover lead feature
- Editorial Mention: by Anthony DeBlase aka Fledermaus of "Master of Sleaze" Fritscher as video-photographer of Roger Earl and Terry LeGrand's six-video series, *Bound for Europe* (1989), p. 34

- Editorial Mention: by Kevin Wolff of Fritscher as cinematographer and collaborator with Roger Earl and Terry LeGrand on the six-video series, *Bound for Europe* (1989), p. 43
- 7 Photographs (Interior Advertising): "Palm Drive Models Sonny Butts, Dave Gold, Jason Steele, Bruno, Keith Ardent, Mike Welder, Redneck Cowboy," p. 90, by Fritscher dba "Palm Drive Video," display ad, half-page "New S&M Fetish Videos," and "Cop Jock Videos," p. 92, classified ad copy by Fritscher for Palm Drive Video
- 1 Photograph (Interior Editorial, Inside Back Cover): "Palm Drive Model Bobby Stumps," inside back cover, by Fritscher dba "Palm Drive Video"

DRUMMER 134, October 1989
Masthead: Jack Fritscher, Writer, Featured Contributors; Palm Drive Video, Photography, Frequent Contributors
Theme for *Drummer* 134 Created by Fritscher: Brown Leather
1 Piece of Writing by Fritscher
7 Photographs (Interior Editorial, Centerfold) by Fritscher dba "Palm Drive Video"
11 Photographs (Interior Advertising) by Fritscher dba "Palm Drive Video"
2 Pieces of Writing (Advertising) by Fritscher dba "Palm Drive Video"
- "Rear-View Mirror #5: Artist Chuck Arnett—His Life, Our Times," pp. 32-36, GLBT leather history column
- 7 Photographs (Interior Editorial, Centerfold) "Palm Drive Model Bobby Stumps," pp. 50-55 by Fritscher dba "Palm Drive Video"
- 11 Photographs (Interior Advertising) : "Palm Drive Models Redneck Cowboy Curtis James, Mike Welder, Pro-Wrestler Chris Colt, Big Hairy Bruno, Jack Husky, Cigar Sarge, Vigilante, Jason Steele, Dave Gold, Bobby Stumps, Keith Ardent," p. 72, by Fritscher dba "Palm Drive Video," full-page display ad for Christmas
- "New S&M Fetish Videos," and "Cop Jock Videos," p. 92, classified ad copy by Fritscher for Palm Drive Video

DRUMMER 135, December 1989 (First Post-Earthquake Issue)
Masthead: Jack Fritscher, Writer, Featured Contributors; Palm Drive Video, Photography, Frequent Contributors
1 Photograph (Interior Editorial) by Fritscher dba "Palm Drive Video"
3 Photographs (Interior Advertising) by Fritscher dba "Palm Drive Video"
2 Pieces of Writing (Advertising) by Fritscher dba "Palm Drive Video"
- 1 Photograph (Interior Editorial): "Uncut Bear," p. 24, by Fritscher dba "Palm Drive Video" of Ken Wimberly in the Palm Drive Video *Bear in the Woods* illustrating Larry Townsend's "Leather Notebook"
- 3 Photographs (Interior Advertising): "Palm Drive Video Model Rick Conder," p. 82, by Fritscher dba "Palm Drive Video," display ad, "Star Search," a video casting call for grass-roots actors who are not models for roles in Palm Drive "reality TV."
- "New S&M Fetish Videos," and "Cop Jock Videos," p. 94, classified ad copy by Fritscher for Palm Drive Video

DRUMMER 136, January 1990
Masthead: Jack Fritscher, Writer, Featured Contributors; Palm Drive Video, Photography, Frequent Contributors
2 Photographs (Interior Advertising) by Fritscher dba "Palm Drive Video"
1 Photograph (Interior Advertising) by Fritscher for Roger Earl and Terry LeGrand, Marathon Films
2 Pieces of Writing (Advertising) by Fritscher dba "Palm Drive Video"
- 2 Photographs (Interior Advertising): "Palm Drive Models Sonny Butts and Goliath," p. 86, by Fritscher dba "Palm Drive Video," display ad, half-page
- 1 Photograph (Interior Advertising) for *Argos Session*, p. 99, by Fritscher for Roger Earl and Terry LeGrand, Marathon Films: one photograph designed and shot by Fritscher

during videotaping of *The Argos Session* shot and composed in two Hi8 cameras by Mark Hemry and Fritscher for Marathon Films in Amsterdam, June 21, 1989
- "New S&M Fetish Videos," and "Cop Jock Videos," p. 102, classified ad copy by Fritscher for Palm Drive Video

DRUMMER 137, February 1990
Masthead: Jack Fritscher, Writer, Featured Contributors; Palm Drive Video, Photography, Frequent Contributors
1 Photograph (Interior Advertising) by Fritscher for Roger Earl and Terry LeGrand, Marathon Films
2 Photographs (Interior Advertising) by Fritscher dba "Palm Drive Video"
2 Pieces of Writing (Advertising) by Fritscher dba "Palm Drive Video"
2 Editorial Mentions
- Editorial Mention: "Letters to the Editor" regarding Fritscher's Palm Drive Video, p. 6
- Editorial Mention: (Inside Back Cover) with announcement for Fritscher's proposed satirical "topsy-turvy earthquake" special issue of *Drummer* titled "*Dummer* #1, A Desmodus Flip Publication"; see Fritscher concept incorporated into *Drummer* 138.
- 2 Photographs: "Palm Drive Models Sonny Butts and Goliath," p. 87, Palm Drive Video display ad, half-page
- 1 Photograph (Interior Advertising) for *Argos Session*, p. 99, by Fritscher for Roger Earl and Terry LeGrand, Marathon Films
- "New S&M Fetish Videos," and "Cop Jock Videos," p. 98, classified ad copy by Fritscher for Palm Drive Video

DRUMMER 138, March 1990 aka "*Dummer* [*sic*, Satire] 1: A Unique *Drummer* Semi-Publication"
Masthead: Jack Fritscher, Writer, Frequent Contributors; Palm Drive Video, Photography, Frequent Contributors
Theme for *Drummer* 138 Created by Fritscher: Satirical Upside-Down Earthquake Issue of *Drummer* titled "*Dummer*": A Unique Drummer Semi-Publication
1 Editorial Review
2 Photographs (Interior Advertising) by Fritscher dba "Palm Drive Video"
2 Pieces of Writing (Advertising) by Fritscher dba "Palm Drive Video"
- Editorial Review: "Drummedia" by Joseph W. Bean, pp. 36, 37, 38, of three Fritscher "Palm Drive Video" features: *Blond Saddle Tramp, Mud and Oil, The Hun Video Gallery #1: Rainy Night in Georgia*
- 2 Photographs: "Palm Drive Models Sonny Butts and Goliath," p. 58, by Fritscher dba "Palm Drive Video," display ad, half-page
- "New S&M Fetish Videos," and "Cop Jock Videos," p. 80, classified ad copy by Fritscher for Palm Drive Video

DRUMMER 139, May 1990
Masthead: Jack Fritscher, Writer, Frequent Contributors; Palm Drive Video, Photography, Frequent Contributors
Theme for *Drummer* 139 Created by Fritscher: Remembrance of Sleaze Past in the Titanic 70s
1 Piece of Writing (Cover Lead Feature) by Fritscher
2 Photographs (Interior Advertising) by Fritscher dba "Palm Drive Video"
1 Photograph (Interior Advertising) by Fritscher for Roger Earl and Terry LeGrand, Marathon Films
2 Pieces of Writing (Advertising) by Fritscher dba "Palm Drive Video"
3 Editorial Mentions
- Editorial Mention: in Deblase editorial, p. 4, referencing Fritscher as source for issue's theme
- "Remembrance of Sleaze Past...and Present and Future," cover feature article, pp. 7-11
- Editorial Mention: in "Sidebar" by Gayle Rubin, p. 34, concerning her research in

- Fritscher's feature article, "Catacombs," *Drummer* 23, 1978
- Editorial Mention: in Deblase introduction, p. 35, "Remembrance of Sleaze Past" referencing Fritscher as source for issue's theme and for photo shoot by Jim Wigler
- 1 Photograph (Interior Advertising) for *The Argos Session*, p. 77, by Fritscher for Roger Earl and Terry LeGrand, Marathon Films
- 2 Photographs (Interior Advertising): Palm Drive Models Terry Kelly with Jack Fritscher as well as Jack Husky with Chris Colt, p. 85, by Fritscher dba "Palm Drive Video," display ad, half-page, p. 85: one photograph by Hemry and Fritscher of "Terry Kelly with Fritscher" in Hemry-Fritscher video, *Hot Lunch*, and one photograph of "Chris Colt with Jack Husky" in Fritscher's video, *Sex Aggression: Jack Husky's First Night at Chris Colt's Wrestling Academy*
- "New S&M Fetish Videos," and "Cop Jock Videos," p. 89, classified ad copy by Fritscher for Palm Drive Video

DRUMMER 140, June 1990
Masthead: Jack Fritscher, Writer, Featured Contributors; Palm Drive Video, Photography, Frequent Contributors
1 Photograph (Front Cover Portrait) by Fritscher dba "Palm Drive Video"
4 Photographs (Interior Centerfold Editorial) by Fritscher dba "Palm Drive Video"
7 Photographs (Interior Advertising) by Fritscher dba "Palm Drive Video"
1 Photograph (Interior Advertising) by Fritscher for Roger Earl and Terry LeGrand, Marathon Films
2 Pieces of Writing (Advertising) by Fritscher dba "Palm Drive Video"
1 Editorial Mention
- 1 Photograph (Front Cover Portrait): "Palm Drive Video Star of *Daddy's Tools*" by Fritscher dba "Palm Drive Video"
- 2 Photographs (Interior Editorial): "Palm Drive Model Goliath," pp. 20 and 23, by Fritscher dba "Palm Drive Video"
- Editorial Mention: by Joseph W. Bean of Fritscher's memoir-novel, *Some Dance to Remember*, p. 28
- 4 Photographs (Centerfold): "Palm Drive Video: Randy, Carpenter Bear," pp. 55-58, by Fritscher dba "Palm Drive Video" of *Drummer* 140 cover model, Ken Horan
- 7 Photographs (Interior Advertising): "Palm Drive Video Models Sonny Butts, Dave Gold, Keith Ardent, Jason Steele, Big Bruno, Mike Welder, and Curtis James," p. 75, by Fritscher dba "Palm Drive Video," display ad, half-page
- 1 Photograph (Interior Advertising) for *Argos Session*, p. 83, by Fritscher for Roger Earl and Terry LeGrand, Marathon Films
- "New S&M Fetish Videos," and "Cop Jock Videos," p. 88, classified ad copy by Fritscher for Palm Drive Video

DRUMMER 141, August 1990
Masthead: Jack Fritscher, Writer, Featured Contributors; Palm Drive Video, Photography, Frequent Contributors
1 Photograph (Interior Editorial, including Centerfold) by Fritscher dba "Palm Drive Video"
6 Photographs (Interior Editorial) by Fritscher for Roger Earl and Terry LeGrand, Marathon Films
7 Photographs (Interior Advertising) by Fritscher dba "Palm Drive Video"
2 Pieces of Writing (Advertising) by Fritscher dba "Palm Drive Video"
3 Editorial Reviews
- Editorial Book Review by Paul Martin: review of *Some Dance to Remember*, pp. 32-33
- Editorial Video Review by Paul Martin: review of Fritscher's video, *Hot Lunch*, pp. 33-34;
- Editorial Video Review by DeBlase aka Fledermaus: review of *The Argos Session*, p. 34, a feature video shot and composed in two Hi8 cameras by Mark Hemry and Jack Fritscher

for Roger Earl and Terry LeGrand, Marathon Films in Amsterdam, June 21, 1989
- 6 Photographs (Interior Editorial): "*The Argos Session*: Photo Feature and Video Review," pp. 34, 35, 36, 37, 38, shot by Fritscher for Roger Earl and Terry LeGrand, Marathon Films, in the Argos Bar, Amsterdam, June 21, 1989
- 1 Photograph (Interior Editorial): "Palm Drive Model Goliath," p. 47, by Fritscher dba "Palm Drive Video"
- 7 Photographs (Interior Advertising): "Palm Drive Models Sonny Butts, Dave Gold, Keith Ardent, Jason Steele, Big Bruno, Mike Welder, and Curtis James," p. 68, by Fritscher dba "Palm Drive Video," display ad, half page
- "New S&M Fetish Videos," and "Cop Jock Videos," p. 89, classified ad copy by Fritscher for Palm Drive Video

MR. DRUMMER CONTEST FINALS AND SHOW PROGRAM MAGAZINE, September 1990
1 Photograph (Interior Advertising) by Fritscher dba "Palm Drive Video" and David Hurles (Old Reliable)
1 Photograph (Interior Advertising) by Fritscher dba "Palm Drive Video"
- 1 Photograph (Interior Advertising): "How I Write Erotica: Thinking 'XXX' Auto-Photograph of Jack Fritscher," p. 4, by Fritscher dba "Palm Drive Video" and David Hurles (Old Reliable)
- 1 Photograph (Interior Advertising): Insert photograph of Palm Drive Video model Brutus into "How I Write Erotica: Thinking 'XXX,'" Auto-Photograph of Jack Fritscher, p. 4

DRUMMER 143, October 1990
Masthead: Jack Fritscher, Writer, Featured Contributors; Palm Drive Video, Photography, Frequent Contributors
1 Piece of Writing (Cover Lead Feature) by Fritscher
1 Photograph (Interior Advertising) by Fritscher dba "Palm Drive Video" and David Hurles (Old Reliable)
1 Photograph (Interior Advertising) by Fritscher dba "Palm Drive Video"
2 Pieces of Writing (Advertising) by Fritscher dba "Palm Drive Video"
1 Advertising Notice by Malibu Sales of Fritscher books
- "Radical Nipples," pp. 18-22, cover lead feature article
- 1 Photograph (Interior Advertising): "How I Write Erotica: Thinking 'XXX' Auto-Photograph of Jack Fritscher," p. 15, by Fritscher dba "Palm Drive Video" and David Hurles (Old Reliable)
- 1 Photograph (Interior Advertising): Insert photograph of Palm Drive Video model Brutus into "How I Write Erotica: Thinking 'XXX' Auto-Photograph of Jack Fritscher," p. 15
- Advertising Notice by Malibu Sales, p. 87, of two Fritscher books, *Corporal in Charge of Taking Care of Captain O'Malley and Other Stories* and *Stand by Your Man and Other Stories*
- "New S&M Fetish Videos," and "Cop Jock Videos," p. 95, classified ad copy by Fritscher for Palm Drive Video

DRUMMER 144, November 1990
Masthead: Jack Fritscher, Writer, Frequent Contributors; Palm Drive Video, Photography, Frequent Contributors
1 Piece of Writing
3 Photographs (Interior Editorial) by Fritscher
1 Photograph (Interior Advertising) by Fritscher dba "Palm Drive Video"
2 Pieces of Writing (Advertising) by Fritscher dba "Palm Drive Video"
1 Editorial Mention

- 3 Photographs (Interior Editorial): "The Training Center: The Academy," pp. 29, 30, and p. 98, by Fritscher dba "Palm Drive Video"
- "I, Brutus: Muscle-Cop Road Warrior," poem, p. 73
- 1 Photograph (Interior Advertising): "Palm Drive Model Brutus," p. 73, by Fritscher dba "Palm Drive Video." display ad, half-page
- "New S&M Fetish Videos," and "Cop Jock Videos," p. 93-94, classified ad copy by Fritscher for Palm Drive Video
- Editorial Mention: "Fritscher Takes You inside the Academy," p. 98

DRUMMER 145, December 1990
Masthead: Jack Fritscher, Writer, Frequent Contributors; Palm Drive Video, Photography, Frequent Contributors
1 Piece of Writing (Cover Lead Feature) by Fritscher
5 Photographs (Interior Editorial) by Fritscher (not as "Palm Drive Video")
1 Photograph (Interior Advertising) by Fritscher dba "Palm Drive Video"
2 Pieces of Writing (Advertising) by Fritscher dba "Palm Drive Video"
1 Editorial Mention

- Editorial Mention (Front Cover Copy): "Incarceration for Pleasure! Jack Fritscher Takes on the Academy"
- "The Academy: Incarceration for Pleasure–Real Cops and Rough Fun in Missouri," pp. 24-29, cover lead feature article
- 5 Photographs (Interior Editorial) by Fritscher solo (not as "Palm Drive Video"), pp. 24-25, 27-29
- 1 Photograph (Interior Advertising): "I, Brutus: Muscle-Cop Road Warrior," p. 70, by Fritscher dba "Palm Drive Video," display ad, half-page
- "New S&M Fetish Videos," and "Cop Jock Videos," p. 95, classified ad copy by Fritscher for Palm Drive Video

DRUMMER 147, March 1991
Masthead: Jack Fritscher, Writer, Frequent Contributors; Palm Drive Video, Photography, Frequent Contributors
1 Photograph (Interior Advertising) by Fritscher dba "Palm Drive Video"
2 Pieces of Writing (Advertising) by Fritscher dba "Palm Drive Video"
1 Editorial Review

- Editorial Review: Review by Joseph W. Bean of video series *Bound for Europe*, six S&M video features shot by Jack Fritscher and Mark Hemry for Roger Earl and Terry LeGrand, Marathon Films, p. 65; display ad, p. 77
- 1 Photograph (Interior Editorial): "Palm Drive Model Brutus," p. 88, by Fritscher dba "Palm Drive Video," display ad, half-page
- "New S&M Fetish Videos," and "Cop Jock Videos," p. 95, classified ad copy by Fritscher for Palm Drive Video

DRUMMER 148, April 1991
Masthead: Jack Fritscher, Writer, Frequent Contributors; Palm Drive Video, Photography, Frequent Contributors
7 Photographs (Interior Editorial, Including Centerfold) by Fritscher dba "Palm Drive Video"
1 Photograph (Interior Advertising) by Fritscher dba "Palm Drive Video"
1 Photography Feature (by DeBlase) Produced by Fritscher
2 Pieces of Writing (Advertising) by Fritscher dba "Palm Drive Video"
1 Editorial Mention

- Editorial Mention: Contents Page, p. 3, "Slap Happy. What Is the Sound of One Hand Slapping? Palm Drive Video Has the Answer"
- "Steve Parker Photography by Anthony DeBlase," pp. 27-30, produced by Fritscher who cast his Palm Drive Video model Steve Parker with DeBlase at DeBlase's request

- 3 Photographs (Interior Editorial, Centerfold): "Slap Happy," pp. 50-51, by Fritscher dba "Palm Drive Video"
- 4 Photographs (Interior Editorial): "Wes Decker in *Sodbuster*," p. 60-62, by Fritscher dba "Palm Drive Video"
- 1 Photograph (Interior Advertising): "Brutus," p. 92, by Fritscher dba "Palm Drive Video," display ad, half-page
- "New S&M Fetish Videos," and "Cop Jock Videos," p. 96, classified ad copy by Fritscher for Palm Drive Video

DRUMMER 155, May 1992
Masthead: Jack Fritscher, Writer, Frequent Contributors; Palm Drive Video, Photography, Frequent Contributors
10 Photographs (Interior Editorial) by Fritscher dba "Palm Drive Video"
1 Photograph (Interior Advertising) by Fritscher dba "Palm Drive Video"
2 Pieces of Writing (Advertising) by Fritscher dba "Palm Drive Video"
1 Editorial Mention
- Editorial Mention: Contents Page Caption, p. 3, "Latino Attitude! Photography by Fritscher dba "Palm Drive Video"
- 10 Photographs (Interior Editorial): "Attitude Latino," pp. 18-22, cover photo essay by Fritscher dba "Jack Fritscher/Palm Drive Video"
- 1 Photograph (Interior Advertising): "Redneck Cowboy Curtis James," p. 73, by Fritscher dba "Palm Drive Video," display ad, half-page
- "New S&M Fetish Videos," and "Cop Jock Videos," p. 81, classified ad copy by Fritscher for Palm Drive Video

DRUMMER 157, August 1992
Masthead: Jack Fritscher, Writer, Frequent Contributors; Palm Drive Video, Photography, Frequent Contributors
1 Photograph (Front Cover Portrait Insert) by Fritscher dba "Palm Drive Video"
1 Photograph (Interior Editorial) by Fritscher dba "Palm Drive Video"
1 Photograph (Interior Advertising) by Fritscher dba "Palm Drive Video"
2 Pieces of Writing (Advertising) by Fritscher dba "Palm Drive Video"
- 1 Photograph (Front Cover Portrait Insert): "Moustached Bodybuilder," by Fritscher dba "Palm Drive Video"
- 1 Photograph (Interior Editorial): "Moustached Bodybuilder: Double Biceps Pose," p. 10, by Fritscher dba "Palm Drive Video"
- 1 Photograph (Interior Advertising): "Brutus," p. 77, by Fritscher dba "Palm Drive Video," display ad, half-page
- "New S&M Fetish Videos," and "Cop Jock Videos," p. 77, classified ad copy by Fritscher for Palm Drive Video

DRUMMER 159, December 1992
Masthead: Jack Fritscher, Writer, Frequent Contributors; Palm Drive Video, Photography, Frequent Contributors
1 Photograph (Front Cover Portrait Insert) by Fritscher dba "Palm Drive Video"
8 Photographs (Interior Editorial) by Fritscher dba "Palm Drive Video"
1 Photograph (Interior Advertising) by Fritscher dba "Palm Drive Video"
2 Pieces of Writing (Advertising) by Fritscher dba "Palm Drive Video"
1 Editorial Mention
- 1 Photograph (Front Cover Portrait Insert): "Larry Perry," cover photograph by Fritscher dba "Palm Drive Video"
- Editorial Mention: Contents Page Caption, p. 3, "Barman Larry Perry"
- 8 Photographs (Interior Editorial): "Palm Drive Model Larry Perry," pp. 14-18, photo feature by Fritscher dba "Palm Drive Video"

- 1 Photograph (Interior Advertising): "Brutus," p. 60, by Fritscher dba "Palm Drive Video," display ad, half-page
- "New S&M Fetish Videos," and "Cop Jock Videos," p. 78, classified ad copy by Fritscher for Palm Drive Video

DRUMMER 169, November 1993
Masthead: Jack Fritscher, Writer, Frequent Contributors; Palm Drive Video, Photographer, Frequent Contributors
1 Photograph (Interior Editorial) by Fritscher dba "Palm Drive Video"
1 Photograph (Interior Advertising) by Fritscher dba "Palm Drive Video"
1 Piece of Writing (Advertising) by Fritscher dba "Palm Drive Video"
- 1 Photograph (Interior Advertising): "Donnie Russo," p. 67, by Fritscher dba "Palm Drive Video," display ad, quarter page
- "Cop Jock Videos," p. 78, classified ad copy by Fritscher for Palm Drive Video
- 1 Photograph (Interior Editorial): "Donnie Russo," p. 82, by Fritscher dba "Palm Drive Video"

DRUMMER 170, December 1993
Masthead: Jack Fritscher, Writer, Frequent Contributors; Palm Drive Video, Photography, Frequent Contributors
Theme for *Drummer* 170 Created by Fritscher: Russomania—Shooting Porn
1 Photograph (Front Cover Portrait) by Fritscher dba "Palm Drive Video"
1 Piece of Writing (Cover Lead Feature Article) by Fritscher
13 Photographs (Interior Editorial, Centerfold) by Fritscher dba "Palm Drive Video"
1 Photograph (Interior Advertising) by Fritscher dba "Palm Drive Video"
1 Piece of Writing (Advertising) by Fritscher dba "Palm Drive Video"
- 1 Photograph (Front Cover Portrait): "Donnie Russo" by Fritscher dba "Palm Drive Video"
- "Russomania: Inside Porn Star Donnie Russo," pp. 39-46, cover lead feature article
- 13 Photographs (Interior Editorial, Centerfold): "Donnie Russo," pp. 39-46, centerfold by Fritscher dba "Palm Drive Video"
- 1 Photograph: "Donnie Russo," p. 66, by Fritscher dba "Palm Drive Video," display ad, quarter page
- "Cop Jock Videos," p. 74, classified ad copy by Fritscher for Palm Drive Video

DRUMMER 186, July 1995
Masthead: Jack Fritscher, Writer; Palm Drive Video, Photography
3 Pieces of Writing (Two: Cover Fiction) by Fritscher
1 Drawing by Skipper Produced by Fritscher
2 Editorial Mentions
- Editorial Mention: Contents Page, p. 5, cover fiction, "Uncut Lust, "My Foreskin Fetish"
- Editorial Mention: Contents Page, p. 5, "'Foreskin Prison Blues,' Story and Illustration by Jack Fritscher"
- "Uncut Lust: Foreskin Fetish," pp. 19-20, cover fiction
- "Foreskin Prison Blues," pp. 26-27, feature fiction (published foreshortened in an unauthorized edit)
- Drawing: "Foreskin Mask," p. 27, by Skipper, commissioned and produced by Fritscher for "Foreskin Prison Blues"; copyright 1995 and 2007 Jack Fritscher
- "Digital Mapplethorpe," p. 59

DRUMMER 188, September 1995
20th Anniversary Issue
Masthead: Jack Fritscher, Writer; Palm Drive Video, Photography
1 Piece of Writing (Historical Essay) Fritscher

1 Photograph (Interior Advertising) by Fritscher dba "Palm Drive Video"
5 Editorial Mentions
- Editorial Mention: Contents Page, p. 5, "Cover Story, '*Drummer*, The Magazine with Balls' by Jack Fritscher,"
- Editorial Mention: "Mapplethorpe cover, shot by Mapplethorpe, designed and cast by Jack Fritscher," p. 17
- Editorial Mention: Joseph W. Bean and Anthony DeBlase re Fritscher, pp. 18, 19
- Editorial Mention: Cover of *Drummer* 100, p. 21
- "20 Years of *Drummer* History: The Magazine with Balls," pp. 21-22, excerpt of a longer historical feature essay by founding San Francisco editor-in-chief Fritscher
- Editorial Mention: John Embry, p. 23, "What happened in 1977 could fill a book. We hired A. Jay's friend Jack Fritscher as editor-in-chief and bought a building on Harriet Street...."
- 1 Photograph: "Donnie Russo," p. 48, by Fritscher dba "Palm Drive Video," display ad, quarter page

DRUMMER **204, June 1997**
Masthead: Jack Fritscher, Writer; Palm Drive Video, Photography
1 Piece of Writing (Short Story) by Fritscher dba "www.JackFritscher.com"
19 Photographs (Interior Editorial) from a Video by Fritscher dba "Palm Drive Video"
1 Photograph (Interior Editorial) by Fritscher dba "www.JackFritscher.com"
- 19 Photographs (Interior Editorial): "Gym Jock from Palm Drive Video," pp. 22-25, pictorial essay of color video frames chosen and printed as underground new-tech art by *Drummer* art director from Fritscher's video, *Dave Gold's Gym Workout*
- "Hustler Bars: Tricks of the Trade," pp. 36-37, short story, by Fritscher dba "www.JackFritscher.com"
- 1 Photograph (Interior Editorial): "Mike Welder," p. 36, by Fritscher dba "www.JackFritscher.com"
  [Editor's Note: Palm Drive Video display ad and classified ad, despite trade agreement, not honored by editor Wickie Stamps, and so not inserted.]

FORESKIN QUARTERLY **12, August 1989**
Masthead: Publisher Anthony F. DeBlase; Managing Editor Joseph W. Bean
6 Photographs (Interior Editorial) by Fritscher dba "Palm Drive Video"
7 Photographs (Interior Advertising) by Fritscher dba "Palm Drive Video"
- 6 Photographs (Interior Editorial): "*Cheesiest Uncut Cowboy in West Texas,*" pp. 10-15, photo essay
- 7 Photographs (Interior Advertising): "Palm Drive Models Sonny Butts, Dave Gold, Keith Ardent, Jason Steele, Big Bruno, Mike Welder, and Curtis James," p. 63, by Fritscher dba "Palm Drive Video," display ad, half page

MACH **20 — A *DRUMMER SUPER PUBLICATION*, April 1990**
Masthead: Publisher Anthony F. DeBlase; Managing Editor Joseph W. Bean
1 Photograph (Front Cover Portrait) by Fritscher for Roger Earl and Terry LeGrand, Marathon Films
12 Photographs (Interior Editorial, Including Inside Front Cover) by Fritscher for Roger Earl and Terry LeGrand, Marathon Films
- 1 Photograph (Front Cover Portrait): "Argos," one photograph designed and shot on set by Fritscher during videotaping of *The Argos Session* shot and composed in two Hi8 cameras by Mark Hemry and Jack Fritscher for Roger Earl and Terry LeGrand, Marathon Films in the Argos Bar, Amsterdam, June 21, 1989
- 1 Photograph (Inside Front Cover), "*Argos,*" color photograph shot on set by Fritscher of *The Argos Session* for Roger Earl and Terry LeGrand, Marathon Films.
- 1 Photograph (Contents Page), "*Argos,*" shot by Fritscher on set of two actors during

taping of *The Argos Session* for Roger Earl and Terry LeGrand, Marathon Films.
- 10 Photographs (Interior Editorial): "*The Argos Session*, Photographic Essay," pp. 41-45, ten photographs shot by Fritscher on set during taping of *The Argos Session* for Roger Earl and Terry LeGrand, Marathon Films.

MACH 22 — A *DRUMMER* SUPER PUBLICATION, December 1990
Masthead: Publisher Anthony F. DeBlase; Managing Editor Joseph W. Bean
1 Piece of Writing by Fritscher
10 Photographs (Interior Editorial) by Fritscher dba "Palm Drive Video"
1 Photograph (Interior Advertising) by Fritscher dba "Palm Drive Video"
1 Editorial Mention
- Editorial Mention (Front Cover Copy): "A Palm Drive Boy in Bondage"
- 10 Photographs: "The Excellent Adventure of Peter Longdicker," pp. 53-59, ten color photographs shot July 5, 1989, in Germany by Fritscher dba "Palm Drive Video"
- "Muscle-Cop Road Warrior," p. 79, poem
- 1 Photograph: "Palm Drive Model Brutus," p. 79, by Fritscher dba "Palm Drive Video," display ad

MACH 25 — A *DRUMMER* SUPER PUBLICATION, April 1992
Masthead: Publisher Anthony F. DeBlase; Editor Joseph W. Bean
1 Piece of Writing by Fritscher
10 Photographs (Interior Editorial) by Fritscher dba "Palm Drive Video"
2 Photographs (Interior Advertising) by Fritscher dba "Palm Drive Video"
1 Editorial Mention
- Editorial Mention (Contents Page): p. 3, "Wes Decker in Photography by Palm Drive Video"
- 4 Photographs (Interior Editorial): "Wes Decker," pp. 56-57, by Fritscher dba "Palm Drive Video"
- 2 Photographs (Interior Advertising): "Mr. *Drummer* Contestant Larry Perry," p. 51, by Fritscher dba "Palm Drive Video," display ad, half-page

MACH 29 — A *DRUMMER* SUPER PUBLICATION, July 1993
Masthead: Publisher Anthony F. DeBlase; Editor Joseph W. Bean
1 Photograph (Front Cover Portrait) by Fritscher dba "Palm Drive Video"
1 Piece of Writing by Fritscher
11 Photographs (Interior Editorial) by Fritscher dba "Palm Drive Video"
2 Photographs (Interior Advertising) by Fritscher dba "Palm Drive Video"
   [Editor's Note: Surviving long past Embry, Fritscher's fiction continued to be published in *Mach* by managing editor Joseph W. Bean at *Drummer* rival, Brush Creek Media: *Titanic: The Novella*, *Mach* 35 (March 1997) and by managing editor Peter Millar: "Father and Son Tag Team," *Mach* 38 (January 1998)]
- 1 Photograph (Front Cover Portrait): "Terry Kelly," shot by Fritscher dba "Palm Drive Video"
- 11 Photographs (Interior Editorial): "Terry Kelly, The Biker Next Door, Photo Essay," pp. 5-9, by Fritscher dba "Palm Drive Video"
- 1 Photograph (Interior Advertising): "Palm Drive Model Curtis James," p. 51, by Fritscher dba "Palm Drive Video," display ad, half-page

DRUMMER: TOUGH CUSTOMERS 1, July 1990
Masthead: Publisher/Editor Anthony F. DeBlase; Managing Editor/Art Director Joseph W. Bean
1 Photograph (Front Cover Portrait) reprint of *Mach* 20 cover, p. 12, shot by Fritscher for Roger Earl and Terry LeGrand, Marathon Films
- Palm Drive Video Display Ad, "Casting Call: Document Yourself Forever!" p. 75, by

Fritscher dba "Palm Drive Video," half page

DUNGEONMASTER 47 — A *DRUMMER*-DESMODUS, INC, PUBLICATION, January 1994
Masthead: Publisher Martijn Bakker, Editor Anthony F. DeBlase
1 Piece of Writing by Fritscher
1 Photograph (Front Cover) by Fritscher dba "Palm Drive Video"
2 Photographs (Interior Editorial) by Fritscher dba "Palm Drive Video"
Editorial Review of four videos produced, directed, and photographed by Fritscher dba "Palm Drive Video"
- 1 Photograph (Front Cover Portrait): *Slap Happy* by Fritscher dba "Palm Drive Video"
- Editorial Mention: Contents Page, p. 3, Fritscher and Palm Drive Video
- "USMC Slapcaptain," pp. 9-10
- 2 Photographs (Interior Editorial): "Terry Kelly" and "Gut Punchers in Action," pp. 24-25, by Fritscher dba "Palm Drive Video"
- Editorial Video Review by Tony DeBlase of four videos produced, directed, and photographed by Fritscher dba "Palm Drive Video," pp. 24-25

DRUMMER: TOUGH CUSTOMERS 12, 1996
Masthead: Publisher/Editor Anthony F. DeBlase; Managing Editor/Art Director Joseph W. Bean
4 Photographs (Interior Editorial) by Fritscher dba "Palm Drive Video"
- 4 Photographs (Interior Editorial): "Mickey Squires: How to Be a Tough Customer," pp. 6-7, by Fritscher dba "Palm Drive Video"

DRUMMER

INTERNATIONAL DRUMMER 214 (CHEAP!) $6.95 SLAVES

SLAVES!
AND SERVITUDE

INSIDE:
- How to Find a Master
- Slaves Throughout History
- You Be The Judge: The Newest Entries In The Drummer Fiction Competition
- Slaves or Masters In The World's Most Complete Kinky Classifieds

DISTRIBUTION TO MINORS PROHIBITED

INDEX

120 Days of Sodom: 174
Aardvark Theater: 121
AAU: 326, 392
ABA (see American Booksellers Association)
ABC-TV Closeup: 326
Abduction, The: 131
Absolut Vodka: 63
Academy Award: 110, 116, 300, 304, 372, 436, 495
Academy Training Center: 77, 80, 199, 231, 292, 293, 457, 526
ACLU (see American Civil Liberties Union)
ACT UP: 122
Acton, Sir Harold: 206
Adam-12: 77
Adult Video News: 122, 195, 203
Adventures of Denny Sargent: 281, 511
Advocate, The: 9, 19, 25, 26, 31, 32, 35, 40, 51, 53, 54, 77, 81-83, 85, 86, 91, 92, 94, 95, 99, 112, 115, 116, 125, 130, 143, 167, 185, 186, 223, 239, 260, 262, 263, 265, 330, 355-358, 360, 365, 366, 371, 372, 379, 380, 382, 389-391, 404-409, 411, 416, 421, 433, 435-441, 444, 447-449, 452, 457, 477, 487, 494
Advocate Experience: 54, 357, 358, 379, 380, 382, 421, 437
AEF Breast Cancer Emergency Fund: 293
African-American: 32, 33, 113, 117, 118, 136, 283, 300, 340, 349, 402
After Dark (mag): 115, 462
Ageism: 232, 438
AIDS: xv, 11, 18, 29, 35, 48, 54, 59, 83, 112, 120-123, 127, 135, 137, 164, 169, 173, 196, 197, 203, 209, 212, 214, 217, 224, 236, 259, 278, 282, 285, 291, 292, 294, 295, 300, 304, 307, 309, 312, 322, 346, 350, 356, 361, 377, 413, 414, 416, 418, 419, 422, 425, 432, 434, 445, 449, 450, 458, 463, 479, 486, 487, 489, 490, 502, 503
AIDS Memorial Quilt: 450
Ainsworth, Tom: 272
Albee, Edward: 300
Albright, Frank: 453
Alexander, Mark: 309
Algonquin Club: 60, 413
All-American Boy: 380, 382
Allen, Sam: 53
Allen, Woody: 373
Alligator Shirts: 382, 384
Allison, Dorothy: 316
Alternate, The: 53, 54, 134, 161, 218, 229, 239, 245-247, 262, 276, 324, 355, 358, 391, 395, 430, 437, 440, 441, 443, 455, 456, 465, 472, 473, 489, 504
Alternate Book Series: 452
Alternate Hawke Publishing: 482
Alternate Marketing: 236
Alternate Publishing: 47, 65, 75, 98, 114, 133, 188, 195, 202, 204, 217, 237, 239, 245-247, 255, 266, 306, 307, 355, 379, 391, 398, 416, 428, 446, 465, 466, 469, 471, 484, 503
Alternate Reader: 18
Alton, Lou: 468
Alyson, Sasha: 159, 167, 411, 417, 418, 420, 422, 438, 449
Alyson Publishing: 85, 170, 380, 416, 420, 421, 438, 440
Amaya, Mario: 130, 297, 299, 305
Ambush bar: 275, 283, 350
American Booksellers Association: 167, 372, 417, 419, 420, 422, 423
American Christians: 136
American Civil Liberties Union: 38, 108, 127, 220
American Civil War: 458
American Concentration Camps: 135
American Empire: 321
American Gigolo: 397
American Indian: 180
American Jewish Leaders: 259
American Leather Festival: 46
American Man, The: 369
American Men: 107, 123, 208, 339, 464
American Mores: 103
American Photography: 244
American Popular Culture Association: 3, 10, 29, 138, 280, 376, 394
American Psychiatric Association: 17
American Review of Gay Popular Culture: xv, 3, 39, 135, 138, 139, 177, 280, 283, 472, 510
American Revolution: 58, 402
American South: 375
American Studies Association: 138
Americans For Truth, President of: 106
AMG Studio (see Athletic Model Guild)
Amoebiasis: 325, 512
Amsterdam: 29, 46, 47, 49, 74, 120, 142, 199, 223, 257, 285, 307, 358, 484, 523, 525, 529
Anderson, Marge: 220, 224, 262, 462
Andros, Phil (see Sam Steward)
Angel of Death: 137
Angelou, Maya: 74, 187
Anger, Kenneth: 121, 159, 162, 164, 190, 234, 370, 495
Anglo-Saxon: 127
Answer, Scott: 252
Anthology of Gay History: 170, 317
Anthony, Susan, B: 364
Antoinette, Marie: 42, 392
Antoniou, Laura: 449
Anvil (bar): 298, 367, 487
Apartheid: 167, 365, 366, 378-380
Aquinas, Thomas: 30
Arab Death: 324, 468, 511
Ardent, Keith: 44, 56, 71, 72, 197, 252, 348, 505, 517-522, 524, 525, 529
Argentina: 11, 20, 33
Argos Bar: 120, 200, 522-525, 529, 530
Argos Hotel: 200
Argosy (mag): 7, 31, 157, 235, 356, 468
Arizona: 16, 230, 394
Arm-Wrestling Championships: 71
Arnett, Chuck: ix, 6, 57, 111, 210, 214, 226, 280, 316, 328, 369, 377, 440, 522

533

Arnold, Karl: 89
Aroma Room Freshener: 47, 235, 237
Arseneaux, Bill: 116
Art Deco: 66
Art of Motorcycle Maintenance: 390
Arthur, Gavin: 297
Aryan: 131, 370
Asians: 32, 392
Ask Larry: 98
Associated Press: 200, 339
Astrologic: 75, 133, 323, 325, 326, 508-512, 516
Athletic Model Guild: 217, 233, 234, 237, 243-245, 326, 370
Atlanta: 80, 169, 415, 458
Attias, Ben: 38
Austen, Jane: 16, 246, 423
Australia: 265, 271, 272
Authentic Biker-for-Hire: 464
Authentic Men: 114, 320, 324, 370, 510
AVN (see Adult Video News)
Avocado Experience (see Advocate Experience)
AWOL: 313, 482
Aznavour, Charles: 304
B-List: 255
B-Movie: 362, 363
B.A.R. (see Bay Area Reporter)
Badger Flats: 369
Bag of Toys: Sex, Scandal, and the Death Mask Murder: 342
Bailey, Fenton: 11, 84, 269
Bailey, Toby: 112, 438
Baim, Tracy: 213
Bakker, Martijn: 2, 15, 18, 29, 46-49, 72-74, 98, 138-142, 144, 146-150, 153, 218, 257, 258, 275-277, 285, 294, 307, 353, 354, 358, 360, 424, 433, 481, 493, 499, 502, 531
Balcony (bar): 272
Baldwin, Guy: ix, 6, 122, 302, 317, 366, 470
Baldwin, James: 3, 315, 418
Bales, Mikal: ix, 6, 68, 115, 140, 155, 199, 225, 252, 343, 456
Bangkok: 334
Bannon, Race: ix, 294
Barbato, Randy: 11, 84, 269
Barnes, Ike: 58, 62, 66, 253, 308, 476, 479
Barney, Jeanne Chelsey: i, ix, xiv, 6, 7, 12, 18-21, 23, 24, 26, 28, 31, 34, 37, 38, 47, 49, 50, 52-54, 61, 65, 68, 89, 98-102, 106, 117, 125, 127, 128, 134, 137, 140-142, 145, 148, 166, 182, 194-196, 200-202, 222, 230, 233, 243, 246, 251, 257, 261-266, 281, 285, 308, 335, 346, 354-356, 390, 396, 398, 399, 404, 411, 413, 416, 422, 427, 428, 430, 434-436, 438, 440, 442-446, 453-455, 460, 462, 469-471, 475, 485, 496, 497, 500, 501
Barnhill, Gary: 125
Barnum, P. T.: 475
Baron, Kurt: 334
Barracks (bath): 111, 212, 226, 259, 344-347, 361, 458, 496
Barrie, Dennis: 84
Barrus, Timothy Patrick: ix, 6, 45, 142, 171, 179-181, 253, 266, 269, 317, 411, 415, 417, 422-427, 429, 430, 501

Bartlett, James: 55
Barton, Crawford: 438, 476
Bates, Alan: 110
Batt, Patrick: 215, 238
Battered Lex Barker, The: 326, 512
Baus, Dan: 25
Bawer, Bruce: 372
Baxter, Dr. Earl: 156
Bay Area Reporter: i, 144, 209, 213, 214, 293, 294, 359, 360, 458, 459, 499
Bay Area Society of Technical Communicators: 329
BDSM: 2, 6, 77-80, 105, 120, 129, 136, 138, 140, 141, 147, 151, 188, 198-200, 209, 231, 240, 252, 254, 270, 337, 371, 395, 422, 426
BEA (see Book Expo America)
Bean, Joseph W.: ix, 6, 17, 29, 72, 73, 76, 80, 112, 113, 139, 140, 142, 193, 214, 220, 230, 253, 266, 270, 275, 283, 286-289, 292, 316, 317, 353, 357, 395, 436, 438, 456, 490, 491, 501, 502, 523, 524, 526, 529-531
Bear(s): ii, 44, 231, 232, 267, 270, 426, 469, 505, 509, 518, 522, 524
Bear (mag): 46, 214, 251, 270, 271, 417, 464, 469
Bear Omnimedia LLC: 271
Beat Punks: 314
Beatles: 73, 90
Beaton, Cecil: 79
Beattie, Ann: 418
Beautiful Room Is Empty, The: 173, 179
Begelman, David: 217, 219-222
Beltane: 301
Bemis Street: 156
Benedict, George: 349
Bennett, Alan: 487
Bergman, David: 168
Berkeley, Bud: 468
Berkeley CA: 60, 200, 341, 379, 391
Berlin: 28, 52, 120, 122, 123, 199, 270, 350
Berlin, Peter: ii, 198
Berlin Wall: 122, 225, 336
Bermuda: 176
Bernhard, Irvin Townsend (see Larry Townsend)
Bernstein, Carl: 35
Beseman, Scott: 72
Bestiality: 17, 28, 108, 162, 398, 474
Bianchi, Tom: 353, 359
Bible: ii, 5, 30, 348, 490
Biezeveld, Nicolaas: 344
Biezevelt, Dick: 344
Bijou Video: 285
Birds, The: 259
Birdsong, Bob: 370
Birimisa, George: 6, 141, 190, 256, 343
Biron, Lionel: 328, 389, 405, 406
Bitter End West: 16
Black, Dustin Lance: 436
Black Leather: 44, 234, 252, 458
Black Magic: 162, 163, 238
Black Mass: 240
Black Pipe (bar): 81, 89-91, 95, 99, 101, 102, 106, 124, 403
Black Pipe H. E. L. P.: 99, 101
Black Room: 475
Black Rubber: 44, 71, 154, 197, 517

Blackbird: 268
Blacklist: xiii, 7, 23, 25, 36, 40, 49, 65, 94, 160, 193, 201, 204, 205, 243, 245, 246, 249, 251, 258, 259, 261, 266, 282, 287, 306, 312, 316, 317, 379, 420, 424, 426, 428, 430, 433-435, 437, 438, 444, 445, 447, 450, 452-454, 458, 459, 467, 470, 475, 476, 480, 485, 497
Blake, Blue: 123
Blake Twins Raw: 123
Blanche, Anthony: 79
Blank Road: 66
Blass, Kevin: 168
Blogging: 262, 277
Blood Crucifixion: 66
Blood Feud: 15, 46
Blood Runs Like a River through My Dreams: 180
Bloody Penis: 479
Bloody Sunday: 300
Bloomsbury: 59, 461
Blue, Solly: 242, 268
Blue Light: 282
Blue Meanies: 102
Blueboy: 183, 347, 370, 371, 462, 463, 471, 473-477, 495
Body Alchemy: 115
Bodybuilding: 45, 268, 321, 464, 486, 496, 508, 519
Bokris, Victor: 314
Bolt (bar): 47
Bolton, Rick: 141
Bond Street (see Mapplethorpe)
Bondage (themed article): 231, 308, 324, 335, 404, 488, 514
Bonn: 89
Book Expo America: 167, 172, 182
Born to Raise Hell: 33, 57, 105, 118, 119, 154, 198, 270, 292, 356, 396, 401, 435, 442, 463
Boston: 69, 111, 147, 170, 230, 416, 419
Boudreaux, Gable: 237
Boujaklian, Jack: 270
Boulder CO: 395
Bound for Europe: 105, 119-121, 521, 522, 526
Bowers, Scotty: 233
Bowles, Sally: 31
Bowling Green State University Press: 186
Boy (mag): 110
Boy Scouts: 131
Boyd, Malcolm: 85, 163, 317
Boyes, Malcolm: 85
Boys in the Band, The: 15, 41, 49, 60, 130, 185, 219, 342, 368
Brackett, Bob: 226
Bradburn, Mike: 238
Bradford, William: 136
Bram, Christopher: 311, 315
Branding: 56, 109
Brando, Marlon: 33, 234
Brandon, Kyle: 360, 361
Bratman, Gary: 231
Brazil: 363, 397
Brian, J.: 205, 350
Brick (artist): 452
Brideshead Revisited: 79, 417
Bridgeport CT: 85
Bridgeton MO: 80

Brig (bar): 156, 349
Brig, The (play): 453
Briggs, Don: 400
Briggs, John: 83, 389-391
Briggs Initiative: 82
Bright, Susie: 7, 8, 353, 359
British: 40, 57, 64, 85, 107, 110, 120, 123, 159, 160, 164, 208, 218, 237, 306, 307, 314, 339, 362, 367, 402, 403
Britt, Don: 400
Broadway: 19, 118, 130, 193, 226, 256, 304, 340, 399, 436
Broberg, Lenny: 72
Brokeback Mountain: 339
Bromilow, Peter: 40, 403
Bronski, Michael: 69, 418, 419
Brooklyn Heights: 478
Brooks, Mel: 128, 131
Brothel Hotel: 335, 514
Brough, Tim: 359
Brown, Ellen F.: 169, 414
Brown, Jeffrey: 239
Brown, Mayor Willie: 17
Brown Shirts: 131
Brown University: 11, 172
Brush Creek Media: 46, 251, 270, 271, 457, 530
Brut, Art: 120
Brutus: 72, 478, 525-528, 530
Bryant, Anita: 11, 77, 81, 82, 85, 127, 300, 338, 347, 348, 387, 389-391
Buck, Joe: 70
Buckley, Jeff: 94
Buckskin Mountain Men: 44
Buckskin Musclemen: 268
Buddy Riders (mag): 69
Buena Vista Park: 66
Buena Vista West Avenue: 66
Buffalo Bill: 121
Buffalo Enterprises: 465
Bukowski, Charles: 168
Bulger, Richard: 225, 417, 469
Bullenhochzeit: 319
Bullwhips: 114
Burbank: 403
Burch, Guy: 307
Burden, Chris: 367
Burke, Bill: 452
Burning Pen, The: 179
Burns, Chris: 389, 409, 410
Burroughs, William: 370
Bush, Prescott: 25
Bush, President George: 25
Bush, President George W.: 25
Butch Enough: 129, 325, 374, 380, 381, 511
Butch Media Ltd: 271
Butler, Rhett: 170, 414
Butterfield Theater Chain: 401
Byfield, Greg: 277
Cabaret (film): 123, 128, 186, 304
Caen, Herb: 474
Café, BlaBla: 444
Café Flore: 144, 145, 276, 290, 330
Cahuenga Boulevard: 119

Calamusbooks: 190
Calendo, John: 356, 362
Califia, Patrick: ix, 6, 7, 25, 33, 54, 146, 148, 160, 179, 188, 225, 239, 316, 371, 375, 437, 439, 440, 485, 487, 488
California Action Guide: 72, 243, 348, 350, 461, 485, 488
California Committee for Sexual Freedom: 93
California Consensual Sex Act: 437
California Consenting Adults Law: 17
California State University: 38
California Street: 22, 26, 500
California Voice: 247
Callard, Roger: 370
Callas, Maria: 429
Camelot: v, 40, 403
Cameron, Loren: 115
Cameron, Peter: 173
Camp Pendleton: 326
Camp Street: 350
Campbell, Joseph: 79
Campus Theater: 401
Canada: 69, 107, 112, 334, 476
Cancer: 20, 22, 28, 49, 52, 67, 124, 135-137, 144, 157, 165, 191, 200, 227, 246, 257, 258, 261, 293, 304, 312, 313, 324, 329, 346, 348, 397, 463, 481, 482, 497, 500
Candle Power: 324, 511
Canter's Deli: 182
Canyon One Road: 155, 465
Capezio: 398
Capote, Truman: 49, 50, 132, 358, 418
Caracole: 330
Carmel CA: 332
Carney, Bill: 126, 160
Carney, William: 160
Carpenter, Edward: 297
Carrey, Jim: 489
Carter, President Jimmy: 300, 437
Casablanca: 175, 213
Cassidy, Jim: 370
Castro, Fidel: 206
Castro, Rick: 6, 453
Castro, The: 6, 56, 58, 122, 138, 164, 171, 173, 177, 186, 206, 209, 213, 214, 231, 272, 278, 280, 283, 320, 321, 324, 333-336, 344-346, 348, 349, 361-363, 368, 378, 381-387, 413, 414, 419, 420, 450, 453, 458, 465, 466, 510
Castro Alternate Publishing: 466
Castro Blues (article): 280
Castro Camera: 56, 386
Castro Street (see Castro, The)
Castro Street Blues (article): 177, 324, 382, 383, 510
Castro Street Fair: 280, 378, 510
Castro Theater: 138, 231, 334, 383, 458
Caswell, Craig: 336
Catacombs: 194, 210, 266, 271, 272, 279, 280, 323, 345, 371, 377, 393, 475, 487, 504, 510, 524
Catacombs Wedding: 251
Cathedral City CA: 236
Catholic Church: 189, 209
Catholic Seminary: 333, 433
Catholicism: 160, 165, 186, 189

Caucasian: 334
Caudillo, Richard: 219-222
Cavani, Liliana: 129, 366, 367
Cavelo: 343, 345, 515
Celebration of Leather Sexuality: 168
Celtic: xiv, 288, 301
Censorship: x, 10, 23, 77, 84-87, 105, 107-109, 114, 121, 122, 128, 132, 135, 152, 155, 159-162, 174, 175, 199, 204, 218, 224, 225, 230, 238, 261, 324, 328, 337, 338, 406, 434, 452, 476, 493, 505, 511, 521
Censorship: A World Encyclopedia: 84, 107
Centurion: 164
Century Plaza Hotel: 222
Chaikivsky, Andrew: 180, 424
Champ, Adam: 195
Chaplin, Charlie: 128
Charles, Andrew: ix, xi, 24, 25, 29, 40, 41, 122, 179, 183, 218, 224, 252, 253, 255, 287, 304, 306, 307, 309, 427, 446, 485, 489, 493, 498, 499, 516
Charles Street: 71, 327
Charlton Street: 57, 251
Chartres Street: 377
Chase, Hy: 402
Chaucer: 30, 211, 322
Chawton: 16
Checkmate (mag): 146, 485, 490
Checkpoint Charlie: 123
Chelsea: 69
Chelsea Girls: 348
Chelsea Hotel: 109, 184, 314
Chesley, Robert: 416
Chester, Mark I.: ix, 6, 33, 41, 225, 253, 347, 370, 409, 487, 501
Chicago: 11, 13, 18, 24, 51, 68, 121, 164, 199, 213-215, 234, 238, 241, 252, 283-285, 287, 289, 299, 300, 373, 376, 392, 394, 405, 431, 445, 446, 477, 486, 487, 489, 490
Chicago Loop: 300
Chicago Machine: 213
Chicago Police: 25, 297, 299, 300
Chicago Public Library: 280
Chicago Seven: 58, 301
Child of the Sun: 118
China Basin: 403
Chinatown: 77, 107
Chorus Line, A: 243, 281, 304
Christ (see Jesus Christ)
Christ the Lord: Out of Egypt: 189
Christensen, Sam: 109
Christian, M.: 179
Christianity: 136, 159, 163, 164, 189, 389, 471
Christmas: 20, 23, 66, 129, 195, 196, 224, 231, 272, 319, 325, 328, 338, 343, 346, 375, 393, 508, 522
Christopher Street: 10, 101, 171, 172, 179, 183, 377, 488
Christopher Street West: 101
Church of Satan: 164
Cigar Blues: 18, 317, 426, 463, 466, 509
Cincinnati: 77, 84, 333
Cinematography: 120, 300
City of Angels: 78
Civic Center Plaza: 337
Civil Disobedience: 33

Civil Rights: 136, 298, 299, 337, 376, 406
Civil War Between Women: 379
Claeys, Pieter: 74
Clayton, Rob: 308, 402
Clendinen, Dudley: 82
Clinton, Kate: 372
Clinton, President Bill: 74
Clone: 194, 303, 380, 382, 384
Clute, Ron: 331
CMC (see Cycle Motorcycle Club)
CMC Carnival: 275, 308, 317, 326, 402, 508, 512
Cock Casting: 66, 507
Cockette: ii, 55, 340
Cohn, Roy: 208, 209, 325
Colacello, Bob: 9, 53, 167
Cold War: 123
Cole, Rob: 53
Colorado: 301, 395
Colorado Springs CO: 58
Colt Men: 195, 319
Colt Model: 71, 142, 224, 309, 311, 318, 319, 325, 333, 336, 370, 486
Colt Studio: 66, 69, 70, 195, 238, 268, 298, 309, 319, 320, 333, 336, 370, 433, 476, 477, 487, 488, 522, 524
Columbia Pictures: 219, 221
Columbia University: 375
Communist: 94, 123
Conder, Rick: 197, 293, 522
Confidential Drummer Dossier: 23, 342, 343, 515
Confidential Journal of Old Reliable Hustler Videos: 409
Connecticut: 171, 415
Connection (bar): 123
Connection (mag): 20, 37, 100, 102, 397
Conrad, Robert: 340
Constanza, Midge: 437
Contemporary Arts Center: 84
Continental Baths: 193
Cooper, Anderson: 49, 50
Cooper, Phil: 32, 95
Coppola, Francis Ford: 208
Copyright Law: vii, viii, x, 17, 18, 21, 37, 42, 73-76, 80, 93, 94, 100, 105, 108, 133, 143, 165, 170, 187, 202, 217, 227-230, 236, 251, 281, 285, 292, 295, 305-307, 329, 330, 345, 354, 392, 415, 456, 478, 502, 507, 514, 516, 528
Copyright War: 217, 227
Cordova, Jeanne: 437
Corinne, Tee: 353, 359
Corleone, Don: 208
Corona Heights: 321, 346
Countrywide Publications: 440
Covered Wagon: 195
Cow Palace: 161, 340
Cowboys: 234, 240, 311, 339, 340, 504, 512
Cox, Harold: 302, 485, 490
Crimes Against Nature: 474, 508
Crisp, Quentin: 367
Crispo Case, The: 342
Cross, Frank: 58
Crowley, Aleister: 162
Crowley, Mart: 185, 219
Crucifixion: 66, 163-165, 240, 260

Cruising (film): 185, 207, 342, 368
Cuba: 206, 465
Cultural Revolution: 297
Culture War: vii, xiii, 11, 15, 28, 77, 81, 82, 84, 113, 127, 161, 173, 300, 316, 338, 348, 389
Curran Theater: 337
Curson, N.: 323
Curzon, Daniel: 217, 246, 249
Cushing, Bill: 327
CYA - Up Your Ass (club): 367
Cycle Motorcycle Club: 69, 283, 308
Cycle Sluts: 68, 114, 115, 191, 464, 476
Daddy Mystique: 44, 114, 197, 217, 231, 232, 267, 426, 469, 486, 516, 517, 520
Daddy Zeus (see Mikal Bales)
Dade County: 82, 85
Dagion, John: 228
Dakota, Bill: 221
Dallesandro, Joe: 24
Damron, Bob: 194, 215
Damron Guide: 194, 195
Daniel, Luke: 238
Dansky, Steven: 129, 130
Dante, Nicholas: 304
Data Boy: 224
Dateline Colorado: 58, 301
Dateline News Magazine: 442
Davis, Chief Edward M.: 17, 34, 77-79, 81, 82, 101, 103, 105-108, 110, 114, 116, 117, 119, 124, 128, 130, 132, 308, 389, 392, 396, 401, 434, 435, 460, 475, 496, 497
Davolt, Robert: ix, 6, 16, 46, 47, 74, 75, 135, 139, 142, 144-147, 149-153, 155, 156, 193, 204, 229, 251, 257, 258, 261-264, 266, 275-281, 284-286, 288-291, 293-295, 302-305, 353, 358-360, 394, 464, 469, 482-485, 493, 502
Dawn Media: 441
Dawson, Brian: 225
Day, Greg: 349
De Logt, Martin Van: 340
De Sade, Marquis: 109, 135, 163, 174, 260
De Suede, Marquis: 367
Dean, James: 234
Dean, Roy: 68, 117, 402
DeBlase, Dr. Anthony F.: ix, 2, 6, 9, 12, 15, 18, 23-25, 29, 40, 41, 43-50, 54, 56, 65, 67-69, 72, 76, 80, 84, 108, 111, 114, 119-122, 127, 131, 133, 134, 140, 143, 145, 150, 151, 155, 160, 179, 199-201, 212, 214, 217, 218, 224, 228, 231, 236, 245, 252-255, 257, 265, 266, 275-277, 282-285, 287, 288, 292, 297, 303, 305-307, 309, 312, 317, 320, 341, 353, 403, 404, 415, 421, 425-427, 431, 433, 437, 442, 446, 456, 460, 461, 472, 479-481, 485, 487-493, 497-502, 516, 520, 521, 523, 524, 526, 529-531
DeCelle, Edward Brooks: 349
Decker, Wes: 197, 293, 527, 530
Deddino, Gino: 323, 517
Deer Hunter, The: 331, 513
Dehner, Durk: 9, 112, 116, 440, 507
Del Norte, Jose: 33
Delta Run: 302, 490
Democratic National Convention: 297, 299, 435
Democratic Party: 103, 213, 297, 299, 435

Denbigh Street: 367
DeNiro, Robert: 208
Denmark: 110
Dennenny, Michael: 169, 170, 174, 183, 418
Denver CO: 156
Descartes: 30
Desmodus Earthquake Relief Fund: 490
Desmodus Publishing: 40, 133, 226, 252, 255, 277, 288, 306, 307, 479, 489, 492, 498, 501, 507, 516, 523
Desmodus Style Guide: 127
Detroit MI: 359
Devil: 132, 165, 449, 468
Diamond Heights: 349, 384
Dick, Dr.: 156, 191, 325, 331, 509, 512
Diethelm, Hank: 156, 212, 349
Different Drum, A: 269, 270
Different Light, A: 39, 40
Dillard, Gavin: 246
Dinakos, Ed: 71, 325, 463, 511, 512, 515
Dirty Pictures: 84
Dirty Poole: 171, 327, 513
Dirty Sally's (bar): 195
Divisadero Street: 67, 137, 154, 157, 196, 203, 219, 263, 272, 282, 305, 307, 325, 342, 398, 500
Dix, Otto: 350
Domino (see Don Merrick)
Domino Video Gallery, The: 228, 319
Doors, The: 31
Dore Alley Street Fair: 214
Double-F: A Magazine of Effeminism: 129
Douglas, Barry: 122
Downer, Ted: 74
Drag Show: 301
Dreesen, Christian: 123
Druidism: 159
Drum: 31, 42, 43, 51-53, 57, 64, 75, 82, 101, 117, 118, 140, 220, 229, 269, 270, 307, 314, 402, 443, 457, 462, 492
Drum Media: 141
Drumbeats: 75, 486, 512
Drummer Action Guide: 194
Drummer Anniversary Issue(s): 74, 112, 139, 141, 149, 189, 308, 335, 336, 442, 445, 485, 500
Drummer Archives: 151, 285-287, 295, 305, 345
Drummer Bibliography: 281
Drummer Blacklist: xiii, 7, 433, 480
Drummer Christmas Gift Guide: 346
Drummer Contests International: 483
Drummer Curse: xiii, 251, 257
Drummer Daddies: 114, 232
Drummer Desk Calendar: 311, 312
Drummer Editor: 17, 29, 50, 55, 62, 76, 113, 122, 171, 178, 193, 214, 230, 262, 269, 270, 275, 283, 303, 415, 423, 436, 442, 449, 491
Drummer Editor Emeritus: 50
Drummer Editorial: 4, 55, 146, 171, 224, 280, 281, 374, 403, 444, 454
Drummer Editorial Director: 7, 138, 144, 146
Drummer Eyewitness Timeline: 312
Drummer Fiction: 69, 281, 328, 452, 467
Drummer Forum: 47, 48
Drummer Gift Guide: 325, 511, 515
Drummer Key Club: 194, 195, 247, 252, 516

Drummer Newsletter: 27
Drummer Outreach: 56, 76
Drummer Photographer: 57, 59, 200, 223, 242, 275, 286, 288, 325, 337, 389, 400, 448, 479, 495
Drummer Publications: 75, 341, 355, 452
Drummer Publisher: 17, 24, 40, 50, 61, 76, 122, 156, 199, 200, 231, 236, 329, 342, 360, 433, 479
Drummer Questionnaire: 133
Drummer Restoration Dinner Party: 41
Drummer Rides Again: 195, 313, 340, 343, 345, 403, 478, 491, 507, 515
Drummer Salon: iii, xiii, 6, 25, 41, 55, 59, 60, 98, 113-115, 145, 152, 156, 159, 164, 168, 173, 189, 226, 242, 253, 265, 268, 282, 284, 317, 327, 331, 335, 349, 397, 413, 430, 446, 448, 452, 476, 478, 498, 514
Drummer Slave Auction: 15, 17, 21, 31, 34, 38, 52, 77, 78, 81, 90, 99, 102, 106, 117, 183, 219, 239, 275, 313, 391, 404, 484, 500
Drummer Super Publication: 120, 486, 529, 530
Drummer Tests Community Standards: 105
Drummer Timeline: 27, 38, 311, 495, 499
Drummerboy: 483
Drummerboy Contest: 483
Drummerman: 112, 399, 402
Drummermania: 73
Drummond, Jake: 404
Drumsticks: 53, 75, 381, 510, 513
Duberman, Martin: 259
DuBois, Blanche: 47, 79, 161, 408, 414, 459
Dubovsky, Anthony: 29
Duffy, Chris: 258, 462-465
Dufort, Dan: 317, 318, 322, 323, 509, 517
DungeonMaster (mag): 255, 403, 485, 487, 489, 490, 492, 507, 531
Dungeons: 66, 120, 391
Dungeons of San Francisco: 58, 66
Dunphy, Trent: 41, 225, 243, 253
Duplechan, Larry: 268
Dureau, George: 33, 62, 176, 198, 466
DuskPeterson: 188, 447
Dusseldorf: 120
Dutch: xiii, 4, 18, 46, 73, 74, 98, 113, 123, 135, 142, 143, 153, 194, 255, 257, 258, 261, 270, 275-277, 279, 285, 289, 291, 292, 353, 360, 424, 499, 502
Dutch Connection: 353
Dutch International Drummer: 46, 73, 113, 123, 142, 143, 258, 261, 291
Dworkin, Andrea: 114
Dyer, Kate: 417
Dyllon, Rue: 356, 358
Dyrk (artist): 141
Eagle (bar): 111, 215, 234, 294, 367
Eagle Magazine: 208
Eagles (band): 112, 201, 202
Earl, Roger: 6, 105, 118-121, 156, 195, 197, 225, 270, 292, 401, 435, 521-526, 529, 530
East Berlin: 28, 52, 123
East Coast: 35, 125, 143, 162, 166-169, 171-173, 179-181, 185, 320, 329, 334, 368, 380, 416, 417, 421, 447, 451-453, 467
Easy Rider (film): 234
Easy Rider (mag): 161
Eau de Parfum Spray: 477

Ebert, Roger: 348
Ecstasy: 79, 328, 373
Eddy, Nelson: 370
Edmonds, Don: 367
Edmund Pettus Bridge: 299, 300
Edwardian: 252
Effeminist Manifesto: 129, 130
Effeminists: 105, 129, 130
Egypt: 189, 226
Eighner, Lars: 188, 265, 330, 447
Eisenhower, David: 382
El Paso Wrecking Corp: 70, 508
Elephant Walk (bar): 334, 348, 385, 514
Elesser, Kenneth: 99
Eliot, T. S.: 10, 184
Embarcadero YMCA: 474
Embinder, Don: 183, 347, 370, 371, 474-476, 495
Embry, John Henry: i, ix, 2, 3, 5, 12, 15-22, 25, 26, 28, 32, 33, 37, 38, 40, 42, 46, 48-53, 56, 61, 63, 65-67, 75, 77-79, 89, 90, 95, 96, 99, 105-107, 109, 122, 133-135, 139, 146, 150, 153-155, 160, 171, 181-183, 187, 195, 200, 203-205, 218, 222, 224, 229, 233, 235-238, 241, 246, 247, 254-257, 261, 263, 264, 275, 277, 281, 285, 297, 298, 312, 313, 329, 335, 340, 342, 345, 346, 353, 354, 371, 379, 389, 390, 394, 395, 404, 411-414, 421, 424, 430, 434, 449, 452-455, 457, 459, 462, 465, 467-469, 474, 478, 480-483, 485, 491, 493-496, 499-503, 508, 514-516, 529
Embry Blacklists: 428
Emerson, Ralph Waldo: 117, 318, 373
Emersonian: 71
Empire City (club): 367
Enger, Jim: 237, 311, 317-323, 326-329, 331-333, 336, 345, 349-351, 486, 495
England: 25, 94, 136, 164, 199, 206, 306, 307, 489
English: 198, 205, 341, 397, 398
Enquirer: 77, 85, 86, 441, 474
Enquirer Slave Auction: 85
Eons Gallery: 59, 64, 367
Epilogue (Embry memoir): 38, 133, 136, 154, 400, 412, 413, 493
Epstein, Joseph: 369
Epstein, Rob: 269
Equus: 187, 512
Erhard, Werner: 357, 358, 421, 437
Erickson, McCann: 63
ESPN: 464
Esquire (mag): 7, 31, 49, 50, 177, 180, 411, 424
Essem Enterprises: 69
EST (Erhard Seminars Training): 357, 437
Etat Libre d'Orange: 477
Etienne (see Dom Orejudos)
Europe: 4, 105, 119-122, 224, 270, 292, 301, 373, 521, 522, 526
European: 22, 64, 119, 120, 142, 223, 253, 483
Eustace Chisholm and the Works: 166, 167
Evans, Arthur: 105, 128, 129, 365, 368, 374, 375, 378, 380-382, 447
Evansville IN: 68, 288
Evergreen Review: 7, 31, 127
Everitt, Miles: 62
Evita: 340, 341, 389, 399
Exchange, The: 237

Facebook: 51, 54, 135, 146, 147, 157
Faderman, Lillian: 21
Falco, Joe: 309
Falcon Video: 119, 131, 153, 154
Falwell, Jerry: 127, 389
Fame for 15: 116
Fantasia Fair Provincetown: 68
Fascists: 122, 129, 390
Faulkner, William: 30, 54
FBI (see U.S. Federal Bureau of Investigation)
Feinstein, Dianne: 132, 325, 345
Felix, Maria: 398
Feminism: viii, 11, 74, 130, 146, 164, 232, 259, 264, 301, 302, 366, 376, 377
Feminist: 7, 114, 131, 141, 146, 148, 159, 186, 187, 259, 279, 301, 304, 368, 372, 375, 418, 421, 423, 448, 457-459
Feminist Separatist: 297
Ferdinand, Archduke: 373
Ferlinghetti, Lawrence: 239
Ferro, Robert: 453
Fey-Way Gallery: iii, 59, 60, 110, 116, 117, 214, 328, 331, 332, 337, 452, 495, 497
Fiction Quarterly: 207, 373
Fictitious Business Name: 338
Fierstein, Harvey: 177, 259
Fifty Shades of Gray: 188, 408
Film Associates: 370
Fin de Siecle: xiv, 73, 141, 153, 285, 365
Finger (mag): 116
Finland, Tom of (see Tom of Finland)
Firbank, Ronald: 487
First Amendment: 30, 83, 122
FirstHand Events: 395
Fish, Doris: 272
Fiske, Peter: 302, 344, 349, 487
Fist Fuckers of America: 111
Fisting: 66, 71, 105, 111, 121, 173, 209, 210, 308, 335, 367, 402, 408, 498
Five in the Training Room: 107
Flaming Creatures (film): 121
Flashbacks (film): 205, 350
Fledermaus (see Anthony DeBlase)
Fleischer, Matthew: 180
Florida: 5, 31, 82, 85, 347, 481
Florida Orange Juice: 127, 300
Flowers of Evil: 45, 84, 121, 349, 521
Flynt, Larry: 40, 84, 252, 253
Flyte, Lord Sebastian: 167, 417
Folkers, Dan: 344
Folsom Attitude: 194
Folsom Fire (Barracks): 346, 347
Folsom Street: 3, 39, 48, 57, 110, 111, 129, 156, 174, 193-195, 210-212, 214, 226, 252, 259, 278, 280, 283, 294, 311, 323, 324, 328, 344, 350, 368, 378, 382-385, 387, 391, 393, 400, 402, 412-414, 420, 440, 456, 458, 500, 503
Folsom Street Blues: 280
Folsom Street Fair: 2, 3, 23, 38, 39, 41, 46, 144, 215, 421
Fonda, Peter: 234
Fontaine, Richard: 456
Fonteyn, Margot: 175

Forbes (mag): 13
Forbidden Planet: 132
Foreign Legion: 468
Foreplay: 290
Foreskin: 211, 468, 528
Foreskin Prison Blues: 143, 144, 528
Foreskin Quarterly: 237, 255, 468, 489, 492, 504, 507, 529
Forestville CA: 459, 465
Forster, E. M.: 174, 206
Foucault, Michel: 174, 259, 368, 391
Foucault Who (film): 113
Fouts, Denham: 49
Fox (news): 87
FQ (see Foreskin Quarterly)
Frameline San Francisco: 117
Framing Keywords of Queer Popular Culture: 113, 127
France, David: 342
Francis, Jack: 360
Frank O'Rourke: 80, 155, 206, 328, 453, 465
Frankenstein, Dr.: 370
Franklin, Ed: 160, 220, 230, 438, 476
Freedom of Speech: 106
Freezer, W. Jay: 47
French: 102, 127, 198, 398, 423
French, Jim: 69, 238, 298, 319, 320, 391, 433, 476-478
French Quarter Restaurant: 195, 413, 414
Freud, Dr. Sigmund: 132, 232, 400
Frey, James: 180
Friedkin, William: 185, 207, 342, 368
Friedman, Jeffrey: 269
Frontier Bulletin Gazette: 397
Fry, Mikael: 272
Fundamentalist: 11, 17, 78, 81, 94, 101, 127, 161, 191, 225, 259, 300, 302, 375, 378, 389, 391, 405, 421, 449, 489
Funny Girl: 372
Furstenfelder Hof: 132
Future Farmers of America: 111
Gage Brothers: 70, 109, 197, 292, 322, 508
Gallagher, Joe: 304
Garber, Eric (see Andrew Holleran)
Garden of Gethsemane: 346
Gardner, Gerald: 159, 160
Garland, Judy: 51, 163, 220, 373, 491
Gata, Gina: 195
Gauntlet: 35, 115, 122, 179, 416, 458
Gay Activists Alliance: 376, 380, 405
Gay Alley: 418
Gay Cancer: 346
Gay Cannibalism: 89, 96
Gay Civil War: 159, 297, 302, 374, 437, 453, 458
Gay Community: x, 16, 21, 38, 69, 81, 90, 93, 96, 102, 147, 164, 178, 185, 217, 224, 369, 378, 381, 391, 404, 413, 473
Gay Community Services Center: 93
Gay Counterculture: 129, 376
Gay Deteriorata: 177, 382, 463, 509
Gay Erotic Literature: 179, 450
Gay Games (Olympics): 73, 231, 268, 318, 323, 407
Gay Ghetto: 167, 329
Gay History Business: 259, 369

Gay Jock Sports: 318, 508
Gay Justice: 337
Gay Liberation Front: 38, 130, 131
Gay Mafia: 168
Gay Mail-Order: 217, 237, 241, 242, 412
Gay Marriage: 55, 57, 86, 132, 322, 334, 335, 495
Gay Masculine Identity: 303, 389, 417
Gay Metropolis: 427
Gay Nazi Party: 105, 127, 128, 130, 260
Gay Popular Culture: ii, iii, vii, x, xiv, xv, 2, 3, 5, 9, 19, 39, 46, 63, 83, 135, 138, 139, 177-179, 183, 190, 198, 217, 234, 240, 242, 269, 280, 283, 317, 319, 323, 342, 371, 381, 394, 460, 472-474, 504, 510, 512
Gay Presses of New York: 167, 169
Gay Pride Parade: 82, 300, 337, 385, 405
Gay Publishers: 167, 411
Gay Rights Movement: 82
Gay Rights National Lobby: 437
Gay Rodeo: 339
Gay Roots: 132, 170, 317
Gay Saints: 159, 162
Gay San Francisco: v, 9, 12, 21, 113, 127, 229, 301, 308, 342, 495
Gay Separatist: 367
Gay Sports: 66, 231, 242, 408, 504, 508
Gay Sunshine Press: 41, 69, 168, 170, 190, 232, 249, 317, 405, 406, 415, 452, 458
Gay Times (newspaper): 435
Gay Vice Cop: 124
Gay Victims: 117
Gay Writers: 172, 179, 284, 311, 418, 511, 512, 514
Geary Boulevard: 325
Gender Identity: 15, 50, 114, 115, 160, 231, 232, 267, 365, 374-376, 378, 497, 498
Gender of Homomasculinity: 193
Gender Separatists: 366
Gender War: 130, 297, 302, 365, 372, 374, 405, 407, 417, 437, 458, 487
Genet, Jean: 126, 317
Gengle, Dan: 54
Gengle, Dean: 358
Genocide: 425, 429
Genovese Family: 207
Gentle Warriors: 425
Geppetto: 201
Gere, Richard: 397
German: 59, 89, 90, 122, 123, 131, 245, 319, 468
German Bundest: 94
German Consul General: 89, 90
Germany: 119, 123, 128, 156, 223, 382, 530
Geronimo: 180
Gerrior, Paul: 66, 336
Gershman, Elizabeth: 159, 167, 170, 171, 225, 411, 415-417, 419, 420, 422
Gershman, Jim: 422
Gestapo: 299
Getting Off: xv, 19, 20, 208, 257, 381, 443, 454, 472, 500
Giant (film): 234
Ginsberg, Allen: 259, 297, 298
Giovanni's Room: 268
Glass, Philip: 184
Glass Onion: 16

Glassman, Mike: 71, 325, 463
GLBT Center Rainbow Room: 353, 360
GLBT Historical Society of San Francisco: ii, 2, 11, 66, 209, 353, 359, 360
Gloeden, Wilhelm von: 206, 207
Gloster, Tom: 323, 324, 327
Gluck, Robert: 175
GMSMA (Gay Mens SM Assoc): 122, 310, 487, 488
Gmunder: 477
Godfather, The: 203, 492
Godfather II: 208
Godfather III: 208
Gold, Dave: 44, 142, 224, 517-522, 524, 525, 529
Gold Coast (bar): 210, 213, 214, 299, 329
Golden Age of Drummer: 153, 196, 257, 258, 413, 424, 461, 478
Golden Age of Leather: 1, 27-29, 297, 301, 503
Golden Age of Promiscuity: 184
Golden Drumsticks Award: 381
Golden Gate Bridge: 29, 71, 324, 402, 465, 491
Golden Gate Distributors: 338
Golden Gate Park: 171
Golden Gloves: 177, 325, 333, 513
Golden Shower Festival: 109
Goldstein, Richard: 129, 185, 259, 260, 365, 366, 380, 389, 405
Goliath: 403, 522-525
Golub, Leon: 260
Gomez, Jewelle: 418
Gone With the Wind: 169, 358, 414, 415, 420, 457, 458
Gonzo: 80, 121, 138, 194, 200, 231, 242, 278, 279, 300, 378
Gooch, Brad: 184
Goodstein, David B.: 25, 35, 53, 54, 82, 83, 91, 116, 157, 239, 260, 355, 357, 358, 379, 380, 382, 404-408, 411, 421, 433, 435-442, 447, 477, 494
Google: 262, 272, 291, 368, 457
Gordon, Albert L.: 20, 21, 358
Gordon, Rachel: 450
Goth: 110
Götterdämmerung: 144, 410
Grand National Rodeo: 340
Grand National Rodeo Blues: 326, 340, 512
Granger, Thomas: 136
Great Danes: 363
Great Depression: 165
Great Dictator, The (film): 128
Great Dying (from AIDS): 145, 226, 258, 279
Great Slave Auction: 18, 20, 37, 79, 81, 82, 85, 100, 102, 390, 435, 443, 463, 484, 496
Great Slave Video Adventure, The: 155
Greece: 91, 223, 468
Greenwich Village: 8, 101, 185, 327, 342, 377, 452
Grey, Joel: 186
Griffith Park: 323
Grossman, Nancy: 367
Grove Press: 170
Grunge: 44
Guardian, The: 175, 285
Guerneville CA: 465
Guggenheim, January: 326
Guild Association of H. E. L. P. Inc: 93

Guild Press: 242, 244
Gunn, Thom: 126, 164, 212, 263, 298, 350, 393, 487, 488
Gut Punchers: 45, 318, 322, 323, 531
Guyana: 324, 497
Gypsy (musical): 337
H. E. L. P.: 16, 32, 81, 90-97, 99, 101, 220, 235, 358, 406, 444
H. E. L. P., President of: 32, 90-92
H. E. L. P. Board of Directors: 91
H. E. L. P. Center: 93
H. E. L. P. Drummer: 27, 53, 89, 91-96, 183, 229, 235, 236, 444
H. E. L. P. Drummer Newsletter: 27
H. E. L. P. Incorporated: 32, 92, 93
H. E. L. P. Member: 96
H. E. L. P. Newsletter: 89-91, 235, 252, 355, 444
Haag: 340, 344
Haber, Artie: 487
Hadden, Briton: 276
Hai Karate: 398
Haight-Ashbury: 210, 413
Haight Street: 272, 385, 485, 486
Halloween: 127, 314, 322, 340, 403, 476
Halsted, Fred: ix, 6, 34, 36, 57, 105, 109-111, 116, 126, 197, 198, 219, 230, 243, 266, 292, 308, 370, 396, 401, 404, 408, 409, 413, 435, 439, 453, 476
Hamburg: 120
Hamburger Mary: 350
Hamilton, Dr. Richard: ix, 156, 331, 509, 512
Handball Express: 272
Handkerchief Color Code: 125
Handley, John: 242
Happenings: 393
Hardman, Paul D.: 247
Hardy, Andy: 51
Harper's (mag): 369, 441
Harriet Street: 3, 122, 196, 203, 204, 206, 264, 282, 305, 500, 529
Harrington, Eve: 353
Harrington Gay Men's Literary Quarterly: 301
Harris, Ron: 53, 96
Harry Bush: 244
Harry Chess: 42, 43, 201-203, 398, 481
Harvard University: 168, 459
Hastings House: 421
Hatfield, Frank: 80, 155, 206, 327, 328, 433, 453, 465, 466, 494
Hauck, Donald: 441
Hawaii: 16, 230, 235, 394, 443
Hawke, Terrance: 482
Hawks (bike club): 308, 403
Hay, Harry: 417
Hayden, Tom: 300
Hearst, Patty: 77-79, 106
Hefner, Hugh: 252, 441
Hells Angels: 177
Helms, Senator Jesse: 87, 121, 207, 225, 390
Helsinki: 63, 64
Heltsley, Paul Martin (see Paul Martin)
Hemry, Mark: vii, x, xiv, xv, 9, 10, 41, 49, 119-121, 123, 131, 142, 144, 154, 161, 182, 198, 231, 253, 254, 266, 270, 276, 288, 290, 291, 311, 334, 339, 340, 345,

350, 351, 356, 357, 360, 361, 413, 417, 418, 421, 422, 457, 466, 471, 486, 487, 492, 495, 496, 507, 523, 524, 526, 529
Henry, Patrick: 35
Hepburn, Katharine: 372, 494
Hercules (film): 276
Herlihy, James Leo: 70
Hernandez, Marcus: i, ix, 6, 46, 144, 147, 148, 212, 214, 225, 275, 293, 294, 353, 358-360, 499
Herschberg, Charles: 487
Hertz, Dr. Richard: 89, 90
Hewitt, Chris: 142
Hibernia Bank: 164, 385
Higgins, Henry: 449, 452
High Priest of Calumny: 92
High Times (mag): 370
Hinde, Tom: ix, 22, 328, 507
Hippie: 163, 169, 300, 344, 463
Hispanic: 20, 86
Hitchcock, Alfred: 259
Hitler: 128, 129, 132, 344, 490
Hitler Youth: 156
HIV: 4, 11, 41, 49, 55, 56, 71, 184, 188, 191, 193, 196, 224, 275, 291, 327, 330, 365, 376, 377, 458, 493, 498
Hodo, David: 113
Hoffman, Abbie: 300, 301
Hoffman, Beardog: 46, 70, 270, 457
Hogarth Press: 161
Hole, Gloria: 68
Holiday, Douglas: 37
Holland: 119, 340, 342, 344, 424, 514
Holleran, Andrew: 172, 174, 268, 449, 453
Holliday, Douglas: 404
Hollywood: 27, 29, 33, 37, 47, 51, 78, 85, 89, 98, 100, 101, 107, 115, 118, 119, 155, 163, 169, 174, 175, 220-222, 233-235, 252, 254, 270, 300, 323, 341, 355, 358, 378, 383, 397, 403, 413, 415, 422, 439, 442, 459
Hollywood-Burbank: 323
Hollywood Boulevard: 117, 233, 323
Hollywood Hills: 90, 320, 414, 436, 444
Hollywood Hills Democratic Club: 90, 444
Hollywood Star: 221
Hollywood Strip: 266
Holocaust: 282, 286, 294
Holy Mountain, The: 66
Homomasculine Archetype: 336
Homomasculine Men: 110, 213, 302, 372, 487, 493
Homomasculinity: ii, viii, 7, 105, 111-114, 127, 160, 170, 193-195, 205, 231, 237, 238, 254, 267, 297, 302, 304, 318, 323, 326, 365, 366, 370, 371, 373, 374, 395, 405, 408, 422, 437, 438, 458, 469, 477, 487, 496, 504, 511
Homophile: 16, 81, 90, 444
Homophile Effort for Legal Protection (see H.E.L.P.)
Homosex: 85, 198
Homosexual: 21, 58, 59, 78, 82, 106, 111, 132, 136, 182, 186, 208, 237, 259, 301, 309, 326, 365, 369, 371, 391, 423
Homosexual Matrix: 371
Homosexual Revolution: 391
Homosexuality: viii, 6, 17, 105, 106, 111, 130, 132, 159, 179, 186, 259, 302, 316, 318, 365, 366, 369-371, 376, 380, 385, 407, 425, 471
Honcho (mag): 98, 205, 265, 350, 441, 471, 476, 477
Hoover, J. Edgar: 94
Hopper, Dennis: 234
Horner, Lance: 118
Horseman: 340, 512
Horsemaster: 325, 466, 512
Horses: 108, 325
Hotel California (recording): 112, 201, 202, 469
House of Dominance, The: 119
House Un-American Activities Committee: 208, 209
Houston: 241, 457
Howard, Jerry: 93, 95
Howard, Tom: 152
Howard Street: 357
HRC (see Human Rights Commission)
HUAC (see House Un-American Activities Committee)
Hudson, Dr. Fred: 327
Hudson, Rock: 350
Hudson River: 181
Hughes, Fred: 166
Hughes, Glenn: 113
Human Rights Commission: 437
Hun (artist): ix, 6, 140, 225, 228, 328, 395, 466
Hun Video Gallery: 228, 523
Hungry Project: 381
Hunt, Larry: 323, 328
Hunter, Richard: 5, 231
Hurles, David: ii, ix, 6, 70, 140, 141, 154, 217, 242-245, 266, 268, 281, 355, 362, 395, 409, 410, 441, 476, 486, 502, 509, 510, 512, 515, 516, 525
Hustler (mag): 84, 252, 253
Hustler Bars: 142, 243, 529
Hyslop, Bob: 23, 71, 333, 335, 342, 402, 514
Ianniello, Marry: 207
Iconic Dinner Party Hosting Tom of Finland: 55
Icons: 9, 60, 177, 234, 238, 294, 414
ICU (see Intensive Care Unit)
Illinois: 29, 284, 377
Illinois Institute of Technology: 164
Ilsa: She Wolf of the SS: 129, 367
IMD (see International Mr. Drummer)
IML (see International Mr. Leather)
In Hot Blood: Ex-Cons: 324, 325, 510, 512
In Passing (column): 20, 75, 84, 124, 248, 313, 343, 512, 515, 517
In Praise of Older Men: 114, 232, 469
In Touch (mag): 149, 232, 315, 356, 362, 471
Inches (mag): 69, 205, 244, 265, 266, 268, 326, 467
Indecent Exposure: 220
Index on Censorship for Free Expression: 107
Indiana: 68, 288
Inferno (BDSM gathering): 302
Inge, William: 278
Inner Tube, The (mag): 69
Inquisition: 129, 240
Intensive Care Unit: 48, 182, 212, 255, 256, 347
International Drummer: 46, 270, 354, 499
International Leatherman (mag): 270, 464
International Mr. Drummer: 5, 33, 67, 360, 481, 483
International Mr. Leather: i, 13, 23, 72, 113, 197, 213-215, 238, 302, 306, 342, 389, 392, 394-396, 438, 445, 477, 486, 489, 514

International Workers Day: 301
Interview (mag): 9, 53, 164, 166
Ionesco, Eugene: 61
Ireland: 113, 331, 377
Irish-American: 409, 474
Irish-Catholic: 189, 259
Iron Man (mag): 321
Ironman Gym: 328
IRS (see U.S. Internal Revenue Service)
Isherwood, Christopher: 199, 315, 386
Islam: 159, 164
Italian: 205-207, 209, 211, 350, 396, 397, 442, 467
Ivory, James: 173
Jack Tar Hotel: 437
Jackson, Glenda: 403
James, Curtis: 44, 522, 524, 525, 527, 529, 530
James, E. L.: 188
Janssen, Volker: 244
Janus, Society of (SF): 7, 58, 59, 66, 156, 308, 327, 371, 375, 504, 513
Janus Society of Philadelphia: 51
Japan: 66, 399
Japan Center Theater: 399
Japanese: 33, 92
Javert, Inspector: 17
Jaws: 36, 408
A. Jay (see Allen Shapiro)
A. Jay Video Gallery: 228
Jebe, Walt: 318
Jersey Shore: 208
Jesuit: 30
Jesus Christ: 163, 164, 186, 189, 471
Jesus Christ Superstar: 159, 163
JFK (see John F. Kennedy)
Jhabvala, Ruth Prawer: 173
Jocks: 385, 407, 408, 510, 511
Jockstrap: 43
Jockstrap Gym: 73, 208, 403
John Hay Library: 11, 172
Johnson, Bob: 203, 205, 244, 265, 266, 357, 467
Johnson, Ron: 212, 283, 393
Jones, Cleve: 449, 450
Jones, Coleman: 71
Jones, Douglas: 369
Jones, James: 174
Jones, Jim: 324, 497
Jonestown Massacre: 325, 497
Joralemon Street: 478
Journal of Popular Culture, The: 31
Joy of Atheism, The: 246
Joy of Gay Sex, The: 174
Joyce, James: 161, 378
Judaism: 159, 164, 209, 259, 260
Judas: 163, 444
Jumbo Jet: 199, 200
Jung, Karl: 30, 232, 366
Just Men (mag): 244, 266, 467
Justice Weekly (mag): 69
Kahlo, Frieda: 63
Kaiser Engineers: 29, 58, 59, 254, 279, 329, 332, 333, 348, 434
Kalamazoo MI: 401
Kampsville IL: 377

Kane, Reverend James H. (Jim): 6, 55, 58-60, 62, 65, 66, 156, 241, 251, 253, 265, 298, 299, 301, 308, 329, 403, 445, 476, 478, 487, 495
Kansas City Trucking Company: 109
Kantrowitz, Arnie: 316, 405, 487
Karate Kock Warrior: 410
Karr, John F.: i, 131, 316, 317, 453, 457-459, 499
Katsam (studio): 422
Kay, Vee: 424, 425
Keats, John: 449
Keehnen, Owen: 213, 449
Keller's (bar): 198, 367
Kennedy, Jacqueline (see Jacqueline Bouvier Kennedy Onassis)
Kennedy, President John F.: 11, 298, 326
Kennedy, Robert: 130, 297-299
Kennedy, Senator Teddy: 168, 420, 422
Kennedy Family: 86, 411, 420
Kent State University: 301
Key West Writers Conference: 169, 181, 411, 418
Keyhole Studio: 242
Keystone Cops: 100, 124
Kight, Morris: 38, 91, 437
Kilt: 231, 325, 512
Kincaid, Jeff: 131
Kincaid, Tim: 109
King (cartoon): 109
King, Dagmar: 17
King, Martin Luther Jr.: 297, 298
Kinser, Jeremy: 207
Kinsey, Alfred: i, 11, 125, 215, 371
Kinsey Scale: 301, 366
Kirkup, James: 164
Kirkwood, James: 304
Kiwanis Club: 194
Knast (bar): 120, 123
Knight, Heather: 450
Knights Press: 121, 159, 167, 168, 171, 269, 415-419, 421-423, 425
Knoebel, John: 130
Koffka, Kurt: 317
Koontz, Rod: 326
Kopay, Dave: 405-408
Kramer, Larry: 3, 110, 159, 173, 174, 177, 181, 259, 309, 411, 418
Kriegmont, Dick: 41, 228, 253, 335
Kris Studio Chicago: 213, 217, 234, 238, 370, 392, 394, 477
Kurosawa, Akira: 1, 92
Kushner, Tony: 173, 174, 209, 259, 418
KY Flats: 478
La Brea Avenue: 119
La Cienega Blvd.: 91
La Côte Basque: 50
La Crescenta CA: 428, 470
LA Cycle Sluts: 68
LA Tool and Die: 322
Laaksonen, Touko (see Tom of Finland)
LaBarbera, Peter: 106
Labonté, Richard: 39, 40
Lackey, Ken: ix, 127
Lackey, Peter: 353
Lambda Book Report: 143

Lambda Literary Award: 143, 170, 317, 378, 380, 416
Lambda Rising: 416
Lamble, David: 247, 248
LaMotta, Jake: 208
Langley-Porter Hospital: 349
Lansky, Meyer: 206, 465
LAPD (see Los Angeles Police Dept.)
Las Vegas: 167, 271, 417, 422
Lasley, Jerry: 462
Last Rites: 197
Last Taboo: 327, 513
Last Word, The: 10, 98, 396, 473
Latinos: 32, 396, 398, 399
Laurent, Aristede: 53, 54, 133, 416, 440, 516
Laurila, Norman: 39
Lavender Standard: 101
LaVey, Anton: 164
Law, Bernard Cardinal: 230
Lawrence, D. H.: 110, 175
Lawrence, Michael: 89
Lawson-DeCelle Gallery: 349
Lawson YMCA: 392
Le Salon: 202, 203, 456
Leather-Heritage: 46, 302, 360, 367, 395, 452, 488
Leather Archives & Museum: i, ix, 9, 11, 13, 16, 18, 20, 31, 35, 65, 67, 70, 81, 101, 105, 110, 117-119, 124, 126, 155, 163, 183, 193, 200, 203, 213, 214, 221, 230, 241, 257, 263, 265, 267; 275, 279, 282, 283, 289, 292, 297, 305, 306, 318, 326, 337, 345, 356, 395, 396, 398, 431, 434-436, 445, 456, 474, 477, 482, 487, 490, 493, 513
Leather Bazaar: 46
Leather Blues (novel): v, 30, 68, 69, 107, 190, 249, 281, 324, 367, 415, 447, 452, 467, 511, 516
Leather Bulletin Board: 359
Leather Calendar: 68
Leather Christmas: 231, 375, 508
Leather Community: 11, 35, 82, 112, 140, 151-153, 197, 226, 230, 279, 304, 306, 375, 404, 406, 425, 435, 483, 490
Leather Contests: 197, 279, 294, 389, 393, 413, 501
Leather Culture: i, ii, 7, 13, 15, 17, 18, 26, 27, 30, 35, 80, 125, 128, 142, 145, 146, 151, 167, 193, 214, 259, 269, 280, 284, 291, 311, 344, 359, 366, 368, 371, 373, 377, 380, 389, 390, 406, 431, 435, 436, 438, 456, 495
Leather Decade: 346, 496
Leather Discipline Duo: 293
Leather Disco: 399
Leather Dolce Vita (essay): 451
Leather Elder: 359
Leather Emporium: 229
Leather Family: 177, 209
Leather Fraternity and Newsletter: 16, 20, 47, 53, 57, 68, 81, 96, 99, 100, 111, 118, 138, 157, 161, 222, 223, 229, 233, 239-241, 245, 375, 391, 392, 428, 444, 470, 471, 486
Leather Fringe of Gay Culture: 251
Leather Heritage: 10, 152, 237, 240, 251, 298, 306, 487
Leather Heritage GLBT Society: 102
Leather Historian: 74, 310, 360
Leather Immigrant: 389
Leather Journal (column): 112, 438

Leather Journal (newspaper): 208
Leather Lifestyles: 231
Leather Mafia: 454
Leather Man (mag): 268-270
Leather Nazi: 131
Leather Notebook: 98, 522
Leather Pride Flag: 214, 489
Leather Sabbat: 110, 308, 403
Leather Saddle Cowboy Bondage: 197, 293
Leather Timeline: 275, 279, 282, 283, 297, 298, 395, 431
Leather Times (mag): 193, 230, 436
Leather Verite: 232
Leather Wedding: 132
Leather Week: 360
Leatherati: 145, 152
Leatherfolk: 4, 6, 7, 10, 17, 18, 39, 46, 57, 79, 125-127, 187, 190, 197, 226, 259, 261, 280, 283, 303, 316, 361, 365, 367, 368, 390, 422, 440, 489
Leathergender: 303
LeatherLit: 179, 415, 425
Leatherman: The Legend of Chuck Renslow: 213, 215, 238
Leatherneck (bar): 22, 195, 331, 400, 508
Leathers, Dane (see Rick Leathers)
Leathers, Mike (see Rick Leathers)
Leathers, Rick: 6, 114, 193, 200, 204, 205, 372, 400, 433, 465, 466, 493
Leatherwoman: 303
Leaves of Grass: 232
Leavitt, David: 418
Ledermeister (see Paul Gerrior)
Lee, Gypsy Rose: 391
LeGrand, Terry: 34, 105, 118-120, 195, 197, 219, 225, 270, 401, 435, 521-526, 529, 530
Leighton, Robert: 435
Leno, Assemblyman Mark: 86
LeRoy, JT: 180
Les Liaisons Dangereuse: 321
Les Pirates Associes: 367
Lesbian Feminists: 94
Lesbian Film Festival: 117
Lesbian Literary Heritage: 415, 451, 455
Lesbian Review: 459
Lesbian Separatist: 130
Lesbian Task Force: 372
Lettieri, Cliff: 93
Lewis, David: 487
Lewis, Jackie: 395
Lewis, Jerry: 398
Leyland, Winston: 168, 170, 190, 232, 249, 317, 411, 415, 452
Leyland Publications: 232
Liberation Publications: 379, 421, 438
Libertarian: 34
Libertarian Party: 404
Life (mag): 214, 280, 369
Likens, David: 324
Limited Editions Club: 165
Lincoln Park: 300
Lind, Dennis: 442
Linotti, Ed: 71, 333, 334
Lion Pub (bar): 108, 109, 372

Locke, Richard: 217, 232, 511
Lockner, Clint: 319, 321, 333, 486
Loma Prieta Earthquake: 29, 122, 225, 275, 291, 489, 499
Loman, Willy: 412
London: 120, 164, 199, 307, 357, 367, 464, 489
Lone Star (bar): 393
Long, Thomas Lawrence: 301
Lord Jim: 241
Lords of Leather, The: 85, 516
Los Angeles Advocate: 53, 239, 380
Los Angeles Algonquin Club: 60, 413
Los Angeles City Council: 103
Los Angeles County Board of Supervisors: 103
Los Angeles Free Press: 84, 124
Los Angeles Herald-Examiner: 221, 474
Los Angeles Magazine: 92, 101, 106, 117, 166
Los Angeles Police Department: 10, 16-20, 25, 27, 28, 31-35, 37, 38, 51, 52, 65, 67, 77-83, 89-91, 95, 97, 99-103, 105-107, 112, 114, 117-119, 124, 125, 127, 128, 133, 135, 137, 155, 157, 161, 165, 183, 224, 238, 239, 257, 308, 313, 319, 325, 335, 356, 389, 390, 392, 395-397, 401, 403, 404, 413, 433-435, 439, 440, 444, 474, 475, 484, 489, 496, 497, 500
Los Angeles Police Department Vice Squad: 34, 403, 435
Los Angeles Postal Inspector: 89
Los Angeles Times: 21, 89, 341, 474
Los Angeles Weekly: 180
Loud Family: 177
Love Story (film): 137
Love That Dares to Speak Its Name: 164
Lovett, Joseph F.: 309
Lowery, Allan: 195, 400
Loyola University: 30, 299, 375
LT Publishing: 98, 217, 241, 459
Luce, Henry: 276
Lucie-Smith, Edward: 107, 123, 173
Lumbleau, Vince: 400
Lupone, Patty: 340
Lurch: 148, 393
Lure, The (book): 172
Lurie, Dan: 321, 328
Lynch, David: 403
Lynes, George Platt: 62
Lyon, Lisa: 349
M2M (see Man2Man Quarterly)
Maccubbin, Deacon: 143
Mach (mag): 56, 119, 120, 134, 237, 255, 372, 411, 430, 431, 442, 455, 472, 489, 492, 504, 507, 529, 530
Machiavelli: 361, 411, 429, 431
Macho (mag): 441, 442
Mad Magazine: 485, 489, 490
Mad Men (television): 63
Maddox, Bob: 164
Madonna: 146, 498
Madrid: 399
Mafia: xiii, 35, 40, 122, 172, 193, 199, 201, 203, 205-209, 213, 220, 325, 340, 419, 420, 465, 492
Magaldi, Augustin: 341, 399
Magazine, The (business): 41
Magcorp: 69
Magdalene, Mary: 163

Maggiore, Santa Maria: 230
Mahoney, Bob: 272
Mail-Order: 16, 25, 46-48, 57, 81, 95, 96, 98, 107, 154, 155, 157, 162, 183, 184, 199, 200, 206, 217, 229, 233-238, 241-243, 245, 252, 254, 269, 270, 306, 307, 317, 327, 328, 390, 391, 399, 412, 413, 440, 443, 452, 465, 473, 476, 477, 486, 487
Mailer, Norman: 6, 177
Mainardi, Robert: 41, 253, 477
Mains, Geoff: 85, 122, 168, 316, 415, 425
Maison Europeenne de la Photographie: 466
Male Nude: 244
Male Rape: 105, 110, 111
Male Slave: 452, 453, 478
Malebox: 486
Maletta, Michael: 171
Man2Man Personals: 161, 471, 486
Man2Man Quarterly (mag): 69, 142, 159, 161, 245, 254, 269, 321, 338, 345, 351, 356, 357, 361-364, 441, 442, 461, 471, 472, 485-488
Mandela, Nelson: 322
Mandingo (film): 33, 117, 118, 163, 314
Maneuvers (mag): 170, 269, 270
Manhattan Review of Unnatural Acts: 487, 488
Manhattanite A-Group: 176
Manhattanization of San Francisco: 159, 171, 176, 366, 474
Manhood Rituals (article): 114
Manhood Rituals (mag): 23, 114, 134, 461-464, 466
Manifest Reader (mag): 3, 23, 28, 50-52, 65, 114, 115, 131, 133, 134, 150, 154-156, 194, 217, 236, 237, 306, 307, 316, 317, 356, 372, 394, 396, 398, 399, 413, 424, 426, 427, 429, 430, 441, 446, 453, 454, 457, 461, 465, 471, 476, 479, 493, 498, 501, 503
Manifesto: 112, 129, 130, 269, 297, 299, 305, 366, 405, 406, 437
Mannespielen: 177, 367
Manson, Charles: 77, 106, 363
Manson Family: 77, 105, 106
Mapplethorpe, Robert: ii, iii, v, ix, 6, 11, 32, 45, 55-57, 59-63, 66, 70, 71, 77, 84, 86, 87, 99, 107, 109, 121, 140, 141, 159, 162, 163, 165, 166, 171-173, 175, 176, 184, 185, 190, 198, 200, 207, 208, 212, 214, 227, 243, 244, 251, 253, 260, 263, 266, 268, 288, 290, 293-295, 298, 309, 311, 314-320, 323-326, 328, 331, 336, 342, 343, 349-351, 354, 361, 362, 365, 367, 371-373, 380, 390, 415, 416, 419, 421, 426, 429, 433, 438, 440, 448-450, 452, 453, 457, 460, 464, 475, 476, 478, 479, 487, 491, 495, 496, 498, 503-505, 510, 511, 521, 528, 529
Mapplethorpe Cover: 140, 161, 314, 324, 464, 478, 510, 529
Mapplethorpe Foundation: 228
Marathon Films: 119-121, 522-526, 529, 530
Marcus, Bruce: 342
Mardi Gras: 481
Marin CA: 344, 384
Marines Memorial Auditorium: 409
Mariposa Foundation: 48
Mark IV Bath: 18, 21, 34, 37, 38, 89, 101, 102, 391, 404
Marks of Pleasure: 120
Marlboro Man: 8, 9, 340, 424
Mars (mag): 238

Marsh, Glenn: 123
Martin, Douglas: 60, 62
Martin, Lloyd: 34
Martin, Paul: 85, 319, 353, 456, 521, 524
Martin, Val: ix, 15, 20, 23, 33, 34, 36, 37, 42, 57, 68, 71, 100, 102, 109, 229, 333, 335, 342, 389, 396-398, 401-404, 514, 515
Martin of Holland: 340, 342, 514
Martinelli, Vallot (see Val Martin)
Marxist: 11, 30, 82, 164, 259, 302, 379, 421, 487
Mary Queen of Scots: 403
Masculinist: 130, 131, 376
Masculinist Manifesto: 112, 130, 269, 299, 305, 437
Masculinity: viii, 7, 23, 33, 105, 106, 111, 112, 114, 115, 117, 129, 130, 138, 157, 170, 235, 267, 301-305, 318, 333, 342, 366, 369, 370, 372-375, 404, 406, 437, 438, 457, 469, 487, 497, 501, 514
Masi, Carlo: 195
Masochism: 438
Masochist: 33, 430, 452
Masochist Stomp: 70
Mason Street SF: ix, 190, 453
Masquerade Books: 448
Master of Falconhurst: 118
Masters, Scott: 107, 438
Matlovich, Leonard: 338, 369, 407
Maupin, Armistead: 418, 437
Maurice: xi, 174
Mavety, George: 203, 205, 244, 266, 357, 467, 476
Mavety Media Group: 262, 467
McCabe, Charles: 474
McCarren Act: 135, 136
McCarthy, Senator Joe: 6, 7, 209
McCarthyism: 225
McClintick, David: 220
McCormick, Tyler: 213, 302
McDonald, Boyd: 317
McDonald, Jeannette: 370, 490, 491, 494
McDonald, Malcolm: 317
McEachern, Steve: 210, 266, 271, 487
Mckee, Sally: 199
McKenzie, Scott: 176
McNally, Terrence: 193
McQueen, Butterfly: 229
MDA: 373
MDMA: 373
Mead, Margaret: 125, 280
Meatpacking District NY: 368
Medium Cool: 300
Men South of Market: 22, 507
Menerth, Ed: ix, 65, 266, 438, 439, 487
Merchant-Ivory: 41
Merman, Ethel: 337
Merrick, Don: 6, 42, 225, 228, 311, 319, 320, 331, 333, 395, 487, 513
Mesmerist, The: 172
Methodist: 16, 165, 260, 454
Metro-Goldwyn-Mayer: 132
Metropolitan Community Church: 21
Metz, Roger: 326, 328
Mexican: 23, 33, 43, 398
Meyer, Russ: 348
MGM: 411, 422

Miami FL: 183, 206, 463
Michaels, Dick: 53, 92, 239, 439
Michigan: 242, 279, 280, 332
Midler, Bette: 193, 459
Midnight Cowboy: 70
Midwestern: 174, 214, 224, 238, 257, 279, 288
Milk, Supervisor Harvey: 56, 83, 126, 171, 213, 308, 311, 324-326, 334, 348, 368, 386, 436, 449, 450, 497, 512
Millennial: 138, 141, 144, 153
Millennium: 154, 155
Miller, Ann: 411, 422
Miller, Edmund: 451, 455
Mineshaft: 71, 176, 177, 184, 185, 199, 207, 342, 362, 373, 429, 508
Minnelli, Liza: 123, 304
Misa, G. B.: 343
Mishima, Yukio: 33, 317, 346, 496
Miss America: 85
Miss Scarlett: 169, 414
Missabu, Rumi: 55
Mississippi: 377
Missouri: 80, 161, 261, 264, 292, 303, 526
Mister Benson: 8, 23, 25, 69, 188, 239, 249, 265, 329, 330, 333, 335, 342, 346, 413, 415, 433, 447, 448, 451-453, 455, 513-516
Mister Marcus (see Marcus Hernandez)
Mitch, Richard: 53
Mitchell, Margaret: 169, 414, 415, 458
Mitchum, Robert: 340
Mizer, Bob: 217, 233, 234, 237, 242-245
Modernismo Publishing: 203, 205, 244, 265, 266, 357, 441, 476
Monroe, Marilyn: 398
Monteagudo, Jesse: 449
Moral Majority: 127, 389
Morales, Max: ix, 66, 401
Morgan, Captain: 453
Moriarty, Dean: 297
Moritz, B.: 308
Mormons: 159
Morrison, Don: 487
Morrison, Jim: 31, 85
Morrison, Peter: 309
Morrisroe, Patricia: 184, 314, 315, 460
Moscone, Mayor George: 126, 324, 325, 497
Most Dangerous Game: 324, 331, 333, 350, 513
Mother Jones: 225
Mountain Men: ii, 44, 518
Movie Mayhem: 163
Movie Movie: 327, 513
Mr. America: 268, 385, 464, 518
Mr. CMC Carnival: 402
Mr. Colt: 488
Mr. Detour Leather: 197
Mr. Drummer: 5, 15, 20, 33, 112, 113, 117, 153, 197, 251, 258, 293, 303, 309, 318, 325, 360, 389, 394, 396, 402, 403, 430, 445, 464, 483, 498, 501-503, 512, 530
Mr. Drummer Contest: 67, 112, 113, 118, 153, 193, 196, 197, 215, 229, 238, 252, 285, 293, 294, 306, 360, 392-394, 396, 399, 445, 446, 475, 477, 481, 484, 492, 502, 507, 519, 525
Mr. Drummer Southern California: 197

Mr. Drummer Southwest: 293
Mr. Germany Drummer: 123
Mr. Groovey: 402
Mr. Leather: i, 13, 113, 197, 213, 238, 302, 306, 389, 392, 394-396, 403, 438, 445, 477, 486, 489, 514
Mr. Manifest: 131, 396, 446
Mr. Northern California Drummer: 293
Mr. Physique USA: 332
Mr. S Leather Company: 5, 231, 283, 367
Mr. Southeast Drummer: 197
Mr. Southwest Drummer: 197
Mr. UK Drummer: 123
Mr. Universe: 268
Mr. USA: 117, 402
Mr. West Coast: 326
Mr. Western California: 332
Mr. World: 268
Mrs. Drummer: 340, 389, 396
Ms. Benson: 448
Mud Pillow Fight: 44, 518
Muni Metro (see San Francisco Municipal Railway)
Munich: 132
Muralist Movement: 214
Murray Hill Station: 69
Muscle Beach: 333
Muscle Training Illustrated: 321, 328
Muscle Works Gym: 380, 381
Musgrave, Charles: 469, 470
Music Theater of Ventura County: 399
Mussolini, Benito: 207
Nagourney, Adam: 82
Narrow Rooms: 339
Nasdijj (see Tim Barrus)
National Book Expo America: 167, 172, 182
National Endowment for the Arts: 84, 390
National Enquirer: 77, 85, 86, 441, 474
National Gay Task Force: 48, 437
National Geographic: 116
National Guard: 301
National Lampoon: 163, 490
National Magazine Award: 180
National Mirror: 441
National Pornographic: 116
National Socialist League: 127, 128, 260
Native Americans: 136
Natoma Street: 154, 401, 500
Naugahyde: 198, 229, 269, 382
Navajo: 180
Nazi: 32, 105, 128-131, 156, 344, 365
Naziphile: 367
Necrophilia: 17, 108, 162, 474, 475
New Age: 213, 231, 418, 422, 337
New England: 25, 94, 136, 167, 168
New Homosexuals: 326
New Jersey: 203, 206, 422, 467
New Journalism: 6, 7, 60, 123, 138, 157, 175, 177, 231, 344, 434
New Media: 56, 127, 141, 254
New Orleans: 5, 198, 377, 466
New Republic, The: 268, 372
New Testament: 164, 260
New York Art: 83, 141, 178, 324, 504, 511
New York City: 58, 63, 396, 397

New York Hellfire Club: 342
New York Magazine: 166, 315, 365, 371
New York Police Department: 34, 35, 207, 396
New York Review of Books: 168
New York Times: 42, 162, 174, 180, 315
New York Wrestling Club: 242
New Yorker: 42, 62, 109, 168, 169, 173, 184, 314, 378
New Yorker, The (mag): 63, 181, 298, 334, 441
Newman, Alfred E.: 489
Newsletter of Personal Rights: 239
NewsMagazine of Gay America: 443, 500
Newsom, Mayor Gavin: 334
Newsweek (mag): 56
NewsWest: 53, 54
Newton-John, Olivia: 327
Newton, Wayne: 341
Nichols Canyon Road: 333
Nicholson, Jack: 78
Night Flight: 171, 194, 508, 509
Night of the Iguana: 135
Night Porter, The: 108, 129, 189, 323, 355, 367, 501
Niven, David: 116
Nixon, President Richard: 300
No Name (bar): 156, 393
Nobile, Philip: 365, 371
Noebel, D.A.: 391
Norse Cove: 138, 361, 383
Norsemen, The: 325
North Beach: 66
Norton, Ken: 117
Not Butch Enough: 129, 325, 381, 511
Nureyev, Rudolf: 175, 320
O'Brien, Glenn: 166, 370
O'Brien, Howard Allen (see Anne Rice)
O'Connor, Flannery: 375
O'Grady, Camille: iii, 116, 117, 146, 331, 332, 337
O'Hara, Scarlett: 169, 170, 414, 457, 458
O'Hara, Scott: 108, 141, 154, 198, 204, 223, 389, 409, 445, 449, 467
O'Rourke, Frank (see Frank Hatfield)
Oakland CA: 29, 215, 279, 329
Oceanside CA: 210, 326-328, 332
Odegaard, Olaf: 20, 36, 37, 100, 102, 397
Olander, Jim: 487
Old Chelsea Station: 69
Old Crow (bar): 243
Old Guard: i, 4, 112, 126, 193
Old Reliable Studio: ii, ix, 6, 70, 140, 154, 190, 217, 242-245, 268, 395, 409, 410, 441, 457, 476, 486, 502, 515, 516, 525
Old Religion: 159, 160
Old Testament: 260
Olson, Frank: 487
On Target: 70, 333, 514
Onassis, Jacqueline Bouvier Kennedy: 49, 298, 326
ONE Archive: 103
One Way (bar): 35, 111
Onstott, Kyle: 118, 314
Opel, Robert: ii, iii, ix, 6, 35, 36, 55, 57, 59, 60, 62, 63, 68, 99, 105, 110, 112, 115-117, 132, 212, 214, 230, 243, 251, 253, 263, 264, 308, 311, 328, 331, 332, 337, 340, 342, 347, 348, 409, 435, 452-454, 457, 476, 495-497, 509, 510, 515

Opelthorpe, Robert: 99, 496
Oppel, Robert: 117
Oprah: 180
Orange County Register: 78
Orange County Torso Murders: 101
Orejudos, Dom (Etienne): 6, 65, 131, 164, 210, 213, 214, 217, 238, 244, 295, 392, 395, 396, 495, 508
Original Joe: 45
Orpheum Theater: 340, 399
Orton, Joe: 311
Oscar Streaker: 60, 110, 115, 214, 263
Our Times (newspaper): 57, 522
Outing Gay Cowboys: 311, 339
Outlaw Motorcycle Gangs: 177
Outspoken: Oral Histories from LGBTQ Pioneers: 130
Oxnard Street: 262, 341, 399
Oz: 28, 433
P. R. I. D. E.: 239
Pace, Dan (see Daniel Pacella)
Pacella, Daniel D: 311, 321, 322, 333
Pacific Drill Patrol: 71
Pacino, Al: 207
Package (mag): 34, 110, 116, 126, 308, 370, 404, 408, 409, 439
Paglia, Camille: 365
Palm Drive Video: vii, viii, 6, 23, 24, 44-46, 56, 71, 72, 119-121, 123, 142, 152-155, 197, 208, 224, 236, 245, 254, 258, 267, 268, 270, 293, 319, 395, 403, 409, 410, 457, 461-466, 488, 492, 517-531
Palm Springs: 384, 468
Pan Am: 199, 373
Pantages Theater: 117
Paris: 16, 198, 199, 304, 326, 367, 377, 453, 466
Paris, Orlando: 109
Parker, Dorothy: 146
Parker, Durk (see Durk Dehner)
Party Animal Raw: 152
Pasolini, Pier Paolo: 129, 174, 334, 455, 508
Patent Law Division: 94
Patient Zero: 445
Patinkin, Mandy: 340
Patrick, Robert: 425
Payne, Arnie: 237
Payne, Robert (see John Embry)
PBS: 177, 239, 368
PCA (see American Popular Culture Assoc.)
PCP: 331, 509
Pearce, David: 120
Pearl Street SF: 65, 265, 445
Pec Stud in Black Rubber: 44, 71, 154, 197, 517
Penis Envy: 392, 478
Pentimento: 45, 84, 121, 315, 316, 349, 440, 449, 521
Peoria IL: 29, 30, 161
Pere-Lachaise: 337
Pereya, Michael: 112, 113
Perles, Anthony: 58
Perrott, Andy: 116
Perry, David: 457
Perry, Larry: 72, 197, 293, 527, 530
Perry, Reverend Troy: 21, 35, 91
Peterson, Dusk: 285
Philadelphia PA: 31, 51, 57
Phillips, Lou: 221

Photography: viii, 2, 6, 10, 18, 22-24, 26, 56, 59, 66, 71, 142, 143, 150, 153, 161, 173, 177, 178, 197, 205, 213, 214, 229, 233, 238, 240, 242-244, 263, 271, 281, 286-288, 311, 312, 319, 338, 343, 345, 367, 456, 464, 486, 495, 498, 505, 507, 508, 511, 513-515, 517-530
Physique Contest: 231, 268, 318, 320, 326, 332
Physique Pictorial: 233, 237, 242, 244
Piaf, Edith: 50, 309
Picano, Felice: 159, 167-172, 174, 177-179, 181, 453, 457, 458
Piercing: 109, 122, 332
Pilgrims: 136, 302
Pink Flamingos: 422
Pink Section (Advocate): 125, 239, 360, 436
Pinocchio: 201, 454
Pirami, Mario: 393
Pitchford, Kenneth: 130
Pittsburgh PA: 484
PlanetOut: 494
Plaster Casting: 66
Platonic Ideal: 8, 9, 29, 143, 318, 319, 323, 375
Playboy: 51, 247, 252, 441, 463
Playboy Bunnies: 252
Playguy: 205, 476
Pleasure Chest: 367, 402
Plewik, Tony: 23, 342, 514, 515
Plimpton, George: 6, 177
Plunge, The (bar): 195, 400
Plymouth Rock: 136
Pohl, Gerhard: 59, 468
Polak, Clark: 31, 42, 51, 443, 462
Polanski, Roman: 77, 78
Political Censorship: 77
Politically Correct: iii, 4, 11, 74, 84, 105, 123, 129, 131, 132, 164, 170, 180, 187, 259, 260, 302, 304, 357, 365, 366, 368, 372, 375, 378, 379, 390, 405, 421, 425, 426, 457, 458, 487, 498
Polk Street SF: 202, 243, 383, 385, 456
Pomona CA: 195
Pontifical College Josephinum: 30, 230
Poole, Wakefield: ii, ix, 171, 197, 198, 326, 327, 348, 487, 513
Pop Culture: iii, xv, 46, 63, 83, 86, 87, 108, 152, 323, 408, 451, 472-474, 504, 510, 512
Pope: 30, 230
Popper: 16, 42, 47, 48, 184, 194, 235, 236, 252, 269, 355, 386, 390, 391, 473, 477
Popular Witchcraft: v, 107, 110, 129, 132, 136, 160, 186, 240, 241, 376, 439
Porn Stars: 141, 360, 498
Pornographer: 168, 205, 242
Pornography: 84, 180, 207, 356, 426, 496
Porter, Cole: 100
Portland OR: 255, 306
Portrait of Dorian Gray, The: 174, 462
Post-Homophobic Stress Disorder: 135
Post-Traumatic Stress Disorder: 135
Post, Emily: 457
Powell Street SF: 119
Powell Theater: 118, 119
Powerhouse (bar): 156, 188
Powerhouse Productions: 338
Powerplay (mag): 270

Praetorians (club): 367
Prague Spring: 297
Prairie Avenue Productions: 213
Pratt Institute: 244
Prescott, Jack (see John Preston)
Preston, Jack (see John Preston)
Preston, John: ii, ix, 8, 23, 25, 54, 61, 69, 148, 149, 168, 172, 174, 185, 187, 188, 239, 249, 263-266, 284, 316, 329, 330, 333, 335, 342, 343, 346, 412, 413, 415, 416, 418, 429, 433, 439, 440, 445, 447-455, 467, 469, 513-516
Pride Foundation: 53
Prince, James: 448
Prison Blues: 67, 80, 123, 143, 144, 231, 242, 463, 466, 509, 528
Prison Punk: 80, 113, 117, 155, 328
Prison Tour Junkie: 80
Prock, Bernie: 112, 438
Producers, The: 128, 129, 490
Pronger, Brian: 318
Protestant: 136, 160, 163, 165, 386, 454
Proust, Marcel: 12, 13, 45, 336
Provincetown MA: 68, 448
Prufrock, J. Alfred: 2, 10, 184
Pruzan, Robert: 399
Prynne, Hester: 445, 485
PSA: 323, 384
Pseudonyms: 25, 287
Psychology Today: 370
Public Sex: 112
Puerto Rican: 398
Purdy, James: 166, 167, 172, 339
Puritan: 77, 84, 94, 136, 138, 172, 309, 361, 362
Pussy Pussy Bang Bang: 348
QQ (see Queens Quarterly)
Quaalude: 108
Quality Inn: 332
Quarters, The: 40, 195, 247, 324, 327, 345, 364, 511, 515, 516
Queen, Carol A.: 449
Queen Cougar: 214, 275, 294
Queen Kong: 490
Queen of Disco: 340
Queening of America, The: ii, 176, 268, 374
Queens Quarterly: 43, 57, 183, 202, 203, 490
Queer Studies: 35, 259, 379, 477
Queer Theory: 259, 304, 389, 459
Querelle de Brest: 126
Questionnaire, The: 94, 133, 233, 237, 240, 241
Quinlan, Chuck: 402
Radcliffe Publishing Program: 168
Radical Faeries: 440
Radziwill, Princess Lee Bouvier: 49
Rage, Christopher: 71
Raging Bull: 208
Rainbow County: v, 85, 339, 511
Rainbow Motorcycle Club: 393
Ram Studios: 74
Ramirez, Efren: ix, 479
Rampling, Anne: 186, 189
Rampling, Charlotte: 189
Ramrod (bar): 129
Rand, Bill: 53, 92, 239, 439

Rand Daily Mail: 37
Random House: 315, 460
Rann, Randy: 72
Rape: 105, 110, 111, 118
Rashomon: 1, 12, 34, 92, 99, 168, 259, 276, 354, 412, 417, 433, 440, 476
Rather, Dan: 299
Rau, Bill: 53
Raven, Cliff: 68, 164, 402
Raw Hide: 371
Ray, Johnny: 230
Reagan, President Ronald: 300, 312, 346, 449
Real Thing, The: 126, 160, 269
Reality TV: 120, 522
Rear-View Mirror: 141, 142, 282, 309, 312, 375, 393, 460, 519-522
Rebel Without a Cause: 234
Rechy, John: 3, 26, 418, 476
Rector, Ron: 238
Red Queen (see Arthur Evans)
Red Star Saloon: 111, 212
Redford, Robert: 340
Redgrave, Vanessa: 403
Redman, Michael: 348
Redneck Biker: 323, 510
Redneck Cowboy: 44, 518-522, 527
Reed, Oliver: 110
Reeves, Steve: 43, 276, 508
Reh, Larry: 356
Reich, Steve: 184
Religious Right: 390
Rembrandt: 437
Remembrance of Sleaze Past: 45, 184, 231, 505, 523, 524
Reno Gay Rodeo: 339
Reno NV: 114, 339
Renslow, Chuck: i, ix, 9, 13, 18, 68, 164, 209, 210, 213-215, 217, 234, 238, 283, 299, 302, 305, 306, 329, 370, 392, 394, 445, 477, 487, 490, 495
Republican: 86, 209, 225, 332
Republican Party: 70, 86
Revisionism: x, 187, 229, 259, 260, 428, 431, 454
Revisionists: 258, 282
Rex (artist): ii, iv, ix, 6, 32, 41, 47, 69, 84, 111, 140, 141, 176, 177, 184, 225, 228, 243, 253, 260, 324, 328, 367, 368, 395, 476, 486, 504, 511
Rex Video Gallery: 228
RFM Productions: 109, 284
Rhodes, Dave: i, 208
Ricardo, Caro: 331
Rice, Anne: 7, 25, 141, 149, 159, 186-189, 450
Rice, Christopher: 189
Richmond Hill NY: 488
Richter, Ralph: 318
Rimbaud, Arthur: 165, 450
Rimshots: 343
Rinehart, Mary Roberts: 451
Rink (photographer): 345, 349, 515
Rio Nido CA: 328, 465
Rip Colt: 319
Ritz: 193
Riverside Drive: 315
Rob of Amsterdam: 49, 255, 307

Robbins, Harold: 84
Robert Gets His Nipple Pierced: 109
Robert Mapplethorpe Gallery: 324, 511
Robert Payne Production: 155
Robert Ripoff (also John Embry): 68, 223, 224, 233, 355, 430
Robertson, Cliff: 220
Robertson, Pat: 389
Rocco, Pat: 402
Rock 'n' Roll: 153, 379
Rocky Horror Picture Show: 114, 383, 387
Rofes, Eric: 35
Roger of San Francisco: 58
Rolling Stone (mag): 177
Roman Catholic Church: 209
Roman Poems: 334
Roman Spring of Mrs Stone: 206
Romanoff, Noodles: 333
Romanski, Chuck: 311, 319, 321, 322, 333
Rome: 118, 168, 230, 281, 377, 385
Roquelaure, A. N. (also Anne Rice): 25, 186-189, 450
Rorer 714 (see Quaalude)
Rorschach: 33, 34, 295
Rose, Bob: 223, 224
Rose, The (film): 459
Rose Bowl: 58
Rose Tattoo, The: 206
Roshomon: 312
Ross, Betsy: 255
Ross, Bob: 294
Rotterdam: 57
Rough Stuff: 35
Rough Trade: 142, 190, 232
Rowberry, John W.: 8, 36, 52, 75, 108, 117, 122, 182, 204, 205, 244, 246, 247, 251, 261, 262, 264, 265, 277, 282, 308, 353-355, 358, 395, 416, 433, 440, 445, 454, 455, 462, 469, 495, 498, 501, 516
Rowland, Craig: 416
Rubber: 44, 71, 154, 156, 197, 252, 362, 505, 517, 518
Rubberotica: 44, 197, 517, 518
Rubell, Steve: 325
Rubin, Gayle S.: 122, 259, 279, 280, 289, 375, 412, 523
Rudolph, Lou: 211, 328, 350
Rue Keller: 198
Rush (popper): 47, 48
Russell, Ken: 110
Russell, Thomas Hunter: 38, 66
Russian: 122, 123, 175
Russian River: 49, 155, 195, 238, 255, 261, 270, 328, 434, 465, 466
Russo, Donnie: 73, 74, 208, 359, 405, 409, 528, 529
Russomania: 73, 74, 359, 505, 528
Rutherford, John: 195
Ryan, Congressman Leo: 325
Saint Isidore: 336
Saint Patrick: 45, 329
Saint Sebastian: 270
Saint Valentine: 334, 416
Salo: 129, 130, 455, 508
Sammut, Frank: 251, 265, 266, 271
Samois: 371, 375

Samurai: 66
San Carlos Institute: 418
San Diego: 117, 205, 441
San Franciscan: 65, 67, 118, 171, 181, 182, 222, 252, 314, 324, 350, 358, 413, 447, 497
San Francisco Alamo Square: 416, 417
San Francisco Bay Bridge: 28, 225, 474
San Francisco Century Theater: 119
San Francisco Chronicle: 112, 339, 381, 385, 419, 472, 474, 515
San Francisco City Hall: 334
San Francisco Creative Power Foundation: 171
San Francisco Deputy Sheriff: 335, 347
San Francisco Eagle (bar): 294
San Francisco Focus Magazine: 368
San Francisco Gate (newspaper): 450
San Francisco General Hospital: 48, 212, 347, 496
San Francisco GLBT Historical Society: 2, 11, 353, 359
San Francisco Health Department: 135
San Francisco International Airport: 176, 214, 383-387
San Francisco Market Street: 113, 119, 122, 210, 243, 262, 272, 276, 330, 344, 367, 489
San Francisco Municipal Railway: 58, 59, 332, 384, 434
San Francisco PBS: 368
San Francisco Pleasure Guide: 348
San Francisco Police Department: 122, 206, 210, 325, 334, 335, 337, 348
San Francisco Union Square: 243
San Jose: 87, 326
San Mateo: 239, 439
San Quentin: 123, 199, 327, 465
Sanchez, Sam: 138, 140, 148
SandMutopia Guardian: 255, 489
SandMutopia Supply Co.: 491, 492
Sands, Dave: 402, 478
Santa Monica Boulevard LA: 101, 195, 413, 442, 501
Santa Rosa CA: 131, 329
Santa Rosa Junior College: 461
Saroyan, William: 203, 204
Sashes: 193, 197
Satan: 108, 109, 159, 164, 389, 391, 450, 478
Satanic Coven: 240
Satyr (photographer): 288
Saunders, Dick: 397, 454
Saunders, Jameo: 481
Savage, Steve: 72
Saylor, Steven: ix, 6, 118, 162, 168, 169, 193, 204, 248, 249, 267, 281, 282, 429, 455, 467, 516
Scarlet Letter: 470, 485
Scat: 109, 363, 367
Schaaf, Al: 59, 332
Schadenfreude, King of: 134, 137, 245, 270, 356, 494
Schjeldahl, Peter: 63
Schmidt, Kenneth: 99
Schoch, Steve: 89, 92-97
Schrager, Ian: 325
Schwarzenegger, Arnold: 77, 86, 87, 370, 420, 490
Scorpio Rising: 121, 164, 234, 495
Scottish Games: 325, 512
Scrooge: 174
SCUM (see Society to Cut Up Men)
SCUM Manifesto: 130, 297, 299, 305

Seahorse Press: 167, 169
Season in Hell, A: 165
Seattle WA: 62, 115
Sebastopol CA: 66, 270, 334, 465
Secret Historian: 61, 394
Segal, Erich: 137
Segregation: 316, 365, 366, 412, 418
Selan, Bob: 124
Selby, Alan: 225, 283, 367
Sentinel, The: 474, 487
Seven Beauties: 129, 367
Sex Art: 59, 141, 365, 367
Sex Classifieds: 239, 360, 362
Sex Offender: 90
Sex Personals Ads: 191
Sex Slaves: 77, 100, 105, 106
Sex Writing: 175, 179, 267
Sextool (film): 57, 105, 109-111, 198, 292, 396, 401, 435
Sexual Freedom: 93
Sexual Identity: 179, 303, 369, 437
Sgt. Pepper's Lonely Hearts Club Band: 2, 39
Shadow Soldiers, The: 33, 85, 520, 521
Shaffer, Peter: 187
Shakespeare, William: 132, 275, 290
Shanti Project: 35
Shapiro, Allen J.: ii, ix, xv, 3, 6, 20, 26, 28, 41-43, 50, 52, 55, 59, 60, 62, 63, 65, 67, 70, 138, 140, 141, 165, 183, 196, 200-204, 214, 219, 227-230, 253, 260, 263, 264, 266, 286, 293, 307, 308, 319, 327, 328, 335, 337, 338, 340, 342, 345, 347, 355, 357, 395, 398, 399, 402, 426, 443, 455, 456, 460, 462, 463, 476, 478-482, 486, 487, 490, 491, 496-498, 500, 502, 507, 508, 510, 513, 514, 516, 529
Sheppard, Simon: 85
Shilts, Randy: 9, 311, 339, 437
Shipley Street: 292, 500
Shoch, Steve: 32, 94
Shotgun Video: 58
Shriver, Maria: 86, 420
Shulgin, Alexander: 373
Sicilian: 206, 211
Siegal, Elliot: 56, 71, 326
Silver Lake: 39, 40
Silverstein, Shel: 51
Simon, Mario: 32, 100, 137, 223, 236, 261, 262, 340, 341, 389, 396, 398-400, 427, 434
Singleton, Jim: 349
Sipes, Chuck: 268, 518
Sitwell, Edith: 166
Skinflicks (mag): 205, 266, 322, 467
Skipper (artist): ix, 144, 395, 520, 528
Skulls of Akron: 199
SLA (see Symbionese Liberation Army)
Slap Happy: 403, 526, 527, 531
Slater, Cynthia: 7, 66, 251, 265, 271, 375, 445
Slave Auction: 15, 17, 18, 20, 21, 28, 31, 33-38, 52, 61, 75, 77-79, 81, 82, 84, 85, 89, 90, 95, 99-103, 106, 107, 110, 117, 124, 128, 137, 160, 183, 219, 239, 275, 291, 313, 319, 325, 338, 358, 389-392, 397, 398, 404, 405, 408, 435-437, 443, 444, 463, 474, 484, 489, 493, 496, 500, 510
Slave Boys: 353

Slavery of Words, The: 113
Sleep in Heavenly Peace: 325, 512
SMADS (mag): 69
Smith, Jack: 121
Smith, Joseph: 159
Smith, Patti: 109, 116, 263, 314
Smith, Scott: 141, 242, 509
Smith, William: 235
Socialist Workers Party: 94
Society to Cut Up Men: 299
Sodbuster: 44, 197, 527
Sodom: 174, 207, 383, 466, 489
Solanas, Valerie: 130, 297, 299, 305
Soldier of Fortune (mag): 7, 161
Solo Sex: 44, 519, 520
Solomon, King: 372
SOMA (see South of Market)
Some Dance to Remember: v, 4, 12, 26, 45, 66, 68, 85, 112, 116, 120, 121, 130, 146, 167, 169, 171, 176, 182, 185, 202, 226, 242, 263, 265, 268-270, 278, 290, 293, 299, 300, 302, 305, 310, 318, 321, 324-327, 345-347, 350, 361, 366, 376, 378, 414-416, 419-421, 425, 454, 457-459, 494, 503, 505, 519, 521, 524
Son of Drummer: 33, 45, 69, 84, 141, 142, 176, 178, 184, 227, 258, 281, 307, 316, 318, 324, 343, 415, 446, 455, 468, 475, 478, 489, 491, 500, 504, 507, 511
Sondheim, Stephen: 135, 415
Sonoma County: 71, 113, 329, 334, 402
Sorenson, Kick: 170, 321, 419
Sorenson, Paul: 272
Sorenson Farm: 66
South Africa Gay Scene: 37
South African: 38
South America: 396
South of Market: i, 22, 91, 116, 154, 195, 196, 203, 210, 212-214, 244, 247, 262, 292, 323, 327, 328, 345, 355, 357, 378, 384, 385, 400, 401, 403, 458, 467, 489, 490, 495, 497, 499, 503, 507
South San Francisco: 161, 442
South Side of Chicago: 299
Southern Belle: 419
Southern California: 11, 91, 102, 103, 197, 220, 224, 239, 358, 390, 399, 400, 435
Spaghetti Factory: 320
Spain: 32, 340, 389, 398-400, 494
Spanish: 219, 223, 397, 398
Sparrow, David: ix, 6, 25, 55-59, 65, 68, 71, 133, 156, 195, 200, 213, 226, 241, 242, 251, 254, 263, 266, 275, 286-289, 308, 311, 325, 328, 329, 331-333, 335, 336, 338, 343, 400, 402, 403, 426, 463, 464, 476, 478, 495, 508-516
Sparrow, Philip: 68, 287, 495
Sparrow Photography: 6, 287, 288, 338, 343, 345, 508, 511, 513-515
Speeding: 4, 214, 243, 433, 486
Speer, Manfred: 476
Speier, Jackie: 325
Spike (barj): 72, 367
Spit: 71, 90, 342, 356, 364, 402, 403, 458, 505, 514
Sprague, Ken: 370
Spring, Justin: 61, 62, 394
Squires, Mickey: 142, 319, 531
St. Mark's Baths: 327

St. Martin's Press: 169
Stables (bar): 195
Staley, Jake: 482-484
Stamford: 171, 415
Stamps, Wickie: 6, 7, 74, 113, 135, 138, 144-147, 151, 156, 186, 189, 422, 449, 529
Standish, Miles: 136
Stanford University: 29
Stanton, Bull: 462
Star Pharmacy: 345, 385, 386
Stars Magazine: 122, 203
Steam (mag): 108, 162, 204, 409, 467
Steele, Jason: 44, 517-522, 524, 525, 529
Stein, David L.: 310, 368, 487, 488
Stein, Gertrude: 1, 6, 60, 62, 203, 204, 211, 310, 337, 368, 487, 488, 495
Steinbeck, John: 168
Steinberg, Saul: 181
Stemigin, Barbara: 85
Sterling, Jan: 199
Steward, Samuel: ii, ix, 6, 22, 28, 55, 58-62, 68, 69, 126, 164, 166, 215, 227, 253, 287, 316, 319, 321, 337, 340, 341, 357, 394, 457, 476, 478, 495, 509
Stewart-Addison, M. J.: 357
Stewart, Jim: ix, 6, 242, 263, 280, 328, 331, 337, 357, 400, 401, 412, 457, 478, 495, 507
Stockholm Syndrome: 79
Stockman, Thor: 479
Stompers (store): 410, 452
Stompers Gallery: 63
Stone, Leo: 71
Stone, Robert: 441
Stonewall Inn: 34, 201, 207, 208, 377
Stonewall Myth: 372
Stonewall Rebellion: 16, 20, 297, 301, 334, 373, 436
Story of Q, The: 107
Straight Society: 186, 268, 374
Straight to Hell (mag): 488
Strand: 22, 332, 333, 338, 367, 383
Streetcar Named Desire, A: 33, 234, 414
Streisand, Barbra: 1, 372
Strom, Greg: 139
Stubble (newsletter): 114
Stud (bar): 100, 210, 363, 396, 444
Student Prince, The: 131
Studflix (mag): 266, 267, 467
Studio City: 16
Studio Royale: 367
Sturman, Reuben: 122, 203
Suicide: 2, 30, 49, 82, 156, 324, 331, 410, 475, 497, 509
Summer of Love: 334
Summers, Claude: 415
Sunset Boulevard: 266, 410
Sunset Bull: 258, 463-465
Sunset Plaza Drive: 451
Super-8mm: 154, 156, 210, 243, 300, 319, 321, 326, 370, 392, 393
Super Manifest Reader: 23, 28, 38, 46, 47, 49, 50, 52, 67, 75, 79, 114, 134, 144, 145, 182, 219, 223, 251, 255, 257, 258, 286, 398, 430, 434, 444, 453, 461, 463, 464, 466, 481-484, 503, 504
Super MR: 23, 28, 38, 46, 47, 49, 50, 67, 75, 79, 114,
134, 144, 145, 182, 219, 223, 251, 255, 257, 258, 286, 398, 430, 434, 444, 453, 461, 463, 464, 466, 481-484, 503, 504
Superman: 327, 513
Supreme Court: 214, 335
Sykes, Bill: 183
Sylvester: 214, 340
Sylvestri, Leonard: 350
Symbionese Liberation Army: 78, 79, 105, 106
Tallwing, Judith: 6, 7
Tan, Celia: 449
Tanny, Armand: 369, 370
Taormina: 206, 207
Target, Jon: 69
Target Album: 70
Target Men: 323, 510
Target Studio: 69, 70, 238, 281, 295, 298, 305, 323, 440, 477, 487, 511
Tarlton, Ed: 241
Taschen: 319
Tate, Sharon: 77
Tattooing: 61, 68, 215, 234, 287
Tavarossi, Tony: 48, 193, 206, 209, 212, 311, 347, 496, 521
Tavern Guild: 93, 206, 210
Taylor, Elizabeth: 116
Taylor, Paul: 315
Teddy Bear: 167, 417
Teddy of Paris: 453, 466
Tehama County: 327
Tehtaankatu: 64
Telegraph Hill: 474
Tempest, The: 132, 270
Tenderloin: 206, 209, 210, 243
Tennant, Stephen: 79
Terror Is My Only Hardon: 243, 245
Theater of Cruelty: 413
Thirteenth Amendment: 78
Thomas, Lou: ix, 6, 55, 69, 70, 140, 238, 295, 298, 305, 357, 440, 476-478, 487
Thompson, Hunter: 177
Thompson, JimEd: ix, 142, 389, 409, 480, 481
Thompson, Mark: ix, 9, 57, 85, 116, 117, 148, 225, 226, 263, 280, 303, 316, 371, 408, 409, 439, 440, 480
Thoreau, Henry David: 4, 31-33, 51, 53, 187, 232, 392, 502
Thornton, Graylin: 33, 113
Thrasher: 403
Thrust (mag): 464
Tiffenbach, Joe: 468
Time (mag): 31, 56, 276, 369, 370
Timmons, Stuart: 21, 417
Timmy (book): 109
Tingle, Ralph J: 90, 91
Tit Torture Blues: 44, 335, 514
Titanic 1970s: xi, 4, 12, 26, 45, 55, 184, 198, 201, 210, 212, 237, 264, 280, 282, 316, 334, 336, 346, 361, 365, 374, 376, 505, 523
Titian: 336
Toad Hall (bar): 272, 383
Toklas, Alice: 62, 337, 495
Tokyo: 66, 199
Tom of Finland: ii, iii, 6, 8, 32, 55, 57, 59-65, 112,

129, 131, 140, 156, 176, 214, 244, 253, 260, 295, 319, 331, 367, 476, 477, 509, 510
Tom of Finland Foundation: 9, 63, 112, 116, 440, 477
Toner, Patrick: 214
Tool Box (bar): 111, 112, 210, 214, 226, 280, 377
Torre, Jerry: 298
Torso (mag): 246, 476
Tough Customer: 55, 56, 65, 75, 76, 141-143, 178, 196, 232, 325-327, 331, 333, 335, 342, 346, 396, 454, 456, 457, 472, 507, 512-516, 519, 520, 530, 531
Tough Shit: 55, 75, 76, 323, 324, 326, 327, 331, 333-335, 342, 346, 510-516
Toulouse-Lautrec, Henri de: 57, 214
Toushin, Steve: 105, 121, 122
Townsend, Larry: ii, ix, xiv, 6, 15, 17, 25, 32, 51, 65, 81, 89-99, 126, 140, 143, 149, 160, 162, 182, 183, 188, 194-196, 200, 201, 205, 217, 230, 234, 235, 237, 240, 241, 244, 255, 256, 266, 284, 285, 317, 355, 398, 406, 411, 413, 418, 433, 440, 444-446, 449-451, 453, 459, 470, 476, 487, 500, 522
Tracy, Spencer: 91, 213
Trademark: 75, 76, 228, 251, 277, 425, 441, 484
Trader Dick: 435, 436
Transbay Bus Terminal: 243
Trash (club): 367
Trash (mag): 228
Travis, Aaron: 25, 168, 188, 204, 267, 282, 453, 455, 467, 516
Treib, Marc: 29
Tribeca Film Festival: 181
Tripp, Dr. C. A.: 365, 371
Tristram, John: 237, 326
Triumph Gym: 213, 214, 238, 392
Trocadero: 328
Trocadero Transfer: 385, 446
Trojan Horse: 114, 161, 366
Trojanski, John: 58, 263, 333, 512
Trowbridge, John: 70, 509
Truck Stop (bar): 119
Tucker, Cole: 361
Tucker, Scott: 316, 371
Turkish Delight: 324, 511
Turner, Glenn: 122, 203, 206
Turngren, John: 474
Twain, Mark: 484
Twin Peaks (bar): 319
Twinkie Defense: 126, 334
Twist, Oliver: 183
Tzu, Sun: 32
Ulysses: 161
Uncircumcised Society of America: 468
Uncle Bob: 117
Uncut (mag): 205, 357, 468
Underwear: 30, 43, 44, 517
United Kingdom: 123, 160, 307
United Parcel Service: 290
United States Air Force: 89, 94
United States Air Force Intelligence Service: 94
United States Army: 16, 78, 106, 301, 319, 344, 368, 397, 503
United States Coast Guard: 240
United States Congress: viii, 135, 136
United States Constitution: 17, 78, 159

United States Federal Bureau of Investigation: 90, 94
United States Marine Corps: 205, 210, 240, 292, 319, 326, 327, 344, 403, 509, 531
United States Navy: 278
United States Olympic Committee: 73
United States Postal Inspector: 89, 99
United States Postal Service: 240
United States Senate: 225, 449
United States Trademark Office: 228
Universal Studios Amphitheater: 163
University College Dublin: 113
University of California: 268, 374
University of California Berkeley: 29, 461
University of California Los Angeles: 89, 240, 469
University of Michigan: 280
University of Missouri: 264, 303
University of Southern California: 11, 103
University of Wisconsin Press: 136
Unzipped (mag): 360
Urban Aboriginals: 122, 168, 415
US Steel Tower: 474
USMC (see US Marine Corps)
USMC Slap Captain: 403
USSM video series: 155, 199, 252
***V4_Wordlist_2F
Vader, Darth: 284
Vaid, Urvashi: 365, 372
Valentino, Rudolph: 61, 62, 337
Valjean, Jean: 17
Valley Girl: 417
Van Leer, David: ii, 176, 268, 374
Van Leer, Russell: 66
Van Nuys: 262
Van Sant, Gus: 436
Vanderbilt, Gloria: 50
Vangelis: 184
Variety (mag): 110, 173
Vatican: 230, 278
Vatican II: 230
VCR: 163, 225, 312, 319, 458, 493, 498
Vee, Kay: 424
Velvet Underground: 164
Venice Beach: 40, 91, 309, 310, 333
Ventura: 399, 491
Verlaine, Paul: 165, 450
Vermont: 334
Versace, Gianni: 49
Vesti, Eigil: 342
VHS: 154
Viagra: 175
Vickers, Frank: 268
Vidal, Gore: 49, 166, 268, 315, 409, 459
Vietnam: 407, 521
Vietnam Veteran: 378
Vietnam War: 297, 299
Viking: 449
Village People: 2, 113, 397
Village Voice (newspaper): 129, 185, 260, 365, 366, 380, 389, 390, 405
Violet Hour: 168
Violet Quill: 159, 167-169, 172, 179, 453
Virtual Drummer: xiii, 116, 119, 134, 159, 161, 205, 237, 243, 321, 322, 351, 396, 442, 461, 485-487

Voeller, Dr. Bruce: 48
Vogue (mag): 473
Voight, Jon: 70
Waddell, Dr. Tom: 73, 407
Wagner, Richard: 144, 290
Wait Till Your Father Gets Home: 466
Walden: 4, 31
Walker, Willie: ii, 2, 353, 359
Wall Street: 53, 220
Wallace, Wally: 184, 373
Waller Street: 156
Ward, Bill: 6, 42, 57, 64, 108, 109, 140, 218, 237, 295, 306, 307, 343, 453
Ward, Brendan: 359
Ward, Jim: 122
Warfield Theater: 113
Warhol, Andy: 9, 24, 51, 53, 130, 134, 154, 162, 164, 166, 167, 190, 253, 297, 299, 305, 348
Warner Brothers: 403
Washington DC: 94, 243, 244
Washington Street NYC: 373
WASP: 396
Water King: 109
Waters, John: 78, 184, 186, 243, 422
Watts Riots: 117
Waugh, Evelyn: 79, 206
We Abuse Fags: 113, 324, 325
Webber, Andrew Lloyd: 163
Weber, Gene: ix, 59, 66, 308, 508
WeHo: 358, 414, 501
Weichelt, Chip (also Academy Trng Cntr): 80, 292, 457
Weider, Joe: 370
Weimar Republic: 123, 350
Weimaraners: 363
Weingarden, Lou: 452
Wertmueller, Lina: 129, 367
West Berlin: 120, 122, 123, 199, 270
West Coast: 35, 42, 125, 143, 162, 166-170, 173, 179, 183, 190, 245, 326, 334, 380, 417, 418, 421, 447, 453
West Coast Drummer: 171, 452
West Coast Stonewall: 35
West Hollywood: 27, 89, 101, 235, 252, 270, 323, 355, 383, 413, 439, 442
West Los Angeles: 90, 91, 117
West Side (NY): 207
Western Civilization: 370
Western Michigan University: 332
Wet Stough: 329, 331, 513
Wexler, Haskell: 300
What They Did to the Kid: v, 164
Wheels (club): 367
Wheels (mag): 69
When Bodybuilders Collide: 73
Whipcrack (mag): 318
Whipping: 115, 163, 313, 314, 345, 451
Whips: 34, 117
Whistle-blowers: 414
White, Dan: 116, 126, 325, 333, 334, 337, 346
White, Edmund: 3, 168, 174, 175, 177, 179, 185, 373, 411, 419, 425, 453
White Crane Journal: 129
White Death: 308, 356, 475
White House: 437

White Night Riot: 334
White Party: 171, 214
Whitehead, Bill: 265
Whitman-Radclyffe Foundation: 91, 93
Whitman, Meg: 86
Whitman, Walt: 232, 297, 302, 317
Whitney, Helen: 326
Who's Afraid of Virginia Woolf: 300
Who's Your Big Daddy: 213
Why Bondage: 488
Wiegert, Leland: 107, 108
Wife of Bath: 322
Wigler, Jim: 6, 33, 223, 524
Wild One, The: 30, 33, 234
Wild Thing: 424
Wilde, Oscar: 174, 222, 337
Wilde, Parker: 41
Wilder, Thornton: 211, 309
Wiley, John: 169, 414, 425, 511
Willhoite, Michael: 417
Williams, Tennessee: 30, 33, 135, 161, 178, 206, 280, 309, 315, 376, 414, 418, 459
Willmore, Judy: 435
Wilshire Blvd LA: 90
Wilson, Captain Jack: 38, 391
Wilson, Dave: 339
Wilson, President Woodrow: 326
Wings: 154, 200, 258, 399, 465
Wings Catalog: 155, 464
Wings Distributing: 155, 245, 399, 465
Wings Galleria: 466
Winslow AZ: 16, 230
Winter of Love: 334
Witch: 110, 136, 159, 160, 186, 376
Witch Trial: 240
Witchcraft: v, 107, 110, 129, 132, 136, 155, 160, 186, 240, 241, 376, 439
Witchcraft and the Gay Counterculture: 129, 376
Witches Sabbath: 240
Without Reservation: 335, 349
Witomski, T. R.: 114, 343, 422, 424, 429
Wolfe, Tom: 6, 177
Womack, Dr. H. Lynn: 242, 243
Woman: 8, 18, 89, 100, 132, 138, 145, 148, 167, 175, 196, 232, 246, 279, 302, 303, 372, 428, 444, 475, 500
Women: v, 6-8, 86, 94, 108, 114, 118, 129, 136, 145, 146, 148, 160, 171, 185, 186, 303, 348, 366, 372, 379, 392, 404, 423, 437, 459, 469, 487
Women in Love (film): 110
Wonacott, Marcus-Jay: 73, 147, 148, 501
Woodstock: 372, 373
Woodward, Bob: 35
Woolf, Virginia: 161, 173, 300, 461
Wordsworth, William: xi, 278
World Encyclopedia: 84, 107
World Series: 225
World War I: 373
World War II: 30, 66, 94, 233, 280, 374
World Wide Federation for Nature: 74
World Wrestling Entertainment: 74
World Wrestling Federation: 73, 74, 502
Worst of Drummer: 83, 108, 117, 132, 133, 136, 154, 227, 402, 491

Wrangler, Jack: 402
Wrestlemania: 73, 74, 502
Wrestling: 73, 74, 110, 242, 324, 331, 502, 508, 511, 513
Wrestling Academy: 524
Wuthering Heights: 321, 346
WWE (see World Wrestling Entertainment)
WWF (see World Wrestling Federation)
Wyoming: 260
XYZ Enterprises: 465
Yale, Joey: 109, 126, 370
Yerkes, Fred: 183
Yippies: 300
YMCA: 40, 392, 474
York, Michael: 123
Young, Ian: 246, 370
Young Research Library: 469
Young Turks Dream of Derek Jarman: 142
Your Ass Is Falling Out: 325, 512
Zee Hotel: 243
Zehel, Ron: 112, 113
Zelig: 373
Zen and the Art of Motorcycle Maintenance: 390
Zeus Studio: 68, 71, 115, 140, 155, 199, 252, 321, 335, 343, 345, 456, 514, 515
Zodiac Killer: 323, 324
Zombie Works: 380-382
Zuckerberg, Mark: 54
Zuhl, Mike: 294, 481-484
Zygarlicki, Bob: ix, 263, 508

www.ingramcontent.com/pod-product-compliance
Lightning Source LLC
Chambersburg PA
CBHW021050080526
44587CB00010B/191